Vespa Scooters
Service and Repair Manual

by Matthew Coombs

with additional information on the 2012-on LX/LXV and S 3v models by Phil Mather

Models covered

LX125ie 2009-on (inc. Touring model)
LX150ie 2009-on (inc. Touring model)
LXV125ie 2010-on
S125ie 2009 to 2013 (inc. College model)
S150ie 2009 to 2013 (inc. College model)
GTS125ie Super 2009-on
GTS250ie 2005 to 2009 (inc. GT250ie 60° anniversary model)
GTS300ie Super 2008-on
GTS300ie SuperSport 2010-on
GTV250ie 2007 to 2010 (inc. Navy model)
GTV300ie 2010-on

(4898 - 288 - 2AN1)

© Haynes Publishing 2014

ABCDE
FGHIJ
KLMNO
PQ

A book in the **Haynes Service and Repair Manual Series**

ISBN **978 0 85733 736 8**

British Library Cataloguing in Publication Data
A catalogue record for this book is available from the British Library.

Library of Congress Control Number 2013954586

Printed in the USA

Haynes Publishing
Sparkford, Yeovil, Somerset BA22 7JJ, England

Haynes North America, Inc
861 Lawrence Drive, Newbury Park, California 91320, USA

Haynes Publishing Nordiska AB
Box 1504, 751 45 UPPSALA, Sverige

Printed using 33-lb Resolute Book 65 4.0 from Resolute Forest Products Calhoun, TN mill. Resolute is a member of World Wildlife Fund's Climate Savers programme committed to significantly reducing GHG emissions. This paper uses 50% less wood fibre than traditional offset. The Calhoun Mill is certified to the following sustainable forest management and chain of custody standards: SFI, PEFC and FSC Controlled Wood.

Contents

LIVING WITH YOUR SCOOTER

Introduction

Pre-ride checks

MAINTENANCE

Routine maintenance and servicing

Contents

REPAIRS AND OVERHAUL

Engine, transmission and associated systems

Chassis components

Electrical system

Wiring diagrams

REFERENCE

Index

The Piaggio Story

by Julian Ryder

Outside of its native Italy, Piaggio is in a strange position. Everyone has heard of one of its products while comparatively few know the name of the parent company itself. That products is, of course, the Vespa, the first mass-produced scooter and the vehicle that got Italy mobile after World War II before becoming a style icon for generations all over the world.

The first Vespa was completed in April 1946, after just three months design work by the gifted aeronautical engineer Corradino d'Ascanio. Piaggio itself was founded as long ago as 1884 by Rinaldo Piaggio, then only 20 years of age, to manufacture components for naval and railway applications. At the outbreak of World War I, Piaggio branched out into aeronautical parts and by 1923 had built a monoplane fighter with cantilever wing. He also started Italy's first airline and became a member of the Italian Senate. In 1924 the company took over the Pontedera factory near Pisa to build seaplanes and bombers. Today, it is the Piaggio group's biggest manufacturing facility.

After Rinaldo Piaggio died in 1938, his sons Armando and Enrico took over the company, and it was Enrico who, with d'Ascanio, developed the first Vespa. He was responsible for redeveloping the Pontedera plant, which had been blown up by the retreating Germans and bombed by the advancing allies. He realised that the country was crying out for mobility, and it would have to be mobility at the lowest possible price and with the toughness and ease of use that could cope with the prevailing conditions. Enrico had already started thinking about this problem before the end of the War, he stared with a small motorcycle built for parachute troops which was modified with unsatisfactory results. This prototype, the MP5 or Paperino – Italian for Donald Duck – was then handed over to d'Ascanio, a man who did not like motorcycles because of their bulk, the difficulty involved in changing wheels and the fact that exposed drive chains made them dirty.

In an astonishingly short period of time (around three months) d'Ascanio had refined his ideas and laid out a totally new and original vehicle that is still recognisable today. He attached the motor to a load-bearing single-sided swinging arm with direct gearing to the rear wheel, he put the gearchange on the handlebar, he used an aircraft-undercarriage strut design for the stub-axle front suspension thus allowing instant wheel changing both front and rear, and he clothed the whole thing in lightweight bodywork that protected the rider from the elements.

It was christened when Piaggio himself saw the first prototype, the MP6, and he remarked that with its wide engine housing and narrow central 'waist' it looked like a wasp.

The Italian word for wasp is *vespa*.

The first 98 cc Vespa was an instant success. In the first year 2484 were sold, 10,535 in the following year, and in 1948 just under 20,000 were built. Piaggio did his first deal for licensed-production in 1950 with Germany. Already, the Vespa was becoming a cult object. By 1953 there were 10,000 Piaggio dealers all over the World, and that same year production passed the half-million mark. The millionth Vespa left the production line in June 1956, the two-millionth in 1960, the four-millionth in 1970, the ten-millionth in 1980, and production is now past 15,000,000 in eighty-nine different models. Worldwide, the Vespa is still Piaggio's top-selling two-wheeler.

But it would be wrong to think that Piaggio is nothing but Vespa. In 1967 the company started making mopeds and in '69 took over one of the Italian motorcycle industry's greatest names – Gilera. In 1980 it absorbed Bianchi one of the greatest names in the Italian bicycle industry (as well as an occasional motorcycle manufacturer) and seven years later took-over the Austrian company Steyr-Daimler-Puch. And that's just the two-wheeled business: there are also Piaggio companies involved in chemicals, textiles, mechanical engineering (which supplied machinery to Toyota's new plant in Derby, England), powder technology, automation, and industrial plant, to name but a few.

The Vespa 150 Sportique of 1964

The main Piaggio company, Piaggio Veicoli Europei SpA, is the biggest manufacturer of two and three-wheeled vehicles in Europe and the third biggest in the World, marketing vehicles under the Piaggio, Gilera and Puch banners. It runs Motovespa SA in Spain which manufactures as well as markets mopeds and scooters, and national distributors Vespa GmbH in Germany, Vespa Diffusion SA in France, and Piaggio Ltd in the UK. Piaggio VE SpA also controls 25% of LML Ltd of Kampur, India's second largest scooter manufacturer and owns 51% of P&D SpA, a joint venture with Daihatsu of Japan to co-ordinate the manufacture and marketing of lightweight three- and four-wheeled light commercial vehicles worldwide. In some countries they're sold as Daihatsus, in others as Piaggios.

Piaggio is a big company, a major player on the world scene, but you can trace it all back to that revolutionary little scooter – the Vespa.

Of course the original 98 cc Vespa has developed over the years. It grew to 125 cc as early as 1948 and the 150 cc model of 1955 was the first of the really modern scooters. A few years ago, scooters were thought of, in the UK at least, as only of interest to born-again mods. Nothing of course is further from the truth. Great chunks of Europe, mainly the southern half, gained mobility thanks to the Vespa. In more remote areas, a scooter can still be the mainstay of a family's transport. Now, the northern half of Europe is starting to cotton on.

Much of the thanks for that must go to the Italian industry in general and Piaggio in particular. In the UK, the big four Japanese manufacturers had effectively given up on what used to be called the 'soft bike' market. Can you remember any publicity for any Japan's soft bikes since the days of the Honda Express as demonstrated by Twiggy and the line "You meet the nicest people on a Honda". Thought not.

At the start of the '90s, Piaggio UK gave the rest of the industry a lesson in marketing. The accepted wisdom was that the British wouldn't buy scooters because of the country's less than two-wheeler friendly weather. Piaggio were already selling vast numbers of scooters in Germany and didn't really see any difference between the climate of Manchester and Dusseldorf, so with a minimal budget and cleverly targeted marketing they started pointing out to people that modern scooters were the most convenient form of inner-city transport yet invented. More to the point they were very affordable, reliable and clean.

Piaggio UK got the non-motorcycling press to ride these twist-and-go scooters and the word started to spread. Scooter

Scooters are a familiar sight in European cities

tests appeared in the motoring pages of the daily press, fashionable young things from the fashion and music world were pictured on their new transport. The message got across. Increasing concern over congestion and pollution in cities isn't confined to the UK. Back in Italy, there are many medieval city centres that are particularly unsuited to or suffer badly from modern traffic. Vehicles powered by internal combustion engines are banned from many of them, so Piaggio came up with what may be the first compound-engined vehicle offered for sale. The 'Zip & Zip' looks like any other 50 cc scooter but

The traditional styled semi-automatic PX125 T5

The S125 College

On Vespa's 50th anniversary in 1996, Piaggio unveiled the Vespa ET2 Injection, an attempt to make two-stroke motors cleaner by using fuel injection. So far the Injection, or Purejet as it is now known, has only been launched in a few European markets but shows graphically how you don't have to be building 150 hp rocketships to be at the forefront of two-wheel technology.

But these are side issues, Piaggio's core business is scooters, and they make them in a seemingly bewildering variety of specifications. The good old Vespa still lives on of course in 50, 80, 125 and 200 cc forms plus a special classic edition for the Japanese home market where it is the most successful European two-wheeler. Modern Vespas look very like their ancestors but nowadays have such refinements as electric starters, electronic ignition and fuel injection. Vespas still use steel bodywork whereas all other scooters produced by the Piaggio group are based on a tubular and sheet steel frame and plastic bodywork. The original left-handlebar mounted gearshifter is still a feature of the PX125 models, but every scooter covered by this manual uses the modern constantly variable automatic transmission that makes them such easy bikes to ride, especially in city traffic.

as well as Piaggio's conventional two-stroke motor it also has an electric motor. The rider selects which engine he or she wants to use by a conventional switch on the handlebar. When you reach the perimeter of the old town where petrol-burning motors are prohibited, you stop and switch to the electric motor.

The GTS250ie was the first four-stroke engined Vespa to be fitted with fuel injection. Ever-tightening emission legislation would soon lead to the end of their carburettor engined models and the factory needed a replacement which would carry them through into the future. The GTS was launched in 2005 and featured the 4-valve liquid-cooled Quasar engine. In most other respects the steel frame, leading link front suspension and monoshock rear end of previous Vespas were deliberately retained, and from the outside the new model looked little different. This was, however, the first Vespa larger than the old PX200, and one which would in three years time be enlarged to 300cc.

A derivitive of the GTS Sport model was the vintage series. It was possible to buy a Vespa in GTV form, 250 or 300, which took on the look of the company's original models characterised by a low level headlight mounted on the front mudguard, tubular chromed-plated handlebars and simplied instruments with an analogue display. A leather seat, designed to look like the two-piece units of older models was fitted, and a flyscreen at the front and chrome rear carrier at the rear completed the retro look. The Vintage series models were a little more expensive and sometimes only available to special order. The first Vespa to appear in Vintage trim was the 60th anniversary GT250 60° model.

The GTS300ie Super Sport

In 2009 125 and 150cc fuel injected GTS, LX and S models were introduced, which eventually superseded their carburettor engined predecessors. The GTS adopted the same cycle parts as the established GTS250 and 300, but used an injected version of Piaggio's 125/150cc 4v liquid-cooled Leader engine. The cheaper LX and S models, used a 2-valve air-cooled Leader engine and had a rear drum brake instead of the rear disc fitted to all other models. The LX and S are slightly smaller bodied than the GTS, but still retain the steel bodywork design – the S can be distinguished by its rectangular headlight. Special edition versions of both models followed and the LX could be obtained in vintage livery (LXV) with an individual headlight unit, fly screen, chrome bars and two-piece design seat. A touring version of the LX was available with flyscreen and front luggage rack.

In 2012 the 125 and 150 LX, LXV and S models were fitted with a new 3-valve (two intake and one exhaust) engine with increased bhp and torque, plus improved fuel economy.

The GTV300ie 'Via Montenapoleone'

Acknowledgements

Our thanks are due to Bridge Motorcycles of Exeter and Fowlers of Bristol who supplied the scooters featured in the photographs throughout this manual. We would also like to thank NGK Spark Plugs (UK) Ltd for supplying the colour spark plug condition photos, the Avon Tyres for supplying the tyre sidewall illustration and Draper Tools Ltd for some of the workshop tools shown.

About this Manual

The aim of this manual is to help you get the best value from your scooter. It can do so in several ways. It can help you decide what work must be done, even if you choose to have it done by a dealer; it provides information and procedures for routine maintenance and servicing; and it offers diagnostic and repair procedures to follow when trouble occurs.

We hope you use the manual to tackle the work yourself. For many simpler jobs, doing it yourself may be quicker than arranging an appointment to get the scooter into a dealer and making the trips to leave it and pick it up. More importantly, a lot of money can be saved by avoiding the expense the shop must pass on to you to cover its labour and overhead costs. An added benefit is the sense of satisfaction and accomplishment that you feel after doing the job yourself.

References to the left or right side of the scooter assume you are sitting on the seat, facing forward.

We take great pride in the accuracy of information given in this manual, but manufacturers make alterations and design changes during the production run of machines about which they do not inform us. No liability can be accepted by the authors or publishers for loss, damage or injury caused by any errors in, or omissions from, the information given.
insert illegal copying clause

Frame and engine numbers

The frame serial number, or VIN (Vehicle Identification Number) as it is often known, is stamped into the frame at the back of the storage compartment, and also appears on the VIN plate. The engine number is stamped into the rear of the transmission casing. Both of these numbers should be recorded and kept in a safe place so they can be furnished to law enforcement officials in the event of a theft.

The frame and engine numbers should also be kept in a handy place (such as with your driving licence) so they are always available when purchasing or ordering parts for your scooter.

A label with the colour code and frame number is stuck to the inside of the body behind the storage compartment – this will be needed if ordering colour matched parts.

The procedures in this manual identify models by their model name (e.g. GTS), and if necessary by their engine size (e.g. GTS250ie), and if also necessary (to differentiate between variants of a model during its production run) also by production year (e.g. 2003 GTS250ie), or by engine type (e.g. air-cooled or liquid-cooled). The model code and production year are on the VIN plate.

Model name	Engine No. prefix	Frame No. prefix	Production years
LX125ie 2v	M681M	ZAPM68100	2009 to 2011
LX125ie 3v	M687M	ZAPM68300	2012
LX125ie 3v	M68AM	ZAPM68303	2013-on
LX150ie 2v	–	ZAPM68200	2009-on
LX150ie 3v	M688M	ZAPM68400	2012
LX150ie 3v	M68BM	ZAPM68402	2013-on
LXV125ie 2v	M444M	ZAPM44300	2010-on
LXV125ie 3v	M669M	ZAPM68102	2012
S125ie 2v	M681M	ZAPM68101	2009 to 2011
S125ie 3v	M687M	ZAPM68301	2012-on
S150ie 2v	–	–	2009 to 2011
S150ie 3v	M688M	ZAPM68401	2012-on
GTS125ie Super	M455M	ZAPM45300	2009-on
GTS250ie	M451M	ZAPM45100	2005 to 2009
GTS250ie ABS	M451M	ZAPM45101	2005 to 2009
GTS300ie Super	M454M	ZAPM45200	2008-on
GTV250ie	M451M	ZAPM45102	2007 to 2009
GTV300ie	–	–	2010-on
GT250ie 60°	M451M	ZAPM45102	2008

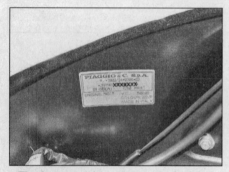

The frame number appears on the label with the colour code . . .

. . . and is stamped into the frame behind the storage compartment

The engine number is stamped into the rear of the transmission casing

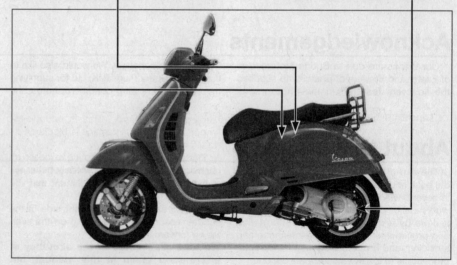

Buying spare parts

When ordering replacement parts, it is essential to identify exactly the model for which the parts are required. While in some cases it is sufficient to identify the machine by its title e.g. 'LX125ie', any modifications made to components mean that it is usually essential to identify the scooter by its year of production, or better still by its frame or engine number.

To be absolutely certain of receiving the correct part, not only is it essential to have the scooter engine or frame number to hand, but it is also useful to take the old part for comparison (where possible). Note that where a modified component has superseded the original, a careful check must be made that there are no related parts which have also been modified and must be used to enable the replacement to be correctly refitted; where such a situation is found, purchase all the necessary parts and fit them, even if this means replacing apparently unworn items.

Purchase replacement parts from an authorised Vespa (Piaggio) dealer or someone who specialises in scooter parts; they are more likely to have the parts in stock or can order them quickly from the importer. Pattern parts may be available for certain components; if used, ensure these are of recognised quality brands which will perform as well as the original.

Expendable items such as lubricants, spark plugs, bearings, bulbs and tyres can usually be obtained at lower prices from accessory shops, motor factors or from specialists advertising in the national motorcycle press.

Professional mechanics are trained in safe working procedures. However enthusiastic you may be about getting on with the job at hand, take the time to ensure that your safety is not put at risk. A moment's lack of attention can result in an accident, as can failure to observe simple precautions.

There will always be new ways of having accidents, and the following is not a comprehensive list of all dangers; it is intended rather to make you aware of the risks and to encourage a safe approach to all work you carry out on your bike.

Asbestos

● Certain friction, insulating, sealing and other products - such as brake pads, clutch linings, gaskets, etc. - contain asbestos. Extreme care must be taken to avoid inhalation of dust from such products since it is hazardous to health. If in doubt, assume that they do contain asbestos.

Fire

● Remember at all times that petrol is highly flammable. Never smoke or have any kind of naked flame around, when working on the vehicle. But the risk does not end there - a spark caused by an electrical short-circuit, by two metal surfaces contacting each other, by careless use of tools, or even by static electricity built up in your body under certain conditions, can ignite petrol vapour, which in a confined space is highly explosive. Never use petrol as a cleaning solvent. Use an approved safety solvent.

● Always disconnect the battery earth terminal before working on any part of the fuel or electrical system, and never risk spilling fuel on to a hot engine or exhaust.

● It is recommended that a fire extinguisher of a type suitable for fuel and electrical fires is kept handy in the garage or workplace at all times. Never try to extinguish a fuel or electrical fire with water.

Fumes

● Certain fumes are highly toxic and can quickly cause unconsciousness and even death if inhaled to any extent. Petrol vapour comes into this category, as do the vapours from certain solvents such as trichloroethylene. Any draining or pouring of such volatile fluids should be done in a well ventilated area.

● When using cleaning fluids and solvents, read the instructions carefully. Never use materials from unmarked containers - they may give off poisonous vapours.

● Never run the engine of a motor vehicle in an enclosed space such as a garage. Exhaust fumes contain carbon monoxide which is extremely poisonous; if you need to run the engine, always do so in the open air or at least have the rear of the vehicle outside the workplace.

The battery

● Never cause a spark, or allow a naked light near the vehicle's battery. It will normally be giving off a certain amount of hydrogen gas, which is highly explosive.

● Always disconnect the battery ground (earth) terminal before working on the fuel or electrical systems (except where noted).

● If possible, loosen the filler plugs or cover when charging the battery from an external source. Do not charge at an excessive rate or the battery may burst.

● Take care when topping up, cleaning or carrying the battery. The acid electrolyte, evenwhen diluted, is very corrosive and should not be allowed to contact the eyes or skin. Always wear rubber gloves and goggles or a face shield. If you ever need to prepare electrolyte yourself, always add the acid slowly to the water; never add the water to the acid.

Electricity

● When using an electric power tool, inspection light etc., always ensure that the appliance is correctly connected to its plug and that, where necessary, it is properly grounded (earthed). Do not use such appliances in damp conditions and, again, beware of creating a spark or applying excessive heat in the vicinity of fuel or fuel vapour. Also ensure that the appliances meet national safety standards.

● A severe electric shock can result from touching certain parts of the electrical system, such as the spark plug wires (HT leads), when the engine is running or being cranked, particularly if components are damp or the insulation is defective. Where an electronic ignition system is used, the secondary (HT) voltage is much higher and could prove fatal.

Remember...

✗ **Don't** start the engine without first ascertaining that the transmission is in neutral.

✗ **Don't** suddenly remove the pressure cap from a hot cooling system - cover it with a cloth and release the pressure gradually first, or you may get scalded by escaping coolant.

✗ **Don't** attempt to drain oil until you are sure it has cooled sufficiently to avoid scalding you.

✗ **Don't** grasp any part of the engine or exhaust system without first ascertaining that it is cool enough not to burn you.

✗ **Don't** allow brake fluid or antifreeze to contact the machine's paintwork or plastic components.

✗ **Don't** siphon toxic liquids such as fuel, hydraulic fluid or antifreeze by mouth, or allow them to remain on your skin.

✗ **Don't** inhale dust - it may be injurious to health (see Asbestos heading).

✗ **Don't** allow any spilled oil or grease to remain on the floor - wipe it up right away, before someone slips on it.

✗ **Don't** use ill-fitting spanners or other tools which may slip and cause injury.

✗ **Don't** lift a heavy component which may be beyond your capability - get assistance.

✗ **Don't** rush to finish a job or take unverified short cuts.

✗ **Don't** allow children or animals in or around an unattended vehicle.

✗ **Don't** inflate a tyre above the recommended pressure. Apart from overstressing the carcass, in extreme cases the tyre may blow off forcibly.

✔ **Do** ensure that the machine is supported securely at all times. This is especially important when the machine is blocked up to aid wheel or fork removal.

✔ **Do** take care when attempting to loosen a stubborn nut or bolt. It is generally better to pull on a spanner, rather than push, so that if you slip, you fall away from the machine rather than onto it.

✔ **Do** wear eye protection when using power tools such as drill, sander, bench grinder etc.

✔ **Do** use a barrier cream on your hands prior to undertaking dirty jobs - it will protect your skin from infection as well as making the dirt easier to remove afterwards; but make sure your hands aren't left slippery. Note that long-term contact with used engine oil can be a health hazard.

✔ **Do** keep loose clothing (cuffs, ties etc. and long hair) well out of the way of moving mechanical parts.

✔ **Do** remove rings, wristwatch etc., before working on the vehicle - especially the electrical system.

✔ **Do** keep your work area tidy - it is only too easy to fall over articles left lying around.

✔ **Do** exercise caution when compressing springs for removal or installation. Ensure that the tension is applied and released in a controlled manner, using suitable tools which preclude the possibility of the spring escaping violently.

✔ **Do** ensure that any lifting tackle used has a safe working load rating adequate for the job.

✔ **Do** get someone to check periodically that all is well, when working alone on the vehicle.

✔ **Do** carry out work in a logical sequence and check that everything is correctly assembled and tightened afterwards.

✔ **Do** remember that your vehicle's safety affects that of yourself and others. If in doubt on any point, get professional advice.

● If in spite of following these precautions, you are unfortunate enough to injure yourself, seek medical attention as soon as possible.

Engine oil level check

The correct oil

● Engines place great demands on their oil. It is very important that the correct oil is used.

● Always top up with a good quality motorcycle/scooter oil of the specified type and viscosity and do not overfill the engine. Do not use oil designed for use in car engines.

Oil type	API grade SL, ACEA A3, JASO grade MA
Oil viscosity –	
2012-on 3v engines	SAE 10W-40 semi synthetic
All other engines	SAE 5W-40 fully synthetic

Caution: Do not use chemical additives or oils labelled 'ENERGY CONSERVING'.

Before you start

✔ Support the scooter on its centre stand on level ground.

✔ Check the oil level when the engine is cold.

✔ If the engine is hot wait at least ten minutes after stopping it before checking the level to get a true reading.

Scooter care

● If you have to add oil frequently, check the engine joints, oil seals and gaskets for oil leakage. If not, the engine could be burning oil, in which case there will be white smoke coming out of the exhaust (see *Fault Finding*).

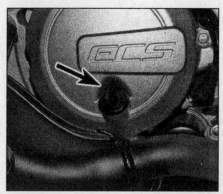

1 Unscrew the oil filler cap/level dipstick (arrowed) from the right-hand side of the engine on GTS125ie models . . .

2 . . . and LX, LXV and S 2012-on 3v models.

3 The oil filler cap is on the left-hand side on all other models.

4 Wipe the dipstick clean.

5 Insert the dipstick and screw the cap fully in.

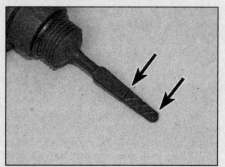

6 Remove the dipstick and check the oil mark – it should lie between the MAX and MIN level lines (arrowed).

7 If the level is on or below the MIN line, top up the engine with the recommended grade and type of oil to bring the level almost up to the upper line. Do not overfill. To raise the level from MIN to MAX requires about 200ml of oil.

8 Before fitting the cap make sure the O-ring (arrowed) on the underside is in good condition and properly seated. Fit a new one if necessary. Wipe it clean and smear new oil onto it. Fit the cap and tighten it by hand.

Coolant level check (liquid-cooled models)

 Warning: Do not remove the cap from the reservoir when the engine is hot. Scalding hot coolant and steam may be blown out under pressure, which could cause serious injury. When the engine has cooled slowly remove the cap allowing any residual pressure to escape.

 Warning: DO NOT leave open containers of coolant about, as it is poisonous.

Before you start

✔ The coolant reservoir is located behind the access panel to the right of the ignition switch.

✔ Make sure you have a supply of premix coolant available or prepare some yourself (a mixture of 50% distilled water and 50% corrosion inhibited ethylene glycol anti-freeze is needed).

✔ Support the scooter on its centre stand on level ground.

✔ Check the coolant level when the engine is cold.

Bike care

● Use only the specified coolant mixture. It is important that anti-freeze is used in the system all year round, and not just in the winter. Do not top-up the system with water only, as the coolant will become too diluted.

● Do not overfill the reservoir tank. The coolant level should be just below the MAX level line. Any surplus should be siphoned or drained off to prevent the possibility of it being expelled when the engine is hot.

● If the coolant level falls steadily, check the system for leaks (see Chapter 1). If no leaks are found and the level continues to fall, it is recommended that the machine is taken to a Vespa dealer for a pressure test.

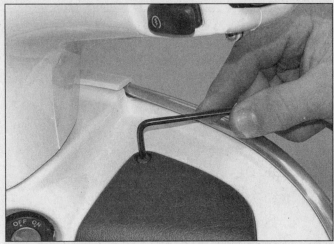

1 Undo the screw and remove the reservoir access panel.

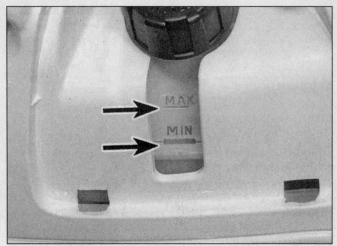

2 Check the level of coolant in the reservoir – it should lie between the MAX and MIN level lines (arrowed).

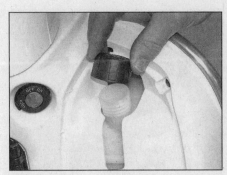

3 If the level is on or below the MIN line, slowly unscrew the reservoir cap – if you hear a hissing sound (indicating there is still pressure in the system), wait until it stops before fully removing the cap.

4 Top-up with the specified coolant mixture to bring the level almost up to the MAX line, using a funnel if required. **Do not overfill**. Fit the reservoir cap.

5 Fit the access panel, making sure the tabs at the bottom locate correctly.

Brake fluid level check

⚠ *Warning: Brake fluid can harm your eyes and damage painted surfaces, so use extreme caution when handling and pouring it and cover surrounding surfaces with rag. Do not use fluid that has been standing open for some time, as it absorbs moisture from the air which can cause a dangerous loss of braking effectiveness.*

Before you start

✔ Support the scooter on its centrestand on level ground. Turn the handlebars until the brake reservoir is as level as possible – remember to check both reservoirs if your scooter is equipped with a rear disc brake.

✔ Make sure you have a supply of DOT 4 brake fluid.

✔ If top-up is required wrap a rag around the reservoir to ensure that any spillage does not come into contact with painted or plastic surfaces. If any fluid is spilt, wash it off immediately with cold water.

Bike care

● The fluid in the brake master cylinder reservoir(s) will drop as the brake pads wear. If the fluid level is low check the brake pads for wear (see Chapter 1), and replace them with new ones if necessary before topping the reservoir up (see Chapter 8). After the new pads have been fitted check to see if topping up is still necessary – when the pistons are pushed back into the caliper to accommodate the extra thickness of the pads some fluid will be displaced back into the reservoir.

● If the reservoir requires repeated topping-up this is an indication of a fluid leak somewhere in the system, which should be investigated immediately.

● Check for signs of fluid leakage from the brake hoses and components – if found, rectify immediately.

● Check the operation of the brakes before riding the machine. If there is evidence of air in the system (a spongy feel to the lever), bleed the brake as described in Chapter 8.

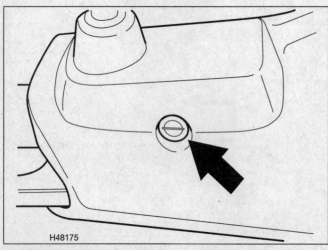

1 **Check – LX and S models**
Check the fluid level in the window in the reservoir body via the aperture in the front handlebar cover (arrowed) – the fluid level must be visible in the window. If it is not visible remove the front handlebar cover (see Chapter 9), then follow Steps 7 to 10.

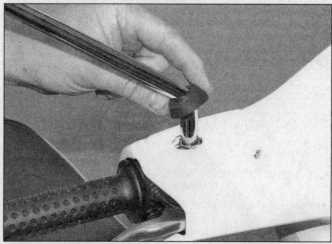

2 **Check – GTS models**
Displace the rubber grommet for the mirror stem from each reservoir access panel and slide it up the stem.

3 Undo the access panel screw . . .

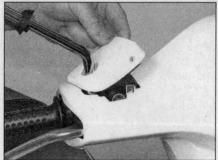

4 . . . then displace the panel and slide it up the stem – secure it in place with some tape or using the rubber grommet.

5 Check the fluid level in the window (arrowed) in the reservoir body – it must be visible in the window. If it is not visible, follow Steps 7 to 10.

6 **Check – GTV, GT and LXV models**
Check the fluid level in the window (arrowed) in each reservoir body – it must be visible in the window. If it is not visible, follow Steps 7 to 10.

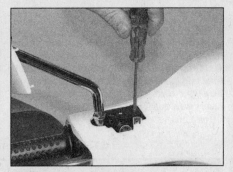

7 **Top-up – all models**
Undo the reservoir cover screws and remove the cover and diaphragm.

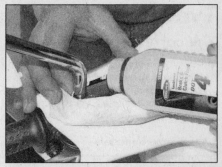

8 Top up with new clean DOT 4 hydraulic fluid, until the level is up to the top of the window. Do not overfill and take care to avoid spills (see *Warning* on page 0•12).

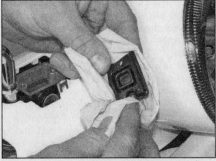

9 Wipe any moisture out of the diaphragm with a tissue.

10 Ensure that the diaphragm is correctly seated before fitting the cover. Secure the cover with its screws. Fit the handlebar cover or access panel according to model.

Suspension and steering checks

● Check that the front and rear suspension operates smoothly without binding.

● Check that the steering moves smoothly from lock-to-lock.

Legal and safety checks

Lighting and signalling
● Take a minute to check that the headlight, tail light, brake light, instrument lights and turn signals all work correctly.
● Check that the horn sounds when the button is pushed.
● A working speedometer graduated in mph is a statutory requirement in the UK.

Safety
● Check that the throttle grip rotates smoothly and snaps shut when released, in all steering positions.

● Check that stand return springs hold the stand(s) securely up when retracted.

● Check that both brakes work correctly when applied and free off when released.

Fuel
● This may seem obvious, but check that you have enough fuel to complete your journey. Do not wait until the fuel gauge or warning light tells you that the level in the tank is low before filling up.

● If you notice signs of leakage you must rectify the cause immediately.

● Ensure you use the correct grade unleaded petrol, minimum 91 octane (RON) – 95 octane is the standard rating for premium unleaded in the UK.

Tyre checks

The correct pressures

● The tyres must be checked when cold, not immediately after riding. Note that low tyre pressures may cause the tyre to slip on the rim or come off. High tyre pressures will cause abnormal tread wear and unsafe handling.

● Use an accurate pressure gauge. Many forecourt gauges are wildly inaccurate. If you buy your own, spend as much as you can justify on a quality gauge.

● Proper air pressure will increase tyre life and provide maximum stability and ride comfort.

● Refer to the tables below for the correct tyre pressures for your model.

LX, LXV and S models

	Front	Rear
Rider only	23 psi (1.6 Bar)	29 psi (2.0 Bar)
Rider and passenger	23 psi (1.6 Bar)	33 psi (2.3 Bar)

GTS, GTV and GT models

	Front	Rear
Rider only	26 psi (1.8 Bar)	29 psi (2.0 Bar)
Rider and passenger	26 psi (1.8 Bar)	32 psi (2.2 Bar)

Tyre care

● Check the tyres carefully for cuts, tears, embedded nails or other sharp objects and excessive wear. Operation of the scooter with excessively worn tyres is extremely hazardous, as traction and handling are directly affected.

● Check the condition of the tyre valve and ensure the dust cap is in place.

● Pick out any stones or other objects which may have become embedded in the tyre tread. If left, they could eventually penetrate through the casing and cause a puncture. If there are any nails or metal shards check for any air leakage from the hole after removing them (a dab of soapy water over the hole will bubble up if any air is leaking), and also check the tyre pressure a few hours later. Any puncture, however slow, must be dealt with.

● If tyre damage is apparent, or unexplained loss of pressure is experienced, seek the advice of a tyre fitting specialist without delay.

Tyre tread depth

● At the time of writing UK law requires that tread depth must be at least 1 mm over 3/4 of the tread breadth all the way around the tyre, with no bald patches. Many riders, however, consider 2 mm tread depth minimum to be a safer limit. Vespa recommend a minimum of 1.5 mm on the front and 2 mm on the rear. Refer to the tyre tread legislation in your country.

● Many tyres now incorporate wear indicators in the tread grooves. Identify the location marking(s) (usually an arrow, a triangle or the letters TWI) on the tyre sidewall to locate the indicator bars and replace the tyre if the tread has worn down to the bars.

1 Remove the dust cap (arrowed) from the valve and do not forget to fit it after checking the pressure.

2 Check the tyre pressures when the tyres are cold.

3 Measure tread depth at the centre of the tyre using a tread depth gauge.

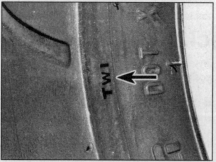

4 Tyre tread wear indicator bar location marking (in this case the letters TWI) (arrowed) . . .

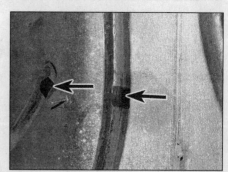

5 . . . and indicator bars (arrowed) in the tread groove.

Chapter 1
Routine maintenance and servicing

Contents

Degrees of difficulty

Easy, suitable for novice with little experience	**Fairly easy,** suitable for beginner with some experience	**Fairly difficult,** suitable for competent DIY mechanic	**Difficult,** suitable for experienced DIY mechanic	**Very difficult,** suitable for expert DIY or professional

Introduction

1 This Chapter is designed to help the home mechanic maintain his/her scooter for safety, economy, long life and peak performance.

2 Deciding where to start or plug into a service schedule depends on several factors. If the warranty period on your scooter has just expired, and if it has been maintained according to the warranty standards, you will want to pick up routine maintenance as it coincides with the next mileage or calendar interval. If you have owned the machine for some time but have never performed any maintenance on it, or if you have just purchased a used scooter and have no knowledge of its history or maintenance record, then you should carry out all checks and perform all necessary procedures in one big service to ensure that nothing is overlooked, then start the regular maintenance schedule from that point. If you have just had a major engine overhaul, then you will want to start the schedule from the beginning as with a new machine.

3 Before beginning any maintenance or repair, clean your scooter thoroughly, especially around the suspension, brakes, engine and gearbox covers. Cleaning will help ensure that dirt does not contaminate the working parts and will allow you to detect wear and damage that could otherwise easily go unnoticed.

4 Certain maintenance information is sometimes printed on decals attached to the scooter. If the information on the decals differs from that included here, use the information on the decal.

Note 1: *Pre-ride checks are listed at the beginning of this manual. Always perform the pre-ride inspection at every maintenance interval (in addition to the procedures listed).*

Note 2: *The intervals listed below are the intervals recommended by the manufacturer.*

Note 3: *An initial (one-off) service should be performed by a Vespa dealer after the first 600 miles (1000 km) from new. Thereafter, the scooter should be serviced according to the intervals specified in the service schedules which follow.*

LXV125ie

LX125/150ie and LXV125/150ie – 2009 to 2011

Model identification

Engine . . . . .124/151cc 2v single cylinder, air-cooled, four-stroke
Gearbox. . . . . Variable speed automatic, belt driven
Ignition. . . . . Capacitor discharge ignition (CDI)
Fuel system. . . . . .Fuel injection
Front suspension . . . . Trailing link and monoshock
Rear suspension. . . . . .Swingarm and monoshock
Front brake . . . . .Hydraulic disc
Rear brake. . . . . .Drum
Front tyre size 110/70-11
Rear tyre size 120/70-10
Overall length . . . . .1770 mm
Overall width . . . . .740 mm
Overall height . . . . .1140 mm
Wheelbase. . . . . .1280 mm
Curb weight. . . . . .114 ± 5 kg
Fuel tank capacity
  Total. . . . . 8.2 litres
  Reserve . . . . .2 litres
Introduced
  LX125/150ie 2009
  LX125/150ie Touring. 2010
  LXV125/150ie. 2010

Servicing specifications and lubricants

Battery. 12V-10Ah
Spark plug type
  125 engine . . . . NGK CR8EB
  150 engine . . . . NGK CR7EB
Spark plug electrode gap . . . . 0.7 to 0.8 mm
Idle speed . . . . .1700 to 1800 rpm
Front brake pad and rear drum brake shoe wear limit . . . . 1.5 mm
Rear brake lever freeplay. . . . . see Section 4
Throttle twistgrip freeplay. 2 to 6 mm
Valve clearances (engine COLD)
  Intake valve . . . . 0.10 mm
  Exhaust valve . . . . 0.15 mm
Fuel . . . . .Petrol (unleaded) min 91 octane
Engine oil type . . SAE 5W-40 synthetic. API SL, ACEA A3, JASO MA
Engine oil capacity
  After draining . . . . approx 1.0 litre
  Dry fill capacity . . . . 1.1 litre
Gearbox oil . . . . SAE 80W-90 API GL3 gear oil
Gearbox oil capacity . . . . .100 ml
Brake fluid. . . . . DOT 4

Torque settings

Engine oil drain plug. . . . . 24 to 30 Nm
Gearbox oil drain plug . . . . 15 to 17 Nm
Spark plug. . . . . 12 to 14 Nm

LX125ie

LX125ie Touring

Service schedule – LX125/150ie and LXV125/150ie (09-11)

Note: *Always perform the Pre-ride checks before every service interval – see the beginning of this Manual.*

	Text section in this Chapter	Every 3750 miles (6000 km) or 12 months	Every 7500 miles (12,000 km) or 2 years	Every 11,250 miles (18,000 km)	Every 15,000 miles (24,000 km)
Air filter – clean*	1	✔			
Battery – check	2	✔			
Brake pad and shoe – wear check	3	✔			
Brake system – check**	4	✔			
Cooling system – check	5		✔		
Crankcase breather – clean	6				✔
Drive belt and transmission – check	7	✔			
Drive belt and transmission – replace belt and variator components	7		✔		
Engine oil and filter – change	8	✔			
Fuel system – check	9		✔		
Gearbox oil level – check	10	✔			
Gearbox oil – change	10				✔
Headlight aim – check	11		✔		
Idle speed – check	12		✔		
Nuts and bolts – tightness check	13		✔		
Spark plug – check	14	✔			
Spark plug – replace	14		✔		
Stand(s) – check and lubricate	15	✔			
Speedometer cable and drive gear – lubricate	16		✔		
Steering head bearings – check	17		✔		
Suspension – check	18		✔		
Throttle – check and adjust	19		✔		
Valve clearances – check	20	**First check at 3750 miles (6000 km)**		✔	
Wheels and tyres – check	21	✔			

* Clean the air filter more often if the scooter is ridden in constantly wet or dusty conditions.
** The brake fluid must be changed every 2 years, irrespective of mileage.

LX125/150ie and LXV125/150ie 3v 2012-on

Model identification

Engine . . . . . 124.5/154.8cc 3v single cylinder, air-cooled, four-stroke
Gearbox . . . . Variable speed automatic, belt driven
Ignition . . . . Capacitor discharge ignition (CDI)
Fuel system . . . . Fuel injection
Front suspension . . . . Trailing link and monoshock
Rear suspension . . . . Swingarm and monoshock
Front brake . . . . Hydraulic disc
Rear brake . . . . Drum
Front tyre size 110/70-11
Rear tyre size 120/70-10
Overall length . . . . 1770 mm
Overall width . . . . 740 mm
Overall height
  LX125/150 . . . . 1140 mm
  LXV125/150 . . . . 1225 mm
Wheelbase . . . . 1280 mm
Curb weight
  LX125/150 . . . . 114 kg
  LXV125/150 . . . . 122 kg
Fuel tank capacity
  LX125/150
    Total . . . . 8.2 litres
    Reserve . . . . 2 litres
  LXV125/150
    Total . . . . 7.0 litres
    Reserve . . . . 2.5 litres
Introduced 2012
Engine number prefix (125) M669M
Engine number prefix (150) M66AM
Frame number prefix RP8M66500

Servicing specifications and lubricants

Battery . . . . 12V-10Ah, (12V-6Ah from June 2013)
Spark plug type . . . . NGK CR8EB
Spark plug electrode gap . . . . 0.7 to 0.8 mm
Idle speed . . . . 1700 to 1800 rpm
Front brake pad and rear drum brake shoe wear limit . . . 1.5 mm
Rear brake lever freeplay . . . . see Section 4
Throttle twistgrip freeplay . . . . 2 to 6 mm
Valve clearances (engine COLD)
  Intake valve . . . . 0.08 mm
  Exhaust valve . . . . 0.08 mm
Fuel . . . . Petrol (unleaded) min 95 octane
Engine oil type . . . SAE 10W-40 synthetic-based. API SL, ACEA A3,
                                               JASO MA, MA2
Engine oil capacity . . . . 1.34 litre
Gearbox oil . . . . SAE 80W-90 API GL4 gear oil
Gearbox oil capacity . . . . 200 ml
Brake fluid . . . . DOT 43

Torque settings

Engine oil drain plug . . . . 15 to 17 Nm
Engine oil filter cartridge . . . . 5 to 6 Nm
Gearbox oil filler plug . . . . 15 to 17 Nm
Spark plug . . . . 10 to 12 Nm

Service schedule – LX125/150ie and LXV125/150ie 3v – 2012-on

Note: *Always perform the Pre-ride checks before every service interval – see the beginning of this Manual.*

	Text section in this Chapter	Every 3000 miles (5000 km) or 5 months	Every 6200 miles (10,000 km) or 10 months	Every 12,400 miles (20,000 km) or 20 months
Air filter – clean*	1		✔	
Battery – check	2	✔		
Brake pad and shoe – wear check	3	✔		
Brake system – check**	4	✔		
Cooling system – check	5	✔		
Crankcase breather – clean	6			✔
Drive belt 125 cc models	7		✔ Inspect	✔ Renew
Drive belt 150 cc models	7		✔ Renew	
Variator components	7		✔	
Engine oil and filter – change	8		✔	
Fuel system – check	9	✔		
Gearbox oil level – check	10		✔	
Headlight aim – check	11		✔	
Idle speed – check	12		✔	
Nuts and bolts – tightness check	13		✔	
Spark plug LX125/150	14		✔ Inspect	✔ Renew
Spark plug LXV125/150	14	✔ Inspect	✔ Renew	
Stand – check and lubricate	15	✔		
Speedometer cable and drive gear – lubricate	16		✔	
Steering head bearings – check	17		✔	
Suspension – check	18		✔	
Throttle – check and adjust	19		✔	
Valve clearances – check	20		✔	
Wheels and tyres – check	21	✔		

Clean the air filter more often if the scooter is ridden in constantly wet or dusty conditions. Fit a new filter element at 18,600 miles (30,000 km).
** *The brake fluid must be changed every 2 years, irrespective of mileage.*

S125ie

S125ie and S150ie – 2009 to 2011

Model identification

Engine . . . . 124/151 cc 2v single cylinder, air-cooled four-stroke
Gearbox . . . . Variable speed automatic, belt driven
Ignition . . . . Capacitor discharge ignition (CDI)
Fuel system . . . . Fuel injection
Front suspension . . . . Trailing link and monoshock
Rear suspension . . . . Swingarm and monoshock
Front brake . . . . Hydraulic disc
Rear brake . . . . Drum
Front tyre size 110/70-11
Rear tyre size 120/70-10
Overall length . . . . .1770 mm
Overall width . . . . .740 mm
Overall height . . . . .1140 mm
Wheelbase . . . . .1280 mm
Curb weight . . . . .114 ± 5 kg
Fuel tank capacity
    Total . . . . 8.3 litres
    Reserve . . . . 2.5 litres
Introduced
    S125/150ie 2009
    College model 2010

Servicing specifications and lubricants

Battery 12V-10Ah
Spark plug type
    125 engine . . . . NGK CR8EB
    150 engine . . . . NGK CR7EB
Spark plug electrode gap . . . . 0.7 to 0.8 mm
Idle speed . . . . .1700 to 1800 rpm
Front brake pad and rear drum brake shoe wear limit . . . . . 1.5 mm
Rear brake lever freeplay . . . . see Section 4
Throttle twistgrip freeplay . . . . 2 to 6 mm
Valve clearances (engine COLD)
    Inlet valve . . . . 0.10 mm
    Exhaust valve . . . . 0.15 mm
Fuel . . . . Petrol (unleaded) min 91 octane
Engine oil type . . SAE 5W-40 synthetic. API SL, ACEA A3, JASO MA
Engine oil capacity
    After draining . . . . approx 1.0 litre
    Dry fill capacity . . . . 1.1 litre
Gearbox oil . . . . SAE 80W-90 API GL3 gear oil
Gearbox oil capacity . . . . .100 ml
Brake fluid . . . . DOT 4

Torque settings

Engine oil drain plug . . . . 24 to 30 Nm
Gearbox oil drain plug . . . . 15 to 17 Nm
Spark plug . . . . 12 to 14 Nm

S125ie College

Service schedule – S125ie and S150ie (09-11)

Note: *Always perform the Pre-ride checks before every service interval – see the beginning of this Manual.*

	Text section in this Chapter	Every 3750 miles (6000 km) or 12 months	Every 7500 miles (12,000 km) or 2 years	Every 11,250 miles (18,000 km)	Every 15,000 miles (24,000 km)
Air filter – clean*	1	✔			
Battery – check	2	✔			
Brake pad and shoe – wear check	3	✔			
Brake system – check**	4	✔			
Cooling system – check	5		✔		
Crankcase breather – clean	6				✔
Drive belt and transmission – check	7	✔			
Drive belt and transmission – replace belt and variator components	7		✔		
Engine oil and filter – change	8	✔			
Fuel system – check	9		✔		
Gearbox oil level – check	10	✔			
Gearbox oil – change	10				✔
Headlight aim – check	11		✔		
Idle speed – check	12		✔		
Nuts and bolts – tightness check	13		✔		
Spark plug – check	14	✔			
Spark plug – replace	14		✔		
Stand(s) – check and lubricate	15	✔			
Speedometer cable and drive gear – lubricate	16		✔		
Steering head bearings – check	17		✔		
Suspension – check	18		✔		
Throttle – check and adjust	19		✔		
Valve clearances – check	20	**First check at 3750 miles (6000 km)**		✔	
Wheels and tyres – check	21	✔			

* Clean the air filter more often if the scooter is ridden in constantly wet or dusty conditions.
** The brake fluid must be changed every 2 years, irrespective of mileage.

S125ie and S150ie 3v – 2012-on

Model identification

Engine . . . .124.5/154.8 cc 3v single cylinder, air-cooled four-stroke
Gearbox . . . . Variable speed automatic, belt driven
Ignition . . . . Capacitor discharge ignition (CDI)
Fuel system . . . . .Fuel injection
Front suspension . . . . Trailing link and monoshock
Rear suspension . . . . .Swingarm and monoshock
Front brake . . . . Hydraulic disc
Rear brake . . . . .Drum
Front tyre size 110/70-11
Rear tyre size 120/70-10
Overall length . . . . .1770 mm
Overall width . . . . .740 mm
Overall height . . . . .1140 mm
Wheelbase . . . . .1280 mm
Curb weight . . . . .114 kg
Fuel tank capacity
    Total . . . . 8.2 litres
    Reserve . . . . 2.5 litres
Introduced 2012
    Engine number prefix (125) M669M
    Engine number prefix (150) M66AM
    Frame number prefix (125) RP8M66501
    Frame number prefix (150) RP8M66601

Servicing specifications and lubricants

Battery 12V-10Ah
Spark plug type . . . . NGK CR8EB
Spark plug electrode gap . . . . 0.7 to 0.8 mm
Idle speed . . . . 1700 to 1800 rpm
Front brake pad and rear drum brake shoe wear limit . . . . . 1.5 mm
Rear brake lever freeplay . . . . see Section 4
Throttle twistgrip freeplay . . . . 2 to 6 mm
Valve clearances (engine COLD)
    Inlet valve . . . . 0.08 mm
    Exhaust valve . . . . 0.08 mm
Fuel . . . . .Petrol (unleaded) min 95 octane
Engine oil type . . . . SAE 10W-40 synthetic-based. API SL, ACEA A3,
                                                           JASO MA, MA2
Engine oil capacity . . . . 1.34 litre
Gearbox oil . . . . SAE 80W-90 API GL4 gear oil
Gearbox oil capacity . . . . .200 ml
Brake fluid . . . . DOT 4

Torque settings

Engine oil drain plug . . . . 15 to 17 Nm
Engine oil filter cartridge . . . . 5 to 6 Nm
Gearbox oil filler plug . . . . 15 to 17 Nm
Spark plug . . . . 10 to 12 Nm

Service schedule – S125ie and S150ie 3v (2012-on)

Note: *Always perform the Pre-ride checks before every service interval – see the beginning of this Manual.*

	Text section in this Chapter	Every 3000 miles (5000 km) or 5 months	Every 6200 miles (10,000 km) or 10 months	Every 12,400 miles (20,000 km) or 20 months
Air filter – clean*	1		✔	
Battery – check	2	✔		
Brake pad and shoe – wear check	3	✔		
Brake system – check**	4	✔		
Cooling system – check	5	✔		
Crankcase breather – clean	6			✔
Drive belt 125 cc models	7		✔ Inspect	✔ Renew
Drive belt 150 cc models	7		✔ Renew	
Variator components	7		✔	
Engine oil and filter – change	8		✔	
Fuel system – check	9	✔		
Gearbox oil level – check	10		✔	
Headlight aim – check	11		✔	
Idle speed – check	12	✔		
Nuts and bolts – tightness check	13		✔	
Spark plug	14	✔ Inspect	✔ Renew	
Stands – check and lubricate	15	✔		
Speedometer cable and drive gear – lubricate	16		✔	
Steering head bearings – check	17		✔	
Suspension – check	18		✔	
Throttle – check and adjust	19		✔	
Valve clearances – check	20		✔	
Wheels and tyres – check	21	✔		

* *Clean the air filter more often if the scooter is ridden in constantly wet or dusty conditions. Fit a new filter element at 18,600 miles (30,000 km).*
** *The brake fluid must be changed every 2 years, irrespective of mileage.*

GTS125ie Super

Model identification

Engine . . . . 124cc 4v single cylinder, liquid-cooled, four-stroke
Gearbox . . . . Variable speed automatic, belt driven
Ignition . . . . Capacitor discharge ignition (CDI)
Fuel system . . . . Fuel injection
Front suspension . . . . Trailing link and monoshock
Rear suspension . . . . Swingarm and twin shock
Front brake . . . . Hydraulic disc
Rear brake . . . . Hydraulic disc
Front tyre size 120/70-12
Rear tyre size 130/70-12
Overall length . . . . 1930 mm
Overall width . . . . 755 mm
Overall height . . . . 1170 mm
Wheelbase . . . . 1370 mm
Curb weight . . . . 158 ± 5 kg
Fuel tank capacity
  Total . . . . 9.2 litres
  Reserve . . . . 2 litres
Introduced 2009

Servicing specifications and lubricants

Battery 12V-12Ah
Spark plug type . . . . NGK CR8EKB
Spark plug electrode gap . . . . 0.7 to 0.8 mm
Idle speed . . . . 1700 to 1800 rpm
Brake pad wear limit . . . . 1.5 mm
Throttle twistgrip freeplay . . . . 2 to 6 mm
Valve clearances (engine COLD)
  Inlet valves . . . . 0.10 mm
  Exhaust valves . . . . 0.15 mm
Fuel . . . . Petrol (unleaded) min 91 octane
Engine oil type . . SAE 5W-40 synthetic. API SL, ACEA A3, JASO MA
Engine oil capacity . . . . approx 1.3 litre
Gearbox oil . . . . SAE 80W-90 API GL3 gear oil
Gearbox oil capacity . . . . 250 ml
Coolant type . . . . Pre-mix coolant, or 50/50 distilled water
              and corrosion-inhibited ethylene glycol anti-freeze
Cooling system capacity . . . . 2.1 to 2.15 litre
Brake fluid . . . . DOT 4

Torque settings

Engine oil drain plug . . . . 24 to 30 Nm
Gearbox oil drain plug . . . . 15 to 17 Nm
Spark plug . . . . 12 to 14 Nm

Service schedule – GTS125ie Super

Note: *Always perform the Pre-ride checks before every service interval – see the beginning of this Manual.*

	Text section in this Chapter	Every 3000 miles (5000 km)	Every 6000 miles (10,000 km) or 12 months	Every 9000 miles (15,000 km) or 2 years	Every 15,000 miles (20,000 km) or 2 years
Air filter – clean*	1		✔		
Battery – check	2		✔		
Brake pad – wear check	3	✔			
Brake system – check**	4		✔		
Cooling system – check***	5		✔		
Crankcase breather – check	6				✔
Drive belt – check	7		✔		
Drive belt – replace	7			✔	
Engine oil and filter – change	8		✔		
Fuel system – check	9		✔		
Gearbox oil level – check	10		✔		
Gearbox oil – change	10				✔
Headlight aim – check	11			✔	
Idle speed – check	12		✔		
Nuts and bolts – tightness check	13		✔		
Spark plug – replace	14		✔		
Stand(s) – check and lubricate	15		✔		
Speedometer cable and drive gear – lubricate	16		✔		
Steering head bearings – check	17		✔		
Suspension – check	18		✔		
Throttle – check and adjust	19		✔		
Transmission case filter – clean	1		✔		
Valve clearances – check	20		**After first 6000 miles (10,000 km)**		✔
Variator rollers and ramp guides – replace	7		✔		
Wheels and tyres – check	21	✔			

* Clean the air filter more often if the scooter is ridden in constantly wet or dusty conditions.
** The brake fluid must be changed every 2 years, irrespective of mileage.
*** Drain and refill with fresh coolant every 2 years, irrespective of mileage

GTS250ie

Model identification

Engine	244.3cc 4v single cylinder, liquid-cooled four-stroke
Gearbox	Variable speed automatic, belt driven
Ignition	Capacitor discharge ignition (CDI)
Fuel system	Fuel injection
Front suspension	Trailing link and monoshock
Rear suspension	Swingarm and twin shock
Front brake	Hydraulic disc
Rear brake	Hydraulic disc
Front tyre size	120/70-12
Rear tyre size	130/70-12
Overall length	1930 mm
Overall width	755 mm
Saddle height	800 mm
Wheelbase	1370 mm
Curb weight	151 ± 5 kg

Fuel tank capacity

Total	9.2 litres
Reserve	2 litres
Introduced	2005

Servicing specifications and lubricants

Battery	12V-12Ah
Spark plug type	Champion RG4PHP
Spark plug electrode gap	0.7 to 0.8 mm
Idle speed	1600 to 1700 rpm
Brake pad wear limit	1.5 mm
Throttle twistgrip freeplay	2 to 6 mm

Valve clearances (engine COLD)

Intake valves	0.10 mm
Exhaust valves	0.15 mm
Fuel	Petrol (unleaded) min 91 octane
Engine oil type	SAE 5W-40 synthetic. API SL, ACEA A3, JASO MA
Engine oil capacity	approx 1.3 litre
Gearbox oil	SAE 80W-90 API GL3 gear oil
Gearbox oil capacity	250 ml
Coolant type	Pre-mix coolant, or 50/50 distilled water and corrosion-inhibited ethylene glycol anti-freeze
Cooling system capacity	2.1 to 2.15 litre
Brake fluid	DOT 4

Torque settings

Engine oil drain plug	24 to 30 Nm
Gearbox oil drain plug	15 to 17 Nm
Spark plug	12 to 14 Nm

Service schedule – GTS250ie

Note: *Always perform the Pre-ride checks before every service interval – see the beginning of this Manual.*

	Text section in this Chapter	Every 3000 miles (5000 km)	Every 6000 miles (10,000 km) or 12 months	Every 9000 miles (15,000 km) or 2 years	Every 15,000 miles (20,000 km) or 2 years
Air filter – clean*	1		✔		
Battery – check	2		✔		
Brake pad – wear check	3	✔			
Brake system – check**	4		✔		
Cooling system – check***	5		✔		
Crankcase breather – check	6				✔
Drive belt – replace	7			✔	
Engine oil and filter – change	8		✔		
Fuel system – check	9		✔		
Gearbox oil level – check	10		✔		
Gearbox oil – change	10				✔
Headlight aim – check	11			✔	
Idle speed – check	12		✔		
Nuts and bolts – tightness check	13		✔		
Spark plug – replace	14		✔		
Stand(s) – check and lubricate	15		✔		
Speedometer cable and drive gear – lubricate	16		✔		
Steering head bearings – check	17		✔		
Suspension – check	18		✔		
Throttle – check and adjust	19		✔		
Transmission case air filter – clean	1		✔		
Transmission – check	7		✔		
Valve clearances – check	20				✔
Variator rollers and ramp guides – replace	7		✔		
Wheels and tyres – check	21	✔			

* Clean the air filter more often if the scooter is ridden in constantly wet or dusty conditions.
** The brake fluid must be changed every 2 years, irrespective of mileage.
*** Drain and refill with fresh coolant every 2 years, irrespective of mileage

GTV250ie and GT250 60°

Model identification

Engine . . . . 244.3cc 4v single cylinder, liquid-cooled, four-stroke
Gearbox . . . . Variable speed automatic, belt driven
Ignition . . . . Capacitor discharge ignition (CDI)
Fuel system . . . . Fuel injection
Front suspension . . . . Trailing link and monoshock
Rear suspension . . . . Swingarm and twin shock
Front brake . . . . Hydraulic disc
Rear brake . . . . Hydraulic disc
Front tyre size 120/70-12
Rear tyre size 130/70-12
Overall length . . . . 1930 mm
Overall width . . . . 770 mm
Overall height . . . . 1170 mm
Saddle height . . . . 800 mm
Wheelbase . . . . 1370 mm
Curb weight . . . . 146 ± 5 kg
Fuel tank capacity
   Total . . . . 9.2 litres
   Reserve . . . . 2 litres
Introduced
   GTV250ie 2007
   GTV250ie Navy 2009
   GT250ie 60° Anniversary model 2008

Servicing specifications and lubricants

Battery 12V-12Ah
Spark plug type . . . . Champion RG4PHP
Spark plug electrode gap . . . . 0.7 to 0.8 mm
Idle speed . . . . 1600 to 1800 rpm
Brake pad wear limit . . . . 1.5 mm
Throttle twistgrip freeplay . . . . 2 to 6 mm
Valve clearances (engine COLD)
   Intake valves . . . . 0.10 mm
   Exhaust valves . . . . 0.15 mm
Fuel . . . . Petrol (unleaded) min 91 octane
Engine oil type . . SAE 5W-40 synthetic. API SL, ACEA A3, JASO MA
Engine oil capacity . . . . approx 1.3 litre
Gearbox oil . . . . SAE 80W-90 API GL3 gear oil
Gearbox oil capacity . . . . 250 ml
Coolant type . . . . Pre-mix coolant, or 50/50 distilled water
          and corrosion-inhibited ethylene glycol anti-freeze
Cooling system capacity . . . . 2.1 to 2.15 litre
Brake fluid . . . . DOT 4

Torque settings

Engine oil drain plug . . . . 24 to 30 Nm
Gearbox oil drain plug . . . . 15 to 17 Nm
Spark plug . . . . 12 to 14 Nm

Service schedule – GTV250ie and GT250 60°

Note: *Always perform the Pre-ride checks before every service interval – see the beginning of this Manual.*

	Text section in this Chapter	Every 3000 miles (5000 km)	Every 6000 miles (10,000 km) or 12 months	Every 9000 miles (15,000 km) or 2 years	Every 15,000 miles (20,000 km) or 2 years
Air filter – clean*	1		✔		
Battery – check	2		✔		
Brake pad – wear check	3	✔			
Brake system – check**	4		✔		
Cooling system – check***	5		✔		
Crankcase breather – check	6				✔
Drive belt – replace	7			✔	
Engine oil and filter – change	8		✔		
Fuel system – check	9		✔		
Gearbox oil level – check	10		✔		
Gearbox oil – change	10				✔
Headlight aim – check	11			✔	
Idle speed – check	12		✔		
Nuts and bolts – tightness check	13		✔		
Spark plug – replace	14		✔		
Stand(s) – check and lubricate	15		✔		
Speedometer cable and drive gear – lubricate	16		✔		
Steering head bearings – check	17		✔		
Suspension – check	18		✔		
Throttle – check and adjust	19		✔		
Transmission case air filter – clean	1		✔		
Transmission – check	7		✔		
Valve clearances – check	20				✔
Variator rollers and ramp guides – replace	7		✔		
Wheels and tyres – check	21	✔			

* Clean the air filter more often if the scooter is ridden in constantly wet or dusty conditions.
** The brake fluid must be changed every 2 years, irrespective of mileage.
*** Drain and refill with fresh coolant every 2 years, irrespective of mileage

GTS300ie

GTS300ie Super and GTV300ie

Model identification

Engine . . . . 278.3cc 4v single cylinder, liquid-cooled, four-stroke
Gearbox. . . . . Variable speed automatic, belt driven
Ignition. Capacitor discharge ignition (CDI)
Fuel system. . . . . .Fuel injection
Front suspension . . . . Trailing link and monoshock
Rear suspension. . . . . Swingarm and twin shock
Front brake . . . . .Hydraulic disc
Rear brake. . . . . .Hydraulic disc
Front tyre size. 120/70-12
Rear tyre size 130/70-12
Overall length . . . . 2230 mm (GTS), 1930 mm (GTV)
Overall width. . . . . 755 mm (GTS), 770 mm (GTV)
Overall height (GTS) . . . . .1170 mm
Saddle height (GTV) . . . . .800 mm
Wheelbase. . . . . .1370 mm
Curb weight. . . . . .158 ± 5 kg
Fuel tank capacity
   Total . . . . 9.2 litres
   Reserve . . . . 2 litres
Introduced
   GTS300ie Super 2008
   GTS300ie Super Sport 2010
   GTV300ie 2010

Servicing specifications and lubricants

Battery. 12V-12Ah
Spark plug type. . . . . NGK CR8EKB
Spark plug electrode gap . . . . 0.7 to 0.8 mm
Idle speed . . . . 1600 to 1700 rpm
Brake pad wear limit . . . . 1.5 mm
Throttle twistgrip freeplay . . . . 2 to 6 mm
Valve clearances (engine COLD)
   Intake valves . . . . 0.10 mm
   Exhaust valves . . . . 0.15 mm
Fuel . . . . Petrol (unleaded) min 91 octane
Engine oil type . . SAE 5W-40 synthetic. API SL, ACEA A3, JASO MA
Engine oil capacity. approx 1.3 litre
Gearbox oil . . . . SAE 80W-90 API GL3 gear oil
Gearbox oil capacity . . . . .250 ml
Coolant type . . . . Pre-mix coolant, or 50/50 distilled water
      and corrosion-inhibited ethylene glycol anti-freeze
Cooling system capacity . . . . 2.1 to 2.15 litre
Brake fluid. . . . . DOT 4

Torque settings

Engine oil drain plug. . . . . 24 to 30 Nm
Gearbox oil drain plug . . . . 15 to 17 Nm
Spark plug. . . . . 12 to 14 Nm

GTV300ie

Service schedule – GTS300ie Super and GTV300ie

Note: *Always perform the Pre-ride checks before every service interval – see the beginning of this Manual.*

	Text section in this Chapter	Every 3000 miles (5000 km)	Every 6000 miles (10,000 km) or 12 months	Every 9000 miles (15,000 km) or 2 years	Every 15,000 miles (20,000 km) or 2 years
Air filter – clean*	1		✔		
Battery – check	2		✔		
Brake pad – wear check	3	✔			
Brake system – check**	4		✔		
Cooling system – check***	5		✔		
Crankcase breather – check	6				✔
Drive belt – replace	7			✔	
Engine oil and filter – change	8		✔		
Fuel system – check	9		✔		
Gearbox oil level – check	10		✔		
Gearbox oil – change	10				✔
Headlight aim – check	11			✔	
Idle speed – check	12		✔		
Nuts and bolts – tightness check	13		✔		
Spark plug – replace	14		✔		
Stand(s) – check and lubricate	15		✔		
Speedometer cable and drive gear – lubricate	16		✔		
Steering head bearings – check	17		✔		
Suspension – check	18		✔		
Throttle – check and adjust	19		✔		
Transmission case air filter – clean	1		✔		
Transmission – check	7		✔		
Valve clearances – check	20				✔
Variator rollers and ramp guides – replace	7		✔		
Wheels and tyres – check	21	✔			

* Clean the air filter more often if the scooter is ridden in constantly wet or dusty conditions.
** The brake fluid must be changed every 2 years, irrespective of mileage.
*** Drain and refill with fresh coolant every 2 years, irrespective of mileage

Note: *Refer to the model specifications at the beginning of this Chapter for service intervals*

1 Air filters

Engine air filter

1 Remove the left-hand side panel and the storage compartment (see Chapter 9).

2 Where fitted, release the cable-tie securing the intake hose to the air filter cover and disconnect the hose **(see illustrations)**. Locate either one or two cover screws with knurled heads accessed from inside the bodywork, then undo the cover screws and remove the cover **(see illustrations)**.

3 Remove the filter element, noting how it fits. Two types of filter element are used, paper or foam. Undo the screws securing the paper element assembly and lift it out **(see illustrations)**. Lift the foam element out from the cover **(see illustration)**. Follow the appropriate procedure to clean the element.

Foam element

4 Wash the element in hot soapy water, then rinse out the soap. Gently squeeze out the excess water – DO NOT wring it out – then dry the element with an absorbent towel, and short blasts of compressed air if available.

5 When dry, soak the element in a 50/50 mixture of air filter oil and petrol (gasoline) – air filter oil is available from dealers and should be used instead of any other oil as it is specially formulated with adhesive properties to retain dust and other particles. Gently squeeze out any excess liquid, then allow the element to drip-dry for a while.

Paper element

6 Tap the filter on a hard surface to dislodge any dirt. If available, use low pressure compressed air directed from the inside. If the element is damaged or extremely dirty, fit a new one.

Both types of element

7 Clean the inside of the filter housing and the cover. If necessary remove the drain hole cap(s) and clean out any deposits. Make sure the rubber sealing ring is in good condition and properly seated – replace it with a new if damaged, deformed or deteriorated.

8 Fit the filter element, making sure it is properly seated **(see illustrations 1.3c, or b and a)**.

9 Fit the filter cover and secure it with its screws **(see illustrations 1.2d, c and b)**.

10 Connect the intake hose and secure it with a new cable tie.

11 Install the storage compartment and left-hand side panel (see Chapter 9).

⚠️ *Warning: Petrol is extremely flammable, so take extra precautions when you work on any part of the fuel system. Don't smoke or allow open flames or bare light bulbs near the work area, and don't work in a garage where a natural gas-type appliance is present. If you spill any fuel on your skin, rinse it off immediately with soap and water. When you perform any kind of work on the fuel system, wear safety glasses and have a fire extinguisher suitable for a Class B type fire (flammable liquids) on hand.*

Transmission case air filter – GTS, GTV and GT models

12 On 125 and 150 models remove the outer trans- mission cover.

1.2a Release the cable-tie (arrowed)

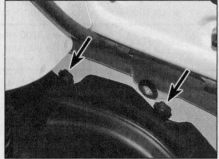

1.2b Undo the two knurled screws (arrowed) from inside the bodywork

1.2c Undo the cover screws . . .

1.2d . . . and remove the cover

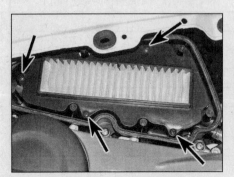

1.3a Undo the screws (arrowed) . . .

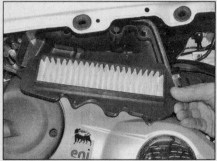

1.3b . . . and lift out the paper element

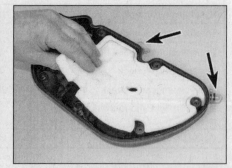

1.3c Remove the foam filter element from the cover. Note the drain hole caps (arrowed)

1.13 Remove the filler cap . . .

1.14 . . . then undo the screws and remove the cover . . .

1.15 . . . then remove the filter

13 On 250 and 300 models remove the oil filler cap/dipstick **(see illustration)**.

14 Undo the filter cover screws and remove the cover **(see illustration)**.

15 Remove the filter, noting how it fits **(see illustration)**.

16 Clean the filter (see Step 4). Check the condition of the filter and replace it with a new one if damaged, deformed or deteriorated.

17 Install the new or cleaned filter in a reverse of the removal procedure.

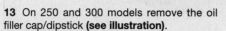

2 Battery

Caution: Be extremely careful when handling or working around the battery. The electrolyte is very caustic and an explosive gas (hydrogen) is given off when the battery is charging.

Note: A maintenance free (MF) battery is fitted as standard on all models.

1 Refer to Chapter 10, Section 3, for access to the battery.

2 Check the battery terminals and leads are tight and clean. If corrosion is evident, clean the terminals and lead ends with a wire brush or knife and emery paper. Apply a thin coat of petroleum jelly (Vaseline) or a dedicated battery terminal spray to the connections to slow further corrosion.

3 If the machine is not in regular use, disconnect the battery and give it a refresher charge every month to six weeks (see Chapter 10).

4 The condition of the battery can be assessed by measuring its specific gravity and open-circuit voltage (see Chapter 10).

5 Do not attempt to remove the battery cap(s) to check the electrolyte level or battery specific gravity. Removal will damage the cap(s), resulting in electrolyte leakage and battery damage.

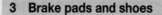

3 Brake pads and shoes

Note: All models are fitted with an hydraulic disc brake at the front. At the rear LX, LXV and S models have a drum brake, and GTS, GTV and GT models have an hydraulic disc brake. The right-hand brake lever operates the front brake. The left-hand brake lever operates the rear brake.

Disc brake pad wear check

1 Some brake pads have wear indicators, either in the form of cut-outs in the face of the friction material, or in the form of a groove in the side of the friction material **(see illustration)**. The wear indicators should be plainly visible by looking at the edges of the friction material from the best vantage point, but note that an accumulation of road dirt and brake dust could make them difficult to see.

2 If the indicators aren't present or visible, then the amount of friction material remaining should be, and it will be obvious when the pads need replacing. Vespa specify a minimum thickness of 1.5 mm for the friction material, and anything less than 1 mm is critical **(see illustration)**. On twin piston calipers also check that the pads are wearing evenly – uneven wear is indicative of a sticking piston, in which case the caliper should be overhauled (see Chapter 8). On all models Vespa specify that if there is a difference of more than 0.5 mm in the thickness across the friction material new pads should be installed.

3 If the pads are dirty or if you are in doubt as to the amount of friction material remaining, remove them for inspection (see Chapter 8). If the pads are excessively worn, check the brake discs (see Chapter 8).

4 If the pads are worn to or beyond the wear indicator (i.e. the bottom of the cut-out or the beginning of the groove) or to the minimum thickness specified, they must be replaced with new ones, though it is advisable to fit new pads before they become this worn.

5 Refer to Chapter 8 for details of pad removal and installation.

Drum brake shoe and drum wear check

6 Make sure the amount of rear brake lever freeplay is correct (see Section 4).

7 As the brake shoes wear and the freeplay is adjusted to compensate, the wear indicator on the brake arm moves closer to the wear limit line, which is the lower of the two lines on the casing.

8 Have an assistant apply the brake, or tie the lever to the handlebar so the brake is applied, and check the position of the wear indicator on the arm in relation to the lower line on the casing **(see illustration)**. If the indicator has reached the line replace the brake shoes with new ones (see Chapter 8).

9 With the wheel removed check the condition of the drum lining (see Chapter 8).

3.1 Front brake pad wear indicator cut-out (arrowed) – GTS, GTV and GT models

3.2 If necessary measure the amount of friction material remaining

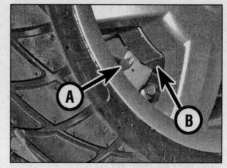

3.8 Drum brake shoe wear indicator (A) and limit line (B)

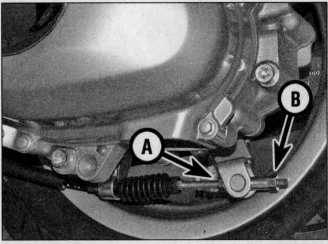

4.8 To adjust lever freeplay slacken the locknut (A) and turn the adjuster nut (B) as required

4.11 Check the banjo union (arrowed) at each end of the hose

4 Brake system

Note: *All models are fitted with an hydraulic disc brake at the front. At the rear LX, LXV and S models have a drum brake, and GTS, GTV and GT models have an hydraulic disc brake. The right-hand brake lever operates the front brake. The left-hand brake lever operates the rear brake.*

1 A routine check of the brake system will ensure that any problems are discovered and remedied before the rider's safety is jeopardised.
2 Make sure all brake fasteners, including the reservoir cover screws, brake hose banjo bolts and caliper mounting bolts, are tight.
3 Make sure the brake light operates when each brake lever is pulled in. The brake light switches are not adjustable. If they fail to operate properly, check them (see Chapter 10).

Brake levers

4 Check the brake levers for looseness, rough action, excessive play and other damage. Replace any worn or damaged parts with new ones (see Chapter 7).
5 The lever pivots should be lubricated periodically to reduce wear and ensure safe and trouble-free operation. Vespa recommend a calcium complex soap-based grease with NLGI 2 and ISO-L-XBCIB2 ratings, which is available as an aerosol spray.
6 In order for the lubricant to be applied where it will do the most good, the lever should be removed (see Chapter 7). However, if an aerosol lubricant is being used, it can be applied to the pivot joint gaps and will usually work its way into the areas where friction occurs. If motor oil or light grease is being used, apply it sparingly as it may attract dirt (which could cause the controls to bind or wear at an accelerated rate). **Note:** *One of the*

best lubricants for the control lever pivots is a dry-film lubricant.
7 Where disc brakes are fitted, if the lever action is spongy (i.e. the lever does not come up hard and can travel all the way to the handlebar, first check the fluid level (see *Pre-ride checks*), then bleed the brakes (see Chapter 8).
8 Where a rear drum brake is fitted check the amount of free travel in the left-hand brake lever before the brake comes on – it should be about 1/3 of the distance between the end of the lever and the handlebar, but you may prefer slightly less. Make sure freeplay is not excessive to ensure efficient braking, and also that there is not too little – the wheel must spin freely with the lever at rest. To adjust the amount of free travel slacken the locknut where the cable goes through the arm on the drum, and turn the adjuster nut as required until the freeplay is correct – to reduce freeplay in the lever, turn the nut clockwise; to increase freeplay, turn the nut anti-clockwise **(see illustration)**. Make sure the adjuster nut is set so its cut-out seats around the pivot bush in the arm. After adjustment turn the rear wheel and check that there is no brake drag. Don't forget to tighten the locknut.

Disc brakes

Brake hoses

Note: *For a complete check of all brake hose and pipe connections, especially on models with a rear disc brake, remove the body covers and panels as required according to model for access (see Chapter 9).*
9 Twist and flex each hose looking for cracks, bulges and seeping fluid. Check extra carefully where the hose connects to the banjo fittings as this is a common area for hose failure.
10 Inspect the banjo fittings; if they are rusted, cracked or damaged, fit new hoses.
11 Inspect the banjo union connections for leaking fluid **(see illustration)**. If they leak when tightened securely, refer to Chapter 8 and fit new sealing washers, then bleed the system.

12 Flexible hydraulic hoses will deteriorate with age and should be replaced with new ones every three years or so regardless of their apparent condition (see Chapter 8).

Brake fluid

13 The fluid level in the master cylinder reservoir(s) should be checked before riding the machine (see *Pre-ride checks*).
14 Brake fluid will degrade over a period of time. Vespa recommends that it should be changed every 2 years, or whenever a new master cylinder or caliper is fitted. Refer to the brake bleeding and fluid change section in Chapter 8.

Brake caliper and master cylinder seals

15 Brake system seals will deteriorate over a period of time and lose their effectiveness. Old master cylinder seals will cause sticky operation of the brake lever; old caliper seals will cause the pistons to stick, and both could cause fluid to leak out.
16 Check the brake master cylinder(s) and caliper(s) for improper action and signs of leaking fluid.
17 Unfortunately caliper and master cylinder rebuild kits are not available from Vespa, so if problems are found a new caliper or master cylinder must be fitted (see Chapter 8).

Drum brakes

Brake cable

18 The rear wheel should spin freely when the brake lever is not activated. If the brake is binding without the handlebar lever being pulled, first check that the lever is moving freely, and that there is the correct amount of freeplay (see Steps 4 to 6, and 8).
19 Disconnect the cable from the left-hand brake lever and the arm on the brake drum (see Chapter 8). Check that the inner cable slides smoothly in the outer cable. If the action is stiff, inspect along the length of the outer cable for splits and kinks, and the ends of the

inner cable for frays, and replace it with a new one if necessary (see Chapter 8).

20 If there are no signs of damage, lubricate the cable (see Steps 21 and 22). If the cable is still stiff after lubrication, replace it with a new one (see Chapter 8).

21 The cable should be lubricated periodically to ensure safe and trouble-free operation. Vespa recommend engine oil, but dedicated cable lubricants in aerosol form are available and are much easier to apply using a pressure adapter, available cheaply from dealers.

22 To lubricate the cable, disconnect it from the lever. If using engine oil suspend the cable upright and drip feed oil from a can into the gap between the inner and outer cables, allowing it time to run down the length of the cable – using warm oil will make the task much easier. If using a spray lubricant and adapter, follow the procedure shown (see illustrations).

23 Reconnect the cable and adjust the freeplay (see Step 8).

24 If the handlebar lever and brake cables are in good condition but there is binding, check the operation of the brake cam (see below).

Brake cam

25 To check the operation of the brake cam, first disconnect the cable from the brake arm (see illustration). Note the fitting of the bush in the arm and the cable return spring where fitted, and make sure the spring is not deformed.

26 Apply the brake using hand pressure on the arm and ensure that the arm returns to the rest position when it is released. If the brake arm is binding in the backplate, follow the procedure in Chapter 8 to remove the brake shoes and inspect the brake cam and the springs on the brake shoes.

27 Apply some copper grease to the bearing surfaces of the cam and its shaft before reassembly. Adjust the freeplay on completion (see Step 8).

Caution: Do not apply too much grease otherwise there is a risk of it contaminating the brake drum and shoe linings.

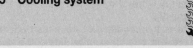

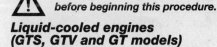

5 Cooling system

⚠️ *Warning: The engine must be cool before beginning this procedure.*

Liquid-cooled engines (GTS, GTV and GT models)

1 Check the coolant level (see *Pre-ride checks*).

2 Remove the right-hand side panel, the kick panel and the floor panel to expose the radiators and the coolant hoses between them and the engine (see Chapters 4 and 9).

3 Check the entire cooling system for evidence of leaks. Examine each coolant hose along its entire length – squeeze the hoses at various points and look for cracks, abrasions and other damage (see illustrations). The hoses should feel firm, yet pliable, and return to their original shape when released. If they

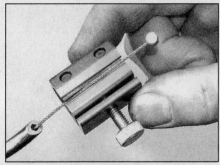

4.22a Fit the cable into the adapter . . .

4.22c . . . then apply the lubricant using the nozzle provided inserted in the hole in the adapter

are hard or perished, replace them with new ones (see Chapter 4).

4 Check each cooling system joint. Ensure that the hoses are pushed fully onto their unions and that the hose clips are tight (see illustration).

5.3a Check the radiators and all cooling system hoses as described . . .

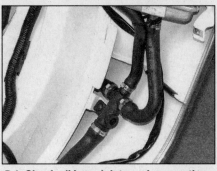

5.4 Check all hose joints and connections

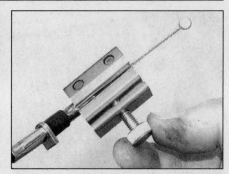

4.22b . . . and tighten the screw to seal it in . . .

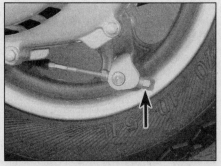

4.25 Fully unscrew the nut (arrowed) and draw the cable out

5 Check the drain spigot in the underside of the alternator cover for evidence of leakage – the spigot drains any coolant should the pump mechanical seal fail (see illustration). If there is evidence of leakage replace the mechanical

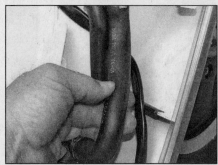

5.3b . . . and squeeze the hoses to check their condition

5.5 Check the drain spigot (arrowed) for leakage

5.7 Straighten any fins that are bent

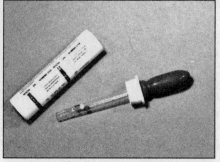

5.9 An anti-freeze hydrometer can be used to check coolant strength

seal with a new one, if there is evidence of oil leakage replace the oil seal with a new one, and if there is a milky emulsion leakage replace both seals with new ones (see Chapter 4).
6 Check the radiators for leaks and other damage. Leaks in the radiator leave tell-tale scale deposits or coolant stains on the outside of the core below the leak. If leaks are noted, remove the radiator (see Chapter 4) and have it repaired or replace it with a new one.
Caution: Do not use a liquid leak stopping compound to try to repair leaks.
7 Inspect the radiator fins for mud, dirt and insects which will impede the flow of air through the radiator. If the fins are dirty, remove the radiator (see Chapter 4) and clean it using water or low pressure compressed air directed through the fins from the back. If the fins are bent or distorted, straighten them carefully with a screwdriver **(see illustration)**. If airflow is restricted by bent or damaged fins

over more than 30% of the radiator's surface area, fit a new radiator.
8 Check the condition of the coolant in the reservoir. If it is rust-coloured or if accumulations of scale are visible, drain, flush and refill the system with new coolant (see Chapter 4). **Note:** *Vespa recommend draining and refilling the cooling system with fresh coolant every 2 years.*
9 Check the antifreeze content of the coolant with an antifreeze hydrometer **(see illustration)**. Sometimes coolant looks like it's in good condition, but is too weak to offer adequate protection. If the hydrometer indicates a weak mixture, drain, flush and refill the system (see Chapter 4).
10 Start the engine and let it reach normal operating temperature, then check for leaks again.
11 If the coolant level consistently drops or overheating occurs, and no evidence of leaks

can be found, replace the reservoir cap with a new one. If this fails to cure the problem have the system pressure-checked by a dealer.

Air-cooled engines (LX, LXV and S models)

12 On air-cooled models a fan mounted on the right-hand side of the engine forces air into the cowling fitted around the cylinder head and block.
13 Check that the air intake in the fan cover is unobstructed and that the cover and cowling sections are correctly fitted together and secure **(see illustration)**. If any sections are missing the engine will not be cooled adequately.
14 Remove the fan cover (see Chapter 2A or 2B) and check the fan. If any of the vanes are broken replace the fan with a new one. On machines with the fan mounted directly onto the alternator rotor, make sure the fan screws are tight **(see illustration)**. Alternatively, check that the fan centre nut is tight **(see illustration)**.
15 Remove the left-hand side panel and trim panel (see Chapter 9).
16 Where fitted, release the cable tie securing the air intake hose to the transmission cooling cover and disconnect the hose **(see illustration)**. Undo the screws securing the cover and remove it, noting the location of the seal **(see illustration)**. Check that the cover and air intake hose are free of obstructions. If necessary, fit a new cover seal on installation.

6 Crankcase breather

Caution: If the machine is continually ridden in wet conditions or at full throttle, the crankcase breather should be drained more frequently. It should also be checked after washing the scooter, or if it has fallen over.

1 Remove the storage compartment (see Chapter 9).
2 Check the condition of the hose between the breather chamber on the side of the valve cover on the engine and the air filter housing

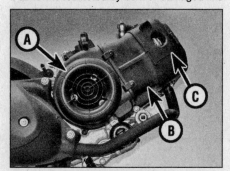

5.13 Fan cover (A) and engine cowling sections (B) and (C)

5.14a Check the fan for broken vanes and make sure the screws (arrowed) are tight

5.14b Check that the centre nut is tight

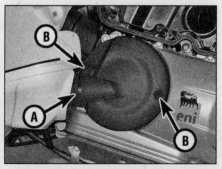

5.16a Air hose tie (A) and cooling cover screws (B)

5.16b Location of cover seal

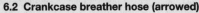

6.2 Crankcase breather hose (arrowed)

7.1 Check the condition of the belt . . .

(see illustration). Make sure it is secure on its union at each end, and there are no cracks, splits or kinks in the hose. Replace the hose with a new one if necessary .

3 Check the drain hole cap(s) on the underside of the air filter cover for deposits. If necessary remove the cap(s) and allow any deposits to drain from the air filter housing.

4 From time to time remove the breather chamber from the valve cover and clean it out (see Chapter 2A, 2B or 2C).

7 Drive belt and variator

Drive belt

1 Remove the drive belt cover (see Chapter 3). Check along the entire length of the belt for cracks, splits, frays and damaged teeth and replace the belt with a new one if any damage is found **(see illustration)**.

2 The edges of the belt will gradually wear away – black dust inside the casing is evidence of belt wear. On 250 and 300 models a minimum of 19.5 mm is specified for the width of the outer face of the belt – measure the width **(see illustration)**. On 125 and 150 models no specification is given, but you could check with your dealer.

3 If the drive belt has worn below the limit, has fraying or is cracked, or is contaminated with oil or grease, it must be replaced with a new one (see Chapter 3). **Note:** *If there is any doubt about the condition of the drive belt, replace it with a new one just in case – a broken belt could cause severe damage to engine or gearbox components. The belt must be renewed at the specified mileage interval, irrespective of condition.*

4 In the event of premature belt wear, the cause should be investigated (see Chapter 3).

5 Oil or grease inside the casing is evidence that a crankshaft, gearbox shaft or clutch assembly seal has failed. Trace the source of the leak and fit a new seal.

6 Clean any dust from inside the casing before installing the drive belt cover.

Variator rollers and ramp guides

7 Refer to Chapter 3, Section 3, and remove the drive pulley and variator components. Check the rollers and ramp guides and replace them with new ones if necessary, or at the specified interval.

8 Engine oil and filter/strainer

⚠ *Warning: Be careful when draining the oil, as the exhaust pipe, the engine, and the oil itself can cause severe burns. To avoid getting oil over your hands it is best to wear some disposable latex or nitrile gloves, cheaply available from most chemists and hardware stores.*

1 Consistent routine oil changes are the single most important maintenance procedure you can perform. The oil not only lubricates the internal parts of the engine, but it also acts as a coolant, a cleaner, a sealant, and a protector. Because of these demands, the oil takes a terrific amount of abuse and should be replaced often with new oil of the recommended grade and type. Saving a little money on the difference in cost between a good oil and a cheap oil won't pay off if the engine is damaged.

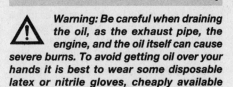

8.2 Oil drain plug (arrowed)

7.2 . . . and measure its width as shown

Caution: Do not run the engine in an enclosed space such as a garage or workshop.

2 Before changing the oil, warm up the engine so the oil will drain easily. Stop the engine and turn the ignition OFF, and wait for a few minutes to allow the oil to drain to the bottom of the engine. Support the scooter on its centrestand, and position a clean drain tray under the oil drain plug on the right-hand side of the engine **(see illustration)** – because the centrestand makes it difficult to position a tray directly below the drain hole it is advisable to make a chute for the oil (see *Tool Tip*).

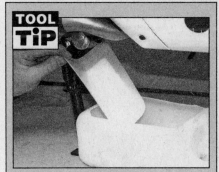

TOOL TIP

A chute can be cut out of the side of an old oil container, or any plastic container, and the container itself can then act as the drain tray.

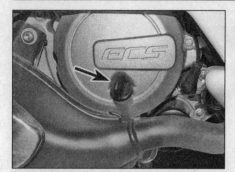

8.3a Oil filler cap (arrowed) is on the right-hand side on GTS125i.e. models . . .

8.3b . . . and on LX, LXV and S 3-valve models . . .

8.3c . . . and on the left-hand side on all other models

8.4a Unscrew the oil drain plug . . .

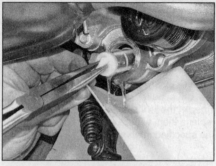

8.4b . . . withdraw the strainer, and allow the oil to completely drain

3 Unscrew the oil filler cap to vent the crankcase and to act as a reminder that there is no oil in the engine **(see illustrations)**.

4 Unscrew the oil drain plug and remove the strainer, and allow the oil to flow into the drain tray **(see illustrations)**. Check the condition of the O-rings on the drain plug and strainer and replace them with new ones if they are in any way damaged or deformed – it is a good idea to use new ones whatever their apparent condition.

5 Unscrew the filter using a large flat-bladed screwdriver, filter pliers, or a filter removing

strap or a chain-wrench, and tip any residual oil into the drain tray **(see illustrations)**. If access to the filter is restricted by the exhaust system (this will depend on model, type of exhaust and the tools available to you), remove the exhaust (see Chapter 5).

6 Clean the strainer in solvent and remove any debris caught in the mesh. Check the mesh for splits or holes and replace it with a new one if necessary.

7 When the oil has completely drained, fit a new O-ring into the groove in the end of the strainer if required, then fit the strainer into the engine with the O-ring innermost **(see illustrations)**. Fit a new O-ring onto the drain plug if required, then fit the plug and tighten it to the torque setting given under the specifications for your model earlier in this Chapter **(see illustrations)**. Do not overtighten the plug as damage to the threads will result.

8 Smear clean engine oil onto the rubber seal on the new filter and thread it onto the engine,

8.5a Unscrew the filter . . .

8.5b . . . and tip any residual oil out

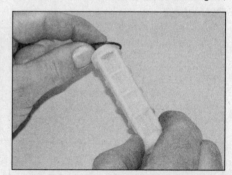

8.7a Fit the O-ring onto the strainer . . .

8.7b . . . then insert the strainer

8.7c Fit the O-ring onto the drain plug . . .

8.7d . . . and tighten it to the specified torque

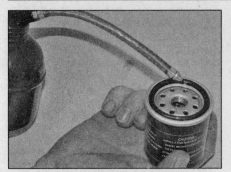

8.8a Smear clean oil onto the filter seal . . .

8.8b . . . and thread it onto the engine

9.2 Check the fuel hose connection(s) to the throttle body (arrowed) and to the tank

tightening it by hand as much as possible, then nipping it up a bit tighter using a bar or screwdriver between the ribs on the end of the filter (but take care not to damage or distort them) **(see illustrations and 8.5a)**. **Note:** *Do not use a strap or chain filter removing tool to tighten the filter as you will damage it.*

9 Refill the engine to the correct level using the recommended type and amount of oil (see *Pre-ride checks*). Make sure the O-ring on the underside of the filler cap is in good condition and properly seated. Fit a new one if necessary. Wipe it clean and smear new oil onto it. Fit the cap and tighten it by hand.

> **HAYNES HiNT**
> *Saving a little money on the difference between good and cheap oils won't pay off if the engine is damaged as a result.*

10 Start the engine and let it run for two or three minutes. Shut it off, wait a few minutes, then check the oil level. If necessary, top-up the oil to the correct level.

11 Check around the drain plug and the oil filter for leaks. If there is a leak around the drain plug and a new O-ring wasn't used, then repeat the procedure using a new one. Otherwise make sure the drain plug is tightened to the specified torque. A leak around the filter probably means it is not tight enough.

12 The old oil drained from the engine cannot be re-used and should be disposed of properly. Check with your local refuse disposal company, disposal facility or environmental agency to see whether they will accept the used oil for recycling. Don't pour used oil into drains or onto the ground.

Note: *It is illegal and anti-social to dump oil down the drain. To find the location of your local oil recycling bank in the UK, call 08708 506 506 or visit www.oilbankline. org.uk.*

> **HAYNES HiNT**
> *Check the old oil carefully – if it is very metallic coloured, then the engine is experiencing wear from break-in (new engine) or from insufficient lubrication. If there are flakes or chips of metal in the oil, then something is drastically wrong internally and the engine will have to be disassembled for inspection and repair.*

9 Fuel system

> ⚠ **Warning:** *Petrol is extremely flammable, so take extra precautions when you work on any part of the fuel system. Don't smoke or allow open flames or bare light bulbs near the work area, and don't work in a garage where a natural gas-type appliance is present. If you spill any fuel on your skin, rinse it off immediately with soap and water. When you perform any kind of work on the fuel system, wear safety glasses and have a fire extinguisher suitable for a Class B type fire (flammable liquids) on hand.*

1 Remove the storage compartment (see Chapter 9).

2 Check the fuel tank, the fuel hose(s) and the hose connections between it and the throttle body for signs of leakage, deterioration or damage **(see illustration)**. Replace the fuel hose(s) if cracked or deteriorated, or if the connectors show signs of leakage. Make sure

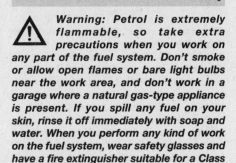

10.2 Location of the oil level plug – LX, LXV and S 2012-on models

that the hose is secure on its union at each end.

3 If there is evidence of leakage from around the fuel pump, remove the pump and replace the seal with a new one (see Chapter 5).

4 Cleaning of the fuel strainer and replacement of the fuel filter is advised after a particularly high mileage has been covered or if fuel starvation is suspected. They are both fitted to the fuel pump – refer to Chapter 5 for details.

5 If fuel starvation is suspected, and if there is a suction on the fuel filler cap caused by a vacuum inside the tank as fuel is used, the tank vent in the filler neck or the vent hose is blocked. Check and clean as required, and if necessary fit a new hose.

6 If the fuel gauge is believed to be faulty, check the operation of the gauge and sensor (see Chapter 5).

10 Gearbox oil

Level check

1 Place the scooter on its centrestand on level ground.

LX, LXV and S 2012-on models

2 Clean around the oil level plug then unscrew it from the gearbox casing **(see illustration)**. The oil should be level with the lower edge of the hole.

3 If required, top-up with the grade and type of oil specified at the beginning of the Chapter, using either a syringe or small funnel **(see illustration)**. Allow any excess oil to drain,

10.3 Topping-up the gearbox oil

10.4 Unscrew the gearbox oil filler cap/ dipstick (arrowed)

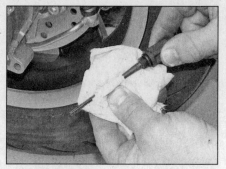

10.5 Wipe the dipstick clean . . .

10.6 . . . then insert it and screw the cap in

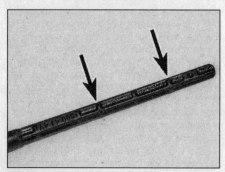

10.7a On LX, LXV and S models the level should lie between the lines arrowed

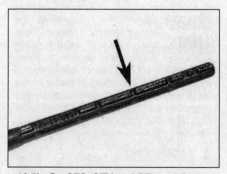

10.7b On GTS, GTV and GT models the level should lie just above the second line (arrowed)

10.8 Topping up the gearbox oil

then fit a new sealing washer to the plug and tighten it to the torque setting specified at the beginning of the Chapter.

All other models

4 Clean around the oil filler cap then unscrew it from the gearbox casing **(see illustration)**.
5 Wipe the dipstick clean **(see illustration)**.
6 Insert the dipstick and screw the cap fully in **(see illustration)**.
7 Unscrew the cap and check the oil mark on the dipstick as follows according to model: on LX, LXV and S models the oil level should lie between the first and third lines up from the bottom of the dipstick **(see illustration)**; on GTS, GTV and GT models the oil level should lie just above the second line up from the bottom of the dipstick **(see illustration)**.
8 If the level is not as it should be, top up with the grade and type of oil specified at

the beginning of the Chapter until it is **(see illustration)**. Do not overfill.
9 Before fitting the cap make sure the O-ring (arrowed) on the underside is in good condition and properly seated **(see illustration)**. Fit a new one if necessary. Wipe it clean and smear new oil onto it. Fit the cap and tighten it by hand.

⚠ *Warning: If the oil level is very low, or oil is leaking from the gearbox, refer to Chapter 3 and inspect the condition of the seals and gaskets and replace them with new ones as necessary.*

Oil change

Note: *Changing the gearbox oil is not a service requirement on 2012-on LX, LXV and S models .*
10 Remove the rear wheel (see Chapter 8).
11 Position a clean drain tray below the

gearbox. Unscrew the filler cap to vent the case and to act as a reminder that there is no oil in it **(see illustration 10.2)**.
12 Unscrew the oil drain plug and allow the oil to drain into the tray **(see illustrations)**. Discard the sealing washer as a new one should be used.
13 When the oil has completely drained, fit the drain plug using a new sealing washer, and tighten it to the torque setting specified at the beginning of the Chapter. Avoid over-tightening as you could damage the casing.
14 Refill the gearbox using the grade and type of oil specified at the beginning of the chapter until it is at the level specified for your model (see above). Fit the filler cap.
15 Check the oil level again after riding the scooter for a few minutes and, if necessary, add more oil. Check around the drain plug for leaks.

10.9 Make sure the O-ring (arrowed) is in good condition

10.12a Unscrew the drain plug (arrowed) . . .

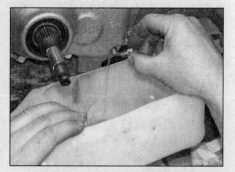

10.12b . . . and allow the oil to drain

11.2 Headlight adjuster screw (arrowed) – LX, S and GTS models

11.3 Headlight adjuster screw (arrowed) – GTV models

11.4 Slacken bolt (arrowed) to allow adjustment on LXV model

16 The old oil drained from the gearbox cannot be re-used and should be disposed of properly. Check with your local refuse disposal company, disposal facility or environmental agency to see whether they will accept the used oil for recycling. Don't pour used oil into drains or onto the ground.

11 Headlight aim

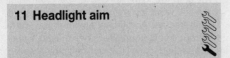

Note: *An improperly adjusted headlight may cause problems for oncoming traffic or provide poor, unsafe illumination of the road ahead. Before adjusting the headlight aim, be sure to consult with local traffic laws and regulations – for UK models refer to MOT Test Checks in the Reference section.*

1 The headlight beam can adjusted vertically. Before making any adjustment, check that the tyre pressures are correct and the suspension is adjusted as required. Make any adjustments to the headlight aim with the machine on level ground, with the fuel tank half full and with an assistant sitting on the seat. If the bike is usually ridden with a passenger on the back, have a second assistant to do this.

2 On LX, S and GTS models the adjuster screw is located below the headlight **(see illustration)**.

3 On GTV models the adjuster screw is on the underside of the front mudguard **(see illustration)**.

4 On LXV models slacken the rear bolt on the

bracket and move the headlight up or down **(see illustration)**.

12 Idle speed

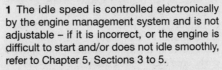

1 The idle speed is controlled electronically by the engine management system and is not adjustable – if it is incorrect, or the engine is difficult to start and/or does not idle smoothly, refer to Chapter 5, Sections 3 to 5.

13 Nuts and bolts

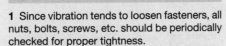

1 Since vibration tends to loosen fasteners, all nuts, bolts, screws, etc. should be periodically checked for proper tightness.

2 Pay particular attention to the following:
- *Spark plug.*
- *Throttle body clamps and intake duct bolts.*
- *Engine oil drain plug.*
- *Gearbox oil drain plug.*
- *Stand pivot bolts.*
- *Engine mounting bolts.*
- *Suspension bolts.*
- *Wheel bolts.*
- *Brake caliper mounting bolts (disc brakes).*
- *Brake hose banjo bolts (disc brakes).*
- *Exhaust system bolts/nuts.*

3 If a torque wrench is available, use it along with the torque specifications given in this manual.

14 Spark plug

1 Make sure your spark plug socket is the correct size (16 mm hex) before attempting to remove the plug – a suitable one is supplied in the Scooter's tool kit.

2 On 2012-on LX, LXV and S models, remove the engine access panel (see Chapter 9). Pull the cap off the spark plug noting how it locates in the recess in the top of the valve cover **(see illustration)**.

3 On all other models, remove the storage compartment (see Chapter 9). On LX, LXV and S models remove the engine access panel (see Chapter 9). On GTS, GTV and GT models remove the battery cover, then release the HT lead from the clip **(see illustrations)**. If a

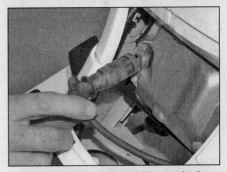

14.2 Note the location of the spark plug cap – 2012-on LX, LXV and S models

14.3a Remove the battery cover . . .

14.3b . . . then release the HT lead clip (arrowed)

14.3c Turn the cap so it is clear of the retainer arm (arrowed)

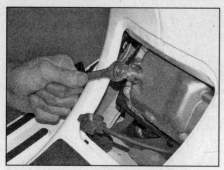

14.5a Unscrewing the spark plug . . .

14.5b . . . using the toolkit box spanner

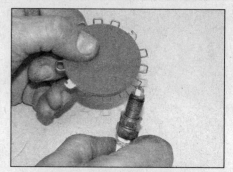

14.7 Using a gauge to measure the electrode gap

spark plug cap retainer is fitted turn the plug cap clockwise so it is clear of the retainer arm **(see illustration)**. Pull the cap off the spark plug. On LX, LXV and S models free the HT lead from its clip and slide the plug access cover off the engine cowl.

4 Clean the area around the base of the spark plug to prevent any dirt falling into the engine.

5 Using either the plug removing tool supplied in the toolkit or a deep spark plug socket, unscrew and remove the plug from the cylinder head **(see illustrations)**.

6 Check the condition of the electrodes, referring to the spark plug reading chart at the end of this manual if signs of contamination are evident.

7 Clean the plug with a wire brush. Examine the tips of the electrodes; if a tip has rounded off, the plug is worn. Measure the gap between the side and centre electrodes using a feeler gauge or a wire type gauge **(see illustration)**. The gap should be as given in the Specifications at the beginning of this chapter; if necessary either adjust the gap by bending the side electrode, or fit a new plug. **Note:** *The original equipment spark plug fitted to the GTS and GTV 250cc engine is a Champion RG4PHP which has a single earth electrode and is of double platinum construction. The OE plug for the GTS 125cc engine, and GTS and GTV 300cc engines is an NGK CR8EKB which has twin earth electrodes. The OE plug for LX, LXV and S engines is a single earth electrode NGK CR7EB or CR8EB – see Specifications at the beginning of this Chapter.*

8 Check the threads, the washer and the ceramic insulator body for cracks and other damage.

9 If the plug is worn or damaged, or if any deposits cannot be cleaned off, replace the plug with a new one. If in any doubt as to the condition of the plug replace with a new one – the expense is minimal. At the prescribed interval, whatever the condition of the existing spark plug, remove the plug as described above and install a new one.

10 Thread the plug into the cylinder head until the washer seats. Since the cylinder head is made of aluminium, which is soft and easily damaged, thread the plug as far as possible by hand. Once the plug is finger-tight, the job can be finished with the tool supplied or a socket drive **(see illustration 14.5a)**. If a new plug is being installed, tighten it by 1/2 a turn

after the washer has seated. If the old plug is being reused, tighten it by 1/8 to 1/4 turn after the washer has seated, or if a torque wrench can be applied, tighten the spark plug to the torque setting specified at the beginning of the Chapter. Otherwise tighten it according to the instructions on the box. Do not over-tighten it.

11 Fit the spark plug cap, making sure it locates correctly onto the plug, and turn it to locate in the retainer where fitted **(see illustrations 14.2 and 3c)**. On 2009 to 2011 LX, LXV and S models fit the plug access cover onto the engine cowl and secure the HT lead in its clip. Fit the engine access panel. On GTS, GTV and GT models fit the HT lead into the clip, then fit the battery cover **(see illustrations 14.3b and a)**.

12 Install the storage compartment (see Chapter 9).

> **HAYNES HiNT**
>
> *Stripped plug threads in the cylinder head can be repaired with a Heli-Coil insert – see 'Tools and Workshop Tips' in the Reference section.*

15 Stand(s)

1 All models are fitted with a centrestand. GTS, GTV and GT models, and certain 2012-on LX and S models, also have a sidestand.

2 The return springs must be capable of retracting the stand(s) fully and holding it/ them retracted when the machine is in use. If a spring has sagged or broken it must be replaced with a new one (see Chapter 9).

3 Since the stand(s) is/are exposed to the elements the pivot should be lubricated periodically to ensure safe and trouble-free operation.

4 In order for the lubricant to be applied where it will do the most good, the stand should be removed and the old grease cleaned off (see Chapter 9). This is particularly important with the centrestand which has O-ring seals on both ends of the pivot spacer located behind the mounting tabs on the stand. Applying lubricant to the outside of the seals will not

lubricate the stand pivot but will attract dirt which will cause the seals to wear.

5 Some sidestand pivot bolts have O-ring seals fitted – remove the bolt to check (see Chapter 9). Again, applying lubricant to the outside of the seals will not lubricate the pivot. If, however, there are no seals on the pivot bolt, lubricant applied to the pivot joint gaps will work its way into the areas where friction occurs. An aerosol lubricant is ideal – if motor oil or light grease is being used, apply it sparingly as it will attract dirt which could cause the pivot bolt to wear at an accelerated rate.

16 Speedometer cable and drive gear

1 Remove the speedometer cable (see Chapter 10).

2 Withdraw the inner cable from the outer cable. Wipe off all old lubricant then apply fresh engine oil or cable lubricant – do not lubricate the upper few inches to prevent it running up into the instrument.

3 Remove the drive gear (see Chapter 10). Clean all the old grease from the drive gear and housing, then lubricate the components with clean grease and reassemble them as described in Chapter 10.

17 Steering head bearings

1 The steering head bearings consist of ball bearings which run in races at the top and bottom of the steering head. The races can become dented or rough during normal use and the balls will gradually wear. In extreme cases, worn or loose steering head bearings can cause steering wobble – a condition that is potentially dangerous.

Check

2 Support the scooter on its centrestand, then have an assistant push down on the rear, or place a jack with a block of wood and plenty of rag under the belly, so the front wheel is off the ground.

17.5 Checking for freeplay in the steering head bearings

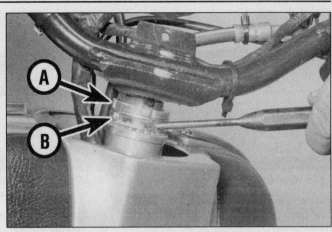

17.8 Slacken the locknut (A) and turn the adjuster nut (B) using a C-spanner or a drift as shown

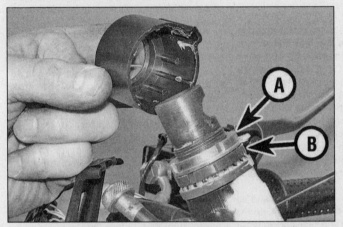

17.9a Remove the bearing cap – steering head bearing locknut (A) and adjuster nut (B)

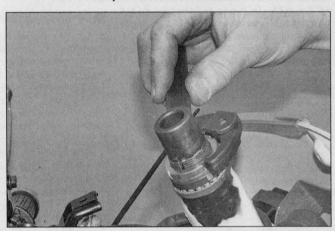

17.9b Using a C-spanner to slacken the locknut

3 Point the front wheel straight-ahead and slowly turn the handlebars from side-to-side. Any dents or roughness in the bearing races will be felt and the bars will not move smoothly and freely. If the bearings are damaged they must be replaced with new ones (see Chapter 7).

4 Again point the wheel straight-ahead, and tap the front of the wheel to one side. The wheel should 'fall' under its own weight to the limit of its lock, indicating that the bearings are not too tight (take into account the restriction that cables and wiring may have). Check for similar movement to the other side.

5 Next, grasp the wheel and front suspension and try to move it forwards and backwards **(see illustration)**. Any freeplay in the steering head bearings will be felt as front-to-rear

> **HAYNES HINT** *Make sure you are not mistaking any movement between the bike and stand, or between the stand and the ground, for freeplay in the bearings. Do not pull and push the wheel too hard – a gentle movement is all that is needed.*

movement of the steering stem. If play is felt in the bearings, follow the procedure described below to adjust them.

6 Over a period of time the grease in the bearings will harden or may be washed out. Follow the procedure in Chapter 7 to disassemble the steering head and re-grease the bearings. If the bearings are damaged they must be replaced with new ones (see Chapter 7).

Adjustment

7 Remove the handlebar cover(s) (see Chapter 9).

8 On LX, LXV and S models slacken the locknut (the upper nut) using either a C-spanner or a suitable drift located in one of the notches **(see illustration)**.

9 On GTS, GTV and GT models displace the handlebars (see Chapter 7). Remove the bearing cap **(see illustration)**. Slacken the locknut (the upper nut) using either a C-spanner or a suitable drift located in one of the notches **(see illustration)**.

10 Turn the adjuster nut (the lower nut) using the same tool, either clockwise to tighten the head bearings or anti-clockwise to loosen them, and only moving it a small amount at

a time. After each small adjustment recheck the freeplay as described in Steps 2 to 5, before making further adjustments. The object is to set the adjuster nut so that the bearings are under a very light loading, just enough to remove any freeplay, but not so much that the steering does not move freely from side-to-side as described in the check procedure above. Note that Vespa specify a torque setting (see Chapter 7), however to apply this a special tool (part no. 00055Y), or a suitable old socket fabricated into a peg spanner, is required, and the handlebars and locknut must be removed.

Caution: Take great care not to apply excessive pressure because this will cause premature failure of the bearings.

11 If the bearings cannot be correctly adjusted, disassemble the steering head and check the bearings and races (see Chapter 7).

12 With the bearings correctly adjusted, hold the adjuster nut to prevent it from moving, then tighten the locknut tight. As with the adjuster nut Vespa specify a torque setting (see Chapter 7, Section 3), however to apply this a special tool (part No. 020055Y), or a suitable old socket fabricated into a peg

18.7 Checking for play in the engine and swingarm mounts

19.4 Throttle cable freeplay is measured in terms of twistgrip rotation

then check again – any freeplay should be more evident. If there is freeplay, inspect the swingarm bushes and/or bearings and all mounting points for wear (see Chapter 7).

9 Reconnect the rear shock absorber(s), then grasp the top of the rear wheel and pull it upwards – there should be no discernible freeplay before the shock begins to compress. Any freeplay indicates a worn shock or shock mountings. The worn components must be identified and replaced with new ones (see Chapter 7).

spanner, is required, and the handlebars must be removed.

13 Check the bearing adjustment as described in steps 2 to 5 and re-adjust if necessary.

14 On GTS, GTV and GT models fit the bearing cap **(see illustration 17.9a)**. Install the handlebars (see Chapter 7).

15 Install the handlebar cover(s) (see Chapter 9).

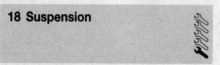

18 Suspension

1 The suspension components must be in good condition to ensure rider safety. Loose, worn or damaged suspension parts decrease the scooter's stability and control.

2 Check the tightness of all suspension nuts and bolts to ensure none have worked loose. Refer to the torque settings specified at the beginning of Chapter 7.

Front suspension

3 While standing alongside the scooter, apply the front brake and push on the handlebars to compress the suspension several times. See if it moves up-and-down smoothly without binding. If binding is felt, the suspension should be disassembled and inspected (see Chapter 7).

4 Inspect the shock absorber for fluid leaks and corrosion on the damper rod. If the shock is faulty it should be replaced with a new one (see Chapter 7).

Rear suspension

5 With the aid of an assistant to support the scooter, compress the rear suspension several times. It should move up and down freely without binding. If any binding is felt, the worn or faulty component must be identified and renewed. The problem could be due to either the shock absorber or the engine front mounting/pivot assembly.

6 Inspect the rear shock absorber(s) for fluid leaks and corrosion on the damper rod. If a shock is faulty it should be renewed (see Chapter 7). Always renew the shocks as a pair on twin-shock models.

7 Support the scooter on its centrestand so that the rear wheel is off the ground. Grip the engine/gearbox unit at the rear and attempt to rock it from side to side – there should be no discernible freeplay **(see illustration)**. If there is movement, refer to Chapters 2A, 2B or 2C and 7 and check the tightness of the bolts securing the front of the engine to the swingarm and the swingarm to the frame.

8 Re-check for movement. If freeplay is felt, disconnect the rear shock absorber lower mounting(s) and displace the shock(s),

19 Throttle

1 Ensure the throttle twistgrip rotates easily from fully closed to fully open with the handlebars turned at various angles, and that the twistgrip returns automatically to the fully closed position when released.

2 If the throttle sticks, this is probably due to a cable fault. Follow the procedure in Chapter 5 and disconnect the cable at the twistgrip end, then lubricate it using a pressure adapter and aerosol cable lubricant **(see illustrations 4.22a, b and c)**.

3 If the throttle action is still stiff, remove the storage compartment, handlebar cover(s), kick panel and floorboard as required to access the cable along its length and check for a trapped or damaged section. If required, follow the procedure in Chapter 5 and install a new cable.

4 With the throttle operating smoothly, make sure there is a small amount of freeplay in the cable, measured in terms of the amount of twistgrip rotation before the throttle opens – Vespa do not specify an amount but generally there should be at least 2 mm and no more than 6 mm freeplay **(see illustration)**.

5 If there is insufficient or excessive freeplay, on S, LX and GTS models remove the front handlebar cover (see Chapter 9). Pull back the boot on the adjuster for the opening (upper or front, according to model) cable at the twistgrip end **(see illustrations)**.

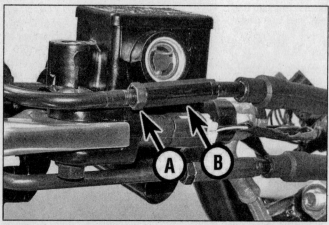

19.5a On LX, S and GTS models pull back the boot, then slacken the adjuster locknut (A) and turn the adjuster (B) as required – throttle end

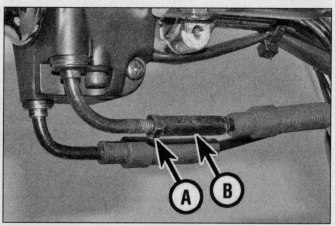

19.5b On LXV, GTV and GT models pull back the boot, then slacken the adjuster locknut (A) and turn the adjuster (B) as required – throttle end

Loosen the locknut on the adjuster, then turn the adjuster until the specified amount of freeplay is evident. Tighten the locknut.

6 If the adjuster has reached its limit of adjustment, reset it so that freeplay is at a maximum. Remove the storage compartment (see Chapter 9). Refer to Chapter 5 and loosen the nuts securing the cable in the throttle body bracket and thread them up or down the cable as required until the freeplay is correct, and tighten the locknut. If the freeplay cannot be set correctly replace the cable (see Chapter 5).

7 Start the engine and check the idle speed. If the idle speed is too high, this could be due to incorrect adjustment of the cable. Loosen the locknut and turn the adjuster in – if the idle speed falls as you do, there is insufficient freeplay in the cable. Reset the adjuster (see Step 5). Turn the handlebars from side to side and check that the idle speed does not change as you do. If it does, the throttle cable is routed incorrectly. Correct the problem before riding the scooter.

20 Valve clearances

1 The engine must be completely cold for this maintenance procedure, so let the machine sit overnight before beginning.

2 Remove the spark plug (see Section 14). Remove the valve cover (see Chapter 2A, 2B or 2C).

GTS, GTV and GT models, 2009 to 2011 LX, LXV and S models

3 On air-cooled engines, remove the cooling fan cover and cooling fan (see Chapter 2A). On liquid-cooled engines, remove the alternator cover (see Chapter 2C).

4 The valve clearances are checked with the piston at top dead centre (TDC) on its compression stroke (all valves are closed and a small clearance can be felt at each rocker arm). Turn the engine clockwise using a socket on the alternator rotor nut until the line next to the upside-down T mark on the alternator rotor aligns with the static timing mark, which is a projection on the crankcase, and the 2V mark on air-cooled two valve engines or the 4V mark on liquid-cooled four valve engines on the camshaft sprocket aligns with the index mark on the camshaft holder **(see illustrations)**. If the mark on the rotor aligns but the mark on the camshaft sprocket does not, turn the engine clockwise one full turn (360°) more – all marks will now be aligned and there should now be some freeplay in each rocker arm (i.e. they are not contacting the valve stem).

LX, LXV and S models 2012-on

Special tool: *A Vespa service tool Part No. 020941Y is required for this procedure (see Step 6).*

5 Remove the cooling fan and alternator cover (see Chapter 2B).

6 The valve clearances are checked with the piston at top dead centre (TDC) on its compression stroke (all valves are closed and a small clearance can be felt at each rocker arm). Turn the engine in the normal direction of rotation until the piston is at TDC – you can do this using a socket on the alternator rotor nut. To confirm that the piston is in the correct position, install the service tool,

20.4a Turn the engine clockwise . . .

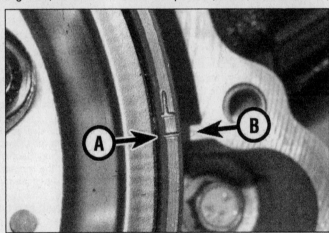

20.4b . . . until the line next to the T mark (A) aligns with the projection (B) . . .

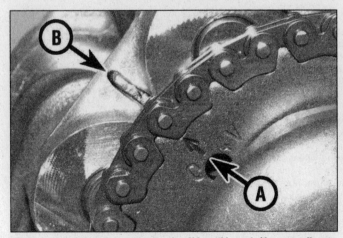

20.4c . . . and the arrow next to the 2V or 4V mark (A, according to model) on the sprocket aligns with the index mark (B)

20.6a Installed position of the TDC service tool

20.6b Check the alignment of the camshaft sprocket timing marks (arrowed)

20.7a Insert the feeler gauge between the base of the adjuster on the arm and the top of the valve stem as shown

20.7b Intake valve clearance can be checked from inside the bodywork

20.8 Slacken the locknut with a spanner then turn the adjuster using a screwdriver until the gap is correct

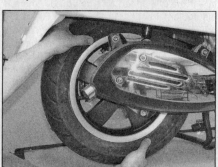

21.2 Checking for play in the rear wheel bearings

locating the curved face in the gap between the ignition timing triggers on the outer surface of the alternator rotor (see illustration). Check that the timing mark on the camshaft sprocket is aligned with the mark on the camshaft holder (see illustration). If the crankshaft and camshaft sprocket are not correctly aligned, turn the engine clockwise one full turn (360°) more – they should now be correctly aligned and there should some freeplay in each rocker arm (i.e. they are not contacting the valve stems).

All models

7 With the engine in this position, check the clearance of each valve by inserting a feeler gauge of the same thickness as the correct valve clearance (refer to the Specifications for your model) in the gap between the rocker arm and the valve stem (see illustrations). The intake valve(s) is/are on the top of the cylinder head and the exhaust valve(s) is/are on the bottom. The gauge should be a firm sliding fit – you should feel a slight drag when you pull the gauge out.

8 If the gap (clearance) is either too wide or too narrow, slacken the locknut on the adjuster in the rocker arm and turn the adjuster as required using a screwdriver until the gap is as specified and the feeler gauge is a firm sliding fit, then hold the adjuster still and tighten the locknut (see illustration). Recheck the clearance after tightening the locknut.

9 When the clearances are correct install the valve cover (see Chapter 2A, 2B or 2C) and the spark plug (Section 14).

10 Install the remaining components in the reverse order of removal.

21 Wheels and tyres

Wheels

1 Cast wheels are virtually maintenance free, but they should be kept clean and checked periodically for cracks and other damage. Also check the wheel runout and alignment (see Chapter 8). Never attempt to repair damaged cast wheels; they must be replaced with new ones.

2 Support the scooter on its centrestand and check for any play in the bearings by pushing and pulling the wheel against the hub (see illustration). Also rotate the wheel and check that it turns smoothly.

3 If any play is detected in the hub, or if the wheel does not rotate smoothly (and this is not due to brake drag), first check that the wheel mountings are tight (see Chapter 8). If they are the wheel bearings must be inspected for wear or damage (see Chapter 8).

4 The front wheel bearings are housed in the

hub assembly as opposed to the wheel itself – see Chapter 8.

5 There are no rear wheel bearings as such – the wheel is mounted directly onto the gearbox output shaft which turns on bearings located inside the gearbox. If any play is detected, refer to Chapter 3 to check the gearbox. Also check that play is not due to a fault or wear in the rear suspension (see Section 18).

Tyres

6 Check the tyre condition and tread depth thoroughly – see Pre-ride checks.

7 Check that the directional arrow on the tyre sidewall is pointing in the normal direction of wheel rotation.

8 Check the valve rubber for signs of damage or deterioration and have it replaced if necessary by a tyre specialist.

9 Make sure the valve stem cap is in place and tight. On some types, the cap doubles as a tool for the valve core. If a tyre loses pressure, and this is not due to damage of the tyre itself, check that the valve core is tight (these caps are available in automotive accessory shops).

10 A dab of soapy water will indicate if the valve is leaking – the leak will show as bubbles in the water. If required, use the valve cap to unscrew the old valve and install a new one.

11 If fitted, check that the wheel balance weights are firmly attached to the rim.

Chapter 2A
Air-cooled two-valve engines (LX, LXV and S models)

See 'Model specifications' at the beginning of the manual for identification details.

Contents

Degrees of difficulty

Easy, suitable for novice with little experience	**Fairly easy,** suitable for beginner with some experience	**Fairly difficult,** suitable for competent DIY mechanic	**Difficult,** suitable for experienced DIY mechanic	**Very difficult,** suitable for expert DIY or professional

Specifications

General

Type	Single cylinder 2v air-cooled four-stroke
Capacity	
125 engine	124 cc
150 engine	151cc
Bore	
125 engine	57.0 mm
150 engine	62.8 mm
Stroke	48.6 mm
Compression ratio	10.1 to 11.1 : 1
Cylinder compression	150 to 200 psi (10 to 14 Bar) @ 600rpm

Camshaft

Intake and exhaust lobe height	
Intake	27.512 mm
Exhaust	27.212 mm
Left-hand journal diameter	
Standard	32.50 mm
Service limit (min)	32.44 mm
Right-hand journal diameter	
Standard	20.00 mm
Service limit (min)	19.95 mm
Camshaft end-float (max)	0.42 mm

Cylinder head

Warpage (max)	0.05 mm
Left-hand camshaft bearing housing diameter (standard)	32.500 to 32.525 mm
Right-hand camshaft journal housing diameter (standard)	20.000 to 20.021 mm
Rocker arm shaft housing (standard)	12.000 to 12.018 mm
Rocker arm shaft diameter (service limit)	11.970 mm (min)
Rocker arm internal diameter (service limit)	12.030 mm (max)

Valves, guides and springs

	Intake valve	Exhaust valve
Valve clearances	See Chapter 1	
Overall standard length	80.6 mm	79.6 mm
Stem diameter		
Service limit (min)	4.960 mm	4.950 mm
Guide bore diameter		
Standard	5.012 mm	5.012 mm
Stem/valve guide clearance		
Standard	0.013 to 0.040 mm	0.025 to 0.052 mm
Service limit	0.062 mm	0.072 mm
Face width	2.4 to 2.8 mm	2.2 to 2.6 mm
Seat width (max)	1.6 mm	1.6 mm
Spring free length	33.9 to 34.4 mm	33.9 to 34.4 mm

Cylinder and piston – 125 engines

Cylinder bore – aluminium cylinder

Bore diameter (measured 38.5 mm down from top edge of the cylinder, at 90° to the piston pin axis)

Standard
- Size-code A .... 56.980 to 56.987 mm
- Size-code B .... 56.987 to 56.994 mm
- Size-code C .... 56.994 to 57.001 mm
- Size-code D .... 57.001 to 57.008 mm

1st oversize
- Size-code A1 .... 57.180 to 57.187 mm
- Size-code B1 .... 57.187 to 57.194 mm
- Size-code C1 .... 57.194 to 57.201 mm
- Size-code D1 .... 57.201 to 57.208 mm

2nd oversize
- Size-code A2 .... 57.380 to 57.387 mm
- Size-code B2 .... 57.387 to 57.394 mm
- Size-code C2 .... 57.394 to 57.401 mm
- Size-code D2 .... 57.401 to 57.408 mm

3rd oversize
- Size-code A3 .... 57.580 to 57.587 mm
- Size-code B3 .... 57.587 to 57.594 mm
- Size-code C3 .... 57.594 to 57.601 mm
- Size-code D3 .... 57.601 to 57.608 mm

Piston – aluminium cylinder

Piston diameter (measured 36.5 mm down from top edge of the piston, at 90° to the piston pin axis)

Standard
- Size-code A .... 56.933 to 56.940 mm
- Size-code B .... 56.940 to 56.947 mm
- Size-code C .... 56.947 to 56.954 mm
- Size-code D .... 56.954 to 56.961 mm

1st oversize
- Size-code A1 .... 57.133 to 57.140 mm
- Size-code B1 .... 57.140 to 57.147 mm
- Size-code C1 .... 57.147 to 57.154 mm
- Size-code D1 .... 57.154 to 57.161 mm

2nd oversize
- Size-code A2 .... 57.333 to 57.340 mm
- Size-code B2 .... 57.340 to 57.347 mm
- Size-code C2 .... 57.347 to 57.354 mm
- Size-code D2 .... 57.354 to 57.361 mm

3rd oversize
- Size-code A3 .... 57.533 to 57.540 mm
- Size-code B3 .... 57.540 to 57.547 mm
- Size-code C3 .... 57.547 to 57.554 mm
- Size-code D3 .... 57.554 to 57.561 mm

Piston-to-bore clearance (when new, all size codes) .... 0.040 to 0.054 mm

Piston pin diameter
- Standard .... 14.996 to 15.000 mm
- Service limit (min) .... 14.994 mm

Piston pin bore diameter in piston .... 15.001 to 15.006 mm

Cylinder bore – cast iron cylinder

Bore diameter (measured 38.5 mm down from top edge of the cylinder, at 90° to the piston pin axis)
Standard
Size-code M .... 56.997 to 57.004 mm
Size-code N .... 57.004 to 57.011 mm
Size-code O .... 57.011 to 57.018 mm
Size-code P .... 57.018 to 57.025 mm
1st oversize
Size-code M1 .... 57.197 to 57.204 mm
Size-code N1 .... 57.204 to 57.211 mm
Size-code O1 .... 57.211 to 57.218 mm
Size-code P1 .... 57.218 to 57.225 mm
2nd oversize
Size-code M2 .... 57.397 to 57.404 mm
Size-code N2 .... 57.404 to 57.411 mm
Size-code O2 .... 57.411 to 57.418 mm
Size-code P2 .... 57.418 to 57.425 mm
3rd oversize
Size-code M3 .... 57.597 to 57.604 mm
Size-code N3 .... 57.604 to 57.611 mm
Size-code O3 .... 57.611 to 57.618 mm
Size-code P3 .... 57.618 to 57.625 mm

Piston – cast iron cylinder

Piston diameter (measured 36.5 mm down from top edge of the piston, at 90° to the piston pin axis)
Standard
Size-code M .... 56.944 to 56.951 mm
Size-code N .... 56.951 to 56.958 mm
Size-code O .... 56.958 to 56.965 mm
Size-code P .... 56.965 to 56.972 mm
1st oversize
Size-code M1 .... 57.144 to 57.151 mm
Size-code N1 .... 57.151 to 57.158 mm
Size-code O1 .... 57.158 to 57.165 mm
Size-code P1 .... 57.165 to 57.172 mm
2nd oversize
Size-code M2 .... 57.344 to 57.351 mm
Size-code N2 .... 57.351 to 57.358 mm
Size-code O2 .... 57.358 to 57.365 mm
Size-code P2 .... 57.365 to 57.372 mm
3rd oversize
Size-code M3 .... 57.544 to 57.551 mm
Size-code N3 .... 57.551 to 57.558 mm
Size-code O3 .... 57.558 to 57.565 mm
Size-code P3 .... 57.565 to 57.572 mm
Piston-to-bore clearance (when new) .... 0.046 to 0.060 mm
Piston pin diameter
Standard .... 14.996 to 15.000 mm
Service limit (min) .... 14.994 mm
Piston pin bore diameter in piston .... 15.001 to 15.006 mm

Cylinder and piston – 150 engines

Cylinder bore

Bore diameter (measured 38.5 mm down from top edge of the cylinder, at 90° to the piston pin axis)
Standard
Size-code A .... 62.580 to 62.587 mm
Size-code B .... 62.587 to 62.594 mm
Size-code C .... 62.594 to 62.601 mm
Size-code D .... 62.601 to 62.608 mm
1st oversize
Size-code A1 .... 62.780 to 62.787 mm
Size-code B1 .... 62.787 to 62.794 mm
Size-code C1 .... 62.794 to 62.801 mm
Size-code D1 .... 62.801 to 62.808 mm
2nd oversize
Size-code A2 .... 62.980 to 62.987 mm
Size-code B2 .... 62.987 to 62.994 mm
Size-code C2 .... 62.994 to 63.001 mm
Size-code D2 .... 63.001 to 63.008 mm

Cylinder and piston – 150 engines (continued)

Cylinder bore (continued)
3rd oversize

Size-code A3	63.180 to 63.187 mm
Size-code B3	63.187 to 63.194 mm
Size-code C3	63.194 to 63.201 mm
Size-code D3	63.201 to 63.208 mm

Piston
Piston diameter (measured 36.5 mm down from top edge of the piston, at 90° to the piston pin axis)
Standard

Size-code A	62.533 to 62.540 mm
Size-code B	62.540 to 62.547 mm
Size-code C	62.547 to 62.554 mm
Size-code D	62.554 to 62.561 mm
1st oversize	
Size-code A1	62.733 to 62.740 mm
Size-code B1	62.740 to 62.747 mm
Size-code C1	62.747 to 62.754 mm
Size-code D1	62.754 to 62.761 mm
2nd oversize	
Size-code A2	62.933 to 62.940 mm
Size-code B2	62.940 to 62.947 mm
Size-code C2	62.947 to 62.954 mm
Size-code D2	62.954 to 62.961 mm
3rd oversize	
Size-code A3	63.133 to 63.140 mm
Size-code B3	63.140 to 63.147 mm
Size-code C3	63.147 to 63.154 mm
Size-code D3	63.154 to 63.161 mm
Piston-to-bore clearance (when new, all size codes)...............	0.040 to 0.054 mm
Piston pin diameter	
Standard..	14.996 to 15.000 mm
Service limit (min)	14.994 mm
Piston pin bore diameter in piston	15.001 to 15.006 mm

Piston rings – 125 engine

Ring end gap (installed)

Top ring..	0.15 to 0.30 mm
2nd ring...	0.10 to 0.30 mm
Oil control ring	0.10 to 0.35 mm

Ring-to-groove clearance
Top ring

Standard..	0.025 to 0.070 mm
Service limit (max).......................................	0.080 mm
2nd ring	
Standard..	0.015 to 0.060 mm
Service limit (max).......................................	0.070 mm
Oil control ring	
Standard..	0.015 to 0.060 mm
Service limit (max).......................................	0.070 mm

Piston rings – 150 engine

Ring end gap (installed)

Top ring..	0.15 to 0.30 mm
2nd ring...	0.20 to 0.40 mm
Oil control ring	0.20 to 0.40 mm

Ring-to-groove clearance
Top ring

Standard..	0.025 to 0.070 mm
Service limit (max).......................................	0.080 mm
2nd ring	
Standard..	0.015 to 0.060 mm
Service limit (max).......................................	0.070 mm
Oil control ring	
Standard..	0.015 to 0.060 mm
Service limit (max).......................................	0.070 mm

Lubrication system

Engine oil pressure (at 90°C)	
At idle	7.25 to 17.5 psi (0.5 to 1.2 Bar)
At 6000 rpm	46.5 to 61 psi (3.2 to 4.2 Bar)
Oil pump	
Inner rotor tip-to-outer rotor clearance (max).	0.12 mm
Outer rotor-to-body clearance (max)	0.20 mm
Rotor end-float (max)	0.09 mm
Relief valve spring free length	54.2 mm

Connecting rod

Small-end internal diameter	
Standard.	15.015 to 15.025 mm
Service limit (max)	15.030 mm
Big-end side clearance	
Standard.	0.20 to 0.50 mm
Big-end radial freeplay	
Standard.	0.036 to 0.054 mm
Service limit (max)	0.25 mm

Crankshaft

Combined width of flywheels and big-end.	55.67 to 55.85 mm
Runout A (max)*	0.15 mm
Runout B (max)*	0.01 mm
Runout C (max)*	0.10 mm
End-float.	0.15 to 0.40 mm

* See illustration 20.18 for runout measurement points

Torque settings

Alternator rotor nut.	52 to 58 Nm
Alternator stator screws/pulse generator coil screws	3 to 4 Nm
Cam chain tensioner blade bolt	10 to 14 Nm
Cam chain tensioner bolts	11 to 13 Nm
Cam chain tensioner spring cap bolt	5 to 6 Nm
Camshaft retaining plate bolts	4 to 6 Nm
Camshaft sprocket bolt	12 to 14 Nm
Crankcase bolts	11 to 13 Nm
Cylinder head bolts	11 to 13 Nm
Cylinder head nuts	28 to 30 Nm
Engine front mounting bolt/nut.	33 to 41 Nm
Oil pressure switch.	12 to 14 Nm
Oil pump cover screws.	0.7 to 0.9 Nm
Oil pump mounting screws	5 to 6 Nm
Oil pump sprocket bolt.	12 to 14 Nm
Sump cover bolts	11 to 13 Nm
Throttle body intake duct screws	11 to 13 Nm
Valve cover bolts	11 to 13 Nm

---

1 General information

The engine unit is a single cylinder four-stroke, with fan-assisted air cooling. The fan is mounted on the alternator rotor, which is on the right-hand end of the crankshaft. The crankshaft assembly is pressed together, incorporating the connecting rod, with the big-end running on the crankpin on a bronze bearing. The crankshaft runs in plain main bearings. The crankcase divides vertically.

The camshaft is chain-driven off the left-hand end of the crankshaft, and operates two valves via rocker arms.

2 Component access

Access to the alternator rotor and stator on the right-hand side and the transmission on the left-hand side is easy and can be done with the engine in place.

Access to the top-end of the engine is very restricted making removal of the valve cover, the first component that needs to be removed, difficult. Removal of the engine is recommended, though it is also possible to just raise the frame up off the engine until there is enough clearance if you have the necessary equipment – refer to Section 5, Step 1, for details.

To access the crankshaft and connecting rod assembly and its bearings, the engine must be removed from the frame and the crankcase halves separated.

3 Engine wear assessment

Cylinder compression test

Special tool: *A compression gauge is required to perform this test.*

1 Poor engine performance may be caused by leaking valves, incorrect valve clearances, a leaking head gasket, or a worn piston, piston rings or cylinder walls. A cylinder compression check will highlight these conditions and can also indicate the presence of excessive carbon deposits in the cylinder head.

2 The only tools required are a compression gauge (there are two types, one with a threaded adapter to fit the spark plug hole in the cylinder head, the other has a rubber seal which is pressed into the spark plug hole to create a seal – the threaded adapter type is preferable), and a spark plug socket. Depending on the outcome of the initial test, a squirt-type oil can may also be needed.

3 Make sure the valve clearances are correctly set (see Chapter 1) and that the cylinder head nuts/bolts are tightened to the correct torque setting (see Section 11).

4 Run the engine until it is at normal operating temperature. Remove the spark plug (see Chapter 1). Fit the plug back into the plug cap and earth the plug against the engine away from the plug hole – if the plug is not grounded the ignition system could be damaged.

5 Fit the gauge into the spark plug hole – if the rubber cone type is used keep the gauge pressed onto the hole throughout the test to maintain a good seal.

6 With the ignition switch ON, the throttle held fully open and the spark plug earthed, turn the engine over on the starter motor until the gauge reading has built up and stabilised.

7 Compare the reading on the gauge to the cylinder compression range specified at the beginning of the Chapter (under General specifications). Note that this is not a range specified by Vespa (they do not provide one), but is a general range acceptable for this engine – if in doubt ask your dealer.

8 If the reading is low, it could be due to a worn cylinder bore, piston or rings, failure of the head gasket, or worn valve seats. To determine which is the cause, pour a small quantity of engine oil into the spark plug hole to seal the rings, then repeat the compression test. If the figures are noticeably higher the cause is worn cylinder, piston or rings. If there is no change the cause is a leaking head gasket or worn valve seats.

9 If the reading is high there could be a build-up of carbon deposits in the combustion chamber. Remove the cylinder head and scrape all deposits off the piston and the cylinder head.

10 While working on the engine also check that the correct base gasket has been fitted under the cylinder block – different thicknesses are available and it is possible that the one fitted is either too thick, which will reduce cylinder compression, or too thin, increasing compression – refer to Section 13 for details.

Oil pressure check

Special tool: *A pressure gauge is required to perform this test.*

11 This engine is fitted with an oil pressure switch and warning light. The function of the circuit is described in Chapter 10.

12 If there is any doubt about the performance of the engine lubrication system, the oil pressure should be checked. The

check provides useful information about the condition of the lubrication system. If you do not have the facilities to check the oil pressure yourself, have it done by a Vespa dealer.

13 To check the oil pressure, a suitable pressure gauge (which screws into the crankcase) will be needed. Vespa can supply a gauge (Part No. 020193Y) for this purpose.

14 Check the engine oil level (see *Pre-ride checks*), then warm the engine up to normal operating temperature and stop it. Support the scooter so that the rear wheel is clear of the ground.

15 Remove the alternator cover (see Section 16). Disconnect the oil pressure switch wiring connector **(see illustration 17.5)**, then unscrew the switch using a deep socket and screw in the gauge adapter. Connect the pressure gauge to the adapter. Discard the pressure switch sealing washer, as a new one must be fitted on reassembly.

⚠️ *Warning: Take great care not to burn your hands on the hot engine unit, exhaust pipe or with engine oil when connecting the gauge adapter to the crankcase. Do not allow exhaust gases to build-up in the work area; either perform the check outside or use an exhaust gas extraction system.*

16 Start the engine and increase the engine speed to 6000 rpm whilst watching the pressure gauge reading. The oil pressure should be within the range given in the Specifications at the beginning of the Chapter.

17 If the pressure is significantly lower than the standard, either the oil strainer or filter is blocked, the pressure relief valve is stuck open, the oil pump is faulty, the piston oil jet in the crankcases has become dislodged, or there is considerable engine main bearing wear. Begin diagnosis by checking the oil filter and strainer (see Chapter 1), then the relief valve and oil pump (see Sections 19 and 20). If those items check out okay, the crankcases will have to be split to check the oil jet and the main bearings (see Section 21).

18 If the pressure is too high, either an oil passage is clogged, the relief valve is stuck closed or the wrong grade of oil is being used.

19 Stop the engine and unscrew the gauge and adapter from the crankcase.

20 Fit a new sealing washer to the oil pressure switch and tighten the switch using a deep socket. Connect the wiring connector. Install the alternator cover (see Section 16). Check the oil level (see *Pre-ride checks*). **Note:** *Rectify any problems before running the engine again.*

4	Major engine repair – general note

1 It is not always easy to determine when or if an engine should be completely overhauled, as a number of factors must be considered.

2 High mileage is not necessarily an indication

that an overhaul is needed, while low mileage, on the other hand, does not preclude the need for an overhaul. Frequency of servicing is probably the single most important consideration. An engine that has regular and frequent oil and filter changes, as well as other required maintenance, will most likely give many miles of reliable service. Conversely, a neglected engine, or one which has not been run-in properly, may require an overhaul very early in its life.

3 Exhaust smoke and excessive oil consumption are both indications that piston rings and/or valve guides are in need of attention, although make sure that the fault is not due to oil leakage.

4 If the engine is making obvious knocking or rumbling noises, the connecting rod and/or main bearings are probably at fault.

5 Loss of power, rough running, excessive valve train noise and high fuel consumption rates may also point to the need for an overhaul, especially if they are all present at the same time. If a complete tune-up does not remedy the situation, major mechanical work is the only solution.

6 A full engine overhaul generally involves restoring the internal parts to the specifications of a new engine. The piston and piston rings are renewed and the cylinder is re-bored. The valve seats are re-ground and new valve springs are fitted. If the connecting rod bearings are worn a new crankshaft assembly is fitted. The end result should be a like-new engine that will give as many trouble-free miles as the original.

7 Before beginning the engine overhaul, read through the related procedures to familiarise yourself with the scope and requirements of the job. Overhauling an engine is not all that difficult, but it is time-consuming. Plan on the scooter being tied up for a minimum of two weeks. Check on the availability of parts and make sure that any necessary special tools, equipment and supplies are obtained in advance.

8 Most work can be done with typical workshop hand tools, although a number of precision measuring tools are required for inspecting parts to determine if they must be renewed. Often a dealer will handle the inspection of parts and offer advice concerning reconditioning and renewal. As a general rule, time is the primary cost of an overhaul so it does not pay to install worn or substandard parts.

9 As a final note, to ensure maximum life and minimum trouble from a rebuilt engine, everything must be assembled with care in a spotlessly-clean environment.

5	Engine/transmission unit removal and installation

Caution: The engine is not heavy, although engine removal and installation should be carried out with the aid of an assistant; personal injury or damage could occur if the engine falls or is dropped.

Removal

1 Wash any accumulated dirt off the engine. Support the scooter securely in an upright position. Note that the centre stand is bolted to the engine so you will need to support the belly of the scooter on axle stands or wooden blocks after the engine has been removed – use adequate protection, and make sure the frame is securely supported so it cannot topple over. Also note that the scooter must be lifted up off the engine to get the necessary clearance for the engine to be then draw back from under it. To do this you will need at least one assistant. Alternatively, as shown you could fabricate a frame with straps that can be used to raise and support the scooter above the engine while the engine is worked on **(see illustration)** – use the method best suited to your workshop set-up and surroundings. Work on the engine can be made easier by raising the machine to a suitable working height on an hydraulic ramp or a suitable platform – again make sure the scooter is secure and will not topple over.

2 Remove the storage compartment, side panels and floor panel (see Chapter 9).

3 If the sump is going to be removed, or the crankcases separated, drain the engine oil (see Chapter 1).

4 Disconnect the battery negative (-) terminal (see Chapter 10).

5 Remove the exhaust system (see Chapter 5).

6 Trace the wiring from the alternator/pulse generator coil on the right-hand side of the engine and disconnect it at the connectors. Free the wiring from any clips and feed it down to the alternator cover, noting its routing. Disconnect the engine temperature sensor wiring connector; the sensor is mounted in the cylinder head.

7 Pull the spark plug cap off the plug.

8 Detach the air intake duct from the air filter housing **(see illustration)**. Clean around the intake duct joint to the cylinder head. Undo the intake duct screws and detach the complete throttle body assembly from the head and tie it to the body so the wiring, hose(s) and cables are not strained. Stuff some clean rag into the head and into the throttle body ducts.

9 If required remove the air filter housing (see Chapter 5) – note that it is easier to do after the scooter has been raised.

10 Disconnect the starter motor lead and engine earth leads **(see illustration)**. If required remove the starter motor.

11 Detach the drive belt air duct from the front of the belt cover.

12 Carefully release the swingarm pre-load spring from its hook on the engine.

13 If required, remove the rear wheel (see Chapter 8). **Note:** *The rear wheel and centrestand provide a convenient support for the engine unit once it is removed from the scooter, so only remove it if necessary. If you want to leave it in place for now but may remove it later loosen the rear wheel nut at this point before disconnecting the rear brake.*

5.1 Fabricated structure to hoist and support the frame above the engine

14 Disconnect the rear brake cable from the brake and free the cable from the clips on the underside of the drive belt cover **(see illustration)**.

15 Unscrew the nut and withdraw the bolt securing the lower end of the rear shock absorber to the transmission casing **(see illustration)**. If the rear wheel has been removed support the back of the engine unit on a wood block. If the rear wheel has not been removed place a piece of wood under the rear tyre.

16 Check that all wiring, cables and hoses are free and clear as required.

17 Prepare your method of raising and supporting the scooter as outlined in Step 1. Unscrew the nut on the front engine mounting bolt **(see illustration)**. Take the weight of the scooter, then withdraw the bolt, and raise the scooter off the engine unit, then support it or move it to its support as required.

5.10 Disconnect the lead (arrowed) from the starter motor

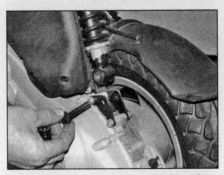

5.15 Unscrew the nut and withdraw the bolt

5.8 Slacken the clamp (arrowed) and detach the duct

18 If the engine is dirty clean it thoroughly before starting any major dismantling work (see Section 6).

Installation

19 Installation is the reverse of removal, noting the following:

- *Make sure no wires, cables or hoses become trapped between the engine and the frame when installing the engine.*
- *Tighten the engine mounting bolt and shock absorber bolt/nut to the torque settings specified at the beginning of this Chapter and Chapter 7.*
- *Make sure all wires, cables and hoses are correctly routed and connected, and secured by any clips or ties.*
- *Tighten the throttle body intake duct screws to the torque setting specified at the beginning of the Chapter.*

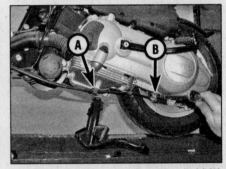

5.14 Free the brake cable from the clip(s) (A) and the clamp(s) (B) as fitted

5.17 Unscrew the nut

7.2 Undo the screws and remove the breather housing, noting the O-ring (arrowed)

- *Adjust the throttle cable and the rear brake cable (see Chapter 1).*
- *Fill the engine with the specified quantity of oil (see Chapter 1 Specifications) and check the oil level as described in Pre-ride checks.*

6 Engine overhaul information

Disassembly

1 Before disassembling the engine, the external surfaces of the unit should be thoroughly cleaned and degreased to rule out the possibility of dirt falling inside. A high flash-point solvent, such as paraffin can be used, or better still, a proprietary engine degreaser. Use old paintbrushes and toothbrushes to work the solvent into the various recesses of the engine casings. Take care to exclude solvent or water from the electrical components and intake and exhaust ports.

 Warning: The use of petrol (gasoline) as a cleaning agent should be avoided because of the risk of fire.

2 When clean and dry, arrange the unit on the workbench, leaving suitable clear area for working. Gather a selection of small containers and plastic bags so that parts can be grouped together in an easily identifiable manner. Some paper notes and a pen should be on hand to permit notes to be made and labels

8.3 Remove the engine cowling sections

attached where necessary. A supply of clean rag is also required.

3 Before commencing work, read through the appropriate section so that some idea of the necessary procedure can be gained. When removing components it should be noted that great force is seldom required, unless specified. In many cases, a component's reluctance to be removed is indicative of an incorrect approach or removal method – if in any doubt, recheck with the text.

4 When disassembling the engine, keep 'mated' parts that have been in contact with each other during engine operation together. These 'mated' parts must be re-used or renewed as an assembly.

5 Complete engine disassembly should be done in the following general order with reference to the appropriate Sections. Refer to Chapter 3 for details of transmission components disassembly.

Remove the valve cover.
Remove the camshaft and rockers.
Remove the cylinder head.
Remove the cylinder.
Remove the piston.
Remove the alternator.
Remove the starter motor (see Chapter 10).
Remove the oil pump.
Remove the variator (see Chapter 3).
Separate the crankcase halves.
Remove the crankshaft.

Reassembly

6 Reassembly is the reverse of the general disassembly sequence.

7.3 Unscrew the bolts and remove the cover

8.5 Unscrew the cap bolt and remove the spring

7 Valve cover

Removal

1 Raise the frame up off the engine (see Section 5).

2 If you want to remove the valve cover completely undo the engine breather housing screws and detach the housing – note the O-ring **(see illustration)**. Otherwise leave the breather cover attached and just displace the valve cover from the head.

3 Unscrew the valve cover bolts, then lift the cover off the cylinder head **(see illustration)**. If it is stuck, do not try to lever it off with a screwdriver. Tap it gently with a rubber hammer or block of wood to dislodge it. Remove and discard the gasket – a new one must be fitted.

Installation

4 Clean the mating surfaces of the cylinder head and the valve cover with a suitable solvent.

5 Fit the new gasket into the groove in the valve cover, making sure it locates correctly – use some dabs of grease to help stick it in place if required.

6 Position the valve cover on the cylinder head, making sure the gasket stays in place, then fit the cover bolts and tighten them evenly and in a criss-cross sequence to the torque setting specified at the beginning of the Chapter **(see illustration 7.3)**.

7 If detached fit the breather cover using a new O-ring if required **(see illustration 7.2)**.

8 Lower the frame down onto the engine (see Section 5).

8 Cam chain tensioner

Removal

1 Remove the valve cover (see Section 7).

2 Pull the cap off the spark plug.

3 Slide the spark plug access panel up off the engine cowling. Undo the screws securing the cowling sections to each other, to the alternator cover and to the crankcase and remove them, noting how they clip together on the left-hand side **(see illustration)**.

4 Remove the cooling fan (see Section 16). Turn the engine in a clockwise direction using the alternator rotor nut, until the timing mark on the rotor aligns with the index mark on the crankcase, and the timing mark (2V) on the camshaft sprocket aligns with the index mark on the camshaft holder **(see illustrations 9.3a and 9.3b)**. At this point the engine is at TDC (top dead centre) on the compression stroke (both valves closed). If the 2V mark is not in alignment, rotate the engine 360° and re-align the timing marks.

5 Unscrew the chain tensioner spring

cap bolt and withdraw the spring from the tensioner body **(see illustration)**. Discard the sealing washer – a new one must be fitted on reassembly

6 Unscrew the two tensioner mounting bolts and withdraw the tensioner from the back of the cylinder **(see illustration)**.

7 Remove the gasket from the base of the tensioner or from the cylinder and discard it – a new one must be used.

Inspection

8 Examine the tensioner components for signs of wear or damage.

9 Release the ratchet mechanism on the tensioner plunger and check that the plunger moves freely in and out of the tensioner body **(see illustration)**.

10 If the tensioner mechanism or the spring are worn or damaged, or if the plunger is seized in the body, the tensioner must be replaced with a new one as an assembly – individual components are not available.

Installation

11 Turn the engine a small amount in a clockwise direction using the alternator rotor nut to take up any slack in the front run of the cam chain between the crankshaft and the camshaft and transfer it to the back run where it will be taken up by the tensioner.

12 Release the ratchet mechanism and press the tensioner plunger all the way into the tensioner body **(see illustration 8.9)**.

13 Place a new gasket on the tensioner body, then install it in the cylinder and tighten the bolts to the torque specified at the beginning of the Chapter **(see illustration 8.6)**.

14 Fit a new sealing washer onto the spring cap bolt. Fit the spring and cap bolt and tighten the bolt to the specified torque **(see illustration 8.5)** – as you thread the bolt in you should hear the plunger extend over the ratchet mechanism and see the chain tension.

8.6 Unscrew the bolts and remove the tensioner

15 Check that the cam chain is tensioned. If it is slack, the tensioner plunger did not release when the cap bolt was tightened. Remove the tensioner and check the operation of the plunger again.

16 Install the engine cowling sections (see Step 3), the cooling fan (see Section 16), and the valve cover (see Section 7).

9 Cam chain, blades and sprockets

Removal

1 Remove the valve cover (see Section 7).

2 If the cam chain and crankshaft sprocket are to be removed, remove the oil pump driven sprocket, drive chain and drive sprocket (see Section 19).

3 Remove the cooling fan (see Section 16). Turn the engine in a clockwise direction using the alternator rotor nut, until the timing mark on the rotor aligns with the index mark on the crankcase, and the timing mark (2V) on the camshaft sprocket aligns with the index mark on the camshaft holder **(see illustrations)**. At this point the engine is at TDC (top dead

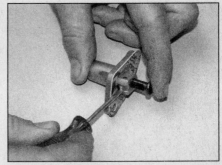

8.9 Check the operation of the ratchet and plunger

centre) on the compression stroke (both valves closed). If the 2V mark is not in alignment, rotate the engine 360° and re-align the timing marks.

4 If your engine is fitted with a decompressor mechanism as shown in illustration 9.3b, refer to Chapter 2C, Section 9, Steps 4 to 6 to remove it. If not, then hold the alternator to prevent the camshaft sprocket from turning and loosen the sprocket centre bolt, noting the washers, and the offset bolt.

5 Remove the cam chain tensioner (see Section 8).

6 Displace the sprocket and its backing plate from the end of the camshaft, noting how they fit, and slip the sprocket out of the chain **(see illustrations)**.

7 If required, secure the chain with a cable-tie to prevent it falling into the engine. If the chain is to be removed, mark it with paint so that if it is re-used it can be fitted the same way round. Remove the thrust washer from the end of the crankshaft, then pass the chain down its tunnel and slip it off the sprocket on the crankshaft **(see illustrations)**. Draw the sprocket off the crankshaft, noting how it locates on the pin **(see illustration)**.

8 To remove the cam chain tensioner blade unscrew its pivot bolt and withdraw the blade,

9.3a Turn the engine clockwise until the mark on the rotor (A) aligns with the mark (B) . . .

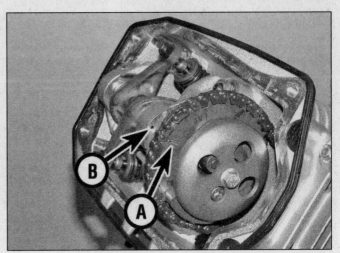

9.3b . . . and the arrow next to the 2V mark (A) on the sprocket aligns with the index mark (B)

9.6a Lift off the sprocket and backing plate . . .

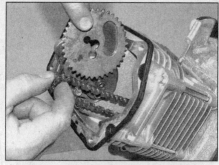

9.6b . . . and disengage the chain

9.7a Remove the thrust washer . . .

9.7b . . . then lift out the cam chain . . .

9.7c . . . and draw the sprocket off

9.8 Unscrew the bolt (arrowed) and remove the tensioner blade

noting which way round it fits, and the spacer (see illustration).

9 To remove cam chain guide blade remove the cylinder head (see Section 11). Lift the blade out, noting how it locates (see illustration).

9.9 Draw the guide blade out of the engine

9.12b . . . and the lugs seat in the cut-outs

Inspection

10 Check the sprockets for wear and damaged teeth, replacing them with new ones if necessary. If the sprocket teeth are worn, a new cam chain should be fitted.

9.12a Make sure the slot locates over the pin . . .

9.13 Make sure the spacer is fitted

11 Check the chain tensioner blade and guide blade for wear or damage and fit new ones if necessary. Damaged or severely worn blades are an indication of a worn or improperly tensioned chain. Check the operation of the cam chain tensioner (see Section 8).

Installation

12 If removed, fit the cam chain guide blade, locating the cut-out in its bottom end over the pin on the crankcase and its lugs in the cut-outs in the cylinder (see illustrations). Install the cylinder head (see Section 11).
13 If removed, fit the tensioner blade with its spacer and tighten the bolt to the torque setting specified at the beginning of the Chapter (see illustration).
14 Slide the sprocket onto the crankshaft, aligning the notch in the sprocket with the pin on the shaft (see illustration 9.7c). Pass the cam chain along the tunnel and fit it onto the sprocket (see illustration 9.7b). If the chain is being re-used, ensure it is fitted the right way round (see Step 7). Slide the thrust washer against the sprocket (see illustration 9.7a).
15 Check that the timing mark on the alternator rotor still aligns with the index mark on the crankcase and that the engine is at TDC on the compression stroke (see Step 3).
16 Fit the camshaft sprocket backing plate onto the end of the camshaft (see illustration). Slip the sprocket into the top of the chain, then take up the slack in the lower run of the chain, making sure it is still engaged around the crankshaft sprocket, and fit the sprocket onto the camshaft, aligning the 2V timing mark with the index mark on the camshaft

holder **(see illustration)**. If your engine is fitted with a decompressor mechanism as shown in illustration 9.3b, refer to Chapter 2C, Section 9, Steps 20 to 22 to install it. If not fit the centre and offset bolts with their spring washers and tighten them finger-tight.

Caution: If the marks are not aligned exactly as described, the valve timing will be incorrect and the valves may strike the piston, causing extensive damage to the engine.

17 Install the cam chain tensioner (see Section 8).

18 Now tighten the decompressor mechanism bolts or camshaft sprocket bolt and offset bolt to the specified torque settings (see Chapter 2C specs for the decompressor where fitted), holding the alternator to prevent the sprocket from turning.

19 Install the oil pump drive sprocket, chain and driven sprocket (see Section 19).

20 Install the remaining components in the reverse order of removal.

10 Camshaft and rockers

Removal

1 Remove the valve cover (see Section 7).

2 Remove the cooling fan (see Section 16). Turn the engine in a clockwise direction using the alternator rotor nut, until the timing mark on the rotor aligns with the index mark on the crankcase, and the timing mark (2V) on the camshaft sprocket aligns with the index mark on the camshaft holder **(see illustrations 9.3a and 9.3b)**. At this point the engine is at TDC (top dead centre) on the compression stroke (both valves closed). If the 2V mark is not in alignment, rotate the engine 360° and re-align the timing marks.

3 Remove the camshaft sprocket (see Section 9, Steps 4, 5 and 6). Secure the cam chain

9.16a Locate the backing plate onto the projections . . .

with a cable-tie or length of wire to prevent it dropping into the engine. Stuff a clean rag into the cam chain tunnel to prevent anything falling into the engine.

4 Undo the two bolts securing the camshaft retaining plate and lift out the plate **(see illustrations)**. Mark the end of the camshaft so that it can be refitted in the same position (TDC, both valves closed), then withdraw the camshaft from its housing **(see illustration)**.

5 Mark the rocker arms so they can be installed in their original positions. Support the intake valve (right-hand) rocker arm and slowly withdraw the rocker shaft until the arm is free and can be removed **(see illustration)**.

10.4a Unscrew the bolts (arrowed) . . .

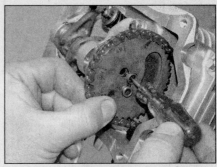

9.16b . . . then fit the sprocket into the chain and onto the camshaft

Withdraw the shaft completely and remove the exhaust valve rocker arm.

Inspection

6 Clean all the components with a suitable solvent and dry them. Inspect the camshaft lobes for heat discoloration (blue appearance), score marks, chipped areas, flat spots and spalling **(see illustration)**. Measure the height of both lobes with a micrometer and compare the results to the Specifications at the beginning of the Chapter **(see illustration)**. If damage is noted or wear is excessive, the camshaft must be replaced with a new one.

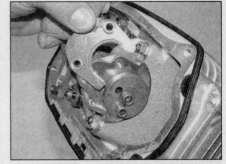

10.4b . . . and lift out the plate

10.4c Withdraw the camshaft

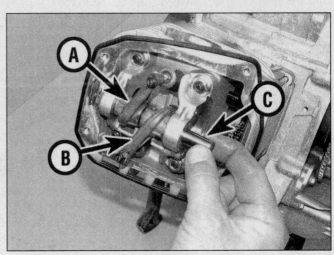

10.5 Intake rocker arm (A), exhaust rocker arm (B), rocker shaft (C)

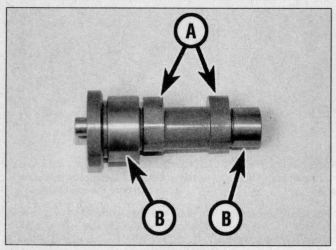

10.6a Check the lobes (A) and camshaft journals (B) for wear and damage . . .

10.6b . . . and measure the height of each lobe

7 Check the condition of the camshaft bearing journals and the housing journals in the cylinder head **(see illustration 10.6a)**. Measure the camshaft journals with a micrometer and, if available, measure the internal diameter of the housing journals with a telescoping gauge and micrometer **(see illustration)**. Compare the results to the Specifications at the beginning of the Chapter and, if damage is noted or wear is excessive, replace any faulty component with a new one.

8 Lubricate the camshaft journals with clean engine oil, fit the camshaft in the cylinder head and secure it with the retaining plate. The camshaft should rotate freely with no discernible up-and-down movement. If available, measure the camshaft end-float with a dial gauge and compare the result to the Specifications at the beginning of the Chapter. If the end-float is excessive, inspect the retaining plate and the slot in the camshaft for wear and replace any worn component with a new one.

9 Blow through the oil passages in the rocker arms with compressed air, if available. Inspect the rocker arm faces for pits and spalling **(see illustration)**. Check the articulated tip of the adjusting screw and the top of each valve stem for wear. The tip should move freely but not be loose. Slip the shaft into the arm and check for freeplay between them. Measure the internal diameter of each rocker arm, the internal diameters of the rocker shaft housings and the diameter of the rocker shaft and compare the results to the Specifications at the beginning of the Chapter. If damage is noted or wear is excessive, replace any faulty component with a new one.

Installation

10 Lubricate the camshaft journals with clean engine oil, then fit the camshaft into the cylinder head **(see illustration 10.4c)**. Ensure the cam lobes are facing the same way as on disassembly (see Step 4).

11 Lubricate the rocker shaft with engine oil. Slide the shaft through the left-hand housing and fit the exhaust valve rocker arm then the intake valve rocker arm and press the shaft fully into place **(see illustration 10.5)**. With the camshaft in the correct position there should be no pressure on the rocker arms. Align the camshaft retaining plate with the slot in the camshaft, slide the plate into position and secure it with the bolts **(see illustrations 10.4b and a)**. Tighten the bolts to the specified torque setting.

12 Follow the procedure in Section 9, Steps 15 to 18, and install the camshaft sprocket and cam chain tensioner, then check the valve timing.

Caution: If the marks are not aligned *exactly as described, the valve timing will be incorrect and the valves may strike the piston, causing extensive damage to the engine.*

13 Check the valve clearances and adjust them if necessary (see Chapter 1).

14 Install the remaining components in the reverse order of removal.

11 Cylinder head removal and installation

Caution: The engine must be completely cool before beginning this procedure or the cylinder head may become warped.

Removal

1 Remove the exhaust system (see Chapter 5).

2 Remove the cam chain tensioner (see Section 8). If there is enough slack in the chain slip it off the sprocket on the camshaft. If not, or if required anyway, remove the camshaft sprocket (see Section 9, Steps 4, 5 and 6). Secure the cam chain with a cable-tie or length of wire to prevent it dropping into the engine. If required remove the camshaft and rockers (see Section 10).

3 Lift off the engine cowling seal **(see illustration)**.

10.7 Check and measure the journals and their housings

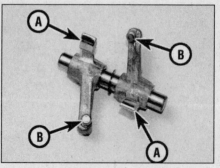

10.9 Inspect the rocker arm faces (A) and adjuster screw tips (B)

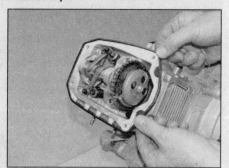

11.3 Remove the cowling seal

11.4a Undo the two external cylinder head bolts (arrowed) . . .

11.4b . . . then the four internal cylinder head nuts (arrowed)

4 Undo the two cylinder head bolts on the left-hand side of the engine **(see illustration)**. Undo the four cylinder head nuts evenly, a little at a time, in a criss-cross pattern and remove them **(see illustration)**.

5 Lift the cylinder head up off the studs, feeding the cam chain down through the tunnel in the head **(see illustration)**. If the head is stuck, tap around the joint face with a soft-faced mallet to free it. Do not attempt to free the head by inserting a screwdriver between the head and cylinder – you'll damage the sealing surfaces. **Note:** *Avoid lifting the cylinder off the crankcase when the head is removed, otherwise a new cylinder base gasket will have to be fitted (see Section 13).*

6 Remove the cylinder head gasket – a new one must be fitted on reassembly **(see illustration)**. Note the two dowels and remove them for safekeeping if they are loose – they could be in the underside of the head or in the top of the cylinder **(see illustration)**.

7 Inspect the gasket and the mating surfaces on the head and cylinder for signs of leakage, which could indicate that the head is warped. Refer to Section 12 and check the head gasket mating surface for warpage.

8 Clean all traces of old gasket material from the cylinder head and cylinder using a suitable scraper and solvent. Take care not to scratch or gouge the soft aluminium. Be careful not to

let any dirt fall into the crankcase, the cylinder bore or the oil passage.

Installation

9 Ensure both cylinder head and cylinder mating surfaces are clean. Fit the dowels into the top of the cylinder if removed. Lay the new gasket onto the cylinder, making sure it locates over the dowels and the oil passage holes are correctly aligned **(see illustration 11.6a)**. Never re-use the old gasket. Make sure the cam chain guide blade is correctly seated.

10 Carefully fit the head over the studs and onto the cylinder, feeding the cam chain up through the tunnel **(see illustration 11.5)**. Make sure the dowels locate correctly.

11 Lubricate the seating surfaces of the cylinder head nuts with clean engine oil, then fit the nuts finger tight **(see illustration 11.4b)**. Tighten the nuts evenly and a little at a time in a criss-cross pattern to the torque setting specified at the beginning of the Chapter.

12 Fit the two cylinder head bolts on the left-hand side of the engine and tighten them to the specified torque setting **(see illustration 11.4a)**.

13 Install the rockers, camshaft, sprocket, tensioner and all other remaining components in the reverse order of removal as required, referring to the relevant Sections and Chapters.

12 Cylinder head and valve overhaul

1 Because of the complex nature of this job and the special tools and equipment required, most owners leave checking and servicing of the valves, valve seats and valve guides to a professional. However, you can make an initial assessment of whether the valves are seating correctly, and therefore sealing, by pouring a small amount of solvent into each of the valve ports. If the solvent leaks past any valve into the combustion chamber area the valve is not seating correctly and sealing.

2 With the correct tools (a valve spring compressor is essential – make sure it is suitable for motorcycle work), you can also remove the valves and associated components from the cylinder head, clean them and check them for wear to assess the extent of the work needed, and grind in the valves and reassemble them in the head.

3 If the valve guides or the valve seats are worn a new cylinder head is required – valve guides are not available and Vespa state that the seats cannot be re-cut.

4 After the valve service has been performed, be sure to clean the head very thoroughly

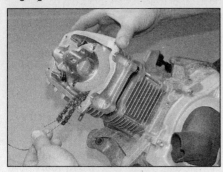

11.5 Lift off the cylinder head

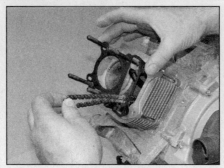

11.6a Remove the gasket . . .

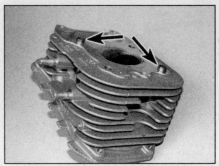

11.6b . . . and the dowels (arrowed) if loose

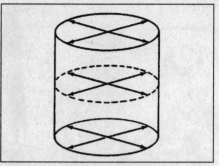

13.7a Measure the cylinder bore in the directions shown . . .

before installation to remove any metal particles or abrasive grit that may still be present from the valve service operations. Use compressed air, if available, to blow out all the holes and passages.

Disassembly, inspection and reassembly

5 Refer to Chapter 2C, Section 12, for procedural details, but use the Specifications at the beginning of this Chapter.

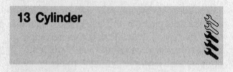

13 Cylinder

Removal

1 Remove the cylinder head (see Section 11).
2 Note how the cam chain guide blade locates in a groove in the front edge of the cam chain tunnel in the cylinder, then lift the blade out, noting which way round it fits.
3 Lift the cylinder up off the studs, feeding the cam chain down through the tunnel and laying it over the front of the engine. Support the piston as it becomes accessible to prevent it hitting the crankcase. If the cylinder is stuck, tap around its joint face with a soft-faced mallet to free it from the crankcase. Don't attempt to free the cylinder by inserting a screwdriver between it and the crankcase – you'll damage the sealing surfaces. When the cylinder is removed, stuff a clean rag around the piston to prevent anything falling into the crankcase.

13.13 Zero the dial gauge on the cylinder top gasket face

13.7b . . . using a telescoping gauge

4 Note the dowel(s) and remove it/them for safekeeping if loose – it could be in the underside of the cylinder or in the crankcase.
5 Remove the gasket and make a note of the thickness (0.4, 0.6 or 0.8) stamped into the material. If the original cylinder and piston are used on reassembly, a new gasket of the same thickness should be used. Discard the old gasket.

Inspection

6 Inspect the cylinder bore carefully for scratches and score marks. A re-bore will be necessary to remove any deep scores (see Step 7).
7 Using telescoping gauges and a micrometer, check the dimensions of the cylinder to assess the amount of wear, taper and ovality. Vespa recommend the bore is measured at 10 mm, 38.5 mm and 75 mm down from the top edge, both parallel to and across the crankshaft axis **(see illustrations)**. Compare the results to the cylinder bore Specifications at the beginning of this Chapter. Note: *Cylinders and pistons are size-coded during manufacture and it is important that they are of the same size-code. Vespa list four size-codes (A to D or M to P) for this engine, in standard size, and first, second and third oversizes (for re-bored cylinders). The size-code is stamped in the gasket surface at the top or base of the cylinder, and in the piston crown. When purchasing a new cylinder or piston, always supply the size-code letter.*
8 Calculate any differences between the measurements to determine any taper or ovality in the bore. Vespa specify a wear limit

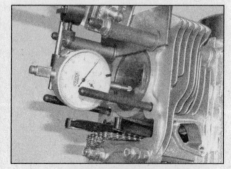

13.15 Take the reading off the piston crown at TDC

of 0.05 mm between any of the measurements. If the cylinder is worn beyond this service limit, badly scratched, scuffed or scored, have it re-bored by a Vespa dealer or motorcycle engineer. If the cylinder is re-bored, it will require an oversize piston and rings. If the cylinder has already been re-bored to the maximum oversize and is worn or damaged, the cylinder must be replaced with a new one. If a re-bore is being done make sure the person doing it is provided with the size and clearance specifications.
9 Measure the cylinder bore diameter 38.5 mm down from the top edge, then calculate the piston-to-bore clearance by subtracting the piston diameter (see Section 14) from the bore diameter. If the cylinder is in good condition and the piston-to-bore clearance is within specifications, the cylinder can be re-used.
10 Check that all the studs are tight in the crankcase. If any are loose, or need to be replaced with new ones, remove them. Clean their threads and smear them with a thread locking compound. Fit them into the crankcase and tighten them using a stud tool, or by threading two of the cylinder head nuts onto the top of the stud and tightening them together so they are locked on the stud, then tighten the stud by turning the upper of the two nuts.

Installation

11 Check that the mating surfaces of the cylinder and crankcase are clean.
12 Three different thicknesses of cylinder base gasket are available from Vespa. If the original cylinder and piston are being re-used, fit a gasket the same thickness as the original (see Step 5). If new components are being used, the cylinder must be assembled on the crankcase and piston (see Steps 17 to 20) without a base gasket, and a dial gauge mounted against the crown of the piston to establish which thickness is required – Vespa have a dial gauge mounting plate especially made for the purpose (part No. 020428Y). Basically what you are trying to do is establish the gap between the top of the piston at TDC and a plane across the cylinder mating surface without a base gasket, and the amount determines the thickness of gasket required. You could achieve the task using a precision straight-edge laid across the cylinder and a good set of feeler blades, but a dial gauge is far more accurate.
13 Mount the dial gauge with its tip resting against the cylinder top gasket face, and zero the gauge dial **(see illustration)**. Rotate the crankshaft so that the piston is part way down the bore.
14 Move the gauge so the tip is in the centre of the cylinder bore.
15 Rotate the crankshaft via the alternator rotor nut so the piston rises to the top of its stroke (TDC) and the gauge tip rests on the centre of the piston crown. At this point read off the dial gauge **(see illustration)**. The further the piston crown is below the top of the cylinder bore, the thinner the base gasket

should be. On 125 engines, if the reading is between 0 and 0.1 mm a 0.8 mm gasket is required, between 0.1 and 0.3 mm a 0.6 mm gasket is required, and between 0.3 and 0.4 mm a 0.4 mm gasket is required. On 150 engines, if the reading is between 1 and 1.1 mm a 0.8 mm gasket is required, between 1.1 and 1.3 mm a 0.6 mm gasket is required, and between 1.3 and 1.4 mm a 0.4 mm gasket is required. If you are in doubt about anything have a Vespa dealer take the measurement.

16 If removed fit the dowel into the crankcase. Fit the new gasket, locating it over the studs and the dowel **(see illustration)**. Never re-use the old gasket.

17 If required, fit a piston ring clamp onto the piston to ease its entry into the bore as the cylinder is lowered. This is not essential as the cylinder has a good lead-in enabling the piston rings to be hand-fed into the bore. If possible, have an assistant to support the cylinder while this is done. Check that the piston ring end gaps are positioned as described in Section 15.

18 Lubricate the cylinder bore, piston and piston rings, and the connecting rod big- and small-ends, with the clean engine oil, then fit the cylinder down over the studs until the piston crown fits into the bore.

19 Gently push down on the cylinder, making sure the piston enters the bore squarely and does not get cocked sideways. If a piston ring clamp is not being used, carefully compress and feed each ring into the bore as the cylinder is lowered **(see illustration)**. If necessary, use a soft mallet to gently tap the cylinder down, but do not use force if it appears to be stuck as the piston and/or rings will be damaged. If a clamp is used, remove it once the piston is in the bore.

20 When the piston is correctly installed in the cylinder, press the cylinder down onto the base gasket, making sure it locates on the dowel.

21 Fit the cam chain guide blade into the tunnel (see Step 2), then install the cylinder head (see Section 11).

14 Piston

Removal

1 Remove the cylinder (see Section 13). Before removing the piston from the connecting rod, stuff a clean rag into the hole around the rod to prevent the circlips or anything else from falling into the crankcase. The piston should have a triangle marked on its crown which should face towards the exhaust valve. If this is not visible, mark the piston accordingly so that it can be installed the correct way round. Note that the arrow may not be visible until the carbon deposits have been scraped off and the piston cleaned.

2 Carefully prise out the circlip on one side of the piston using a pointed instrument or a

13.16 Fit a new cylinder base gasket onto the crankcase

small flat-bladed screwdriver inserted into the notch **(see illustration)**. Push the piston pin out from the other side to free the piston from the connecting rod **(see illustration)**. Remove the other circlip and discard them both, as new ones must be used. Use a socket extension to push the piston pin out if required.

 To prevent the circlip from flying away or from dropping into the crankcase, pass a rod or screwdriver with a greater diameter than the gap between the circlip ends, through the piston pin. This will trap the circlip if it springs out.

 If a piston pin is a tight fit in the piston bosses, heat the piston gently with a hot air gun – this will expand the alloy piston sufficiently to release its grip on the pin.

Inspection

3 Before the inspection process can be carried out, the piston rings must be removed and the piston must be cleaned. Note that if the cylinder is being re-bored, piston inspection can be overlooked, as a new one will be fitted. All three piston rings can be removed by hand; a ring removal and installation tool can be used on the two compression rings if required, but do not use it on the oil control ring **(see illustration 15.7e, d, c and a)**.

14.2a Remove the circlip . . .

13.19 Locate the top of the piston in the bottom of the bore then carefully feed each ring in as you push the cylinder down

Carefully note which way up each ring fits and in which groove as they must be installed in their original positions if being re-used. Do not nick or gouge the piston in the process.

4 Scrape all traces of carbon from the top of the piston. A hand-held wire brush or a piece of fine emery cloth can be used once most of the deposits have been scraped away. Do not, under any circumstances, use a wire brush mounted in a drill motor to remove deposits from the piston; the piston material is soft and will be eroded away by the wire brush.

5 Use a piston ring groove cleaning tool to remove any carbon deposits from the ring grooves. If a tool is not available, a piece broken off an old ring will do the job. Be very careful to remove only the carbon deposits. Do not remove any metal and do not nick or gouge the sides of the ring grooves. Once the deposits have been removed, clean the piston with solvent and dry it thoroughly.

6 Inspect the piston for cracks around the skirt, at the pin bosses and at the ring lands. Normal piston wear appears as even, vertical wear on the thrust surfaces of the piston and slight looseness of the top ring in its groove. If the skirt is scored or scuffed, the engine may have been suffering from overheating and/or abnormal combustion, which caused excessively high operating temperatures. Also check that the circlip grooves are not damaged.

7 A hole in the piston crown is an extreme example that abnormal combustion (pre-ignition) was occurring. Burned areas at the edge of the piston crown are usually evidence

14.2b . . . and push out the piston pin

14.8 Measure the piston diameter as described

14.9a Check for freeplay between the pin and the piston

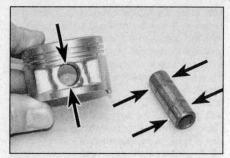

14.9b Measure both ends of the piston pin and the internal diameter of the piston pin boss

14.10 Check for freeplay between the pin and the small-end

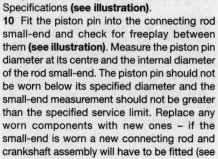
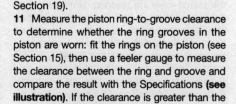

14.11 Measuring piston ring-to-groove clearance

14.13 Secure the piston pin with new circlips

of spark knock (detonation). If any of the above problems exist, the causes must be corrected or the damage will occur again.

8 Check the piston-to-bore clearance by measuring the bore (see Section 13) and the piston diameter. Measure the piston 36.5 mm down from the top edge of the piston and at 90° to the piston pin axis **(see illustration)**. Subtract the piston diameter from the bore diameter to obtain the clearance. If it is greater than the specified figure, the piston must be replaced with a new one (assuming the bore itself is within limits, otherwise a re-bore is necessary). Remember that the piston and cylinder are size-coded (see Section 13, Step 7) – make sure you have matched components.

9 Fit the piston pin into the piston and check for freeplay between them **(see illustration)**. Using a micrometer and a telescoping gauge measure the piston pin diameter at both ends and the internal diameter of each pin boss in

the piston and compare the results with the Specifications **(see illustration)**.

10 Fit the piston pin into the connecting rod small-end and check for freeplay between them **(see illustration)**. Measure the piston pin diameter at its centre and the internal diameter of the rod small-end. The piston pin should not be worn below its specified diameter and the small-end measurement should not be greater than the specified service limit. Replace any worn components with new ones – if the small-end is worn a new connecting rod and crankshaft assembly will have to be fitted (see Section 19).

11 Measure the piston ring-to-groove clearance to determine whether the ring grooves in the piston are worn: fit the rings on the piston (see Section 15), then use a feeler gauge to measure the clearance between the ring and groove and compare the result with the Specifications **(see illustration)**. If the clearance is greater than the

service limit, repeat the check using new rings, if the clearance is still too great, a new piston should be fitted.

Installation

12 Inspect and install the piston rings (see Section 15).

13 Lubricate the piston pin, the piston pin bore and the connecting rod small-end bore with clean engine oil. Fit a new circlip in one side of the piston (do not re-use old circlips). Line up the piston on the connecting rod, making sure the arrow on the piston crown faces down towards the exhaust, and insert the piston pin **(see illustration 14.2b)**. Secure the pin with the other new circlip **(see illustration)**. When fitting the circlips, compress them only just enough to fit them in the piston, and make sure they are properly seated in their grooves with the open end away from the removal notch **(see illustration 14.2a)**.

14 Install the cylinder (see Section 13).

15 Piston rings

1 New piston rings should be fitted whenever an engine is being overhauled. Before fitting the new rings, the end gaps must be checked with the rings installed in an unworn part of the bore.

2 To measure the installed ring end gap, fit the top ring into the bottom of the bore and square it up with the bore walls by pushing it in with the top of the piston **(see illustrations)**.

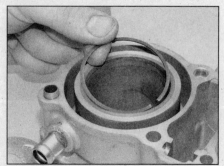

15.2a Fit the ring in its bore . . .

15.2b . . . and set it square using the piston . . .

15.2c . . . then measure the end gap using a feeler gauge

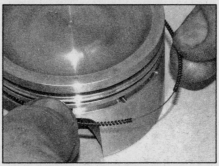

15.7a Fit the oil ring expander in its groove

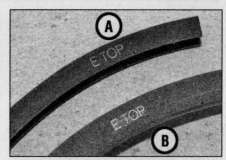

15.7b Make sure the E-TOP marks on the control ring (A) and second ring (B) face the top

15.7c Fit the control ring over the expander

15.7d Fit the second ring into its groove

15.7e Fit the top ring into its groove

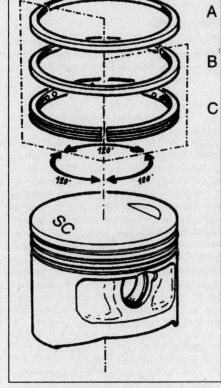

15.8 Stagger the ring end gaps at 120° intervals

A Top ring
B Second ring
C Oil control ring

The ring should be about 15 mm from the bottom of the bore. To measure the end gap, slip a feeler gauge between the ends of the ring and compare the measurement to the Specifications at the beginning of the Chapter (see illustration).

3 If the gap is larger or smaller than specified, double-check to make sure that you have the correct rings before proceeding. If the gap is too small the ends may come in contact with each other during engine operation, which can cause serious damage. Check the piston and bore diameters with the Specifications to confirm whether they are standard or oversize.

4 Excess end gap is not critical unless it exceeds the service limit. Again, double-check to make sure you have the correct rings for your engine and check that the bore is not worn.

5 Repeat the procedure for the other rings.

6 Once the ring end gaps have been checked, the rings can be fitted onto the piston.

7 Fit the oil control ring expander into the bottom groove in the piston (see illustration). Fit the control ring over it with the E-TOP mark facing the top of the piston, and with the expander gap opposite to the ring gap, and do not expand the ring any more than is necessary to slide it into place (see illustrations). Next fit the second (middle) compression ring into the middle groove in the piston with the E-TOP mark facing the top of the piston (see illustration). Finally fit the top ring into its groove with its horizontal section at the bottom so it fits correctly into the stepped groove (see illustration).

8 Once the rings are correctly installed, check

they move freely without snagging and stagger their end gaps as shown (see illustration).

16 Cooling fan

Note: This procedure can be carried out with the engine in the frame. If the engine has been removed, ignore the steps which do not apply.

1 Remove the right-hand side panel, (see Chapter 9).

2 Disconnect the oxygen sensor wiring connector and release the wiring from the clips around the alternator cover.

3 Undo the fan cover screws and bolts and remove the cover, freeing the wiring grommet from its cut-out (see illustration). Note the washers with the bolts, and the bushes in the cover.

16.3 Remove the fan cover

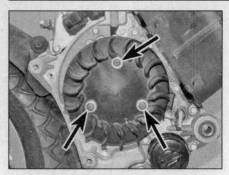

16.4 Undo the screws (arrowed) and remove the fan

4 Undo the three screws securing the cooling fan to the alternator rotor and remove the fan **(see illustration)**.

5 Installation is the reverse of removal.

17 Alternator rotor and stator

Note: *This procedure can be carried out with the engine in the frame. If the engine has been removed, ignore the steps which do not apply.*

Check

1 Refer to Chapter 10.

Removal

2 Remove the cooling fan (see Section 16).

3 To remove the rotor nut it is necessary to stop the rotor from turning. Vespa produces a

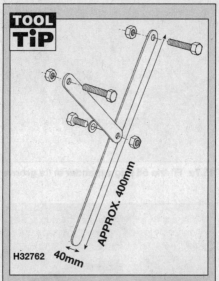

A rotor holding tool can easily be made using two strips of steel bolted together in the middle, with a bolt through each end which locates into the holes in the rotor. Do not allow the bolts to extend too far through the rotor holes otherwise the coils could be damaged.

service tool (Part No. 020656Y) which locates in the holes in the rotor **(see illustration)**. Similar tools can be purchased from aftermarket suppliers, such as a motorcycle clutch holding tool which has pegs on the reverse side – make sure you measure the diameter of the

holes so you can check the pegs on the tool are not too big. A strap wrench can be used around the rotor periphery of the rotor, but be careful not to damage the ignition pulse generator coil – it is best to undo the coil bolts and displace the coil first. Alternatively you could make a tool (see **Tool Tip**). With the rotor held securely, unscrew the nut.

4 To pull the rotor off the crankshaft it is necessary to use the Vespa service tool (Part No. 008564Y), a commercially available equivalent, or a two-legged puller **(see illustration)**. When fitting the tool make sure the centre bolt is backed-out sufficiently to allow the body of the tool to be screwed all the way into the threads in the rotor. With the tool in place, hold the body of the tool using a spanner on its flats while tightening the centre bolt (turn it clockwise) to draw the rotor off the end of the shaft. If using a two-legged puller, assemble the puller legs through the holes in the rotor and tighten the centre bolt down onto the crankshaft end until the rotor is drawn off. If it is loose, remove the Woodruff key from the shaft, noting how it fits.

5 Disconnect the alternator, pulse generator coil and oil pressure switch wiring connectors **(see illustration)**. Free the wiring from any clips and ties and feed it back to the rotor, noting its routing.

6 Undo the wiring guide screw, the pulse generator coil screws and the stator screws and remove the two units together **(see illustration)**.

Installation

7 Fit the stator and pulse generator coil onto the crankcase – make sure that the wiring for the generator coil and the oil pressure switch is correctly positioned **(see illustration 17.6)**. Fit the stator screws, and the generator coil screws unless you need it displaced to fit a rotor strap for tightening the rotor nut, and tighten them to the specified torque.

8 Connect the oil pressure switch and alternator/pulse generator coil wiring connectors, making sure the wiring is correctly routed and secured by any ties and guides.

9 Clean the tapered end of the crankshaft and the corresponding mating surface on the inside of the rotor with a suitable solvent. Make sure that no metal objects have attached themselves to the magnets on the inside of the rotor. If removed, fit the Woodruff key into its slot in the shaft. Fit the rotor onto the shaft, aligning the slot in the rotor with the key.

10 Fit the rotor nut and tighten it to the torque setting specified at the beginning of the Chapter, using the method employed on removal to prevent the rotor from turning **(see illustration 17.3)**. Fit the pulse generator coil screws now if not already done.

11 Turn the rotor so that the raised trigger aligns with the pulse generator coil, then measure the air gap between the rotor and the coil with a feeler gauge **(see illustration)**. The air gap should be between 0.34 to 0.76 mm. If the gap is outside the specified limits inspect

17.3 With the rotor held securely, unscrew the nut

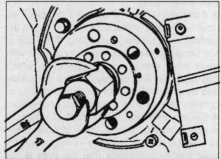

17.4 Screw the rotor puller into the hub then turn the bolt until the rotor is displaced

17.5 Oil pressure switch wiring connector (arrowed)

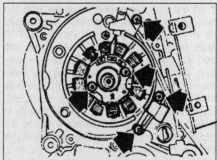

17.6 Undo the screws (arrowed) and remove the stator and pulse coil assembly

17.11 Measure the air gap between the trigger and the pick-up

the coil mounting for distortion. If the gap is too small the rotor may strike to coil and damage it; if the gap is too large the performance of the ignition system will be reduced.

12 Install the cooling fan (see Section 16).

18 Starter pinion assembly

Note: *This procedure can be carried out with the engine in the frame.*

Removal

1 Remove the drive belt cover (see Chapter 3).
2 Lift out the starter pinion assembly, noting how it fits **(see illustration)**.

Inspection

3 Check the starter pinion assembly for any signs of damage or wear, particularly for chipped or broken teeth on either of the pinions. Check the corresponding teeth on the starter motor pinion and the starter driven gear.
4 Rotate the outer pinion and check that it moves smoothly up and down the shaft, and that it returns easily to its rest position **(see illustration)**.
5 The starter pinion assembly is supplied as a complete unit; if any of the component parts are worn or damaged, the unit will have to be renewed.

18.2 Remove the starter pinion (arrowed)

Installation

6 Installation is the reverse of removal. Ensure the inner pinion engages with the starter motor shaft.

19 Oil pump and relief valve

1 Refer to Chapter 2C, Section 18, for procedural details, but use the Specifications at the beginning of this Chapter.

20 Crankcase halves, crankshaft and connecting rod

Note: *To separate the crankcase halves, the engine must be removed from the frame.*

Separation

1 To access the crankshaft and its bearings, the crankcase must be split into two parts.
2 To enable the crankcases to be separated, the engine must be removed from the frame (see Section 5). Before the crankcases can be separated the following components must be removed:
• Cam chain, blades and sprockets (see Section 9).
• Cylinder head (see Section 11).

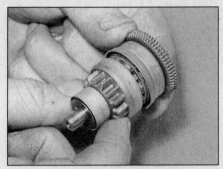

18.4 Outer pinion check

• Cylinder (see Section 13).
• Piston (see Section 14).
• Alternator rotor and stator (see Section 17).
• Variator (see Chapter 3).
• Starter motor (see Chapter 10).
• Oil pump (see Section 19).
• Centrestand (see Chapter 9).

3 Before separating the crankcases, measure the crankshaft end-float with a dial gauge and compare the result with the Specifications at the beginning of the Chapter. Excessive end-float is an indication of wear on the crankshaft or the crankcases and should be investigated when the cases have been separated.
4 Unscrew the eleven crankcase bolts evenly, a little at a time and in a criss-cross sequence until they are all finger-tight, then remove them **(see illustration)**. Support the engine unit on the work surface with the left-hand (transmission) side down. Carefully lift the right-hand crankcase half off the left-hand half, taking care not to score the surface of the right-hand main bearing on the crankshaft **(see illustration)**. If the halves do not separate easily, tap around the joint with a soft-faced mallet. **Note:** *Do not try and separate the halves by levering against the crankcase mating surfaces as they are easily scored and will not seal correctly afterwards.* Note the position of the two crankcase dowels and remove them for safekeeping if they are loose.

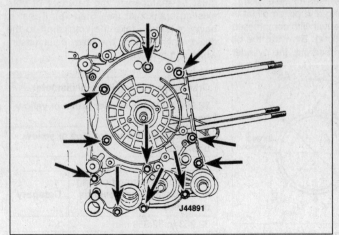

20.4a Unscrew the crankcase bolts (arrowed) . . .

20.4b . . . and lift the right-hand half off

20.5 Lift the crankshaft out

20.7 Unscrew the bolts (arrowed) and remove the plate

20.12 Check the bush (arrowed) in each crankcase half

5 Lift the crankshaft assembly out of the left-hand crankcase, again taking care not to mark the bearing surface **(see illustration)**.

6 Remove and discard the gasket – a new one must be fitted on reassembly **(see illustration 20.22b)**. Note the position of the two crankcase dowels and remove them for safe-keeping if they are loose **(see illustration 20.22a)**. Remove the oil filter insert and discard its O-ring **(see illustrations 20.21b and a)** – a new one must be used.

7 If required remove the baffle plate **(see illustration)**. Clean the crankcases thoroughly with solvent and dry them with compressed air. Clean the crankshaft assembly with solvent. **Note:** *Vespa warn against blowing compressed air through the connecting rod oil passage to avoid the danger of compacting dirt and blocking the passage to the big-end bearing.* Remove all traces of old gasket from the mating surfaces using a suitable scraper and solvent. Take care not to scratch or gouge the soft aluminium.

Caution: Be very careful not to nick or gouge the crankcase mating surfaces, or oil leaks will result. Check both crankcase halves very carefully for cracks and other damage.

8 Note the position of the crankshaft oil seal in the right-hand crankcase half, then drive the seal out with a bearing driver or suitably-sized socket. Take care not to damage the surface of the main bearing.

Inspection

Crankcases

9 Small cracks or holes in aluminium castings can be repaired with an epoxy resin adhesive as a temporary measure. Permanent repairs can only be effected by argon-arc welding, and only a specialist in this process is in a position to advise on the economy or practical aspect of such a repair. If any damage is found that can't be repaired, replace the crankcase halves with a new set.

10 Damaged threads can be economically reclaimed by using a diamond section wire insert, of the Heli-Coil type, which is easily fitted after drilling and re-tapping the affected thread. Sheared studs or screws can usually be removed with stud or screw extractors; if you are in any doubt consult a Vespa dealer or specialist motorcycle engineer.

11 Always wash the crankcases thoroughly after any repair work to ensure no dirt or metal swarf is trapped inside when the engine is rebuilt.

12 Inspect the engine mounting bushes **(see illustration)**. If they show signs of deterioration, replace them both with new ones. To remove a bush, first note its position in the casing. Heat the casing with a hot air gun, then support the casing and drive the bush out with a hammer and a suitably-sized socket. Clean the bush housing with steel wool to remove any corrosion, then reheat the casing and fit the new bush. **Note:** *Always support the casing when removing or fitting bushes to avoid breaking the casing.*

13 Blow out the oil passages for the oil pump, relief valve, main bearing and piston oil jet in the left-hand crankcase half with compressed air **(see illustration 20.14)**. Blow out the oil passages for the main bearing, the cylinder head oil supply and the oil seal drain in the right-hand crankcase half.

Main bearings

14 Check the condition of the main bearings in each crankcase half **(see illustration)**. Each bearing comprises two halves – the surface of the rear half is plain and the front half has an oilway in it. The surface of each bearing should be smooth with no scoring or scuff marks. The condition of the bearings and the corresponding crankshaft journals is vital to the performance of the engine lubrication system. If the bearings are damaged or worn, oil pressure will drop and the oil feed to the connecting rod big end and the cylinder head will be insufficient to prevent rapid wear and possible seizure.

15 Use a telescoping gauge and a micrometer to measure the internal diameter of each bearing in three directions as shown **(see illustration)**. Ensure that the measurements are taken in the centre of the bearing surface, either side of the oilway. Ensure all three measurements for each bearing are within the specifications given below for the colour of the bearing. Vespa do not supply new bearings; if either of the bearings are worn beyond the specifications new crankcase halves will have to be fitted. If there is any doubt about the condition of the bearings consult a Vespa dealer. The category of the new crankcases must be matched to the category of your existing crankshaft (see Step 16), if that is being re-used – take the crankshaft to the dealer when ordering the cases if you unsure which category it is.

Crankcase bearing internal diameter
28.999 to 29.005 mm for green or yellow bearings
29.005 to 29.011 mm for blue or yellow bearings

Crankcase bearing housing internal diameter (bearings removed)	Category
32.953 to 32.959 mm	1
32.959 to 32.965 mm	2

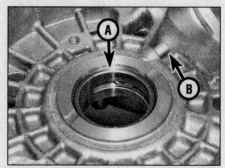

20.14 Check each main bearing (A). Piston oil jet (B)

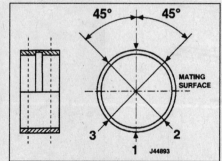

20.15 Measure the main bearings as described

Crankshaft journal diameter	Category
28.998 to 29.004 mm	1
29.004 to 29.010 mm	2

Main bearing colour selection	
Crankshaft category 1 with crankcase category 1	Green bearing
Crankshaft category 1 with crankcase category 2	Yellow bearing
Crankshaft category 2 with crankcase category 1	Yellow bearing
Crankshaft category 2 with crankcase category 2	Blue bearing

Crankshaft

16 Check the condition of the crankshaft journals. The surface of each journal should be smooth with no scoring, pitting or scuff marks. Use a micrometer to measure the diameter of each journal in two positions (A and B) and in two directions as shown **(see illustration)**. There are two size categories for the crankshaft journals. Compare the results with the table and ensure that the journal size is within the specifications. If the crankshaft journals are damaged or worn beyond the specifications a new crankshaft will have to be fitted, but note that it must be matched correctly to the crankcases and the bearings fitted – take the crankcases to the dealer when ordering the new crankshaft to ensure correct fitment.

17 Measure the connecting rod big-end side clearance with a feeler gauge and compare it with the Specifications at the beginning of the Chapter **(see illustration)**. Measure the up-and-down (radial) play on the rod with a dial gauge and measure the width of the flywheels at several points to ensure they are not out of alignment **(see illustrations)**. Compare the results with the Specifications at the beginning of the Chapter.

18 Place the crankshaft assembly on V-blocks and check the runout at the main bearing journals and at the ends of the shafts **(see illustration)**. If the runout exceeds the specified limit, or if either of the connecting rod measurements exceed the limit, the crankshaft assembly must be renewed.

Reassembly

19 Lubricate the new crankshaft oil seal with clean engine oil, then fit it in the right-hand crankcase half in the same position as noted on removal. Use a bearing driver or a suitably-sized socket which contacts only the outer face of the seal to drive it into position. **Note:** *Do not press the oil seal too far into the casing.* If removed fit the baffle plate **(see illustration 20.7)**.

20 Lubricate the main bearings and crank-shaft journals with clean engine oil. Fit the crankshaft all the way into the left-hand crankcase half, positioning the connecting

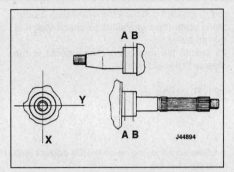

20.16 Measure the crankshaft journals as described

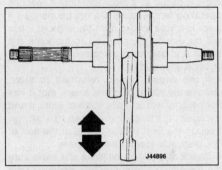

20.17b Measure the radial play on the connecting rod

rod in-line with the crankcase mouth **(see illustration 20.5)**.

21 Fit a new O-ring onto the oil filter insert and fit it into the crankcase **(see illustrations)**.

22 Ensure that the crankcase mating surfaces are clean. Support the left-hand crankcase half

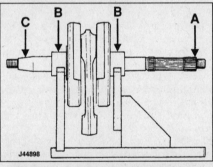

20.18 Check the crankshaft runout as described

20.21b . . . then fit the insert into the crankcase

20.17a Checking the connecting rod big-end bearing side clearance

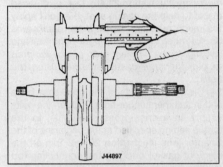

20.17c Measure the width across the flywheels at several points

on the work surface, transmission side down. Check that the crankcase dowels are in place, then fit a new gasket **(see illustrations)**.

23 Guide the crankcase right-hand half over the crankshaft end and press it down, making sure the dowels locate, until the two halves

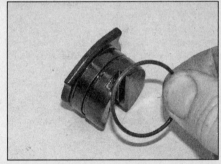

20.21a Fit a new O-ring into the groove . . .

20.22a Fit the dowels (arrowed) if removed . . .

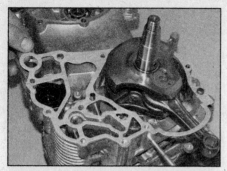

20.22b . . . then lay a new gasket onto the mating surface and over the dowels

meet **(see illustration 20.4b)**. Use a soft-faced mallet to help the casing seat, but don't apply too much pressure. **Note:** *If the crankcases do not meet, remove the right-hand half and investigate the problem – do not be tempted to pull the crankcases together using the bolts.*

24 Clean the threads of the crankcase bolts and install them finger-tight. Tighten the bolts evenly, in a criss-cross sequence, to the torque setting specified at the beginning of the Chapter **(see illustration 20.4a)**. Trim off the piece of gasket bridging the connecting rod mouth with a sharp knife. Hold the connecting rod to prevent it hitting the crankcase mouth, then rotate the crankshaft to check that it is moves freely.

25 Install the remaining components in the reverse order of removal.

21 Running-in

1 Make sure the engine oil level is correct (see *Pre-ride checks*).

2 Make sure there is fuel in the tank.

3 Turn the ignition ON, start the engine and allow it to run at a slow idle until it reaches operating temperature. Do not be alarmed if there is a little smoke from the exhaust – this will be due to the oil used to lubricate the piston and bore during assembly and should subside after a while.

4 If the engine proves reluctant to start, remove the spark plug and check that it has not become wet and oily. If it has, clean it and try again. If the engine refuses to start, go through the fault finding charts at the end of this manual to identify the problem.

5 Check carefully for oil leaks and make sure the transmission and controls, especially the brakes, function properly before road testing the machine.

6 Treat the machine gently for the first few miles to make sure oil has circulated throughout the engine and any new parts installed have started to seat.

7 Even greater care is necessary if the engine has been re-bored or a new crankshaft has been installed. In the case of a re-bore, the machine will have to be run-in as when new. This means a restraining hand on the throttle until at least 600 miles (1000 km) have been covered. There's no point in keeping to any set speed limit – the main idea is to keep from labouring the engine and not to maintain any one speed for too long. Experience is the best guide, since it's easy to tell when an engine is running freely. Once past the 600 mile (1000 km) mark, gradually increase performance, using full throttle for short bursts to begin with.

8 If a lubrication failure is suspected, stop the engine immediately and try to find the cause. If an engine is run without oil, even for a short period of time, severe damage will occur.

9 Upon completion of the road test, and after the engine has cooled down completely, recheck the valve clearances (see Chapter 1) and check the engine oil level (see *Pre-ride checks*).

Chapter 2B
Air-cooled three-valve engines (LX, LXV and S models)

See 'Model specifications' at the beginning of the manual for identification details.

Contents

Degrees of difficulty

Easy, suitable for novice with little experience	Fairly easy, suitable for beginner with some experience	Fairly difficult, suitable for competent DIY mechanic	Difficult, suitable for experienced DIY mechanic	Very difficult, suitable for expert DIY or professional

Specifications

General

Type	Single cylinder 3v air-cooled four-stroke
Capacity	
125 engine	124 cc
150 engine	154.8 cc
Bore	
125 engine	52.0 mm
150 engine	58 mm
Stroke	58.6 mm
Compression ratio	10.1 to 11.1 : 1
Cylinder compression	150 to 200 psi (10 to 14 Bars) @ 600rpm

Camshaft

Left-hand journal diameter	
Standard	25.002 to 25.015 mm
Right-hand journal diameter	
Standard	12.002 to12.013 mm

Cylinder head

Warpage (max)	0.03 mm
Left-hand camshaft bearing housing diameter (standard)	42.000 to 42.034 mm
Right-hand camshaft bearing housing diameter (standard)	28.000 to 28.028 mm
Rocker arm shaft housing (standard)	10.000 to 10.015 mm
Rocker arm shaft diameter	10.015 to 10.023 mm
Rocker arm internal diameter	10.015 to 10.035 mm

Valves, guides and springs

Valve clearances	See Chapter 1
Stem diameter	
Intake valves	4.015 to 4.030 mm
Exhaust valve	4.960 to 4.975 mm
Stem-to-valve guide clearance	
Intake valves	0.10 mm
Exhaust valve	0.15 mm
Face width	1.0 to 1.3 mm
Spring free length	35.8 mm

Cylinder and piston – 125 engine

Standard bore diameter (measured 27.7 mm down from top edge of the cylinder, at 90° to the piston pin axis)	
Size-code A	51.980 to 51.987 mm
Size-code B	51.987 to 51.994 mm
Size-code C	51.994 to 52.001 mm
Size-code D	52.001 to 52.008 mm
Standard piston diameter (measured 27.0 mm down from top edge of the piston, at 90° to the piston pin axis)	
Size-code A	51.947 to 51.954 mm
Size-code B	51.954 to 51.961 mm
Size-code C	51.961 to 51.968 mm
Size-code D	51.968 to 51.975 mm
Piston-to-bore clearance (when new, all size codes)	0.026 to 0.040 mm
Piston pin diameter	14.000 to 14.004 mm
Piston pin bore diameter in piston	14.001 to 14.006 mm

Cylinder and piston – 2012 LX 150 engine from Engine No. M66AM5004083

Standard bore diameter (measured 27.7 mm down from top edge of the cylinder, at 90° to the piston pin axis)	
Size-code A2	57.980 to 57.987 mm
Size-code B2	57.987 to 57.994 mm
Size-code C2	57.994 to 58.001 mm
Size-code D2	58.001 to 58.008 mm
Standard piston diameter (measured 27.0 mm down from top edge of the piston, at 90° to the piston pin axis)	
Size-code A2	57.947 to 57.954 mm
Size-code B2	57.954 to 57.961 mm
Size-code C2	57.961 to 57.968 mm
Size-code D2	57.968 to 57.975 mm
Piston-to-bore clearance (when new, all size codes)	0.026 to 0.040 mm
Piston pin diameter	14.000 to 14.004 mm
Piston pin bore diameter in piston	14.001 to 14.006 mm

Cylinder and piston – 2013-on LX 150 engine

Standard bore diameter (measured 27.7 mm down from top edge of the cylinder, at 90° to the piston pin axis)	
Size-code A	57.980 to 57.987 mm
Size-code B	57.987 to 57.994 mm
Size-code C	57.994 to 58.001 mm
Size-code D	58.001 to 58.008 mm
Standard piston diameter (measured 27.0 mm down from top edge of the piston, at 90° to the piston pin axis)	
Size-code A	57.933 to 57.940 mm
Size-code B	57.940 to 57.947 mm
Size-code C	57.947 to 57.954 mm
Size-code D	57.954 to 57.961 mm
Piston-to-bore clearance (when new, all size codes)	0.040 to 0.054 mm
Piston pin diameter	14.000 to 14.004 mm
Piston pin bore diameter in piston	14.001 to 14.006 mm

Piston rings

Ring end gap (installed)	
Top ring	0.20 to 0.35 mm
2nd ring	0.20 to 0.45 mm
Oil control ring	0.25 to 0.55 mm

Lubrication system

Engine oil pressure (at 90°C)
    At idle .... 7.25 to 17.5 psi (0.5 to 1.2 Bar)
    At 5000 rpm .... 46.5 to 61 psi (3.2 to 4.2 Bars)
Oil pump
    Inner rotor tip-to-outer rotor clearance (max).................... 0.12 mm
    Outer rotor-to-body clearance (max) .... 0.20 mm
    Rotor end-float (max) .... 0.09 mm
Pressure relief valve piston diameter .... 12.843 to 12.861 mm
Pressure relief valve spring free length........................ 52.4 mm

Connecting rod

Small-end internal diameter
    Standard.. 14.015 to 14.025 mm
    Service limit (max) .... 14.030 mm
Big-end side clearance
    Standard.. 0.20 to 0.50 mm
Big-end radial freeplay
    Standard.. 0.036 to 0.054 mm
    Service limit (max) .... 0.25 mm

Crankshaft

Combined width of flywheels and big-end.................... 51.40 to 51.45 mm

Torque settings

Alternator rotor nut... 100 to 110 Nm
Alternator stator screws.................................... 5 to 6 Nm
Cam chain tensioner blade bolt.............................. 10 to 14 Nm
Cam chain tensioner bolts................................... 11 to 13 Nm
Cam chain tensioner spring cap bolt......................... 5 to 6 Nm
Camshaft sprocket bolts .... 4 to 6 Nm
Crankcase bolts.. 11 to 13 Nm
Crankcase cover screws (left-hand side)..................... 11 to 13 Nm
Cylinder head nuts
    Initial setting... 9 to 11 Nm
    Final setting .... 270° (in 3 stages)
Cylinder head bolts .... 11 to 13 Nm
Engine unit front mounting bolt/nut .... 40 to 45 Nm
Engine unit to rear shock bolt .... 40 to 45 Nm
Ignition pulse generator coil screws......................... 3 to 4 Nm
Intake manifold bolts .... 11 to 13 Nm
Oil pressure switch... 12 to 14 Nm
Oil pump cover screws...................................... 0.7 to 0.9 Nm
Oil pump mounting bolts .... 5 to 6 Nm
Oil pump sprocket bolt...................................... 12 to 14 Nm
Sump cover bolts.. 11 to 13 Nm
Valve cover bolts .... 11 to 13 Nm

1 General information

The engine unit is a single cylinder four-stroke, with fan-assisted air cooling. The fan is mounted inside a cowling on the right-hand end of the crankshaft. The crankshaft assembly is pressed together, incorporating the connecting rod, with the big-end running on the crankpin on a bronze bearing. The crankshaft runs in plain main bearings. The crankcase divides vertically.

The camshaft is chain-driven off the left-hand end of the crankshaft, and operates three valves (two intake and one exhaust) via rocker arms.

2 Component access

Access to the alternator rotor and stator on the right-hand side and the transmission on the left-hand side is easy and can be done with the engine in place.

Access to the top-end of the engine is very restricted making removal of the valve cover the only operation that can be achieved with the engine in the frame.

To access the crankshaft and connecting rod assembly and its bearings, the engine must be removed from the frame and the crankcase halves separated.

3 Engine wear assessment

Cylinder compression test

Special tool: *A compression gauge is required to perform this test.*

1 Poor engine performance may be caused by leaking valves, incorrect valve clearances, a leaking head gasket, or a worn piston, piston rings or cylinder walls. A cylinder compression check will highlight these conditions and can also indicate the presence of excessive carbon deposits in the cylinder head.

2 The only tools required are a compression

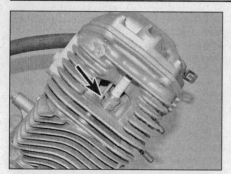

3.5a Note the location of the spark plug hole . . .

3.5b . . . in relation to the access through the valve cover

3.15 Oil pressure switch wiring connector (arrowed)

gauge (there are two types, one with a 10 mm threaded adapter to fit the spark plug hole in the cylinder head, the other has a rubber seal which is pressed into the spark plug hole to create a seal ñ the threaded adapter type is preferable), and a spark plug socket. Depending on the outcome of the initial test, a squirt-type oil can may also be needed.

3 Make sure the valve clearances are correctly set (see Chapter 1) and that the cylinder head nuts and bolts are tightened to the correct torque settings (see Section 11).

4 Run the engine until it is at normal operating temperature. Remove the spark plug (see Chapter 1). Fit the plug back into the plug cap and earth the plug against the engine away from the plug hole ñ if the plug is not earthed the ignition system could be damaged.

5 Fit the gauge into the spark plug hole ñ if the rubber cone type is used keep the gauge pressed onto the hole throughout the test to maintain a good seal. Note that the spark plug hole is deeply recessed and that the cone must seal in the hole, not the valve cover **(see illustrations)**.

6 With the ignition switch ON, the throttle held fully open and the spark plug earthed, turn the engine over on the starter motor until the gauge reading has built up and stabilised.

7 Compare the reading on the gauge to the cylinder compression range specified at the beginning of the Chapter (under General specifications). Note that this is not a range specified by Vespa (they do not provide one), but is a general range acceptable for this engine ñ if in doubt ask your dealer.

8 If the reading is low, it could be due to a worn cylinder bore, piston or rings, failure of the head gasket, or worn valve seats. To determine which is the cause, pour a small quantity of engine oil into the spark plug hole to seal the rings, then repeat the compression test. If the figures are noticeably higher the cause is worn cylinder, piston or rings (see Sections 13 to 15). If there is no change the cause is a leaking head gasket or worn valve seats (see Sections 11 and 12).

9 If the reading is high there could be a build-up of carbon deposits in the combustion chamber. Remove the cylinder head and scrape all deposits off the piston and the cylinder head.

10 While working on the engine also check

that the correct base gasket has been fitted under the cylinder ñ different thicknesses are available and it is possible that the one fitted is either too thick, which will reduce cylinder compression, or too thin, increasing compression ñ refer to Section 13 for details.

Oil pressure check

Special tools: *A pressure gauge and an auxilliary tachometer are required to perform this test.*

11 This engine is fitted with an oil pressure switch and warning light. The function of the circuit is described in Chapter 10.

12 If there is any doubt about the performance of the engine lubrication system, the oil pressure should be checked. The check provides useful information about the condition of the lubrication system. If you do not have the facilities to check the oil pressure yourself, have it done by a Vespa dealer.

13 To check the oil pressure, a suitable pressure gauge (which screws into the crankcase) will be needed. Vespa can supply a gauge (Part No. 020193Y) for this purpose.

14 Check the engine oil level (see *Pre-ride checks*), then warm the engine up to normal operating temperature and stop it. Support the scooter so that the rear wheel is clear of the ground.

15 Remove the cooling fan cover (see Section 16). Disconnect the oil pressure switch wiring connector **(see illustration)**, then unscrew the switch using a deep socket and screw in the gauge adapter. Connect the pressure gauge to the adapter. Discard the pressure switch sealing washer, as a new one must be fitted on reassembly.

⚠️ *Warning: Take great care not to burn your hands on the hot engine unit, exhaust pipe or with engine oil when connecting the gauge adapter to the crankcase. Do not allow exhaust gases to build-up in the work area; either perform the check outside or use an exhaust gas extraction system.*

16 Start the engine, allow it to idle and note the pressure gauge reading. Now increase the engine speed to 5000 rpm whilst watching the pressure gauge. The oil pressure should be within the range given in the Specifications at the beginning of the Chapter.

17 If the pressure is significantly lower than

the standard, either the oil strainer or filter is blocked, the pressure relief valve is stuck open, the oil pump is faulty, the piston oil jet in the crankcases has become dislodged, or there is considerable engine main bearing wear. Begin diagnosis by checking the oil filter and strainer (see Chapter 1), then the relief valve and oil pump (see Section 19). If those items check out okay, the crankcases will have to be split to check the oil jet and the main bearings (see Section 20).

18 If the pressure is too high, either an oil passage is clogged, the relief valve is stuck closed or the wrong grade of oil is being used.

19 Stop the engine and unscrew the gauge and adapter from the crankcase.

20 Fit a new sealing washer to the oil pressure switch and tighten the switch using a deep socket to the specified torque setting. Connect the wiring connector. Install the fan cover (see Section 16). Check the oil level (see *Pre-ride checks*). **Note:** *Rectify any problems before running the engine again.*

4 Major engine repair – general note

1 It is not always easy to determine when or if an engine should be completely overhauled, as a number of factors must be considered.

2 High mileage is not necessarily an indication that an overhaul is needed, while low mileage, on the other hand, does not preclude the need for an overhaul. Frequency of servicing is probably the single most important consideration. An engine that has regular and frequent oil and filter changes, as well as other required maintenance, will most likely give many miles of reliable service. Conversely, a neglected engine, or one which has not been run-in properly, may require an overhaul very early in its life.

3 Exhaust smoke and excessive oil consumption are both indications that piston rings and/or valve guides are in need of attention, although make sure that the fault is not due to oil leakage.

4 If the engine is making obvious knocking or rumbling noises, the connecting rod and/or main bearings are probably at fault.

5.5 Using axle stands underneath the swingarm cross-member

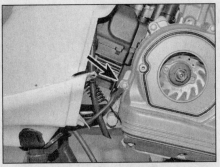

5.7 Location of the crankcase earth terminal

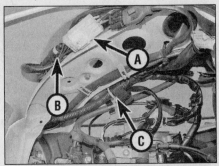

5.10 Alternator (A) and pulse generator coil (B) connectors. Note wiring loom clip (C)

5 Loss of power, rough running, excessive valve train noise and high fuel consumption rates may also point to the need for an overhaul, especially if they are all present at the same time. If a complete tune-up does not remedy the situation, major mechanical work is the only solution.

6 A full engine overhaul generally involves restoring the internal parts to the specifications of a new engine. The piston, piston rings and cylinder are renewed as a set. The valve seats are re-ground and new valve springs are fitted. If the connecting rod bearings are worn a new crankshaft assembly is fitted. The end result should be a like-new engine that will give as many trouble-free miles as the original.

7 Before beginning the engine overhaul, read through the related procedures to familiarise yourself with the scope and requirements of the job. Overhauling an engine is not all that difficult, but it is time-consuming. Plan on the scooter being tied up for a minimum of two weeks. Check on the availability of parts and make sure that any necessary special tools, equipment and supplies are obtained in advance.

8 Most work can be done with typical workshop hand tools, although a number of precision measuring tools are required for inspecting parts to determine if they must be renewed. Often a dealer will handle the inspection of parts and offer advice concerning reconditioning and renewal. As a general rule, time is the primary cost of an overhaul so it does not pay to install worn or substandard parts.

9 As a final note, to ensure maximum life

and minimum trouble from a rebuilt engine, everything must be assembled with care in a spotlessly-clean environment.

5 Engine/transmission unit removal and installation

Caution: The engine is not heavy, although engine removal and installation should be carried out with the aid of an assistant; personal injury or damage could occur if the engine falls or is dropped.

Removal

1 Remove the storage compartment, side panels and floor panel (see Chapter 9).
2 Wash any accumulated dirt off the engine.
3 If the sump is going to be removed, or the crankcases separated, drain the engine oil (see Chapter 1).
4 Disconnect the battery (see Chapter 10).
5 Support the scooter securely in an upright position. Note that the centrestand is bolted to the engine so you will need to support the body of the scooter on axle stands or wooden blocks after the engine has been removed **(see illustration)**. Have an assistant to help with this procedure. Make sure the scooter is securely supported so it cannot topple over. Work on the engine can be made easier by raising the machine to a suitable working height on an hydraulic ramp or a suitable platform ñ again make sure the scooter is secure and will not topple over.

6 Remove the air filter element and the transmission cooling cover (see Chapter 1).
7 Undo the bolt securing the crankcase earth (ground) terminal **(see illustration)** and position the lead clear of the engine unit.
8 Remove the cooling fan cover (see Section 16).
9 Remove the exhaust system (see Chapter 5).
10 Trace the wiring from the alternator and ignition pulse generator coil and oil pressure switch on the right-hand side of the engine and disconnect it at the connectors inside the bodywork **(see illustration)**. Free the wiring from any clips and feed it down to the alternator cover, noting its routing.
11 Undo the bolt securing the fuel hose guide to the throttle body **(see illustration)**. Referring to Chapter 5, place some rag around the fuel hose connector to catch any residual fuel and disconnect the hose from the injector. Disconnect the injector wiring connector.
12 Disconnect the engine temperature sensor wiring connector **(see illustration)**.
13 On machines fitted with a combined throttle body/ECU, pull back the rubber boot and release the retaining clip to disconnect the ECU multi-pin wiring connector **(see illustration)**.
14 On machines fitted with a separate throttle body, disconnect the idle speed control valve wiring connector. Loosen the clip securing the air hose to the valve and disconnect the hose, then ease the valve off its mounting bracket. Disconnect the throttle position sensor wiring connector.

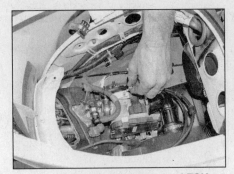

5.11 Release the fuel hose and ECU connector clips

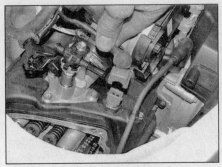

5.12 Disconnect the engine temperature sensor connector

5.13 Release the ECU connector clip

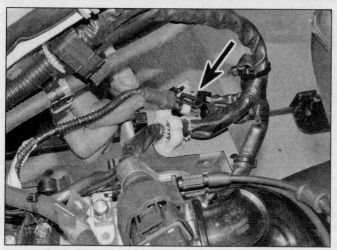

5.15 Location of the ignition coil wiring connector

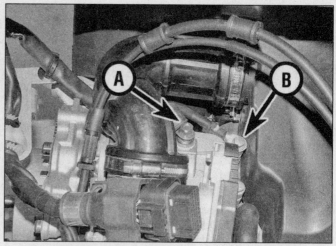

5.16 Starter motor terminal (A) and earth terminal (B)

15 Trace the wiring from the ignition coil located underneath the throttle body and disconnect it at the connector **(see illustration)**.

16 Undo the nut securing the starter motor terminal and the bolt securing the starter motor earth (ground) terminal **(see illustration)** and position the leads clear of the engine unit.

17 Loosen the clips securing the air intake duct between the air filter housing and the throttle body **(see illustration)**. Ease the duct off the throttle body, then draw it out from the back of the housing **(see illustration)**.

18 Loosen the clip securing the throttle body to the intake manifold sleeve and detach the throttle body, noting how it fits (see Chapter 5). Secure the throttle body so the throttle cables are not strained. Stuff some clean rag into the intake manifold and into the open ends of the throttle body.

19 Remove the air filter housing (see Chapter 5).

20 If not already done, raise the scooter and support the body with sufficient room underneath for the engine unit to be lowered out **(see illustration 5.5)**.

21 Remove the rear wheel (see Chapter 8).

22 Disconnect the rear brake cable from the brake arm and cable stop, then free the cable from the clips on the underside of the drive belt cover **(see illustrations)**.

23 Carefully release the swingarm pre-load spring from its hook on the engine **(see illustration)**.

24 Remove the rear mudguard (see Chapter 9).

25 Unscrew the nut and withdraw the bolt securing the lower end of the rear shock absorber to the transmission casing **(see illustration)**. Lower the casing onto some

5.17a Loosen the air intake duct clips . . .

5.17b . . . and remove the duct

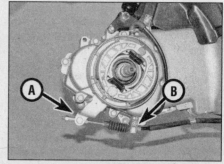

5.22a Rear brake arm (A) and cable stop (B)

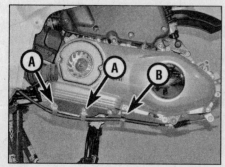

5.22b Undo the bolts (A) and unhook the cable (B)

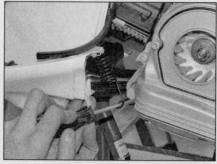

5.23 Unhook the swingarm pre-load spring

5.25a Disconnect the rear shock from the transmission casing

5.25b Support the engine unit with wood blocks

5.27a Unscrew the nut . . .

5.27b . . . and withdraw the front engine mounting bolt

wood blocks and place a wood block underneath the centrestand **(see illustration)**.

26 Check that all wiring, cables and hoses are free and clear of the engine unit.

27 Unscrew the nut on the front engine mounting bolt **(see illustration)**. Ensure the weight of the engine unit is supported, then withdraw the bolt from the left-hand side **(see illustration)**.

28 Draw the engine unit rearwards, then remove the wood blocks and lift the engine clear **(see illustrations)**.

29 If required, clean the engine unit thoroughly before starting any major dismantling work (see Section 6).

Installation

30 Installation is the reverse of removal, noting the following:

● Make sure no wires, cables or hoses become trapped between the engine and the frame when installing the engine.

● Tighten the engine mounting bolt and shock absorber bolt/nut to the torque settings specified at the beginning of this Chapter.

● Make sure all wires, cables and hoses are correctly routed and connected, and secured by any clips or ties.

● Adjust the throttle cable and the rear brake cable (see Chapter 1).

● Fill the engine with the specified quantity of oil (see Chapter 1) and check the oil level as described in Pre-ride checks.

6   Engine overhaul information

Disassembly

1 Before disassembling the engine, the external surfaces of the unit should be thoroughly cleaned and degreased to rule out the possibility of dirt falling inside. A high flash-point solvent, such as paraffin can be used, or better still, a proprietary engine degreaser. Use old paintbrushes and toothbrushes to work the solvent into the various recesses of the engine casings. Take care to exclude solvent or water from the electrical components and intake and exhaust ports.

 Warning: The use of petrol (gasoline) as a cleaning agent should be avoided because of the risk of fire.

2 When clean and dry, arrange the unit on the workbench, leaving suitable clear area for working. Gather a selection of small containers and plastic bags so that parts can be grouped together in an easily identifiable manner. Some paper and a pen should be on hand to permit notes to be made and labels attached where necessary. A supply of clean rag is also required.

3 Before commencing work, read through the appropriate section so that some idea of the necessary procedure can be gained. When removing components it should be noted that great force is seldom required, unless specified. In many cases, a component's reluctance to be removed is indicative of an incorrect approach or removal method – if in any doubt, recheck with the text.

4 When disassembling the engine, keep 'mated' parts that have been in contact with each other during engine operation together. These 'mated' parts must be re-used or renewed as an assembly.

5 Complete engine disassembly should be done in the following general order with reference to the appropriate Sections. Refer to Chapter 3 for details of transmission components disassembly.

Remove the valve cover.
Remove the camshaft and rockers.
Remove the cylinder head.
Remove the cylinder.
Remove the piston.

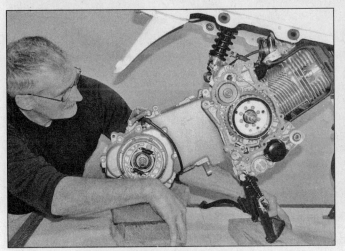

5.28a Draw the engine rearwards . . .

5.28b . . . then lift it clear

Remove the starter motor (see Chapter 10).
Remove the alternator.
Remove the variator (see Chapter 3).
Remove the oil pump.
Separate the crankcase halves.
Remove the crankshaft.

Reassembly

6 Reassembly is the reverse of the general disassembly sequence.

7 Valve cover

Removal

1 Remove the engine access panel and storage compartment (see Chapter 9).
2 Remove the spark plug cap (see Chapter 1). Release the HT lead from the guide on the left-hand side of the valve cover.
3 Release the clip securing the hose from the breather housing and disconnect the hose **(see illustration)**.
4 Unscrew the valve cover bolts **(see illustrations)**.
5 Ease the cover off the cylinder head and manoeuvre it out through the access hatch **(see illustration)**. If the cover is stuck, do not try to lever it off with a screwdriver. Tap it gently with a rubber hammer or block of wood to dislodge it.
6 Remove and discard the cover gasket and spark plug hole seal – new ones must be fitted **(see illustrations)**.
7 Inspect the breather hose – if it is cracked or perished a new one must be fitted.
8 If required, undo the screws securing the breather housing and detach the housing – note the gasket **(see illustrations)**. Clean the inside of the housing prior to reassembly.

Installation

9 If removed, install the breather housing using a new gasket if required **(see illustration 7.8b)**. Tighten the housing screws securely.
10 Clean the mating surfaces of the cylinder head and the valve cover with a suitable solvent.
11 Fit the new gasket into the groove in the valve cover, making sure it locates correctly **(see illustration 7.6a)** – use some dabs of grease to hold it in place if required. Fit the new spark plug seal **(see illustration 7.6b)**.
12 Position the valve cover on the cylinder head, making sure the gasket stays in place, then fit the cover bolts and tighten them evenly and in a criss-cross sequence to the torque setting specified at the beginning of the Chapter **(see illustrations 7.4a, b and c)**.
13 Install the remaining components in the reverse order of removal.

7.3 Disconnect the breather housing hose

7.4a Access the cover bolts . . .

7.4b . . . through the access hatch . . .

7.4c . . . and from inside the scooter body

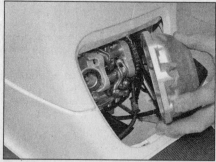

7.5 Remove the cover through the access hatch

7.6a Discard the old cover gasket . . .

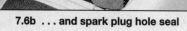

7.6b . . . and spark plug hole seal

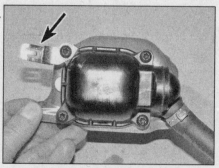

7.8a Breather housing is secured by four screws – note HT lead guide (arrowed)

7.8b Location of breather housing gasket

8 Cam chain tensioner

Removal

Special tool: *A T30 tamper-proof Torx bit is required to undo the intake manifold bolts (see Step 8).*

1 Remove the engine from the frame (see Section 5).
2 Remove the valve cover (see Section 7).
3 Remove the spark plug (see Chapter 1).
4 Remove the lower section of the engine cowling (see Section 16).
5 Unscrew the engine coolant temperature sensor (**see illustration**).
6 Remove the starter motor (see Chapter 10).
7 Remove the ignition coil (see Chapter 6).

8 Using a T30 tamper-proof Torx bit, unscrew the intake manifold bolts and lift the manifold off (**see illustrations**). Discard the manifold gasket as a new one must be fitted (see Chapter 5).
9 Remove the upper section of the engine cowling (see Section 16).
10 Turn the engine in the normal direction of rotation until the piston is at top dead centre (TDC) on its compression stroke (all valves are closed and a small clearance can be felt at each rocker arm) – you can do this by rotating the crankshaft via the cooling fan. To confirm that the piston is in the correct position, ensure that the timing mark on the camshaft sprocket is aligned with the mark on the camshaft holder (see Chapter 1, Section 20).
11 Unscrew the chain tensioner cap bolt and withdraw the spring from the tensioner body (**see illustrations**). Discard the O-ring seal – a new one must be fitted on reassembly.

12 Unscrew the tensioner mounting bolts and withdraw the tensioner from the back of the cylinder (**see illustration**).
13 Remove the gasket from the base of the tensioner or from the cylinder and discard it – a new one must be used (**see illustration**).
Caution: Don't rotate the crankshaft while the cam chain tensioner is removed – the cam chain could slip around one of its sprockets and disturb the valve timing.

Inspection

14 Examine the tensioner components for signs of wear or damage (**see illustration**).
15 Release the ratchet mechanism on the tensioner plunger and check that the plunger moves freely in and out of the tensioner body (**see illustration**).
16 If the tensioner mechanism or the spring are worn or damaged, or if the plunger is seized in the body, a new tensioner assembly

8.5 Location of the engine coolant temperature sensor

8.8a Unscrew the intake manifold bolts . . .

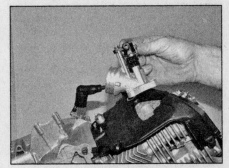

8.8b . . . and lift off the manifold

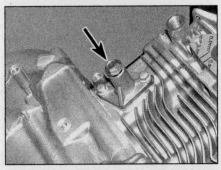
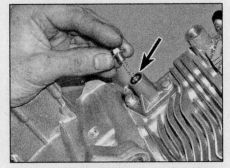
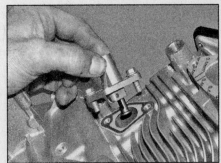

8.11a Unscrew the chain tensioner cap bolt . . .

8.11b . . . and withdraw the spring. Note O-ring (arrowed)

8.12 Withdraw the tensioner from the cylinder

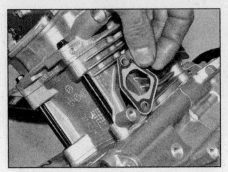

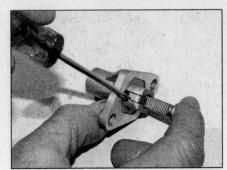

8.13 Note location of the tensioner gasket

8.14 Inspect the ratchet teeth and plunger

8.15 Press the catch to release the ratchet

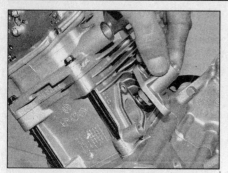

8.19 Install the tensioner with the plunger retracted

9.4 Installed position of the TDC service tool

1 Remove the engine from the frame (see Section 5).

2 Remove the cooling fan and the alternator cover (see Sections 16 and 17).

3 Remove the cam chain tensioner (see Section 8).

4 With the engine still at TDC, install the service tool, locating the curved face in the gap between the ignition timing triggers on the outer surface of the alternator rotor **(see illustration)**.

5 To loosen the camshaft sprocket bolts, hold the sprocket by passing a pin punch through the hole in the sprocket and locate it in the hole in the camshaft holder behind **(see illustration)**. Unscrew the bolts and lift off the sprocket, noting how it fits over the offset peg on the end of the camshaft **(see illustrations)**. Slip the sprocket out of the chain and secure the chain with a cable-tie or length of wire to prevent it falling into the engine.

6 If the cam chain and crankshaft sprocket are to be removed, first remove the drive pulley and variator for access (see Chapter 3). Remove the oil pump driven sprocket, drive chain and drive sprocket (see Section 19). Remove the flat washer from behind the pump drive sprocket **(see illustration)**.

7 Before the cam chain is removed, mark it with paint so that if it is re-used it can be fitted the same way round, then pass the chain down its tunnel and slip it off the sprocket on the crankshaft **(see illustration)**.

8 Draw the sprocket off the crankshaft, noting how it locates on the peg on the shaft **(see illustration)**. Note that the inner face

must be fitted – individual components are not available.

Installation

17 Using the cooling fan, turn the engine a small amount in a clockwise direction to take up any slack in the front run of the cam chain between the crankshaft and the camshaft and transfer it to the back run where it will be taken up by the tensioner.

18 Press the tensioner plunger all the way into the tensioner body.

19 Place a new gasket on the cylinder, then install the tensioner and tighten the bolts to the torque specified at the beginning of the Chapter **(see illustration)**.

20 Fit a new O-ring into the open end of the tensioner body, then fit the spring and tighten the cap bolt to the specified torque **(see illustration 8.11b)** – as you thread the

bolt in you should hear the plunger extend over the ratchet mechanism and see the cam chain tension.

21 Check that the cam chain is tensioned. If it is slack, the tensioner plunger did not release when the cap bolt was tightened. Remove the tensioner and check the operation of the plunger again.

22 Install the remaining components in the reverse order of removal.

9 Cam chain, blades and sprockets

Removal

Special Tool: *A Vespa service tool Part No. 020941Y is required for this procedure (see Step 4).*

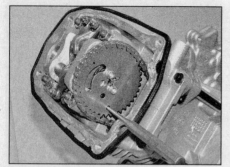

9.5a Holding the camshaft sprocket with a pin punch

9.5b Unscrew the sprocket bolts . . .

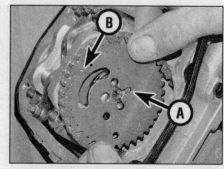

9.5c . . . and remove the sprocket. Note offset peg (A) and timing mark (B)

9.6 Slide off the flat washer

9.7 Remove the cam chain

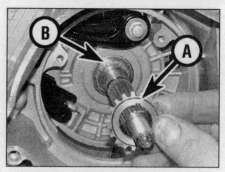

9.8a Slot in sprocket (A) aligns with peg (B)

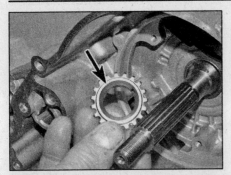

9.8b Chamfered edge (arrowed) is on the inside edge

of the sprocket has a chamfered edge **(see illustration)**.

9 To remove cam chain guide and tensioner blades, first remove the cylinder head (see Section 11). Lift the guide blade out, noting how it locates **(see illustrations)**.

10 To remove the cam chain tensioner blade, unscrew the pivot bolt and lift the blade out noting which way round it fits **(see illustration)**. Note the location of the sleeve in the end of the blade **(see illustration)**.

Inspection

11 Check the sprockets for wear and damaged teeth, replacing them with new ones if necessary **(see illustration)**. If the sprocket teeth are worn, a new cam chain should be fitted.

12 Check the chain tensioner blade and guide blade for wear or damage and fit new ones if necessary. Damaged or severely worn blades are an indication of a worn or improperly tensioned chain. Check the operation of the cam chain tensioner (see Section 8).

Installation

13 If removed, fit the tensioner blade with its sleeve and tighten the bolt to the torque setting specified at the beginning of the Chapter **(see illustration 9.10b and a)**

14 If removed, fit the cam chain guide blade, locating the cut-out in the lower end over the peg on the crankcase and its lugs in the cut-outs in the cylinder **(see illustrations 9.9b and a)**.

15 Install the cylinder head (see Section 11).

16 Slide the sprocket onto the crankshaft with the chamfered edge innermost and align the slot in the sprocket with the peg on the shaft **(see illustrations 9.8b and a)**. Pass the cam chain through the tunnel and fit it onto the sprocket **(see illustration 9.7)**. If the chain is being re-used, ensure it is fitted the right way round (see Step 7). Secure the chain to prevent it falling back into the tunnel.

17 Slide the thrust washer against the sprocket **(see illustration 9.6)**. If required, the oil pump chain and sprockets and transmission components can be installed at this point.

18 Check that the engine is at TDC on the compression stroke – if removed, install the service tool (see Step 4).Check that the camshaft is in the TDC compression position with all valves closed and a small clearance between each rocker arm and valve stem **(see illustration)**.

19 Slip the camshaft sprocket into the top of the chain, then take up the slack in the lower run of the chain, making sure it is still engaged around the crankshaft sprocket, and fit the sprocket onto the camshaft **(see illustration 9.5c)**. Ensure that the timing mark on the camshaft sprocket is aligned with the mark on the camshaft holder. Install the sprocket bolts finger-tight.

Caution: If the marks are not aligned exactly as described, the valve timing will be incorrect and the valves may strike the piston, causing extensive damage to the engine.

20 Install the cam chain tensioner (see Section 8).

21 Check that the camshaft sprocket timing marks are still aligned – if not, remove the tensioner and reposition the chain on the sprocket. With the timing marks aligned, hold the sprocket as on removal and tighten the sprocket bolts to the specified torque setting **(see illustration 9.5a)**.

22 Remove the service tool from the alternator and rotate the engine a few times, then check the alignment of the timing marks. If all is well, install the remaining components in the reverse order of removal.

9.9a Guide blade locates in cut-out in top of cylinder . . .

9.9b . . . and on peg on the crankcase

9.10a Cam chain tensioner blade pivot bolt

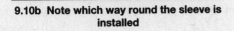
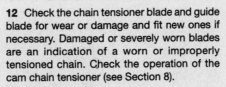

9.10b Note which way round the sleeve is installed

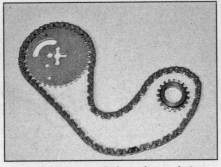

9.11 Fit new cam chain and sprockets as a set

9.18 Check for a small amount of freeplay in the rocker arms

10.7 Remove the camshaft retaining plate

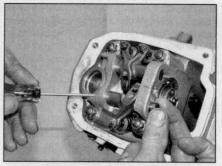

10.9a Ease the rocker shaft out . . .

10.9b . . . and remove the exhaust rocker arm

10 Camshaft and rockers

Removal

Special Tool: *A Vespa service tool Part No. 020941Y is required for this procedure (see Step 4).*

1 Remove the engine from the frame (see Section 5).

2 Remove the cooling fan and the alternator cover (see Sections 16 and 17).

3 Remove the cam chain tensioner (see Section 8).

4 With the engine still at TDC, install the service tool (see illustration 9.4).

5 Follow the procedure in Section 9 to remove the camshaft sprocket. Don't forget to secure the cam chain to prevent it falling into the engine. Stuff a clean rag into the cam chain tunnel to prevent anything falling into the engine.

6 Note the orientation of the camshaft in the TDC compression position (see illustration 9.18). If required, mark the end of the camshaft so that it can be refitted in the same position.

7 Undo the screw securing the camshaft

10.10 Remove the intake rocker arm and shaft

retaining plate and lift off the plate, noting how it fits (see illustration).

8 Mark the rocker shafts so they can be installed in their original positions.

9 Working on the exhaust rocker arm first, press the shaft out from the right-hand side, then support the rocker arm and withdraw the shaft completely (see illustrations). Slide the arm back onto the shaft to avoid mixing components up.

10 Follow the same procedure to remove the intake shaft and rocker arm (see illustration).

11 Withdraw the camshaft with bearings from its housing (see illustration).

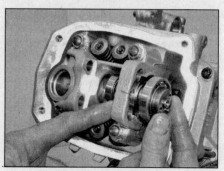

10.11 Remove the camshaft and bearings

Inspection

12 Clean all the components with a suitable solvent and dry them.

13 Inspect the camshaft lobes for heat discoloration (blue appearance), score marks, chipped areas, flat spots and spalling (see illustration). If damage is noted or wear is excessive, the camshaft must be replaced with a new one.

14 Inspect the rocker arm rollers for wear (see illustration). The rollers should turn freely but there should be no play between the rollers and the arm. Check the tip of

10.13 Inspect the camshaft lobes (arrowed)

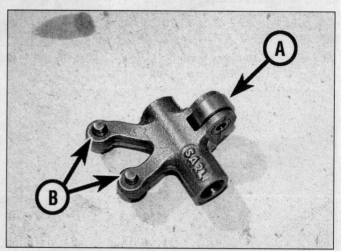

10.14 Rocker arm roller (A) and adjusting screw tips (B)

10.15a Measuring the internal diameter of the rocker arm . . .

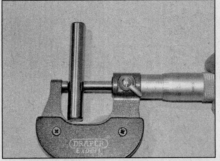

10.15b . . . and the external diameter of the rocker shaft

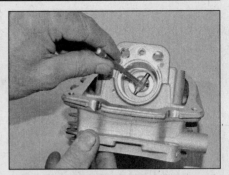

10.17 Measuring the internal diameter of the bearing housings

each adjusting screw and the top of each corresponding valve stem (see Section 12) for wear. If required, new adjusting screws or rocker arm assemblies should be fitted.

15 Lubricate the rocker arms and shafts with engine oil and assemble them in the cylinder head. The components should be a sliding fit with no discernable freeplay. If freeplay is noted, measure the internal diameter of each rocker arm, the internal diameters of the rocker shaft housings in the cylinder head and the external diameters of the rocker shafts **(see illustrations)**. Compare the results to the Specifications at the beginning of the Chapter – any worn components should be replaced with new ones.

16 Check the condition of the camshaft bearings (see *Tools and Workshop Tips* in the Reference section). If new bearings need to be fitted, use a puller to remove the old ones being careful to avoid damage to the camshaft. Note which way round the bearings are fitted. Prior to installing the new bearings, measure the diameter of the camshaft journals and compare the results with the specifications at the beginning of the Chapter. If the journals are worn or damaged a new camshaft will have to be fitted. **Note:** *New camshafts are supplied with bearings as an assembly.*

17 Check the bearing housings in the cylinder head for score marks and spalling. Measure the internal diameter of the housings and compare the results with the specifications **(see illustration)**. Any damage is an indication that the bearing has seized on the camshaft and turned inside its housing. Prior to reassembly, check that the outer races are a tight fit in the

housings, otherwise use some bearing locking compound to hold them in position.

Installation

18 Lubricate the camshaft bearings with clean engine oil, then fit the camshaft into the cylinder head **(see illustration 10.11)**. Ensure the camshaft is pressed all the way in. Ensure the cam lobes are facing the same way as on disassembly (see Step 6).

19 Lubricate the rocker shafts with engine oil. Hold the intake rocker arm in position and press the shaft through from the left-hand side **(see illustration 10.10)**. Ensure the shaft is pressed all the way in. Follow the same procedure to install the exhaust rocker arm. With the camshaft in the correct position there should be no pressure on the rocker arms.

20 Hold the camshaft retaining plate in position with the countersink for the retaining screw on the outside **(see illustration 10.7)**, then tighten the screw securely.

21 Follow the procedure in Sections 9 and 8 to install the camshaft sprocket and cam chain tensioner, then check the valve timing with both the service tool located on the alternator rotor and the timing marks on the camshaft sprocket and camshaft holder in alignment. **Caution:** *If the marks are not aligned exactly as described, the valve timing will be incorrect and the valves may strike the piston, causing extensive damage to the engine.*

22 Check the valve clearances and adjust them if necessary (see Chapter 1).

23 Install the remaining components in the reverse order of removal.

11 Cylinder head removal and installation

Caution: The engine must be completely cool before beginning this procedure or the cylinder head may become warped.

Removal

Special Tool: *A dial gauge is required for tightening the cylinder head nuts to the specified torque setting.*

1 Remove the engine unit from the frame (see Section 5).

2 Remove the cooling fan and the alternator cover (see Sections 16 and 17).

3 Remove the cam chain tensioner (see Section 8).

4 Follow the procedure in Section 9 to remove the camshaft sprocket. Don't forget to secure the cam chain to prevent it falling into the engine. Stuff a clean rag into the cam chain tunnel to prevent anything falling into the engine.

5 If required, remove the camshaft and rockers (see Chapter 10).

6 Remove the engine cowling seal (see Section 16).

7 Undo the two external cylinder head bolts on the left-hand side **(see illustration)**. Undo the four cylinder head nuts evenly, a little at a time, in a criss-cross pattern and remove them **(see illustration)**.

8 Lift the cylinder head up off the studs, feeding the cam chain down through the tunnel in the head **(see illustration)**. If the head is stuck, tap

11.7a Remove the external bolts

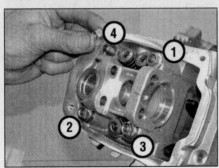

11.7b Cylinder head nuts – tightening order shown

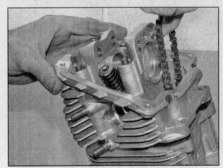

11.8 Keep the cam chain taut while lifting the head

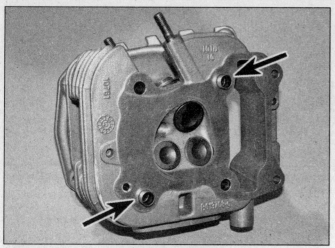

11.9a Check security of the cylinder head dowels (arrowed)

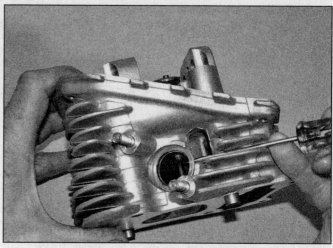

11.9b Prise out the exhaust gasket

around the joint face with a soft-faced mallet to free it. Do not attempt to free the head by inserting a screwdriver between the head and cylinder – you'll damage the sealing surfaces. **Note:** *Avoid lifting the cylinder off the crankcase when the head is removed, otherwise a new cylinder base gasket will have to be fitted (see Section 13).*

9 Note the two dowels and remove them for safekeeping if they are loose – they could be in the underside of the head or in the top of the cylinder **(see illustration)**. Prise the exhaust gasket out from the exhaust port and discard it **(see illustration)**.

10 Remove the cylinder head gasket – a new one must be fitted on reassembly **(see illustration)**. Inspect the gasket and the mating surfaces on the head and cylinder for signs of leakage, which could indicate that the head is warped. Refer to Section 12 and check the head gasket mating surface for warpage. Once it has been inspected, discard the old gasket and fit a new one on reassembly – never re-use the old gasket.

11 Clean all traces of old gasket material from the cylinder head and cylinder using a suitable scraper and solvent. Take care not to scratch or gouge the soft aluminium. Be careful not to let any dirt fall into the crankcase, the cylinder bore or the oil passage.

Installation

12 Ensure both cylinder head and cylinder mating surfaces are clean. Fit the dowels into the top of the cylinder if removed. Check that the cam chain guide blade is correctly located in the front edge of the cam chain tunnel (see Section 13).

13 Lay the new gasket onto the cylinder, making sure it locates over the dowels and the oil passage channel. Make sure the cam chain guide blade is correctly seated.

14 Carefully fit the head over the studs and onto the cylinder, feeding the cam chain up through the tunnel **(see illustration 11.8)**. Make sure the dowels locate correctly.

15 Lubricate the stud threads and seating surfaces of the cylinder head nuts with clean engine oil, then fit the nuts finger tight . Tighten the nuts evenly and a little at a time in a criss-cross pattern to the initial torque setting specified at the beginning of the Chapter.

16 Using a dial gauge, tighten the nuts in three equal stages, 90° at a time, to the final torque setting in the sequence shown **(see illustration 11.7b)**.

17 Tighten the two external cylinder head bolts to the specified torque setting **(see illustration 11.7a)**.

18 Install the remaining components in the reverse order of removal.

12 Cylinder head and valve overhaul

1 Because of the complex nature of this job and the special tools and equipment required, most owners leave checking and servicing of the valves, valve seats and valve guides to a professional. However, you can make an initial assessment of whether the valves are seating correctly, and therefore sealing, by pouring a small amount of solvent into each of the valve ports. If the solvent leaks past any valve into the combustion chamber area the valve is not seating correctly.

2 With the correct tools (a valve spring compressor is essential – make sure it is suitable for motorcycle work), you can remove the valves and associated components from the cylinder head, clean them and check them for wear to assess the extent of the work needed. If required, the valves can be ground-in prior to reassembly.

3 If the valve guides or the valve seats are worn a new cylinder head is required – valve guides are not available and Vespa state that the seats cannot be re-cut.

4 After the valve service has been performed, be sure to clean the head very thoroughly before installation to remove any metal particles or abrasive grit that may still be present from the valve service operations. Use compressed air, if available, to blow out all the holes and passages.

Disassembly

5 Before you start, arrange to label and store the valves and their related components so that they can be returned to their original locations without getting mixed up **(see illustration)**.

11.10 Note how the head gasket fits

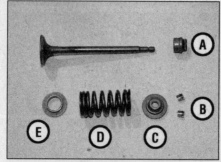

12.5 Valve components – stem seal (A), collets (B), spring retainer (C), spring (D) and spring seat (E)

12.7a Install the spring compressor carefully . . .

12.7b . . . on both ends of the valve . . .

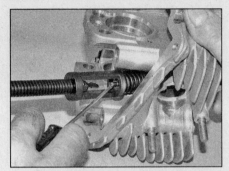

12.7c . . . then remove the collets

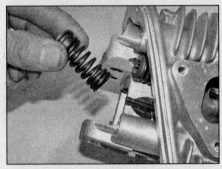

12.8 Remove the spring retainer and spring

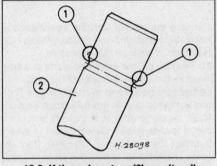

12.9 If the valve stem (2) won't pull through the guide, deburr the area (1) above the collet groove

12.10a Pull off the stem seal . . .

6 If not already done, follow the procedure in Section 10 to remove the camshaft and rockers.

7 Compress the valve spring on the first valve with a spring compressor, making sure it is correctly located onto each end of the valve assembly **(see illustrations)**. Do not compress the spring any more than is absolutely necessary to release the collets, then remove the collets, using either needle-nose pliers, a magnet or a screwdriver with a dab of grease on it **(see illustration)**.

8 Carefully release the valve spring compressor and remove the spring retainer and valve spring **(see illustration). Note:** *On some engines the valve springs have closer-wound coils that are fitted next to the cylinder head. On the engine photographed, the upper ends of the springs were marked with a dab of paint.*

9 Turn the head over and withdraw the valve – if it binds in the guide (won't pull through), push it back into the head and deburr the area around the collet groove with a very fine file **(see illustration)**.

10 When working on an intake valve, once the valve has been removed, pull the valve stem oil seal off the top of the valve guide with pliers, then lift out the spring seat **(see illustrations)**. On the exhaust valve, the stem seal and spring seat are integral **(see illustration)**. Discard the stem seals as new ones must be used on reassembly.

11 Repeat the procedure for the remaining valves. Remember to keep the parts for each valve together and in order so they can be reinstalled in the correct location.

12 Next, clean the cylinder head with solvent and dry it thoroughly. Compressed air will speed the drying process and ensure that all

holes and recessed areas are clean.

13 Clean the valve springs, collets, retainers and spring seats with solvent. Work on the parts from one valve at a time so as not to mix them up.

14 Scrape off any heavy carbon deposits that may have formed on the valve or in the exhaust port, then use a motorised wire brush to remove any residual carbon. Again, make sure the valves do not get mixed up.

Inspection

15 Inspect the head very carefully for cracks and other damage, especially around the spark plug hole and valve seats **(see illustration)**. If cracks are found, a new head will be required.

16 Inspect the threads in the spark plug hole. Damaged or worn threads can be reclaimed using a thread insert (see *Tools and Workshop*

12.10b . . . and lift out the intake valve spring seat

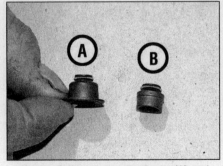

12.10c Comparison of exhaust (A) and intake (B) valve stem seals

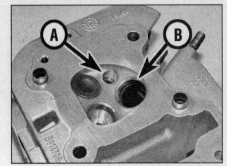

12.15 Check for cracks around spark plug hole (A) and valve seats (B)

12.18 Valve seats (arrowed) should be a uniform width

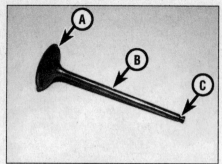

12.19 Check the valve face (A), stem (B) and collet groove (C) for signs of wear and damage

12.20 Measure the valve stem diameter

Tips in the Reference section). Most small engineering firms offer a service of this kind.

17 Using a precision straight-edge and a feeler gauge, check the head mating surface for warpage. Lay the straight-edge across the surface and measure any gap under it with feeler gauges. Check vertically, horizontally and diagonally across the head, making four checks in all. Warpage should not exceed the service limit specified at the beginning of the Chapter – if it does, have the cylinder head machined flat or replace it with a new one. If there is any doubt about the condition of the head consult an automotive engineer.

18 Examine the valve seats in the combustion chamber – they should be a uniform width all the way round **(see illustration)**. If they are deeply pitted, cracked or burned, a new head will be required.

19 Inspect the valve face for cracks, pits and burned spots, and check the valve stem and the collet groove area for score marks and cracks **(see illustration)**. Measure the valve face width and compare the result with the specification. Rotate the valve and check for any obvious indication that it is bent. Check the end of the stem for pitting and excessive wear. If any of the above conditions are found, fit a new valve. If the stem end is pitted or worn, also check the contact area of the adjuster screw in the rocker arm (see Section 10).

20 If available, use a micrometer to measure the valve stem diameter in several places along the stem length **(see illustration)** and compare the results with the specifications. **Note:** *Any variation in the measurements is an indication of wear on the valve stem.*

21 Working on one valve and guide at a time, measure the inside diameter of the guide with a small hole gauge and micrometer (see *Tools and workshop tips* in the *Reference* section). Make measurements at both ends and in the centre to determine if they are worn unevenly. Subtract the valve stem diameter from the guide diameter to obtain the stem-to-guide clearance and compare the results with the specifications. If the valve guides are worn excessively a new cylinder head will have to be fitted – valve guides are not listed as separate items. **Note:** *Carbon build-up inside the guide is an indication of wear.*

22 Check the end of each valve spring for wear. Stand the spring upright on a flat surface and check it for bend by placing a square against it. Valve springs will take a permanent set (sag) after a long period of use. Their free length can be measured to determine if they need to be renewed – compare the results with the specifications **(see illustration)**. If the spring is worn, or the bend is excessive, or the spring has sagged, it must be renewed. **Note:** *It is good practice to fit new springs when the head has been disassembled for valve servicing. Always fit new valve springs as a set.*

23 Check the spring retainers and collets for obvious wear and cracks. Any questionable parts should not be reused, as extensive damage will occur in the event of failure during engine operation.

Reassembly

24 Before installing the valves in the head they should be ground-in (lapped) to ensure a positive seal between the valves and seats – refer to the procedure in Chapter 2C, Section 12.

25 Once all the components are ready for assembly, install the valves one at a time. When working on an intake valve, lay the spring seat in place in the cylinder head, then install a new seal onto the guide. Use an appropriate size deep socket to push the seal over the end of the valve guide until it is felt to clip into place **(see illustrations)**. Don't twist or cock the seal sideways, or it will not seal properly against the valve stem. Also, don't remove it again or it will be damaged. Fit an integral stem seal and valve seat on the exhaust guide.

26 Lubricate the valve stem with clean engine oil, then install it into its guide, rotating it slowly to avoid damaging the seal. Check that the valve moves up and down freely in the guide.

27 Install the valve spring as noted on removal (see Step 8). Install the spring retainer, with its shouldered side facing down so that it fits into the top of the springs.

28 Apply a small amount of grease to the collets to hold them in place, then compress the spring and install the collets. Compress the

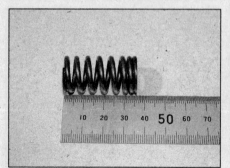

12.22 Measure the valve spring free length

12.25a Press the stem seal into place squarely

12.25b Correct installation of the valve stem seal

spring only as far as is absolutely necessary to slip the collets into place **(see illustration)**. Once installed, make certain that the collets are securely locked in their retaining grooves.

29 Repeat the procedure for the remaining valves.

30 Support the cylinder head on blocks so the valves can't contact the workbench top, then very gently tap each of the valve stems with a soft-faced hammer. This will help seat the collets in their grooves.

13 Cylinder

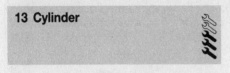

Removal

Special Tools: *If a new cylinder and/or piston are required specialist measuring equipment will be needed to determine the correct thickness of the new cylinder gasket (see Step 13 and 18).*

1 Remove the cylinder head (see Section 11).
2 Note how the cam chain guide blade locates in the front edge of the cam chain tunnel, then lift the blade out, noting which way round it fits **(see illustration 9.9a)**.
3 Lift the cylinder up off the studs, feeding the cam chain down through the tunnel and laying it over the front of the engine. Support the piston as it becomes accessible to prevent it hitting the crankcase **(see illustration)**. If the cylinder is stuck, tap around its joint face with a soft-faced mallet to free it from the crankcase. Don't attempt to free the cylinder by inserting

12.28 A dab of grease will hold the collets in place

a screwdriver between it and the crankcase – you'll damage the sealing surfaces. When the cylinder is removed, stuff a clean rag around the piston to prevent anything falling into the crankcase.
4 Note the location of the dowels and remove them for safekeeping if loose – they could be in the underside of the cylinder or in the crankcase **(see illustration)**.
5 Remove the gasket and make a note of the thickness printed onto the material **(see illustrations)**. If the original cylinder and piston are used on reassembly, a new gasket of the same thickness should be used. If new components are used the height of the piston at TDC in relation to the cylinder will have to be measured (see Step 13). Discard the old gasket and fit a new one on reassembly – never re-use the old gasket.

Inspection

6 Inspect the cylinder bore carefully for

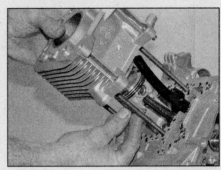

13.3 Support the piston as the cylinder is lifted off

scratches and score marks. A new cylinder and piston will be required if there are any deep scores.
7 Using telescoping gauges and a micrometer, check the dimensions of the cylinder to assess the amount of wear, taper and ovality. Measure the bore diameter just below the top edge, at the centre and just above the bottom edge, both parallel to and across the crankshaft axis **(see illustrations)**. Calculate any differences between the measurements to determine any taper or ovality in the bore.
8 Measure the bore diameter 27.7 mm down from the top edge at the point of most wear, then compare the results to the cylinder bore Specifications at the beginning of the Chapter.
Note: *Cylinders and pistons are size-coded during manufacture and are assembled in matching pairs. Vespa list four size-codes (A to D) for this engine. The cylinder size-code is stamped at the top of the cylinder adjacent to the gasket surface (see illustration).*

13.4 Note location of the cylinder dowels

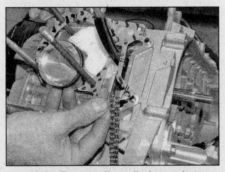

13.5a Remove the cylinder gasket

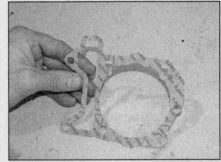

13.5b Printed thickness of the gasket

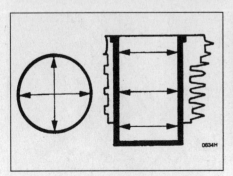

13.7a Measure the cylinder bore in the directions shown . . .

13.7b . . . using a telescoping gauge

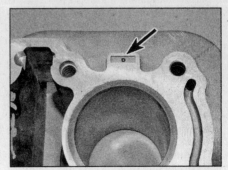

13.8 Location of the cylinder size code

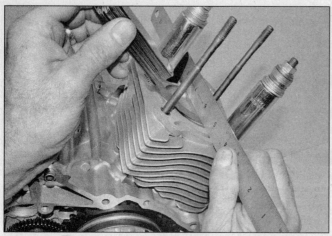

13.18 Measuring piston height with a straight-edge and feeler gauge

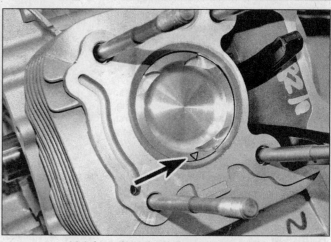

14.1 Location of arrow on piston crown

9 If the cylinder is deeply scored or wear is excessive a new cylinder and piston kit will have to be fitted – cylinders are not listed as separate items.

10 Calculate the piston-to-bore clearance by subtracting the piston diameter (see Section 14) from the bore diameter. If the cylinder is in good condition and the piston-to-bore clearance is within specifications, the cylinder can be re-used. If the piston-to-bore clearance indicates a worn piston, one of the correct size code will have to be fitted (see Section 14).

11 Check that all the studs are tight in the crankcase. If any are loose, or need to be replaced with new ones, unscrew them fully. Clean their threads and apply a thread locking compound. Fit the studs into the crankcase and tighten them using a stud tool, or by threading two of the cylinder head nuts onto the top of the stud and tightening them together so they are locked on the stud, then tighten the stud by turning the upper of the two nuts. The installed height of the studs, measured from the cylinder to crankcase mating surface, is 170 mm.

Installation

12 Check that the mating surfaces of the cylinder and crankcase are clean.

13 Three different thicknesses of cylinder base gasket are available from Vespa (0.4, 0.6 or 0.8 mm). It is important to fit the correct gasket to ensure that the engine compression ratio is maintained. If the original cylinder and piston are being re-used, fit a gasket the same thickness as the original (see Step 5). If new components are being used, the cylinder must first be assembled on the piston and crankcase (see Steps 21 to 23) without a base gasket and the height of the piston at TDC (top dead centre) in relation to the top edge of the cylinder measured. Vespa produce a dial gauge mounting plate especially made for the purpose (Part No. 020942Y).

14 Ensure that the cylinder is pressed firmly against the crankcase during this procedure by fitting spacers over the cylinder studs and tightening the cylinder head nuts lightly.

15 Mount the dial gauge with its tip resting against the cylinder top gasket face, and zero the gauge dial (see illustration 13.13 in Chapter 2A). Rotate the crankshaft so that the piston is part way down the bore.

16 Move the gauge so the tip is inside the edge of the cylinder bore, then rotate the crankshaft to bring the piston up to TDC with the tip of the gauge resting on the outside rim of the piston crown (see illustration 13.15 in Chapter 2A). The gauge reading will determine the thickness of gasket required.

17 The further the piston is below the top of the cylinder bore, the thinner the base gasket should be. If the reading is between 0 and 0.1 mm a 0.8 mm gasket is required, between 0.1 and 0.3 mm a 0.6 mm gasket is required, and between 0.3 and 0.4 mm a 0.4 mm gasket is required.

18 If a dial gauge is not available, the height of the piston can be measured by laying a precision straight-edge across the top of the cylinder. With the piston at TDC, measure the gap between the outside rim of the piston crown and the underside of the straight-edge with feeler gauges (see illustration). Once again, it is essential to ensure that the cylinder is pressed firmly against the crankcase during the procedure.

19 Once the correct gasket thickness is known, remove the cylinder and install the dowels and new gasket (see illustration 13.4).

20 Check that the piston ring end gaps are positioned as described in Section 15.

21 Lubricate the cylinder bore, piston and piston rings, and the connecting rod big- and small-ends, with the clean engine oil, then lower the cylinder down over the studs until the piston crown fits into the bore. Feed the cam chain up through the tunnel to avoid it getting jammed inside the crankcase.

22 Gently push down on the cylinder, making sure the piston enters the bore squarely and does not get cocked sideways. Carefully compress and feed each ring into the bore as the cylinder is lowered. If necessary, tap the cylinder down, but do not use force if it appears to be stuck as the piston and/or rings will be damaged.

23 When the piston is fully installed in the cylinder, press the cylinder down onto the base gasket, making sure it locates on the dowels.

24 Fit the cam chain guide blade (see Step 2), then install the cylinder head (see Section 11).

14 Piston

Removal

1 Remove the cylinder (see Section 13). Before removing the piston from the connecting rod, stuff a clean rag into the hole around the rod to prevent the circlips or anything else from falling into the crankcase. The piston should have an arrow marked on its crown which should point towards the exhaust port (see illustration). If this is not visible, mark the piston accordingly so that it can be installed the correct way round – the arrow may not be visible until the carbon deposits have been scraped off and the piston cleaned.

2 Carefully prise out the circlip on one side of the piston using a pointed instrument or a small flat-bladed screwdriver inserted into the notch (see illustration). Push the piston

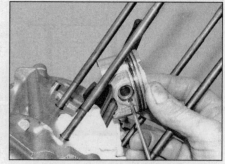

14.2a Remove the circlip . . .

14.2b . . . and push out the piston pin

14.4a Ease the ends of the rings apart . . .

14.4b . . . and lift the rings off the piston

pin out from the other side to free the piston from the connecting rod **(see illustration)**. Remove the other circlip and discard them both, as new ones must be used. Use a socket extension to push the piston pin out if required.

> **HAYNES HiNT**
> *To prevent the circlip from flying away or from dropping into the crankcase, pass a rod or screwdriver with a greater diameter than the gap between the circlip ends, through the piston pin. This will trap the circlip if it springs out.*

> **HAYNES HiNT**
> *If a piston pin is a tight fit in the piston bosses, heat the piston gently with a hot air gun – this will expand the alloy piston sufficiently to release its grip on the pin.*

Inspection

3 Before the inspection process can be carried out, the piston rings must be removed and the piston cleaned. Note that if the cylinder is being renewed, piston inspection can be overlooked as a new piston and rings assembly will be supplied with the new cylinder.
4 All three piston rings can be removed by

hand **(see illustrations)**. If available, a ring removal and installation tool can be used on the two compression rings if required, but do not use it on the oil control ring. Carefully note which way up each ring fits and in which groove as they must be installed in their original positions if being re-used. On the engine photographed the top surface of each ring was marked TOP **(see illustration)**. Do not nick or gouge the piston in the process. Note that a spring wire expander is located behind the oil control ring (see Section 15).
5 Scrape all traces of carbon from the top of the piston. A hand-held wire brush or a piece of fine emery cloth can be used once most of the deposits have been scraped away. Do not, under any circumstances, use a wire brush mounted in a drill motor to remove deposits from the piston; the piston material is soft and will be eroded away by the wire brush. Note the piston size code stamped on the piston crown **(see illustration)**. This should match the cylinder size code **(see illustration 13.8)**.
6 Use a piston ring groove cleaning tool to remove any carbon deposits from the ring grooves. If a tool is not available, a piece broken off an old ring will do the job. Be very careful to remove only the carbon deposits. Do not remove any metal and do not nick or gouge the sides of the ring grooves. Once the deposits have been removed, clean the piston with solvent and dry it thoroughly.

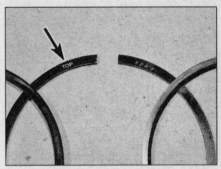
14.4c All piston rings are marked TOP

7 Inspect the piston for cracks around the skirt, at the pin bosses and at the ring lands. Normal piston wear appears as even, vertical wear on the thrust surfaces of the piston and slight looseness of the top ring in its groove. If the skirt is scored or scuffed, the engine may have been suffering from overheating and/or abnormal combustion, which caused excessively high operating temperatures. Also check that the circlip grooves are not damaged.
8 A hole in the piston crown is an extreme example that abnormal combustion (pre-ignition) has been occurring. Burned areas at the edge of the piston crown are usually evidence of spark knock (detonation). If any of the above problems exist, the causes must be corrected or the damage will occur again.
9 Measure the piston diameter 27 mm down from the top edge of the piston and at 90° to the piston pin axis **(see illustration)**. Compare the result to the Specifications at the beginning of the Chapter. **Note:** *Cylinders and pistons are size-coded during manufacture and are assembled in matching pairs. Vespa list four size-codes (A to D) for this engine. The piston size-code is stamped in the top of the piston* **(see illustration 14.5)**.
10 Subtract the piston diameter from the bore diameter (see Section 13) to obtain the clearance.
11 Fit the piston pin into the piston and check for freeplay between them **(see**

14.5 Location of the piston size code

14.9 Measuring the piston diameter

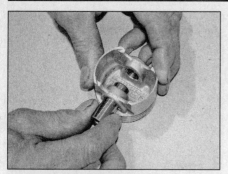

14.11a Checking the piston pin for freeplay

14.11b Measuring piston pin diameter . . .

14.11c . . . and piston boss internal diameter

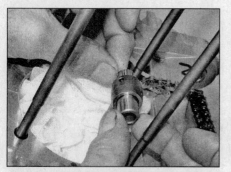

14.12 Checking for pin freeplay in the small-end

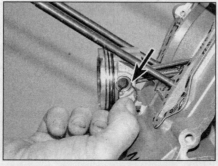

14.15 Fit circlip with open end (arrowed) away from removal notch

insert the piston pin **(see illustration 14.2b)**. Secure the pin with the other new circlip . When fitting the circlips, compress them only just enough to fit them in the piston, and make sure they are properly seated in their grooves with the open end away from the removal notch **(see illustration)**.

16 Install the cylinder (see Section 13).

15 Piston rings

illustration). There should be no freeplay. Using a micrometer and a telescoping gauge measure the piston pin diameter at both ends and the internal diameter of each pin boss in the piston and compare the results with the Specifications **(see illustrations)**.

12 Fit the piston pin into the connecting rod small-end and check for freeplay between them **(see illustration)**. If there is freeplay, measure the piston pin diameter at its centre and the internal diameter of the rod small-end to determine which component is worn.

13 Replace any components that are damaged or worn with new ones – if the small-end is worn a new connecting rod and crankshaft assembly will have to be fitted (see Section 20).

Installation

14 Inspect and install the piston rings (see Section 15).

15 Lubricate the piston pin, the piston pin bore and the connecting rod small-end bore with clean engine oil. Fit a new circlip in one side of the piston (do not re-use old circlips). Line up the piston on the connecting rod, making sure the arrow on the piston crown faces down towards the exhaust port (front of engine), and

1 New piston rings should be fitted whenever an engine is being overhauled (**see illustration)**. Before fitting the new rings, the end gaps must be checked with the rings installed in an unworn part of the bore. Note that the piston rings are marked with a size code letter which must correspond with the size code of the piston and cylinder (see Sections 14 and 13).

2 To measure the installed ring end gap, fit the top ring into the bottom of the bore and square it up with the bore walls by pushing it in with the top of the piston. The ring should be about 15 mm from the bottom of the bore **(see illustration)**. To measure the end gap,

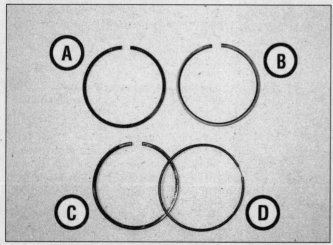

15.1 Piston ring set – Top ring (A), second ring (B), oil control ring (C) and ring expander (D)

15.2a Use the piston to fit the piston ring squarely in the bore

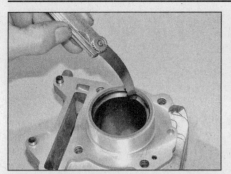

15.2b Measure the end gap with a feeler gauge

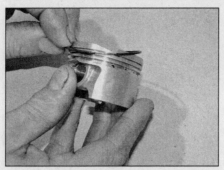

15.7 Ensure the oil ring expander is fitted correctly

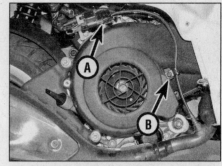

16.2 Oxygen sensor wiring connector (A) and wiring clip (B)

slip a feeler gauge between the ends of the ring and compare the measurement to the Specifications at the beginning of the Chapter **(see illustration)**.

3 If the gap is larger or smaller than specified, double-check to make sure that you have the correct rings before proceeding. If the gap is too small the ends may come in contact with each other during engine operation, which can cause serious damage. Check the piston and bore diameters with the Specifications.

4 Excess end gap is not critical unless it exceeds the maximum. Again, double-check to make sure you have the correct rings for your engine and check that the bore is not worn.

5 Repeat the procedure for the other rings.

6 Once the ring end gaps have been checked, the rings can be fitted onto the piston.

7 Fit the oil control ring expander into the bottom groove in the piston **(see illustration)**. Ensure the central wire fits inside both open ends of the spring wire. Fit the control ring over the expander with the TOP mark (and/or any other lettering) facing the top of the piston, and with the expander gap opposite to the ring gap, and do not expand the ring any more than is necessary to slide it into place **(see illustrations 14.4b and a)**.

8 Next fit the second (middle) compression ring into the middle groove in the piston with the TOP mark facing the top of the piston.

9 Finally fit the top ring into its groove with the TOP mark facing the top of the piston.

10 Once the rings are correctly installed,

check they move freely without snagging and stagger their end gaps as shown **(see illustration 15.8 in Chapter 2A)**.

16 Cooling fan and engine cowling

Cooling fan

1 Remove the right-hand side panel and the storage compartment (see Chapter 9). If required for access, remove the footboard trim panel and footboard.

2 Disconnect the oxygen sensor wiring connector and release the wiring clip from the fan cover **(see illustration)**.

3 Undo the fan cover screws and remove the cover **(see illustrations)**. Note the washers with the screws and the bushes in the cover. Note how the upper end of the cover locates inside the engine cowling.

4 To undo the fan centre nut the fan must be held to prevent the crankshaft turning – there are two holes in the fan hub for this purpose **(see illustration)**. Vespa produce a service tool to do this (Part No. 020442Y). Similar tools can be purchased from aftermarket suppliers. Alternatively, you could make a holding tool (see Section 17). With the fan held securely, undo the centre nut and washer and pull the fan off **(see illustrations)**.

5 Note the location of the pin in the crankshaft and the thrust washer that fits over the pin

16.3a Cooling fan cover screws (arrowed)

16.3b Lift the fan cover off

16.4a Locate holding tool in holes (arrowed)

16.4b Undo the centre nut and washer (arrowed) . . .

16.4c . . . and draw the fan off

16.5a Note the location of the pin

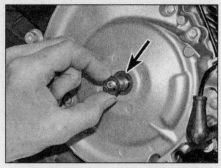

16.5b Remove the thrust washer. Note location of cover oil seal (arrowed)

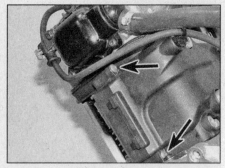

16.10a Cowling screws – left-hand side

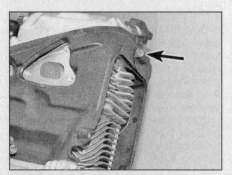

16.10b Cowling screw – right-hand side

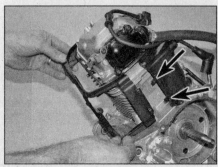

16.11 Disengage the tabs (arrowed) on the left-hand side

16.14a Undo the screw on the left-hand side . . .

(see illustration). Remove the thrust washer for safekeeping **(see illustration).**

6 Installation is the reverse of removal.

Engine cowling

7 Access is extremely limited and it is necessary to remove the engine from the frame (see Section 5) if the upper and lower sections of the cowling are to be removed rather than displaced.

8 Remove the fan cover (see Steps 1 to 3).

9 Remove the exhaust system (see Chapter 5).

10 Undo the screws on the left-hand side and the single screw on the right-hand side securing the two halves of the cowling together **(see illustrations).**

11 Ease the lower half of the cowling away to disengage the tabs on the left-hand side **(see illustration).**

12 Referring to the procedure in Section 8, displace the throttle body and remove the

intake manifold. Disconnect the engine temperature sensor wiring connector and unscrew the sensor.

13 Remove the starter motor (see Chapter 10) and the ignition coil (see Chapter 6).

14 Undo the screw on the left-hand side securing the upper half of the cowling to the crankcase and lift the upper half off **(see illustrations).**

15 A cowling seal is located around the top edge of the cylinder head – ease the seal off, noting how it fits **(see illustration).**

16 Installation is the reverse of removal.

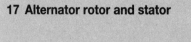

17 Alternator rotor and stator

Note: *This procedure can be carried out with the engine in the frame. If the engine has*

been removed, ignore the steps which do not apply.

Check

1 Refer to Chapter 10.

Removal

2 Drain the engine oil (see Chapter 1).

3 Remove the cooling fan (see Section 16).

4 An oil seal is fitted in the alternator cover where the crankshaft passes through it **(see illustration 16.5b).** Check around the seal for signs of oil leakage – if the seal has been leaking a new one must be fitted once the cover has been removed. **Note:** *It is good practice to renew the oil seal whenever the cover is removed.*

5 Disconnect the wiring connector on the oil pressure switch **(see illustration).**

6 Trace the wiring from the alternator and ignition pulse generator coil on the

16.14b . . . and lift the upper cowling half off

16.15 Remove the cowling seal

17.5 Disconnect the oil pressure switch wiring connector

17.7 Location of the silencer mounting bolts

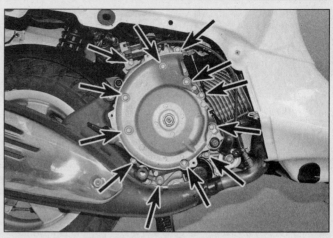

17.8a Undo the cover screws . . .

17.8b . . . and keep them in order to aid reassembly

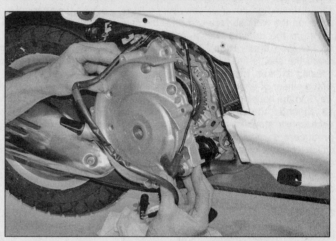

17.9 Pull the cover off, don't lever it

right-hand side of the engine and disconnect it at the connectors inside the bodywork **(see illustration 5.10)**. Free the wiring from any clips and feed it down to the alternator cover, noting its routing.

7 Remove the exhaust system (see Chapter 5). Alternatively, undo the silencer mounting bolts **(see illustration)** and ease the exhaust system away from the alternator cover to allow access to the cover screws and clearance for the cover to be removed.

8 Position a drain tray underneath the engine to catch any residual oil when the cover is removed,

then undo the cover screws in a criss-cross pattern, noting their locations **(see illustrations)**.

> **HAYNES HiNT**
>
> *Make a cardboard template of the crankcase and punch a hole for each screw location. This will ensure that they are all installed correctly on reassembly – this is important as the bolts are of different lengths.*

9 Draw the cover off **(see illustration)**. If the cover is stuck, tap around the joint face

between the cover and the crankcase with a soft-faced mallet to free it. Do not try to lever the cover off as this may damage the sealing surfaces. If fitted, note the location of the thrust washer on the crankshaft and remove it.

10 Remove the gasket and discard it as a new one must be used **(see illustration)**. Note the dowels in the cover or crankcase and remove them for safekeeping if they are loose **(see illustrations)**.

11 The alternator stator and ignition pulse generator coil are located inside the cover

17.10a Discard the old gasket (arrowed)

17.10b Note the location of the upper . . .

17.10c . . . and lower cover dowels (arrowed)

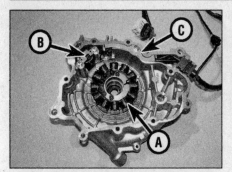

17.11 Alternator stator (A), ignition pulse generator (B) and wiring guide (C)

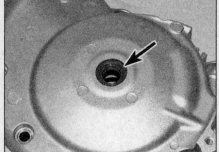

17.12 Note which way round the cover seal is fitted

17.13 Holding the rotor with a strap wrench

(see illustration). If required, undo the screws securing the wiring guide, pulse generator and stator and lift them out as an assembly.

12 To renew the cover oil seal, support the cover on the work surface and drive the seal out from the outside with a suitably-sized socket (see illustration). Note which way round the seal is fitted. Ensure that the seal housing is clean, then lubricate the new seal with a smear of engine oil and press it all the way into the housing from the inside.

13 To undo the alternator rotor nut it is necessary to stop the rotor from turning. Vespa produce a service tool (Part No. 020939Y) which locks the centre of the rotor against the crankcase. Alternatively, the rotor can be held using a commercially available strap wrench, but make sure it does not damage the pulse generator triggers on the outside of the rotor (see illustration).

14 With the rotor held securely, unscrew the nut and remove the washer (see illustration). From 2013 a Belleville (spring) washer is fitted behind the rotor nut ñ note which way round it is fitted before removing it.

15 Before removing the rotor assembly, undo the screw securing the starter driven gear guide and remove the guide (see illustration).

16 To pull the rotor off the crankshaft it is necessary to use the Vespa service tool (Part No. 020933Y), a commercially available equivalent, or a two-legged puller. Thread the rotor nut back on by a few threads to protect the end of the shaft during this procedure.

17 When fitting the service tool make sure the centre bolt is backed-out sufficiently to allow the body of the tool to be screwed all the way onto the threads on the rotor hub. With the tool in place, hold the body of the tool using a

spanner on its flats while tightening the centre bolt to draw the rotor off the end of the shaft.

18 If using a two-legged puller, fit a thick washer against the rotor nut, then slide a deep socket or tube over the shaft (see illustration). Ensure the legs of the puller are located securely behind the rotor before tightening the centre bolt (see illustration).

19 When the rotor is free, remove the tool and unscrew the rotor nut. Remove the rotor and the starter reduction gear (see illustration). If it is loose, remove the Woodruff key from the shaft, noting how it fits (see illustration).

20 If required, remove the starter driven gear from the starter clutch on the back of the rotor (see Section 18).

Installation

21 Prior to installation, clean the mating surfaces of the cover and the crankcase with

17.14 Unscrew the nut and remove the washer (arrowed)

17.15 Remove the starter driven gear guide

17.18a Slide a thick washer (arrowed) and deep socket over the shaft

17.18b Removing the rotor with a two-legged puller

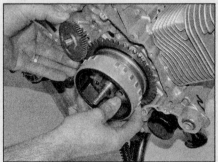

17.19a Remove the rotor and starter reduction gear together

17.19b Remove the Woodruff key

a suitable solvent to remove any traces of old gasket or sealant. Take care not to scratch or gouge the soft aluminium.

22 Fit the stator, pulse generator coil and wiring guide into the cover – make sure that the wiring grommet is correctly positioned **(see illustration 17.11)**. Clean the threads of the fixing screws and apply a suitable non-permanent thread-locking compound (Vespa recommends Loctite 242). Fit the screws and tighten them to the torque setting specified at the beginning of the Chapter.

23 If removed, assemble the starter clutch and driven gear on the back of the rotor (see Section 18).

24 Clean the tapered end of the crankshaft and the corresponding mating surface on the inside of the rotor with a suitable solvent. Make sure that no metal objects have attached themselves to the magnets on the inside of the rotor. If removed, fit the Woodruff key into its slot in the shaft. Install the rotor and starter reduction gear together **(see illustration 17.19a)** aligning the slot in the rotor with the key.

25 Fit the washer (see Step 14) and rotor nut and tighten the nut to the torque setting specified at the beginning of the Chapter, using the method employed on removal to prevent the rotor from turning **(see illustration 17.13)**. If applicable, fit the thrust washer onto the crankshaft.

26 Fit the guide for the starter driven gear and tighten the securing screw securely **(see illustration 17.15)**.

27 If removed, fit the dowels into the crankcase, then fit a new cover gasket, making sure it locates correctly onto the dowels **(see illustrations 17.10c, b and a)**. If necessary, use a dab of grease to hold the gasket in position.

28 Lubricate the inside of the cover oil seal with engine oil, then install the cover taking care not to damage the seal on the crankshaft threads.

29 Install the cover screws, making sure they are in the correct locations, then tighten them evenly and in a criss-cross sequence to the specified torque setting **(see illustration 17.8a)**.

30 Install the remaining components in the reverse order of removal. Ensure the wiring is

18.2 Starter driven gear (A) should rotate freely anti-clockwise. Note location of reduction gear (B)

correctly routed and secured by any ties and guides. If the exhaust system was displaced, don't forget to tighten the mounting bolts **(see illustration 17.7)**.

31 Fill the engine with the correct type and quantity of oil (see Chapter 1 and *Pre-ride checks*)

18 Starter clutch and gears

Note: *This procedure can be carried out with the engine in the frame.*

Check

1 The starter (one-way) clutch is located on the back of the alternator rotor. To access the clutch, first follow the procedure in Section 17 to remove the alternator cover.

2 The operation of the starter clutch can be checked with the alternator in place. The starter driven gear should rotate freely in the *opposite* direction to crankshaft rotation (anti-clockwise), but lock when rotated clockwise **(see illustration)**. If not, the starter clutch is faulty and should be removed for inspection.

Removal

3 Follow the procedure in Section 17 to remove the starter reduction gear and the alternator rotor.

Inspection

4 If not already done, check the operation

18.4 Starter driven gear should rotate freely clockwise

of the starter clutch. With the alternator rotor face down on the workbench, check that the starter gear rotates freely clockwise and locks against the rotor anti-clockwise **(see illustration)**. If it doesn't, the starter clutch should be dismantled for further investigation.

5 Withdraw the driven gear from the starter clutch, rotating it clockwise to ease removal.

6 Inspect the ring of sprags in the one-way mechanism for wear and damage and ensure they are free to move **(see illustration)**. Wash the assembly in suitable solvent and dry it with compressed air, if available. Lubricate the sprags with clean engine oil and check the operation of the clutch again (see Step 4). If the starter clutch still does not operate correctly a new clutch ring will have to be fitted.

7 On 2012 S models, the starter clutch is integral with the alternator rotor and is not available as a separate item.

8 On LX models, the clutch ring is secured to the back of the alternator rotor by a spring pin. Lever the clutch ring off evenly, then pull out the spring pin and discard it as a new one must be fitted. Note the location of the spacer between the back of the rotor and the clutch ring. Clean the components then assemble the spacer and new clutch ring on the rotor and secure them with a new spring pin.

9 Check the surface of the driven gear hub for wear and damage **(see illustration)**.

10 Check the teeth on the reduction gear and the corresponding teeth on the driven gear and starter motor drive shaft **(see illustration)**.

18.6 Inspect the starter clutch sprags (arrowed)

18.9 Inspect the driven gear hub (arrowed)

18.10 Check the gear teeth for wear and damage

Renew the gears and/or the starter motor if any wear or damage is found.

Installation

11 Lubricate the clutch sprags and install the driven gear, then fit the alternator rotor and reduction gear (see Section 17). Ensure the reduction gear engages with the driven gear and the starter motor shaft. **(see illustration 18.2).**

12 Install the remaining components in the reverse order of removal.

19 Oil pump and relief valve

Removal

1 Drain the engine oil (see Chapter 1).

2 Remove the drive pulley and variator (see Chapter 3).

3 An oil seal is fitted in the left-hand crankcase cover where the crankshaft passes through it **(see illustration)**. Check around the seal for signs of oil leakage – if the seal has been leaking a new one must be fitted once the cover has been removed. **Note:** *It is good practice to renew the oil seal whenever the cover is removed.* An O-ring seal is fitted around the outside edge of the cover – this should also be renewed when the cover removed (see Step 7).

19.3 Left-hand cover screws (arrowed). Note location of cover seal (A)

4 Undo the screws securing the left-hand crankcase cover and remove the copper sealing washers **(see illustration 19.3)**. If the washers are damaged new ones must be fitted on reassembly.

5 Note how the cover is fitted, then pull it out from the crankcase using the tabs provided **(see illustration)**. Do not lever the cover out as this will damage the sealing lip.

6 Note the location of the oil pump drive chain guide on the back of the cover **(see illustration)**. If the guide is worn a new one should be fitted.

7 Remove the O-ring from the groove around the outside of the cover **(see illustration)**. To renew the centre seal, first note which way round it is fitted, then press it out from the inside with a suitably-sized socket.

19.5 Pull cover using the tabs provided

Lubricate the new seal with engine oil, then press it in and level it with the outer edge of its housing using a small block of wood **(see illustrations)**.

8 Position a drain tray underneath the engine to catch any residual oil, then undo the sump cover bolts in a criss-cross pattern, noting their locations **(see illustration)**. Note the position of the rear brake cable guide.

9 Draw the cover off, noting the location of the oil pressure relief valve spring **(see illustration)**. If the cover is stuck, tap around the joint face between the cover and the crankcase with a soft-faced mallet to free it. Do not try to lever the cover off as this may damage the sealing surfaces.

10 Withdraw the oil pressure relief valve from

19.6 Location of the oil pump chain guide

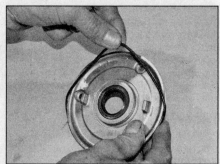

19.7a O-ring fits in the outer groove

19.7b Note how the seal is fitted

19.7c Level the seal using a block of wood

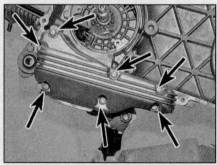

19.8 Undo the sump cover bolts (arrowed)

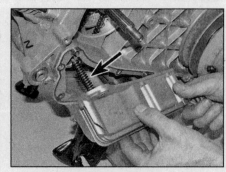

19.9 Oil pressure relief valve spring

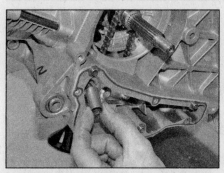

19.10 Location of the oil pressure relief valve

19.11a Remove the sump cover gasket

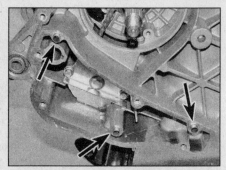

19.11b Location of the sump cover dowels

19.12a Undo the bolts . . .

19.12b . . . and lift off the plate

19.13a Undo the sprocket bolt . . .

the housing in the front of the sump **(see illustration)**.

11 Remove the gasket and discard it as a new one must be used **(see illustration)**. Note the dowels in the cover or crankcase and remove them for safekeeping if they are loose **(see illustration)**.

12 Undo the bolts securing the oil pump sprocket plate and remove the plate **(see illustrations)**.

13 Insert a pin punch through one of the holes in the pump sprocket and locate it in one of the recesses in the pump body to prevent the sprocket turning, then unscrew the sprocket bolt **(see illustrations)**. Remove the bolt and Belleville washer, noting how the washer fits. Draw the sprocket off the pump shaft and slip it out of the chain. Note how the sprocket locates on the pump shaft **(see illustration)**.

14 If required, lift the chain up and off the drive sprocket on the crankshaft **(see illustration)**.

19.13b . . . and remove the bolt and washer

Mark the chain with paint so that if it is re-used it can be fitted the same way round.

15 Draw the drive sprocket off the crankshaft, noting how it fits **(see illustration)**. Note the

19.13c Note how flat (arrowed) locates on pump shaft

location of the O-ring on the crankshaft and remove it **(see illustration)**. A new O-ring must be fitted on reassembly.

16 Undo the bolts securing the oil pump

19.14 Lifting the chain off the drive sprocket

19.15a Draw off the drive sprocket . . .

19.15b . . . and the O-ring

19.16a Oil pump mounting bolts

19.16b Note how the pump gasket fits

and remove the pump, noting how it fits **(see illustration)**. Remove the pump gasket and discard it as a new one must be fitted **(see illustration)**.

Inspection

17 Follow the procedure in Chapter 2C, Section 18, for inspection details, but use the Specifications at the beginning of this Chapter. If available, use a micrometer to measure the diameter of the pressure relief valve piston to assess it for wear.

Installation

18 Clean the mating surfaces of the sump cover and the crankcase with a suitable solvent to remove any traces of old gasket or sealant. Take care not to scratch or gouge the soft aluminium.

19 Clean all traces of old gasket off the mating surfaces of the crankcase and oil pump. Take great care not to scratch the mating surfaces.

20 Fit a new pump gasket into the crankcase making sure it aligns correctly **(see illustration 19.16b)**.

21 Install the oil pump ensuring it is correctly aligned with the recess in the crankcase **(see illustration)**. Tighten the mounting bolts to the torque setting specified at the beginning of the Chapter.

22 Lubricate a new O-ring with engine oil and slide it into the groove in the crankshaft **(see illustration)**. Slide on the drive sprocket then install the drive chain around the sprocket **(see illustrations 19.15a and 14)**.

23 Fit the pump sprocket into the chain, then align the centre of the sprocket with the flat on the pump shaft **(see illustration 19.13c)**. Secure the sprocket with the Belleville washer and bolt. The raised outer edge of the washer should face the pump sprocket. Hold the sprocket to prevent it turning as on removal and tighten the bolt to the specified torque setting.

24 Install the pump sprocket plate and tighten the bolts securely **(see illustration 19.12a)**.

25 Lubricate the pressure relief valve with engine oil, then fit the valve into its housing closed end first **(see illustration 19.10)**.

26 Ensure the sump cover dowels are in place, then fit a new cover gasket **(see illustrations 19.11b and a)**. Fit the pressure relief valve spring onto the stud on the inside of the cover, then align the cover with the sump carefully to ensure the spring enters the open end of the valve as the cover is installed **(see illustration)**. Install the cover bolts and brake cable guide **(see illustration 19.8)**, then tighten the bolts in a criss-cross pattern to the specified torque setting.

27 Fit a new O-ring into the groove around the outside of the left-hand crankcase cover **(see illustration 19.7a)**. Lubricate the O-ring and centre seal with engine oil, then slide the cover carefully over the crankshaft to avoid damaging the seal. Align the holes in the cover with the threads for the mounting screws and press the cover firmly into place.

28 If required, fit new copper washers onto the mounting screws, then install the screws and tighten them evenly to the specified torque setting.

29 Install the drive pulley and variator (see Chapter 3).

30 Fill the engine with the correct type and quantity of oil (see Chapter 1 and *Pre-ride checks*).

20 Crankcase halves, crankshaft and connecting rod

Note: *To separate the crankcase halves, the engine must be removed from the frame.*

Separation

1 To access the crankshaft and its bearings, the crankcase must be split into two parts.

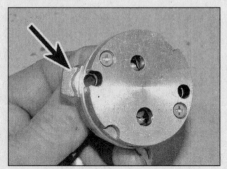

19.21 Align pump body (arrowed) with crankcase recess

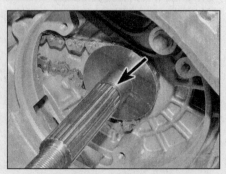

19.22 Installed location of the O-ring (arrowed)

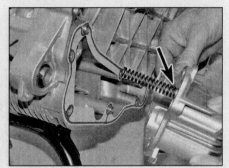

19.26 Fit the spring onto the stud on the cover

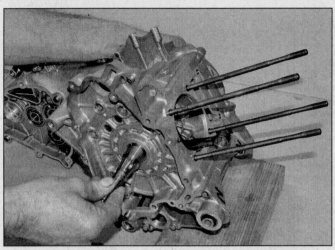

20.3 Push-and-pull the crankshaft to check the end-float

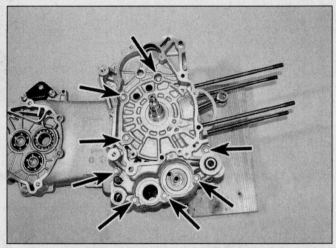

20.4 Location of the crankcase bolts

20.5 Separate the crankcase halves carefully

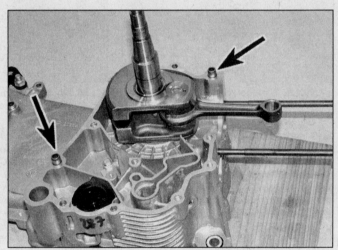

20.6 Location of the crankcase dowels

2 To enable the crankcases to be separated, the engine must be removed from the frame (see Section 5). Before the crankcases can be separated the following components must be removed:

Cylinder head (see Section 11).
Cylinder (see Section 13).
Piston (see Section 14).
Alternator rotor (see Section 17).
Starter motor (see Chapter 10).
Drive pulley and variator (see Chapter 3).
Oil pump (see Section 19).
Cam chain, blades and sprockets (see
    Section 9).
Centrestand (see Chapter 9).

3 Before separating the crankcases, check the crankshaft end-float **(see illustration)**. Excessive end-float is an indication of wear on the crankshaft or the crankcases and should be investigated when the cases have been separated. Also check for up-and-down movement between the crankshaft and the crankcase main bearings. The crankshaft should turn freely but there should be no up-and-down movement, otherwise engine oil pressure will be impaired (see Step 18).

4 Support the engine unit on the work surface with the left-hand (transmission) side down. Unscrew the crankcase bolts evenly, a little at a time and in a criss-cross sequence until they are all finger-tight, then remove them **(see illustration)**.

5 Carefully lift the right-hand crankcase half off the left-hand half, taking care not to score the surface of the right-hand main bearing on the crankshaft **(see illustration)**. If the halves do not separate easily, tap around the joint with a soft-faced mallet. **Note:** *Do not try and separate the halves by levering against the crankcase mating surfaces as they are easily scored and will not seal correctly afterwards.*

6 Remove and discard the gasket – a new one must be fitted on reassembly. Note the position of the two crankcase dowels and remove them for safekeeping if they are loose **(see illustration)**.

7 Lift the crankshaft assembly out of the left-hand crankcase, again taking care not to mark the bearing surface **(see illustration)**.

8 Remove the oil filter insert and discard

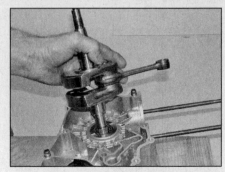

20.7 Lifting out the crankshaft assembly

20.8a Ease out the oil filter insert . . .

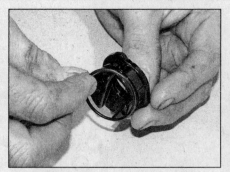

20.8b . . . and remove the O-ring

20.9 Location of the crankcase baffle plate

20.12a Location of the piston oil jet (arrowed)

20.12b Ensure the cylinder head oil passage (arrowed) is clear

its O-ring as a new one must be fitted on reassembly **(see illustrations)**.

9 If required, undo the bolts securing the baffle plate in the left-hand crankcase half **(see illustration)**.

10 Remove all traces of old gasket from the mating surfaces using a suitable scraper and solvent. Take care not to scratch or gouge the soft aluminium.

11 Clean the crankcases thoroughly with solvent and dry them with compressed air.

12 Blow out the oil passages for the oil pump, relief valve, main bearing and piston oil jet in the left-hand crankcase half with compressed air **(see illustration)**. Blow out the oil passages for the main bearing and the cylinder head oil supply in the right-hand crankcase half **(see illustration)**.

Caution: Be very careful not to nick or gouge the crankcase mating surfaces, or oil leaks will result. Check both crankcase halves very carefully for cracks and other damage.

13 Clean the crankshaft assembly with solvent. **Note:** *Vespa warn against blowing compressed air through the connecting rod oil passage to avoid the danger of compacting dirt and blocking the passage to the big-end bearing.*

Inspection

Crankcases

14 Small cracks or holes in aluminium castings can be repaired with an epoxy resin adhesive as a temporary measure. Permanent repairs can only be effected by

argon-arc welding, and only a specialist in this process is in a position to advise on the economy or practical aspect of such a repair. If any damage is found that can't be repaired, replace the crankcase halves with a new set.

15 Damaged threads can be economically reclaimed by using a diamond section wire insert, of the Heli-Coil type, which is easily fitted after drilling and re-tapping the affected thread. Sheared studs or screws can usually be removed with stud or screw extractors; if you are in any doubt consult a Vespa dealer or specialist motorcycle engineer.

16 Always wash the crankcases thoroughly after any repair work to ensure no dirt or metal swarf is trapped inside when the engine is rebuilt.

17 Inspect the engine mounting bushes **(see illustration)**. If they show signs of deterioration, replace them both with new ones. To remove a bush, first note its position in the casing. Heat the casing with a hot air gun, then support the casing and drive the bush out with a hammer and a suitably-sized socket. Clean the bush housing with steel wool to remove any corrosion, then reheat the casing and fit the new bush. **Note:** *Always support the casing when removing or fitting bushes to avoid breaking the casing.*

Main bearings and crankshaft

18 Check the condition of the main bearings in each crankcase half **(see illustration)**. Each bearing comprises two halves – the surface of the lower half is plain and the upper half has an oilway in it. The surface of each bearing should be smooth with no scoring or scuff marks. The condition of the bearings and the corresponding crankshaft journals is vital to the performance of the engine lubrication system. If the bearings are damaged or worn, oil pressure will drop and the oil feed to the connecting rod big-end and the cylinder head will be insufficient to prevent rapid wear and possible seizure. The procedure for checking the oil pressure is described in Section 3.

19 The main bearings are a very tight fit in the crankcases and should not be removed. They are not supplied as separate items – if any of the bearings show signs of wear or damage new crankcase halves will have to be fitted. If

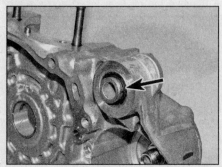

20.17 Engine mounting bush – right-hand front shown

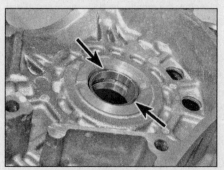

20.18 Main bearings are fitted in two halves. Note colour coding (arrowed) on bearing edge

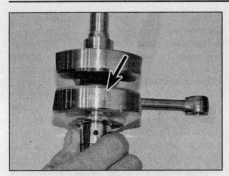

20.20 Counterweight marked with crankshaft category

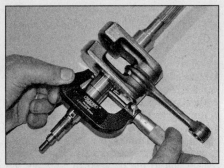

20.21a Measure the crankshaft journals . . .

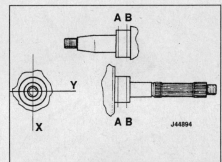

20.21b . . . in the positions and directions indicated

there is any doubt about the condition of the bearings consult a Vespa dealer.

20 Crankcases and crankshafts are supplied as either Category 1 or Category 2. The crankshaft category is marked on one of the counterweights (see illustration). The appropriate main bearings are colour coded on the edge of the bearing shells (see illustration 20.18). Use the information in Table 2 to determine the crankcase category.

21 Check the condition of the crankshaft journals. The surface of each journal should be smooth with no scoring, pitting or scuff marks. Use a micrometer to measure the diameter of each journal in two positions (A and B) and in two directions (X and Y) as shown (see illustrations). Compare the results with Table 1 and ensure that the journal size is within the specifications.

22 If the crankshaft journals are good, but the check in Step 3 indicated up-and-down movement, then the main bearings are worn. If the crankshaft journals are damaged or worn beyond the specifications a new crankshaft will have to be fitted, but note that it must be matched correctly to the crankcases and the bearings fitted as shown in Table 2. It is advisable to take the crankcases to the dealer when ordering the new crankshaft to ensure correct fitment.

Table 1: Crankshaft journal diameter	Crankshaft category
26.998 to 27.004 mm	1
27.004 to 27.010 mm	2

Table 2: Crankshaft, crankcase and main bearing selection	
Crankshaft category 1 with crankcase category 1	GREEN bearing
Crankshaft category 2 with crankcase category 2	BLUE bearing
Crankshaft category 1 with crankcase category 2	YELLOW bearing
Crankshaft category 2 with crankcase category 1	YELLOW bearing

23 Measure the connecting rod big-end side clearance with a feeler gauge and compare it with the Specifications at the beginning

of the Chapter (see illustration). Check for up-and-down (radial) play on the rod (see illustration). If available, use a dial gauge to measure the radial play and compare the result with the specification. Measure the width of the flywheels at several points to ensure they are not out of alignment (see illustration). Compare the result with the specification. If any of the results exceed the limit, the crankshaft assembly must be renewed.

Reassembly

24 Support the engine unit on the work surface with the left-hand (transmission) side down.

25 If removed fit the baffle plate and tighten the bolts securely (see illustration 20.9).

26 Fit a new O-ring onto the oil filter insert and fit it into the crankcase (see illustrations 20.8b and a).

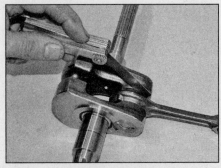

20.23a Measuring connecting rod big-end side clearance

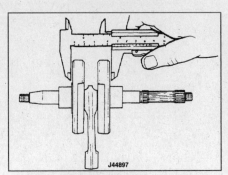

20.23c Measure the width across the flywheels at several points

27 Lubricate the main bearings and crankshaft journals with clean engine oil. Fit the crankshaft all the way into the left-hand crankcase half, positioning the connecting rod in-line with the crankcase mouth (see illustration 20.7).

28 Ensure that the crankcase mating surfaces are clean. Check that the crankcase dowels are in place, then fit a new gasket (see illustration).

29 Guide the crankcase right-hand half over the crankshaft end and press it down, making sure the dowels locate, until the two halves meet (see illustration 20.5). Use a soft-faced mallet to help the casing seat, but don't apply too much pressure. **Note:** *If the crankcases do not meet, remove the right-hand half and investigate the problem – do not be tempted to pull the crankcases together using the bolts.*

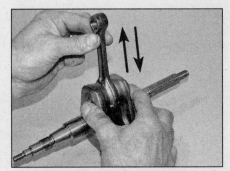

20.23b Checking for radial play

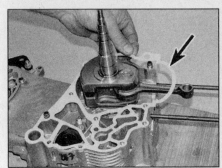

20.28 Leave the bridging section (arrowed) of the new gasket in place during assembly

20.30 Trim off the excess gasket

30 Clean the threads of the crankcase bolts and install them finger-tight. Tighten the bolts evenly, in a criss-cross sequence, to the torque setting specified at the beginning of the Chapter **(see illustration 20.4)**. Trim off the piece of gasket bridging the crankcase mouth with a sharp knife **(see illustration)**.

31 Hold the connecting rod to prevent it hitting the crankcase mouth, then rotate the crankshaft to check that it is turns freely.

32 Install the remaining components in the reverse order of removal.

21 Running-in

1 Make sure the engine oil level is correct (see *Pre-ride checks*).

2 Make sure there is fuel in the tank.

3 Turn the ignition ON, start the engine and allow it to run at a slow idle until it reaches operating temperature. Do not be alarmed if there is a little smoke from the exhaust – this will be due to the oil used to lubricate the piston and bore during assembly and should subside after a while.

 Warning: If the oil pressure warning light doesn't go off, or it comes on while the engine is running, stop the engine immediately.

4 If the engine proves reluctant to start, remove the spark plug and check that it has not become wet and oily. If it has, clean it and try again. If the engine refuses to start, go through the fault finding charts at the end of this manual to identify the problem.

5 Check carefully for oil leaks and make sure the transmission and controls, especially the brakes, function properly before road testing the machine.

6 Treat the machine gently for the first few miles to make sure oil has circulated throughout the engine and any new parts installed have started to seat.

7 Even greater care is necessary if the engine has been re-bored or a new crankshaft has been installed. In the case of a re-bore, the machine will have to be run-in as when new. This means a restraining hand on the throttle until at least 600 miles (1000 km) have been covered. There's no point in keeping to any set speed limit – the main idea is to keep from labouring the engine and not to maintain any one speed for too long. Experience is the best guide, since it's easy to tell when an engine is running freely. Once past the 600 mile (1000 km) mark, gradually increase performance, using full throttle for short bursts to begin with.

8 If a lubrication failure is suspected, stop the engine immediately and try to find the cause. If an engine is run without oil, even for a short period of time, severe damage will occur.

9 Upon completion of the road test, and after the engine has cooled down completely, recheck the valve clearances (see Chapter 1) and check the engine oil level (see *Pre-ride checks*).

Chapter 2C
Liquid-cooled four-valve engines (GTS, GTV and GT models)

Contents

Degrees of difficulty

Easy, suitable for novice with little experience 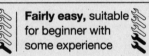	**Fairly easy,** suitable for beginner with some experience	**Fairly difficult,** suitable for competent DIY mechanic	**Difficult,** suitable for experienced DIY mechanic	**Very difficult,** suitable for expert DIY or professional

Specifications

General

Type	Single cylinder 4v liquid-cooled four-stroke
Capacity	
125 engine	124 cc
250 engine	244.3 cc
300 engine	278.3 cc
Bore	
125 engine	57.0 mm
250 engine	72.0 mm
300 engine	75.0 mm
Stroke	
125 engine	48.6 mm
250 engine	60.0 mm
300 engine	63.0 mm
Compression ratio	
125 engine	11.5:1 to 12.5:1
250 engine	10.5:1 to 11.5:1
300 engine	10.5:1 to 11.5:1

Camshaft

Intake lobe height
  125 engine
    Standard... 17.382 mm
    Service limit .... 17.130 mm
  250 and 300 engine
    Standard... 30.285 mm
    Service limit .... not available
Exhaust lobe height
  125 engine
    Standard... 16.563 mm
    Service limit .... 16.310 mm
  250 and 300 engine
    Standard... 29.209 mm
    Service limit .... not available
Left-hand journal diameter
  Standard... 36.950 to 36.975 mm
  Service limit (min) .... 36.940 mm
Right-hand journal diameter
  Standard... 19.959 to 19.980 mm
  Service limit (min) .... 19.950 mm
Camshaft end-float
  Standard... 0.11 to 0.41 mm
  Service limit .... 0.42 mm

Cylinder head

Warpage (max)
  125 engine .... 0.09 mm
  250 engine .... 0.05 mm
  300 engine .... 0.10 mm
Left-hand camshaft bearing housing diameter .... 37.000 to 37.025 mm
Right-hand camshaft journal housing diameter................... 20.000 to 20.021 mm
Rocker arm shaft housing .... 12.000 to 12.018 mm
Rocker arm shaft diameter............................... 11.977 to 11.985 mm
Rocker arm internal diameter............................. 12.000 to 12.011 mm

Valves, guides and springs

Valve clearances.................................... see Chapter 1
Intake valve
  Overall standard length .... 94.6 mm
  Stem diameter
    Standard... 4.972 to 4.987 mm
    Service limit (min) .... 4.960 mm
  Guide bore diameter
    Standard... 5.000 to 5.012 mm
    Service limit (max)................................... 5.022 mm
  Stem/valve guide clearance
    Standard... 0.013 to 0.040 mm
    Service limit
      125 engine .... 0.080 mm
      250 and 300 engine .... 0.062 mm
  Face width
    Standard... 0.99 to 1.27 mm
    Service limit (max)................................... 1.6 mm
  Seat width (max)..................................... 1.6 mm
  Spring free length
    125 engine
      Standard... 40.5 mm
      Service limit (max)................................... 39.7 mm
    250 engine .... not available
    300 engine
      Standard... 40.2 mm
      Service limit (max)................................... 38.2 mm
Exhaust valve
  Overall standard length .... 94.4 mm
  Stem diameter
    Standard... 4.960 to 4.975 mm
    Service limit (min) .... 4.950 mm

Valves, guides and springs (continued)

Exhaust valve (continued)
  Guide bore diameter
    Standard . . . .   5.000 to 5.012 mm
    Service limit (max). . . . .   5.022 mm
  Stem/valve guide clearance
    Standard . . . .   0.025 to 0.052 mm
    Service limit
      125 and 300 engine . . . .   0.090 mm
      250 engine . . . .   0.072 mm
  Face width
    Standard . . . .   0.99 to 1.27 mm
    Service limit (max). . . . .   1.6 mm
  Seat width (max). . . . .   1.6 mm
  Spring free length
    125 engine
      Standard . . . .   40.5 mm
      Service limit (max). . . . .   39.7 mm
    250 engine . . . .   not available
    300 engine
      Standard . . . .   40.2 mm
      Service limit (max). . . . .   38.2 mm

Cylinder bore

125 cc engine bore diameter (measured 41 mm down from top edge of the cylinder, at 90° to the piston pin axis)
  Standard
    Size code A. . . . .   56.997 to 57.004 mm
    Size code B. . . . .   57.004 to 57.011 mm
    Size code C . . . .   57.011 to 57.018 mm
    Size code D. . . . .   57.018 to 57.025 mm
  1st oversize
    Size code A1. . . . .   57.197 to 57.204 mm
    Size code B1. . . . .   57.204 to 57.211 mm
    Size code C1 . . . .   57.211 to 57.218 mm
    Size code D1. . . . .   57.218 to 57.225 mm
  2nd oversize
    Size code A2. . . . .   57.397 to 57.404 mm
    Size code B2. . . . .   57.404 to 57.411 mm
    Size code C2 . . . .   57.411 to 57.418 mm
    Size code D2. . . . .   57.418 to 57.425 mm
  3rd oversize
    Size code A3. . . . .   57.597 to 57.604 mm
    Size code B3. . . . .   57.604 to 57.611 mm
    Size code C3 . . . .   57.611 to 57.618 mm
    Size code D3. . . . .   57.618 to 57.625 mm
250 cc engine bore diameter (measured 33 mm down from top edge of the cylinder, at 90° to the piston pin axis)
    Size code M . . . .   72.010 to 72.017 mm
    Size code N . . . .   72.017 to 72.024 mm
    Size code O . . . .   72.024 to 72.031 mm
    Size code P. . . . .   72.031 to 72.038 mm
300 cc engine bore diameter (measured 33 mm down from top edge of the cylinder, at 90° to the piston pin axis)
    Size code M . . . .   75.010 to 75.017 mm
    Size code N . . . .   75.017 to 75.024 mm
    Size code O . . . .   75.024 to 75.031 mm
    Size code P. . . . .   75.031 to 75.038 mm

Piston – 125 cc engine

Piston diameter (measured 41 mm down from top edge of the piston, at 90° to the piston pin axis)
  Standard
    Size code A. . . . .   56.945 to 56.952 mm
    Size code B. . . . .   56.952 to 56.959 mm
    Size code C . . . .   56.959 to 56.966 mm
    Size code D. . . . .   56.966 to 56.973 mm
  1st oversize
    Size code A1. . . . .   57.145 to 57.152 mm
    Size code B1. . . . .   57.152 to 57.159 mm
    Size code C1 . . . .   57.159 to 57.166 mm
    Size code D1. . . . .   57.166 to 57.173 mm

Piston – 125 cc engine (continued)

2nd oversize
Size code A2	57.345 to 57.352 mm
Size code B2	57.352 to 57.359 mm
Size code C2	57.359 to 57.366 mm
Size code D2	57.366 to 57.373 mm

3rd oversize
Size code A3	57.545 to 57.552 mm
Size code B3	57.552 to 57.559 mm
Size code C3	57.559 to 57.566 mm
Size code D3	57.566 to 57.573 mm
Piston-to-bore clearance (when new)	0.045 to 0.059 mm
Piston pin diameter	14.996 to 15.000 mm
Piston pin bore diameter in piston	15.001 to 15.006 mm
Piston pin-to-piston clearance (when new)	0.001 to 0.010 mm

Piston – 250 cc engine

Piston diameter (measured 33 mm down from top edge of the piston, at 90° to the piston pin axis)
Size code M	71.953 to 71.960 mm
Size code N	71.960 to 71.967 mm
Size code O	71.967 to 71.974 mm
Size code P	71.974 to 71.981 mm
Piston-to-bore clearance (when new)	0.050 to 0.064 mm
Piston pin diameter	14.996 to 15.000 mm
Piston pin bore diameter in piston	15.001 to 15.006 mm
Piston pin-to-piston clearance (when new)	0.015 to 0.029 mm

Piston – 300 cc engine

Piston diameter (measured 33 mm down from top edge of the piston, at 90° to the piston pin axis)
Size code M	74.953 to 74.960 mm
Size code N	74.960 to 74.967 mm
Size code O	74.967 to 74.974 mm
Size code P	74.974 to 74.981 mm
Piston-to-bore clearance (when new)	0.050 to 0.064 mm
Piston pin diameter	15.996 to 16.000 mm
Piston pin bore diameter in piston	16.001 to 16.006 mm
Piston pin-to-piston clearance (when new)	0.001 to 0.010 mm

Piston rings – 125 cc engine

Ring end gap (installed)

Top ring
Standard	0.15 to 0.30 mm
Service limit (max)	0.5 mm

2nd ring
Standard	0.10 to 0.30 mm
Service limit (max)	0.65 mm

Oil control ring
Standard	0.15 to 0.35 mm
Service limit (max)	0.65 mm

Ring-to-groove clearance (all rings)
Standard	0.015 to 0.060 mm
Service limit (max)	0.070 mm

Piston rings – 250 and 300 cc engine

Ring end gap (installed)

Top ring
Standard	0.15 to 0.30 mm
Service limit (max)	0.5 mm

2nd ring
Standard	0.20 to 0.40 mm
Service limit (max)	0.65 mm

Oil control ring
Standard	0.20 to 0.40 mm
Service limit (max)	0.65 mm

Ring-to-groove clearance (all rings)
Standard	0.015 to 0.060 mm
Service limit (max)	0.070 mm

Lubrication system

Engine oil pressure (at 90°C)
    At idle . . . .   7.25 to 17.5 psi (0.5 to 1.2 Bar)
    At 6000 rpm . . . .   46.5 to 61 psi (3.2 to 4.2 Bar)
Oil pump
    Inner rotor tip-to-outer rotor clearance (max) . . . .   0.12 mm
    Outer rotor-to-body clearance (max) . . . .   0.20 mm
    Rotor end-float (max) . . . .   0.09 mm
Relief valve spring free length . . . .   54.2 mm

Connecting rod

Small-end internal diameter
    150 and 250 engines
        Standard . . . .   15.015 to 15.025 mm
        Service limit (max) . . . .   15.030 mm
    300 engine
        Standard . . . .   16.015 to 16.025 mm
        Service limit (max) . . . .   16.030 mm
Big-end side clearance . . . .   0.20 to 0.50 mm
Big-end radial play . . . .   0.036 to 0.054 mm

Crankshaft

Combined width of flywheels and big-end
    150 and 300 engines . . . .   51.40 to 51.45 mm
    250 engine . . . .   55.67 to 55.85 mm
Runout A (max) . . . .   0.15 mm
Runout B (max) . . . .   0.01 mm
Runout C (max) . . . .   0.10 mm
End-float . . . .   0.15 to 0.40 mm

Torque settings

Alternator cover bolts . . . .   11 to 13 Nm
Alternator rotor nut . . . .   94 to 102 Nm
Cam chain tensioner blade bolt . . . .   10 to 14 Nm
Cam chain tensioner bolts . . . .   11 to 13 Nm
Cam chain tensioner spring cap bolt . . . .   5 to 6 Nm
Camshaft retaining plate bolts . . . .   4 to 6 Nm
Camshaft sprocket bolt . . . .   11 to 15 Nm
Crankcase bolts . . . .   11 to 13 Nm
Cylinder head bolts . . . .   11 to 13 Nm
Cylinder head nuts
    Initial setting . . . .   7 Nm
    Middle setting . . . .   10 Nm
    Final setting . . . .   angle tighten through 270°
Decompressor mechanism cover bolt . . . .   7 to 8.5 Nm
Decompressor mechanism static weight bolt . . . .   11 to 15 Nm
Engine front mounting bolt . . . .   64 to 72 Nm
Intake duct screws . . . .   11 to 13 Nm
Oil pressure switch . . . .   12 to 14 Nm
Oil pump drive chain cover bolts . . . .   0.7 to 0.9 Nm
Oil pump driven sprocket bolt . . . .   10 to 14 Nm
Oil pump mounting bolts . . . .   5 to 6 Nm
Starter clutch bolts . . . .   13 to 15 Nm
Sump cover bolts . . . .   10 to 14 Nm
Valve cover bolts . . . .   6 to 7 Nm

1 General information

The engine unit is a liquid-cooled, single cylinder four-stroke. The crankshaft assembly is pressed together, incorporating the connecting rod, with the big-end running on the crankpin on a bronze bearing. The crankshaft runs in plain main bearings. The crankcase divides vertically. On 250 and 300 cc engines the water pump is mounted in the alternator cover and is driven off the right-hand end of the crankshaft. On 125 cc engines the pump is electric.

The camshaft is chain-driven off the left-hand end of the crankshaft, and operates four valves via rocker arms.

2 Component access

Access to the alternator rotor and stator on the right-hand side and the transmission on the left-hand side is easy and can be done with the engine in place.

Access to the top-end of the engine is

very restricted making removal of the valve cover, the first component that needs to be removed, difficult. Removal of the engine is recommended, though it is also possible to just raise the frame up off the engine until there is enough clearance if you have the necessary equipment – refer to Section 5, Step 1, for details.

To access the crankshaft and connecting rod assembly and its bearings, the engine must be removed from the frame and the crankcase halves separated.

3 Engine wear assessment

Cylinder compression test

Special tool: *A compression gauge is required to perform this test.*

1 Poor engine performance may be caused by leaking valves, incorrect valve clearances, a leaking head gasket, or worn piston, piston rings or cylinder walls. A cylinder compression check will highlight these conditions and can also indicate the presence of excessive carbon deposits in the cylinder head.

2 The only tools required are a compression gauge (there are two types, one with a threaded adapter to fit the spark plug hole in the cylinder head, the other has a rubber seal which is pressed into the spark plug hole to create a seal – the threaded adapter type is preferable), and a spark plug socket. Depending on the outcome of the initial test, a squirt-type oil can may also be needed.

3 Make sure the valve clearances are correctly set (see Chapter 1) and that the cylinder head nuts/bolts are tightened to the correct torque setting (see Section 11).

4 Run the engine until it is at normal operating temperature. Remove the spark plug (see Chapter 1). Fit the plug back into the plug cap and earth the plug against the engine away from the plug hole – if the plug is not earthed the ignition system could be damaged.

5 Fit the gauge into the spark plug hole – if the rubber cone type is used keep the gauge pressed onto the hole throughout the test to maintain a good seal.

6 With the ignition switch ON, the throttle held fully open and the spark plug grounded, turn the engine over on the starter motor until the gauge reading has built up and stabilised.

7 Compare the reading on the gauge to the cylinder compression range specified at the beginning of the Chapter (under General specifications). Note that this is not a range specified by Vespa (they do not provide one), but is a general range acceptable for this engine – if in doubt ask your dealer.

8 If the reading is low, it could be due to a worn cylinder bore, piston or rings, failure of the head gasket, or worn valve seats. To determine which is the cause, pour a small quantity of engine oil into the spark plug hole

to seal the rings, then repeat the compression test. If the figures are noticeably higher the cause is worn cylinder, piston or rings. If there is no change the cause is a leaking head gasket or worn valve seats.

9 If the reading is high there could be a build-up of carbon deposits in the combustion chamber. Remove the cylinder head and scrape all deposits off the piston and the cylinder head.

10 While working on the engine also check that the correct base gasket has been fitted under the cylinder block – different thicknesses are available and it is possible that the one fitted is either too thick, which will reduce cylinder compression, or too thin, increasing compression – refer to Section 13 for details.

Oil pressure check

Special tool: *A pressure gauge is required to perform this test.*

11 This engine is fitted with an oil pressure switch and warning light. The function of the circuit is described in Chapter 10.

12 If there is any doubt about the performance of the engine lubrication system, the oil pressure should be checked. The check provides useful information about the condition of the lubrication system. If you do not have the facilities to check the oil pressure yourself, have it done by a Vespa dealer.

13 To check the oil pressure, a suitable pressure gauge (which screws into the crankcase) will be needed. Vespa can supply a gauge (Part No. 020193Y) for this purpose.

14 Check the engine oil level (see *Pre-ride checks*), then warm the engine up to normal operating temperature and stop it. Support the scooter so that the rear wheel is clear of the ground.

15 Remove the right-hand side panel (see Chapter 9). Remove the oil pressure switch (see Chapter 10) and screw in the gauge adapter. Connect the pressure gauge to the adapter.

⚠ **Warning: Take great care not to burn your hands on the hot engine unit, exhaust pipe or with engine oil when connecting the gauge adapter to the crankcase. Do not allow exhaust gases to build-up in the work area; either perform the check outside or use an exhaust gas extraction system.**

16 Start the engine and increase the engine speed to 6000 rpm whilst watching the pressure gauge reading. The oil pressure should be within the range given in the Specifications at the beginning of the Chapter.

17 If the pressure is significantly lower than the standard, either the oil strainer or filter is blocked, the pressure relief valve is stuck open, the oil pump is faulty, the piston oil jet in the crankcases has become dislodged, or there is considerable engine main bearing wear. Begin diagnosis by checking the oil filter and strainer (see Chapter 1), then the relief valve and oil pump (see Section 18). If

those items check out okay, the crankcases will have to be split to check the oil jet and the main bearings (see Section 19).

18 If the pressure is too high, either an oil passage is clogged, the relief valve is stuck closed or the wrong grade of oil is being used.

19 Stop the engine and unscrew the gauge and adapter from the crankcase.

20 Install the oil pressure switch (see Chapter 10). Check the oil level (see *Pre-ride checks*). **Note:** *Rectify any problems before running the engine again.* Install the side panel (see Chapter 9).

4 Major engine repair –
general note

1 It is not always easy to determine when or if an engine should be completely overhauled, as a number of factors must be considered.

2 High mileage is not necessarily an indication that an overhaul is needed, while low mileage, on the other hand, does not preclude the need for an overhaul. Frequency of servicing is probably the single most important consideration. An engine that has regular and frequent oil and filter changes, as well as other required maintenance, will most likely give many miles of reliable service. Conversely, a neglected engine, or one which has not been run-in properly, may require an overhaul very early in its life.

3 Exhaust smoke and excessive oil consumption are both indications that piston rings and/or valve guides are in need of attention, although make sure that the fault is not due to oil leakage.

4 If the engine is making obvious knocking or rumbling noises, the connecting rod and/or main bearings are probably at fault.

5 Loss of power, rough running, excessive valve train noise and high fuel consumption rates may also point to the need for an overhaul, especially if they are all present at the same time. If a complete tune-up does not remedy the situation, major mechanical work is the only solution.

6 A full engine overhaul generally involves restoring the internal parts to the specifications of a new engine. The piston and piston rings are renewed; addtionally on 125 cc engines the cylinder is re-bored if necessary. The valve seats are re-ground and new valve springs are fitted. If the connecting rod bearings are worn a new crankshaft assembly is fitted. The end result should be a like-new engine that will give as many trouble-free miles as the original.

7 Before beginning the engine overhaul, read through the related procedures to familiarise yourself with the scope and requirements of the job. Overhauling an engine is not all that difficult, but it is time-consuming. Plan on the scooter being tied up for a minimum of two weeks. Check on the availability of parts and make sure that any necessary special tools, equipment and supplies are obtained in advance.

8 Most work can be done with typical workshop hand tools, although a number of precision measuring tools are required for inspecting parts to determine if they must be renewed. Often a dealer will handle the inspection of parts and offer advice concerning reconditioning and renewal. As a general rule, time is the primary cost of an overhaul so it does not pay to install worn or substandard parts.

9 As a final note, to ensure maximum life and minimum trouble from a rebuilt engine, everything must be assembled with care in a spotlessly-clean environment.

5 Engine/transmission unit removal and installation

Caution: The engine is not heavy, however engine removal and installation should be carried out with the aid of an assistant; personal injury or damage could occur if the engine falls or is dropped.

Removal

1 Wash any accumulated dirt off the engine. Support the scooter securely in an upright position. Note that the centre stand is bolted to the engine so you will need to support the belly of the scooter on axle stands or wooden blocks after the engine has been removed – use adequate protection, and make sure the frame is securely supported so it cannot topple over. Also note that the scooter must be lifted up off the engine to get the necessary clearance for the engine to be then draw back from under it. To do this you will need at least one assistant. Alternatively, as shown you could fabricate a frame with straps that can be used to raise and support the scooter above the engine while the engine is worked on **(see illustration)** – use the method best suited to your workshop set-up and surroundings. Work on the engine can be made easier by raising the machine to a suitable working height on an hydraulic ramp or a suitable platform – again make sure the scooter is secure and will not topple over.

5.1 Fabricated structure to hoist and support the scooter's frame above the engine

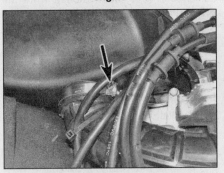

5.8a Slacken the clamp (arrowed) and detach the duct

2 Remove the storage compartment, side panels and floor panel (see Chapter 9).

3 If the sump is going to be removed, or the crankcases separated, drain the engine oil (see Chapter 1).

4 Drain the cooling system, then disconnect the coolant hoses from the engine (see Chapter 4).

5 Disconnect the battery negative (-) terminal (see Chapter 10).

6 Remove the exhaust system (see Chapter 5).

7 Disconnect the temperature sensor wiring connector **(see illustration)**.

8 Detach the air intake duct from the air filter housing **(see illustration)**. Clean around the intake duct joint to the cylinder head. Undo the intake duct screws and detach the complete throttle body assembly from the head and tie it to the body so the wiring, hose(s) and cables are not strained **(see illustration)**. Stuff some clean rag into the head and into the throttle body ducts.

5.7 Disconnect the temperature sensor wiring connector

5.8b Unscrew the bolts (arrowed) and detach the throttle body assembly

9 If required remove the air filter housing (see Chapter 5) – note that it is easier to do after the scooter has been raised.

10 Disconnect the starter motor lead and engine earth lead **(see illustration)**. If required remove the starter motor.

11 Trace the wiring from the alternator/pulse generator coil on the right-hand side of the engine and disconnect it at the connectors **(see illustration)**. Free the wiring from any clips and feed it down to the alternator cover, noting its routing.

12 Remove the rear wheel (see Chapter 8).

13 Free the rear brake hose from the underside of the drive belt cover **(see illustration)**. Displace the rear brake caliper and secure it clear.

14 If required, remove the wheel spacer then pull the disc and hub off the driveshaft and support the rear of the engine unit on a wood block to prevent damage to the casing

5.10 Disconnect the leads (arrowed) from the starter motor

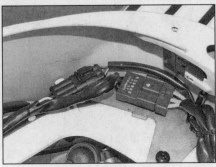

5.11 Disconnect the alternator sub-loom wiring connectors

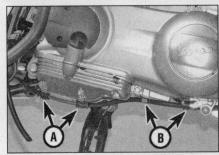

5.13 Free the brake hose from the front clips (A) and release the rear clips (B) from the cover

5.14a Remove the spacer . . .

5.14b . . . and the disc/hub unit

5.15 Unscrew the nut and withdraw the bolt

(see illustrations). Alternatively, temporarily reinstall the wheel, but leave the right-hand shock absorber free. Note: The rear wheel and centrestand provide a convenient support for the engine unit once it is removed from the scooter.

15 Unscrew the nut and withdraw the bolt securing the bottom of the left-hand shock (see illustration). If the rear wheel has been removed support the back of the engine unit on a wood block. If the rear wheel has not been removed place a piece of wood under the rear tyre.

16 Check that all wiring, cables and hoses are free and clear as required.

17 Prepare your method of raising and supporting the scooter as outlined in Step 1. Unscrew the nut on the front engine mounting bolt (see illustration). Take the weight of the scooter, then withdraw the bolt, remove the spacer, and raise the scooter off the engine unit, then support it or move it to its support

as required (see illustrations). Note the collars in the bottom of the left-hand shock absorber and remove them for safekeeping (see illustration).

18 If the engine is dirty clean it thoroughly before starting any major dismantling work (see Section 6).

Installation

19 Installation is the reverse of removal, noting the following:

• Make sure no wires, cables or hoses become trapped between the engine and the frame when installing the engine. Do not forget the collars in the bottom of the left-hand shock absorber (see illustration 5.17e).

• Tighten the engine mounting bolt and shock absorber bolt/nuts to the torque settings specified at the beginning of this Chapter and Chapter 7.

• Make sure all wires, cables and hoses are correctly routed and connected, and secured by any clips or ties, using new ones where necessary.

• Tighten the throttle body intake duct screws to the torque setting specified at the beginning of the Chapter.

• Adjust the throttle cable (see Chapter 1).

• If required, fill the engine with the specified quantity of oil (see Chapter 1 Specifications) and check the oil level as described in Pre-ride checks.

• Fill the cooling system (see Chapter 4).

6 Engine overhaul information

Disassembly

1 Before disassembling the engine, the external surfaces of the unit should be thoroughly cleaned and degreased to avoid the possibility of dirt falling inside. A high flash-point solvent, such as paraffin can be used, or better still, a proprietary engine degreaser such as Gunk. Use old paintbrushes and toothbrushes to work the solvent into the various recesses of the engine casings. Take care to exclude solvent or water from the electrical components and intake and exhaust ports.

⚠️ Warning: The use of petrol (gasoline) as a cleaning agent should be avoided because of the risk of fire.

2 When clean and dry, arrange the unit on the workbench, leaving suitable clear area for

5.17a Unscrew the nut

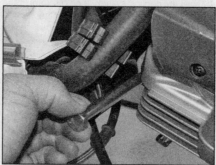

5.17b Withdraw the bolt . . .

5.17c . . . and remove the spacer . . .

5.17d . . . then lift the scooter up off the engine

5.17e Retrieve the collars from the shock absorber

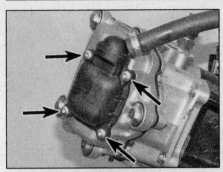

7.2 Undo the screws (arrowed) and remove the breather housing

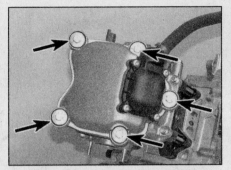

7.3 Unscrew the bolts (arrowed) and remove the cover

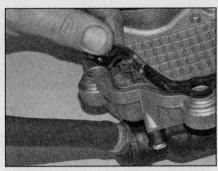

7.5 Make sure the gasket seats in the groove

working. Gather a selection of small containers and plastic bags so that parts can be grouped together in an easily identifiable manner. Some paper and a pen should be on hand to permit notes to be made and labels attached where necessary. A supply of clean rag is also required.

3 Before commencing work, read through the appropriate section so that some idea of the necessary procedure can be gained. When removing components it should be noted that great force is seldom required, unless specified. In many cases, a component's reluctance to be removed is indicative of an incorrect approach or removal method – if in any doubt, re-check with the text.

4 When disassembling the engine, keep 'mated' parts that have been in contact with each other during engine operation together. These 'mated' parts must be reused or renewed as an assembly.

5 Complete engine disassembly should be done in the following general order with reference to the appropriate Sections. Refer to Chapter 3 for details of transmission components disassembly.

- *Remove the valve cover.*
- *Remove the camshaft and rockers.*
- *Remove the cylinder head.*
- *Remove the cylinder.*
- *Remove the piston.*
- *Remove the alternator.*
- *Remove the starter motor (see Chapter 10).*
- *Remove the oil pump.*
- *Remove the variator (see Chapter 3).*
- *Separate the crankcase halves.*
- *Remove the crankshaft.*

Reassembly

6 Reassembly is the reverse of the general disassembly sequence.

7 Valve cover

Removal

1 Raise the scooter up off the engine (see Section 5).

2 If you want to remove the valve cover completely undo the engine breather housing screws and detach the cover – note the

O-ring **(see illustration)**. Otherwise leave the breather cover attached and just displace the valve cover from the head.

3 Unscrew the valve cover bolts, then lift the cover off the cylinder head **(see illustration)**. If it is stuck, do not try to lever it off with a screwdriver. Tap it gently with a rubber hammer or block of wood to dislodge it. Remove and discard the gasket – a new one must be fitted. Check the condition of the cover bolt seals and replace them with new ones if necessary **(see illustration 7.6b)**.

Installation

4 Clean the mating surfaces of the cylinder head and the valve cover with a suitable solvent.

5 Fit the new gasket into the groove in the valve cover, making sure it locates correctly **(see illustration)** – use some dabs of grease to help stick it in place if required.

6 Position the valve cover on the cylinder

7.6a Locate the cover on the head . . .

head, making sure the gasket stays in place **(see illustration)**. Fit the cover bolts, using new seals if necessary, and tighten the bolts evenly and in a criss-cross sequence to the torque setting specified at the beginning of the Chapter **(see illustration)**.

7 If detached fit the breather housing using a new O-ring if required **(see illustrations)**. Install the remaining components in the reverse order of removal.

8 Lower the scooter down onto the engine (see Section 5).

8 Cam chain tensioner

Removal

1 Remove the valve cover (see Section 7).

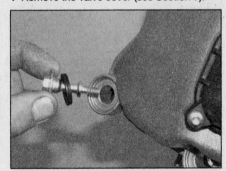

7.6b . . . then fit the bolts with their seals

7.7a Seat the O-ring in its groove . . .

7.7b . . . then fit the breather housing

8.3a Turn the engine clockwise . . .

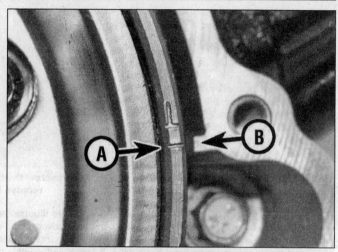

8.3b . . . until the line next to the T mark (A) aligns with the projection (B) . . .

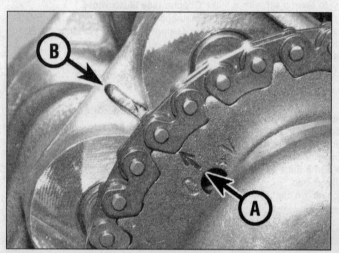

8.3c . . . and the arrow next to the 4V mark (A) on the sprocket aligns with the index mark (B)

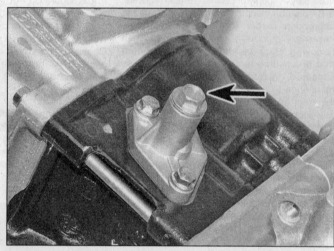

8.4 Unscrew the cap bolt and remove the spring

2 Remove the alternator cover (see Section 16).
3 Turn the engine in a clockwise direction using the alternator rotor nut, until the timing mark on the rotor aligns with the index mark on the crankcase, and the timing mark (4V) on the camshaft sprocket aligns with the index mark on the camshaft holder (see illustrations). At this point the engine is at TDC (top dead centre) on the compression stroke (all valves closed). If the 4V arrow is not in alignment, rotate the engine 360° and re-align the timing marks. **Note:** *On some engines there is no timing mark on the alternator rotor. To ensure correct reassembly, paint a mark on the rotor aligned with the index mark on the crankcase.*
4 Unscrew the chain tensioner spring cap bolt and withdraw the spring from the tensioner body (see illustration). Discard the sealing washer as a new one must be fitted on reassembly
5 Unscrew the two tensioner mounting bolts and withdraw the tensioner from the back of the cylinder (see illustration).
6 Remove the gasket from the base of the tensioner or from the cylinder and discard it (see illustration 8.12) – a new one must be used.

Inspection

7 Examine the tensioner components for signs of wear or damage.
8 Use a small screwdriver to release the ratchet mechanism on the tensioner plunger and check that the plunger moves freely in and out of the tensioner body (see illustration).
9 If the tensioner mechanism or the spring are worn or damaged, or if the plunger is seized in the body, the tensioner assembly must be replaced with a new one – individual components are not available.

Installation

10 Turn the engine a small amount in a

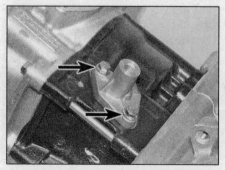

8.5 Unscrew the bolts (arrowed) and remove the tensioner

8.8 Check the operation of the ratchet and plunger

clockwise direction using the alternator rotor nut **(see illustration 8.3a)** to take up any slack in the front run of the cam chain between the crankshaft and the camshaft and transfer it to the back run where it will be taken up by the tensioner.

11 Release the ratchet mechanism and press the tensioner plunger all the way into the tensioner body **(see illustration 8.8).**

12 Place a new gasket on the tensioner body, then install it in the cylinder and tighten the bolts to the torque specified at the beginning of the Chapter **(see illustration).**

13 Fit a new sealing washer onto the spring cap bolt. Fit the spring and cap bolt and tighten the bolt to the specified torque **(see illustration)** – as you thread the bolt in you should hear the plunger extend over the ratchet mechanism and see the chain tension.

14 Check that the cam chain is tensioned. If it is slack, the tensioner plunger did not release when the cap bolt was tightened. Remove the tensioner and check the operation of the plunger again.

15 Install the alternator cover (see Section 16) and the valve cover (see Section 7).

9 Cam chain, blades and sprockets

Removal

1 Remove the valve cover (see Section 7). Remove the alternator cover (see Section 16).

2 If the cam chain and crankshaft sprocket

8.12 Fit the tensioner using a new gasket

are to be removed, remove the oil pump driven sprocket, drive chain and drive sprocket (see Section 18).

3 Turn the engine in a clockwise direction using the alternator rotor nut, until the timing mark on the rotor aligns with the index mark on the crankcase, and the timing mark (4V) on the camshaft sprocket aligns with the index mark on the camshaft holder **(see illustrations 8.3a, b and c).** At this point the engine is at TDC (top dead centre) on the compression stroke (all valves closed). If the 4V mark is not in alignment, rotate the engine 360° and re-align the timing marks.

4 Hold the alternator to prevent the camshaft sprocket from turning and undo the decompressor mechanism cover bolt, noting the washer(s) where fitted **(see illustration).**

5 Release the bob weight return spring end from the static weight **(see illustration).** Remove the bob weight, noting how the shaft

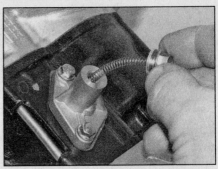

8.13 Fit the spring and the cap bolt, using a new sealing washer

locates in the slot in the cam chain sprocket **(see illustration).** Note the nylon bush on the back of the weight, and remove it for safekeeping **(see illustration).**

6 Undo the static weight bolt and remove the weight, noting how it locates **(see illustration).**

7 Remove the cam chain tensioner (see Section 8).

8 Lift the sprocket and its backing plate off the end of the camshaft, then disengage it from the cam chain **(see illustration).**

9 If required, secure the chain with a cable-tie to prevent it falling into the engine. If the chain is to be removed, mark it with paint so that if it is re-used it can be fitted the same way round. Remove the thrust washer from the end of the crankshaft, then lower the chain down its tunnel and slip it off the sprocket on the crankshaft **(see illustrations).** Draw the sprocket off the crankshaft, noting how it locates on the pin **(see illustration).**

9.4 Unscrew the bolt (arrowed) and remove the cover

9.5a Release the spring end . . .

9.5b . . . then remove the bob weight . . .

9.5c . . . noting the nylon bush

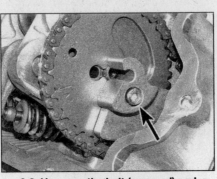

9.6 Unscrew the bolt (arrowed) and remove the weight

9.8 Lift off the sprocket and backing plate and disengage the chain

9.9a Remove the thrust washer . . .

9.9b . . . then lift out the cam chain . . .

9.9c . . . and draw the sprocket off – note notch and pin (arrowed)

9.10 Unscrew the bolt (arrowed) and remove the tensioner blade

9.11 Draw the guide blade out of the engine

10 To remove the cam chain tensioner blade unscrew its pivot bolt and withdraw the blade, noting which way round it fits, and the spacer (see illustration).

11 To remove cam chain guide blade remove the cylinder head (see Section 11).

Inspection

12 Check the sprockets for wear and damaged teeth, replacing them with new ones

Lift the blade out, noting how it locates (see illustration).

if necessary. If the sprocket teeth are worn, a new cam chain should be fitted.

13 Check the chain tensioner blade and guide blade for wear or damage and fit new ones if necessary. Damaged or severely worn blades are an indication of a worn or improperly tensioned chain. Check the operation of the cam chain tensioner (see Section 8). Fit a new chain if necessary.

14 Inspect the components of the decompressor mechanism. Check the nylon bush for wear and flat spots and replace it with a new one if necessary (see illustration 9.5c). Temporarily assemble the mechanism on the camshaft (see below) and check its operation – check the spring tension and ensure the bob weight does not bind on the cover.

Installation

15 If removed, fit the cam chain guide blade, locating the slot in its bottom end over the pin on the crankcase and its lugs in the cut-outs in the cylinder (see illustrations). Install the cylinder head (see Section 11).

16 If removed, fit the tensioner blade with its spacer and tighten the bolt to the torque setting specified at the beginning of the Chapter (see illustration).

17 Slide the sprocket onto the crankshaft (see illustration 9.9c) – align the notch in the sprocket with the pin on the shaft. Pass the cam chain along the tunnel and fit it onto the sprocket (see illustration 9.9b). If the original chain is being re-used, ensure it is fitted the right way round (see Step 9). Slide the thrust washer against the sprocket (see illustration 9.9a).

18 Check that the timing mark on the alternator rotor still aligns with the index mark on the crankcase and that the engine is at TDC on the compression stroke (see Step 3).

19 Fit the camshaft sprocket backing plate on the end of the camshaft (see illustration). Slip the camshaft sprocket into the top of the chain, then take up the slack in the lower run of the chain, making sure it is still engaged around the crankshaft sprocket, and fit the sprocket onto the camshaft, aligning the timing mark (4V) with the index mark on the camshaft holder (see illustration).

Caution: If the marks are not aligned exactly as described, the valve timing will be incorrect and the valves may strike the

9.15a Make sure the slot locates over the pin . . .

9.15b . . . and the lugs seat in the cut-outs

9.16 Make sure the spacer is fitted

9.19a Locate the backing plate onto the projections . . .

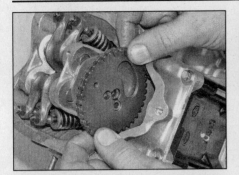

9.19b . . . then fit the sprocket into the chain and onto the camshaft

9.20 Fit the static weight and thread the bolt into the offset hole

9.21a Fit the return spring as shown

9.21b Make sure the return spring ends (arrowed) are correctly located

9.22 Fit the cover and finger-tighten tighten the bolt

9.24 Counter-hold the alternator and tighten the bolts (arrowed)

piston, causing extensive damage to the engine.

20 Fit the static weight for the decompressor mechanism, making sure it locates correctly around the centre projection **(see illustration)**. Tighten the decompressor mechanism bolt finger-tight **(see illustration 9.6)**.

21 Apply some grease to the nylon bush and fit it onto the back of the bob weight **(see illustration 9.5c)**. Fit the return spring onto the weight as shown if removed **(see illustration)**. Fit the bob weight – ensure the bush locates in the slot in the cam chain sprocket **(see illustration 9.5b)**. Hook the outer return spring end round and onto the static weight **(see illustration 9.5a)** – the spring ends should be located as shown **(see illustrations)**. Check the operation of the mechanism – the bob weight should move freely on its spindle and return to the rest position under the tension of the spring.

22 Fit the decompressor mechanism cover, aligning the small hole with the head of the static weight bolt, and tighten the bolt finger-tight **(see illustration)**.

23 Install the cam chain tensioner (see Section 8).

24 Tighten the decompressor mechanism cover bolt and the static weight bolt to the specified torque settings **(see illustration)**. Hold the alternator to prevent the assembly turning.

25 Install the oil pump drive sprocket, chain and driven sprocket (see Section 18).

26 Install the alternator cover (see Section 16), the valve cover (see Section 7), and all remaining components in the reverse order of removal.

10 Camshaft and rockers

Removal

1 Remove the valve cover (see Section 7). Remove the alternator cover (see Section 16).

2 Turn the engine in a clockwise direction using the alternator rotor nut, until the timing mark on the rotor aligns with the index mark on the crankcase, and the timing mark (4V) on the camshaft sprocket aligns with the index mark on the camshaft holder **(see illustrations 8.3a, b and c)**. At this point the engine is at TDC (top dead centre) on the compression stroke (all valves closed). If the 4V mark is not in alignment, rotate the engine 360° and re-align the timing marks.

3 Where fitted, remove the decompressor mechanism (see Section 9).

4 Remove the camshaft sprocket (see Section 9), then secure the cam chain with a cable-tie or length of wire to prevent it dropping into the engine. Stuff a clean rag into the cam chain tunnel to prevent anything falling into the engine.

5 Undo the two bolts securing the camshaft retaining plate and lift out the plate **(see illustration)**.

6 The rocker arms are fitted on two separate shafts. The intake rocker arm is on the throttle body side of the cylinder head, and the exhaust arm is on the exhaust side of the head. Mark the ends of the shafts and the rocker arms so that they can be installed in their original positions.

7 Support each rocker arm in turn and withdraw its shaft **(see illustration)**. Do not mix the rocker arms and shafts up – they must be installed in their original positions.

10.5 Unscrew the bolts (arrowed) and lift out the plate

10.7 Withdraw the rocker shafts and remove the arms

10.8 Withdraw the camshaft

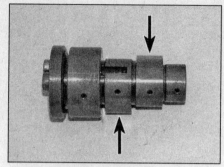

10.10a Check the lobes (arrowed) for wear and damage . . .

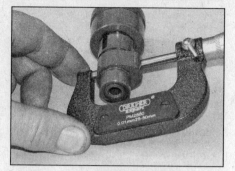

10.10b . . . and measure the height of each lobe

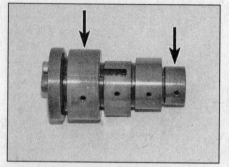

10.11a Check and measure the journals (arrowed) . . .

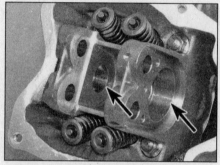

10.11b . . . and their housings (arrowed)

8 Withdraw the camshaft from its housing (see illustration).

Inspection

9 Clean all the components with a suitable solvent and dry them.

10 Inspect the camshaft lobes for heat discoloration (blue appearance), score marks, chipped areas, flat spots and spalling (see illustration). Measure the height of both lobes with a micrometer and compare the results to the Specifications at the beginning of the

Chapter (see illustration). If damage is noted or wear is excessive, the camshaft must be replaced with a new one.

11 Check the condition of the camshaft bearing journals and the housing journals in the cylinder head (see illustrations). Measure the camshaft journals with a micrometer and, if available, measure the internal diameter of the housing journals with a telescoping gauge and micrometer. Compare the results to the Specifications at the beginning of the Chapter and, if damage is noted or wear is excessive, replace any faulty component with a new one.

12 Lubricate the camshaft journals with clean engine oil, fit the camshaft into the cylinder head and secure it with the retaining plate (see illustrations 10.8 and 10.5). The camshaft should rotate freely with no discernible up-and-down movement. If available, measure the camshaft end-float with a dial gauge and compare the result to the Specifications at the beginning of the Chapter. If the end-float is excessive, inspect the retaining plate and the slot in the camshaft for wear and replace any worn component with a new one.

13 Inspect the rocker arm faces for pits and spalling (see illustration). Check the articulated tip of the adjusting screw and the top of each valve for wear. The tip should move freely but not be loose. Slip the shaft into the arm and check for freeplay between them (see illustration). Measure the internal diameter of each rocker arm, the internal diameters of the rocker shaft housings and the diameter of the rocker shaft and compare the results to the Specifications at the beginning of the Chapter (see illustration). If damage is noted or wear is excessive, replace any faulty component with a new one.

Installation

14 Lubricate the camshaft journals with clean engine oil, then fit the camshaft in the cylinder head with the end holes positioned as shown (see illustration 10.8).

15 Lubricate the rocker shafts with engine oil. Hold the exhaust rocker arm in position, then slide the exhaust shaft through its housing and the arm (see illustration 10.7). Press the shaft fully into place. Follow the same procedure and install the intake rocker arm (see illustration). With the camshaft in the

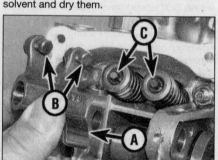

10.13a Inspect the rocker arm faces (A), adjuster screw tips (B) and valve stem ends (C)

10.13b Check for freeplay between the each arm and its shaft . . .

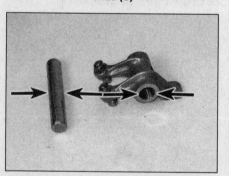

10.13c . . . and measure the OD of the shaft and the ID of the arm

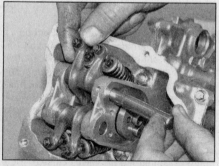

10.15 Locate each rocker arm and slide its shaft through

correct position there should be no pressure on the rocker arms.

16 Align the camshaft retaining plate with the slot in the camshaft, slide the plate into position and secure it with the bolts **(see illustration)**. Tighten the bolts to the specified torque setting.

17 Follow the procedure in Section 9 to install the camshaft sprocket, decompressor mechanism and cam chain tensioner, then check the valve timing.

Caution: If the marks are not aligned exactly as described, the valve timing will be incorrect and the valves may strike the piston, causing extensive damage to the engine.

18 Check the valve clearances and adjust them if necessary (see Chapter 1).

19 Install the remaining components in the reverse order of removal.

11 Cylinder head removal and installation

Caution: The engine must be completely cool before beginning this procedure or the cylinder head may become warped.

Removal

1 Remove the exhaust system (see Chapter 5).
2 Remove the valve cover (see Section 7).
3 Remove the cam chain tensioner (see Section 8). If there is enough slack in the chain slip it off the sprocket on the camshaft. If not, or if required anyway, remove the camshaft

10.16 Fit the plate into its slot

sprocket (see Section 9). Secure the cam chain with a cable-tie or length of wire to prevent it dropping into the engine. If required remove the camshaft and rockers (see Section 10).

4 Undo the two cylinder head bolts on the left-hand side of the engine **(see illustration)**. Undo the four cylinder head nuts evenly, a little at a time, in a criss-cross pattern and remove them **(see illustration)**.

5 Lift the cylinder head up off the studs, feeding the cam chain down through the tunnel in the head **(see illustration)**. If the head is stuck, tap around the joint face with a soft-faced mallet to free it. Do not attempt to free the head by inserting a screwdriver between the head and cylinder – you'll damage the sealing surfaces. **Note:** *Avoid lifting the cylinder off the crankcase when the head is removed, otherwise a new cylinder base gasket will have to be fitted (see Section 13).*

6 Remove the cylinder head gasket – a

new one must be fitted on reassembly **(see illustration 11.9b)**. Note the two dowels and remove them for safekeeping if they are loose – they could be in the underside of the head or in the top of the cylinder **(see illustration)**. Remove the O-rings from the studs – discard them as new ones must be fitted **(see illustration)**.

7 Inspect the gasket and the mating surfaces on the head and cylinder for signs of leakage, which could indicate that the head is warped. Refer to Section 12 and check the head gasket mating surface for warpage.

8 Clean all traces of old gasket material from the cylinder head and cylinder using a suitable scraper and solvent. Take care not to scratch or gouge the soft aluminium. Be careful not to let any dirt fall into the crankcase, the cylinder bore or the oil passage.

Installation

9 Ensure both cylinder head and cylinder mating surfaces are clean. Fit a new O-ring around the base of each stud **(see illustration)**. Fit the two dowels if removed **(see illustration 11.6a)**. Lay the new gasket in place on the cylinder **(see illustration)**. Never re-use the old gasket. Make sure the cam chain guide blade is correctly seated **(see illustration 9.15b)**.

10 Carefully fit the head over the studs and onto the cylinder, feeding the cam chain up through the tunnel **(see illustration 11.5)**. Make sure the dowels locate correctly.

11 Smear some oil onto the stud threads. Fit the cylinder head nuts finger-tight, then

11.4a Undo the two external cylinder head bolts (arrowed) . . .

11.4b . . . then the four internal cylinder head nuts (arrowed)

11.5 Lift off the cylinder head

11.6a Remove the dowels (arrowed) if loose

11.6b Dig the O-rings out from around the studs

11.9a Fit a new O-ring over each stud and into the hole in the cylinder

11.9b Fit the new head gasket

11.11 Tighten the cylinder head nuts as described – this shows a degree disc for the final angle tightening

11.12 Fit the two side bolts and tighten to the specified torque

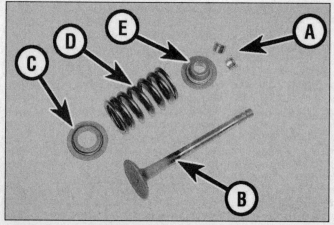

12.5 Valve components – collets (A), valve (B), spring seat (C), spring (D) and spring retainer (E)

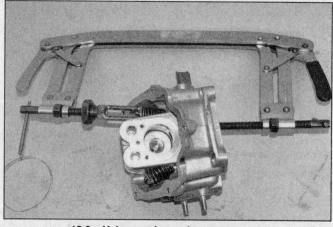

12.6a Using a valve spring compressor

tighten them in the sequence shown first to the initial torque setting specified at the beginning of this Chapter, then in the same sequence to the middle torque setting, and then for the final setting tighten them through the specified angle using a degree disc (see illustration).

12 Fit the two cylinder head bolts on the left-hand side of the engine and tighten them to the specified torque setting (see illustration).

13 Install the rockers, camshaft, sprocket, tensioner and all other remaining components in the reverse order of removal as required, referring to the relevant Sections and Chapters.

12 Cylinder head and valve overhaul

1 Because of the complex nature of this job and the special tools and equipment required, most owners leave checking and servicing of the valves, valve seats and valve guides to a professional. However, you can make an initial assessment of whether the valves are seating correctly, and therefore sealing, by pouring a small amount of solvent into each of the valve ports. If the solvent leaks past any valve into the combustion chamber area the valve is not seating correctly and sealing.

2 With the correct tools (a valve spring compressor is essential – make sure it is suitable for motorcycle work), you can also remove the valves and associated components from the cylinder head, clean them and check them for wear to assess the extent of the work needed, and grind in the valves and reassemble them in the head.

3 If the valve guides or the valve seats are worn a new cylinder head is required – valve guides are not available and Vespa state that the seats cannot be re-cut.

4 After the valve service has been performed, be sure to clean the head very thoroughly before installation to remove any metal particles or abrasive grit that may still be present from the valve service operations. Use compressed air, if available, to blow out all the holes and passages.

Disassembly

5 Before proceeding, arrange to label and store the valves along with their related components in such a way that they can be returned to their original locations without getting mixed up (see illustration). Labelled plastic bags or a plastic container with two compartments are ideal.

6 Compress the valve spring on the first valve with a spring compressor, making sure it is correctly located onto each end of the valve assembly (see illustration). On the top of the

12.6b Make sure the compressor locates correctly both on the top of the spring retainer . . .

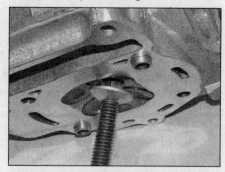

12.6c . . . and on the bottom of the valve

valve the adaptor needs to be about the same size as the spring retainer – if it is too small it will be difficult to remove and install the collets **(see illustration)**. On the underside of the head make sure the plate on the compressor only contacts the valve and not the soft aluminium of the head **(see illustration)** – if the plate is too big for the valve, use a spacer between them as shown. Do not compress the springs any more than is absolutely necessary.

7 Remove the collets, using a magnet or a screwdriver with a dab of grease on it **(see illustration)**. Carefully release the valve spring compressor and remove the spring retainer, noting which way up it fits, the spring and the valve **(see illustrations 12.30b, 12.30a and 12.27)**. If the valve binds in the guide and won't pull through, push it back into the head and deburr the area around the collet groove with a very fine file or whetstone **(see illustration)**.

8 Pull the valve stem seal off the top of the valve guide with pliers and discard it (the old seals should never be reused), then remove the spring seat noting which way up it fits **(see illustrations 12.28 and 12.29a)**.

9 Repeat the procedure for the other valve. Remember to keep the parts for each valve together so they can be reinstalled in the same location.

10 Clean the cylinder head with solvent and dry it thoroughly. Compressed air will speed the drying process and ensure that all holes and recessed areas are clean. **Note:** *Do not use a wire brush mounted in a drill motor to clean the combustion chambers as the head material is soft and may be scratched or eroded away by the wire brush.*

11 Clean the valve springs, collets, retainers and spring seats with solvent and dry them thoroughly. Do the parts from one valve at a time so that no mixing of parts between valves occurs.

12 Scrape off any deposits that may have formed on the valve, then use a motorised wire brush to remove deposits from the valve heads and stems. Again, make sure the valves do not get mixed up.

Inspection

13 Inspect the head very carefully for cracks and other damage. If cracks are found, a new head is required.

14 Using a precision straight-edge and a feeler gauge set to the warpage limit listed in the specifications at the beginning of the Chapter, check the head gasket mating surface for warpage. Take six measurements, one along each side and two diagonally across. If the head is warped beyond the limit specified at the beginning of this Chapter, consult a Vespa dealer or take it to a specialist repair shop for an opinion, though be prepared to have to buy a new one.

15 Examine the valve seats in the combustion chamber and the corresponding surface on each valve. If they are pitted, cracked or burned, a new head must be fitted. Measure

12.7a Compress the valve spring and remove the collets

the valve seat width and compare it to this Chapter's Specifications **(see illustration)**. If it exceeds the service limit, or if it varies around its circumference, a new head is required.

16 Working on one valve and guide at a time, measure the valve stem diameter in three places along the stem **(see illustration)**. Clean the valve's guide using a guide reamer to remove any carbon build-up. Now measure the inside diameter of the guide with a small bore gauge, then measure the gauge with a micrometer **(see illustration)**. Measure the guide at the ends and at the centre to determine if they are worn in a bell-mouth pattern (more wear at the ends). Subtract the stem diameter from the valve guide diameter to obtain the valve stem-to-guide clearance. Repeat for the other valve. If the stem-to-guide clearance is greater than the service limit

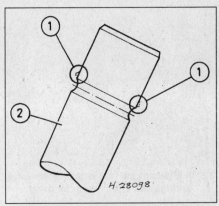

12.7b If the valve stem (2) won't pull through the guide, deburr the area (1) above the collet groove

listed in this Chapter's Specifications, but the guides are within their limit, replace the valves with new ones. If the guides are worn fit a new head – it will come assembled with new valves.

17 Carefully inspect each valve face, stem and collet groove area for cracks, pits and burned spots **(see illustration)**.

18 Rotate the valve and check for any obvious indication that it is bent, in which case it must be replaced with a new one. Check the end of the stem for pitting and excessive wear, and replace with a new one if necessary.

19 Check the end of each valve spring for wear and pitting. Measure the spring free

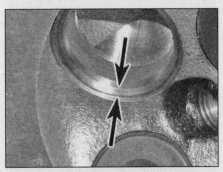

12.15 Measure the valve seat width

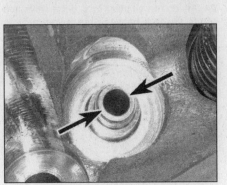

12.16b Measure the valve guide with a small bore gauge, then measure the bore gauge with a micrometer

12.16a Measure the valve stem diameter with a micrometer

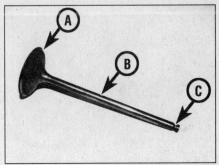

12.17 Check the valve face (A), stem (B) and collet groove (C) for signs of wear and damage

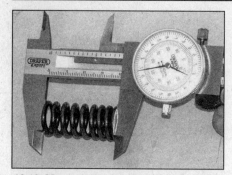

12.19 Measure the free length of the valve springs and check them for bend

12.23 Apply small dabs of the paste around the circumference of the valve

12.24 Using a valve lapping tool

12.27 Slide the valve up into its guide

12.28 Fit the spring seat

length and compare it to the specifications **(see illustration)**. If the spring is shorter than specified it has sagged and must be replaced with a new one. Also place the spring upright on a flat surface and check it for bend by placing a ruler against it, or alternatively lay it against a set square. If the bend in any spring is excessive, it must be replaced with a new one.

20 Check the spring seats, retainers and collets for obvious wear and cracks **(see illustration 12.5)**. Any questionable parts should not be reused, as extensive damage will occur in the event of failure during engine operation.

21 If the inspection indicates that no overhaul work is required, the valve components can be reinstalled in the head.

Reassembly

22 Unless a valve service has been

performed, before installing the valves in the head they should be ground in (lapped) to ensure a positive seal between the valves and seats. This procedure requires fine valve grinding compound and a valve grinding tool (either hand-held or drill driven). If a grinding tool is not available, a piece of rubber or plastic hose can be slipped over the valve stem (after the valve has been installed in the guide) and used to turn the valve.

23 Apply a small amount of fine grinding compound to the valve face **(see illustration)**. Smear some molybdenum disulphide oil (a 50/50 mixture of molybdenum disulphide grease and engine oil) to the valve stem, then slip the valve into the guide **(see illustration 12.27)**. **Note:** *Make sure each valve is installed in its correct guide and be careful not to get any grinding compound on the valve stem.*

24 Attach the grinding tool to the valve and rotate the tool between the palms of your

hands **(see illustration)**. Use a back-and-forth motion (as though rubbing your hands together) rather than a circular motion (i.e. so that the valve rotates alternately clockwise and anti-clockwise rather than in one direction only). If a motorised tool is being used, take note of the correct drive speed for it – if your drill runs too fast and is not variable, use a hand tool instead. Lift the valve off the seat and turn it at regular intervals to distribute the grinding compound properly. Continue the grinding procedure until the valve face and seat contact area are of uniform width, and unbroken around the entire circumference **(see illustration 12.15)**.

25 Remove the valve and wipe off all traces of grinding compound, making sure none gets in the guide. Use solvent to clean the valve and valve seat, and flush the guide.

26 Repeat the entire procedure for the other valves. On completion thoroughly clean the entire head again, then blow through all passages with compressed air. Make sure all traces of the grinding compound have been removed before assembling the head.

27 Coat the valve stem with molybdenum disulphide oil (a 50/50 mixture of molybdenum disulphide grease and engine oil), then fit it into its guide **(see illustration)**. Check that the valve moves up-and-down freely.

28 Working on one valve at a time, lay the spring seat in place in the cylinder head with its shouldered side facing up **(see illustration)**.

29 Fit a new valve stem seal over the valve stem and onto the guide, using finger pressure, a stem seal fitting tool or an appropriate size deep socket, to push the seal squarely onto the end of the valve guide until it is felt to clip into place **(see illustrations)**.

30 Next fit the spring, then fit the spring retainer, with its shouldered side facing down so that it fits into the top of the spring **(see illustrations)**.

31 Apply a small amount of grease to the inside of the collets to help hold them in place. Compress the valve spring with a spring compressor, making sure it is correctly located onto each end of the valve assembly (see Step 6) **(see illustrations 12.6a, b and c)**. Do not compress the spring any more than is necessary to slip the collets into place. Locate each collet in turn into the groove in the valve

12.29a Fit a new valve stem seal . . .

12.29b . . . and press it squarely into place using a deep socket of the appropriate size

12.30a Fit the spring . . .

12.30b . . . and the retainer

12.31a Compress the spring and fit the collets, locating them in the groove

stem using a screwdriver with a dab of grease on it (see illustration). Carefully release the compressor, making sure the collets seat and lock in the retaining groove (see illustration).
32 Repeat the procedure for the other valves.
33 Support the cylinder head on blocks so the valves can't contact the work surface, then tap the end of each valve stem lightly using a copper or plastic hammer to seat the collets in their grooves (see illustration).

 HAYNES HiNT *Check for proper sealing of the valves by pouring a small amount of solvent into each of the valve ports. If the solvent leaks past any valve into the combustion chamber the valve grinding operation on that valve should be repeated.*

34 After the cylinder head and all related components have been installed, check the valve clearances and adjust as required (see Chapter 1).

13 Cylinder

Removal

1 Remove the cylinder head (see Section 11).
2 Remove the cam chain guide blade (see illustration 9.11).

12.31b Slowly release the spring and make sure each collet has located in its groove in the top of the valve stem

3 Lift the cylinder up off the studs, feeding the cam chain down through the tunnel and laying it over the front of the engine (see illustration). Support the piston as it becomes accessible to prevent it hitting the crankcase. If the cylinder is stuck, tap around its joint face with a soft-faced mallet to free it from the crankcase. Don't attempt to free the cylinder by inserting a screwdriver between it and the crankcase – you'll damage the sealing surfaces. When the cylinder is removed, stuff a clean rag around the piston to prevent anything falling into the crankcase.
4 Note the two dowels and remove them for safekeeping if they are loose – they could be in the underside of the cylinder or in the crankcase (see illustration).
5 Remove the gasket and make a note of the thickness (0.4, 0.6 or 0.8) stamped into the material (see illustration 13.16). If the original

12.33 Tap the top of the valve stem to ensure correct seating of the collets

cylinder and piston are used on reassembly, a new gasket of the same thickness should be used. Discard the old gasket.

Inspection

6 Inspect the cylinder bore carefully for scratches and score marks. A re-bore (125 cc engine) or new cylinder (250/300 cc engines) will be necessary if the cylinder is deeply scored.
7 Using a telescoping gauge and micrometer, check the dimensions of the cylinder to assess the amount of wear, taper and ovality. Vespa recommend the bore is measured at 6 mm, 33 mm and 78 mm stages down from the top edge, both parallel to and across the crankshaft axis (see illustrations). Compare the results to the cylinder bore specifications at the beginning of this Chapter. **Note:** *Cylinders and pistons are size coded during*

13.3 Lift the cylinder up off the piston and studs

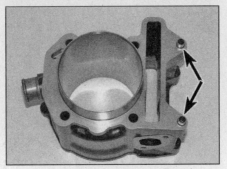

13.4 Remove the dowels (arrowed) if loose

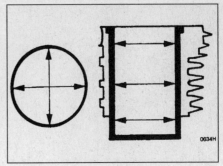

13.7a Measure the cylinder bore in the directions shown . . .

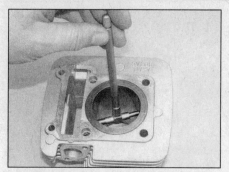

13.7b . . . using a telescoping gauge

13.13 Zero the dial gauge on the cylinder top gasket face

13.15 Take the reading off the piston crown at TDC

manufacture and it is important that they are of the same size code. Vespa list four standard size codes, A to D for the 125, and M to P for the 250 and 300 cc engines, but first, second and third oversizes (re-bored cylinders) are only listed for the 125 cc engine. The size code is stamped into the lower edge of the cylinder, and in the piston crown. When purchasing a new cylinder or piston, always supply the size code.

8 Calculate any differences between the measurements to determine any taper or ovality in the bore. Vespa specify a wear limit of 0.05 mm between any of the measurements. If the cylinder is worn beyond this service limit, badly scratched, scuffed or scored, on 125 engines have it re-bored by a Vespa dealer or motorcycle engineer or fit a new cylinder, and on 250 and 300 engines fit a new cylinder. If the cylinder is re-bored (125 cc engine), it will require an oversize piston and rings. If the cylinder has already been re-bored to the maximum oversize and is worn or damaged, the cylinder must be replaced with a new one. If a re-bore is being done make sure the person doing it is provided with the size and clearance specifications.

9 Measure the cylinder bore diameter 33 mm down from the top edge, then calculate the piston-to-bore clearance by subtracting the piston diameter (see Section 14) from the bore diameter. If the cylinder is in good condition and the piston-to-bore clearance is within specifications, the cylinder can be re-used.

10 Check that all the studs are tight in

the crankcase. If any are loose, or need to be replaced with new ones, remove them. Clean their threads and smear them with a thread locking compound. Fit them into the crankcase and tighten them using a stud tool, or by threading two of the cylinder head nuts onto the top of the stud and tightening them together so they are locked on the stud, then tighten the stud by turning the upper of the two nuts.

Installation

11 Check that the mating surfaces of the cylinder and crankcase are clean.

12 Two different thicknesses of cylinder base gasket are available for 125 engines, and three for 250 and 300 engines. If the original cylinder and piston are being re-used, use a gasket the same thickness as the original (see Step 5). If new components are being used, the cylinder must be assembled on the crankcase and piston (see Steps 17 to 21) without a base gasket, and a dial gauge mounted against the crown of the piston to establish which thickness is required – Vespa have a dial gauge mounting plate especially made for the purpose (part No. 020428Y). Basically what you are trying to do is establish the gap between the top of the piston at TDC and a plane across the cylinder mating surface without a base gasket, and the amount determines the thickness of gasket required. You could achieve the task using a precision straight-edge laid across the cylinder and a good set of feeler blades, but a dial gauge is far more accurate.

13 Mount the dial gauge with its tip resting against the cylinder top gasket face, and zero the gauge dial **(see illustration)**. Rotate the crankshaft so that the piston is part way down the bore.

14 Move the gauge so the tip is in the centre of the cylinder bore.

15 Rotate the crankshaft via the alternator rotor nut so the piston rises to the top of its stroke (TDC) and the gauge tip rests on the centre of the piston crown. At this point read off the dial gauge **(see illustration)**. The further the piston crown is below the top of the cylinder bore, the thinner the base gasket should be. On 125 engines, if the reading is between 1.6 and 1.8 mm a 0.8 mm gasket is required, and between 1.4 and 1.6 a 0.6 mm gasket is required. On 250 and 300 engines, if the reading is between 3.3 and 3.4 mm a 0.8 mm gasket is required, between 3.4 and 3.6 mm a 0.6 mm gasket is required, and between 3.6 and 3.7 mm a 0.4 mm gasket is required. If you are in doubt about anything have a Vespa dealer take the measurement.

16 If removed fit the dowels into the crankcase or the underside of the block **(see illustration 13.4)**. Fit the new gasket, locating it over the studs and the dowel **(see illustration)**. Never re-use the old gasket.

17 If required, fit a piston ring clamp onto the piston to ease its entry into the bore as the cylinder is lowered. This is not essential as the cylinder has a good lead-in enabling the piston rings to be hand-fed into the bore. If possible, have an assistant to support the cylinder while this is done. Check that the piston ring end gaps are positioned as described in Section 15.

18 Lubricate the cylinder bore, piston and piston rings, and the connecting rod big- and small-ends, with the clean engine oil, then fit the cylinder down over the studs until the piston crown fits into the bore **(see illustration)**.

19 Gently push down on the cylinder, making sure the piston enters the bore squarely and does not get cocked sideways. If a piston ring clamp is not being used, carefully compress and feed each ring into the bore as the cylinder is lowered **(see illustration)**. If necessary, use a soft mallet to gently tap the cylinder down, but do not use force if it appears to be stuck

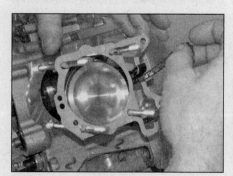

13.16 Fit a new cylinder base gasket onto the crankcase

13.18 Locate the top of the piston in the bottom of the bore . . .

as the piston and/or rings will be damaged. If a clamp is used, remove it once the piston is in the bore.

20 When the piston is correctly installed in the cylinder, press the cylinder down onto the base gasket, making sure it locates on the dowels.

21 Fit the cam chain guide blade, locating the slot in its bottom end over the pin on the crankcase and its lugs in the cut-outs in the cylinder **(see illustrations 9.15a and b)**. Install the cylinder head **(see Section 11)**.

14 Piston

Removal

1 Remove the cylinder (see Section 13). Before removing the piston from the connecting rod, stuff a clean rag into the hole around the rod to prevent the circlips or anything else from falling into the crankcase. The piston should have a triangle marked on its crown which should face towards the exhaust. If this is not visible, mark the piston accordingly so that it can be installed the correct way round. Note that the arrow may not be visible until the carbon deposits have been scraped off and the piston cleaned.

2 Carefully prise out the circlip on one side of the piston using a pointed instrument or a small flat-bladed screwdriver inserted into the notch **(see illustration)**. Push the piston pin out from the other side to free the piston from the connecting rod **(see illustration)**. Remove the other circlip and discard them both as new ones must be used. Use a socket extension to push the piston pin out if required.

 HAYNES HINT *To prevent the circlip from flying away or from dropping into the crankcase, pass a rod or screwdriver with a greater diameter than the gap between the circlip ends, through the piston pin. This will trap the circlip if it springs out.*

 HAYNES HINT *If a piston pin is a tight fit in the piston bosses, heat the piston gently with a hot air gun – this will expand the alloy piston sufficiently to release its grip on the pin.*

Inspection

3 Before the inspection process can be carried out, the piston rings must be removed and the piston must be cleaned. Note that if the cylinder is being re-bored (125 cc engine only), piston inspection can be overlooked as a new one will be fitted. All three piston rings can be removed by hand; a ring removal and installation tool can be used on the two compression rings, but do not use it on the

13.19 . . . then carefully feed each ring in as you push the cylinder down

oil control ring **(see illustrations 15.7e, d, c, and a)**. Carefully note which way up each ring fits and in which groove as they must be installed in their original positions if being re-used. Do not nick or gouge the piston in the process.

4 Scrape all traces of carbon from the top of the piston. A hand-held wire brush or a piece of fine emery cloth can be used once most of the deposits have been scraped away. Do not, under any circumstances, use a wire brush mounted in a drill motor to remove deposits from the piston; the piston material is soft and will be eroded away.

5 Use a piston ring groove cleaning tool to remove any carbon deposits from the ring grooves. If a tool is not available, a piece broken off an old ring will do the job. Be very careful to remove only the carbon deposits. Do not remove any metal and do not nick or gouge the sides of the ring grooves. Once the

14.2a Remove the circlip . . .

14.8 Measure the piston diameter as described

deposits have been removed, clean the piston with solvent and dry it thoroughly.

6 Inspect the piston for cracks around the skirt, at the pin bosses and at the ring lands. Normal piston wear appears as even, vertical wear on the thrust surfaces of the piston and slight looseness of the top ring in its groove. If the skirt is scored or scuffed, the engine may have been suffering from overheating and/or abnormal combustion, which caused excessively high operating temperatures. Also check that the circlip grooves are not damaged.

7 A hole in the piston crown is an extreme example that abnormal combustion (pre-ignition) was occurring. Burned areas at the edge of the piston crown are usually evidence of spark knock (detonation). If any of the above problems exist, the causes must be corrected or the damage will occur again.

8 Check the piston-to-bore clearance by measuring the bore (see Section 13) and the piston diameter. Measure the piston the specified distance (see Specifications) down from the top edge and at 90° to the piston pin axis **(see illustration)**. Subtract the piston diameter from the bore diameter to obtain the clearance. If it is greater than the specified figure, the piston must be replaced with a new one (assuming the bore itself is within limits, otherwise a re-bore (125 cc engine only) or new piston and cylinder (250/300 cc engines) is necessary). Remember that the piston and cylinder are size-coded (see Section 13, Step 7) – make sure you have matched components.

9 Fit the piston pin into the piston and check for freeplay between them **(see illustration)**.

14.2b . . . and push out the piston pin

14.9a Check for freeplay between the pin and the piston

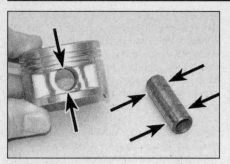

14.9b Measure both ends of the piston pin and the internal diameter of the piston pin boss

14.10 Check for freeplay between the pin and the small-end

Secure the pin with the other new circlip **(see illustration)**. When installing the circlips, compress them only just enough to fit them in the piston, and make sure they are properly seated in their grooves with the open end away from the removal notch **(see illustration 14.2a)**.

14 Install the cylinder (see Section 13).

15 Piston rings

1 New piston rings should be fitted whenever an engine is being overhauled. Before fitting the new rings, the end gaps must be checked with the rings installed in an unworn part of the bore.

2 To measure the installed ring end gap, fit the top ring into the bottom of the bore and square it up with the bore walls by pushing it in with the top of the piston **(see illustrations)**. The ring should be about 15 mm from the bottom of the bore. To measure the end gap, slip a feeler gauge between the ends of the ring and compare the measurement to the Specifications at the beginning of the Chapter **(see illustration)**.

3 If the gap is larger or smaller than specified, double-check to make sure that you have the correct rings before proceeding. If the gap is too small the ends may come in contact with each other during engine operation, which can cause serious damage. If working on a 125 cc engine, check the piston and bore diameters with the Specifications to confirm whether they are standard or oversize.

4 Excess end gap is not critical unless it exceeds the service limit. Again, double-check to make sure you have the correct rings for your engine and check that the bore is not worn.

5 Repeat the procedure for the other rings.

6 Once the ring end gaps have been checked, the rings can be fitted onto the piston.

7 Fit the oil control ring expander into the bottom groove in the piston **(see illustration)**. Fit the control ring over it with the E-TOP mark facing the top of the piston, and with the expander gap opposite to the ring gap, and do not expand the ring any more

14.11 Measuring piston ring-to-groove clearance

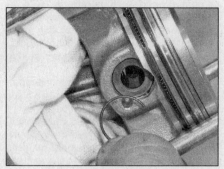

14.13 Secure the piston pin with new circlips

Using a micrometer and a telescoping gauge measure the piston pin diameter at both ends and the internal diameter of each pin boss in the piston and compare the results with the Specifications **(see illustration)**.

10 Fit the piston pin into the connecting rod small-end and check for freeplay between them **(see illustration)**. Measure the piston pin diameter at its centre and the internal diameter of the rod small-end. The piston pin should not be worn below its specified diameter and the small-end measurement should not be greater than the specified service limit. Replace any worn components with new ones – if the small-end is worn a new connecting rod and crankshaft assembly will have to be fitted (see Section 19).

11 Measure the piston ring-to-groove clearance to determine whether the ring grooves in the piston are worn: fit the rings on

the piston (see Section 15), then use a feeler gauge to measure the clearance between the ring and groove and compare the result with the Specifications **(see illustration)**. If the clearance is greater than the service limit, repeat the check using new rings, if the clearance is still too great, a new piston should be fitted.

Installation

12 Inspect and install the piston rings (see Section 15).

13 Lubricate the piston pin, the piston pin bore and the connecting rod small-end bore with clean engine oil. Install a new circlip in one side of the piston (do not re-use old circlips). Line up the piston on the connecting rod, making sure the arrow on the piston crown faces down towards the exhaust, and insert the piston pin **(see illustration 14.2b)**.

15.2a Fit the ring in its bore . . .

15.2b . . . and set it square using the piston . . .

15.2c . . . then measure the end gap using a feeler gauge

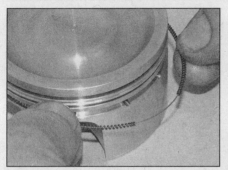

15.7a Fit the oil ring expander in its groove

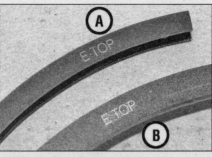

15.7b Make sure the E-TOP marks on the control ring (A) and second ring (B) face the top

15.7c Fit the control ring over the expander

15.7d Fit the second ring into its groove

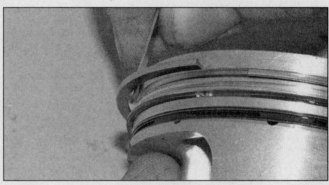

15.7e Fit the top ring into its groove

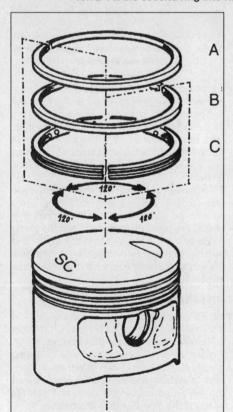

15.8 Stagger the ring end gaps at 120° intervals

A   Top ring
B   Second ring
C   Oil control ring

than is necessary to slide it into place **(see illustrations)**. Next fit the 2nd (middle) compression ring into the middle groove in the piston with the E-TOP mark facing the top of the piston **(see illustration)**. Finally fit the top ring into its groove with its horizontal section at the bottom so it fits correctly into the stepped groove **(see illustration)**.

8 Once the rings are correctly installed, check they move freely without snagging and stagger their end gaps at 120° intervals as shown **(see illustration)**.

16 Alternator rotor and stator

Note: *This procedure can be carried out with the engine in the frame. If the engine has been removed, ignore the steps which do not apply.*

Check

1 Refer to Chapter 10.

Removal

2 Drain the engine oil (see Chapter 1). Remove the exhaust silencer (see Chapter 5).

3 Either raise the scooter up off the engine until the bottom of the fuel tank is clear of the alternator cover (see Section 5), or remove the fuel tank (see Chapter 5).

4 On 250 and 300 cc engines, if not already done drain the cooling system and disconnect the coolant hoses from the water pump (see Chapter 4).

5 Trace the wiring from the alternator/pulse generator coil and disconnect it at the connectors **(see illustration 5.11)**. Disconnect the wire from the oil pressure switch **(see illustration)**. Free the wiring from any clips and feed it down to the alternator cover, noting its routing. Free any other hoses and wiring from the clips on the cover.

6 Working evenly in a criss-cross pattern, unscrew the alternator cover bolts, noting which length bolts fit where **(see illustration)**. **Note:** *As each bolt is removed, store it in its relative position in a cardboard template of the cover, along with any washer, cable guide or bracket. This will ensure all bolts and any related parts are returned to their original locations on reassembly.* Remove the cover, on 250 and 300 engines noting how the drive mechanism for the water pump engages. On 250 and 300 engines remove the water pump drive spline clip from the end

16.5 Lift the boot and disconnect the oil pressure switch wire

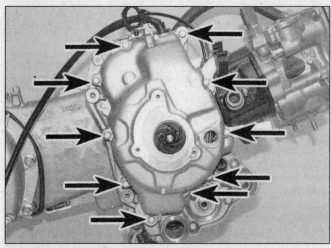

16.6a Unscrew the bolts (arrowed) and remove the cover

16.6b Remove the pump drive spline clip

16.7 With the rotor held securely, unscrew the nut

16.8a Fit the rotor puller onto the hub then turn the bolt (arrowed) until the rotor is displaced

16.8b Using a commercial legged puller to release the rotor

of the crankshaft, noting how it locates (see illustration). Remove and discard the gasket – a new one must be used (see illustration 16.16a). Remove the dowels if loose.

7 To undo the alternator rotor nut it is necessary to stop the rotor from turning. Use a commercially available strap wrench to hold the rotor, but make sure it does not locate over the pulse generator coil triggers (see illustration). With the rotor held securely, unscrew the nut, and remove the washer. Thread the nut back on by a few threads, leaving its outer rim proud of the end of the shaft – this protects the shaft and prevents the rotor dropping when it is pulled off.

8 To remove the rotor from the crankshaft it is necessary to use either the Vespa service tool (Part No. 020467Y), or a commercially available legged puller. If using the tool make sure that its centre bolt is backed-out sufficiently to allow the body of the tool to be screwed all the way onto the threads provided on the rotor hub (see illustration). With the tool in place, hold the body of the tool using a spanner on its flats while tightening the centre bolt (turn it clockwise) to displace the rotor from the end of the shaft – note that it could be quite tight, and may release its grip suddenly. If using a legged puller make sure the legs are securely located behind the rotor before tightening the

centre bolt (see illustration). When the rotor is free, remove the tool, unscrew the rotor nut and remove the rotor. If it is loose, remove the Woodruff key from the shaft, noting how it fits (see illustration 16.12). If required remove the starter clutch from the back of the rotor, and the idle/reduction and driven gears (see Section 17).

9 To remove the stator, it is also necessary to remove the pulse generator coil as they come as a linked assembly. Undo the screws that secure the pulse generator coil and the wiring guide and the bolts securing the stator and remove the two units together, noting how the wiring grommet locates in the cover (see illustration).

Installation

10 Fit the stator and pulse generator coil into the cover, aligning the rubber wiring grommet with the groove (see illustration 16.9). Tighten the screws and bolts. Press the wiring grommet into the cut-out in the cover, then apply a suitable sealant into the gap between the cut-out sections in the cover so that it fills all round the grommet (see illustration).

11 Remove any traces of old gasket from the alternator cover and crankcase mating surfaces using a suitable scraper and solvent. Take care not to scratch or gouge the soft aluminium.

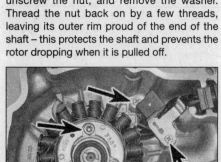

16.9 Undo the screws and bolts (arrowed) and free the wiring guide

16.10 Fit the grommet then apply the sealant in the gap

12 Clean the tapered end of the crankshaft and the corresponding mating surface on the inside of the rotor with a suitable solvent. Fit the Woodruff key into its slot in the crankshaft if removed **(see illustration)**.

13 If removed fit the starter clutch onto the back of the rotor, and install the starter driven and idle/reduction gears (see Section 17). Lubricate the outside of the starter driven gear hub and the starter clutch sprags with clean engine oil.

14 Make sure that no metal objects have attached themselves to the magnets on the inside of the rotor. Slide the rotor onto the shaft, making sure the groove on the inside of the rotor is aligned with and fits over the Woodruff key, and turn the starter driven gear anti-clockwise with your finger to ease entry of the hub into the starter clutch **(see illustration)**. Make sure the Woodruff key does not become dislodged.

15 Fit the rotor nut with its washer and tighten it to the torque setting specified at the beginning of the Chapter, using the method employed on removal to prevent the rotor from turning **(see illustrations)**. On 250 and 300 engines fit the water pump drive spline clip onto the end of the crankshaft, making sure it locates correctly **(see illustration 16.6b)**.

16 Fit the dowels into the crankcase if removed, then locate a new gasket onto the dowels **(see illustration)**. Smear a suitable sealant onto the wiring grommet. On 250 and 300 engines align the drive spline with the pump drive **(see illustration)**. Fit the alternator cover, noting that the rotor magnets

will forcibly draw the stator on, making sure it locates onto the dowels, and on 250 and 300 engines the pump drive engages correctly **(see illustration)**. On 250 and 300 engines try to turn the impeller to make sure it has engaged

– you should not be able to turn it easily **(see illustration)**. Fit the cover bolts and tighten them evenly in a criss-cross sequence to the specified torque setting **(see illustrations)**.

17 Connect the oil pressure switch, pulse

16.12 Make sure the Woodruff key (arrowed) is in its slot

16.14 Fit the rotor, turning the driven gear as you do to ease engagement

16.15a Fit the washer and the nut . . .

16.15b . . . and tighten the nut to the specified torque

16.16a Fit the new gasket onto the dowels (arrowed)

16.16b Locate the drive clip (A) into the cut-out (B)

16.16c Take care when fitting the cover as the magnets draw it on

16.16d If the pump drive has engaged you won't be able to turn the impeller

16.16e The longer bolt fits in the hole shown . . .

16.16f . . . and make sure the brackets/ clips (arrowed) are correctly positioned

17.3a Remove the idle/reduction gear

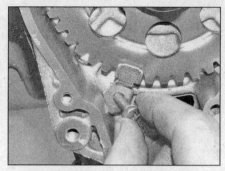

17.3b Undo the screw and remove the plate . . .

17.3c . . . then draw the gear off the shaft

17.4 Fit the gear into the starter clutch . . .

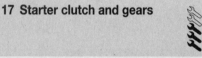

17.5 . . . and make sure it rotates freely clockwise and locks anti-clockwise

generator coil and alternator wiring connectors **(see illustrations 6.5 and 5.11)** – make sure the wiring is correctly routed and secured by any clips.

18 Lower the scooter onto the engine (see Section 5) or install the fuel tank (see Chapter 5) according to your removal method. On 250 and 300 engines connect the coolant hoses to the unions on the water pump and refill the cooling system (see Chapter 4).

19 Install the exhaust silencer (see Chapter 5). Refill the engine with oil (see Chapter 1).

17 Starter clutch and gears

Note: *The starter clutch can be removed with*

the engine in the frame. If the engine has been removed, ignore the steps which do not apply.

Check

1 The operation of the starter clutch can be checked while it is in situ. Remove the starter motor (see Chapter 10). Check that the idle/reduction gear is able to rotate freely anti-clockwise as you look at it via the starter motor aperture, but locks when rotated clockwise. If not, the starter clutch is faulty and should be removed for inspection.

Removal

2 Remove the alternator rotor (see Section 16) – the starter clutch is bolted to the back of it.
3 Remove the idle/reduction gear **(see illustration)**. Undo the starter driven gear retaining plate screw and remove the plate

(see illustration). Slide the starter driven gear off the crankshaft **(see illustration)**.

Inspection

4 Fit the starter driven gear into the starter clutch, rotating it clockwise as you do **(see illustration)**.
5 With the alternator face down on a workbench, check that the starter driven gear rotates freely clockwise and locks against the rotor anti-clockwise **(see illustration)**. If it doesn't, the starter clutch should be dismantled for further investigation.
6 Withdraw the starter driven gear from the starter clutch, rotating it clockwise as you do.
7 Check the condition of the sprags inside the clutch body and the corresponding surface on the driven gear hub **(see illustration)**. If they are damaged, marked or flattened at any point, they should be replaced with new ones.
8 To remove the starter clutch assembly, hold the alternator rotor using a holding strap and unscrew the bolts inside the rotor, noting the washers where fitted **(see illustration)**. Remove the clutch form the rotor noting which way round it fits. Install the new assembly in a reverse sequence – clean the threads of the bolts and apply a suitable non-permanent thread locking compound, then tighten them to the torque setting specified at the beginning of the Chapter.
9 Check the bush in the starter driven gear hub and its bearing surface on the crankshaft. If the bush shows signs of excessive wear (the

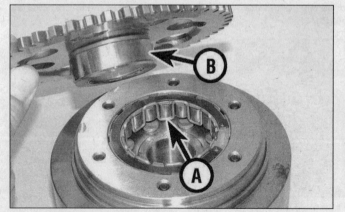

17.7 Check the sprags (A) and the hub (B) for wear and damage

17.8 Starter clutch bolts (arrowed)

holes or groove in the surface of the bush for holding the oil will be barely visible) replace the driven gear with a new one.

10 Check the teeth of the reduction and idle gears and the corresponding teeth of the starter driven gear and starter motor drive shaft. Replace the gears and/or starter motor if worn or chipped teeth are discovered on related gears. Also check the idle gear shaft for damage, and check that the gear is not a loose fit on it. Check the reduction gear shaft ends and the bores they run in for wear.

Installation

11 Lubricate the flat section of the crankshaft that the starter driven gear turns on with engine oil. Slide the gear onto the crankshaft (**see illustration 17.3c**).

12 Lubricate the idle/reduction gear shaft with clean engine oil, then locate the gear, meshing the small inner gear teeth with those on the driven gear (**see illustration 17.3a**). Fit the driven gear retainer plate and tighten the screw (**see illustration 17.3b**).

13. Install the alternator rotor (see Section 16).

18 Oil pump and relief valve

Note 1: *This procedure can be carried out with the engine in the frame.*

Note 2: *The crankcase seal plate is a tight fit in the crankcase and needs to be pulled out. Piaggio produce a special tool (Part No. 20622Y) to remove and install the plate – it is not too expensive (ask your dealer), but may not be easy to get hold of (**see illustration**). While the plate can be removed using a home-made puller set-up as described in Step 4, the tool is essential for installation of the plate as it must be aligned exactly in order for the oil pump drive chain to be correctly tensioned by the rubbing strip on the inner face of the plate. The plate is easily distorted (particularly if using the method described in Step 4 – this is not a problem as a*

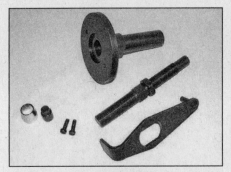

18.00 Components of the Piaggio special Tool No. 20622Y

new plate must be fitted whether the old one distorts or not), and the tool ensures that no distortion can take place on installation. To save having to buy the tool, you could remove the plate as described in Step 4, and then when ready take the engine to a dealer equipped with the tool and have them install the new plate – it should be cheaper than buying the tool. If however you decide to buy the tool, the procedure for using it is described and shown in Steps 3 and 28.

Removal

1 Drain the engine oil (see Chapter 1).

2 Remove the drive pulley and variator (see Chapter 3).

3 To remove the crankcase seal plate using the Piaggio tool (see **Note 2** above), fit the tool base over the crankshaft and against the plate and tighten the two screws provided to secure it (**see illustrations**). Now screw the end of the bar with the external threads into the shaft of the tool base until it butts against the end of the crankshaft. Keep turning the bar using a spanner on the hex section until the plate is drawn out of the crankcase – you can counter-hold the base using another spanner on the flats of the boss if required. Remove the tool and discard the plate – a new one must be used.

4 To remove the crankcase seal plate without

18.3a To remove the seal plate (arrowed) . . .

18.3b . . . fit the tool and tighten the screws (arrowed), then fit the bar and tighten it against the crankshaft using the hex

the Piaggio tool, thread two pieces of stud of the correct size and thread pitch into the holes in the plate (**see illustration**). Obtain a suitable piece of steel plate and drill two holes through so it can be fitted over the studs and against the end of the crankshaft, but fit a piece of copper or aluminium between them to act as a cushion. Thread a nut onto each stud and against the bar. Now tighten the nuts evenly and a little at a time until the plate is drawn out of the crankcase. Discard the seal plate – a new one must be fitted (see **Note 2** above).

5 Undo the bolts securing the sump cover and remove the cover (**see illustration**). Note the positions of the guides for the rear brake hose

18.4 Removing the seal plate using the Haynes method

18.5 Undo the bolts (arrowed) and remove the cover

18.6 Undo the bolts (arrowed) and remove the plate

18.7a Lock the sprocket and unscrew the bolt . . .

18.7b . . . then remove the sprocket

18.9a Undo the bolts (arrowed) and remove the pump . . .

18.9b . . . then remove the gasket

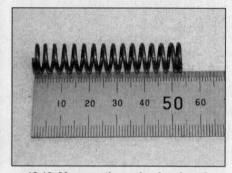
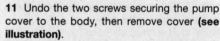

18.10 Measure the spring free length

or cable. Discard the gasket, as a new one must be used. Remove the relief valve spring and withdraw the relief valve from the sump (see illustration 18.26a). Note the location of the cover dowels and remove them for safekeeping if loose (see illustration 18.26b).

6 Undo the pump sprocket plate bolts and remove the plate, noting how it fits (see illustration).

7 Insert a pin punch or screwdriver through one of the holes in the pump sprocket and locate it against the pump body to stop the sprocket turning, then unscrew the sprocket bolt (see illustration). Note the Belleville washer on the bolt. Draw the sprocket off the pump and slip it out of the chain (see illustration).

8 If required, draw the chain up into the transmission housing and remove it from the drive sprocket (see illustration 18.22c). Note: Before the chain is removed, mark it so that it can be fitted the same way round. Slide the

drive sprocket off the end of the crankshaft (see illustration 18.22b). Remove the O-ring from its groove and discard it (see illustration 18.22a) – a new one must be used.

9 Undo the two screws securing the oil pump and remove the pump, noting how it fits (see illustration). Remove the gasket and discard it – a new one must be fitted (see illustration).

Inspection

10 Clean the relief valve and spring in solvent. Inspect the surface of the valve for wear and scoring. Measure the free length of the spring and compare the result with the Specifications at the beginning of the Chapter (see illustration). If the valve is worn or the spring has shortened, fit new ones. Inspect the valve housing in the casing; any dirt lodged in the housing will prevent the valve from seating properly and must be cleaned out carefully to avoid scratching the surface of the housing.

11 Undo the two screws securing the pump cover to the body, then remove cover (see illustration).

12 It is not be necessary to disassemble the pump (individual components are not available) but, if required, remove the central circlip with circlip pliers, then lift out the rotors, noting that the punch marks face the cover (see illustration). Clean the pump body and rotors in solvent and dry them with compressed air, if available. Inspect the body and rotors for scoring and wear. If any damage, scoring, uneven or excessive wear is evident, fit a new pump. If the pump has been disassembled, fit the rotors back into the body, ensuring that the punch marks face out, and install the circlip.

13 Measure the clearance between the inner rotor tip and the outer rotor with a feeler gauge as shown, and compare the result to the Specifications at the beginning of the Chapter (see illustration).

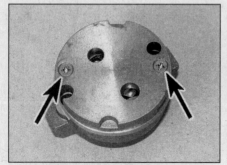

18.11 Undo the screws (arrowed) and remove the cover

18.12 Remove the circlip (arrowed) to free the inner rotor – note the punch marks

18.13 Measure inner-to-outer rotor clearance . . .

18.14 . . . outer rotor-to-body clearance . . .

18.15 . . . and rotor end-float

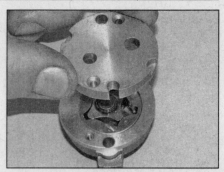

18.18 Fit the cover and tighten the screws

14 Measure the clearance between the outer rotor and the pump body and compare the result to the Specifications at the beginning of the Chapter **(see illustration)**. If either clearance measured is greater than the maximum listed, fit a new pump.

15 Lay a straight-edge across the rotors and the pump body and, using a feeler gauge, measure the rotor end-float (the gap between the rotors and the straight-edge **(see illustration)**. If the clearance measured is greater than the maximum listed, fit a new pump.

16 Check the pump drive chain and sprockets for wear or damage, and replace them with a new set if necessary.

17 If the pump is good, make sure all the components are clean, then lubricate them with clean engine oil.

18 Fit the cover, noting that it can only be fitted one way, and tighten the screws **(see illustration)**.

19 Rotate the pump shaft by hand and check that the rotors turn smoothly.

Installation

20 Fit a new pump gasket onto the crankcase, making sure the holes align correctly and the tab locates in the cut-out **(see illustration 18.9b)**.

21 Fit the pump, noting that it can only go one way round or the bolt holes do not align – as a guide there is a rounded section on the pump that aligns with a cut-out in the crankcase **(see illustration)**. Tighten the bolts to the torque setting specified at the beginning of the Chapter.

22 Fit a new O-ring smeared with oil into the groove on the crankshaft **(see illustration)**. Slide the drive sprocket, with its shouldered end facing out, onto the crankshaft, then fit the drive chain around the sprocket and slip it down into the sump **(see illustrations)**.

23 Fit the pump sprocket into the chain, then fit the sprocket onto the pump, aligning the flat with that on the pump shaft **(see illustration)**. Fit the Belleville washer onto the sprocket bolt so that the raised outer edge of the washer faces the pump sprocket, then fit the bolt. Use the method employed on removal to stop the sprocket turning and tighten the bolt to the specified torque **(see illustration 18.7a)**.

24 Install the pump sprocket plate and tighten its screws **(see illustration 18.6)**.

25 Remove any traces of old gasket from the sump cover and crankcase mating surfaces using a suitable scraper and solvent. Take care not to scratch or gouge the soft aluminium.

26 Lubricate the relief valve with clean engine oil, then fit the valve, closed end first, and the spring, fitted into the open end of the valve, into the casing **(see illustration)**. Ensure the dowels for the sump cover are in place then fit the cover using a new gasket, locating the

18.21 Fit the pump, aligning it as described, and tighten the bolts

18.22a Fit a new O-ring (arrowed)

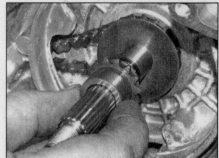

18.22b Slide the sprocket on . . .

18.22c . . . then loop the chain round it

18.23 Fit the sprocket onto the pump, aligning the flats, then fit the bolt with its washer

18.26a Fit the relief valve and plunger

18.26b Fit a new gasket onto the dowels (arrowed) . . .

18.26c . . . then fit the cover . . .

18.26d . . . locating the spring end over the lug (arrowed)

spring end over the lug **(see illustrations)**. Fit the cover bolts and the clips for the rear brake hose or cable, then tighten the bolts to the specified torque **(see illustration 18.5)**.

27 If you do not have the Piaggio tool to fit the new crankcase seal plate (see **Note 2** above) take the engine to a dealer equipped with the tool and have them fit it.

28 If you have the Piaggio tool, first lubricate the crankshaft seal lips in the centre of the plate with new engine oil – DO NOT lubricate the crankcase seal around the rim of the plate **(see illustration)**. Fit the tool base onto the plate and tighten the two screws provided to secure it **(see illustrations)**. Fit the alignment plate over the flats of the tool with the peg section at the top of the seal plate and the flat section at the bottom between the chain guide strips, then fit the seal guide into the seal **(see illustration)**. Fit the adaptor bushing into the hole in the top of the crankcase **(see illustration)**. Fit the assembly onto the crankshaft, with the oil pump drive chain guide strips on the back of the seal plate aligned with the chain, and seat it lightly against the crankcase, locating the peg on the top of the alignment plate in the adaptor bush **(see illustrations)**. Now fit the plain end of the bar with the internal threads into the shaft of the

18.28a Lubricate the seal lips

18.28b Fit the tool onto the plate . . .

18.28c . . . and secure it with the screws

18.28d Fit the alignment plate as shown, then fit the seal guide with the tapered end going into the seal

18.28e Fit the adaptor bush into the hole

18.28f Fit the plate and assembled tool over the crankshaft . . .

18.28g . . . locating the peg on the alignment plate in the adaptor bush

18.28h Fit the bar into the tool . . .

18.28i . . . and thread it onto the crankshaft until it seats

18.28j Now tighten the loose nut against the tool to press the seal plate in

tool and thread it onto the crankshaft as far as it will go **(see illustrations)**. Tighten the loose nut on the threaded bar against the tool to press the seal plate into position and fully home **(see illustration)**. Remove the tool.

29 Install the drive pulley and variator (see Chapter 3).

30 Fill the engine with the correct type and quantity of oil (see Chapter 1). Start the engine and check that there are no leaks around the sump.

19 Crankcase halves, crankcase and connecting rod

Note: *To separate the crankcase halves, the engine must be removed from the frame.*

Separation

1 To access the main bearings and crankshaft assembly, the crankcase halves must be separated.

2 Remove the engine from the frame (see Section 5). Before the crankcases can be separated the following components must be removed:

• *Cam chain, blades and sprockets (see Section 9).*
• *Cylinder head (see Section 11).*
• *Cylinder (see Section 13).*
• *Piston (see Section 14).*
• *Alternator rotor and stator (see Section 16).*
• *Variator (see Chapter 3).*
• *Starter motor (see Chapter 10).*
• *Oil pump (see Section 18).*
• *Centrestand (see Chapter 9).*

3 Before separating the crankcases, measure the crankshaft end-float with a dial gauge and compare the result with the specifications at the beginning of this Chapter. Excessive end-float is an indication of wear on the crankshaft or the crankcases and should be investigated when the cases have been separated.

4 Unscrew the ten crankcase bolts evenly, a little at a time and in a criss-cross sequence

until they are all finger-tight, then remove them **(see illustration)**. Support the engine unit on the work surface, left-hand (transmission) side down. Carefully lift the right-hand crankcase half off the left-hand half, taking care not to score the surface of the right-hand main bearing on the crankshaft **(see illustration)**. If the halves do not separate easily, tap around the joint with a soft-faced mallet. **Note:** *Do not try and separate the halves by levering against the crankcase mating surfaces as they are easily scored and will not seal correctly afterwards.*

5 Lift the crankshaft assembly out of the left-hand crankcase, again taking care not to mark the bearing surface **(see illustration)**.

6 Remove and discard the gasket – a new one must be fitted on reassembly **(see illustration 19.21b)**. Note the position of the two crankcase dowels and remove them for safekeeping if they are loose **(see illustration 19.21a)**. Remove the oil filter insert and discard its O-ring **(see illustrations 19.20b and a)** – a new one must be used.

19.4a Unscrew the crankcase bolts (arrowed) . . .

19.4b . . . and lift the right-hand half off

19.5 Lift the crankshaft out

19.7 Unscrew the bolts (arrowed) and remove the plate

19.12 Check the bush (arrowed) in each crankcase half

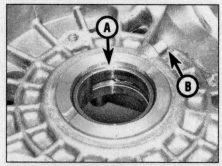

19.14 Check each main bearing (A). Piston oil jet (B)

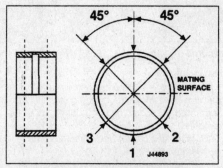

19.15 Measure the main bearings as described

7 If required remove the baffle plate **(see illustration)**. Clean the crankcases thoroughly with solvent and dry them with compressed air. Clean the crankshaft assembly with solvent. **Note:** *Vespa warn against blowing compressed air through the connecting rod oil passage to avoid the danger of compacting dirt and blocking the passage to the big-end bearing.*

8 Remove all traces of old gasket from the mating surfaces with solvent. Take care not to scratch or gouge the soft aluminium.
Caution: Be very careful not to nick or gouge the crankcase mating surfaces, or oil leaks will result. Check both crankcase halves very carefully for cracks and other damage.

Inspection

Crankcases

9 Small cracks or holes in aluminium castings can be repaired with an epoxy resin adhesive as a temporary measure. Permanent repairs can only be effected by argon-arc welding, and only a specialist in this process is in a position

to advise on the economy or practical aspect of such a repair. Low temperature repair kits are available for repair of aluminium castings. If any damage is found that can't be repaired, renew the crankcase halves as a set.

10 Damaged threads can be economically reclaimed by using a diamond section wire insert, of the Heli-Coil type, which is easily fitted after drilling and re-tapping the affected thread. Sheared studs or screws can usually be removed with stud or screw extractors; if you are in any doubt consult a Vespa dealer or specialist motorcycle engineer.

11 Always wash the crankcases thoroughly after any repair work to ensure no dirt or metal swarf is trapped inside when the engine is rebuilt.

12 Inspect the engine mounting bushes **(see illustration)**. If they show signs of deterioration renew them both at the same time. To remove a bush, first note its position in the casing. Heat the casing with a hot air gun, then support the casing and drive the bush out with a hammer and a suitably sized socket. Clean the bush housing with steel

wool to remove any corrosion, then reheat the casing and fit the new bush. **Note:** *Always support the casing when removing or fitting bushes to avoid breaking the casing.*

13 Blow out the oil passages for the oil pump, relief valve, main bearing and piston oil jet **(see illustration 19.14)** in the left-hand crankcase half with compressed air. Blow out the oil passages for the main bearing, the cylinder head oil supply and the oil seal drain in the right-hand crankcase half.

Main bearings

14 Check the condition of the main bearings **(see illustration)**. Each bearing comprises two halves – the surface of the rear half is plain and the front half has an oilway in it. The surface of each bearing should be smooth with no scoring or scuff marks. The condition of the bearings and the corresponding crankshaft journals is vital to the performance of the lubrication system. If the bearings are damaged or worn, oil pressure will drop and the oil feed to the connecting rod big-end and the cylinder head will be insufficient to prevent rapid wear and possible seizure.

15 Use a telescoping gauge and a micrometer to measure the internal diameter of each bearing in three directions as shown **(see illustration)**. Ensure that the measurements are taken in the centre of each bearing surface. The bearings are colour-coded red, blue or yellow; ensure all three measurements for each bearing are within the specifications in the table below. Vespa do not supply new bearings; if any of the bearings are worn beyond the specifications new crankcase halves will have to be fitted. If there is any doubt about the condition of the bearings consult a Vespa dealer.

Crankshaft and connecting rod

16 Check the condition of the crankshaft journals. The surface of each journal should be smooth with no scoring, pitting or scuff marks. Use a micrometer to measure the diameter of each journal in two positions (A and B), and in two directions as shown **(see illustration)**. There are two size categories for the crankshaft journals, Class 1 and Class 2, which match the colour coding of the crankcase bearings. Compare the results with the table and ensure that the journal size is within the specifications

Main bearing size table		
Crankcase main bearing	**Crankshaft journal**	**Bearing colour**
A (29.025 to 29.040 mm)	1 (28.994 to 29.000 mm)	Red
B (29.019 to 29.034 mm)	1 (28.994 to 29.000 mm)	Blue
B (29.028 to 29.043 mm)	2 (29.000 to 29.006 mm)	Blue
C (29.022 to 29.037 mm)	2 (29.000 to 29.006 mm)	Yellow

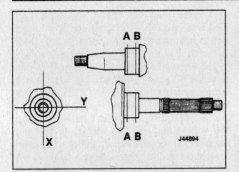

19.16 Measure the crankshaft journals as described

19.17a Checking the connecting rod big-end bearing side clearance

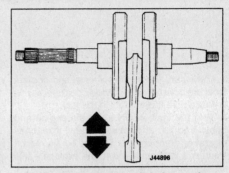

19.17b Measure the radial play on the connecting rod

for the appropriate bearing. If the crankshaft journals are damaged or worn beyond the specifications a new crankshaft will have to be fitted.

17 Measure the connecting rod big-end side clearance with a feeler gauge and compare it with the specifications at the beginning of this Chapter **(see illustration)**. Measure the up-and-down (radial) play on the rod with a dial gauge and measure the width of the flywheels at several points to ensure they are not out of alignment **(see illustrations)**. Compare the results with the specifications at the beginning of this Chapter.

18 Place the crankshaft assembly on V-blocks and check the runout at the main bearing journals and at the ends of the shafts **(see illustration)**. If the runout exceeds the specified limit, or if either of the connecting

rod measurements exceed the limit, the crankshaft assembly must be renewed.

Reassembly

19 If removed fit the baffle plate **(see illustration 19.7)**. Lubricate the main bearings and crankshaft journals with clean engine oil. Fit the crankshaft all the way into the left-hand crankcase half, positioning the connecting rod in-line with the crankcase mouth **(see illustration 19.5)**.

20 Fit a new O-ring onto the oil filter insert and fit it into the crankcase **(see illustrations)**.

21 Ensure that the crankcase mating surfaces are clean. Support the left-hand crankcase half on the work surface, transmission side down. Check that the crankcase dowels are in place, then fit a new gasket **(see illustrations)**.

22 Guide the crankcase right-hand half over

the crankshaft end and press it down, making sure the dowels locate, until the two halves meet **(see illustration 19.4b)**. Use a soft-faced mallet to help the casing seat, but don't apply too much pressure. **Note:** *If the crankcases do not meet, remove the right-hand half and investigate the problem – do not be tempted to pull the crankcases together using the bolts.*

23 Clean the threads of the crankcase bolts and install them finger-tight. Tighten the bolts evenly, in a criss-cross sequence, to the torque setting specified at the beginning of the Chapter **(see illustration 19.4a)**. Trim off the piece of gasket bridging the connecting rod mouth with a sharp knife. Hold the connecting rod to prevent it hitting the crankcase mouth, then rotate the crankshaft to check that it is moves freely.

24 Install the remaining components in the reverse order of removal.

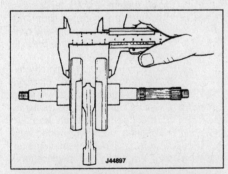

19.17c Measure the width across the flywheels at several points

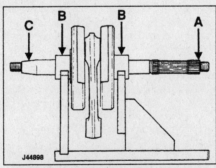

19.18 Check the crankshaft runout as described

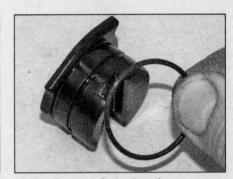

19.20a Fit a new O-ring into the groove . . .

19.20b . . . then fit the insert into the crankcase

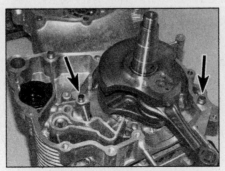

19.21a Fit the dowels (arrowed) if removed . . .

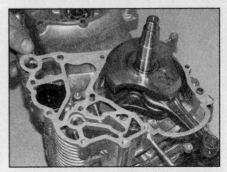

19.21b . . . then lay a new gasket onto the mating surface and over the dowels

20 Running-in

1 Make sure the engine oil level and coolant level are correct (see *Pre-ride checks*).
2 Make sure there is fuel in the tank.
3 Turn the ignition ON, start the engine and allow it to run at a slow idle until it reaches operating temperature. Do not be alarmed if there is a little smoke from the exhaust – this will be due to the oil used to lubricate the piston and bore during assembly and should subside after a while.
4 If the engine proves reluctant to start, remove the spark plug and check that it has not become wet and oily. If it has, clean it and

try again. If the engine refuses to start, go through the fault finding charts at the end of this manual to identify the problem.
5 Check carefully for oil leaks and make sure the transmission and controls, especially the brakes, function properly before road testing the machine.
6 Treat the machine gently for the first few miles to make sure oil has circulated throughout the engine and any new parts installed have started to seat.
7 Even greater care is necessary if a new piston/cylinder has been fitted, or in the case of the 125 cc engine, if the cylinder has been rebored. The machine will have to be run-in as when new. This means a restraining hand on the throttle until at least 600 miles (1000 km) have been covered. There's no point

in keeping to any set speed limit – the main idea is to keep from labouring the engine and not to maintain any one speed for too long. Experience is the best guide, since it's easy to tell when an engine is running freely. Once past the 600 mile (1000 km) mark, gradually increase performance, using full throttle for short bursts to begin with.
8 If a lubrication failure is suspected, stop the engine immediately and try to find the cause. If an engine is run without oil, even for a short period of time, severe damage will occur.
9 Upon completion of the road test, and after the engine has cooled down completely, recheck the valve clearances (see Chapter 1) and check the engine oil level and coolant level (see *Pre-ride checks*).

Chapter 3
Transmission

Contents

Degrees of difficulty

Easy, suitable for novice with little experience	**Fairly easy,** suitable for beginner with some experience	**Fairly difficult,** suitable for competent DIY mechanic	**Difficult,** suitable for experienced DIY mechanic	**Very difficult,** suitable for expert DIY or professional

Specifications

Variator – all GTS, GTV and GT models, 2009 to 2011 LX, LXV and S models

Roller diameter (min)
LX, LXV and S models	18.4 mm
GTS125 model	19.0 mm
250 and 300 models	20.0 mm
Sleeve diameter (min)	25.95 mm
Bush diameter (max)	26.12 mm

Variator – 2012-on LX, LXV and S models

Roller diameter
Standard	19.0 mm
Service limit (min)	18.4 mm

Sleeve diameter
Standard	25.959 to 25.98 mm
Service limit (min)	25.950 mm

Clutch and driven pulley – all GTS, GTV and GT models, 2009 to 2011 LX, LXV and S models

Clutch drum diameter (max)	134.5 mm
Clutch drum out-of-round (max)	0.15 mm
Inner pulley shaft diameter (min)	40.96 mm
Outer pulley bore diameter (max)	41.08 mm

Spring free length (min)
LX, LXV and S models	105.5 mm
GTS125 model	140 mm
250 and 300 models	118 mm
Clutch lining material thickness (min)	1 mm

Clutch and driven pulley – 2012-on LX, LXV and S models

Clutch drum diameter
Standard	134 to 134.2 mm
Service limit (max)	134.5 mm
Clutch drum out-of-round (max)	0.15 mm
Inner pulley shaft diameter	40.05 to 40.15 mm
Spring free length (standard)	106 mm
Clutch lining material thickness (min)	1 mm

Drive belt

Minimum width of outer run	see Chapter 1

Torque settings

Drive belt cover bolts	11 to 13 Nm
Drive belt support roller centre bolt (250 and 300 models)	12 to 13 Nm
Drive pulley nut	75 to 83 Nm
Clutch nut	
GTS, GTV, GT and 2009 to 2011 LX, LXV and S models	45 to 50 Nm
2012-on LX, LXV and S models	53 to 59 Nm
Gearbox input shaft nut	54 to 60 Nm
Gearbox cover bolts	24 to 27 Nm
Gearbox oil drain plug	15 to 17 Nm

1 General information

The transmission on all models is fully automatic in operation. Power is transmitted from the engine to the rear wheel by belt, via a variator on the drive pulley, which automatically varies the gearing with engine speed, an automatic clutch on the driven pulley, and a reduction gearbox. Both the variator and the automatic clutch work on the principal of centrifugal force.
Note: *On some models the internal components of the transmission may differ slightly to those components described or shown. When dismantling, always note the* fitted position, order and way round of each component as it is removed.

2 Drive belt cover

Removal

1 If the engine is still in the frame, remove the left-hand side cover and floor panel (see Chapter 9).
2 Remove the air filter housing (see Chapter 5).
3 On LX, LXV and S models detach the air cooling duct.
4 Unclip the plastic cap from the back of the cover **(see illustration)**.
5 The gearbox input shaft passes through the drive belt cover and is supported by a bearing in the cover. To undo the nut on the outer end of the shaft, the clutch drum must be locked against the belt cover to prevent the shaft turning while the nut is undone; Vespa produce a service tool (Part No. 020423Y) to do this, or alternatively use a commercially available or home-made equivalent as shown, then unscrew the nut and remove washer **(see illustration)**.
6 If located on the left-hand side of the engine, remove the oil filler cap **(see illustration)**.
7 Unscrew the bolts securing the drive belt cover, noting the position of the clips and which bolts fit where for correct installation (make a cardboard template of the cover and fit the bolts accordingly to avoid confusion) **(see illustrations)**. Remove the cover, taking care that the clutch drum does not fall off the end of the shaft.

2.4 Unclip and remove the cap

2.5 Lock the clutch drum as described and unscrew the nut (arrowed)

2.6 Remove the oil filler cap

2.7a Unscrew the bolts (arrowed) . . .

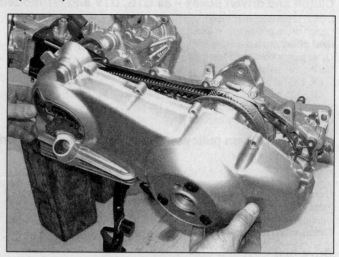

2.7b . . . and remove the cover

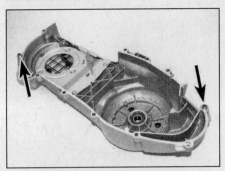

2.8 The cover has two dowels

2.9 The bearing is secured by a circlip (arrowed)

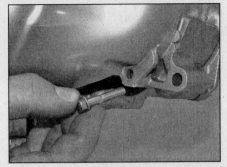

2.10a Fit the shouldered bolts in the dowel holes . . .

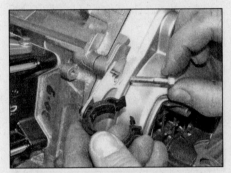

2.10b . . . and fit all clips with the bolts

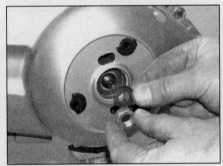

2.10c Fit the washer and nut . . .

2.10d . . . then lock the clutch and tighten the nut to the specified torque

8 Note the dowels and remove them if loose **(see illustration)**.

Inspection

9 Check the condition of the bearing in the cover **(see illustration)**. The bearing should turn smoothly and freely without excessive play between the inner and outer races. If there is any doubt about the condition of the bearing, replace it with a new one: remove the circlip on the inside of the cover, then drive the bearing out from the outside with a driver or suitably sized socket. If necessary, heat the cover on the inside around the bearing housing with a hot air gun to aid removal. Note which way round the bearing is fitted. Drive the new bearing in with a socket that contacts the outer race only, then fit a new circlip.

Installation

10 Installation is the reverse of removal.

Make sure the cover dowels are fitted **(see illustration 2.8)**, and that the shouldered bolts (where present) are fitted in the dowel locations **(see illustrations)**. Tighten the cover bolts to the torque setting specified at the beginning of the Chapter. Lock the shaft as on removal, then fit the washer and tighten the input shaft nut to the specified torque **(see illustrations)**. Do not forget the oil filler cap **(see illustration 2.6)**.

3 Drive pulley and variator

Removal

1 Remove the drive belt cover (see Section 2).
2 To remove the drive pulley nut, the pulley must be locked to prevent it turning. Vespa produce a service tool (Part No. 020368Y, 020626Y or 020938Y depending on model) to

hold the pulley. Alternatively, hold the pulley around the rim using a rubber rotor strap **(see illustration)** or fabricate a forked holding tool with squared ends to fit into the holes in the pulley **(see illustrations)**. If you can't hold the pulley tight enough you will have to remove the

3.2a Holding the pulley with a rotor strap to undo the nut (arrowed)

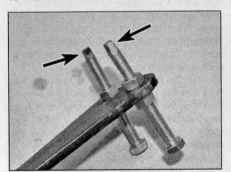

3.2b Fabricate a forked tool with squared ends . . .

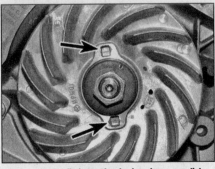

3.2c . . . to fit into the holes (arrowed) in the pulley . . .

3.2d . . . to hold it while undoing the nut

3.3a Slide the variator and the collar off the shaft, noting the rollers in the variator . . .

3.3b . . . then draw the ramp plate off

3.6 Check and measure the sleeve and the bush (arrowed)

3.9a Fit the rollers into the ramp plate as shown

3.9b Make sure the guide shoes are in place . . .

3.9c . . . then fit the ramp plate

alternator cover and hold the alternator with a socket on the nut to prevent rotation. With the pulley locked, unscrew the nut and remove the washers, noting their order and which way round they fit (see illustrations 3.13c, b and a). On 2012-on LX, LXV and S models, a Belleville washer is fitted between the thin washer and the pulley nut. On earlier LX, LXV and S models, Vespa specify that a new nut is used on assembly. Slide the outer half of the drive pulley off the shaft (see illustration 3.12b).

3 Remove the washer from the end of the shaft where fitted (see illustration 3.12a). Move the drive belt aside, or if required slip it out of the driven pulley and remove it. Note: If the belt is removed from the machine, note any directional arrows or mark the belt so that it can be installed the same way round. Slide the variator, the centre sleeve and the ramp plate off the crankshaft as an assembly if

possible, or if separately taking care not to let the rollers drop out (see illustrations).

4 Lift out the ramp plate (if not already separated), then remove the rollers, noting which fits where – unless new ones are used, they should be installed in their original locations (see illustrations 3.9c and a). Also note that each side of the roller is different, with the covered side facing the direction of thrust. Clean all the components.

Inspection

5 Check the rollers and the corresponding ramps in the variator housing and ramp plate for damage, wear and flat spots, and replace the rollers, the housing and the plate with new ones if necessary (see illustration 3.9a). Measure the diameter of the rollers and compare the result to the Specifications at the beginning of the Chapter. Replace the rollers as a set if any are worn below the minimum diameter.

6 Check the centre sleeve and its bush in the housing for wear and damage and replace them with new ones if necessary (see illustration). Measure the external diameter of the sleeve and the internal diameter of the bush and compare the results to the Specifications at the beginning of the Chapter. Replace either or both if they are worn beyond their limit.

7 Check the condition of the guide shoes on the ramp plate and replace them with new ones if they are worn or damaged (see illustration 3.9b). Also check the splines on the plate and fit a new plate if they are worn.

Installation

8 Make sure the inner surfaces of both pulley halves, the sleeve, the rollers and the ramps are clean and oil-free.

9 Fit the rollers into the housing, making sure they are in their original positions (unless new ones are used), and that the covered side faces the direction of thrust as shown (see illustration). Check that the guide shoes are correctly fitted on the ramp plate, then fit the plate (see illustrations).

10 Grip the variator so that the ramp plate is held into the housing and insert the sleeve, then slide the variator onto the crankshaft (see illustration). Note: If the ramp plate moves and the rollers are dislodged, disassemble the variator and reposition the rollers correctly.

11 Position the drive belt around the driven pulley if removed from it, and around the end of the shaft (see illustration). If fitting a new belt, make sure any directional arrows point

3.10 Slide the variator assembly onto the shaft

3.11 Fit the belt over the shaft

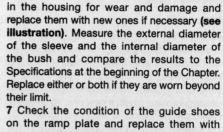

in the direction of normal rotation (see illustration 5.5). Ensure there is sufficient slack in the belt to avoid it being trapped when the outer half of the pulley is installed – if necessary, grasp the driven pulley and pull it towards the clutch to compress the spring and press the drive belt into the pulley to create slack at the front to ease fitting of the drive pulley (see illustration 4.2b).

12 Fit the washer where removed (see illustration). Slide the outer half of the drive pulley onto the crankshaft (see illustration).

13 Fit the washers as noted on removal, then fit the nut and tighten it finger-tight (see illustrations). On 2009 to 2011 LX, LXV and S models, use a new nut and apply a suitable non-permanent thread-locking compound to the threads. Make sure the outer pulley half butts against the centre sleeve and is not skewed by the drive belt. Use the method employed on removal to prevent the pulley turning and tighten the nut to the torque setting specified at the beginning of the Chapter (see illustration).

14 Ease the drive belt out of the driven pulley to reduce the slack in the belt.

15 Install the drive belt cover (see Section 2).

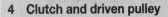

4 Clutch and driven pulley

Removal

1 Remove the drive belt cover (see Section 2).

2 Remove the clutch drum, then draw the clutch/driven pulley assembly off the shaft and disengage the drive belt from it (see illustrations). Note: *If the belt is removed from the machine, note any directional arrows or mark the belt so that it can be installed the same way round.*

3 To disassemble the clutch and pulley assembly, it is necessary first to hold it using a holding tool to initially slacken the nut, then to compress and hold the clutch spring while the nut is undone and removed. Lay the clutch on a flat surface, fit a holding tool and loosen the nut (see illustration). Now have an assistant

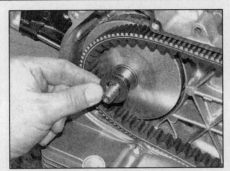
3.12a Slide on the washer . . .

3.12b . . . and the outer half of the pulley

3.13a Fit the thin washer . . .

3.13b . . . the thick washer or Belleville washer . . .

3.13c . . . and the nut . . .

3.13d . . . and tighten it to the specified torque

4.2a Remove the clutch drum . . .

4.2b . . . then draw the assembly off the shaft and disengage the belt

4.3a Hold the clutch and slacken the nut (arrowed) . . .

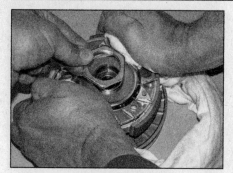

4.3b . . . then press down on the clutch and unscrew it

4.4 Release and remove the clutch . . .

4.5a . . . then remove the collar . . .

press down on the clutch to compress the clutch spring while the nut is finally unscrewed by hand and removed **(see illustration)**.

 Warning: The clutch assembly is under pressure from the centre spring – take care to maintain downwards pressure to avoid damage or injury.

4 Carefully release the downward pressure on the clutch, allowing the spring to relax, and remove the clutch **(see illustration)**.
5 Remove the collar and the spring **(see illustrations)**. On 2012-on LX, LXV and S models, remove the spring seat and washer.
6 Simultaneously turn and pull the spring sleeve off the boss **(see illustration)**. Draw out the guide pins, noting how they fit **(see illustration)**. Separate the pulley halves **(see illustration)**. Note the location of the O-rings and the seals in the boss **(see illustrations 4.15a and b)** – new

O-rings should be fitted on reassembly, and new seals must be fitted if there is any evidence of grease having worked its way past them and onto the shaft on the inner half of the pulley.
7 Clean all the components with a suitable solvent.

Inspection

8 Check the inner surface of the clutch drum for damage and scoring and inspect the splines in the centre and those on the shafts **(see illustrations)** – the clutch drum should be a firm fit on the gearbox input shaft, with no backlash between the drum and the shaft. Measure the internal diameter of the drum at several points to determine if it is worn or out-of-round. If the drum is out-of-round, or if the results are outside the specifications listed at the beginning of this Chapter, replace it with a new one.

4.5b . . . and the spring

9 Check the amount of friction material remaining on the clutch shoes is equal and within the limit specified **(see illustration)**. Check the springs and make sure the shoes are not seized on their pivot pins **(see**

4.6a Remove the spring sleeve as described . . .

4.6b . . . then remove the guide pins

4.6c Slide the outer half of the pulley off the inner half

4.8a Check and measure the drum lining . . .

4.8b . . . and check the splines (arrowed) for wear

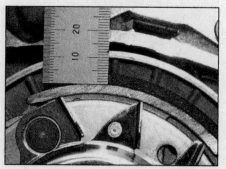

4.9a Check the friction material on the shoes . . .

4.9b . . . and check the springs and pivots

4.11a Measure the diameter of the inner pulley shaft . . .

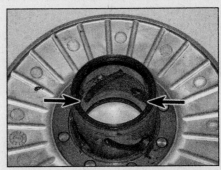

4.11b . . . and of the outer pulley boss

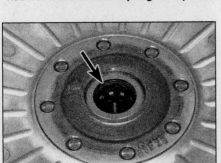

4.12a Check the needle bearing (arrowed) . . .

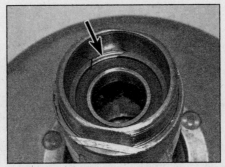

4.12b . . . and the ball bearing (arrowed)

4.13 Check the guide pins and slots for wear

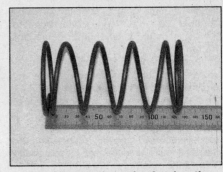

4.14 Measure the spring free length

illustration). If the shoes are worn to the limit, worn unevenly or contaminated with grease, or there is evidence of damage replace the clutch shoe assembly with a new one – individual parts are not available.

10 Inspect the inner faces of the driven pulley for signs of overheating or blueing, caused by the pulley running out of alignment. If the pulley has run out of alignment, first check the condition of the bearings in the hub of the pulley inner half (see Step 12), then check the gearbox input shaft for play in the bearings (see Section 6).

11 Measure the external diameter of the shaft on the inner half of the pulley and the internal diameter of the boss on the outer half and compare the results to the specifications at the beginning of the Chapter **(see illustrations)**. Replace either or both halves if worn beyond their limits.

12 A needle roller bearing and a sealed ball bearing are fitted in the hub of the pulley inner

half **(see illustrations)**. Inspect the bearing rollers for flat spots and pitting and check that the ball bearing turns smoothly. If either bearing is worn or damaged replace them both with new ones. First remove the needle bearing using a puller, then remove the circlip retaining the ball bearing and drive the bearing out – refer to the reference section for more information on bearing removal and installation methods and tools.

13 Inspect the guide pins and their slots in the pulley outer boss and replace any components that are worn with new ones **(see illustration)**.

14 Check the condition of the spring. Measure its free length and compare the result with the figure in the Specifications **(see illustration)**. Replace the spring with a new one if it is bent or has sagged to less than the service limit.

Installation

15 Fit new O-rings smeared with grease onto the pulley outer half boss, and fit new oil seals

if required **(see illustrations)**. Lubricate the oil seal lips with grease.

16 Fit the outer half of the pulley onto the inner half **(see illustration 4.6c)**. Fit the guide pins **(see illustration 4.6b)**. Push grease into the guide pin slots and holes **(see illustration)**. Fit

4.15a Fit new O-rings (arrowed) . . .

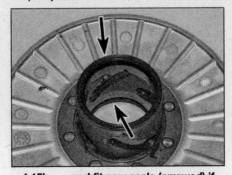

4.15b . . . and fit new seals (arrowed) if necessary

4.16 Apply grease to the slots

4.18 Hold the clutch and tighten the nut to the specified torque

4.21 Recess the belt in the pulley by pulling the outer half up against the clutch

5.2 Belt support roller (arrowed)

the spring sleeve over the boss with its flanged end facing down **(see illustration 4.6a)**.

17 On 2012-on LX, LXV and S models, fit the washer and spring seat. On all models, fit the spring and the collar **(see illustrations 4.5b and a)**.

18 Position the clutch assembly over the spring, then press it down to compress the spring, making sure that the flats on the clutch drive plate are aligned with the flats on the end of the shaft, and hold it there while an assistant threads the nut finger-tight onto the shaft **(see illustrations 4.4 and 4.3b)**. Fit the holding tool as on disassembly and tighten the nut to the torque setting specified at the beginning of this Chapter **(see illustration)**.

19 Lubricate the needle bearing inside the pulley inner half with grease **(see illustration 4.12a)**.

20 Ensure the inner surfaces of both pulley halves and the inside surface of the clutch drum are clean and grease-free.

21 If the drive pulley has been removed fit the belt around and into the driven pulley on the bench, forcing the pulleys halves apart so the belt sits recessed **(see illustration)**, then slide the driven pulley onto the shaft **(see illustration 4.2b)**. If the drive pulley has not been removed fit the drive belt around the driven pulley halves and ease the belt into the pulley, forcing the halves apart clutch. When there is sufficient slack in the belt, slide the assembly onto the gearbox input shaft **(see illustration 4.2b)**.

22 Fit the clutch drum, aligning the splines with those on the shaft **(see illustration 4.2a)**.

23 Install the drive belt cover (see Section 2).

5 Drive belt and support roller

Inspection

1 The belt should be inspected regularly, according to the service interval (see Chapter 1). **Note:** *Oil or grease inside the casing will contaminate the belt and prevent it gripping the pulleys. Any evidence of oil inside the casing suggests a worn seal on either the crankshaft or the gearbox input shaft; evidence of grease suggests worn seals in the clutch centre.*

2 On 250 and 300 cc models, a belt support roller is fitted midway between the variator and the clutch pulley. Check that the roller turns smoothly and freely, and that the outer surface is not damaged. If the roller centre bearing is worn or the roller is damaged, undo the centre bolt and remove the roller **(see illustration)**. Replace the roller with a new one, fitting it with the flanged edge innermost. Tighten the bolt to the torque setting specified at the beginning of the Chapter.

Renewal

3 Follow the procedure in Section 3 and remove the outer half of the drive pulley – hold the variator in position on the crankshaft as you remove it to avoid dislodging the rollers (if the ramp plate moves and the rollers are dislodged, disassemble the variator and reposition the rollers correctly).

4 Lift the belt off the crankshaft and ease it

out of the driven pulley**(see illustration)** – if necessary, pull the outer pulley half back against the spring tension and manoeuvre the belt out.

5 Fit the new belt, making sure any directional arrows point in the direction of normal rotation **(see illustration)**. Ease the belt into the driven pulley by pulling the outer half up against the clutch to ensure there is sufficient slack to avoid the belt being trapped when the outer half of the drive pulley is installed **(see illustration 4.2b)**.

6 Install the outer half of the drive pulley (see Section 3).

6 Gearbox

Removal

1 Remove the clutch and driven pulley (see Section 4). Remove the rear wheel (see Chapter 8). On 2012-on LX, LXV and S models, slide the large thrust washer off the output shaft **(see illustration)**.

2 Where possible, drain the gearbox oil (see Chapter 1).

3 On LX, LXV and S models release the drum brake cable from its rear holders, then unscrew the adjustment nut and draw the cable out of the arm **(see illustration)**. Note the bush in the arm and remove it for safekeeping if. Remove the brake shoes (see Chapter 8).

4 On GTS, GTV and GT models displace the

5.4 Remove the belt

5.5 Arrows should point in the normal direction of rotation

6.1 Slide off the large thrust washer

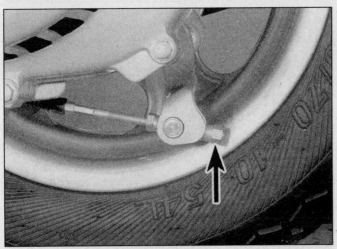

6.3 Unscrew the nut (arrowed) and draw the cable out of the arm

6.5a Undo the bolts (arrowed) . . .

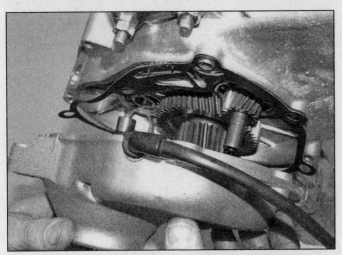

6.5b . . . and remove the cover with the output shaft

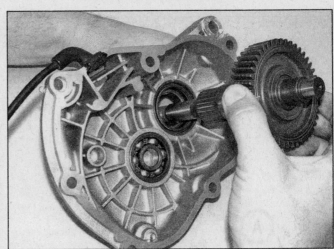

6.6 Remove the output shaft from the cover

rear brake caliper and remove the rear hub (see Chapter 8).

2009 to 2011 LX, LXV and S models and all GTS models

5 Undo the gearbox cover bolts and remove the cover – hold the end of the output shaft so that comes away with the cover, leaving the intermediate and input shafts in place (see illustrations). Remove the gasket and discard it – a new one must be fitted (see illustration 6.23). Note the location of the dowels and remove them for safekeeping if they are loose.

6 Remove the output shaft from the cover (see illustration).

7 Remove the intermediate shaft (see illustration).

8 Remove the input shaft (see illustration).

2012-on LX, LXV and S models

9 Release the clip securing the gearbox breather hose and disconnect the hose (see illustration)

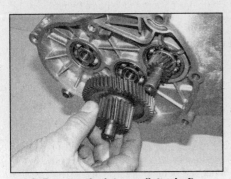

6.7 Remove the intermediate shaft . . .

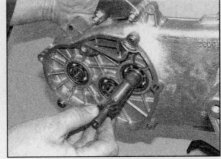

6.8 . . . then the input shaft

6.9 Disconnect the breather hose

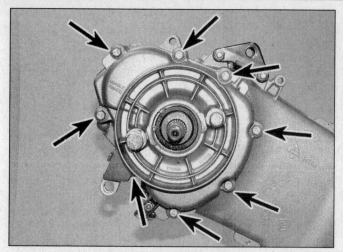

6.10a Undo the cover bolts . . .

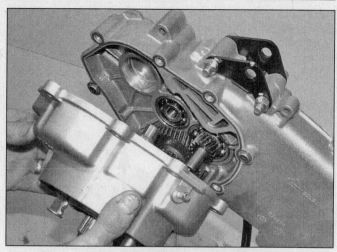

6.10b . . . and remove the cover

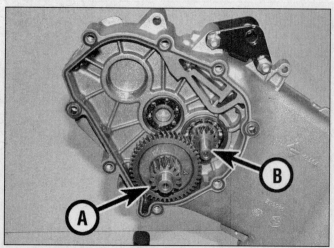

6.11 Gearbox intermediate shaft (A) and input shaft (B)

6.16a New oil seals (arrowed) must be fitted . . .

10 Undo the gearbox cover bolts and remove the cover – hold the end of the output shaft so that it comes away with the cover **(see illustrations)**.

11 Lift out the intermediate shaft then draw out the input shaft **(see illustration)**. If necessary, tap the left-hand end of the input shaft with a soft-faced mallet to ease it out of the bearing. Remove the output shaft from the cover.

12 Remove the gasket and discard it – a new one must be fitted **(see illustration 6.32)**. Note the location of the dowels and remove them for safekeeping if they are loose.

Inspection

13 Remove all traces of old gasket from the gearbox and cover mating surfaces, taking care not to nick or gouge the soft aluminium if a scraper is used. Wash all of the components in clean solvent and dry them off.

14 Check the pinion teeth for cracking, chipping, pitting and other obvious wear or damage. Check the splines on the shafts for wear and damage. Replace worn or damaged components with new ones.

15 Check for signs of scoring or bluing on the pinions and shaft. This could be caused by overheating due to inadequate lubrication.

16 Note which way round the input and output shaft oil seals are fitted, then lever them out and discard them – new ones must be used **(see illustrations)**.

17 Check that all the bearings turn smoothly and freely without excessive play between the inner and outer races. The bearings should be a tight fit in the casing; if a bearing is loose, and the casing is not damaged, use a suitable

6.16b . . . lever out the old seal . . .

6.16c . . . using a seal hook or screwdriver . . .

6.18 This bearing is secured by a circlip (arrowed)

6.19a Fit the puller jaws behind the bearing inner race and expand them . . .

6.19b . . . then attach the slide-hammer and jar the bearings out

6.20 A socket can be used to drive the bearings out and in

6.21a Drive the new seal in using a seal driver . . .

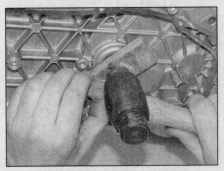

6.21b . . . or a piece of wood

bearing locking compound to hold it in place.

18. To remove a bearing from a housing open on both sides, first remove the circlip where fitted **(see illustration)**. Note the position of the bearing, then heat the housing using a hot air gun and drive the bearing out with a bearing driver or suitably-sized socket **(see illustration 6.20)**.

19 Bearings fitted in blind holes require an internal bearing puller to extract them **(see illustrations)** – again heat the housing before drawing the bearing out.

20 Fit the new bearing with a bearing driver or socket large enough to contact the outer race of the bearing **(see illustration)**. Fit a new circlip as required.

21 Fit new oil seals, making sure they are the

correct way round **(see illustration 6.16a)**. Drive them in until flush with their housing, and grease the lips **(see illustrations)**.

Installation

2009 to 2011 LX, LXV and S models and all GTS models

22 Fit the input shaft, then the intermediate shaft, then fit the output shaft into the cover **(see illustrations 6.8, 6.7 and 6.6)**.

23 If removed, fit the dowels, then locate the new gasket onto them **(see illustration)**.

24 Apply a smear of sealant to the breather hose grommet **(see illustration)**. Fit the cover, ensuring the shafts engage fully with their bearings **(see illustration)**. Fit the cover bolts and tighten them evenly and in a criss-cross

pattern to the torque setting specified at the beginning of this Chapter **(see illustration 6.5a)**. Check that the input and output shafts turn freely.

25 Fill the gearbox with the specified amount and type of oil (see Chapter 1).

26 On LX, LXV and S models install the brake shoes and connect the cable (see Chapter 8) **(see illustration 6.3)**.

27 On GTS, GTV and GT models install the rear hub and the rear brake caliper (see Chapter 8).

28 Install the rear wheel (see Chapter 8). On LX, LXV and S models adjust brake cable freeplay (see Chapter 1).

29 Install the clutch and driven pulley (see Section 4).

6.23 Fit a new gasket onto the dowels (arrowed)

6.24a Do not forget the breather hose and apply sealant to the grommet

6.24b Fit the cover, making sure everything locates and seats correctly

6.30a Install the input shaft carefully . . .

6.30b . . . to avoid damaging the seal (arrowed)

6.31a Install the intermediate shaft . . .

6.31b . . . and the output shaft

6.31c Ensure the pinions are fully engaged

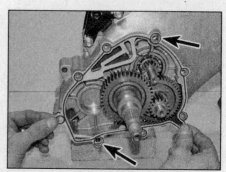

6.32 Fit the new gasket over the dowels (arrowed)

6.33 Take care not to damage the output shaft seal

2012-on LX, LXV and S models

30 Fit the input shaft, taking care not to damage the lips of the seal **(see illustrations)**. Ensure the shaft is pressed all the way in.

31 Install the intermediate shaft and the output shaft, ensuring the shaft pinions are correctly engaged **(see illustrations)**.

32 If removed, fit the dowels, then locate the new gasket onto them **(see illustration)**.

33 Fit the cover, taking care not to damage the output shaft seal **(see illustration)**. Ensure the shafts engage fully with their bearings. Fit the cover bolts and tighten them evenly and in a criss-cross pattern to the torque setting specified at the beginning of this Chapter **(see illustration 6.10a)**. Check that the input and output shafts turn freely.

34 Fit the breather hose and secure it with the clip **(see illustration 6.9)**.

35 Fill the gearbox with the specified amount and type of oil (see Chapter 1).

36 Install the brake shoes and connect the cable (see Chapter 8). Don't forget to install the large thrust washer off the output shaft **(see illustration 6.1)**.

37 Install the rear wheel (see Chapter 8). Adjust brake cable freeplay (see Chapter 1).

38 Install the clutch and driven pulley (see Section 4).

Chapter 4
Cooling system

Contents

Degrees of difficulty

Easy, suitable for novice with little experience	**Fairly easy,** suitable for beginner with some experience	**Fairly difficult,** suitable for competent DIY mechanic	**Difficult,** suitable for experienced DIY mechanic	**Very difficult,** suitable for expert DIY or professional

Specifications

Coolant

Mixture type	Pre-mix coolant or 50% distilled water / 50% corrosion inhibited ethylene glycol anti-freeze
Coolant capacity	2.1 to 2.15 litres

Engine temperature sensor – GTS, GTV and GT models

Resistance @ 0°C	5.9 K-ohms
Resistance @ 10°C	3.8 K-ohms
Resistance @ 20°C	2.5 K-ohms
Resistance @ 30°C	1.7 K-ohms
Resistance @ 80°C	300 ohms

Thermostat

Opening temperature	
GTV250ie, GT250ie and GTS250ie	69.5 to 72.5°C
GTS125ie and GTS/GTV300ie	85 to 87°C

Radiator

Cap valve opening pressure	13 psi (0.9 Bar)

Torque setting

Thermostat cover screws	3 to 4 Nm

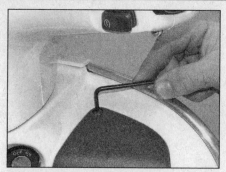

2.1 Undo the screw and remove the panel

1 General information

The cooling system uses a water and anti-freeze coolant mixture to carry away excess heat from the engine and maintain as constant a temperature as possible. The cylinder is surrounded by a water jacket from which the heated coolant is circulated through the cylinder head by thermo-syphonic action in conjunction with a water pump. On GTS125ie models the pump is electric. On all other GTS models and GTV and GT models the pump is mechanical, driven directly off the crankshaft and housed in the alternator cover. The hot coolant from the engine passes via the thermostat on the cylinder head to the radiators. The coolant then flows across the core of the radiators to the water pump and back to the engine where the cycle is repeated.

A thermostat is fitted in the system to prevent the coolant flowing through the radiator when the engine is cold, therefore accelerating the speed at which the engine reaches normal operating temperature. On all models a temperature sensor mounted in the cylinder head transmits engine temperature information to the engine management system; on GTS models the sensor also operates the temperature gauge in the instrument cluster.

On GTV and GT models a thermo-switch transmits engine temperature information to a warning light in the instrument cluster.

A cooling fan fitted to the back of the radiator aids cooling in extreme conditions by drawing extra air through. The fan motor is controlled by a relay that itself is controlled by the ECU based on the information from the temperature sensor.

The complete cooling system is partially sealed and pressurised, the pressure being controlled by a valve contained in the reservoir cap. By pressurising the coolant the boiling point is raised, preventing premature boiling in adverse conditions. The overflow pipe from the system is connected to a reservoir into which excess coolant is expelled under pressure. The discharged coolant automatically returns to the radiator by the vacuum created when the engine cools.

⚠️ **Warning: Do not remove the cap from the reservoir when the engine is hot. Scalding hot coolant and steam may be blown out under pressure, which could cause serious injury. When the engine has cooled slowly remove the cap allowing any residual pressure to escape.**

Caution: Do not allow anti-freeze to come in contact with your skin or painted surfaces of the motorcycle. Rinse off any spills immediately with plenty of water. Anti-freeze is highly toxic if ingested. Never leave anti-freeze lying around in an open container or in puddles on the floor; children and pets are attracted by its sweet smell and may drink it. Check with the local authorities about disposing of used anti-freeze. Many communities will have collection centres which will see that anti-freeze is disposed of safely.

Caution: At all times use the specified type of anti-freeze, and always mix it with distilled water in the correct proportion, or purchase pre-mix coolant. The anti-freeze contains corrosion inhibitors which are essential to avoid damage to the cooling system. A lack of these inhibitors could

lead to a build-up of corrosion which would block the coolant passages, resulting in overheating and severe engine damage. Distilled water must be used as opposed to tap water to avoid a build-up of scale which would also block the passages.

2 Coolant change

⚠️ **Warning: Allow the engine to cool completely before performing this maintenance operation. Also, don't allow anti-freeze to come into contact with your skin or the painted surfaces of the motorcycle. Rinse off spills immediately with plenty of water. Anti-freeze is highly toxic if ingested. Never leave anti-freeze lying around in an open container or in puddles on the floor; children and pets are attracted by its sweet smell and may drink it. Check with local authorities (councils) about disposing of anti-freeze. Many communities have collection centres which will see that anti-freeze is disposed of safely. Anti-freeze is also combustible, so don't store it near open flames.**

Draining

1 Support the scooter on its centrestand on a level surface. Remove the right-hand side panel, and on GTS125ie models the storage compartment (see Chapter 9). Remove the reservoir access panel **(see illustration)**.

2 Slowly unscrew the reservoir cap **(see illustration)** – if you hear a hissing sound (indicating there is still pressure in the system), wait until it stops before fully removing the cap.

3 Position a suitable container beneath the engine on the right-hand side. On GTS125ie models release the clip securing the hose to the cylinder, detach the hose and allow the coolant to completely drain from the system **(see illustration)** – to release the clip see illustrations 2.3b and c. On all other models

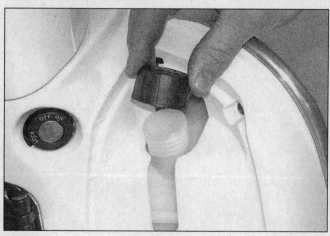

2.2 Unscrew the cap

2.3a On GTS125 models detach the hose (arrowed) from the cylinder

2.3b Expand the centre of the clip . . .

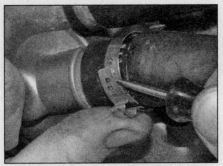

2.3c . . . then unhook the end . . .

2.3d . . . detach the hose from its union . . .

release the clip securing the hose to the bottom union on the water pump, detach the hose and allow the coolant to completely drain from the system **(see illustrations)**. In each case place the hose low down so it is the lowest point of the system to ensure complete draining. Note that the clips fitted as standard cannot be re-used – it is best to replace them with widely available screw-type Jubilee clips that can be re-used **(see illustration)**.

Flushing

4 Flush the system with clean tap water by inserting a hose in the reservoir filler neck. Allow the water to run through the system until it is clear and flows out cleanly. If the radiators are extremely corroded, remove them (see Section 6) and have them cleaned by a specialist.

5 Refit the coolant hose to its union **(see illustration 2.3a or 2.3d)**.

6 Using a suitable funnel inserted in the reservoir, fill the system to the upper level line with clean water mixed with a flushing compound **(see illustration 2.12b)**. Make sure the flushing compound is compatible with aluminium components, and follow the manufacturer's instructions carefully. Fit the reservoir cap.

7 Start the engine and allow it to reach normal operating temperature. Let it run for about ten minutes.

8 Stop the engine. Let it cool for a while, then cover the reservoir cap with a heavy rag and slowly unscrew it – if you hear a hissing sound (indicating there is still pressure in the system), wait until it stops before fully removing the cap.

9 Drain the system once again.

10 Fill the system with clean water, then fit the reservoir cap and repeat the procedure.

Refilling

11 Refit the coolant hose to its union using a new clip – if using a Jubilee clip as a replacement **(see illustration 2.3f)** tighten its screw; if using a new clip of the original type you need special pliers to secure it – make sure the open end is hooked onto the tangs **(see illustration 2.3c)**, then fit the pliers over the raised section of the clip, and squeeze the pliers to tighten the clip **(see illustrations)**.

2.3e . . . and hold it down to allow the system to drain

12 Using a suitable funnel if required, fill the system via the reservoir almost up to the MAX level line with the proper coolant mixture (see this Chapter's Specifications)

2.11a Locate the special pliers over the bridge . . .

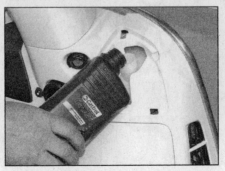

2.12a Fill the system with coolant . . .

2.3f Single use clips can be replaced with multi-use Jubilee clips

(see illustrations). Note: *Pour the coolant in slowly to minimise the amount of air entering the system.* Carefully shake the scooter to dislodge any trapped air.

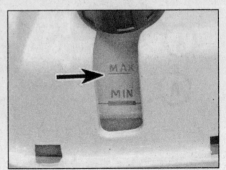

2.11b . . . then squeeze the pliers

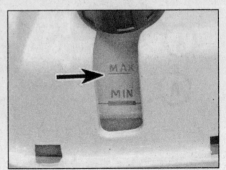

2.12b . . . to the MAX line on the reservoir

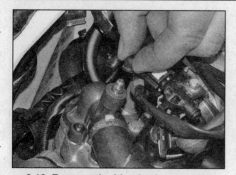

2.13 Remove the bleed valve cap and bleed the system as described

13 Remove the rubber cap from the bleed valve on the thermostat housing **(see illustration)**. Prepare a suitable hose long enough to reach from the valve to the reservoir. Connect the hose to the valve and place the other end in the reservoir. Start the engine and allow it to idle until it reaches normal operating temperature – flick the throttle twistgrip part open 3 or 4 times, so that the engine speed rises to approximately 4000 to 5000 rpm. Stop the engine. Open the bleed valve two full turns – any air trapped in the system should bleed through the hose to the reservoir, after which coolant should flow. When there is no more air in the coolant close the valve.

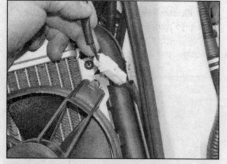

3.2 Disconnect the fan wiring connector

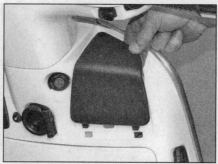

2.16 Locate the tabs along the bottom in the slots

14 If necessary, top up the coolant to the MAX level line if necessary.
15 Let the engine cool then check that the coolant level is still up to the line.
16 Check the system for leaks. Install the body panels (see Chapter 9). Fit the reservoir access panel, making sure the tabs locate correctly **(see illustration)**.
17 Do not dispose of the old coolant by pouring it down the drain. Instead pour it into a heavy plastic container, cap it tightly and take it into an authorised disposal site or service station – see *Warning* in Section 1.

3 Cooling fan and fan relay

Cooling fan

Check

1 If the engine is overheating and the cooling fan isn't coming on, first check the fan fuse (see Chapter 10). If the fuse is good, check the relay, as described in Steps 8 to 14.
2 To test the cooling fan motor, remove the kick panel (see Chapter 9). Trace the wiring from the fan motor and disconnect it at the connector **(see illustration)**. Using a 12 volt battery and

two jumper wires with suitable connectors, connect the battery positive (+) lead to the red wire terminal on the fan side of the motor wiring connector, and the battery negative (–) lead to the black wire terminal in the connector. Once connected the fan should operate. If it does not, and the wiring and connectors are all good, then the fan motor is faulty – replace the fan assembly with a new one.

Replacement

⚠️ *Warning: The engine must be completely cool before carrying out this procedure.*

3 Remove the kick panel (see Chapter 9).
4 Trace the wiring from the fan motor and disconnect it at the connector **(see illustration 3.2)**. Release the wiring from any clips or guides not attached to the fan assembly.
5 Undo the fan assembly screws, release the peg and remove the fan **(see illustration)**.
6 Installation is the reverse of removal. Make sure the peg locates correctly **(see illustration)**.

Cooling fan relay

Check

7 If the engine is overheating and the cooling fan isn't coming on, first check the cooling fan fuse (see Chapter 10). If the fuse is blown, check the fan circuit for a short to earth (refer to *Electrical System Fault Finding* and the *Wiring Diagrams* in Chapter 10).
8 If the fuse is good, remove the front panel grille to access the relay (see Chapter 9) **(see illustrations)**.
9 Pull the relay out of its socket **(see illustration)**. Using a jumper wire short between the grey and red wire terminals in the socket with the ignition ON – the fan should come on. If it does, the wiring between the relay and the fan and the circuit to earth is all good, so go to Step 10 and check the relay, then if the relay is good go to Step 11 to check the power supply to it. If the fan doesn't come on, go to Step 12.
10 Set a multimeter to the ohms x 1 scale and

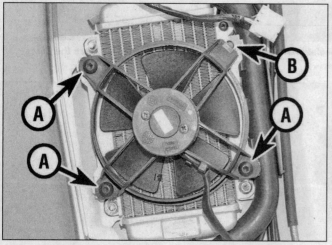

3.5 Undo the screws (A) and release the peg (B)

3.6 Make sure the peg locates correctly

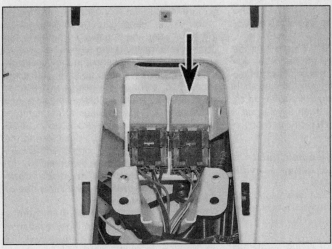

3.8a Cooling fan relay (arrowed) – GTS models

3.8b Cooling fan relay (arrowed) – GTV/GT models

connect it between the 87 and 30 terminals on the relay **(see illustration)**. There should be no continuity (infinite resistance). Using a fully-charged 12 volt battery and two insulated jumper wires, connect the positive (+) terminal of the battery to the 86 terminal, and the negative (–) terminal to the 85 terminal. At this point the relay should be heard to click and the multimeter read 0 ohms (continuity). If this is the case the relay is proved good. If the relay does not click when battery voltage is applied and still indicates no continuity (infinite resistance) across its terminals, it is faulty and must be replaced with a new one.

11 If the relay is good, check for battery voltage first at the grey wire in the relay socket, then at the red/white wire, with the ignition switch ON. If there is no voltage, check the wiring between the relay and the fuse for continuity, referring to the relevant wiring diagram at the end of Chapter 10. Also check for continuity in the blue/yellow wire to the ECU.

12 Check that there is continuity in the red wire from the relay socket to the fan wiring connector, and in the black wire from the fan wiring connector to earth. If there is no continuity, check all the wiring in the circuit, looking for loose connections and broken wires, referring to *Electrical System Fault Finding* and the *Wiring Diagrams* in Chapter 10.

13 If the fan is on the whole time, pull the

relay off its socket. The fan should stop. If it does, the relay is faulty and must be replaced with a new one.

14 If the fan works but is suspected of cutting in at the wrong temperature, check the temperature sensor (see Section 4).

Removal and installation

15 Remove the front panel grille to access the relay (see Chapter 9) **(see illustration 3.8a or b)**.

16 Pull the relay out of its socket **(see illustration 3.9)**.

17 Installation is the reverse of removal.

---

4 Temperature gauge or warning light and temperature sensor or thermo-switch ⚙

Temperature gauge – GTS models

Check

1 The circuit consists of the sensor mounted in the cylinder head, and the gauge in the instrument cluster. If the gauge does not work as the engine warms up first check the relevant fuse (see Chapter 10). If the gauge is on H all the time that the ignition is on, there is a short circuit in the wire from the instrument cluster

to the sensor – locate and repair the break, referring to *Electrical System Fault Finding* and the *Wiring Diagrams* in Chapter 10.

2 Remove the storage compartment (see Chapter 9). Disconnect the wiring connector from the temperature sensor **(see illustration)**. With the ignition on, using an auxiliary piece or wire earth the green/yellow (250 and 300 models) or grey/black (125 models) wire terminal in the loom side of the connector against the engine and check that the needle moves to H on the gauge, then quickly disconnect the wire to avoid damaging the gauge. If the gauge moves, check for continuity to earth first between the sensor hex and the battery negative (–) terminal, and then in the black wire. If there is none make sure the earth connectors on the engine and frame are tight. If all is good remove the sensor and check it (Steps 9 to 12).

3 If the gauge does not move, check the wiring and connectors between the sensor and the instrument cluster for continuity, referring to Chapter 10 for access to the instrument cluster wiring and for the wiring diagrams. If the wiring is good the instrument cluster power circuit or the gauge is faulty. First check the power circuit (see Chapter 10).

Replacement

4 The temperature gauge is part of the instrument cluster and is covered in Chapter 10.

3.9 Pull the relay out

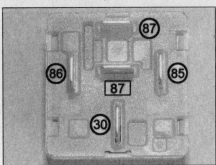

3.10 Terminal numbers are marked on the underside of the relay

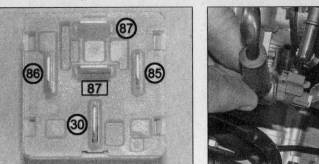

4.2 Disconnect the wiring connector from the temperature sensor

Warning light – GTV and GT models

Check

5 The circuit consists of the thermo-switch mounted in the joint in the coolant hose running along the left-hand side under the floor panel on GTV250ie Navy models and mounted in the right-hand radiator on all other models, and the warning light in the instrument cluster. If the warning light does not come on momentarily when the ignition is switched on first check the fuse, and then check the instrument cluster (see Chapter 10). If the light is on all the time that the ignition is on, there is a short circuit in the wire from the instrument cluster to the sensor or switch – locate and repair the break, referring to *Electrical System Fault Finding* and the *Wiring Diagrams* in Chapter 10.

6 Next, on GTV250ie Navy models remove the floor panel, and on all other models remove the kick panel (see Chapter 9). Disconnect the wiring connector from the thermo-switch. With the ignition on, using an auxiliary piece or wire earth the green/yellow wire terminal in the loom side of the connector against the engine or frame (according to model) and check that the warning light comes on. If the light comes on check for continuity to earth in the black wire. If there is none make sure the earth connectors on the engine and frame are tight. If all is good remove the switch and check it (Steps 21 and 22).

7 If the light does not come on, check the wiring and connectors between the switch and the instrument cluster for continuity, referring to Chapter 10 for access to the instrument cluster wiring and for the wiring diagrams. If the wiring is good the instrument cluster power circuit or the gauge is faulty. First check the power circuit (see Chapter 10).

Replacement

8 The warning light LED is part of the instrument cluster and is covered in Chapter 10.

Temperature gauge sensor – GTS models

Check

9 Drain the cooling system (see Section 2).
10 Remove the sensor (see Steps 13 and 14).
11 Fill a small heatproof container with coolant and place it on a stove. Using an ohmmeter, connect the positive (+) probe of the meter to the green/yellow (GTS250 and 300 models) or grey/black (GTS125 models) wire terminal on the sensor, and the negative (–) probe to the black wire terminal. Using some wire or other support suspend the sensor in the coolant so that just the sensing head up to the threads is submerged, and with the head a minimum of 40 mm above the bottom of the container **(see illustration)**. Also place a thermometer capable of reading temperatures up to 120°C in the coolant so that its bulb is close to the sensor. **Note:** *None of the components should be allowed to directly touch the container.*

 Warning: This must be done very carefully to avoid the risk of personal injury.

12 Heat the coolant, stirring it gently. As the temperature rises the meter resistance reading should be as specified at the beginning of the Chapter at the various temperatures given. If the meter readings obtained are different by a margin of 10% or more, then the sensor is faulty and must be replaced with a new one.

Replacement

 Warning: The engine must be completely cool before carrying out this procedure.

13 Drain the cooling system (see Section 2). Remove the storage compartment (see Chapter 9). The sensor is mounted in the cylinder head.
14 Disconnect the sensor wiring connector **(see illustration 4.2)**. Unscrew and remove the sensor. Where fitted remove and discard the sealing washer – a new one must be used.
15 Apply a suitable sealant to the thread of the sensor, making sure none gets on the sensor head. Fit the sensor and tighten it. Connect the wiring.
16 Install the storage compartment (see Chapter 9). Refill the cooling system (see Section 2).

Thermo-switch – GTV and GT models

Check

17 Drain the cooling system (see Section 2).
18 Remove the switch (see Steps 21 and 22).
19 Fill a small heatproof container with coolant and place it on a stove. Using an ohmmeter

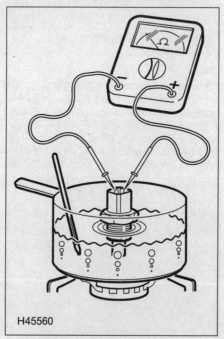

4.11 Temperature sensor test set-up

or continuity tester, connect the positive (+) probe to the green/yellow wire terminal on the sensor and the negative (–) probe to the black wire terminal. Using some wire or other support suspend the sensor in the coolant so that just the sensing head up to the threads is submerged, and with the head a minimum of 40 mm above the bottom of the container **(see illustration 4.11)**. Also place a thermometer capable of reading temperatures up to 130°C in the coolant so that its bulb is close to the sensor. **Note:** *None of the components should be allowed to directly touch the container.*

 Warning: This must be done very carefully to avoid the risk of personal injury.

20 Heat the coolant, stirring it gently. Initially there should be infinite resistance or no continuity (switch open). When the temperature is high (Vespa do not give a figure, but it will be approaching 100°C, the switch should close and the meter show no resistance or continuity. If not, then the switch is faulty and must be replaced with a new one.

Replacement

 Warning: The engine must be completely cool before carrying out this procedure.

21 Drain the cooling system (see Section 2). The thermo switch is mounted in the joint in the coolant hose running along the left-hand side under the floor panel on GTV250ie Navy models and mounted in the right-hand radiator on all other models – remove the floor panel or kick panel accordingly (see Chapter 9).
22 Disconnect the wiring connector. Unscrew and remove the switch.
23 Apply a suitable sealant to the thread of the switch, making sure none gets on the sensor head. Fit the switch and tighten it. Connect the wiring.
24 Install the floor panel or kick panel (see Chapter 9). Refill the cooling system (see Section 2).

5 Thermostat

1 The thermostat is automatic in operation and should give many years service without requiring attention. In the event of a failure, the valve will probably jam open, in which case the engine will take much longer than normal to warm up. Conversely, if the valve jams shut, the coolant will be unable to circulate and the engine will overheat. Neither condition is acceptable, and the fault must be investigated promptly.

Removal

 Warning: The engine must be completely cool before carrying out this procedure.

2 Drain the coolant (see Section 2). The thermostat housing is on the cylinder head.

5.3a Undo the screws (arrowed) and detach the cover . . .

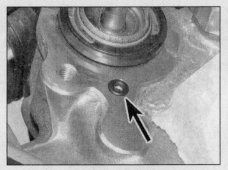

5.3b . . . then remove the O-ring (arrowed) . . .

5.3c . . . and the thermostat

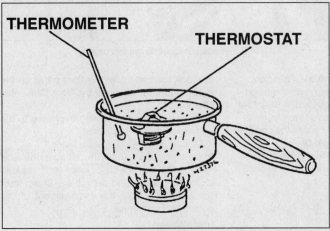

5.5 Thermostat testing set-up

5.7 Check the condition of the sealing ring (arrowed) and make sure it is correctly seated

Remove the storage compartment (see Chapter 9).

3 Undo the screws securing the cover and detach it from the head **(see illustration)**. Remove the small O-ring – check its condition and replace it with a new one if necessary on installation **(see illustration)**. Withdraw the thermostat, noting how it fits **(see illustration)**.

Check

4 Examine the thermostat visually before carrying out the test. If it remains in the open position at room temperature, it should be replaced with a new one. Check the condition of the rubber seal around the thermostat and replace it with a new one if it is damaged, deformed or deteriorated.

5 Suspend the thermostat by a piece of wire in a container of cold water. Place a thermometer capable of reading temperatures up to 110°C in the water so that the bulb is close to the thermostat **(see illustration)**. Heat the water, noting the temperature when the thermostat opens, and compare it to that listed in the Specifications at the beginning of the Chapter for your model. Also check the valve opens fully after it has been heated for a few minutes. If the thermostat does not behave as described replace it with a new one.

6 In the event of thermostat failure, as an emergency measure only, it can be removed and the machine used without it (this is better than leaving a permanently closed thermostat in, but if it is permanently open, you might as well leave it in). **Note:** *Take care when starting the engine from cold as it will take much longer than usual to warm up.* Ensure that a new unit is installed as soon as possible.

Installation

7 Make sure the thermostat seal is fitted and is in good condition, otherwise fit a new thermostat – smear some fresh coolant over it **(see illustration)**. Install the thermostat,

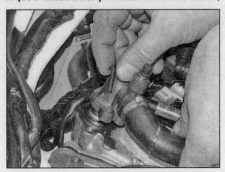

5.8 Fit the cover and tighten the screws

making sure it locates correctly **(see illustration 5.3c)**.

8 Fit the O-ring, using a new one if necessary. Fit the cover and tighten the screws to the torque setting specified at the beginning of the Chapter **(see illustration)**.

9 Install the storage compartment (see Chapter 9). Refill the cooling system with fresh coolant (see Section 2).

6 Radiators

Removal

 Warning: The engine must be completely cool before carrying out this procedure.

1 Remove the kick panel and floor panel (see Chapter 9). Drain the coolant (see Section 2).

2 If removing the left-hand radiator, if required first remove the cooling fan (see Section 3), otherwise just disconnect the fan motor wiring connector and feed the wiring to the radiator, noting its routing **(see illustration 3.2)**.

3 If removing the right-hand radiator on GTV and GT models (except Navy version), disconnect the wiring connector from the thermo-switch.

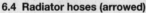

6.4 Radiator hoses (arrowed)

6.5 Radiator mountings (arrowed)

4 Release the clips securing the hoses to the radiator and detach them, noting which fits where **(see illustration)** – to release the clip see illustrations 2.3b and c. Note that the clips fitted as standard cannot be re-used – it is best to replace them with widely available screw-type Jubilee clips that can be re-used **(see illustration 2.3f)**.

5 Unscrew the radiator mounting screw and nuts **(see illustration)**. Ease the radiator out, noting how it locates.

6 If required and not already done, remove the cooling fan from the left-hand radiator (see Section 3). If required remove the radiator shroud. Check the radiator for signs of damage and clear any dirt or debris that might obstruct airflow and inhibit cooling. If the radiator fins are badly damaged or broken the radiator must be replaced with a new one.

Installation

7 Installation is the reverse of removal, noting the following.
- Make sure that the fan wiring is correctly connected.
- Ensure the coolant hoses are in good condition (see Chapter 1), and are securely retained by their clips – if using a Jubilee clip as a replacement **(see illustration 2.3f)** tighten its screw; if using a new clip of the original type you need

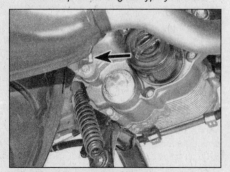

7.11 Water pump drain spigot (arrowed)

special pliers to secure it – make sure the open end is hooked onto the tangs **(see illustration 2.3c)**, then fit the pliers over the raised section of the clip, and squeeze the pliers to tighten the clip **(see illustrations 2.11a and b)**.
- On completion refill the cooling system with fresh coolant as described in Section 2.

7 Water pump

GTS125 model
Check

1 The pump is located under the floor panel on the right-hand side. Remove the floor panel (see Chapter 9). Visually check the area around the pump for signs of leakage – tighten the hose clips or fit new ones as required, or fit new hoses if there is any leakage from the hose unions.

2 If the pump does not run first check the pump circuit fuse (see Chapter 10). Next check the pump wiring connector for loose wires or damaged terminals. Also check the pump earth wire is secure.

3 The pump gets its power from the same circuit as the fuel pump, fuel injector and ignition coil, so if the engine runs then the power circuit is good and the water pump is probably faulty. If the engine does not run check the load relay (see Chapter 5).

4 To test the pump disconnect the wiring connector, then connect the positive (+) terminal of an auxiliary battery to both the black/green wire terminals on the pump using two auxiliary leads, and connect the battery negative (-) terminal to the black wire terminal. If the pump does not run replace it with a new one.

Removal

5 Drain the coolant (see Section 2). The

pump is located under the floor panel on the right-hand side. Remove the floor panel (see Chapter 9).

6 Release the clips securing the hoses to the pump and detach the hoses.

7 Disconnect the wiring connector.

8 Unscrew the pump mounting bolts and remove the pump with its bracket. If required undo the screws and detach the pump from the bracket – note the arrangement of the collars and grommets.

Installation

9 Installation is the reverse of removal. Make sure the rubber mounting grommets are in good condition. Certain types of hose clip are re-usable, others are not – fit new clips if necessary. Refill the system with the specified coolant (see Section 2).

250 and 300 models

Special Tool: If the pump mechanical seal, bearings or driveshaft require renewal, a special Vespa service tool will be required.

Check

10 The pump is located in the alternator cover on the right-hand side of the engine. Remove the right-hand side panel (see Chapter 9). Visually check the area around the pump for signs of leakage – tighten the hose clips or fit new ones as required, or if necessary fit new hoses.

11 To prevent leakage of water from the cooling system to the lubrication system and vice versa, two seals are fitted on the pump shaft. Below the pump housing there is a drain spigot **(see illustration)**. If either seal fails, the drain allows the coolant or oil to escape and prevents them mixing.

12 The seal on the water pump side is of the mechanical type. The second seal, which is mounted behind the mechanical seal, is of the normal feathered lip type. If on inspection the drain shows signs of coolant leakage fit a new mechanical seal (see Steps 15 to 25). If there is oil leakage fit a new oil seal (see Steps 26

7.13 Undo the screws (arrowed) and displace the cover

7.14a Check the impeller as described

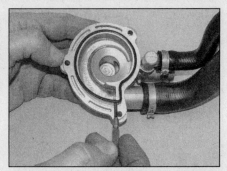

7.14b Fit a new O-ring into the groove in the cover

Components of the special tool needed for mechanical seal replacement

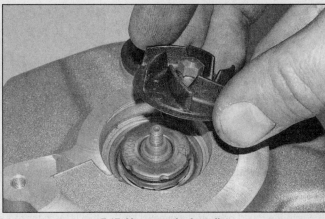

7.17 Unscrew the impeller

to 29). If the leakage is an emulsion-like mix of coolant and oil replace both seals with new ones. Note that whenever a mechanical seal fails it will allow coolant to wash into contact with the bearings, which could then become contaminated, so be sure to check them and fit new ones as well if necessary or if in doubt (see Steps 13 and 14).

13 If the pump is noisy and you suspect the bearings have failed drain the coolant (see Section 2). Undo the pump cover screws and displace the cover **(see illustration)**. Discard the O-ring as a new one must be used.

14 Wiggle the pump impeller back-and-forth and in-and-out **(see illustration)**. If there is excessive movement when wiggling it, replace the shaft and bearings, which come as an assembly, with a new one (see Steps 30 to 35). If you are not sure remove the alternator cover (see Chapter 2B), and rotate the impeller, checking for excessive noise and roughness in the bearings. If the bearings are good fit the cover using a new O-ring smeared with petroleum jelly (Vaseline) – do not use a mineral grease **(see illustration)**. Connect the hose and refill the system with the specified coolant (see Section 2).

Mechanical seal replacement

Note: *Do not remove the seal unless it needs to be replaced with a new one – once removed it cannot be re-used. A special Vespa service tool is essential for this procedure – there is no*

alternative way of doing it (see illustration). The tool is not cheap and may be difficult to get hold of. It is probably best to get a Vespa dealer equipped with the tool to perform the task. When assessing and costing the task bear in mind that you can buy a new alternator cover that comes fitted with a complete new water pump assembly (impeller, seals, shaft and bearings) – if in doubt seek advice from a Vespa dealer as to the relative costs of the options and availability of the part(s) needed and the tool. If you decide to buy the tool the procedure for using it is given as follows.

15 Refer to Chapter 2B and remove the alternator cover, then remove the stator from the cover.

16 Undo the pump cover screws and remove

the cover **(see illustration 7.13)**. Discard the O-ring as a new one must be used.

17 Unscrew the impeller – it has a left-hand thread so it must be unscrewed clockwise **(see illustration)**.

18 Get two flat-bladed screwdrivers and two strips of Teflon, hard plastic or nylon, or suitable pieces of wood. Using the screwdrivers as levers and the pieces of whatever material you are using as protection for the pump cover mating surface and as leverage fulcrums, carefully prise the centre moving piece of the mechanical seal off the body of the seal **(see illustration)**. Remove the black ring of material from the seal **(see illustration)** – it is brittle and will break away in pieces.

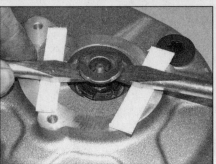

7.18a Lever up the centre piece of the seal . . .

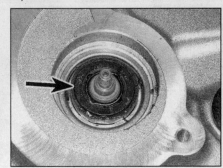

7.18b . . . then remove the black ring (arrowed)

7.19a Fit the body of the tool . . .

7.19b . . . then fit the punch into the first hole . . .

7.19c . . . and strike it home

7.19d Fit and tighten the screw

7.21a Fit the puller onto the body . . .

7.21b . . . then thread the bolt into the body

19 Place the round body of the removal tool over the body of the seal, then fit the punch provided into one of the holes and strike it with a hammer using enough conviction and force so it penetrates and makes a hole in the metal base of the seal – it is no good if the pin only deforms the seal rather than penetrates it **(see illustrations)**. Remove the punch, and keeping the tool in place fit one of the screws and tighten it **(see illustration)** – do not overtighten as you will strip the holes in the seal and the screws will lose purchase.
20 Punch holes through the seal via the two

other holes in the tool and fit the two remaining screws.
21 Fit the puller section of the tool onto the body of the tool and fit the bolt, with the nut on it, through the hole in the puller and thread it into the body **(see illustrations)**. Counter-hold the head of the bolt and turn the nut down onto the puller using a spanner and keep turning it until the seal is pulled out of its housing **(see illustrations)**.
22 Remove the puller from the body, then undo the screws and detach the body from the seal. Discard the seal. If you are going to fit a

new shaft/bearing assembly do so now before fitting the new seal (see Steps 30 to 35).
23 Lubricate the pump shaft with new engine oil **(see illustration)**. Fit the new seal onto the shaft **(see illustration)**. Two rods are provided with the tool – thread the rod with the 5 mm ID left-handed thread onto the shaft by hand as far as it will go **(see illustrations)**. Fit the installation tool then thread the nut onto the rod **(see illustrations)**. Counter-hold the rod using a hex key and tighten the nut as far as it will go – as you tighten it the tool sets the body of the seal into the housing and the

7.21c Hold the bolt head and turn the nut . . .

7.21d . . . until the seal comes out

7.23a Lubricate the shaft . . .

7.23b . . . then fit the seal onto it

7.23c Thread the correct rod onto the shaft . . .

moving part of the seal to the correct position on the pump shaft **(see illustrations)**. Remove the tool.

24 Thread the impeller onto the shaft and tighten it – it has a left-hand thread so it must be screwed on anti-clockwise **(see illustration 7.17)**.

25 Fit the cover using a new O-ring smeared with petroleum jelly (Vaseline) – do not use a mineral grease **(see illustration 7.14b)**. Refer to Chapter 2B and install the alternator stator and cover.

Oil seal replacement

Note: *Do not remove the seal unless it needs to be replaced with a new one – once removed it cannot be re-used.*

26 Refer to Chapter 2B and remove the alternator cover, then remove the stator from the cover.

27 Dig the old seal out using a pointed tool **(see illustration)**.

7.23d . . . until it seats

7.23e Fit the installation tool . . .

7.23f . . . then thread the nut on

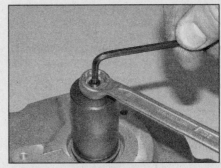

7.23g Counter-hold the end of the rod and tighten the nut . . .

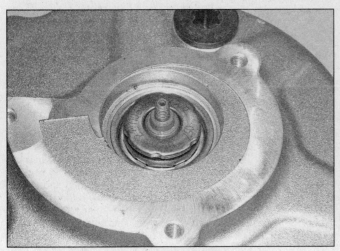

7.23h . . . until the seal seats

7.27 Dig the oil seal out using a pointed tool

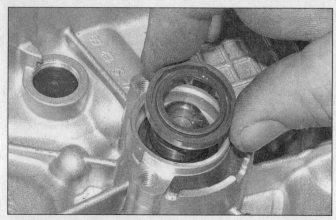

7.28a Make sure the new seal is the correct way round . . .

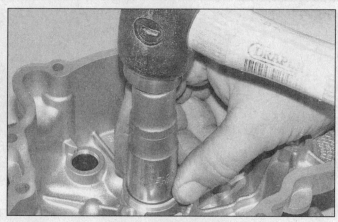

7.28b . . . then drive it in . . .

7.28c . . . until it seats

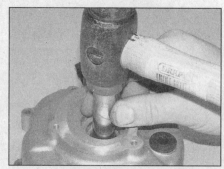

7.31a Drive the assembly out using a suitable socket . . .

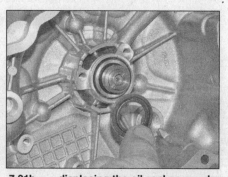

7.31b . . . displacing the oil seal as you do

28 Fit the new seal with its marked face towards the bearings **(see illustration)**. Drive it in using a suitable socket on the edge of the seal until it seats **(see illustrations)**.

29 Refer to Chapter 2B and install the alternator stator and cover.

Bearing replacement

Note: *Do not remove the shaft/bearings unless the assembly needs to be replaced with a new one – once removed it cannot be re-used.*

30 Remove the mechanical seal (see Steps 15 to 22, and make sure you read the **Note**).

31 The driveshaft bearings are a tight fit in their housing – to ease removal heat the bearing housing section of the cover using a hot air gun **(see illustration 7.33a)**. When the casing is hot drive the shaft and bearing assembly out of the cover from the outside using a suitable socket **(see illustration)** – doing so will displace the oil seal **(see illustration)**.

32 The drive piece must be drawn off the old driveshaft and pressed onto the new shaft **(see illustrations)**. The face of the drive piece is tapered so you need to use a puller which can locate securely against it – a legged puller may not work.

33 To ease entry of the new shaft and bearing assembly heat the bearing housing section of the cover using a hot air gun and freeze the shaft/bearing assembly either by using a freeze spray or by putting the assembly in a freezer for an hour before fitting it **(see illustration)**. Drive the assembly into the cover from the inside using a suitable socket that bears only on the outer race of the bearing **(see illustrations)**.

7.32a Pull the drive piece off the old shaft . . .

7.32b . . . then press it onto the new one (arrowed) until it seats

7.33a Heat the bearing housing . . .

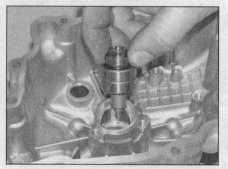

7.33b . . . then fit the shaft/bearing assembly . . .

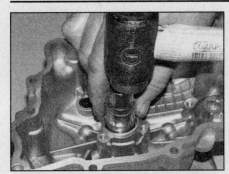

7.33c . . . and drive it in until it seats

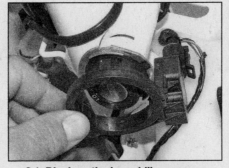

8.1 Displace the immobiliser sensor

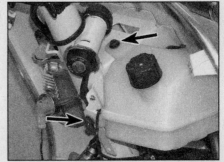

8.3 Undo the screws (arrowed) and drain the reservoir

34 When the housing has cooled fit a new oil seal (see Step 28).
35 Install a new mechanical seal (see Steps 23 to 25).

8 Coolant reservoir

Removal

1 Remove the kick panel (see Chapter 9). Where fitted displace the immobiliser sensor from around the front of the switch – it is a clip-fit **(see illustration)**.
2 Get a suitable container for holding the coolant.
3 Undo the reservoir screws, then remove the cap and drain the reservoir into the container **(see illustration)**.
4 Release the clips and detach the hoses – to release the clip see illustrations 2.3b and c. Note that the clips fitted as standard cannot be re-used – it is best to replace them with screw-type Jubilee clips that can be re-used **(see illustration 2.3f)**.

Installation

5 Installation is the reverse of removal. Make sure the coolant hoses are in good condition (see Chapter 1), and are securely retained

using new clips – if using a Jubilee clip as a replacement **(see illustration 2.3f)** tighten its screw; if using a new clip of the original type you need special pliers to secure it – make sure the open end is hooked onto the tangs **(see illustration 2.3c)**, then fit the pliers over the raised section of the clip, and squeeze the pliers to tighten the clip **(see illustrations 2.11a and b)**. On completion refill the reservoir to the MAX level line with the specified coolant mixture (see *Pre-ride checks*).

9 Coolant hoses

Removal

1 Remove the kick panel, side panels, storage compartment and floor panel (see Chapter 9). Drain the coolant (see Section 2).
2 Release the hose clips, then slide them back along the hose and clear of the union spigot – to release the clips see illustrations 2.3b and c. Note that the clips fitted as standard cannot be re-used – it is best to replace them with screw-type Jubilee clips that can be re-used **(see illustration 2.3f)**.
Caution: The radiator unions are fragile. Do not use excessive force when attempting to remove the hoses.

3 If a hose proves stubborn, release it by rotating it on its union before working it off. If all else fails, cut the hose with a sharp knife. Whilst this means replacing the hose with a new one, it is preferable to buying a new radiator.

Installation

4 Slide the clips onto the hose and then work the hose on to its union as far as the spigot where present.

HAYNES HiNT *If the hose is difficult to push on its union, soften it by soaking it in very hot water, or alternatively a little soapy water on the union can be used as a lubricant.*

5 Rotate the hose on its unions to settle it in position before sliding the clips into place and securing them. If using a Jubilee clip as a replacement **(see illustration 2.3f)** tighten its screw; if using a new clip of the original type you need special pliers to secure it – make sure the open end is hooked onto the tangs **(see illustration 2.3c)**, then fit the pliers over the raised section of the clip, and squeeze the pliers to tighten the clip **(see illustrations 2.11a and b)**.
6 Refill the cooling system with fresh coolant (see Section 2).

Chapter 5
Fuel injection system and exhaust

Contents

Degrees of difficulty

Easy, suitable for novice with little experience | **Fairly easy,** suitable for beginner with some experience | **Fairly difficult,** suitable for competent DIY mechanic | **Difficult,** suitable for experienced DIY mechanic | **Very difficult,** suitable for expert DIY or professional

Specifications

Fuel

Grade . . . . Unleaded. Minimum 91 RON (Research Octane Number)
Fuel tank capacity . . . . see Chapter 1 Specifications

Fuel injection system

Idle speed . . . . see Chapter 1 Specifications
Fuel pressure at idle speed . . . . 36 psi (2.5 Bar)
Fuel pump winding resistance . . . . 1.5 ohms
Engine temperature sensor resistance
  LX, LXV and S models (2009 to 2011 models)
    Resistance @ 0°C . . . . 9.4 K-ohms
    Resistance @ 10°C . . . . 5.6 K-ohms
    Resistance @ 20°C . . . . 3.5 K-ohms
    Resistance @ 30°C . . . . 2.2 K-ohms
    Resistance @ 80°C . . . . 3.5 K-ohms
  GTS, GTV and GT models
    Resistance @ 0°C . . . . 5.9 K-ohms
    Resistance @ 10°C . . . . 3.8 K-ohms
    Resistance @ 20°C . . . . 2.5 K-ohms
    Resistance @ 30°C . . . . 1.7 K-ohms
    Resistance @ 80°C . . . . 300 ohms
Fuel injector resistance . . . . 13.7 to 15.2 ohms
Oxygen sensor heater resistance . . . . approx. 9 ohms
Load relay resistance . . . . 40 to 80 ohms

Torque settings

Exhaust header pipe nuts . . . . 16 to 18 Nm
Intake duct bolts . . . . 11 to 13 Nm
Oxygen sensor . . . . 40 to 50 Nm
Silencer bolts
  LX, LXV and S models . . . . 24 to 27 Nm
  GTS, GTV and GT models . . . . 20 to 25 Nm

1 General information and precautions

General information

The fuel supply system consists of the fuel tank with internal and integral fuel pump, filter and pressure regulator, the fuel hose, the throttle body, the injector, and the throttle cable(s). The fuel pump is switched on and off with the engine via a relay. Idle speed and fast idle speed for cold starting are set automatically by the electronic control unit (ECU). The injection system supplies fuel and air to the engine via a single throttle body with one injector. The injector is operated by the ECU using the information obtained from the various sensors it monitors. On most of the machines covered in this manual the ECU and throttle body are an integrated assembly. From mid 2013-on, some LX models were fitted with separate ECU and throttle body units. On the integrated assembly, the intake air temperature (IAT) sensor, idle speed adjuster and throttle position (TP) sensor are integral with the ECU. Refer to Section 3 for more information on the operation of the fuel injection system.

All models have a fuel gauge incorporated in the instrument cluster, actuated by a level sensor inside the fuel tank.

A catalytic converter is incorporated in the exhaust system to minimise the level of exhaust pollutants released into the atmosphere.

Note: *Electronic components can be checked but not repaired. If system troubles* occur, and the faulty component can be isolated, the only cure for the problem in most cases is to replace the part with a new one. Keep in mind that most electronic parts, once purchased, cannot be returned. To avoid unnecessary expense, make very sure the faulty component has been positively identified before buying a new part.

Precautions

⚠️ **Warning: Petrol (gasoline) is extremely flammable, so take extra precautions when you work on any part of the fuel system. Always disconnect the battery (see Chapter 10). Don't smoke or allow open flames or bare light bulbs near the work area, and don't work in a garage where a natural gas-type appliance is present. If you spill any fuel on your skin, rinse it off immediately with soap and water. When you perform any kind of work on the fuel system, wear safety glasses and have a fire extinguisher suitable for a class B type fire (flammable liquids) on hand.**

With the fuel injection system, some residual pressure will remain in the fuel feed hose and injector after the engine has been stopped. Before disconnecting the fuel hose, ensure the ignition is switched OFF and make sure you have some clean rag to catch and mop up the fuel. It is vital that no dirt or debris is allowed to enter any part of the system while a fuel hose is disconnected. Any foreign matter in the fuel system components could result in injector damage or malfunction. Ensure the ignition is switched OFF before disconnecting or reconnecting any fuel injection system wiring connector. If a connector is disconnected or reconnected with the ignition switched ON, the engine control unit (ECU) may be damaged.

Always perform service procedures in a well-ventilated area to prevent a build-up of fumes.

Never work in a building containing a gas appliance with a pilot light, or any other form of naked flame. Ensure that there are no naked light bulbs or any sources of flame or sparks nearby.

Do not smoke (or allow anyone else to smoke) while in the vicinity of petrol (gasoline) or of components containing it. Remember the possible presence of vapour from these sources and move well clear before smoking.

Check all electrical equipment belonging to the house, garage or workshop where work is being undertaken (see the *Safety first!* section of this manual). Remember that certain electrical appliances such as drills, cutters etc, create sparks in the normal course of operation and must not be used near petrol (gasoline) or any component containing it. Again, remember the possible presence of fumes before using electrical equipment.

Always mop up any spilt fuel and safely dispose of the rag used.

Any stored fuel that is drained off during servicing work must be kept in sealed containers that are suitable for holding petrol (gasoline), and clearly marked as such; the containers themselves should be kept in a safe place. Note that this last point applies equally to the fuel tank if it is removed from the machine; also remember to keep its filler cap closed at all times.

Read the *Safety first!* section of this manual carefully before starting work.

2 Air filter housing

1 Remove the storage compartment and the left-hand side panel (see Chapter 9).
2 Detach the crankcase breather hose from its union **(see illustration)**. Slacken the clamp securing the air duct to the back of the housing then draw the duct out, noting how it seats **(see illustrations)**.
3 Undo the screws or bolts securing the air filter housing to the transmission casing and manoeuvre the housing away, noting how it fits **(see illustrations)**. Note the arrangement

2.2a Detach the crankcase breather hose (arrowed)

2.2b Slacken the air duct clamp screw (arrowed) . . .

2.2c . . . then draw the duct out, noting how it locates

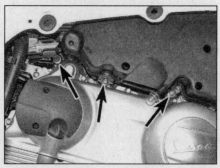

2.3a Undo the screws (arrowed) . . .

2.3b . . . and manoeuvre the housing out

of the washers and the collars and grommets where fitted.

4 Installation is the reverse of removal. Where fitted make sure the grommets are in good condition and the collars are fitted.

3 Fuel injection system description

1 All models are equipped with Vespa's fuel injection system. It is controlled by an electronic control unit (ECU) that operates both the injection and ignition systems (refer to Chapter 6 for the ignition system).

2 The engine control unit (ECU) monitors signals from the following sensors:

- *Throttle position (TP) sensor – informs the ECU of the throttle position, and the rate of throttle opening or closing.*
- *Engine temperature (ET) sensor – informs the ECU of engine temperature. It also actuates the temperature gauge on GTS models (see Chapter 4).*
- *Intake air temperature (IAT) sensor – informs the ECU of the temperature of the air entering the throttle body.*
- *Ignition pulse generator coil – informs the ECU of engine speed and crankshaft position (see Chapter 6).*
- *Oxygen sensor – informs the ECU of the oxygen content of the exhaust gases.*

3 All the information from the sensors is analysed by the ECU, and from that it determines the appropriate ignition and fuelling requirements of the engine. The ECU controls the fuel injector by varying its pulse width – the length of time the injector is held open – to provide more or less fuel, as appropriate for cold starting, warm up, idle, cruising, and acceleration.

4 Cold starting and warm up idle speeds are controlled automatically by the ECU via a stepper motor that controls a throttle valve by-pass circuit.

4 Fuel injection system fault diagnosis

1 When the ignition is switched on the fuel injection indicator light (with an engine-shaped symbol) in the instrument cluster will come on for a few seconds, then go out. When the engine is started the fuel injection system automatically performs a self-diagnosis check. If all is good the indicator light remains off. If there is an abnormality in any of the readings obtained from any sensor, the indicator light will come on, and the ECU enters its back-up mode. In back-up mode the ECU ignores the abnormal sensor signal, and assumes a pre-programmed value which may, depending on the sensor in question and the fault detected, allow the engine to continue running (albeit at reduced efficiency). Otherwise the engine will

stop, or will not be able to be restarted once it has been stopped. In each case the relevant fault code will be stored in the ECU memory. The fault can be identified by reading the fault code or codes. To do this the Vespa diagnostic tester is essential; a data link connector from the ECU is provided for this purpose. The diagnostic tester is also essential for adjusting engine idle speed and throttle position sensor parameters.

2 If a fault appears, first check the relevant fuse(s) (see Chapter 10). Next refer to the appropriate Section in this Chapter and make sure that the relevant system wiring connectors are securely connected and free of corrosion, and that none of the pins are bent – poor connections are the cause of the majority of problems. Also check the wiring itself for any obvious faults or breaks, and use a continuity tester to check the wiring between the component, its connectors and the ECU, referring to *Electrical System Fault Finding* and the *Wiring Diagrams* in Chapter 10. Also check the injection system load relay (see Section 5) – this relay controls power to the fuel pump, fuel injector and ignition coil. Next refer to Section 5 to see if there are any other specific checks that can be made on that particular component – some of the components and sensors can be checked using home equipment, but there are others which can only be tested using the Vespa diagnostic tester. If this fails to reveal the cause of the problem, the motorcycle should be taken to a Vespa dealer – they will have the tester which should locate the fault quickly and simply.

3 Also ensure that the fault is not due to poor maintenance – i.e. check that the air filter element is clean, that the spark plug is in good condition, that the valve clearances are correctly adjusted, the cylinder compression pressure is correct, and the ignition timing is correct (refer to Chapters 1, 2 and 6). It is also worth removing the component in question where possible (see Section 5) and checking that the sensing tip or head is clean and not obstructed by anything.

5 Fuel injection system components

Caution: Ensure the ignition is switched OFF before disconnecting/reconnecting any fuel injection system wiring. If a connector is disconnected/reconnected with the ignition switched ON the engine control unit (ECU) could be damaged.

1 If a fault is indicated in any of the system components, first check the relevant fuse(s) (see Chapter 10), then the wiring and connectors between the appropriate component and the ECU and/or instrument cluster (refer to *Electrical system fault finding* at the beginning of Chapter 10, and to *Wiring diagrams* at the end of it). Make sure the

5.3 Disconnect the ET sensor wiring connector

ignition is off before disconnecting any wiring connector. A continuity test of all wires will locate a break or short in any circuit. Inspect the terminals inside the wiring connectors and ensure they are not loose, bent or corroded. Spray the inside of the connectors with a proprietary electrical terminal cleaner before reconnection.

Engine temperature (ET) sensor

Check

2 Check the fuse(s), wiring and connectors as in Step 1.

3 Remove the storage compartment (see Chapter 9). Disconnect the wiring connector from the sensor **(see illustration)**. With the engine cold, connect an ohmmeter between the light blue/green and grey/green wire terminals on the sensor and measure its resistance. Compare the reading obtained to that given in the Specifications relevant to the current temperature. If the resistance reading differs greatly from that specified, the sensor is probably faulty.

4 If the sensor appears to be functioning correctly, check its power supply. Connect the positive (+) lead of a voltmeter to the light blue/green wire terminal in the sensor wiring connector, then connect the negative (–) lead to a good earth. Turn the ignition switch ON and check that a voltage is present (the particular value is not specified, but most systems run on less than 12 volts, typically around 5 – the important factor is whether there is any voltage or not).

5 If there is no voltage, there is a fault in the light blue/green wire or the ECU. If voltage is present, now connect the negative lead to the grey/green terminal of the connector and check that the same voltage is present. If it isn't, there is a fault in the grey/green wire or the ECU. If there is voltage, the ECU is probably faulty.

6 If all appears good so far, follow Steps 9 and 10 and remove the sensor for further testing.

7 Fill a small heatproof container with coolant and place it on a stove. Using an ohmmeter, connect the positive (+) probe of the meter to the light blue/green wire terminal on the sensor, and the negative (–) probe to the grey/green wire terminal. Using some wire or other support suspend the sensor in the coolant so

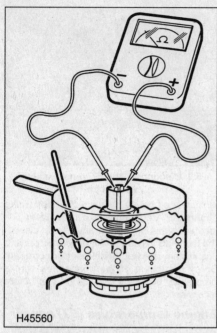

H45560

5.7 Temperature sensor test set-up

that just the sensing head up to the threads is submerged, and with the head a minimum of 40 mm above the bottom of the container **(see illustration)**. Also place a thermometer capable of reading temperatures up to 120°C in the coolant so that its bulb is close to the sensor. **Note:** *None of the components should be allowed to directly touch the container.*

5.10a Disconnect the wiring connector . . .

5.18a Disconnect the wiring connector from the injector

5.9 Location of the engine temperature sensor

⚠ *Warning: This must be done very carefully to avoid the risk of personal injury.*

8 Heat the coolant, stirring it gently. As the temperature rises the meter resistance reading should be as specified at the beginning of the Chapter at the various temperatures given. If the meter readings obtained are different by a margin of 10% or more, then the sensor is faulty and must be replaced with a new one.

Removal and installation

⚠ *Warning: The engine must be completely cool before carrying out this procedure.*

9 Remove the storage compartment for access (see Chapter 9). The sensor is mounted in the cylinder head **(see illustration)**. On liquid-cooled engines, drain the cooling system (see Chapter 4). If required, disconnect

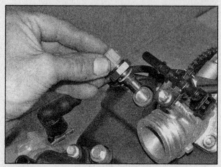

5.10b . . . then unscrew the temperature sensor

5.18b Checking injector resistance

the fuel hose from the union on the injector (see Step 22).
10 Disconnect the sensor wiring connector **(see illustration)**. Unscrew and remove the sensor **(see illustration)**. Where fitted remove and discard the sealing washer – a new one must be used.
11 On liquid-cooled engines, apply a suitable sealant to the thread of the sensor, making sure none gets on the sensor head. Fit the sensor, with a new sealing washer if applicable, and tighten it securely. Connect the wiring connector and the fuel hose if applicable.
12 Install the storage compartment (see Chapter 9). On liquid-cooled engines, refill the cooling system (see Chapter 4).

Throttle position (TP) sensor

13 On most of the machines covered in this manual the TP sensor is an integral part of the ECU/throttle body assembly. However, from mid 2013-on, some LX models were fitted with a separate ECU and the TP sensor is located on the left-hand side of the throttle body. The TP sensor can only be checked using the Vespa diagnostic test pin box.
14 On all machines, the TP sensor is not available separately.

Intake air temperature (IAT) sensor

15 The IAT sensor is part of the throttle body/ECU assembly and can only be checked using the Vespa diagnostic test pin box.
16 The sensor is not available separately from the throttle body. If the sensor is faulty, a complete new throttle body assembly will have to be installed (see Section 7).

Fuel injector

⚠ *Warning: Refer to the precautions given in Section 1 before starting work.*

Check

17 Check the fuse(s), wiring and connectors as in Step 1.
18 Remove the storage compartment (see Chapter 9). Disconnect the wiring connector from the injector **(see illustration)**. Connect an ohmmeter between the terminals and measure the resistance **(see illustration)**. Compare the reading to that given in the Specifications. If the resistance of the injector differs greatly from that specified, a new injector should be fitted.
19 Next check for battery voltage at the black/green wire terminal in the wiring connector – there should be voltage present for about 2 seconds after switching the ignition ON. If there is no voltage, check the load relay (Steps 36 to 39) and other components in the circuit and the wiring and connectors between them, referring to the wiring diagrams at the end of Chapter 10.

Removal

20 Remove the storage compartment (see Chapter 9). Disconnect the battery (see Chapter 10).

5.22a Press in the clips . . .

5.22b . . . and pull the fuel hose(s) off

5.23 Unscrew the bolt (arrowed) and carefully pull the injector out

5.28 Oxygen sensor (arrowed)

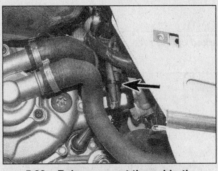

5.30a Release or cut the cable-tie (arrowed) . . .

5.30b . . . then pull the connector off its clip and disconnect it

21 Disconnect the wiring connector from the injector **(see illustration 5.18a)**.

22 Have some rag to hand to catch residual fuel. Release and detach the hose(s) from the union(s) on the injector, noting which fits where on models with supply and return hoses **(see illustrations)**.

23 Unscrew the injector bolt **(see illustration)**. Carefully remove the injector. Note that the injector seal is not available separately so take care not to damage it.

Installation

24 Apply a smear of grease to the seal. Ease the injector into the intake manifold, making sure the seal does not get dislodged, then fit the bolt **(see illustration 5.23)**.

25 Fit the fuel hose(s) onto the injector, making sure it/they locate(s) correctly and click(s) into place **(see illustration 5.22b)**. Check the hose(s) is/are secure by trying to pull it/them off.

26 Connect the wiring connector **(see illustration 5.18a)**. Connect the battery (see Chapter 10).

27 Run the engine and check there are no leaks from the injector and that the fuel system is working correctly before taking the machine out on the road.

Oxygen sensor

Check

28 The oxygen sensor is located in the exhaust header pipe **(see illustration)**. The operation of the sensor itself can only be checked using the Vespa diagnostic test pin box.

29 Check the fuse(s), wiring and connectors as in Step 1.

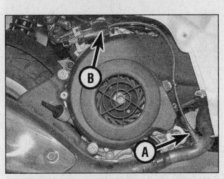

5.30c Location of the oxygen sensor (A) and wiring connector (B) – air-cooled model

30 To check the sensor heater resistance it must be cold. Remove the right-hand side panel (see Chapter 9). Release and disconnect the sensor wiring connector **(see illustrations)**. Referring to the wiring diagram for your machine, connect an ohmmeter between the black/green and green/yellow, or between the light/blue and red wire terminals on the sensor side of the connector and check that the resistance is as specified at the beginning of the Chapter. If the resistance is not as specified, replace the sensor with a new one. Note that only models with a 4-pin connector to the sensor have a heater element.

31 Next check for battery voltage at the black/green (+) wire terminal in the wiring connector – there should be voltage present for about 2 seconds after switching the ignition ON. If there is no voltage, check the load relay and the other

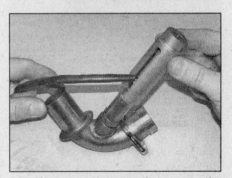

5.33 Unscrew and remove the sensor – the socket shown is specifically for oxygen sensors and enables it to be tightened to the correct torque

components in the power circuit and the wiring and connectors between them, referring to the wiring diagrams at the end of Chapter 10.

Removal and installation

Note: *The oxygen sensor is delicate and will not work if it is dropped or knocked, or if any cleaning materials are used on it. Ensure the exhaust system is cold before proceeding.*

32 If required, remove the exhaust system (see Section 13). Otherwise, remove the right-hand trim panel to improve access to the sensor **(see illustration 5.30c)**. Trace the wiring from the sensor and release it from any clips, then disconnect the sensor wiring connector.

33 Unscrew and remove the sensor **(see illustration)**.

34 Installation is the reverse of removal.

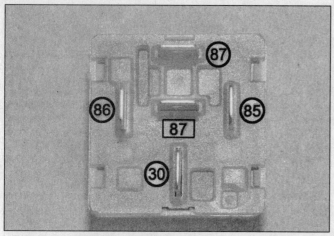

5.37 Terminal identification numbers are marked on the relay

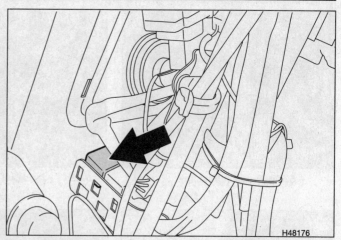

5.40a Load relay (arrowed) – LX, LXV and S models

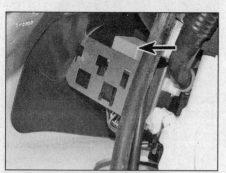

5.40b Load relay (arrowed) – 2012-on LX, LXV and S models

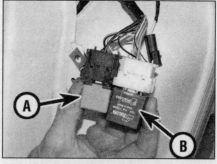

5.40c Injection load relay (A) and headlight relay (B)

5.41 Removing the load relay – GTS, GTV and GT models

Tighten the sensor to the torque setting specified at the beginning of the Chapter – note that a special socket designed for oxygen sensors is required, you should be able to get one from most automotive tool suppliers (see illustration 5.33).

Load relay

Check

35 Check the fuse(s), wiring and connectors as in Step 1.

36 Remove the relay (see below).

37 Set a multimeter to the ohms x 10 scale and connect it between the 86 and 85 terminals on the relay (see illustration) – the resistance should be as specified at the beginning of the Chapter. If not replace the relay with a new one.

38 Set the multimeter to the ohms x 1 scale and connect it between the 87 and 30 terminals on the relay. There should be no continuity (infinite resistance). Using a fully-charged 12 volt battery and two insulated jumper wires, connect the positive (+) terminal of the battery to the 86 terminal, and the negative (–) terminal to the 85 terminal. At this point the relay should be heard to click and the multimeter read 0 ohms (continuity). If this is the case the relay is proved good. If the relay does not click when battery voltage is

applied and still indicates no continuity (infinite resistance) across its terminals, it is faulty and must be replaced with a new one.

39 If the relay is good check for battery voltage at the red/white wire terminal in the relay connector – there should be voltage present for about 2 seconds after switching the ignition ON. Also check for voltage at the grey/black wire terminal in the relay wiring connector with the ignition on. There should be constant voltage. If there is no voltage check the wiring to the relay, referring to the wiring diagram for your model in Chapter 10.

Removal and installation

40 On 2009 to 2011 LX, LXV and S models, remove the front panel grille (see Chapter 9) – the relay is the front one of the two mounted below the horn (see illustration). On 2012-on LX, LXV and S models, remove the kick panel (see Chapter 9) – the relay is mounted on a bracket behind the horn (see illustration). Displace the bracket to access the relay (see illustration). On GTS, GTV and GT models remove the storage compartment (see Chapter 9) – the relay is on the left-hand side.

41 Pull the relay off its socket (see illustration).

42 Installation is the reverse of removal.

Idle speed adjuster/control valve

43 On most of the machines covered in this manual the idle speed adjuster is an integral part of the ECU/throttle body assembly. However, from mid 2013-on, some LX models were fitted with a separate ECU and an idle speed control valve is located on a bracket above the throttle body. The valve can only be checked using the Vespa diagnostic test pin box.

44 On all machines, the idle speed adjuster/ idle speed control valve is not available separately. If it is faulty a complete new throttle body assembly will have to be installed (see Section 7).

6 Electronic Control Unit (ECU)

Check

1 If the tests shown in the preceding or following Sections have failed to isolate the cause of an ignition fault, it is possible that the electronic control unit (ECU) itself is faulty. No details are available for testing the ECU. On most of the machines covered in this manual the ECU is an integral part of the throttle

6.2a Undo the screw (arrowed) to free the clip . . .

6.2b . . . then disconnect and check the wiring connector

7.7 Slacken the clamp screw (arrowed)

body assembly. However, from mid 2013-on, some LX models were fitted with a separate ECU mounted on a bracket inside the rear right-hand side of the bodywork. Remove the ECU, ECU/throttle body assembly and take it to a Vespa dealer for assessment.

2 Before condemning the ECU remove the storage compartment (see Chapter 9). Disconnect the battery (see Chapter 10). Disconnect the wiring connector and check the terminals are clean, and none of the pins are bent or wires have detached **(see illustrations)**.

3 Next reconnect the battery and check for constant battery voltage (even with ignition OFF) at the grey/black or orange/black (according to model) wire terminal (PIN No. 6) of the connector. Next check for battery voltage at the red/white wire terminal (PIN No. 5), with the ignition on. Also check for continuity to earth in the black wire (PIN No. 26). If there is no power in either or both check the relevant fuses and circuit, referring to *Electrical System Fault Finding* at the beginning of Chapter 10 and to the *Wiring Diagrams* at the end of it.

4 Make sure the connector is secure after reconnecting it.

Removal and installation

5 Make sure the ignition is off. Disconnect the battery (see Chapter 10).

6 If the ECU is an integral part of the throttle body assembly, remove the throttle body (see Section 7). To remove the separate ECU, disconnect the wiring connector, then undo the screws securing the ECU and lift it off.

7 Installation is the reverse of removal. Make sure the wiring connector is securely connected.

7 Throttle body assembly

> ⚠️ **Warning: Refer to the precautions given in Section 1 before starting work.**

Removal

Special tool: *On 2012-on LX, LXV and S models, a T30 tamper-proof Torx bit is required to undo the intake manifold bolts (see Step 8).*

1 Remove the storage compartment (see Chapter 9).

2 Disconnect the battery (see Chapter 10).

3 Undo the clamp screw to free the fuel hose and ECU wiring **(see illustration 6.2a)**.

4 Have some rag to hand to catch residual fuel. Release and detach the hose(s) from the union(s) on the injector, noting which fits where on models with supply and return hoses **(see illustrations 5.22a and b)**.

5 Disconnect the wiring connector from the injector **(see illustration 5.18a)**.

6 If the ECU is an integral part of the throttle body assembly, disconnect the ECU wiring connector **(see illustration 6.2b)**. On machines fitted with a separate throttle body, disconnect the idle speed control valve wiring connector. Loosen the clip securing the air hose to the valve and disconnect the hose, then ease the valve off its mounting bracket.

Disconnect the throttle position sensor wiring connector.

7 Fully slacken the air intake duct clamp screw on the throttle body **(see illustration)**.

8 Clean around the intake manifold joint to the cylinder head. Undo the intake manifold bolts **(see illustration)**. Displace the complete throttle body assembly and manifold from the head and air intake duct.

Caution: Tape over or stuff clean rag into the intake duct and manifold after removing the throttle body assembly to prevent anything from falling in.

9 Disconnect the throttle cables – slacken the nut(s) securing the cable(s) in the bracket on the throttle body and thread it/them off the end of the cable(s), then free the cable(s) from the bracket **(see illustrations)**.

Caution: Do not snap the throttle from fully open to fully closed once the cable has been disconnected because this can lead to engine idle speed problems.

10 If required slacken the intake manifold sleeve clamp screw and detach the manifold from the throttle body. If required remove the injector from the manifold (see Section 5).

11 If the air intake duct shows signs of cracking or deterioration a new one must be fitted.

Caution: The throttle body assembly must be treated as a sealed unit. DO NOT attempt to take it apart.

Installation

12 Installation is the reverse of removal, noting the following:

7.8 Unscrew the bolts (arrowed)

7.9a Slacken the nuts securing the cables in the bracket . . .

7.9b . . . and detach them from the pulley, noting which fits where

• Refer to Section 5 for installation of the injector if removed. Make sure the throttle body is fully engaged in the manifold sleeve before tightening the clamp.

• Tighten the intake manifold bolts to the torque setting specified at the beginning of the Chapter.

• Make sure the air intake duct is fully engaged around the throttle body before tightening the clamp screw.

• Make sure all wiring connectors are securely connected.

• Fit the fuel hose(s) onto the injector, making sure it/they locate(s) correctly and click(s) into place. Check the hose(s) is/are secure by trying to pull it/them off.

• Adjust the throttle cable (see Chapter 1).

• Run the engine and check there are no leaks from the injector and that the fuel system is working correctly before taking the machine out on the road.

8 Throttle cable(s)

 Warning: Refer to the precautions given in Section 1 before proceeding.

LX, S and GTS models
Removal

1 Remove the handlebar covers, storage compartment, kick panel, and floor panel to expose the cable from the handlebar to the throttle body (see Chapter 9).

2 On models with two cables mark each cable according to its position on the throttle body if necessary, though the bottom (opening) cable should have chrome nuts while those on the upper (closing) cable are black. Slacken the nut(s) securing the cable(s) in the bracket on the throttle body and thread it/them off the end of the cable(s), then free the cable(s) from the bracket **(see illustration 7.8b)**. Free the cable end(s) from the pulley **(see illustration 7.8c)**.

3 Draw the cable(s) out, noting the routing.

4 Unscrew the opening cable elbow nut from the throttle pulley housing **(see illustration)**. Undo the housing screws and detach the cover **(see illustration)**. Detach the cable end(s) from the pulley and detach the cable housing **(see illustration)**. On models with a closing cable turn the elbow 90° and draw it out of the housing **(see illustration)**. Thread the housing off the opening cable elbow **(see illustration)**.

Installation

5 Thread the upper (threaded) hole in the throttle pulley housing onto the upper end of the opening cable elbow without it becoming tight – the elbow must stay loose so that it aligns itself **(see illustration 8.4e)**. Where fitted fit the closing cable into the housing and turn it 90° to secure it, making sure the opening cable is above the brake lever and the closing cable is below it **(see illustration 8.4d)**. Lubricate the cable end(s) with multi-purpose grease, then locate the housing on the

handlebar and fit the end(s) into the throttle pulley **(see illustration 8.4c)**. Fit the cover onto the housing, then fit the screws and tighten them, aligning the housing mating surfaces with those of the master cylinder clamp **(see illustration 8.4b)**.

6 Feed the cable(s) through to the throttle body, making sure the routing is correct. The cable(s) must not interfere with any other component and should not be kinked or bent sharply. Now tighten the opening cable elbow nut on the housing **(see illustration 8.4a)**.

7 Lubricate the cable end(s) with multi-purpose grease and fit it/them into the pulley on the throttle body **(see illustration 7.8c)** – on models with one cable fit it into the bottom socket on the bracket and pulley, and on models with two cables the opening cable with the chrome nuts goes on the bottom **(see illustration 7.8b)**. Locate the cable(s) in the bracket, turning the pulley as required by hand, then set the nuts so the cable freeplay is as specified (see Chapter 1).

8 Operate the throttle to check that it opens and closes freely.

9 Turn the handlebars back-and-forth to make sure the cable doesn't cause the steering to bind.

10 Install the body panels (see Chapter 9).

11 Start the engine and check that the idle speed does not rise as the handlebars are turned. If it does, the throttle cable is routed incorrectly. Correct the problem before riding the motorcycle.

LXV, GTV and GT models
Removal

12 Remove the handlebar cover/instrument housing, storage compartment, kick panel, and floor panel to expose the cable from the handlebar to the throttle body (see Chapter 9). Displace the front brake master cylinder assembly from the handlebar (see Chapter 8).

13 On models with two cables mark each cable according to its position on the throttle body if necessary, though the bottom (opening) cable should have chrome nuts while those on the upper (closing) cable are black. Slacken the nut(s) securing the cable(s) in the bracket on the throttle body and thread it/them off the end of the cable(s), then free the cable(s) from the

8.4a Unscrew the nut (arrowed)

8.4b Undo the screws (arrowed) and remove the cover

8.4c Detach the cable ends then displace the housing

8.4d Turn and release the closing cable . . .

8.4e . . . then thread the housing off the opening cable

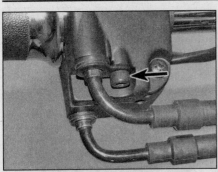

8.15a Undo the screw (arrowed)

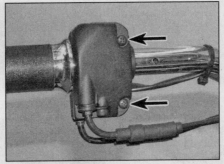

8.15b Undo the screws (arrowed) . . .

8.15c . . . displace the switch face and detach the cable

8.15d Undo the screws (arrowed) . . .

8.15e . . . displace the switch back and detach the cable

8.15f Turn and release the cable

bracket (see illustration 7.8b). Free the cable end(s) from the pulley (see illustration 7.8c).
14 Draw the cable(s) out, noting the routing.
15 Undo the opening cable elbow retainer screw from the throttle pulley housing (see illustration). Undo the switch housing screws and detach the switch face, where fitted freeing the closing cable end from the pulley (see illustrations). Undo the clamp screws and detach the back of the switch, freeing the cable end from the pulley (see illustrations). Turn the cable elbow 90° to release it from its housing and draw it out (see illustration).

Installation

16 Lubricate the cable end(s) with multi-purpose grease. Fit the opening cable into the back of the switch and connect its end to the throttle pulley (see illustration 8.15e), then locate the back of the switch on the

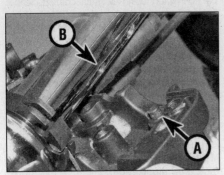

8.16 Locate the peg (A) in the hole (B)

handlebar, fitting the peg into the hole, fit the clamp and tighten the screws (see illustration and 8.15d). Where fitted, fit the closing cable into the switch face and turn it 90° to lock it, then connect end to the throttle pulley (see illustrations 8.15f and 8.15c). Locate the switch face on the handlebar, fit the screws and tighten them (see illustration 8.15b).
17 Feed the cable(s) through to the throttle body, making sure the routing is correct. The cable(s) must not interfere with any other component and should not be kinked or bent sharply. Now locate the opening cable retainer and tighten the screw (see illustration 8.15a).
18 Lubricate the cable end(s) with multi-purpose grease and fit it/them into the pulley on the throttle body (see illustration 7.8c) – on models with one cable fit it into the bottom socket on the bracket and pulley, and on models with two cables the opening cable with the chrome nuts goes on the bottom (see illustration 7.8b). Locate the cable(s) in the bracket, turning the pulley as required by hand, then set the nuts so the cable freeplay is as specified (see Chapter 1).
19 Operate the throttle to check that it opens and closes freely.
20 Turn the handlebars back-and-forth to make sure the cable doesn't cause the steering to bind.
21 Install the body panels (see Chapter 9).
22 Start the engine and check that the idle speed does not rise as the handlebars are turned. If it does, the throttle cable is routed incorrectly. Correct the problem before riding the motorcycle.

9 Fuel pressure check

Warning: Refer to the precautions given in Section 1 before starting work.
Special Tool: *A pressure gauge is required for this check. Vespa specify the use of their gauge (Pt. No. 020480Y), that connects to the fuel supply hose between the fuel pump and the injector.*
1 Remove the storage compartment (see Chapter 9). Disconnect the battery negative (–) lead (see Chapter 10).
2 Release the fuel supply hose from the union on the injector (see illustrations 5.22a and b). On machines with a supply and return hose, disconnect the right-hand hose. Fit the gauge between the fuel supply hose and injector.
3 Connect the battery negative (–) lead. Start the engine and allow it to idle. Note the pressure present in the fuel system by reading the gauge, then turn the engine off. Compare the reading obtained to that given in the Specifications.
4 If the fuel pressure is higher than specified, the pressure regulator in the fuel pump is faulty and so the pump must be replaced with a new one – the regulator is not available separately.
5 If the fuel pressure is lower than specified, likely causes are.
• *Leaking fuel hose union, (which should be obvious).*
• *Blocked fuel filter or strainer.*
• *Faulty fuel pump.*

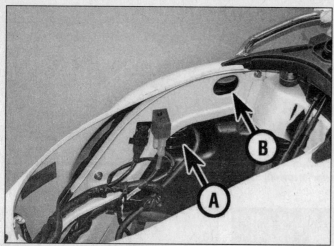

10.2a Access to the wiring connectors for the pump (A) and the level sensor (B) is restricted . . .

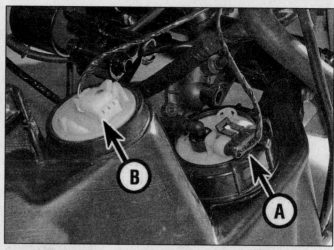

10.2b . . . if necessary displace the tank to access them

6 If necessary remove the fuel pump (see Section 10), clean the strainer and fit a new filter. If the strainer and filter are clean and there are no leaks evident a new pump assembly must be installed.

7 On completion, disconnect the battery again. Remove the fuel gauge assembly, being prepared to catch the residual fuel. Fit the fuel hose onto the injector, making sure it clicks into place **(see illustration 5.22b)** – check it is secure by trying to pull it off.

8 Reconnect the battery then start the engine and check that there is no sign of fuel leakage. If all is well, install the body panels (see Chapter 9).

10 Fuel pump

⚠ **Warning: Refer to the precautions given in Section 1 before starting work.**

Check

Note: *Certain GTS250 and GTS300 models have had problems with the fuel pump cutting out when the engine is warm for no apparent reason (symptoms are of running out of fuel), then working again when the engine has cooled.*

If this is the case seek advice from your dealer.

1 The fuel pump is fitted inside the fuel tank. The fuel pump runs for a few seconds when the ignition is switched ON to pressurise the fuel system, and then cuts out until the engine is started. Check that it does this. If it doesn't, first check the relevant fuses (see Chapter 10). If they are OK proceed as follows.

2 Ensure the ignition is switched OFF then disconnect the fuel pump wiring connector **(see illustration)** – access is difficult, so if necessary displace the fuel tank to access the connector **(see illustration)** (see Section 12).

3 Check the connector for loose or broken terminal pins and wires. Connect the positive (+) lead of a voltmeter to the black/green wire terminal on the loom side of the connector and the negative (–) lead to the green wire terminal. Switch the ignition ON whilst noting the reading obtained on the meter.

4 If battery voltage is present for a few seconds, the fuel pump circuit is operating correctly and the fuel pump itself is faulty and must be replaced with a new one.

5 If no reading is obtained, check the load relay and its circuit (see Section 5). If that is good check the black wire in the pump wiring connector has continuity to earth, and the black/green wire has continuity to the load relay wiring connector. Repair/replace the wiring as necessary and clean the connectors using electrical contact cleaner. If this fails to reveal the fault, the ECU could be faulty – at this point it may be best to have the system checked by a Vespa dealer.

Removal

6 Remove the fuel tank (see Section 12).

7 Release the fuel hose(s) from the tank where necessary **(see illustration)**.

8 Unscrew the pump retaining ring – you may be able to do it by hand, but if not use a special tool as shown, a suitable pair of grips or a drift located against one of the tabs **(see illustration)**. Carefully lift the pump out of the tank **(see illustration)**. Remove the rubber seal from the pump or tank and discard it – a new one must be used **(see illustration)**.

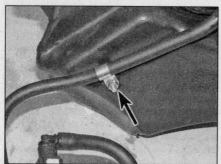

10.7 Undo the nut (arrowed) to free the hose

10.8a Unscrewing the pump retaining ring using a special tool

10.8b Carefully draw the pump out of the tank

10.8c Remove and discard the seal

10.9a Disconnect the wiring (arrowed) . . .

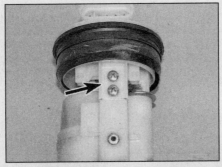

10.9b . . . then undo the screws (arrowed) . . .

10.9c . . . and detach the fuel hose (arrowed)

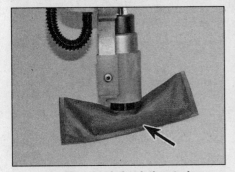

10.10 Clean and check the strainer (arrowed)

10.11a Align the pump as shown and make sure the seal seats . . .

10.11b . . . then fit and tighten the retaining ring as described

9 To remove the filter disconnect the wiring from the pump motor **(see illustration)**. Undo the filter bracket screws **(see illustration)**. Release the clamp securing the hose to the filter **(see illustration)**. Draw the lower half of the filter support off. Pull the filter out of the pump. Fit the new filter in reverse order. Make sure the hose is secure, and use a new clamp if necessary.

10 Make sure the fuel strainer is clean **(see illustration)**.

Installation

11 Fit a new rubber seal onto the pump **(see illustration 10.8c)**. Fit the pump into the tank **(see illustration 10.8b)** – make sure it is correctly aligned and seated **(see illustration)**. Fit the retaining ring and tighten by hand as much as possible, then tighten a little further using a tool as on removal **(see illustration)**.

12 Install the tank (see Section 12).

11 Fuel gauge, warning light and level sensor

Check

Note: *GTS300 models should have a wiring connector on the level sensor with three wires, while GTS250 models should have two wires. Some models may have been incorrectly fitted at the factory, and as a result false fuel level readings may be given. If this is the case seek advice from your dealer.*

1 The circuit consists of the level sensor

in the fuel tank, and the gauge and the low fuel warning light in the instrument cluster. If the instruments malfunction first check the instrument cluster fuse (see Chapter 10).

2 If the gauge or light do not work, remove the storage compartment and handlebar/instrument cover(s) as required according to model (see Chapter 9). Ensure the ignition is switched OFF then disconnect the instrument wiring connector(s) (see Chapter 10). Disconnect the fuel level sensor wiring connector **(see illustration 10.2a)** – access is difficult, so if necessary displace the fuel tank to access the connector **(see illustration 10.2b)** (see Section 12).

3 Check the wiring between the sensor connector and the relevant connector on the back of the instrument cluster for continuity, and check for continuity to earth in the black wire (where present), referring to *Electrical System Fault Finding* and the *Wiring Diagrams* Chapter 10. If that is good check for voltage at the white/green wire to the gauge, and where present in the yellow/green wire. Make sure the connector and terminal pins are not bent or broken and all wires are secure. If the wiring is good the gauge or sensor is faulty.

4 To check the sensor, test its resistance when the tank is full and again when it is empty, or alternatively remove the sensor and test it in the upside down position (so the float is effectively at the top of the sensor, representing a full tank), and again the right way up to represent and empty tank: connect the probes of an ohmmeter to the white/green and black or grey/black (according to model) terminals on the sensor. When the tank is full or upside

down there should be about 7 ohms **(see illustration)**. When the tank is empty or the right way up there should be about 90 to 100 ohms **(see illustration overleaf)**. If not replace the sensor with a new one (see Step 8).

5 If the wiring and sensor are good connect between the relevant terminals of the sensor wiring connector (refer to the wiring diagram for your model, and on models with three wires select the terminals according to whether you are testing the warning light or the gauge) using a suitable wire, then turn the ignition on – the gauge needle should move to the full position or the warning light should come on, according to model and the test being carried out. Disconnect the wire.

11.4a Testing resistance with the level sensor removed and upside down (full tank) . . .

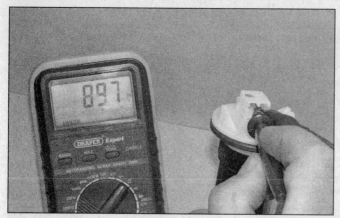

11.4b ... and the right way up (empty tank)

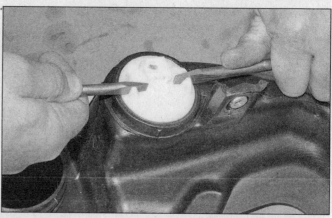

11.8a Turn the sensor using screwdrivers ...

11.8b ... then draw it out of the tank

12.3 Undo the screws (arrowed) and remove the battery panel

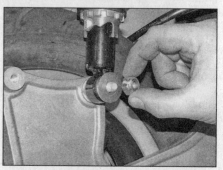

12.9a Unscrew the nut and remove the washer ...

Removal and installation

⚠ **Warning: Refer to the precautions given in Section 1 before starting work.**

6 The fuel gauge and warning light are part of the instrument cluster which is covered in Chapter 10.

7 To remove the sensor remove the fuel tank (see Section 12).

8 Turn the sensor 1/8 of a turn using two screwdrivers in the lugs as shown, then withdraw it from the tank **(see illustrations)**.

9 Fit the sensor into the tank and tighten by hand, then tighten a little further using the screwdrivers as on removal **(see illustrations 11.8b and a)**.

10 Install the tank (see Section 12).

12 Fuel tank

⚠ **Warning: Refer to the precautions given in Section 1 before starting work.**

Removal

LX, LXV and S models

1 Remove the storage compartment (see Chapter 9). Remove the battery (see Chapter 10).

2 Remove the fuel filler cap and its seal.

3 Undo the screws securing the battery panel and lift it up, noting how it locates at the back, then detach the fuse holder and remove the

panel **(see illustration)**. Temporarily install the fuel filler cap.

4 Remove the exhaust system (see Section 13).

5 Unscrew the nut and withdraw the bolt securing the bottom of the shock absorber **(see illustration 12.9a)**.

GTS, GTV and GT models

6 Disconnect the battery (see Chapter 10).

7 Remove the storage compartment and the side panels (see Chapter 9).

8 Remove the exhaust silencer (see Section 13).

9 Unscrew the nut and remove the washer from the bottom the right-hand shock absorber, then pull the shock off its mount **(see illustrations)**. Unscrew the nut and withdraw the bolt securing the bottom of the left-hand shock **(see illustration)**. Note the collars in the bush **(see illustration)**.

12.9b ... then draw the shock off

12.9c Unscrew the nut and withdraw the bolt ...

12.9d ... take care not to lose the collars, and make sure they are in place on installation

All models

10 Remove the tail light and rear turn signals (see Chapter 10).

11 Unscrew the bolts securing the tank **(see illustrations)**.

12 Remove the fuel filler cap and its rubber seal **(see illustration)**.

13 With the help of an assistant raise the scooter up off the engine, then manoeuvre the fuel tank down. Install the fuel filler cap.

14 Disconnect the fuel pump and level sensor wiring connectors **(see illustration 10.2b)**.

15 Have some rag to hand to catch residual fuel. Disconnect the fuel hose(s) from the union(s) on the pump, noting which fits where on models with supply and return hoses – if the fuel hose connector is a male type and fitting into a female socket with no obvious clips to release just pull it squarely up out of its socket **(see illustration)**; if the connector is the female type fitting onto a male union with two white clips, press the clips in and pull the hose off.

16 Remove the tank.

Installation

17 Installation is the reverse of removal. Push the hose(s) fully into the socket(s) or onto the union(s), until it/they click(s) into place **(see illustration 12.15)** – check it/they is/are secure by trying to pull it off. Make sure the fuel pump and level sensor wiring connectors are securely connected **(see illustration 10.2b)**.

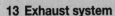
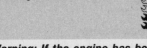

13 Exhaust system

Warning: If the engine has been running the exhaust system will be very hot. Allow the system to cool before carrying out any work.
Caution: Exhaust system fixings tend to become corroded and seized. It is advisable to spray them with penetrating oil before attempting to loosen them.

Removal

LX, LXV and S models

1 Remove the right-hand side panel, trim panel and the access panel (see Chapter 9).

2 Release and disconnect the oxygen sensor wiring connector **(see illustration 5.30b and c)**. Free the wiring from its ties and/or guides and feed it down, noting its routing.

3 Undo the nuts securing the downpipe to the exhaust port in the head, then support the exhaust system and unscrew the silencer mounting bolts **(see illustration)**. Manoeuvre the exhaust system out **(see illustration)**. Note the location of the flange on the downpipe.

4 Pry the gasket out of its groove in exhaust port and discard it as a new one must be used **(see illustration 13.10)**.

5 If required remove the oxygen sensor (see Section 5).

GTS, GTV and GT models

6 Remove the right-hand side panel, and if

12.11a Fuel tank rear bolt . . .

12.12 Remove the filler cap and seal

12.11b . . . and side bolts – GTS/GTV/GT type shown

12.15 Detach the fuel hose – this type just pulls out, but on some you may need to press in some clips

necessary for best access to the header pipe nuts (according to your procedure and tools) remove the floor panel (see Chapter 9).

7 The silencer can be removed independently of the header pipe if required – this is preferable for certain procedures (for example

engine removal, alternator cover removal, rear wheel removal and fuel tank removal), as access to the header pipe nuts is restricted. To remove the silencer slacken the clamp bolt on the silencer-to header pipe joint, then unscrew the silencer bolts and draw the silencer off the

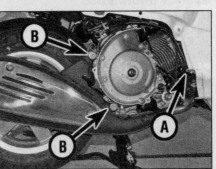

13.3a Exhaust system is retained by nuts (A) and bolts (B)

13.3b Exhaust system is a one-piece assembly

13.7a Slacken the clamp bolt (arrowed) . . .

13.7b . . . then unscrew the bolts . . .

13.7c . . . and remove the silencer

13.8 Unscrew the downpipe nuts (arrowed)

13.10 Dig the old gasket out and discard it

header pipe, taking care not to damage the sealing ring **(see illustrations)**.

8 To remove the header pipe after removing the silencer release and disconnect the oxygen sensor wiring connector **(see illustrations 5.28 and 5.30a and b)**. Free the wiring from its ties and/or guides and feed it down, noting its routing. Undo the nuts securing the downpipe to the exhaust port in the head **(see illustration)**.

9 To remove the complete system in one piece combine Steps 7 and 8 but do not slacken the joint clamp bolt.

10 If the header pipe has been removed, pry the gasket out of its groove in the exhaust port and discard it as a new one must be used **(see illustration)**.

11 If required remove the oxygen sensor (see Section 5).

12 If necessary dig the silencer-to-header pipe sealing ring out and fit a new one on reassembly **(see illustration)**.

Installation

13 Installation is the reverse of removal, noting the following:

• Install the oxygen sensor before fitting the exhaust (see Section 5).
• Clean the exhaust port studs and lubricate them with a suitable copper-based grease before reassembly.
• Use a new header pipe gasket and push it into its groove in the exhaust port – it has small tangs on the perimeter which locate

13.12 Check the sealing ring (arrowed) and fit a new one if necessary

in the groove but also make it tricky to install **(see illustration)**.

• On GTS, GTV and GT models fit a new silencer-to-header pipe sealing ring if necessary **(see illustration 13.12)** – take care when installing it as they are easily damaged.
• Leave all nuts and bolts finger-tight until all have been installed, then tighten the exhaust port nuts first, then the silencer bolts, then on GTS, GTV and GT models the clamp bolt, to the torque settings specified at the beginning of the Chapter.
• Run the engine and check that there are no exhaust gas leaks.

14 Catalytic converter

General information

1 A catalytic converter is incorporated in the exhaust system to minimise the level of exhaust pollutants released into the atmosphere.

2 The catalytic converter consists of a canister containing a fine mesh impregnated with a catalyst material, over which the hot exhaust gases pass. The catalyst speeds up the oxidation of harmful carbon monoxide, unburned hydrocarbons and soot, effectively reducing the quantity of harmful products released into the atmosphere via the exhaust gases.

13.13 Push the new gasket into place, locating the tangs in the groove

3 The catalytic converter is of the closed-loop type with exhaust gas oxygen content information being fed back to the ECU by the oxygen sensor.

4 The oxygen sensor contains a heating element which is controlled by the ECU. When the engine is cold, the ECU switches on the heating element which warms the exhaust gases as they pass over the sensor. This brings the catalytic converter quickly up to its normal operating temperature and decreases the level of exhaust pollutants emitted whilst the engine warms up. Once the engine is sufficiently warmed up, the ECU switches off the heating element.

5 Refer to Section 13 for exhaust system removal and installation, and Section 5 for oxygen sensor removal and installation information.

Precautions

6 The catalytic converter is a reliable and simple device which needs no maintenance in itself, but there are some facts of which an owner should be aware if the converter is to function properly for its full service life.

• DO NOT use leaded or lead replacement petrol (gasoline) – the additives will coat the precious metals, reducing their converting efficiency and will eventually destroy the catalytic converter.
• Always keep the ignition and fuel systems well-maintained in accordance with the manufacturer's schedule – if the fuel/air mixture is suspected of being incorrect have it checked on an exhaust gas analyser.
• If the engine develops a misfire, do not ride the scooter at all (or at least as little as possible) until the fault is cured.
• DO NOT use fuel or engine oil additives – these may contain substances harmful to the catalytic converter.
• DO NOT continue to use the scooter if the engine burns oil to the extent of leaving a visible trail of blue smoke.
• Remember that the catalytic converter and oxygen sensor are FRAGILE – do not strike them with tools during servicing work.

Chapter 6
Ignition system

Contents

Degrees of difficulty

Easy, suitable for novice with little experience 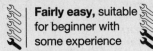	**Fairly easy,** suitable for beginner with some experience	**Fairly difficult,** suitable for competent DIY mechanic	**Difficult,** suitable for experienced DIY mechanic	**Very difficult,** suitable for expert DIY or professional

Specifications

General information
Spark plug . . . .   see Chapter 1

Pulse generator coil
Resistance . . . .   100 to 150 ohms

Ignition coil
Primary winding resistance . . . .   approx. 0.5 to 1.0 ohm
Secondary winding resistance (without plug cap) . . . .   approx. 3.1 K-ohms
Spark plug cap resistance . . . .   approx. 5 K-ohms

Torque wrench settings
Timing inspection cap . . . .   6 Nm

1 General information

All models are fitted with a fully transistorised electronic ignition system which, due to its lack of mechanical parts, is totally maintenance-free. The system comprises a trigger, a pulse generator coil, electronic control unit (ECU) and ignition coil (refer to *Wiring Diagrams* at the end of Chapter 10 for details).

The ignition trigger(s), on the alternator rotor on the right-hand end of the crankshaft, magnetically operate the pulse generator coil as the crankshaft rotates. The pulse generator coil sends a signal to the ECU, which then supplies the ignition coil with the power necessary to produce a spark at the plug. The signal also tells the ECU the speed of the engine.

The ECU incorporates an electronic advance system controlled by signals from the ignition trigger and pulse generator coil.

Because of their nature, the individual ignition system components can be checked but not repaired. If ignition system troubles occur, and the faulty component can be isolated, the only cure for the problem is to replace the part with a new one. Keep in mind that most electrical parts, once purchased, cannot be returned. To avoid unnecessary expense, make very sure the faulty component has been positively identified before buying a replacement part.

Note that there is no provision for adjusting the ignition timing.

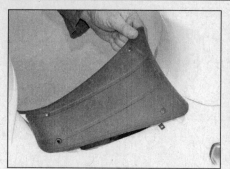

2.2a Remove the battery cover . . .

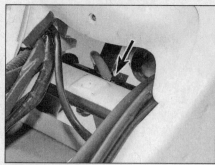

2.2b . . . then release the HT lead clip (arrowed)

2.3 Turn the cap so it is clear of the retainer arm (arrowed)

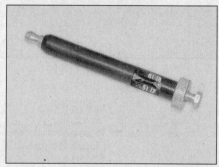

2.5 A typical spark gap testing tool

2 Ignition system check

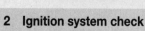

Warning: The energy levels in electronic systems can be very high. On no account should the ignition be switched on whilst the plug or plug cap is being held. Shocks from the HT circuit can be most unpleasant. Secondly, it is vital that the engine is not turned over or run with the plug cap removed, and that the plug is soundly earthed (grounded) when the system is checked for sparking. The ignition system components can be seriously damaged if the HT circuit becomes isolated.

1 As no means of adjustment is available, any failure of the system can be traced to failure of a system component or a simple wiring fault. Of the two possibilities, the latter is by far the most likely. In the event of failure, check the system in a logical fashion, as described below.

2 Remove the storage compartment (see Chapter 9). On LX, LXV and S models remove the engine access panel (see Chapter 9). On GTS, GTV and GT models remove the battery cover, then release the HT lead from the clip **(see illustrations)**.

3 If a spark plug cap retainer is fitted turn the plug cap clockwise so it is clear of the retainer arms **(see illustration)**. Pull the cap off the spark plug. On 2009 to 2011 LX, LXV and S models free the HT lead from its clip and slide the plug access cover off the engine cowl.

Warning: Do not remove the spark plug from the engine to perform this check – atomised fuel being pumped out of the open spark plug hole could ignite, causing severe injury! Make sure the plug is securely held against the engine – if it is not earthed when the engine is turned over, the ECU could be damaged.

4 Turn the ignition switch ON, and turn the engine over on the starter motor. If the system is in good condition a regular, fat blue spark should be seen at the plug electrodes. If the spark appears thin or yellowish, or is non-existent, further investigation is necessary.

5 The ignition system must be able to produce a spark which is capable of jumping a particular size gap – Vespa do not give a specification, but a healthy system should produce a spark capable of jumping at least 6 mm. Simple ignition spark gap testing tools are commercially available – follow the manufacturer's instructions **(see illustration)**.

6 If the test results are good the entire ignition system can be considered good. Fit the spark plug cap, making sure it locates correctly onto the plug, and turn it to locate in the retainer where fitted **(see illustration 2.3)**. On LX, LXV and S models, where applicable, fit the plug access cover onto the engine cowl and secure the HT lead in its clip. Fit the engine access panel. On GTS, GTV and GT models fit the HT lead into the clip, then fit the battery cover **(see illustrations 2.2b and a)**. Install the storage compartment (see Chapter 9).

7 Ignition faults can be divided into two categories, namely those where the ignition system has failed completely, and those which are due to a partial failure. The likely faults are listed below, starting with the most probable source. Work through the list systematically, referring to the subsequent sections for full details of the necessary checks and tests, to electrical system fault finding at the beginning of Chapter 10 and to the *Wiring Diagrams* at the end of it. **Note:** *Before checking the following items ensure that the battery is fully charged and that all fuses are in good condition.*

- *Loose, corroded or damaged wiring and connectors, broken or shorted wiring between any of the component parts of the ignition system (see Chapter 10).*
- *Faulty HT lead or spark plug cap, faulty spark plug, dirty, worn or corroded plug electrodes, or incorrect gap between electrodes.*
- *Faulty pulse generator coil or damaged trigger.*
- *Faulty ignition coil.*
- *Faulty ignition switch (see Chapter 10).*
- *Faulty load relay – see Chapter 5).*
- *Faulty electronic control unit (ECU) – see Chapter 5.*

8 If the above checks don't reveal the cause of the problem, have the ignition system tested by a Vespa dealer.

3 Ignition coil

Check

1 Make sure the ignition is off. Remove the coil (see Steps 9 to 12). Note that on 2012-on LX, LXV and S models, due to extremely restricted access to the coil, initial testing, other than a visual inspection, can be undertaken with the coil *in situ*.

2 Where possible, check the coil visually for loose or damaged connectors and terminals, cracks and other damage.

Primary winding test

3 Set an ohmmeter or multimeter to the ohms x 1 scale and measure the resistance between the primary terminals on the coil **(see illustration)**. This will give a resistance reading of the primary

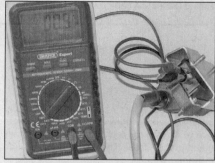

3.3 To test the coil primary resistance, connect the multimeter leads between the primary circuit terminals

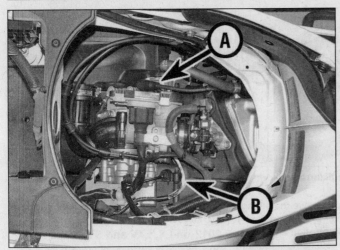

3.4a Location of the HT lead (A) and coil primary wiring (B)

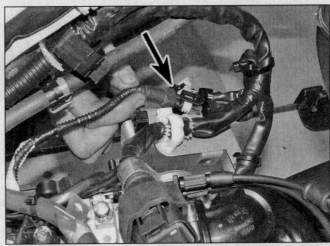

3.4b Disconnect the coil primary wiring connector (arrowed)

windings of the coil and it should be as specified at the beginning of the Chapter.

4 On 2012-on LX, LXV and S models, the coil is located underneath the throttle body assembly with the HT lead accessible on the left-hand side and the primary wiring accessible on the right-hand side (see illustration). Trace the primary wiring to the connector on the inside of the bodywork on the right-hand side and disconnect the connector (see illustration). Measure the resistance between the terminals on the coil side of the connector. Note that an incorrect reading may be due to damaged wiring or a poor connection at the coil in which case testing directly at the coil terminals will be necessary.

Secondary winding test

5 Set the meter to the K-ohm scale. Unscrew the cap from the HT lead (see illustration). Connect one meter probe to one of the primary terminals on the coil, and insert the other in the end of the lead (see illustration). This will give a resistance reading of the secondary windings of the coil and it should

be as specified at the beginning of the Chapter.

6 On 2012-on LX, LXV and S models, pull the HT lead out from the socket on the left-hand end of the coil (see illustration 3.18). Measure the secondary resistance by connecting one meter probe to one of the primary terminals in the connector and insert the other probe directly into the HT socket. Again, an incorrect reading will require confirmation once the coil is more accessible.

7 If the reading is as specified, measure the resistance of the spark plug cap by connecting the meter probes between the HT lead socket and the spark plug contact (see illustration). On LX, LXV and S models, with the HT lead removed, measure the resistance of the spark plug cap by connecting the meter probes between the HT lead coil terminal and the spark plug contact inside the cap. The reading should be around 5 K-ohms. If not replace the spark plug cap with a new one.

Checking for power to the coil

8 Check the coil wiring connector for loose or

broken terminal pins and wires. Connect the positive (+) lead of a voltmeter to the black/green wire terminal on the loom side of the connector and the negative (−) lead to the pink/black wire terminal. Switch the ignition ON whilst noting the reading obtained on the meter.

9 If battery voltage is present for a few seconds, the fuel injection circuit is operating correctly and there may be a fault with the

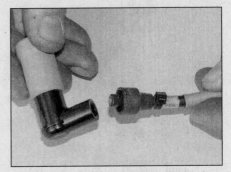

3.5a Unscrew the cap from the lead

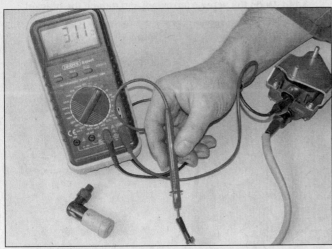

3.5b To test the coil secondary resistance connect the multimeter leads between a primary circuit terminal and the HT lead end

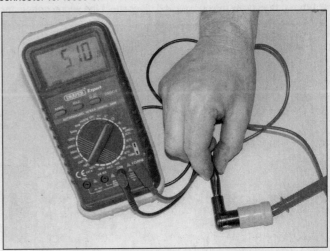

3.7 Measuring the resistance of the spark plug cap

fuel pump (refer to the wiring diagram for your machine at the end of Chapter 10).

10 If no reading is obtained, check the load relay and its circuit (see Chapter 5). If that is good check the black wire in the pump wiring connector has continuity to earth, and the black/green wire has continuity to the load relay wiring connector. Repair/replace the wiring as necessary and clean the connectors using electrical contact cleaner. If this fails to reveal the fault, the ECU could be faulty – at this point it may be best to have the system checked by a Vespa dealer.

Removal and installation

2009 to 2011 LX, LXV and S models and all GTS, GTV and GT models

11 On LX, LXV and S models, the coil is mounted above the alternator cover on the right-hand side of the engine – remove the storage compartment to access it, and also remove the outer access panel (see Chapter 9).
12 On GTS, GTV and GT models the coil is mounted under the floor panel on the right-hand side (see illustration) – remove the floor panel and the battery to access it (see

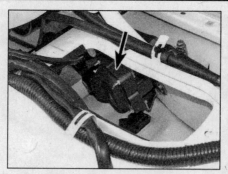

3.12 Ignition coil (arrowed)

Chapters 9 and 10). Also remove the storage compartment (see Chapter 9). Release the HT lead from the clip (see illustration 2.2b).
13 If a spark plug cap retainer is fitted turn the plug cap clockwise so it is clear of the retainer arms (see illustration 2.3). Pull the cap off the spark plug.
14 Unscrew the nuts securing the coil and remove the washers (see illustration). Displace the coil, then disconnect the primary wiring connector (see illustration). If required separate

3.14a Unscrew the nuts and remove the washers . . .

the coil from its bracket (see illustration).
15 Installation is the reverse of removal.

2012-on LX, LXV and S models

16 The coil is located underneath the throttle body assembly (see illustration 3.4a). First remove the storage compartment (see Chapter 9).
17 Follow the procedure in Chapter 5 to remove the intake duct and displace the throttle body from the intake manifold – it is not necessary to remove the manifold (see illustrations).

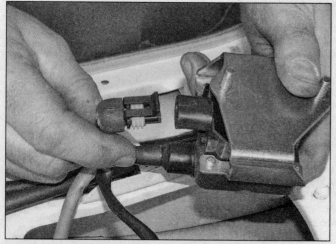

3.14b . . . then draw the coil out and disconnect the wiring connector

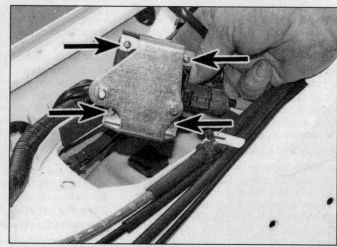

3.14c Undo the screws (arrowed) and detach the bracket

3.17a Displace the throttle body (arrowed) . . .

3.17b . . . to access the ignition coil (arrowed)

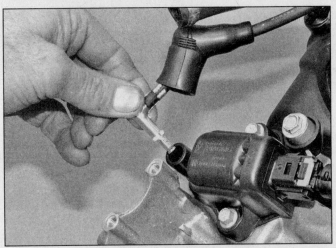

3.19 Pull out the HT lead terminal

3.21a Bolts (arrowed) secure the ignition coil

3.21b Release the catch on the wiring connector

4.1 Pulse generator coil connector (arrowed) – GTS/GTV/GT location shown

18 If required, remove the starter motor (see Chapter 10).

19 Pull the HT lead out from the socket on the left-hand end of the coil (see illustration).

20 Trace the coil primary wiring to the connector on the inside of the bodywork on the right-hand side and disconnect the connector (see illustration 3.4b).

21 Undo the bolts securing the coil and lift it off (see illustration). Release the catch on the primary wiring connector and disconnect it (see illustration).

22 The HT lead is secured to the left-hand side of the engine cowling with a tie – cut the tie then feed the lead through to the front of the engine to remove it.

23 Installation is the reverse of removal.

4 Pulse generator coil

Check

1 Remove the right-hand side panel and the storage compartment (see Chapter 9). Trace the wiring from the top of the alternator cover on the right-hand side of the engine and disconnect it at the connector with the red

and brown wires (there is also a pink/white wire) (see illustration).

2 Using a multimeter set to the ohms x 10 scale, measure the resistance between the red and brown wire terminals on the coil side of the connector – it should be as specified at the beginning of the Chapter. The important thing is that you do not get a zero or infinite reading. If the reading obtained is not as described, it is possible that the coil is defective.

3 If the reading is as specified then the fault must be in the wiring to the ECU. Check the wiring for continuity, referring to *Electrical System Fault Finding* at the beginning of Chapter 10 and to the *Wiring Diagrams* at the end of it. If the wiring is good, the ECU could be faulty.

Removal and installation

4 The pulse generator coil and alternator stator come as a unit. If the coil is faulty a new stator must be fitted as well. Refer to Chapter 2A, 2B or 2C according to engine type.

5 Ignition timing

1 Since no provision exists for adjusting the ignition timing and since no component is

subject to mechanical wear, there is no need for regular checks. Only if investigating a fault such as a loss of power or a misfire, should the ignition timing be checked.

2 The ignition timing is checked dynamically (engine running) using a stroboscopic lamp in conjunction with the Piaggio diagnostic tool – this is necessary as no ignition timing marks are provided to check the amount of advance. If you suspect a problem with the ignition timing take the scooter to a Vespa dealer.

6 Immobiliser

General information

1 An immobiliser system is fitted to most models. The system consists of a transponder which is part of the ignition key, a receiver which is fitted to the ignition switch, the ECU, and the LED in the instrument cluster. The system will only allow the scooter to be started if the master key or a correct registered key is used to turn the ignition ON. Under normal circumstances, when the ignition is turned OFF or the engine kill switch is set to OFF the LED flashes as a deterrent showing the system is active. The LED flashes for 48 hours, after which it turns off to save the battery, though obviously the system is still active. If the LED does not appear to be working check the instrument cluster (see Chapter 10).

2 When the ignition is switched ON using a standard registered key, the system performs a self-diagnosis, during which the LED will flash once for 0.7 sec, and when the ECU matches the code of the key being used with that stored in the ECU memory the LED will be off.

3 If the ignition is switched ON using the master key, the LED will flash once for 0.7 sec while diagnosis takes place, and then emit one or more 0.46 sec flashes, with the number of flashes indicating the number of

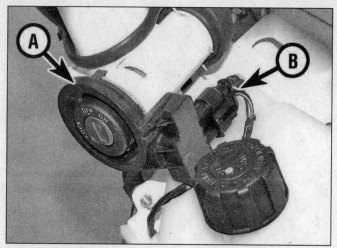

6.7a Immobiliser receiver (A) and its wiring connector (B) . . .

6.7b . . . the receiver simply clips around the ignition switch

keys registered in the system – there can be up to seven keys registered. After the series of flashes the LED will be off.

4 If there is a fault in the system, 2 secs after the initial 0.7 sec flash during diagnosis, the LED will flash for 0.5 sec either once, twice or three times (with a 0.5 sec gap between flashes), and 2 secs thereafter come on. The number of flashes indicates the fault code – see Steps 7 to 9 below.

5 The ECU stores the codes for the registered master key (which has a red head) and up to seven user keys (which have black heads). The master key should be kept in a safe place and not be used – if it is lost it is not possible to register any new user keys, so in the event they are also lost a new ECU must be installed. The user keys should be kept separately (i.e. not on the same key-ring) as the proximity of another key to the one being used in the switch can lead to the signal from it being jammed, and the bike will not start. The key has a built in transponder which can be damaged if the key is dropped or knocked, gets too hot, is too close to a high voltage circuit that is poorly earthed (such as the spark plug lead and/or cap not being properly connected), or a magnetic object, or is submerged in water for too long. Always make sure you have at least one spare key. If a new key is obtained, it must be registered into the system before the bike can be started. For additional security if a key is lost it is best have the key registration invalidated in the ECU – take along your master key and a spare key.

6 If a new throttle body assembly/ECU has

been installed and the ECU has not been programmed with a set of keys, any key can start the engine but engine speed is limited to 2000 rpm. If this is the case when the ignition is turned on the LED will come on for 2 secs, then go out – no self diagnosis is performed and the LED does not flash.

Fault codes

One flash

7 One flash indicates that the ECU has not detected a connection to the receiver. Remove the kick panel (see Chapter 9) and check the receiver wiring connector is securely connected, and check for damaged terminals or wires **(see illustrations)**. If necessary disconnect the battery (see Chapter 10), then remove the storage compartment and check the wiring between the receiver connector and the ECU connector for continuity, referring to *Electrical System Fault Finding* at the beginning of Chapter 10 and to the *Wiring Diagrams* at the end of it.

Two flashes

8 Two flashes indicate that the ECU has not received a signal from the receiver, either due to a faulty key transponder or a faulty receiver. Try using one or more of the other registered keys, and finally if necessary the master key. If the code is only shown with one key then that key is faulty – first try to re-register all keys as described in Step 10, and if that doesn't work obtain a new key and then register the keys. If the code is shown with all keys and the master key, first check the receiver wiring as in Step 7. If the wiring is good, all the keys are good and

the problem persists the ECU could be faulty – at this point consult a Vespa dealer.

Three flashes

9 Three flashes indicate that the ECU does not recognise the key being used. Try using one or more of the other registered keys, and finally if necessary the master key. If the code is only shown with one key then that key is faulty – re-register all keys as described in Step 10, and if that doesn't work obtain a new key and then register the keys. If the code is shown with all keys and the master key the ECU could be faulty – at this point consult a Vespa dealer.

Key registration procedure

10 Insert the master (red) key and turn the ignition on for two seconds (or to be precise no less than one second and no more than three), then turn the ignition off and remove the key. Within ten seconds insert a standard user (blue) key and turn the ignition on for two seconds, then turn the ignition off and remove the key. Repeat for any other user keys, up to a maximum of seven, making sure each is registered within ten seconds of the previous one. When all user keys have been registered insert the master (red) key, again within ten seconds, and turn the ignition on for two seconds, then turn the ignition off and remove the key. If you encounter a problem during the process, or fail to adhere to the time constraints specified, you must start the procedure again from the beginning.

11 If at a later point you need to register another key, the entire process of registering all keys including the master must be repeated along with the new key as described in Step 10.

Chapter 7
Steering and suspension

Contents

Degrees of difficulty

| Easy, suitable for novice with little experience | 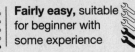 | Fairly easy, suitable for beginner with some experience | | Fairly difficult, suitable for competent DIY mechanic | | Difficult, suitable for experienced DIY mechanic | | Very difficult, suitable for expert DIY or professional | |

Specifications

Torque settings

Front brake master cylinder clamp bolts	10 Nm
Handlebar clamp bolt/nut.	45 to 50 Nm
Steering head bearing adjuster nut	
LX, LXV and S models	8 to 10 Nm
GTS, GTV and GT models	12 to 14 Nm
Steering head bearing locknut	35 to 40 Nm
Front shock absorber upper mounting bolts/nuts	20 to 30 Nm
Front shock absorber lower mounting bolts	20 to 27 Nm
Rear shock absorber upper mounting nut	20 to 25 Nm
Rear shock absorber lower mounting bolt/nut	
LX, LXV and S 2009 to 2011 models	33 to 41 Nm
LX, LXV and S 2012-on models	40 to 45 Nm
All GTS models.	33 to 41 Nm
Swingarm bolts	
LX, LXV and S 2009 to 2011 models	
Front bolt	33 to 41 Nm
Pivot bolt.	44 to 52 Nm
Engine bolt	33 to 41 Nm
LX, LXV and S 2012-on models	
Front bolt	40 to 45 Nm
Pivot bolt.	44 to 52 Nm
Engine bolt	40 to 45 Nm
GTS, GTV and GT models	
Swingarm section centre pivot bolt	33 to 41 Nm
Swingarm-to-frame pivot bolt.	76 to 83 Nm
Swingarm-to-engine pivot bolt.	64 to 72 Nm
Torsion plate bolts	33 to 41 Nm

2.2a Either release the clip and pull the connector out . . .

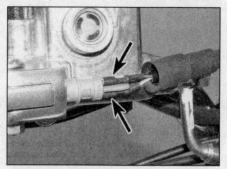

2.2b . . . or pull back the boot and pull the connectors (arrowed) off the terminals, according to model

2.4 Displace the master cylinder(s) from the handlebar

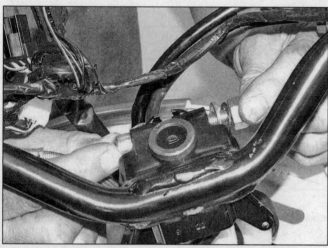

2.7a Unscrew the nut, withdraw the bolt . . .

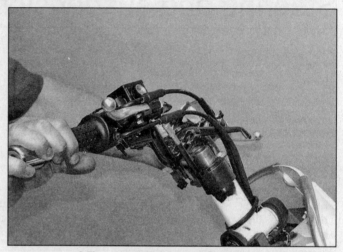

2.7b . . . and lift the handlebars off . . .

1 General information

Front suspension is by a single-sided trailing arm acting on a single shock absorber. The front suspension is not adjustable on any model.

At the rear, single or twin oil-damped shock absorbers are mounted between the engine unit and the frame. The shock absorbers are adjustable for spring preload.

2 Handlebars and levers

Handlebars

Removal

1 Remove the handlebar covers (see Chapter 9). If required, the handlebars can be displaced from the steering head for access to the bearings without having to detach anything – if this is the case, ignore the Steps which do not apply.

2 Disconnect the wiring from each brake light switch **(see illustrations)**.
3 Detach the throttle cable(s) from the twistgrip and slide the twistgrip off the end of the handlebar (see Chapter 5).
4 Unscrew the brake master cylinder clamp bolts and position the assembly clear of the handlebar, making sure no strain is placed on the hydraulic hose(s) **(see illustration)**. Keep the fluid reservoir upright to prevent air entering the system.
5 On models with a cable-operated rear

2.7c . . . resting them securely if required – we lodged a piece of wood as support

brake, remove the left-hand grip (peel the grip off the bar end, or if necessary cut it off), then detach the rear brake cable from the lever (see Chapter 8). Remove the bolt securing the rear brake lever bracket and slide it off the end of the handlebar.

6 If you are removing the handlebars completely, note how any wiring is secured to the handlebar, then release it.
7 Unscrew the clamp bolt nut, then withdraw the bolt, noting the washers, and lift the handlebars off the stem **(see illustrations)**. If the handlebar components have been left attached, position the handlebars so that no strain is placed on the cable(s), hose(s) or wiring **(see illustration)**.

Installation

8 Installation is the reverse of removal, noting the following.
- Tighten the nut on the handlebar clamp bolt to the torque setting specified at the beginning of the Chapter **(see illustration 2.7a)**.
- Do not forget to reconnect the brake light switch wiring connectors **(see illustration 2.2a or b)**.
- Use a suitable adhesive between the left-hand grip and the handlebar.

Brake levers

9 Unscrew the lever pivot bolt locknut, then withdraw the pivot bolt and remove the lever **(see illustrations)**. If applicable, detach the brake cable from the lever as you remove it.
10 Installation is the reverse of removal. Apply grease to the pivot bolt shank and the contact areas between the lever and its bracket, and to the brake cable nipple (where applicable).

3 Steering stem

Special tool: *Either the Vespa service tool (No. 020055Y) or a home-made equivalent is required to apply the torque setting for the steering head bearing adjuster nut.*

Removal

1 Remove the front wheel (see Chapter 8) and the handlebars (see Section 2). If required remove the shock absorber (see Section 5), and the front wheel hub and shock absorber/caliper bracket (see Chapter 8).
2 If not already done displace the brake caliper and secure it with a cable-tie to avoid straining the hydraulic hose (see Chapter 8) – note that there is no need to disconnect the hydraulic hose unless you want to remove the front mudguard. Detach the speedometer cable from the wheel hub (see Chapter 10).
3 Remove the suspension cover **(see illustrations)**. Unscrew the front mudguard nuts **(see illustration)**.

2.9a Unscrew the nut (arrowed) . . .

2.9b . . . and the pivot bolt . . .

2.9c . . . and remove the lever . . .

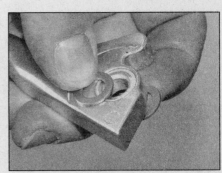

2.9d . . . noting the washers where fitted

4 Release the speedometer cable and brake hose clips.
5 On GTS, GTV and GT models remove the bearing cap **(see illustration)**.
6 Unscrew and remove the bearing adjuster

locknut using either a suitable C-spanner, a peg-spanner or a drift located in one of the notches **(see illustration)**. Remove the washer, noting how it fits **(see illustration)**. Supporting the steering stem, unscrew the

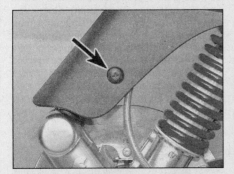

3.3a Undo the screw (arrowed) on the outside . . .

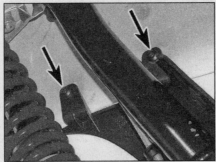

3.3b . . . and the two on the inside and remove the cover

3.3c Unscrew the nuts (arrowed)

3.5 Remove the bearing cap

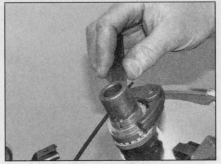

3.6a Unscrew the locknut . . .

3.6b . . . and remove the washer

3.6c Unscrew the adjuster nut . . .

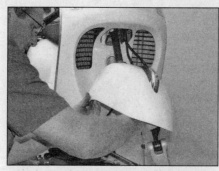

3.7 . . . then carefully lower the steering stem and draw it out of the mudguard

3.8a Remove the upper bearing . . .

3.8b . . . and the lower bearing

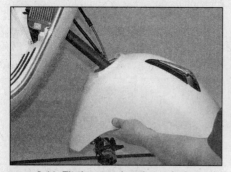

3.11 Fit the steering through the mudguard, secure the mudguard, then fit the stem up through the head

3.12a Fit the adjuster nut . . .

adjuster nut using either a C-spanner, a peg-spanner or a drift located in one of the notches **(see illustration)**.

7 Gently lower the steering stem out of the frame then draw it out of the mudguard and retrieve the screws **(see illustration)**. If the brake hose has been detached from the caliper you can now remove the mudguard.

8 Remove the upper bearing from the top of the steering head and the lower bearing from the steering stem **(see illustrations)**. Remove all traces of old grease from the bearings and races and check them for wear or damage as described in Section 4. **Note:** *Do not attempt to remove the outer races from the frame or the lower bearing inner race from the steering stem unless they are to be replaced with new ones.*

Installation

9 Smear a liberal quantity of grease on the bearing outer races in the frame. Also grease both the upper and lower bearings. Fit the upper and lower bearings **(see illustration 3.8a and b)**.

10 If the mudguard was removed feed the brake hose and speedometer cable through it.

11 Carefully fit the steering stem up through the mudguard, then fit the mudguard screws and finger tighten the nuts **(see illustration)**.

12 Fit the steering stem up through the steering head. Thread the adjuster nut onto the steering stem **(see illustration)**. Tighten the adjuster nut to the torque setting specified at the beginning of the Chapter, using either the Vespa special tool (part No. 020055Y), or a suitable old socket fabricated into a peg spanner **(see illustration)**. Check the adjustment as described in Chapter 1 **(see illustration)**. If it is not possible to apply a torque wrench to the adjuster nut, tighten the nut so the stem is secure (i.e. so any freeplay is just taken up) **(see illustration)**, then adjust the bearings as described in Chapter 1 after the installation of the hub, shock absorber and wheel etc, and on LX, LXV and S models only the handlebars, is complete.

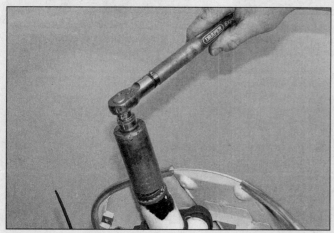

3.12b . . . and tighten it to the specified torque if a tool is available . . .

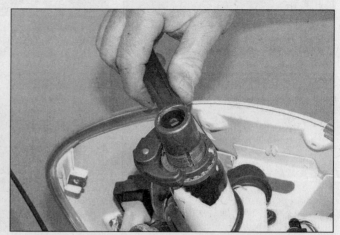

3.12c . . . or using a C-spanner or drift as described if not

Caution: Take great care not to apply excessive pressure because this will cause premature failure of the bearings.

13 When the bearings are correctly adjusted, fit the washer, making sure the tab locates in the slot on the steering stem (see illustration). Fit the locknut and tighten it to the specified torque setting, using the same tool as above, if available (see illustration).

14 Install the remaining components, then carry out a check of the steering head bearing freeplay as described in Chapter 1, and if necessary re-adjust.

4 Steering head bearings

Inspection

1 Remove the steering stem (see Section 3).
2 Remove all traces of old grease from the bearings and races and check them for wear or damage. The races should be polished and free from indentations – the outer races are in the steering head, the inner race for the upper bearing is on the underside of the adjuster nut (see illustration 3.12a), and the inner race for the lower bearing is on the steering stem (see illustrations).
3 Inspect the bearings for signs of wear, damage or discoloration, and examine the bearing cages for signs of cracks or splits (see illustrations 3.8a and b). Fit each bearing onto each of its races and turn it by hand to check for roughness and indentations

3.13a Locate the tab on the inner rim of the washer in the slot in the stem

in the race. If there are any signs of wear on any of the above components both upper and lower bearing assemblies must be renewed as a set. Only remove the races if they are being replaced with new ones – do not re-use them once they have been removed.

Renewal

4 The outer races are an interference fit in the frame and can be tapped from position with a suitable drift (see illustrations). Tap firmly and evenly around each race to ensure that it is driven out squarely. It may prove advantageous to curve the end of the drift slightly to improve access.
5 Alternatively, the races can be pulled out using a slide-hammer with internal expanding extractor.
6 The new outer races can be pressed into the frame using a drawbolt arrangement (see illustration), or by using a large diameter

3.13b Fit and tighten the locknut

tubular drift which bears only on the outer edge of the race. Ensure that the drawbolt washer or drift (as applicable) bears only on the outer edge of the race and does not contact the working surface. Alternatively, have the races installed by a Vespa dealer equipped with the bearing race installing tools.

> **HAYNES HiNT**
> *Installation of new bearing outer races is made much easier if the races are left overnight in the freezer. This causes them to contract slightly making them a looser fit.*

7 To remove the lower bearing inner race from the steering stem, use two screwdrivers placed on opposite sides of the race to work it free. If the bearing is firmly in place it will be necessary to use a bearing puller, or drive a chisel between the underside of the race and

4.2a Check the races (arrowed) . . .

4.2b . . . for wear and damage

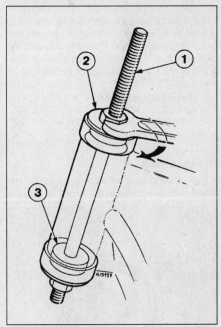

4.6 Drawbolt arrangement for fitting steering stem bearing races

1 Long bolt or threaded bar
2 Thick washer
3 Guide for lower race

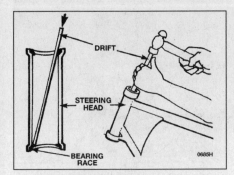

4.4a Drive the bearing races out with a brass drift . . .

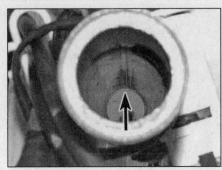

4.4b . . . locating it against the exposed rim (arrowed)

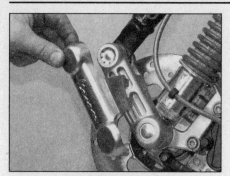

5.1a Remove the trim

5.1b Detach the brake hose guide (arrowed)

5.2a Unscrew the nuts (arrowed) . . .

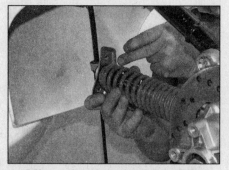

5.2b . . . then draw the shock off the studs . . .

5.2c . . . and unscrew the bolts

the bearing seat. Take the steering stem to a Vespa dealer if required. Check the condition of the seat that fits under the race and fit a new one it if necessary.

8 Fit the new lower inner race bearing onto the steering stem (see illustration 4.2b). A length of tubing with an internal diameter slightly larger than the steering stem will be needed to tap the new bearing into position. Ensure that the drift bears only on the inner edge of the race and does not contact its working surface.

9 Install the steering stem (see Section 3).

5 Front suspension

Disassembly

1 Remove the front wheel and if required the wheel hub (see Chapter 8 – note that there is

no need to remove the hub if only the shock absorber is being removed, but there is if you intend to remove the brake caliper/shock absorber mounting bracket and trailing link arm as well). Remove the suspension cover (see illustrations 3.3a and b). Remove the trailing link trim (see illustration). Release the brake hose guide from the steering stem (see illustration).

2 Slacken the two bolts securing the bottom of the shock absorber to the bracket. Unscrew the two nuts securing the top to the steering stem, noting how one secures the brake hose guide (see illustration). Lower the trailing link, drawing the shock off its upper studs (see illustration). Unscrew the two bolts securing the bottom of the shock absorber to the bracket, noting the washers (see illustration). Remove the shock absorber.

3 Check for any play and roughness in the bearings between the wheel axle and the

brake caliper/shock absorber mounting bracket. If required remove the circlip and inner washer and slide the bracket off the axle (see illustrations). Remove the outer washer and the O-ring.

4 Check for any play and roughness in the bearings between the trailing link arm and the steering stem. If any roughness is felt or the arm does not move smoothly and freely, or play is felt between the arm and the stem, the bearings and spacer pin must be replaced with new ones. If the bearings and pin are good, there is no need to separate the trailing link arm from the steering stem, unless required for other purposes.

5 To remove the trailing link arm, first remove the wheel hub assembly (see Chapter 8) and the brake caliper/shock absorber mounting bracket as described in Step 3. To separate the arm from the steering stem, remove the sprung star washer from each side of the arm (see illustration). The washers can be removed either by hitting them centrally with a suitable punch or drift, which should be wide enough to cover the raised inner section of the washer, or be levering up the outer tangs of the washer with a suitable screwdriver. Discard the washers, as new ones must be used.

6 Drive or press out the bearing spacer pin from the middle of the arm and separate the arm from the stem. Remove the O-rings and dust seals.

Inspection

7 Thoroughly clean all components, removing all traces of dirt, corrosion and grease. Inspect

5.3a Release the circlip (arrowed) and remove the washer behind it . . .

5.3b . . . then draw the bracket off and remove the washer and O-ring (arrowed)

5.5 Remove the star washer (arrowed) from each side as described

5.9 Check the rod (arrowed) for pitting and oil

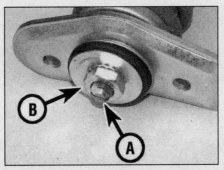

5.10 Hold the stud (A) and unscrew the nut (B)

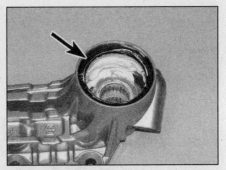

5.11a Check the large seal (arrowed) on the inner side . . .

5.11b . . . the small seal . . .

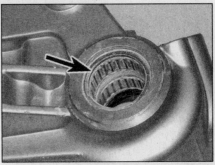

5.11c . . . and the bearings (arrowed)

all components closely, looking for obvious signs of wear such as heavy scoring, or for damage such as cracks or distortion.

8 Inspect the shock absorber for obvious physical damage and the coil spring for looseness, cracks or signs of fatigue.

9 Inspect the damper rod for signs of bending, pitting and oil leakage **(see illustration)**.

10 Inspect the mountings at the top and bottom of the shock for wear or damage. If necessary the top mount can be disassembled for replacement of the rubber bushes, or if a new shock absorber is being fitted. Counter-hold the stud using a screwdriver in the slot and unscrew the nut, then remove the washers, bush, mounting plate and bush, noting their correct fitted order and way round **(see illustration)**.

11 Visually check the condition of the seals and needle roller bearings in the trailing link arm and the brake caliper/shock absorber mounting bracket **(see illustrations)**.

12 Worn bearings can be drifted out of their bores, but note that removal will destroy them; new components should be obtained before work commences. Before removing the bearings, carefully measure or mark their set depth within the bore so that the new ones can be correctly installed. The new ones should be pressed or drawn into their bores rather than driven into position. In the absence of a press, a suitable drawbolt arrangement can be made up as described below.

13 Obtain a long bolt or a length of threaded rod from a local engineering works or some other supplier. The bolt or rod should be about

one inch longer than the combined width of the arm and one bearing. Also required are suitable nuts and two large and robust washers having a larger outside diameter than the bearing housing. In the case of the threaded rod, fit one nut to one end of the rod and stake it in place for convenience.

14 Fit one of the washers over the bolt or rod so that it rests against the head or staked nut, then pass the assembly through the bore. Over the projecting end place the bearing, which should be greased to ease installation, followed by the remaining washer and nut.

15 Holding the bearing to ensure that it is kept square, slowly tighten the nut so that the bearing is drawn into its bore.

16 Once it is fully home, remove the drawbolt arrangement and repeat the procedure to fit the other bearing.

17 Lubricate the needle roller bearings with molybdenum disulphide grease.

18 Fit new seals **(see illustrations 5.11a and b)**.

Reassembly

19 Lubricate the trailing link arm bearing spacer pin with molybdenum disulphide grease. Align the trailing link arm with the steering stem and drive or press the pin through the arm and stem.

20 Fit the new sprung star washers and drive them into place using a piece of tubing that bears only on the section between the raised inner section and the raised outer tangs **(see illustration 5.5)**.

21 Lubricate the axle and bearings in the brake caliper/shock absorber mounting bracket with grease. Fit a new O-ring over the trailing link arm and position it as shown **(see illustration)**. Fit the outer washer **(see illustration)**. Slide the brake caliper/shock absorber mounting bracket onto the axle, then

5.21a Place the new O-ring (arrowed) as shown

5.21b Slide on the outer washer . . .

5.21c . . . the bracket . . .

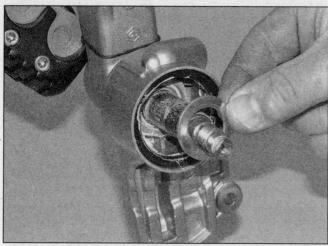

5.21d . . . and the inner washer . . .

5.21e . . . then fit the circlip into the groove

fit the inner washer and the circlip, making sure it sits properly in its groove **(see illustrations)**. Seat the O-ring into the gap between the bracket and the arm **(see illustration)**.

22 Install the shock absorber and tighten the nuts and bolts to the torque settings specified at the beginning of the Chapter **(see illustrations 5.2c, b and a)** – do not forget to secure the brake hose guide with the nut.

23 Refit the brake hose guide onto the steering stem **(see illustration 5.1b)**. Install the hub assembly and the front wheel (see Chapter 8). Fit the trim and covers **(see illustrations 5.1a and 3.3a and b)**.

6 Rear shock absorber(s)

Removal

1 Support the scooter on its centrestand, then position a support under the rear wheel so that the engine does not drop when the shock absorber(s) is/are removed. Check that the weight of the machine is off the rear suspension so that the shock is not compressed. Check for any offset in the bottom mounting lug on the shock absorber(s) and note which way the offset faces for correct installation.

2 On LX, LXV and S models remove the battery (see Chapter 10).

3 On GTS, GTV and GT models remove the grab-rail or rear carrier (see Chapter 9) and the exhaust system (see Chapter 5).

4 The lower end of the shock absorber is secured to the gearbox casing on the left-hand side – unscrew the nut and withdraw the bolt to release it **(see illustration)**.

5 On GTS, GTV and GT models the right-hand shock is secured to a lug on the right-hand sub-frame – unscrew the nut and remove the washer, then pull the shock off the lug **(see illustrations)**.

6 The upper end of the shock absorber is secured to the frame by a nut and washer assembly with a rubber bush. Position a ring spanner on the nut and hold the centre of the stud with a screwdriver to prevent the shock turning, then undo the nut and remove the washer(s) and bush, then lower and remove the shock, noting any washer fitted between the top of the shock and the underside of the body **(see illustration)**. Note the collars fitted in the bottom mount on the left-hand shock on GTS, GTV and GT models **(see illustration 6.10)**.

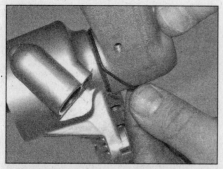

5.21f Now seat the O-ring around the bracket to arm joint

6.4 Unscrew the nut and withdraw the bolt

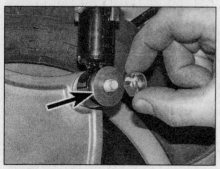

6.5a Unscrew the nut and remove the washer (arrowed) . . .

6.5b . . . then pull the shock off

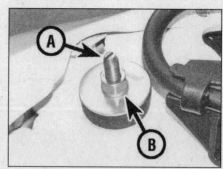

6.6 Hold the stud (A) and unscrew the nut (B)

6.10 Make sure the collars are in place

Inspection

Note: *Always renew shock absorbers as a pair (models with twin shocks).*

7 Inspect the shock absorber for obvious physical damage and the coil spring for looseness, cracks or signs of fatigue, and replace it with a new one if necessary.

8 Inspect the damper rod for signs of bending, pitting and oil leaks, and replace the shock with a new one if necessary **(see illustration 5.9).**

9 Inspect the pivot hardware at the top and bottom of the shock for wear or damage. Check the rubber bush for splits and hardening. The mounting components and rubber bushes are available separately.

Installation

10 Installation is the reverse of removal. Make sure the shock absorber is fitted the correct way round as noted in Step 1. Make sure the collars are fitted in the bottom mount on the left-hand shock on GTS, GTV and GT model **(see illustration).** Tighten the shock absorber mountings to the torque settings specified at the beginning of the Chapter.

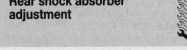

7   Rear shock absorber adjustment

1 Preload adjustment is made using a suitable

7.1 Adjusting the preload with the toolkit C-spanner

C-spanner (one is provided in the toolkit) to turn the spring seat on the bottom of the shock absorber **(see illustration).** Make adjustments when there is no load on the shock.

2 Align the setting required with the adjustment stopper. To increase the preload, turn the spring seat clockwise. To decrease the preload, turn the spring seat anti-clockwise.

3 On twin-shock models, ensure the preload adjustment is the same on both shocks.

8   Swingarm

LX, LXV and S models

Removal

1 Remove the access panel and the floor panel trim panels (see Chapter 9). Remove the rubber blanking caps from the underside and from each side of the scooter.

2 Unscrew the nut and withdraw the front bolt, collecting the washers.

3 Unscrew the nuts on the end of the pivot bolt and engine bolt – note the washer with the pivot bolt. Fit washers between the coils of the spring as shown **(see illustration 8.13a)** –

this holds the spring expanded and makes it easier to remove and install. Carefully unhook the spring.

4 Withdraw the bolts and remove the swing-arm, noting how it fits.

Inspection

5 Thoroughly clean all components, removing all traces of dirt, corrosion and grease.

6 Inspect all components closely, looking for obvious signs of wear such as heavy scoring, and cracks or distortion due to accident damage.

7 Check the bushes and damping rubber for cracks and deterioration. Check the spring for distortion and sag.

8 Check the swingarm pivot bolt and the engine mounting bolt are straight by rolling them on a flat surface such as a piece of plate glass (first wipe off all old grease and remove any corrosion using fine emery cloth).

9 If there are any signs of damage or wear to the swingarm itself or to the bushes fit a new swingarm. Replace other individual components as required.

Installation

10 Installation is the reverse of removal. Smear some grease onto the pivot bolt before assembly and tighten all bolts to the torque settings specified at the beginning of the Chapter.

11 Check the operation of the rear suspension before taking the machine on the road.

GTS, GTV and GT models

Removal

12 Remove the engine (see Chapter 2B).

13 Fit washers between the coils of the spring as shown **(see illustration)** – this holds the spring expanded and makes it easier to remove and install. Carefully unhook the spring. Release the coolant hose from the clips on the left-hand side of the swingarm **(see illustration).**

14 Remove the blanking caps from each side

8.13a Fit washers between the coils to keep the spring extended

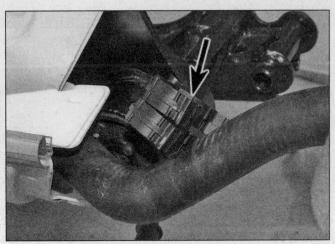

8.13b Release the hose from the clips (arrowed)

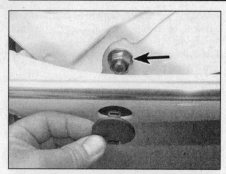

8.14a Remove the cap from each side, then undo the nut (arrowed) . . .

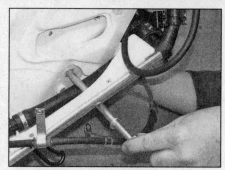

8.14b . . . and withdraw the bolt

8.14c Unscrew the bolts (arrowed) . . .

8.14d . . . and remove the swingarm

8.16 Check the clearance using a feeler gauge

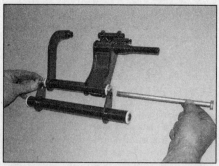

8.18a Unscrew nut, withdraw the centre pivot bolt and separate the sections

of the scooter (see illustration). Undo the nut on the swingarm-to-frame pivot bolt and withdraw the bolt (see illustration). Undo the torsion plate bolts and remove the swingarm (see illustration).

Inspection

15 Thoroughly clean all components, removing all traces of dirt, corrosion and grease.
16 Check the clearance between the two swinging sections using a feeler gauge – the standard amount is 0.4 to 0.6 mm, and the service limit is 1.5 mm (see illustration).
17 Inspect all components closely, looking for obvious signs of wear such as heavy scoring, and cracks or distortion due to accident damage. Make sure the two sections pivot smoothly and freely.
18 If required undo the centre pivot bolt and withdraw it to separate the swinging arm sections (see illustration). Remove the pivot caps and withdraw the long spacer (see illustrations).
19 If required remove the circlip and slide the torsion plate off the main arm (see illustration). Remove the spacing bush (see illustration).
20 Check the various bushes, bearings and seals for wear, cracks and deterioration (see

8.18b Remove the caps . . .

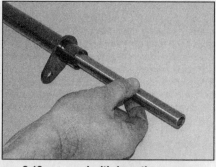

8.18c . . . and withdraw the spacer

8.19a Remove the circlip . . .

8.19b . . . slide the torsion plate off . . .

8.19c . . . and remove the bush

8.20a Check the bearings (arrowed) . . .

8.20b . . . and bushes (arrowed)

illustrations). The silentbloc bush in the torsion plate and all other bushes, bearings and spacers can be replaced with new ones, but check with a Vespa dealer as to the availability of components, and whether it may be cheaper and easier to just fit a complete new swingarm assembly. Bushes and bearings must be driven out, after which they cannot be re-used. A drawbolt arrangement is needed to remove and fit the silentbloc in the torsion plate.

21 Check the swingarm pivot bolt(s) and the engine mounting bolt for straightness by rolling them on a flat surface such as a piece of plate glass (first wipe off all old grease and remove any corrosion using fine emery cloth).

22 Check the spring for distortion and sag.

Installation

23 Assembly and installation is the reverse of removal. Smear some grease onto the spacers, bearings and pivot bolt before

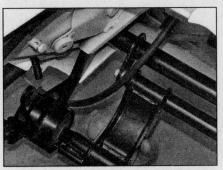

8.23a Make sure the hose is correctly routed . . .

8.23b . . . and the torsion plate and front pivot are correctly aligned

assembly and tighten the bolts to the torque settings specified at the beginning of the Chapter. Make sure the rear brake hose is correctly routed as you fit the swingarm **(see illustration)**, and the holes in the torsion plate and swingarm for the swingarm-to-frame bolt are aligned before inserting the bolt **(see illustration)**.

24 Check the operation of the rear suspension before taking the machine on the road.

Chapter 8
Brakes, wheels and tyres

Contents

Degrees of difficulty

Easy, suitable for novice with little experience	Fairly easy, suitable for beginner with some experience	Fairly difficult, suitable for competent DIY mechanic	Difficult, suitable for experienced DIY mechanic	Very difficult, suitable for expert DIY or professional

Specifications

Disc brakes

Brake fluid type . . . . DOT 4
Brake pad lining minimum thickness . . . . 1.5 mm
Disc diameter
    LX, LXV and S models . . . . 200 mm
    GTS, GTV and GT models (front and rear) . . . . 220 mm
Disc thickness
    Standard . . . . 3.8 to 4.2 mm
    Service limit . . . . 3.5 mm
Disc maximum runout . . . . 0.1 mm

Rear drum brake

Brake shoe lining minimum thickness . . . . 1.5 mm
Drum diameter (standard) . . . . 110 mm

Wheels

Maximum wheel runout (front and rear)
    Axial (side-to-side) . . . . 2 mm
    Radial (out-of-round) . . . . 2 mm
Maximum axle runout (front) . . . . 0.2 mm

Tyres

Tyre pressures . . . . see Pre-ride checks
Tyre sizes*
    LX, LXV and S models
        Front . . . . 110/70-11 45L Tubeless
        Rear . . . . 120/70-10 54L Tubeless
    GTS, GTV and GT models
        Front . . . . 120/70-12 51P Tubeless
        Rear . . . . 130/70-12 62P Tubeless

*Refer to the owners handbook or the tyre information label for approved tyre brands.

Torque settings

Brake disc bolts
   Front . . . . 6 Nm
   Rear . . . . 12 Nm
Brake hose banjo bolts. . . . . 22 Nm
Exhaust bracket bolts (GTS, GTV and GT). . . . . 20 to 25 Nm
Front hub nut . . . . 74 to 88 Nm
Front wheel bolts . . . . 20 to 25 Nm
Front brake caliper mounting bolts
   LX, LXV and S models . . . . 20 to 25 Nm
   GTS, GTV and GT models . . . . 24 to 27 Nm
Front brake pad retaining pins (GTS, GTV and GT) . . . . 20 to 24 Nm
Rear axle nut . . . . 104 to 126 Nm
Rear wheel bolts (GTS, GTV and GT). . . . . 20 to 25 Nm
Rear brake caliper mounting bolts (GTS, GTV and GT) . . . . 20 to 25 Nm
Rear shock absorber lower mounting bolt nut. . . . . 33 to 41 Nm

1 General information

All models covered in this manual have an hydraulically operated front disc brake, with an opposed piston caliper on LX, LXV and S models, and a twin piston sliding caliper on GTS, GTV and GT models. At the rear LX, LXV and S models have a drum brake, and GTS, GTV and GT models have an hydraulic disc brake with an opposed piston caliper. The right-hand brake lever operates the front brake and the left-hand lever operates the rear.

All models are fitted with cast alloy wheels designed for tubeless tyres only.
Caution: Do not disassemble the hydraulic brake caliper(s) or master cylinder(s). Do not loosen or disconnect a brake hose unless absolutely necessary. If a hose is loosened or disconnected, the union sealing washers must be replaced with new ones and the system bled upon reassembly. Use care when working with brake fluid as it can injure your eyes and it will damage painted surfaces and plastic parts.

2 Brake pads

⚠️ **Warning: The dust created by the brake system is harmful to your health. Never blow it out with compressed air and don't inhale any of it. An approved filtering mask should be worn when working on the brakes.**

Removal

LX, LXV and S models – front pads

1 Remove the front wheel (see Section 12).
2 Remove the pad cover where fitted **(see illustration)**. Remove the clip from the pad retaining pin **(see illustration 2.11)**.
3 Partially drive the pin out from the inner side using a suitable drift **(see illustration 2.12)**.
4 Unscrew the caliper mounting bolts and slide the caliper off the disc **(see illustration 2.13)**. Free the brake hose guide to give more freedom of movement if required.
5 Withdraw the pin and remove the spring **(see illustration 2.14a)**. Lift the pads out of the caliper **(see illustration 2.14b)**. **Note:** *Do not operate the brake lever while the pads are out of the caliper.*

GTS, GTV and GT models – front pads

6 Remove the front wheel (see Section 12).
7 Slacken the pad retaining pins **(see illustration)**.
8 Unscrew the caliper mounting bolts and slide the caliper off the disc **(see illustration)**. Free the brake hose guide to give more freedom of movement if required.
9 Unscrew and remove the pad pins, then remove the pads, noting how they fit **(see illustration)**. **Note:** *Do not operate the brake lever while the pads are out of the caliper.*

GTS, GTV and GT models – rear pads

10 Remove the rear wheel (see Section 13). Free the two brake hose guides from the transmission cover **(see illustration)**.

2.2 Remove the pad cover

2.7 Slacken the pins (arrowed)

2.8 Unscrew the bolts (arrowed) and displace the caliper

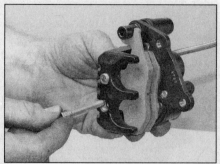

2.9 Withdraw the pad pins and remove the pads

2.10 Unscrew the bolts (arrowed) and free the guides

2.11 Remove the clip from the pin

2.12 Displace the pin using a punch

2.13 Unscrew the bolts (arrowed) and displace the caliper

11 Remove the pad cover where fitted **(see illustration 2.2)**. Remove the clip from the pad retaining pin **(see illustration)**.
12 Partially drive the pin out from the inner side using a suitable drift **(see illustration)**.
13 Unscrew the caliper mounting bolts and slide the caliper off the disc **(see illustration)**.
14 Withdraw the pin and remove the spring **(see illustration)**. Lift the pads out of the caliper **(see illustration)**. Note: *Do not operate the brake lever while the pads are out of the caliper.*

Inspection

15 Inspect the surface of each pad for contamination and check that the friction material has not worn beyond its service limit (see Chapter 1). On GTS, GTV and GT models make sure the pad has worn evenly across its surface – uneven wear is indicative of a sticking piston (see Steps 20 and 21). If either pad is worn down to, or beyond, the service limit wear indicator, is fouled with oil or grease, or heavily scored or damaged, fit a set of new pads. **Note:** *It is not possible to degrease the friction material; if the pads are contaminated in any way they must be replaced with new ones.*
16 If the pads are in good condition clean them carefully, using a fine wire brush which is completely free of oil and grease to remove all traces of road dirt and corrosion. Using a pointed instrument, dig out any embedded particles of foreign matter. If available, spray with a dedicated brake cleaner to remove any dust.
17 Check the condition of the brake disc (see Section 4).
18 Remove all traces of corrosion from the pad pin(s) and check for wear and damage. Where fitted check the clip for distortion and replace it with a new one if necessary.
19 On the front caliper on GTS, GTV and GT models slide the caliper off the bracket **(see illustration)**. Clean off all traces of corrosion and hardened grease from the slider pins and boots. Make sure the slider pins are tight. Apply a smear of silicone-based grease to the boots and slider pins.
20 Clean around the exposed section of each piston to remove any dirt or debris that could cause the seals to be damaged. If new pads

2.14a Withdraw the pin and remove the spring . . .

2.14b . . . then remove the pads

are being fitted, push the pistons all the way back into the caliper to create room for them; if the old pads are still serviceable push the pistons in a little way. To push the pistons back use finger pressure or a piece of wood as leverage, or place the old pads back in the

caliper and use a metal bar or a screwdriver inserted between them, or use grips and a piece of wood, with rag or card to protect the caliper body **(see illustration)**. Alternatively obtain a proper piston-pushing tool from a good tool supplier **(see illustration)**. If there

2.19 Slide the caliper and bracket apart

2.20a Push the pistons in using your fingers . . .

2.20b . . . a suitable improvised tool . . .

2.20c . . . or a proper piston pushing tool

2.29 Make sure the spring (arrowed) is correctly located

2.31b ... then the inner pad, locating the half-circle end against the post

is too much brake fluid in the reservoir it may be necessary to remove the master cylinder reservoir cover and diaphragm and siphon some out (see *Pre-ride checks*). If the pistons are difficult to push back, remove the bleed valve cap, then attach a length of clear hose to the bleed valve and place the open end in a suitable container, then open the valve and try again (see Section 7). Take great care not to draw any air into the system. If in doubt, bleed the brake afterwards.

21 If a piston appears seized, first block or hold the other piston(s) using wood or cable-ties, then apply the brake lever and check whether the piston in question moves at all. If it moves out but can't be pushed back in the chances are there is some hidden corrosion stopping it. If it doesn't move at all, fit a new caliper (see Section 3).

2.38 Make sure the pin passes over the spring

2.31a Fit the outer pad ...

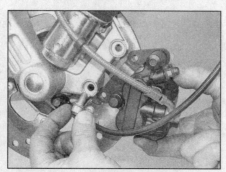

2.32 Slide the caliper onto the disc and fit the bolts

Installation

LX, LXV and S models

22 Lightly smear the back and edges of the pad backing material with copper-based grease, making sure that none gets on the friction material. Smear some copper grease over the pad retaining pin.
23 Fit the pads into the caliper (**see illustration 2.14b**). Locate the pad spring on the pads and insert the pin (**see illustration 2.14a**). Push the pin in as far as possible making sure it fits over the spring and in the groove (**see illustration 2.38**).
24 Slide the caliper onto the disc making sure the pads locate correctly on each side (**see illustration 2.39**). Install the caliper mounting bolts and tighten them to the torque setting specified at the beginning of the Chapter. Fit the brake hose guide if displaced.

2.39 Slide the caliper onto the disc and fit the bolts

25 Drive the pad pin fully home using a suitable drift. Fit the clip, using a new one if necessary, and with the open end facing up (**see illustration 2.11**).
26 Operate the brake lever until the pads contact the disc. Check the level of fluid in the hydraulic reservoir and top-up if necessary (see *Pre-ride checks*).
27 Fit the pad cover (**see illustration 2.2**). Install the wheel (see Section 12).
28 Check the operation of the front brake before riding the scooter.

GTS, GTV and GT models – front pads

29 Make sure the pad spring is correctly located in the caliper (**see illustrations**). Slide the caliper onto the bracket (**see illustration 2.19**) – make sure the rim of each boot locates correctly around the base of its slider pin.
30 Lightly smear the back of each pad, the sliding edges of the inner pad, and the half-circle of the outer pad, with copper-based grease, making sure that none gets on the friction material.
31 Fit the pads into the caliper, making sure they locate correctly (**see illustrations**). Smear some copper grease over the pad retaining pins, and apply a drop of medium strength thread locking compound to the threads. Push the pads up against the spring to align the holes and insert the pins, then tighten them finger-tight (**see illustration 2.9**).
32 Slide the caliper onto the disc making sure the pads locate correctly on each side (**see illustration**). Install the caliper mounting bolts and tighten them to the torque setting specified at the beginning of the Chapter. Fit the brake hose guides if displaced.
33 Tighten the pad pins to the torque setting specified at the beginning of this Chapter (**see illustration 2.7**).
34 Operate the brake lever until the pads contact the disc. Check the level of fluid in the hydraulic reservoir and top-up if necessary (see *Pre-ride checks*).
35 Install the wheel (see Section 12).
36 Check the operation of the front brake before riding the scooter.

GTS, GTV and GT models – rear pads

37 Lightly smear the back and edges of the pad backing material with copper-based grease, making sure that none gets on the friction material. Smear some copper grease over the pad retaining pin.
38 Fit the pads into the caliper (**see illustration 2.14b**). Locate the pad spring on the pads and insert the pin (**see illustration 2.14a**). Push the pin in as far as possible making sure it fits over the spring and in the groove (**see illustration**).
39 Slide the caliper onto the disc making sure the pads locate correctly on each side (**see illustration**). Install the caliper mounting bolts and tighten them to the torque setting specified at the beginning of the Chapter. Fit the brake hose guides (**see illustration 2.10**).
40 Drive the pad pin fully home using a suitable drift. Fit the clip, using a new one if

necessary, and with the open end facing up **(see illustration 2.11)**.

41 Operate the brake lever until the pads contact the disc. Check the level of fluid in the hydraulic reservoir and top-up if necessary (see *Pre-ride checks*).

42 Fit the pad cover where removed. Install the wheel (see Section 13).

43 Check the operation of the rear brake before riding the scooter.

3 Brake caliper

⚠️ *Warning: The dust created by the brake system may be harmful to your health. Never blow it out with compressed air and do not inhale any of it. An approved filtering mask should be worn when working on the brakes.*
Caution: Cover paintwork to prevent damage from spilled brake fluid, and have rag handy to catch fluid when detaching the brake hose.
Note: Individual components and rebuild kits are not available for the brake caliper. If the piston seals are leaking fluid or if a piston has seized in its bore a new caliper must be installed. Do not disassemble and rebuild the caliper using the original seals.

Removal

1 Remove the wheel (see Section 12 or 13).

2 If the caliper is being completely removed, unscrew the brake hose banjo bolt and detach the hose, noting the alignment with the caliper **(see illustrations)**. Wrap plastic foodwrap around the banjo union and secure the hose in an upright position to minimise fluid loss. Discard the sealing washers, as new ones must be fitted on reassembly.

3 If the pads are going to be removed displace or slacken the pad pin(s) now, according to model (see Section 2).

4 Unscrew the caliper mounting bolts and slide the caliper off the disc **(see illustration 2.8 or 2.13)**. If the caliper is just being displaced for removal of the wheel hub or disc, secure it to the scooter with a cable-tie to avoid straining the brake hose. **Note:** *Do not operate the brake lever while the caliper is off the disc.* Free the brake hose guide to give more freedom of movement if required.

5 If required remove the brake pads (see Section 2).

Installation

6 If removed, inspect and install the brake pads (see Section 2).

7 Slide the caliper onto the disc, making sure the pads locate correctly on each side **(see illustration 2.32 or 2.39)**. Install the caliper mounting bolts and tighten them to the torque setting specified at the beginning of the Chapter.

8 If the pads were removed drive the pad pin

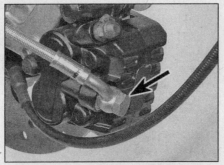

3.2a Brake hose banjo bolt (arrowed) – front caliper GTS/GTV/GT models

in and fit the clip, or tighten the pad pins to the torque setting specified at the beginning of this Chapter, according to model (see Section 2).

9 If detached, connect the brake hose to the caliper, making sure it correctly aligned, and using new sealing washers on each side of the banjo fitting **(see illustration 3.2a or b)**. Tighten the banjo bolt to the specified torque setting.

10 Fit the brake hose guide if displaced.

11 Top up the hydraulic reservoir with DOT 4 brake fluid (see *Pre-ride checks*) and bleed the system as described in Section 7. Check that there are no fluid leaks and test the operation of the brake before riding the scooter.

12 Install the wheel (see Section 12 or 13).

4 Brake disc

Inspection

1 Inspect the surface of the disc for score marks and other damage. Light scratches are normal after use and won't affect brake operation, but deep grooves and heavy score marks will reduce braking efficiency and accelerate pad wear. If a disc is badly grooved it must be replaced with a new one.

2 The disc must not be machined or allowed to wear down to a thickness less than the service limit listed in this Chapter's Specifications. The minimum thickness should also be stamped on the disc. Check the thickness of the disc with a Vernier caliper

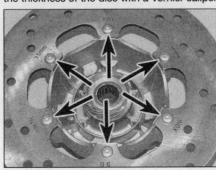

4.5a The front disc is secured by bolts (arrowed)

3.2b Brake hose banjo bolt (arrowed) – rear caliper GTS/GTV/GT models, front caliper LX/LVX/S models

or micrometer and replace it with a new one if necessary.

3 To check if the disc is warped, position the bike on an auxiliary stand with the wheel raised off the ground, and when checking the front with the wheel turned to one side. Mount a dial gauge to the steering stem or transmission casing, with the gauge plunger touching the surface of the disc about 10 mm from the outer edge. When checking the front hold the handlebars against the stop. Rotate the wheel and watch the gauge needle, comparing the reading with the limit listed in the Specifications at the beginning of this Chapter. If the runout is greater than the service limit, check the wheel bearings for play (see Chapter 1). If the bearings are worn, install new ones (see Section 14) and repeat this check. If the disc runout is still excessive, a new disc will have to be fitted.

Removal

4 Remove the wheel and hub (see Section 12 or 13).

5 If you are not replacing the disc with a new one, mark the relationship of the disc to the hub, so it can be installed in the same position. Unscrew the disc bolts, loosening them evenly and a little at a time in a criss-cross pattern to avoid distorting the disc, then remove the disc **(see illustrations)**.

Installation

6 Before installing the disc, make sure there is no dirt or corrosion where the disc seats on the hub. If the disc does not sit flat when it is bolted down, it will appear to be warped when checked or when the front brake is used.

4.5b The bolts securing the rear disc have nuts (arrowed) on the back

5.2a Either release the clip and pull the connector out . . .

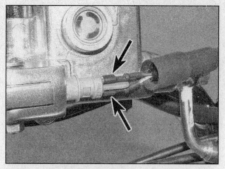

5.2b . . . or pull back the boot and pull the connectors (arrowed) off the terminals, according to model

5.3 Brake hose banjo bolt (arrowed) – note its alignment

7 Fit the disc on the wheel, aligning the previously applied matchmarks (if you're reinstalling the original disc), and making sure the arrow points in the direction of normal rotation.

8 Clean any old locking compound off the bolts and apply fresh compound. Fit the bolts and tighten them evenly and a little at a time in a criss-cross pattern to the torque setting specified at the beginning of this Chapter. Clean the disc using acetone or brake system cleaner. If a new disc has been installed, remove any protective coating from its working surfaces, and fit new brake pads.

9 Install the hub and wheel (see Section 12 or 13).

10 Operate the brake lever several times to bring the pads into contact with the disc. Check the operation of the brake before riding the scooter.

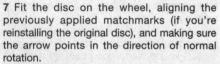

5 Brake master cylinder

Caution: Cover paintwork to prevent damage from spilled brake fluid, and have rag handy to catch fluid when detaching the brake hose.
Note: *Individual components and rebuild kits are not available for the master cylinder. If the piston seals are leaking fluid or if a piston has seized in its bore a new master cylinder must be installed. Do not disassemble and rebuild the master cylinder using the original seals.*

Removal

1 Remove the handlebar covers and the mirror(s) as required according to model (see Chapter 9).

2 Disconnect the brake light switch wiring **(see illustrations)**.

3 If the master cylinder is being completely removed unscrew the brake hose banjo bolt and detach the hose, noting its alignment with the master cylinder **(see illustration)**. Wrap plastic foodwrap around the banjo union and secure the hose in an upright position to minimise fluid loss. Discard the sealing washers as new ones must be fitted on reassembly.

4 If required remove the brake lever (see Chapter 7).

5 If required, unscrew the brake light switch **(see illustration)**.

6 Unscrew the master cylinder clamp bolts and remove the back of the clamp, noting how it fits, then either remove the master cylinder, or secure it clear of the handlebar, making sure no strain is placed on the hydraulic hose **(see illustrations)**. Keep the reservoir upright to prevent air entering the system.

7 If required remove the reservoir cover, diaphragm plate and diaphragm. Drain the brake fluid from the master cylinder and reservoir into a suitable container. Wipe any remaining fluid out of the reservoir with a clean rag.

Installation

8 Attach the master cylinder to the handlebar, locating the peg in the hole **(see illustration)**. Fit the back of the clamp with its UP mark facing up **(see illustration 5.6a or b)**. Tighten the upper bolt first, then the lower bolt.

9 If removed fit the brake light switch **(see illustration 5.5)**.

5.5 The brake light switch screws in

5.6a Master cylinder clamp bolts (arrowed) – front brake, LXV, GTV and GT models

5.6b Master cylinder clamp bolts (arrowed) – rear brake, GTS models

5.6c Remove the clamp and detach the master cylinder

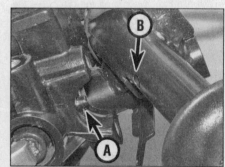

5.8 Locate the peg (A) in the hole (B)

10 If removed install the brake lever (see Chapter 7).

11 Connect the brake hose to the master cylinder, aligning it as noted on removal, and using new sealing washers on each side of the banjo fitting **(see illustration 5.3)**. Tighten the banjo bolt to the torque setting specified at the beginning of this Chapter.

12 Connect the brake light switch wiring **(see illustration 5.2a or b)**.

13 Fill the fluid reservoir with new DOT 4 brake fluid (see *Pre-ride checks*). Refer to Section 7 and bleed the air from the system.

14 Install the mirror(s) and handlebar covers as required (see Chapter 9). Check the operation of the brake before riding the scooter.

6 Brake hoses

Inspection

1 see Chapter 1, Section 4.

Removal and installation

2 The brake hoses have a banjo union on each end, secured by a banjo bolt. Cover the surrounding area with plenty of rag and unscrew the banjo bolt at each end of the hose, noting the alignment of the union **(see illustrations 3.2a or b, and 5.3)**. Free the hose from any clips or guides and remove it, noting its routing. Discard the sealing washers. **Note:** *Do not operate the brake lever while a brake hose is disconnected.*

3 Position the new hose, making sure it isn't twisted or otherwise strained, and ensure that it is correctly routed through any clips or guides and is clear of all moving components.

4 Check that the fittings align correctly, then install the banjo bolts, using a new sealing washer on each side of the union. Tighten the banjo bolts to the torque setting specified at the beginning of this Chapter.

5 Flush the old brake fluid from the system, refill with new DOT 4 brake fluid (see *Pre-ride checks*) and bleed the air from the system (see Section 7).

6 Check the operation of the brakes before riding the scooter.

7 Brake system bleeding and fluid change

Note: *If bleeding the system using the conventional method does not work sufficiently well, it is advisable to obtain a commercially available vacuum-type brake bleeding tool bleeder and repeat the procedure detailed below, following the manufacturer's instructions for using the tool.*

Bleeding

1 Bleeding the brake is simply the process of removing air from the fluid reservoir, master cylinder, hose and caliper. Bleeding is necessary whenever a brake system hydraulic connection is loosened or after a component or hose is replaced with a new one. Leaks in the system may also allow air to enter, but leaking brake fluid will reveal their presence and warn you of the need for repair.

2 To bleed the brakes, you will need some new DOT 4 brake fluid, a length of clear flexible hose, a small container partially filled with clean brake fluid, some rags, a spanner to fit the caliper bleed valve, and help from an assistant **(see illustration)**. Bleeding kits that include the hose, a one-way valve and a container are available relatively cheaply from a good auto store, and simplify the task.

3 Cover painted components to prevent damage in the event that brake fluid is spilled.

4 Refer to 'Pre-ride checks' and remove the reservoir cover and diaphragm and slowly pump the brake lever a few times, until no air bubbles can be seen floating up from the holes in the bottom of the reservoir. This bleeds the air from the master cylinder end of the line. Temporarily refit the reservoir cover.

5 Pull the dust cap off the bleed valve **(see illustrations)**. If using a ring spanner fit it onto the valve. Attach one end of the hose to the bleed valve and, if not using a kit, submerge the other end in the clean brake fluid in the container **(see illustration 7.2)**.

> **HAYNES HINT** *To avoid damaging the bleed valve during the procedure, loosen it and then tighten it temporarily with a ring spanner before attaching the hose. With the hose attached, the valve can then be opened and closed either with an open-ended spanner, or by leaving the ring spanner located on the valve and fitting the hose above it.*

6 Check the fluid level in the reservoir. Do not allow the level to drop below the lower mark during the procedure.

7 Carefully pump the brake lever three or four times and hold it in while opening the bleed valve. When the valve is opened, brake fluid will flow out of the caliper into the clear tubing,

7.2 Set-up for bleeding the brakes

and the lever will move toward the handlebar. If there is air in the system there will be air bubbles in the brake fluid coming out of the caliper.

8 Tighten the bleed valve, then release the brake lever gradually. Repeat the process until no air bubbles are visible in the fluid leaving the caliper, and the lever is firm when applied, topping the reservoir up when necessary. On completion, disconnect the hose, then tighten the bleed valve and fit the dust cap.

> **HAYNES HINT** *If it is not possible to produce a firm feel to the lever, the fluid may be aerated. Let the brake fluid in the system stabilise for a few hours and then repeat the procedure when the tiny bubbles in the system have settled out.*

9 Top-up the reservoir, then install the diaphragm and cover (see *Pre-ride checks*). Wipe up any spilled brake fluid. Check the entire system for fluid leaks.

10 Check the operation of the brakes before riding the scooter.

Fluid change

11 Changing the brake fluid is a similar process to bleeding the brakes and requires the same materials plus a suitable tool (such as a syringe) for siphoning the fluid out of the reservoir. Also ensure that the container is large enough to take all the old fluid when it is flushed out of the system.

12 Follow Steps 3 and 5, then remove the

7.5a Front brake caliper bleed valve (arrowed) – GTS/GTV/GT caliper shown

7.5b Rear brake caliper bleed valve (arrowed)

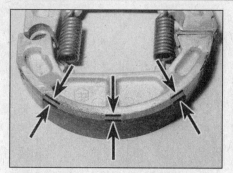

8.2 Check the amount of friction material remaining on each shoe

reservoir cap and diaphragm and siphon the old fluid out of the reservoir. Wipe the reservoir clean. Fill the reservoir with new brake fluid, then carefully pump the brake lever three or four times and hold it in while opening the caliper bleed valve (see Step 5). When the valve is opened, brake fluid will flow out of the caliper into the clear tubing, and the lever will move toward the handlebar.

13 Tighten the bleed valve, then release the brake lever gradually. Keep the reservoir topped-up with new fluid or air may enter the system and greatly increase the length of the task. Repeat the process until new fluid can be seen emerging from the caliper bleed valve.

 HAYNES HINT *Old brake fluid is invariably much darker in colour than new fluid, making it easy to see when all old fluid has been expelled from the system.*

14 Disconnect the hose, then tighten the bleed valve and fit the dust cap.

15 Top-up the reservoir, then fit the diaphragm and cover (see *Pre-ride checks*). Wipe up any spilled brake fluid. Check the entire system for fluid leaks.

16 Check the operation of the brakes before riding the scooter.

Draining the system for overhaul

17 Draining the brake fluid is again a similar process to bleeding the brakes. The quickest and easiest way is to use a commercially available vacuum-type brake bleeding tool

8.6 Check the drum lining for scoring, cracks and wear

– follow the manufacturer's instructions. Otherwise follow the procedure described above for changing the fluid, but quite simply do not put any new fluid into the reservoir – the system fills itself with air instead.

8 Rear drum brake

⚠️ *Warning: The dust created by the brake system may contain asbestos, which is harmful to your health. Never blow it out with compressed air and don't inhale any of it. An approved filtering mask should be worn when working on the brakes.*

Check

1 Remove the rear wheel (see Section 13).
2 Check the condition and amount of friction material on each shoe **(see illustration)**. If there is less than 1.5 mm of material remaining at the cam end replace the shoes with new ones.
3 Inspect the surface of the friction material on each shoe for contamination. If either shoe is fouled with oil or grease, or heavily scored or damaged by dirt and debris, both shoes must be replaced with a new set. Note that it is not possible to degrease the friction material; if the shoes are contaminated in any way they must be replaced with new ones.
4 If the shoes are in good condition clean them carefully, using a fine wire brush which is completely free of oil and grease, or some sandpaper, to remove all traces of road dirt

and corrosion. Using a pointed instrument, dig out any embedded particles of dirt. If the material appears glazed, roughen up the surface using course sandpaper, bearing in mind the *Warning* above.

5 Check the condition of the brake shoe springs and replace them with new ones if they appear weak or are obviously deformed or damaged.

6 Clean the brake drum lining using brake cleaner or a rag soaked in solvent. Examine the surface of the drum lining for scoring and excessive wear **(see illustration)**. While light scratches are expected, any heavy scoring or cracks will impair braking and there is no satisfactory way of removing them – the wheel should be replaced with a new one.

7 Check that the brake cam operates smoothly and to its full limits of travel by operating the lever arm. Clean off all traces of old and hardened grease from the cam and pivot post – remove the shoes to do this. If the bearing surfaces of the cam are worn or damaged it should be replaced with a new one. Remove the brake arm from the brake cam, noting or marking its alignment, then draw the cam out, noting the washer.

8 Check the cable (see Section 9).

Shoe replacement

9 Remove the wheel (see Section 13).
10 Grasp the outer edge of each shoe and fold them upwards and inwards to form a "V", noting that they are under the pressure of the springs, then remove them, noting how they locate around the cam and the pivot post **(see illustration 8.12c)**. Remove the springs from the shoes.
11 Check the shoes and the drum as outlined above.
12 Apply some copper grease to the bearing surfaces on the cam and pivot post. Fit the springs onto the shoes **(see illustration)** – make sure the shoes are the same way round, with their rounded ends together and their flat ends together. Position the shoes so that the rounded end of each shoe fits around the pivot post and the flat end against the flats on the cam **(see illustration)**. Fold the shoes flat, making sure they sit correctly on each side of the pivot and the cam and the springs remain in place **(see illustration)**. Operate the brake

8.12a Apply some copper grease to the cam

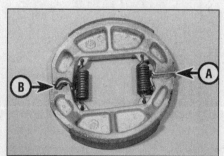

8.12b Fit the springs and locate ends (A) against the cam and the rounded ends (B) against the pivot post

8.12c Locate the shoes and fold them down onto the plate

arm to check that the cam and shoes work correctly.

13 Install the wheel (see Section 13). Check the operation of the brake before riding the scooter.

9 Rear drum brake cable

Note: *For details of cable adjustment and lubrication see Chapter 1.*

1 Remove the kick panel, the floor panel, and the handlebar cover(s) as required according to model (see Chapter 9).

2 Release the cable from the underside of the drive belt cover **(see illustration)**.

3 Fully unscrew the adjuster nut on the brake drum end of the cable, then draw the cable out of the brake arm and the holder on the underside of the drive belt cover **(see illustration)**. Remove the bush from the arm and the return spring from between the arm and casing, noting how it locates.

4 At the handlebar draw the outer cable out of the lever bracket and free the inner cable nipple from its socket in the underside of the lever **(see illustrations)**.

5 Free the cable from any clips or ties, then withdraw it carefully, noting its routing and any guides it passes through.

6 Install the new cables in a reverse of the removal procedure (see **Haynes Hint**). Apply some grease to the ends of the inner cables before fitting them, and to the lever and arm pivot points.

7 Adjust the cable freeplay (see Chapter 1). Check the operation of the rear brake before riding the scooter.

 When fitting a new cable, tape the lower end of the new cable to the upper end of the old cable before removing it from the machine. Slowly pull the lower end of the old cable out, guiding the new cable down into position. Using this method will ensure the cable is routed correctly and could avoid having to remove the bodywork.

10 Wheel inspection and repair

1 In order to carry out a proper inspection of the wheels, it is necessary to support the scooter upright so that the wheel being inspected is raised off the ground. Clean the wheels thoroughly to remove mud and dirt that may interfere with the inspection procedure or mask defects. Make a general check of the wheels and tyres (see Chapter 1 and *Pre-ride checks*).

2 Attach a dial gauge to the fork or the transmission casing and position its tip

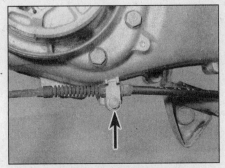

9.2 Unscrew the cable guide bolt (arrowed)

9.4a Draw the outer cable from the bracket . . .

against the side of the wheel rim. Spin the wheel slowly and check the axial (side-to-side) runout of the rim **(see illustration)**.

3 In order to accurately check radial (out of round) runout with the dial gauge, remove the wheel from the scooter and the tyre from the wheel, then refit the wheel. With the dial gauge positioned on the top of the rim, the wheel can be rotated to check the runout **(see illustration 10.2)**.

4 An easier, though slightly less accurate, method is to attach a stiff wire pointer to the fork or the transmission casing and position the end a fraction of an inch from the wheel rim where the wheel and tyre join. If the wheel is true, the distance from the pointer to the rim will be constant as the wheel is rotated.

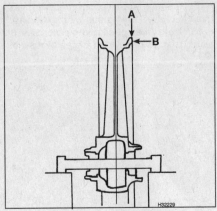

10.2 Check the wheel for radial (out-of-round) runout (A) and axial (side-to-side) runout (B)

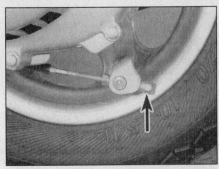

9.3 Unscrew the adjuster nut (arrowed)

9.4b . . . and detach the inner cable end from the lever

Note: *If wheel runout is excessive, check the wheel bearings very carefully before fitting a new wheel.*

5 Inspect the wheels for cracks, flat spots on the rim and other damage. Look very closely for dents in the area where the tyre bead contacts the rim. Dents in this area may prevent complete sealing of the tyre against the rim, which leads to deflation of the tyre over a period of time. If damage is evident, or if runout in either direction is excessive, the wheel will have to be renewed. Never attempt to repair a damaged cast alloy wheel.

11 Wheel alignment check

1 Misalignment of the wheels due to a bent frame, engine hanger or steering stem can cause strange and possibly serious handling problems. If the frame or forks are at fault, repair by a specialist or renewal are the only options.

2 To check wheel alignment you will need an assistant, a length of string or a perfectly straight piece of wood and a ruler. A plumb bob or spirit level for checking that the wheels are vertical will also be required.

3 In order to make a proper check of the wheels it is necessary to support the scooter in an upright position, using an auxiliary stand. First measure the width of both tyres at their widest points. Subtract the smaller measurement from the larger measurement,

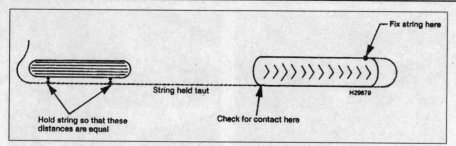

11.5 Wheel alignment check using string

then divide the difference by two. The result is the amount of offset that should exist between the front and rear tyres on both sides of the machine.

4 If a string is used, have your assistant hold one end of it about halfway between the floor and the rear axle, with the string touching the back edge of the rear tyre sidewall.

5 Run the other end of the string forward and pull it tight so that it is roughly parallel to the floor **(see illustration)**. Slowly bring the string into contact with the front edge of the rear tyre sidewall, then turn the front wheel until it is parallel with the string. Measure the distance from the front tyre sidewall to the string.

6 Repeat the procedure on the other side of the scooter. The distance from the front tyre sidewall to the string should be equal on both sides.

7 As previously mentioned, a perfectly straight length of wood or metal bar may be substituted for the string **(see illustration)**.

8 If the distance between the string and tyre is greater on one side, or if the rear wheel appears to be out of alignment, have your machine checked by a Vespa dealer or frame specialist.

9 If the front-to-back alignment is correct, the wheels still may be out of alignment vertically.

10 Using a plumb bob or spirit level, check the rear wheel to make sure it is vertical. To do this, hold the string of the plumb bob against the tyre upper sidewall and allow the weight to settle just off the floor. If the string touches both the upper and lower tyre sidewalls and is perfectly straight, the wheel is vertical. If it is not, adjust the stand until it is.

11 Once the rear wheel is vertical, check the front wheel in the same manner. If both wheels are not perfectly vertical, the frame and/or major suspension components are bent.

12 Front wheel and hub

Wheel

1 Position the scooter on its centrestand and support it so that the front wheel is off the ground.

2 Unscrew the five bolts securing the wheel to the hub and draw the wheel off **(see illustrations)**. Note the washers with the bolts.

3 Fit the wheel, then fit the bolts with their washers and tighten them to the torque setting specified at the beginning of the Chapter **(see illustration)**. **Note:** *If a new tyre has been fitted, make sure the directional arrow on the tyre is pointing in the direction of normal rotation of the wheel.*

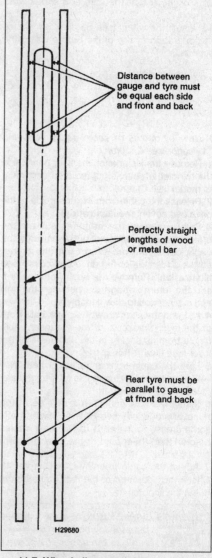

Distance between gauge and tyre must be equal each side and front and back

Perfectly straight lengths of wood or metal bar

Rear tyre must be parallel to gauge at front and back

H29680

11.7 Wheel alignment check using a straight-edge

12.2a Unscrew the bolts (arrowed) . . .

12.2b . . . and remove the wheel

Hub removal

4 Remove the wheel (see Steps 1 and 2). Detach the speedometer cable and withdraw the drive gear (see Chapter 10).

5 Displace the brake caliper (see Section 3).

6 Remove the split pin from the hub cage nut and remove the cage nut **(see illustrations)**. Discard the split pin as a new one must be used.

7 Unscrew the hub nut **(see illustration)**.

8 Draw the hub off the axle **(see illustration)**. The hub may be a tight fit – if it is difficult to remove, fit a strong washer with an external diameter the same as that of the recess in the wheel and with an internal diameter smaller than the diameter of the axle, so that the washer cannot slide over the axle, into the wheel **(see illustration)**. Place the wheel against the axle, then install the wheel bolts and tighten them evenly and a little at a time in a criss-cross sequence until the hub is drawn off **(see illustrations)**.

9 Check the condition of the bearings and seal in the hub (see Section 14), and of those in the shock absorber/caliper bracket (see Chapter 7, Section 5).

Hub installation

10 Installation is the reverse of removal, noting the following:

- *Apply grease to the axle and needle bearing.*
- *Tighten the hub nut to the torque setting specified at the beginning of the Chapter* **(see illustration)**.

- *Use a new split pin to secure the hub nut and cage nut, and bend its ends round to secure it* **(see illustration)**.

- *Grease the speedometer drive gear and fit the cable (see Chapter 10).*

12.3 Make sure the washers are fitted with each bolt

12.6a Straighten the ends of the pin then withdraw it . . .

12.6b . . . and remove the cage nut

12.7 Unscrew the hub nut

12.8a Draw the hub assembly off . . .

12.8b . . . if it is tight fit a washer into the inside of the wheel . . .

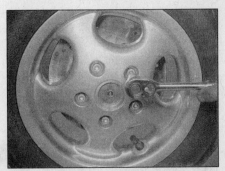

12.8c . . . and use the wheel bolts to draw it off as described . . .

12.8d . . . then separate the wheel and hub

12.10a Tighten the nut to the specified torque setting

12.10b Bend the split ends round to secure the pin

13.3 Note location of the thrust washer

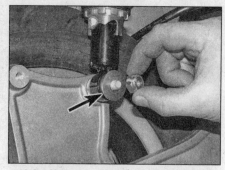

13.6a Unscrew the nut and remove the washer (arrowed) . . .

13.6b . . . then draw the shock off its lug

13.7a Straighten the ends of the pin then withdraw it . . .

13.7b . . . and remove the cage nut

13.7c Unscrew the nut and remove the spacer

13 Rear wheel and hub

Wheel removal

LX, LXV and S models

1 Position the scooter on its centrestand. Remove the exhaust system (see Chapter 5).
2 Remove the split pin from the end of the axle then remove the cage nut (see illustrations 13.7a and b). Discard the split pin as a new one must be used.

3 Unscrew the axle nut, using the rear brake to prevent the wheel from turning, and remove the washer. Draw the wheel off the drive shaft. On 2012-on models, note the location of the large thrust washer on the shaft (see illustration). If necessary, remove the washer for safekeeping.
4 Check the splines on the drive shaft and on the inside of the wheel for wear and damage and replace either or both as required if they are likely to slip over each other.

GTS, GTV and GT models

5 Position the scooter on its centrestand. Remove the exhaust system (see Chapter 5).

6 Unscrew the nut and remove the washer securing the bottom of the right-hand shock absorber, then draw the shock off its lug (see illustrations).
7 Remove the split pin from the end of the axle then remove the cage nut (see illustrations). Discard the split pin as a new one must be used. Unscrew the axle nut, using the rear brake to prevent the wheel from turning (see illustration). Remove the outer spacer.
8 Unscrew the exhaust bracket bolts (see illustration). Draw the bracket off the drive shaft (see illustration).
9 Unscrew the five bolts securing the wheel to the hub, noting the washers, and draw the

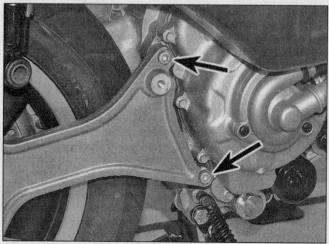

13.8a Unscrew the bolts (arrowed) . . .

13.8b . . . and remove the bracket

13.9a Unscrew the bolts (arrowed) . . .

13.9b . . . and remove the wheel

wheel off **(see illustrations)**. Note the washers with the bolts.

10 Refer to Section 14 and check the condition of the bearing in the exhaust bracket.

Wheel installation

Note: *If a new tyre has been fitted, make sure the directional arrow on the tyre is pointing in the direction of normal rotation of the wheel.*

LX, LXV and S models

11 Installation is the reverse of removal, noting the following:

- *Apply grease to the axle.*
- *Ensure the thrust washer is in position* **(see illustration 13.3)**.
- *Tighten the axle nut to the torque setting*

specified at the beginning of the Chapter.

- *Use a new split pin to secure the axle nut and cage nut and bend its ends round* **(see illustration 13.12d)**.

GTS, GTV and GT models

12 Installation is the reverse of removal, noting the following:

- *Make sure the spacer is on the axle* **(see illustration 13.15a)**. *Fit the wheel, then fit the bolts with their washers and tighten them to the torque setting specified at the beginning of the Chapter* **(see illustration)**.
- *Apply grease to the axle and to the bearing in the exhaust bracket.*
- *Tighten the exhaust bracket bolts, the axle nut and the shock absorber nut to the*

torque settings specified at the beginning of the Chapter.

- *Use a new split pin to secure the axle nut and cage nut and bend its ends round* **(see illustration)**.

Hub (GTS, GTV and GT models)

13 Remove the wheel (see Steps 5 to 8).
14 Displace the brake caliper (see Section 3).
15 Remove the spacer, noting which way round it fits **(see illustration)**. Draw the hub off the axle **(see illustration)**.
16 Installation is the reverse of removal. Check the splines in the centre of the hub and those on the shaft for wear and damage **(see illustrations)**.

13.12a Make sure the washers are on the bolts

13.12b Bend the split ends round to secure the pin

13.15a Slide the spacer off . . .

13.15b . . . then slide the hub off

13.16a Check the splines (arrowed) in the hub . . .

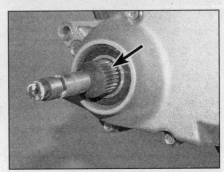

13.16b . . . and on the shaft

14.2 Lever out the seal (arrowed)

14.4 Remove the circlip (arrowed)

14.6 Use a punch to drive the bearings out

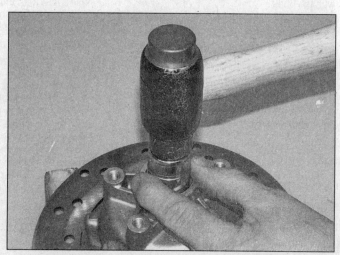

14.10 Using a socket to drive the new ball bearing in

14 Wheel bearings

Note: *Always renew the wheel bearings in sets, never individually. Avoid using a high pressure cleaner on the wheel bearing area.*

Front wheel bearings

1 Remove the wheel and the hub (see Section 12). If required remove the disc (see Section 4). The bearings are housed in the hub – there is a caged ball bearing in the outer side and a needle roller bearing on the inner side.

2 Lever out the grease seal on the inner side of the hub **(see illustration)**. Discard the seal – a new one must be used. Clean the hub and bearings, removing all old grease.

3 Inspect the bearings – check that the inner race of the ball bearing turns smoothly,

quietly and freely and that the outer race is a tight fit in the hub. Check the needle rollers for corrosion and dirt and make sure they turn freely. **Note:** *Do not remove the bearings unless they are going to be replaced with new ones. Once removed they cannot be re-used.*

4 If the bearings are worn, remove the circlip retaining the caged ball bearing using a pair of internal circlip pliers **(see illustration)**.

5 Set the hub assembly on blocks to allow the bearings to be driven out – if the disc has not been removed make sure the hub rests on its rim and not on the disc.

6 Using a metal rod (preferably a brass drift punch) inserted through the centre of the needle roller bearing on the inner side of the hub, tap evenly around the outer race of the caged ball bearing to drive it out **(see illustration)**.

7 Lay the hub on its other side so that the needle roller bearing faces down. Drive the bearing out of the hub using the same technique as above.

8 Thoroughly clean the inside of the hub and inspect the bearing seats for scoring and wear. Fit a new hub if necessary.

9 Apply grease to the outside of the new needle bearing. The bearing should be pressed or drawn rather than driven into position. In the absence of a press, a suitable drawbolt tool can be made up as described in *Tools and Workshop Tips* in the Reference section.

10 Fit the caged ball bearing with the marked or sealed side facing outwards. Using the old bearing (if a new one is being fitted), a bearing driver or a socket large enough to contact the outer race of the bearing, drive it in squarely until it's completely seated **(see illustration)**.

11 Fit the new grease seal **(see illustration 14.2)**. Fit the bearing circlip, making sure it fits properly in its groove **(see illustration 14.4)**.

12 Install the disc if removed (see Section 4). Install the hub and the wheel (see Section 12).

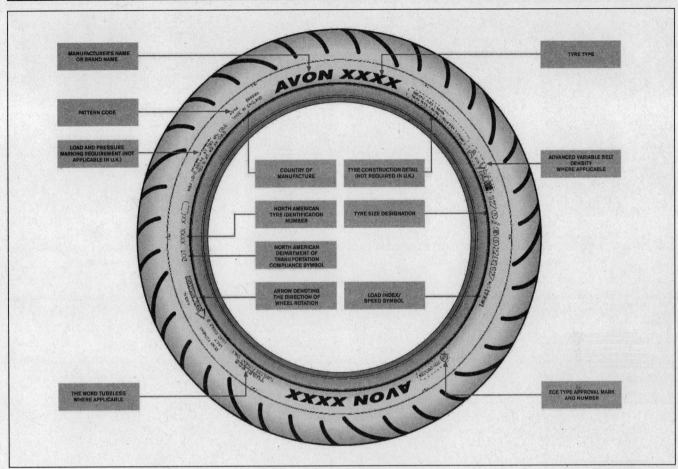

MANUFACTURER'S NAME OR BRAND NAME

PATTERN CODE

LOAD AND PRESSURE MARKING REQUIREMENT (NOT APPLICABLE IN U.K.)

THE WORD TUBELESS WHERE APPLICABLE

TYRE TYPE

ADVANCED VARIABLE BELT DENSITY WHERE APPLICABLE

ECE TYPE APPROVAL MARK AND NUMBER

COUNTRY OF MANUFACTURE

TYRE CONSTRUCTION DETAIL (NOT REQUIRED IN U.K.)

NORTH AMERICAN TYRE IDENTIFICATION NUMBER

TYRE SIZE DESIGNATION

NORTH AMERICAN DEPARTMENT OF TRANSPORTATION COMPLIANCE SYMBOL

ARROW DENOTING THE DIRECTION OF WHEEL ROTATION

LOAD INDEX/ SPEED SYMBOL

15.3 Common tyre sidewall markings

Rear wheel bearings

13 The bearings for the rear wheel axle are fitted on the output shaft in the gearbox (see Chapter 2A, 2B or 2C). On GTS, GTV and GT models there is also a bearing in the exhaust bracket. Refer to Section 13, Steps 5 to 8 and remove the bracket.

14 Inspect the bearing – check that the inner race turns smoothly, quietly and freely and that the outer race is a tight fit in the bracket.

15 If the bearing is worn, set the bracket on blocks. Drive the bearing out from the inside using a driver or socket located on the inner race.

16 Thoroughly clean the inside of the hub and inspect the bearing seat for scoring and wear. Fit a new bracket if necessary.

17 Fit the bearing with the marked or sealed side facing outwards. Using the old bearing

(if a new one is being fitted), a bearing driver or a socket large enough to contact the outer race of the bearing, drive it in squarely until it's completely seated.

18 Install the bracket (see Section 13).

15 Tyres

General information

1 The wheels fitted to all models are designed to take tubeless tyres only. Tyre sizes are given in the Specifications at the start of this Chapter.

2 Refer to the *Pre-ride checks* listed at the beginning of this manual for tyre maintenance.

Fitting new tyres

3 When selecting new tyres, refer to the tyre

information in the Owner's Handbook. Ensure that front and rear tyre types are compatible, the correct size and correct speed rating; if necessary seek advice from a Vespa dealer or tyre fitting specialist **(see illustration)**.

4 It is recommended that tyres are fitted by a motorcycle/scooter tyre specialist rather than attempted in the home workshop. This is particularly relevant in the case of tubeless tyres because the force required to break the seal between the wheel rim and tyre bead is substantial, and is usually beyond the capabilities of an individual working with normal tyre levers. Additionally, the specialist will be able to balance the wheels after tyre fitting.

5 Note that punctured tubeless tyres can in some cases be repaired – seek advice first. Repairs must be carried out by a tyre fitting specialist.

Chapter 9
Frame and bodywork

Contents

Degrees of difficulty

Easy, suitable for novice with little experience		**Fairly easy,** suitable for beginner with some experience		**Fairly difficult,** suitable for competent DIY mechanic		**Difficult,** suitable for experienced DIY mechanic		**Very difficult,** suitable for expert DIY or professional	

Specifications

Torque settings

Centrestand pivot bolt nut	
LX, LXV and S 2009 to 2011 models and all GTS models	32 to 40 Nm
LX, LXV and S 2012-on models	40 to 45 Nm
Sidestand pivot bolt	35 to 40 Nm

---

1 General information

All models are fitted with a monocoque steel body.

The engine and transmission assembly are linked to the frame by a swingarm at the front of the engine and by the rear shock absorber(s), making the engine an integral part of the rear suspension.

All models are fitted with a centrestand, which bolts onto the bottom of the engine. Some models are also fitted with a sidestand which bolts to the frame.

All functional components are enclosed by body panels, including the floor board, making removal of some or all of them a necessary part of most servicing and maintenance procedures. Be sure to follow the advice given in Section 4 before removing the panels.

2 Stands

Centrestand

1 With the stand in the down position, fit washers between the coils of the springs as shown **(see illustration)** – this holds the

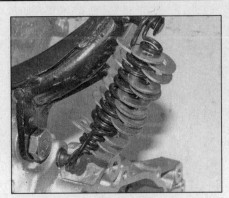

2.1 Fit washers between the coils to keep the spring expanded

2.3 Take care when unhooking the springs

2.4a Unscrew the nut . . .

2.4b . . . withdraw the bolt and remove the stand

2.5a Remove the O-ring from each side . . .

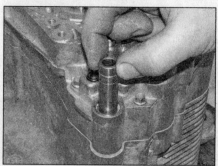

2.5b . . . and withdraw the spacer

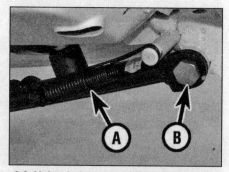

2.8 Unhook the springs (A) then unscrew the bolt (B)

springs expanded and makes them easier to remove and install.

2 Retract the stand and support the scooter on its sidestand where fitted, or securely using an auxiliary stand, making sure that it is not positioned directly against the body panels which could easily break.

3 Carefully unhook the springs **(see illustration)**.

4 Unscrew the nut **(see illustration)**. Withdraw the pivot bolt and remove the stand, noting how it fits **(see illustration)**.

5 Thoroughly clean the stand and the pivot bolt. Remove the O-rings – replace them with new ones if damaged, deformed or deteriorated **(see illustration)**. Withdraw the pivot spacer **(see illustration)**. Clean the spacer.

6 On installation apply grease to the spacer and O-rings, using new ones if necessary. Grease the pivot bolt and all pivot points. Tighten the pivot bolt nut to the torque setting

specified at the beginning of the Chapter. Reconnect the springs and check they hold the stand securely up when not in use – an accident is almost certain to occur if the stand extends while the scooter is being ridden.

Sidestand

7 Support the scooter on the centrestand.

8 With the sidestand down fit washers between the coils of the springs as shown **(see illustration 2.1)** – this holds the springs expanded and makes them easier to remove and install. Retract the stand, then carefully unhook the springs **(see illustration)**.

9 Unscrew the pivot bolt and remove the stand.

10 Where fitted, remove the O-rings and replace them with new ones if necessary. Thoroughly clean the stand and pivot bolt.

11 On installation apply clean grease to the pivot bolt shank and O-rings.

12 Tighten the bolt to the torque setting specified at the beginning of the chapter. Reconnect the springs and check they hold the stand securely up when not in use – an accident is almost certain to occur if the stand extends while the scooter is being ridden.

3 Mirrors

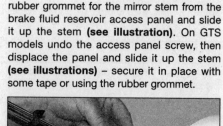

1 On LX, S and GTS models displace the rubber grommet for the mirror stem from the brake fluid reservoir access panel and slide it up the stem **(see illustration)**. On GTS models undo the access panel screw, then displace the panel and slide it up the stem **(see illustrations)** – secure it in place with some tape or using the rubber grommet.

3.1a Displace the rubber grommet

3.1b Undo the screw . . .

3.1c . . . and displace the access panel

2 Slacken the locknut then unscrew the mirror **(see illustrations).**

3 Installation is the reverse of removal. Make sure the rubber grommet and on GTS models the access panel are fitted on the mirror before installing the mirror. Position the mirror as required then tighten the locknut.

4 Body panel removal and installation information

When attempting to remove any body panel, first study it closely, noting any fasteners and associated fittings, to be sure of returning everything to its correct place on installation. In some cases the aid of an assistant will be required when removing panels, to help avoid the risk of damage to paintwork. Once the evident fasteners have been removed, try to withdraw the panel as described but DO NOT FORCE IT – if it will not release, check that all fasteners have been removed and try again. Where a panel engages another by means of tabs, be careful not to break the tab or its mating slot or to damage the paintwork. Remember that a few moments of patience at this stage will save you a lot of money in renewing broken body panels!

When installing a body panel, first study it closely, noting any fasteners and associated fittings removed with it, to be sure of returning everything to its correct place. Check that all fasteners are in good condition, including all trim nuts or clips and damping/rubber mounts; any of these must be renewed if faulty before the panel is reassembled. Check also that all mounting brackets are straight and repair or renew them if necessary before attempting to install the panel. Where assistance was required to remove a panel, make sure your assistant is on hand to install it.

Tighten the fasteners securely, but be careful not to overtighten any of them or the panel may break (not always immediately) due to the uneven stress.

HAYNES HiNT *A small amount of lubricant (liquid soap or similar) applied to rubber mounting grommets will assist the lugs to engage without the need for undue pressure.*

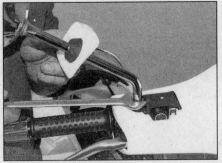
3.2a Slacken the locknut . . .

In the case of damage to the body parts, it is usually necessary to remove the broken component and use a new (or used) one. There are, however, some shops that specialise in 'plastic welding', so it may be worthwhile seeking the advice of one of these specialists before consigning an expensive component to the bin. Additionally proprietary repair kits can be obtained for repair of small components.

5 LX and LXV models – 2009 to 2011

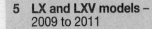

Seat

1 Unlock the seat and swing it upright. Lift the storage compartment out.

2 Undo the screws securing the seat hinge and remove the seat. On LXV models, the passenger seat can be detached from the seat pan by removing its four mounting nuts.

5.4 The storage compartment lifts out

3.2b . . . then unscrew the mirror

3 Installation is a reverse of removal.

Storage compartment – engine access

4 Unlock the seat and swing it upright. Lift the storage compartment out **(see illustration).**

5 Installation is the reverse of removal.

Engine access panel

6 Undo the single screw securing the access panel below the seat and remove the panel **(see illustrations).**

7 Installation is the reverse of removal.

Front panel grille

8 Carefully lever off the badge in the grille **(see illustration 6.3a).** Undo the screw **(see illustration).** Turn the handlebars to one side, then push the panel up to release the hooks from their slots and draw it off, noting how it locates **(see illustration).**

9 Installation is the reverse of removal.

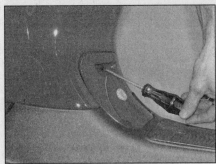
5.6a Undo the screw and remove the panel . . .

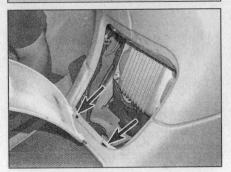
5.6b . . . noting how the tabs locate

5.8a Undo the screw (arrowed) . . .

5.8b . . . and lift the panel, noting how the hooks (arrowed) locate

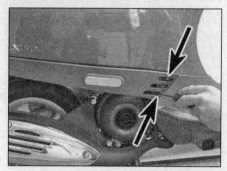

5.10 Undo the screws (arrowed)

5.11a Release the pegs from the grommets (arrowed) . . .

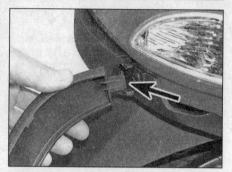

5.11b . . . and release the tab (arrowed) at the back

5.15a Ease the kick panel off . . .

5.15b . . . noting how the catch mechanism (arrowed) aligns

Side panels

10 Undo the screws securing the side panel to the main body **(see illustration)**.

11 Each panel is also secured by two pegs which locate in rubber grommets, and by a tab at the rear. Carefully pull the panel away to release the pegs from the grommets, then pull the panel back to disengage the rear tab **(see illustrations)**.

12 Installation is the reverse of removal. Make sure the tab and pegs are correctly engaged.

Kick panel

13 Remove the front panel grille. Undo the two screws located behind it **(see illustration 7.13)**.

14 Press in the ignition switch to release the glovebox door and swing the door down. Undo the three screws inside the compartment.

15 Ease the kick panel up, then pull it away from the front panel – note how the catch for the glovebox aligns with the catch mechanism around the ignition switch **(see illustrations)**.

16 Installation is the reverse of removal. Check the operation of the glovebox door release mechanism before installing the fixing screws.

Floor panel

17 Remove the kick panel.

18 Remove the side panels.

19 Remove the engine access panel.

20 Undo the two screws on each side securing the floor panel **(see illustration)**.

21 Pull up the floor panel centre mat, then undo the screw underneath the mat **(see illustration)**.

22 Remove the screw on each side securing the lower edge of the front panel chrome trim **(see illustration)**.

23 Draw the floor panel forwards and manoeuvre it off **(see illustration)**.

24 If required, remove the side trim panels, noting how they are secured by the rear floor panel screws **(see illustration)**.

25 Installation is the reverse of removal.

Handlebar covers – LX model

26 Remove the mirrors. Remove the front panel grille.

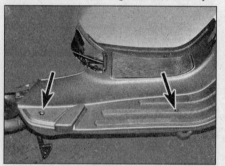

5.20 Undo the two screws (arrowed) on each side . . .

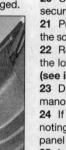

5.21 . . . and the screw (arrowed) under the mat

5.22 Undo the trim fixing screw on each side

5.23 Lift the floor panel off

5.24 Remove the trim panels, noting how they locate

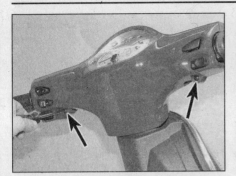

5.27a Undo the screws (arrowed) in the rear cover . . .

5.27b . . . and the screw below the headlight

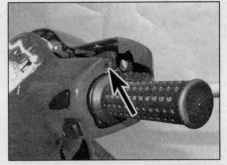

5.27c Pegs locate in both sides of the rear cover . . .

5.27d . . . and in the centre of the top edge

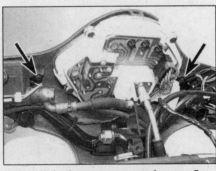

5.28a Undo the cover screws (arrowed) . . .

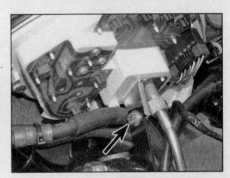

5.28b . . . and the instrument screw (arrowed)

27 To remove the front cover, undo the screws from the rear cover and the screw below the headlight – place a rag under the headlight when undoing the front screw as it is easy to drop it down inside the kick panel (see illustrations). Carefully ease the edge of the front cover away to release the pegs which locate into holes in the top edge and sides of the rear cover (see illustrations). These pegs are quite a tight fit and a certain amount of leverage is required, but take care not to apply excessive force as the cover could break. Once the cover is free, disconnect the headlight wiring connectors and remove the cover. If required, remove the headlight (see Chapter 10).

28 To remove the rear cover, first remove the front cover. Undo the screws securing the rear cover to the brackets on the handlebars (see illustration). Undo the screw securing the instrument cluster to its support bracket (see illustration). If the cover is being completely removed rather than just displaced for access, disconnect the instrument cluster and handlebar switch wiring connectors, noting which fits where, and the speedometer cable, then remove the cover. If required, remove the instrument cluster (see Chapter 10).

29 Installation is the reverse of removal. Make sure the wiring connectors are correctly and securely connected, and check the operation of all switches and lights. Use the rag again to prevent the front screw dropping down.

Handlebar cover/instrument housing – LXV model

30 Detach the windshield by backing-off the grub screw in its two fasteners and pulling the rubber mounting off the chrome support bracket.

31 Undo the two screws in the lower cover, then press the rear edge of the cover inwards to release its tab from the top cover. Draw the top cover up sufficiently to disconnect the speedometer cable – note that this will require a fair amount of dexterity. Disconnect the instrument wiring connector and remove the top cover and instrument cluster. If required, remove the instrument cluster (see Chapter 10).

32 The lower cover can only be removed once the handlebar assembly has been removed (see Chapter 7).

Battery panel and grab handle/rear carrier

33 Remove the storage compartment. Remove the battery (see Chapter 10).

34 Remove the fuel filler cap and its seal.

35 Undo the screws securing the battery panel and lift it up, noting how it locates at the back, then detach the fuse holder and remove the panel (see illustration 6.18). Temporarily install the fuel filler cap.

36 Undo the screw securing the badge to the rear mount (see illustration 7.37).

37 Unscrew the bolts securing the grab handle or rear carrier and lift it off.

38 Installation is the reverse of removal.

Front mudguard

39 Refer to Chapter 7 and follow the procedure for removing and installing the steering stem.

Rear mudguard

40 Remove both side panels.

41 Undo the screws securing the mudguard, displace it and pull the licence plate light bulbholder out (see illustration).

42 Installation is the reverse of removal.

6 S models – 2009 to 2011

Seat and storage compartment – engine access

1 Refer to Section 5 – the procedure is the same as for LX and LXV models.

Engine access panel

2 Refer to Section 5 – the procedure is the same as for LX and LXV models.

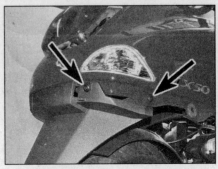

5.41 Undo the two screws (arrowed) on each side

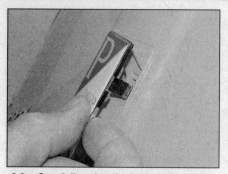

6.3a Carefully prise the badge off using a small screwdriver in the slot

6.3b Undo the top screw . . .

6.3c . . . and the bottom screw . . .

6.3d . . . and remove the panel

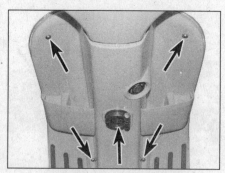

6.7a Undo the five screws (arrowed) . . .

6.7b . . . then lift the outer rubber strip on each side and undo the screw (arrowed)

Front panel grille

3 Carefully lever off the badge in the grille **(see illustration)**. Undo the screw behind it and the screw in the base of the grille **(see illustrations)**. Slide the grille upwards to release the hooks from their slots and remove it.

4 Installation is the reverse of removal – make sure the hooks locate correctly **(see illustration 6.3d)**.

Side panels

5 Refer to Section 5 – the procedure is the same as for LX and LXV models.

Kick panel

6 Remove the front panel grille. Undo the two screws located behind it **(see illustration 7.13)**.
7 Undo the five screws from the kick panel **(see illustration)**. Peel back the outer rubber strip from each side and undo the screw underneath **(see illustration)**.
8 Ease the kick panel rearwards and remove it from the scooter. Take care as the panel may get caught on the chrome trim strip running down each side.
9 Installation is the reverse of removal.

Floor panel

10 Refer to Section 5 – the procedure is the same as for LX and LXV models.

Handlebar covers

11 Remove the mirrors (see Section 3).
12 To remove the front cover (and headlight) undo the two screws from the rear cover and the single screw below the headlight – place a rag under the headlight when undoing the front screw as it is easy to drop it down inside the kick panel **(see illustrations)**. Ease the front cover away, unclipping it from the rear cover at the top and at each side, then disconnect the headlight wiring connector **(see illustrations)**.

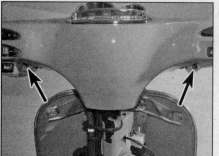

6.12a Undo the screws (arrowed) in the rear cover . . .

6.12b . . . and the screw below the headlight

6.12c Detach the front cover, noting how the tab locates in the slot (arrowed) . . .

6.12d . . . and how the peg (A) locates in the hole (B) on each side

13 To remove the rear cover (and instrument cluster), first remove the front cover. Disconnect the speedometer cable and the switch and instrument wiring connectors. Undo the three screws and remove the rear cover complete with the instrument cluster and switches **(see illustration)**.

14 If required remove the headlight from the front cover and the instrument cluster from the rear cover (see Chapter 10).

15 Installation is the reverse of removal. Use the rag again to prevent the front screw dropping down. Check the operation of all switches and the instruments afterwards.

Battery compartment

16 Remove the storage compartment. Remove the battery (see Chapter 10).

17 Remove the fuel filler cap, and its seal.

18 Undo the screws securing the battery panel and lift it up, noting how it locates at the back, then detach the fuse holder and remove the panel **(see illustration)**. Refit the filler cap.

19 Installation is the reverse of removal.

Front mudguard

20 Refer to Chapter 7 and follow the procedure for removing and installing the steering stem.

Rear mudguard

21 Remove both side panels. Remove the air filter housing (see Chapter 5).

22 Undo the screws securing the mudguard and manoeuvre it out.

23 Installation is the reverse of removal.

---

7 GTS, GTV and GT models

Seat

1 Unlock the seat, using either the electronic release button on the kick panel or the lever inside the glovebox, and swing it upright **(see illustration)**. Lift out the storage compartment **(see illustration 7.4)**.

2 Undo the screws securing the seat hinge and remove the seat **(see illustration)**. Installation is a reverse of removal.

3 On GTV models, the passenger seat can be detached from the seat pan by undoing the four screws. Note that storage is provided for the seat cover in the hole in the underside of the seat pan.

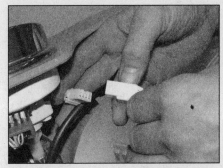

6.12e Disconnect the headlight wiring

Storage compartment – engine access

4 Unlock the seat and swing it upright, then lift out the storage compartment **(see illustration)**.

5 Installation is the reverse of removal.

Front panel grille

6 Carefully lever off the badge in the grille **(see illustration)**. Undo the screw behind it then lift the grille to release the hooks from

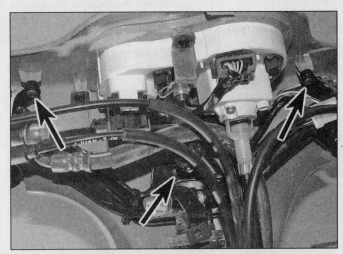

6.13 Disconnect the wiring and cable, then undo the screws (arrowed)

6.18 Battery panel screws (arrowed)

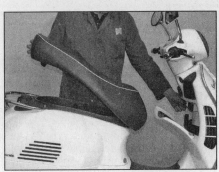

7.1 Unlock the seat and lift it up

7.2 Undo the screws (arrowed) and remove the seat

7.4 Lift the storage compartment out

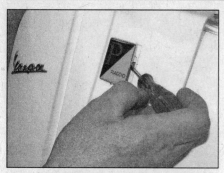

7.6a Carefully prise the badge off using a small screwdriver in the slot

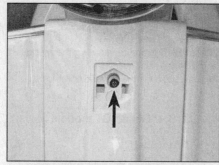

7.6b Undo the screw (arrowed) . . .

which locate in rubber grommets, and two tabs at the front that engage in slots in the floor panel. Carefully pull the panel away to release the pegs from the grommets, then release the tabs **(see illustrations)**.

10 If required undo the remaining screw securing each trim panel and remove the panel **(see illustration)**.

11 Installation is a reverse of removal.

Kick panel

12 Disconnect the battery negative (-) terminal (see Chapter 10).

13 Remove the front panel grille, then undo the two screws located behind it **(see illustration)**.

14 Remove the rear handlebar cover (see below).

15 Undo the screws securing the left and right-hand access panels and remove the panels **(see illustration)**. Undo the screw behind each panel **(see illustration)**.

16 Undo the screws securing the bottom edge of the panel – note that the outer screws are longer than the inner screws **(see illustration)**.

17 Press in the ignition switch to release the glove box door. Undo the screw inside the compartment **(see illustration)**.

18 Unscrew the coolant reservoir filler cap **(see illustration)**.

19 Ease the kick panel up to disengage it from the front edge of the floor panel, then pull it back and when accessible disconnect the seat release button wiring connector, and

7.6c . . . and remove the panel . . .

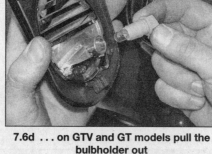

7.6d . . . on GTV and GT models pull the bulbholder out

Side panels

8 Undo the screw at the front and the nut at the rear of each panel **(see illustration)**.

9 Each panel is also secured by three pegs

the slots **(see illustrations)**. On GTV and GT models, pull the sidelight bulbholder out **(see illustration)**.

7 Installation is the reverse of removal.

7.8a Undo the screw (arrowed) . . .

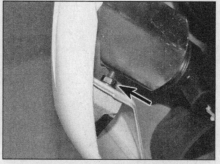

7.8b . . . and the nut (arrowed) . . .

7.9a . . . then pull the panel to release the pegs from the grommets . . .

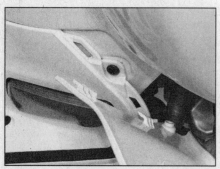

7.9b . . . noting how the tabs at the front locate

7.10 Undo the screw and remove the trim panel

7.13 Undo the screws (arrowed)

7.15a Remove the access panels . . .

7.15b . . . then undo the screw (arrowed) on each side

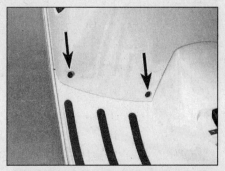

7.16 Undo the screws (arrowed) on each side

unclip the fuse holder from the back of the kick panel **(see illustrations)**.

20 Release the end of the seat opening cable from the lever inside the glove box, then pull the cable stop out of the kick panel **(see illustrations)**. Note how the catch for the glove box aligns with the catch mechanism, then lift the kick panel off. Temporarily refit the coolant reservoir cap.

21 Installation is the reverse of removal. Ensure the ignition immobiliser receiver is correctly positioned on the ignition switch **(see illustration)**. Don't forget to connect the seat release cable and wiring connector and fit the fuseholder in the back of the panel. Check the operation of the seat release and glove box door mechanisms before fitting the screws.

7.17 Undo the screw (arrowed)

Floor panel

22 Remove the side panels and the side trim panels. Undo the four screws and remove the centre mat **(see illustration)**.

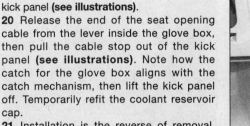

7.18 Remove the cap from the reservoir

23 Remove the kick panel.

24 Undo the screws securing each passenger footrest assembly and remove them **(see illustration)**.

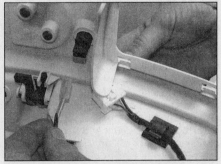

7.19a Disconnect the wiring connector . . .

7.19b . . . and detach the fuse holder

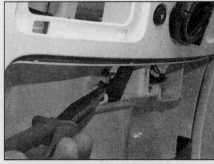

7.20a Detach the cable from the lever . . .

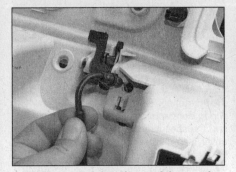

7.20b . . . and draw it out of the panel

7.21 Make sure the receiver (arrowed) is correctly in place

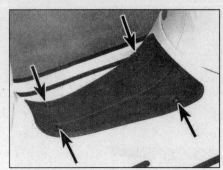

7.22 Undo the screws (arrowed) and remove the mat

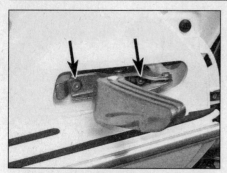

7.24 Undo the screws (arrowed) and remove the footrest

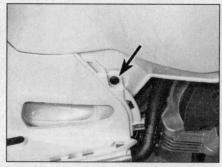

7.25a Undo the screw (arrowed) on each side . . .

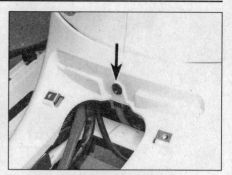

7.25b . . . and the shouldered screw (arrowed) in the centre

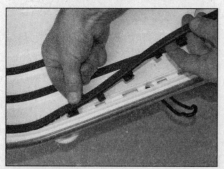

7.26a Pull the rubber strip out . . .

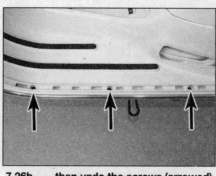

7.26b . . . then undo the screws (arrowed)

7.27 Lift the front and remove the panel

25 Undo the screws securing the back edge of the floor panel, noting that the centre one is shouldered (see illustrations).
26 Pull the outer rubber strip from its channel in each side of the floor panel, noting how it fits (see illustration). Undo the screws along each side (see illustration).
27 Lift up the front of the floor panel and manoeuvre the panel off (see illustration).
28 Installation is the reverse of removal.

Handlebar covers – GTS models

29 Remove the mirrors (see Section 3).
30 Remove the front panel grille.
31 To remove the front cover, undo the screws from the underside of the rear cover and the screw below the headlight – place a rag under the headlight when undoing the front screw as it is easy to drop it down inside the kick panel (see illustrations). Carefully ease away the top edge of the front cover to release the pegs which locate into holes in the top edge of the rear cover (see illustration). The cover is quite a tight fit and a certain amount of leverage is required, but take care not to apply excessive force as the cover could break. Once the cover is free, disconnect the headlight wiring connectors and remove the cover (see illustration). If required, remove the headlight (see Chapter 10).
32 To remove the rear cover, first remove the front cover. Undo the screws securing the rear cover to the brackets on the handlebars (see illustrations). Where fitted undo the screw securing the instrument cluster to its support bracket nest to the speedometer cable. If the cover is being completely removed rather than just displaced for access, disconnect the instrument cluster and handlebar switch wiring connectors, noting which fits where, and the speedometer cable, then remove the cover (see illustrations). If required, remove the instrument cluster (see Chapter 10).
33 Installation is the reverse of removal. Make sure the wiring connectors are correctly and securely connected, and check the operation

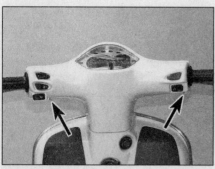

7.31a Undo the screws (arrowed) on the underside . . .

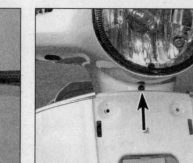

7.31b . . . and the screw (arrowed) below the headlight

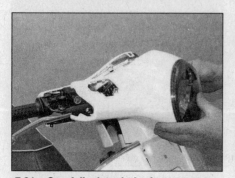

7.31c Carefully detach the front cover . . .

7.31d . . . and disconnect the headlight wiring

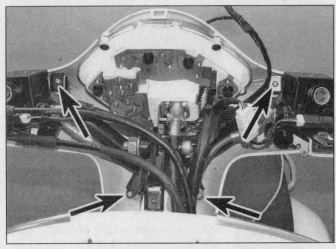

7.32a Undo the screws (arrowed)

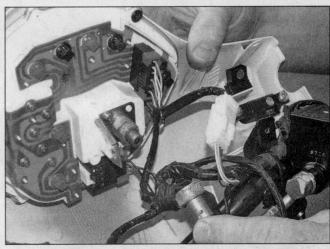

7.32b Disconnect the speedometer cable and all wiring connectors

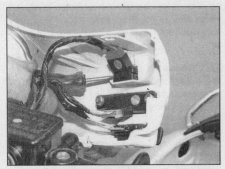

7.32c You need to displace the top switch on the left-hand side . . .

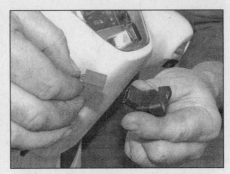

7.32d . . . for clearance to disconnect its connector

7.34a Slacken the screws (arrowed) . . .

of all switches and lights. Use the rag again to prevent the front screw dropping down.

Handlebar covers/instrument housing – GTV and GT models

34 Detach the windshield by backing-off the grub screw in its two fasteners and pulling the rubber mounting off the chrome support bracket **(see illustrations)**. Remove the front panel grille.

35 Slacken the speedometer cable clamp screws and undo the two screws in the lower cover **(see illustration)**, then press the rear edge of the lower cover inwards to release its tab from the top cover **(see illustration)**. Draw the top cover up sufficiently to disconnect the speedometer cable **(see illustration)**. Disconnect the instrument cluster wiring

7.34b . . . then lift the windshield off

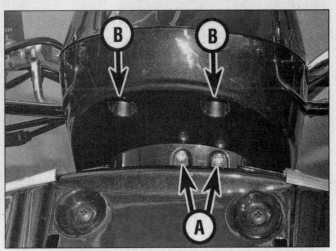

7.35a Slacken the screws (A) and undo the screws (B) . . .

7.35b . . . then release the covers at the back as described

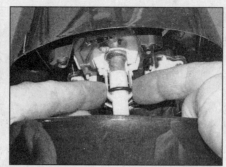

7.35c Lift the front and disconnect the cable . . .

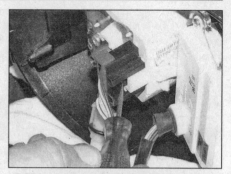

7.35d . . . then push in the tab to release the wiring connector . . .

7.35e . . . and undo the screws (arrowed) securing the warning light panel

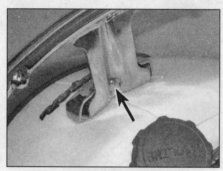

7.37 Undo the screw (arrowed) and remove the badge

connector **(see illustration)**. Undo the warning light panel unit screws and remove the top cover and instrument cluster **(see illustration)**. If required, remove the instrument cluster (see Chapter 10).

36 The lower cover can only be removed once the handlebar assembly has been removed (see Chapter 7).

Grab-rail or rear carrier

37 Remove the storage compartment. Undo the screw securing the badge to the rear mount **(see illustration)**.

38 Remove the fuel filler cap and its seal **(see illustration)**.

39 Undo the tank cover bolts, noting the washers, and remove the cover **(see illustration)**.

40 Undo the rear screws securing the grab rail or rear carrier and lift it off **(see illustration)**.

41 Installation is the reverse of removal.

Front mudguard

42 Refer to Chapter 7 and follow the procedure for removing and installing the steering stem.

Rear mudguard

43 Remove both side panels. Remove the air filter housing (see Chapter 5). Note how two of the bolts also secure the mudguard **(see illustration)**.

44 Undo the screw securing the mudguard and manoeuvre it out **(see illustration)**.

45 Installation is the reverse of removal.

7.38 Unscrew the cap then remove the seal

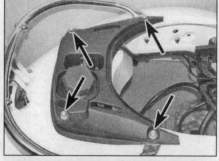

7.39 Unscrew the bolts (arrowed) and remove the cover

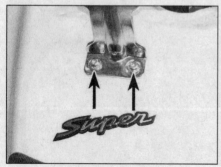

7.40 Undo the screws (arrowed) and remove the rail/carrier

7.43 Note how the mudguard locates (arrows)

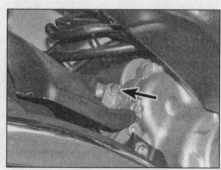

7.44 Undo the screw (arrowed) and remove the mudguard

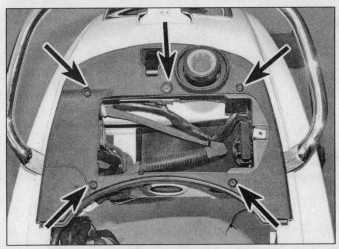

8.10a Undo the screws . . .

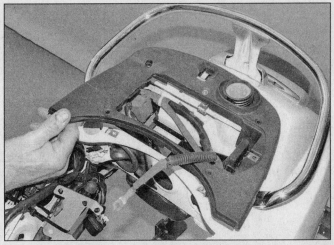

8.10b . . . and lift up the battery panel

8 LX, LXV and S models – 2012-on

Engine access panel

1 Undo the single screw securing the access panel below the front of the seat and remove the panel **(see illustrations 5.6a and b).**
2 Installation is the reverse of removal.

Storage compartment and seat

3 Unlock the seat and swing it upright. Lift the storage compartment out.
4 Undo the screws securing the seat hinge and remove the seat.
5 Installation is a reverse of removal.

Battery panel and grab rail

Note: *On some models a luggage carrier is attached to the grab rail.*
6 Remove the storage compartment (see Steps 3 and 4).
7 Remove the battery (see Chapter 10).
8 Release the clip securing the fuse holder wiring and detach the holder from the battery panel.
9 Remove the fuel filler cap and filler neck seal.
10 Undo the screws securing the battery panel and lift it up, noting how it locates **(see illustrations).** Temporarily install the fuel filler cap.
11 Undo the screw securing the Vespa badge to the centre grab rail mounting **(see illustration 7.37).**
12 Unscrew the bolts securing the grab rail and lift it off.
13 Installation is the reverse of removal.

Side panels and trim panels

14 Working on one side at a time, undo the screws securing the front edge of the panel **(see illustration).**
15 Each panel is secured along the side of

the scooter body by two pegs which locate in rubber grommets, and by a tab at the rear. Carefully pull the panel away to release the pegs from the grommets, then ease the panel back to disengage the rear tab **(see illustration).**
16 Installation is the reverse of removal. Make sure the tab and pegs are correctly engaged. Take care not to over-tighten the screws.
17 To remove a trim panel, first undo the screw in the top of the passenger footrest rubber, then ease the trim panel towards the rear noting how the upper tab locates inside

the bodywork **(see illustrations).** Installation is the reverse of removal.

Front panel grille

18 Carefully lever off the badge in the grille, then undo the screw in the recess behind the badge **(see illustrations 6.3a and b).** On S models, undo the screw at the bottom of the grille **(see illustration 6.3c).** Turn the handlebars to one side, then push the grille up to release the hooks on the back from their slots in the body panel **(see illustration 6.3d).**
19 Installation is the reverse of removal.

8.14 Undo the screws (arrowed) . . .

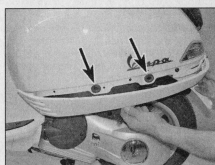

8.15 . . . and release the pegs from the grommets

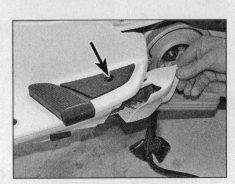

8.17a Screw (arrowed) secures trim panel

8.17b Note location of upper tab (arrowed)

8.20a Undo the screws behind the grille . . .

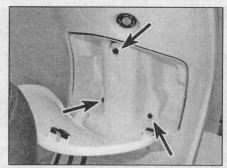

8.20b . . . and inside the glovebox

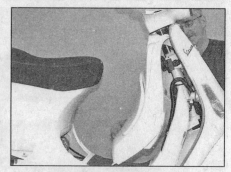

8.22 Lift the kickpanel away

8.27a Undo the screws . . .

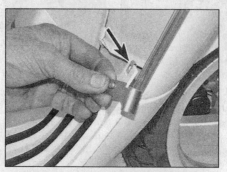

8.27b . . . and remove the trim strip brackets. Note U-clip (arrowed)

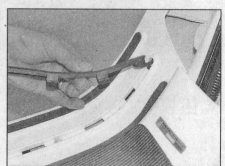

8.28a Remove the rubber runners . . .

Kick panel

20 On LX and LXV models, remove the front panel grille (see Step 18). Undo the two screws located behind it (see illustration). Open the glovebox door. Undo the three screws inside the compartment (see illustration).

21 On S models, undo the five screws securing the kick panel. Pull the left and right-hand outer rubber runners up off the floor, noting how they fit, then undo the screws underneath.

22 Ease the kick panel up, then pull it away from the front panel (see illustration).

23 Installation is the reverse of removal.

Check the operation of the glovebox door release mechanism before installing the fixing screws.

Floor panel

24 Remove the engine access panel (see Step 1).

25 Remove the side panels and trim panels on both sides (see Steps 14, 15 and 17).

26 Remove the kick panel (see Steps 20 to 22).

27 Undo the two screws on each side securing the front edge of the floor panel (see illustration). Note how the brackets secured

by the screws hold the panel trim strip (see illustration). Note the location of the U-clips.

28 Pull the left and right-hand centre rubber runners up off the floor, noting how they fit, then undo the screws underneath (see illustrations).

29 Lift the front edge of the floor panel and manoeuvre it off (see illustration).

30 Installation is the reverse of removal.

Handlebar covers – LX and S model

31 Remove the mirrors (see Section 3). Remove the front panel grille (see Step 18).

32 To remove the front cover, undo the

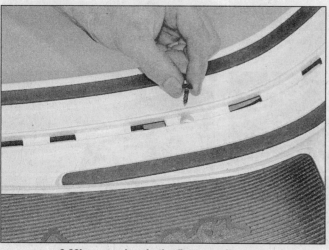

8.28b . . . and undo the floor panel screws

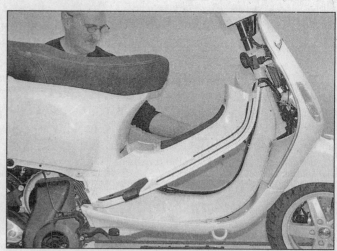

8.29 Manoeuvre the floor panel off

8.32a Undo the screws at the rear . . .

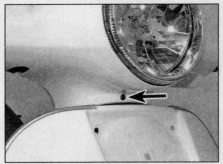

8.32b . . . and the screw at the front

screws from the rear cover and the screw below the headlight – place a rag under the headlight when undoing the front screw as it is easy to drop it down inside the kick panel **(see illustrations)**.

33 Carefully ease the front cover away to release the pegs which secure the top edge **(see illustration)**. These pegs are quite a tight fit and a certain amount of leverage is required, but take care not to apply excessive force as

the cover could break. Once the cover is free, disconnect the headlight wiring connectors **(see illustration)**. If required, remove the headlight (see Chapter 10).

34 To remove the rear cover, first remove the front cover. Undo the screws securing the rear cover to the brackets on the handlebars **(see illustration)**. Unscrew the speedometer cable and ease the cover up off the handlebars **(see illustration)**. If the cover is being completely

removed rather than just displaced for access, disconnect the instrument cluster and handlebar switch wiring connectors, noting which fits where, then remove the cover. If required, remove the instrument cluster (see Chapter 10).

35 Installation is the reverse of removal. Make sure the wiring connectors are correctly and securely connected, and check the operation of all switches and lights before riding the scooter.

Handlebar covers – LXV model

36 Follow the procedure in Section 5.

Front mudguard

37 Refer to Chapter 7 and follow the procedure for removing and installing the steering stem.

Rear mudguard and hugger

38 To remove the mudguard, first remove both side panels (see Steps 14 and 15).

39 Pull the licence plate light bulbholder out

8.33a Ease the front cover away carefully . . .

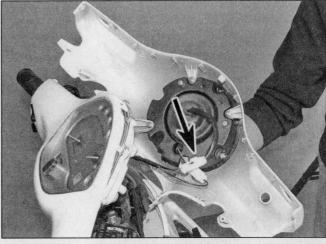

8.33b . . . and disconnect the wiring connectors

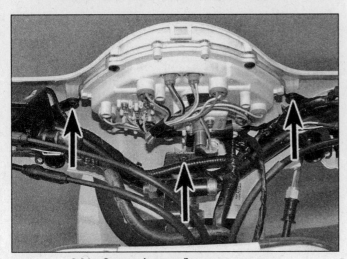

8.34a Screws (arrowed) secure rear cover

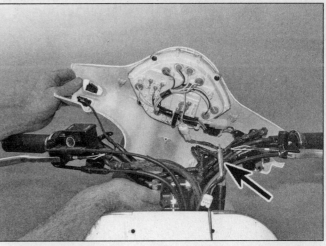

8.34b Raise the cover – note speedometer cable (arrowed)

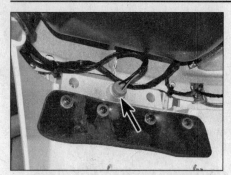

8.39 Pull out the bulbholder (arrowed)

8.43 Undo the screws on left-hand side . . .

8.44 . . . and the screw on the right-hand side

from the back of the light unit **(see illustration)**.
40 Undo the screws on the left and right-hand sides securing the mudguard **(see illustration 5.41)** and lift it off.
41 Installation is the reverse of removal.

42 To remove the hugger, first remove the rear wheel (see Chapter 8).
43 Undo the screws on the lower edge of the air filter housing on the left-hand side **(see illustration)**.

44 Undo the screw on the forward edge of the hugger on the right-hand side **(see illustration)**. Lift the hugger off.
45 Installation is the reverse of removal.

Chapter 10
Electrical system

Contents

Degrees of difficulty

Easy, suitable for novice with little experience 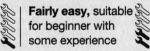 **Fairly easy,** suitable for beginner with some experience **Fairly difficult,** suitable for competent DIY mechanic **Difficult,** suitable for experienced DIY mechanic **Very difficult,** suitable for expert DIY or professional

Specifications

Battery

Capacity
LX, LXV and S models . . . . 12 V, 10 Ah (12V, 6 Ah on LX and LXV from June 2013-on)
GTS, GTV and GT models . . . . 12 V, 12 Ah
Voltage
Fully-charged . . . . 13.0 to 13.2 V
Discharged . . . . below 12.3 V
Charging rate
Normal . . . . 1.0 A for 5 hrs
Quick . . . . 3.0 A for 1 hr

Charging system

Current leakage . . . . 0.5 mA (max)
Alternator stator coil resistance . . . . 0.2 to 1.0 ohms
Regulated voltage output. . . . . 14 to 15 V @ 5000 rpm

Bulbs

Headlight 12V, 60/55W
Sidelight 12V, 5W
Brake light
LX, LXV and S models 2009 to 2011 . . . . 12V, 16W (21W on S)
GTS, GTV and GT models 12V, 16W
Tail light – LX, LXV and S models 2009 to 2011, GTS, GTV and
GT models 12V, 5W
Brake/tail light
LX models 2012-on 12V, 16/5W
LXV models 2012-on 12V, 18/5W
S models 2012-on 12V, 21/5W
Licence plate light 12V, 5W
Turn signal . . . . 12V, 10W (Amber)
Warning lights – LXV and S models
Turn signal, high beam, oil pressure, low fuel, engine check . . . . 12V, 2W (LXV), 1.2W (S)
Instrument illumination 12V, 1.2W

Fuses

Main
LX, LXV and S models . . . .   20 A
GTS, GTV and GT models . . . .   30 A
Others. . . . .   see Section 5 and *Wiring Diagrams*

Torque settings

Starter motor mounting bolts . . . .   12 Nm

---

1 General information

All models have a 12 volt electrical system charged by a three-phase alternator with a separate regulator/rectifier.

The regulator maintains the charging system output within the specified range to prevent overcharging, and the rectifier converts the ac (alternating current) output of the alternator to dc (direct current) to power the lights and other electrical systems and to charge the battery. The alternator rotor is mounted on the right-hand end of the crankshaft.

The starter motor is mounted on the top of the crankcase. The starting system includes the motor, the battery, the relay and the various wires and switches. A safety system, using the brake light switches, prevents the engine from being started unless one of the brake levers is pulled in.

Note: *Keep in mind that electrical parts, once purchased, often cannot be returned. To avoid unnecessary expense, make very sure the faulty component has been positively identified before buying a replacement part.*

2 Electrical system fault finding

1 A typical electrical circuit consists of an electrical component, the switches, relays, etc, related to that component and the wiring and connectors that link the component to the battery and the frame.

2 Before tackling any troublesome electrical circuit, first study the wiring diagram thoroughly to get a complete picture of what makes up that individual circuit. Trouble spots, for instance, can often be narrowed down by noting if other components related to that circuit are operating properly or not. If several components or circuits fail at one time, chances are the fault lies either in the fuse or in the common earth (ground) connection, as several circuits are often routed through the same fuse and earth (ground) connections.

3 Electrical problems often stem from simple causes, such as loose or corroded connections or a blown fuse. Prior to any electrical fault finding, always visually check the condition of the fuse, wires and connections in the problem circuit. Intermittent failures can be especially frustrating, since you can't always duplicate the failure when it's convenient to test. In such situations, a good practice is to clean all connections in the affected circuit, whether or not they appear to be good – where possible use a dedicated electrical cleaning spray along with sandpaper, wire wool or other abrasive material to remove corrosion, and a dedicated electrical protection spray to prevent further problems. All of the connections and wires should also be wiggled to check for looseness which can cause intermittent failure.

4 If you don't have a multimeter it is highly advisable to obtain one – they are not expensive and will enable a full range of electrical tests to be made **(see illustration)**. Go for a modern digital one with LCD display as they are easier to use. A continuity tester and/or test light are useful for certain electrical checks as an alternative, though are limited in their usefulness compared to a multimeter **(see illustrations)**.

Continuity checks

5 The term continuity describes the uninterrupted flow of electricity through an electrical circuit. Continuity can be checked with a multimeter set either to its continuity function (a beep is emitted when continuity is found), or to the resistance (ohms / Ω) function, or with a dedicated continuity tester. Both instruments are powered by an internal battery, therefore the checks are made with the ignition OFF. As a safety precaution, always disconnect the battery negative (–) lead before making continuity checks, particularly if ignition switch checks are being made.

6 If using a multimeter, select the continuity function if it has one, or the resistance (ohms) function. Touch the meter probes together and check that a beep is emitted or the meter reads zero, which indicates continuity. If there is no continuity there will be no beep or the meter will show infinite resistance. After using the meter, always switch it OFF to conserve its battery.

7 A continuity tester can be used in the same way – its light should come on or it should beep to indicate continuity in the switch ON position, but should be off or silent in the OFF position.

8 Note that the polarity of the test probes doesn't matter for continuity checks, although care should be taken to follow specific test procedures if a diode or solid-state component is being checked.

Switch continuity checks

9 If a switch is at fault, trace its wiring to the wiring connectors. Separate the connectors and inspect them for security and condition. A build-up of dirt or corrosion here will most likely be the cause of the problem – clean up and apply a water dispersant such as WD40, or alternatively use a dedicated contact cleaner and protection spray.

10 If using a multimeter, select the continuity function if it has one, or the resistance (ohms) function, and connect its probes to the terminals

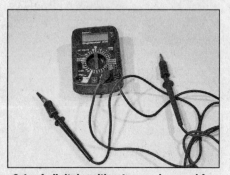

2.4a A digital multimeter can be used for all electrical tests

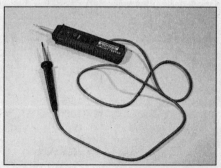

2.4b A battery-powered continuity tester

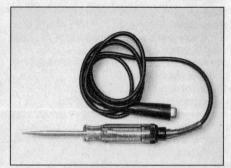

2.4c A simple test light is useful for voltage tests

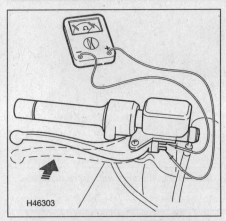

H46303

2.10 Continuity should be indicated across switch terminals when lever is operated

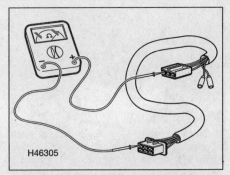

H46305

2.12 Wiring continuity check. Connect the meter probes across each end of the same wire

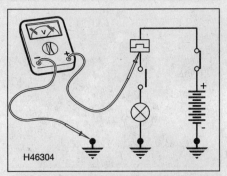

H46304

2.15 Voltage check. Connect the meter positive probe to the component and the negative probe to earth

in the connector **(see illustration)**. Simple ON/OFF type switches, such as brake light switches, only have two wires whereas combination switches, like the handlebar switches, have many wires. Study the wiring diagram to ensure that you are connecting to the correct pair of wires. Continuity should be indicated with the switch ON and no continuity with it OFF.

Wiring continuity checks

11 Many electrical faults are caused by damaged wiring, often due to incorrect routing or chaffing on frame components. Loose, wet or corroded wire connectors can also be the cause of electrical problems.

12 A continuity check can be made on a single length of wire by disconnecting it at each end and connecting the meter or continuity tester probes to each end of the wire **(see illustration)**. Continuity (low or no resistance – 0 ohms) should be indicated if the wire is good. If no continuity (high resistance) is shown, suspect a broken wire.

13 To check for continuity to earth in any earth wire connect one probe of your meter or tester to the earth wire terminal in the connector and the other to the frame, engine, or battery earth (–) terminal. Continuity (low or no resistance – 0 ohms) should be indicated if the wire is good. If no continuity (high resistance) is shown, suspect a broken wire or corroded or loose earth point (see below).

Voltage checks

14 A voltage check can determine whether power is reaching a component. Use a multimeter set to the dc voltage scale, or a test light. The test light is the cheaper component, but the meter has the advantage of being able to give a voltage reading.

15 Connect the meter or test light in parallel, i.e. across the load **(see illustration)**.

16 First identify the relevant wiring circuit by referring to the wiring diagram at the end of this manual. If other electrical components share the same power supply (i.e. are fed from the same fuse), take note whether they are working correctly – this is useful information in deciding where to start checking the circuit.

17 If using a meter, check first that the meter leads are plugged into the correct terminals on the meter (red to positive (+), black to negative (–). Set the meter to the dc volts function, where necessary at a range suitable for the battery voltage – 0 to 20 vdc. Connect the meter red probe (+) to the power supply wire and the black probe to a good metal earth (ground) on the scooter's frame or directly to the battery negative terminal. Battery voltage should be shown on the meter with the ignition switch, and if necessary any other relevant switch, ON.

18 If using a test light, connect its positive (+) probe to the power supply terminal and its negative (–) probe to a good earth (ground) on the scooter's frame. With the switch, and if necessary any other relevant switch, ON, the test light should illuminate.

19 If no voltage is indicated, work back towards the fuse continuing to check for voltage. When you reach a point where there is voltage, you know the problem lies between that point and your last check point.

Earth (ground) checks

20 Earth connections are made either directly to the engine or frame via the mounting of the component, or by a separate wire into the earth circuit of the wiring harness. Alternatively a short earth wire is sometimes run from the component directly to the scooter's frame.

21 Corrosion is a common cause of a poor earth connection, as is a loose earth terminal fastener.

22 If total or multiple component failure is experienced, check the security of the main

earth lead from the negative (–) terminal of the battery, the earth lead bolted to the engine, and the main earth point(s) on the frame. If corroded, dismantle the connection and clean all surfaces back to bare metal. Remake the connection and prevent further corrosion from forming by smearing battery terminal grease over the connection.

23 To check the earth of a component, use an insulated jumper wire to temporarily bypass its earth connection **(see illustration)** – connect one end of the jumper wire to the earth terminal or metal body of the component and the other end to the scooter's frame. If the circuit works with the jumper wire installed, the earth circuit is faulty.

24 To check an earth wire first check for corroded or loose connections, then check the wiring for continuity (Step 13) between each connector in the circuit in turn, and then to its earth point, to locate the break.

3 Battery removal, installation and inspection

Caution: Be extremely careful when handling or working around the battery. The electrolyte is very caustic and an explosive gas (hydrogen) is given off when the battery is charging.

Removal and installation

1 Make sure the ignition is switched OFF.

2 On LX, LXV and S models raise the seat, then remove the battery cover **(see illustration)**.

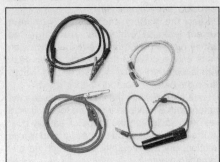

2.23 A selection of insulated jumper wires

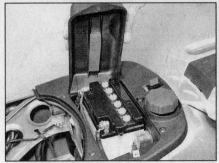

3.2a Remove the battery cover

3.2b Disconnect the negative lead first, then disconnect the positive lead (arrowed) . . .

3.2c . . . and lift the battery out

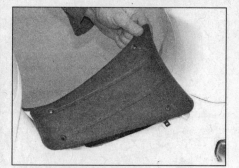

3.3a Undo the screws and remove the mat . . .

3.3b . . . then remove the retainer

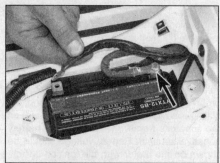

3.3c Disconnect the negative lead first, then disconnect the positive lead (arrowed) . . .

3.3d . . . and lift the battery out

Unscrew the negative (–) terminal bolt first and disconnect the lead from the battery **(see illustration)**. Lift up the red insulating cover to access the positive (+) terminal, then unscrew the bolt and disconnect the lead. Lift the battery out **(see illustration)**.

3 On GTS, GTV and GT models remove the centre mat from the floor panel **(see illustration)**. Remove the battery retainer **(see illustration)**. Unscrew the negative (–) terminal bolt first and disconnect the lead from the battery **(see illustration)**. Lift up the red insulating cover to access the positive (+) terminal, then unscrew the bolt and disconnect the lead. Lift the battery out **(see illustration)**.

4 On installation, clean the battery terminals and lead ends with a wire brush, fine

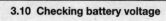

3.10 Checking battery voltage

sandpaper or steel wool. Reconnect the leads, connecting the positive (+) terminal first.

> **HAYNES HINT** *Battery corrosion can be kept to a minimum by applying a layer of battery terminal grease or petroleum jelly (Vaseline) to the terminals after the leads have been connected. DO NOT use a mineral based grease.*

Inspection

5 The battery fitted to all models covered in this manual is of the maintenance-free (sealed) type, therefore requiring no regular maintenance. However, the following checks should still be performed.

6 Check the battery terminals and leads are tight and free of corrosion. If corrosion is evident, clean the terminals as described above, then protect them from further corrosion (see *Haynes Hint*).

7 Keep the battery case clean to prevent current leakage, which can discharge the battery over a period of time (especially when it sits unused). Wash the outside of the case with a solution of baking soda and water. Rinse the battery thoroughly, then dry it.

8 Look for cracks in the case and replace the battery with a new one if any are found. If acid has been spilled on the frame or battery box, neutralise it with a baking soda and water solution, dry it thoroughly, then touch up any damaged paint.

9 If the scooter sits unused for long periods of

time, disconnect the cables from the battery terminals, negative (–) terminal first. Refer to Section 4 and charge the battery once every month to six weeks.

10 Check the condition of the battery by measuring the voltage present at the battery terminals **(see illustration)**. Connect the voltmeter positive (+) probe to the battery positive (+) terminal, and the negative (–) probe to the battery negative (–) terminal. When fully-charged there should be 13.0 to 13.2 volts present. If the voltage falls below 12.3 volts remove the battery (see above), and recharge it as described below in Section 4.

4 Battery charging

Caution: Be extremely careful when handling or working around the battery. The electrolyte is very caustic and an explosive gas (hydrogen) is given off when the battery is charging.

1 Remove the battery (see Section 3). Connect the charger to the battery, making sure that the positive (+) lead on the charger is connected to the positive (+) terminal on the battery, and the negative (–) lead is connected to the negative (–) terminal **(see illustration)**.

2 Vespa recommend that the battery is charged at the normal rate specified at the beginning of the Chapter. Exceeding this figure can cause the battery to overheat, buckling the plates and rendering it useless. Ideally charge the battery using one of the

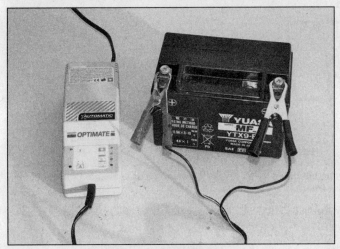

4.1 Battery connected to a charger

5.3a Main and engine management fuses (arrowed) –
LX, LXV and S models

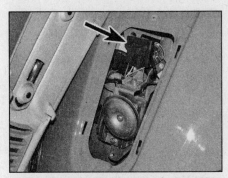

5.3b All other fuses (arrowed) – LX, LXV
and S models

dedicated motorcycle chargers as shown in illustration 4.1. If a normal domestic charger is used check that after a possible initial peak, the charge rate falls to a safe level. If the battery becomes hot during charging **stop**. Further charging will cause damage. **Note:** *In emergencies the battery can be charged at the quick rate specified. However, this is not recommended and the normal charging rate is by far the safer method of charging the battery.*

3 If the recharged battery discharges rapidly if left disconnected it is likely that an internal short caused by physical damage or sulphation has occurred. A new battery will be required. A sound item will tend to lose its charge at about 1% per day.

4 Install the battery (see Section 3).

5 If the scooter sits unused for long periods of time, charge the battery once every month to six weeks and leave it disconnected.

5 Fuses

1 If one particular electrical circuit or component fails to work, i.e. the brake lights or the horn, check the individual fuse for that circuit. If there are no electrical systems working at all, check the main fuse. Refer to your handbook for the location, identity and rating of each fuse.

2 The electrical system is protected by fuses of different ratings.

3 On LX, LXV and S models the main fuse and the fuel injection system fuse are located in the battery compartment – raise the seat, then remove the battery cover to access them **(see illustration)**. All other fuses are located behind the front panel grille **(see illustration)** – remove the grille for access (see Chapter 9).

4 On GTS125ie models the main fuse is located in the battery compartment – remove the centre mat from the floor panel to access it **(see illustration 3.3a)**. All other fuses are located in the left-hand side of the glove compartment **(see illustration 5.5b)** – open the compartment for access (see Chapter 9).

5 On 250/300 GTS models, and on GTV and GT models, the main fuse and the fuel injection system fuses are located in the engine bay **(see illustrations)** – raise the seat and remove

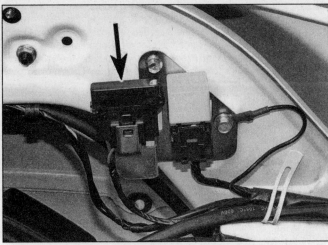

5.5a On GTS, GTV and GT models the main and injection fuses
are located at the side of the engine bay . . .

5.5b . . . and near the seat hinge (arrowed)

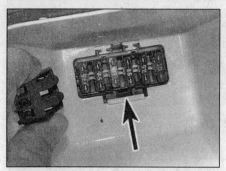

5.5c All other fuses (arrowed) – GTS, GTV and GT models

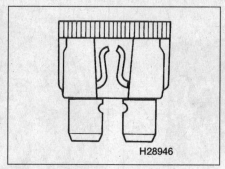

5.6 A blown fuse can be identified by a break in its element

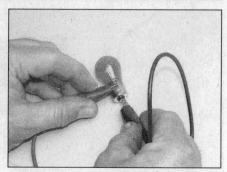

6.1 Checking a bulb filament for continuity

the storage compartment to access them (see Chapter 9). All other fuses are located in the left-hand side of the glove compartment **(see illustration)** – open the compartment for access (see Chapter 9).

6 Where present unclip the fusebox lid to expose the fuses. The fuses can be removed and checked visually. If you can't pull the fuse out with your fingertips, use a pair of suitable pliers. A blown fuse is easily identified by a break in the element **(see illustration)**. Each fuse is clearly marked with its rating and must only be replaced by a fuse of the correct rating.

 Warning: Never put in a fuse of a higher rating or bridge the terminals with any other substitute, however temporary it may be. Serious damage may be done to the circuit, or a fire may start.

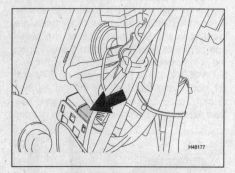

6.4a Headlight relay – 2009 to 2011 LX and S models

7 If the new fuse blows immediately check the wiring circuit very carefully for evidence of a short-circuit. Look for bare wires and chafed, melted or burned insulation.

8 Occasionally a fuse will blow or cause an open-circuit for no obvious reason. Corrosion of the fuse ends and fusebox terminals may occur and cause poor fuse contact. If this happens, remove the corrosion with a wire brush or emery paper, then spray the fuse end and terminals with electrical contact cleaner.

6 Lighting system check

1 The battery provides power for operation of the lights. If a light fails first check the bulb (see relevant Section), and the bulb terminals in the holder. If none of the lights work, always check battery voltage before proceeding. Low battery voltage indicates either a faulty battery or a defective charging system. Refer to Section 3 for battery checks and Section 24 for charging system tests. Also, check the relevant fuse(s) (Section 5) – if there is more than one problem at the same time, it is likely to be a fault relating to a multi-function component, such as one of the fuses governing more than one circuit, or the ignition switch. When checking for a blown filament in a bulb, it is advisable to back up a visual check with a continuity test of the filament as it is not always apparent that a bulb has blown **(see illustration)**. When testing for continuity, remember that on single terminal bulbs it is

the metal body of the bulb that is the earth (ground).

Headlight

2 All models have one twin filament bulb. If one headlight beam fails to work, first check the bulb (see Section 7). If both headlight beams fail to work, first check the fuse (see Section 5), and then the bulb (see Section 7). If they are good, the problem lies in the wiring or connectors, the dimmer switch, or the headlight relay. Refer to *Electrical System Fault Finding* (Section 2), the *Wiring Diagrams* at the end of this Chapter, and Step 3 to check the circuit. Refer to Section 19 for the switch testing procedures. Refer to Step 4 to check the relay(s).

3 If the bulb is good, check for battery voltage at the brown or violet wire terminal (according to beam) on the headlight wiring connector with the ignition ON and the switch set to HI or LO beam as required. If voltage is present, check for continuity to earth (ground) in the black wire from the wiring connector. If no voltage is indicated, check the wiring and connectors in the circuit, referring to *Electrical System Fault Finding* (Section 2) and the *Wiring Diagrams* at the end of this Chapter.

4 Check the headlight relay(s) as follows. On 2009 to 2011 LX, LXV and S models, and all GTS, GTV and GT models, remove the front panel grille (see Chapter 9). On 2012-on LX, LXV and S models, remove the kick panel and displace the bracket supporting the headlight and injection system load relays. Pull the relay off its socket **(see illustrations)**. Note that

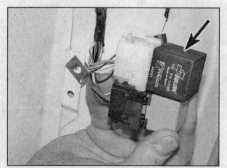

6.4b Headlight relay – 2012-on LX, LXV and S models

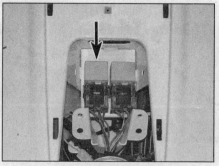

6.4c Headlight relay – GTS models

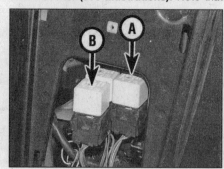

6.4d Headlight relays – GTV and GT models, (A) LO beam, (B) HI beam

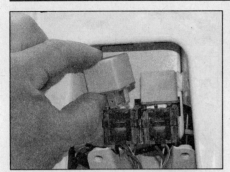

6.4e Pull the relay off its socket

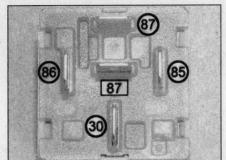

6.5 Terminal numbers are marked on the back

LXV, GTV and GT models have two headlight relays, one for low and another for high beam. Test as follows:

5 Set a multimeter to the ohms x 1 scale and connect it between the 87 and 30 terminals on the relay **(see illustration)**. There should be no continuity (infinite resistance). Using a fully-charged 12 volt battery and two insulated jumper wires, connect the positive (+) terminal of the battery to the 86 terminal, and the negative (–) terminal to the 85 terminal. At this point the relay should be heard to click and the multimeter read 0 ohms (continuity). If this is the case the relay is proved good. If the relay does not click when battery voltage is applied and still indicates no continuity (infinite resistance) across its terminals, it is faulty and must be replaced with a new one. If the relay is good check the wiring to and from the relay, referring to Section 2 and to the wiring diagram for your model at the end of the chapter.

Tail light/sidelight(s), licence plate light

6 If the tail light fails to work, first check the bulb (Section 9 or 7), then the fuse (Section 5). If they are good, disconnect the tail light or sidelight wiring connector, and check for battery voltage at the yellow/black wire terminal on the loom side of the connector with the ignition switch ON. If voltage is present, check for continuity to earth (ground) in the black wire from the wiring connector. If no voltage is indicated, check the wiring and

connectors in the circuit, referring to *Electrical System Fault Finding* (Section 2) and the *Wiring Diagrams* at the end of this Chapter.

Brake light

7 If the brake light fails to work, first check the bulb (Section 9), then the fuse (Section 5). If they are good disconnect the tail light wiring connector, and check for battery voltage at the white/black wire terminal on the loom side of the connector, first with the front brake lever pulled in, then with the rear brake lever pulled in. If voltage is present with one brake on but not the other, then the switch or its wiring is faulty. If voltage is present in both cases, check for continuity to earth (ground) in the black wire from the wiring connector. If no voltage is indicated, check the wiring and connectors between the brake light and the brake switches, the fuse, and the ignition

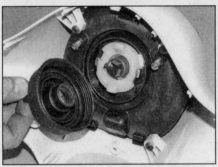

7.1a Remove the dust cover . . .

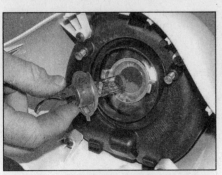

7.1c . . . and remove the bulb from the headlight . . .

7.1d . . . or from the bulbholder

switch, then check the switches themselves. Refer to Section 14 for the switch testing procedures, to *Electrical System Fault Finding* (Section 2) and to the *Wiring Diagrams* at the end of this Chapter.

Turn signals

8 See Section 11.

---

7 Headlight bulb and sidelight bulb

Note: *The headlight bulb is of the quartz-halogen type. Do not touch the bulb glass as skin acids will shorten the bulb's service life. If the bulb is accidentally touched, it should be wiped carefully when cold with a rag soaked in methylated spirit and dried before fitting.*

⚠️ **Warning: Allow the bulb time to cool before removing it if the headlight has just been on.**

Headlight

1 On LX, S and GTS models remove the front handlebar cover (see Chapter 9). Release and remove the bulb according to the type of headlight fitted **(see illustrations)** – where there are individual wiring connectors note which fits on which terminal before disconnecting them.

2 On LXV models release the beam unit from the shell **(see illustrations)**. Disconnect the wiring connectors, noting which fits where

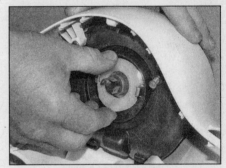

7.1b . . . release the bulb holder or clip . . .

7.2a Unscrew the bolt (arrowed) and tilt the headlight forwards . . .

7.2b ... then undo the screws and detach the beam unit ...

if separate **(see illustration)**. Turn the bulb retainer anti-clockwise. Withdraw the bulb, noting how it locates.

3 On GTV and GT models unscrew the nut and release the beam unit from the shell **(see illustrations)** – retrieve the stud collar if it is

7.2c ... and disconnect the wiring

loose **(see illustration)**. Disconnect the wiring connectors **(see illustration)**. Unscrew the bracket bolts, noting the washers, and remove the bracket **(see illustrations)**. Remove the rubber dust cover **(see illustration)**. Turn the bulb retainer anti-clockwise **(see illustration)**.

Push the bulb in and turn anti-clockwise to release it.
4 Fit the new bulb in reverse order.

 HAYNES HINT *Always use a paper towel or dry cloth when handling new bulbs to prevent injury if the bulb should break and to increase bulb life.*

5 Check the operation of the headlight.

Sidelight

6 On models with the sidelight in the headlight unit either remove the front handlebar cover (see Chapter 9), or release the beam unit from the shell as in Step 2 or 3, according to model. Carefully pull the bulbholder out of the headlight, then pull the bulb out of the holder **(see illustrations)**.
7 On models with the sidelight in the front

7.3a Unscrew the nut ...

7.3b ... and draw the beam unit out

7.3c Retrieve the collar if loose

7.3d Disconnect the wiring

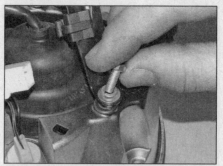

7.3e Unscrew the bolts and remove the bracket

7.3f Remove the rubber cover ...

7.3g ... release the bulb holder ...

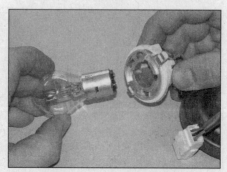

7.3h ... then release the bulb

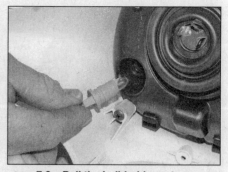

7.6a Pull the bulbholder out ...

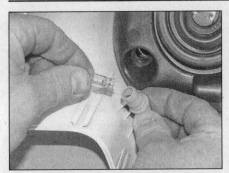

7.6b . . . then remove the bulb

7.7a Pull the bulbholder out when
removing the panel . . .

7.7b . . . then pull the bulb out of the
holder

panel grille remove the grille (see Chapter 9), removing the bulbholder as you do **(see illustration)**. Carefully pull the bulb out of the holder **(see illustration)**.

8 Fit the new bulb in reverse order.

9 Check the operation of the sidelight.

8 Headlight

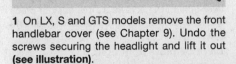

1 On LX, S and GTS models remove the front handlebar cover (see Chapter 9). Undo the screws securing the headlight and lift it out **(see illustration)**.

2 On LXV models release the beam unit

from the shell and disconnect the wiring **(see illustrations 7.2a, b and c)**. Unscrew the shell mounting bolts and remove the light.

3 On GTV and GT models unscrew the nut and release the beam unit from the shell and disconnect the wiring **(see illustrations 7.3a, b, c and d)**. Undo the three screws on the underside of the mudguard and remove the plastic cover **(see illustrations)**. Undo the two front screws and the nut inside the shell, and the two bolts from the underside, and remove the shell **(see illustration)**.

4 If required remove the headlight bulb and the sidelight bulbholder (see Section 7).

5 Installation is the reverse of removal. Make sure all the wiring is correctly routed,

connected and secured. Check the operation of the headlight(s) and sidelight(s). Check the headlight aim.

9 Brake/tail light bulb and licence plate bulb

Note: *It is a good idea to use a paper towel or dry cloth when handling the new bulb to prevent injury if it breaks, and to increase bulb life.*

2009 to 2011 LX, LXV and S models and all GTS, GTV and GT models

8.1 Headlight screws (arrowed) – GTS model shown

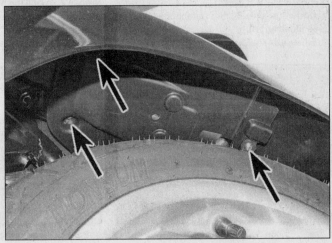

8.3a Undo the screws (arrowed) . . .

8.3b . . . and remove the cover

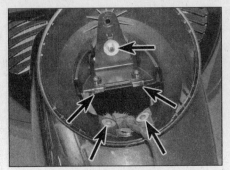

8.3c Undo the nut, bolts and screws to free the shell

9.1 Undo the screw(s) and detach the light unit

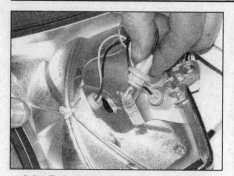

9.2a Twist and release the brake light bulbholder . . .

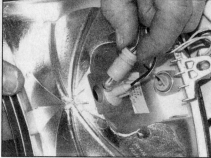

9.2b . . . and pull the tail light bulbholder out . . .

9.3 . . . then remove the bulb

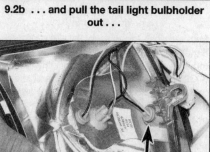

9.6 Licence plate light (arrowed) – GTS, GTV and GT models

Brake/tail light bulb

1 Undo the screw(s) and detach the light unit (see illustration).
2 Either turn the bulbholder anti-clockwise to release it, or pull the bulbholder out, according to model and the bulb being replaced (see illustrations).
3 Carefully remove the bulb, either by

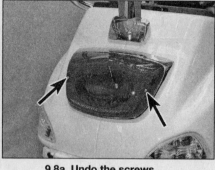

9.8a Undo the screws . . .

9.8b . . . and remove the tail light lens

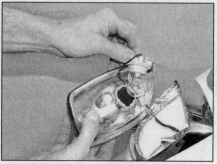

9.9a Remove the bulbholder . . .

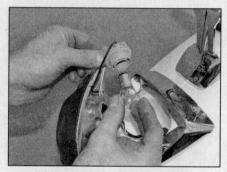

9.9b . . . and release the bulb

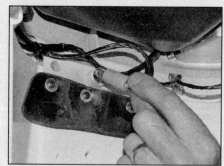

9.11 Licence plate bulbholder and bulb are a push fit

pulling it out or by pushing it in and turning it anti-clockwise, according to type (see illustration).
4 Fit the new bulb in reverse order. Do not over-tighten the screws as it is easy to strip the threads or crack the lens. Check the operation of the tail and brake lights.

Licence plate light bulb

5 On models with the licence plate light in the tail light unit, undo the screw(s) and detach the light unit (see illustration 9.1).
6 Carefully pull the bulbholder out, then pull the bulb out of its socket (see illustration).
7 Fit the new bulb in reverse order. Check the operation of the lights.

2012-on LX, LXV and S models

Brake/tail light bulb

8 Undo the screws and detach the light lens (see illustrations).
9 Turn the bulbholder anti-clockwise to release it, then push the bulb in and turn it anti-clockwise to release it (see illustrations).
10 Fit the new bulb in reverse order. Do not over-tighten the screws as it is easy to crack the lens. Check the operation of the tail and brake lights.

Licence plate light bulb

11 The licence plate light bulbholder is pressed into the back of the light unit. Clean the area around the bulbholder to prevent dirt falling into the light unit. Pull the bulbholder out, then pull the bulb out of the bulbholder (see illustration).
12 Fit the new bulb in reverse order. Check the operation of the lights.

10 Tail light

2009 to 2011 LX, LXV and S models and all GTS, GTV and GT models

1 Undo the screw(s) and detach the light unit (see illustration 9.1).
2 Disconnect the wiring connector(s), and/

or remove the bulbholders, as required **(see illustration)**.

3 Installation is the reverse of removal. Check the operation of the tail and brake lights.

2012-on LX, LXV and S models

4 Undo the screws and detach the light lens **(see illustrations 9.8a and b)**. Disconnect the wiring connector, noting how it fits **(see illustration 10.2)**.

5 If required, undo the screws securing the bezel and lift it off **(see illustration)**.

6 Installation is the reverse of removal. Check the operation of the tail and brake lights.

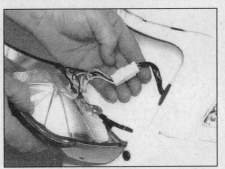

10.2 Disconnect the wiring connector(s)

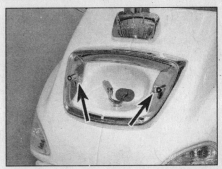

10.5 Bezel is secured by screws (arrowed)

11 Turn signal circuit check

1 Most turn signal problems are the result of a burned out bulb or corroded socket. This is especially true when the turn signals function on one side (although possibly too quickly), but fail to work on the other side. If this is the case, first check the bulbs, the sockets and the wiring connectors (see Section 12). If all the turn signals fail to work, check the fuse (see Section 5). Next check the wiring and connectors, and the switch. Refer to Section 19 for the switch testing procedures, and also to the wiring diagrams at the end of this Chapter.

2 If all is good so far, remove the front handlebar cover and disconnect the wire to the turn signal switch. Connect the positive (+) probe of a voltmeter to the blue/black wire terminal in the connector and the negative (–) probe to earth. With the ignition ON check for a pulsing battery voltage. If voltage is present the relay is working, and the fault lies in the switch itself or the circuit from the switch to the turn signals, or their earth. If there is no pulsing voltage check the wire from the switch connector to the turn signal relay for continuity. On GTS250 and GTV250 models the relay is integrated with the instrument cluster. On 2009 to 2011 LX, LXV and S models remove the storage compartment to access the relay. On 2012-on LX, LXV and S models the

relay is located behind the front grille panel on the left-hand side of the fusebox **(see illustration)**. On all other models remove the left-hand access panel from the kick panel **(see illustrations)**.

3 If continuity is shown, on GTS250 and GTV250 models check the instrument cluster (see Section 15), and on all other models check for battery voltage at the white wire to the relay with the ignition ON. If there is no voltage check the white wire, and if there is voltage replace the relay with a new one.

4 Pull the turn signal relay out of its holder and disconnect the wiring connector **(see illustrations)**. Installation is the reverse of removal.

11.2a Displace the fusebox to access the turn signal relay (arrowed) – 2012-on LX model shown

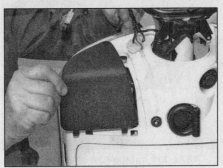

11.2b Remove the panel . . .

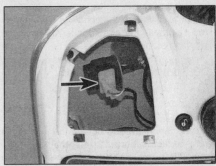

11.2c . . . to access the turn signal relay (arrowed) – GTS125 shown

11.4a Lift the relay out . . .

11.4b . . . and disconnect the wiring connector

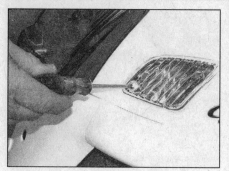

12.1a Undo the screw . . .

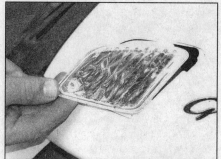

12.1b . . . and detach the turn signal

12.2a Pull the boot back . . .

12 Turn signal bulbs

Note: *It is a good idea to use a paper towel or dry cloth when handling the new bulb to prevent injury if the bulb should break and to increase bulb life.*

1 Undo the screw and detach the turn signal unit **(see illustrations)**.

2 Where fitted, pull back the rubber boot **(see illustration)**. Turn the bulbholder anti-clockwise to release it (see illustration).

3 Push the bulb into the holder and twist it anti-clockwise to remove it **(see illustration)**.

4 Fit the new bulb in reverse order, noting that the pins on amber bulbs are slightly offset. Do not over-tighten the screw as it is easy to strip the threads or crack the lens. Check the operation of the turn signals.

13 Turn signal assemblies

1 Undo the screw and detach the turn signal unit **(see illustrations 12.1a and b)**.

2 On 2012-on LX, LXV and S models, lift the unit out and disconnect the wiring connector from the bulbholder **(see illustrations)**.

3 On all other models, pull the rubber boot back **(see illustration 12.2a)**. Turn the bulbholder anti-clockwise to release it **(see illustration 12.2b)**.

4 Installation is the reverse of removal. Check the operation of the turn signals.

14 Brake light/ starter inhibitor switches

1 The switches, one in each lever housing, are dual function, operating the brake light and preventing the engine from starting unless a brake lever is pulled in.

Circuit check

2 Before checking the switches, and if not already done, check the brake light circuit (see Section 6).

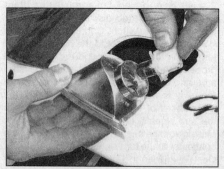

12.2b . . . then release the bulbholder . . .

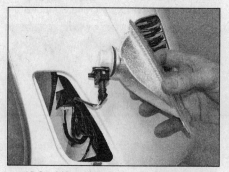

13.2a Lift out the turn signal unit . . .

3 A switch is fitted in the brake master cylinder(s) or in the lever housing on models with a rear drum brake. On LX, S and GTS models remove the front handlebar cover (see Chapter 9), then push in the retaining

14.3a Push the tab in and pull the connector out

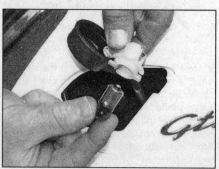

12.3 . . . and remove the bulb

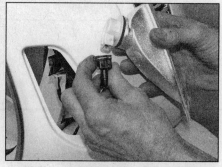

13.2b . . . and disconnect the wiring connector

tab using a small screwdriver to release the connector **(see illustration)**. On LXV, GTV and GT models pull the boot off the switch then disconnect the wires **(see illustration)**.

4 Using a continuity tester, connect the probes

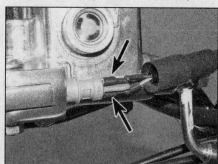

14.3b Pull the boot back and disconnect each wire

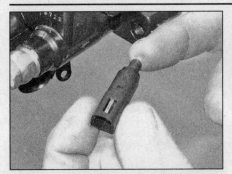

14.4 Check the plunger moves in and out freely and return spring pressure is good

14.7 Unscrew and remove the switch

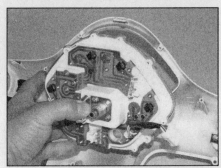

15.9 Undo the screws and lift the cluster from the cover

to the terminals of the switch. With the brake lever at rest, there should be no continuity. With the brake lever applied, there should be continuity. If the switch does not behave as described, unscrew it **(see illustration 14.7)**, then check the plunger is not clogged with dirt and moves in and out freely, returning under spring pressure after being pushed in **(see illustration)**. Otherwise replace the switch with a new one.

5 If the switches are good, check for voltage at the white or red (according to model) wire terminal on the loom side with the ignition switch ON – there should be battery voltage. If there's no voltage present, check the wiring between the connector and the ignition switch via the fuse (see the wiring diagrams at the end of this Chapter). If voltage is present, check the white/black wire for continuity to the brake light wiring connector, referring to the relevant wiring diagram. Repair or replace the wiring or connectors as necessary.

Switch replacement

6 A switch is fitted in the brake master cylinder(s) or in the lever housing on models with a rear drum brake. On LX, S and GTS models remove the front handlebar cover (see Chapter 9), then push in the retaining tab using a small screwdriver to release the connector **(see illustration 14.3a)**. On LXV, GTV and GT models pull the boot off the switch then disconnect the wires **(see illustration 14.3b)**.

7 Unscrew the switch using your fingers **(see illustration)**.

8 Installation is the reverse of removal.

15 Instrument cluster

Check

1 If none of the instruments or displays are working, first check the relevant fuse(s) (see Section 5).

2 Next remove the handlebar cover(s) or displace the instrument housing as required according to model (see Chapter 9). Disconnect the instrument wiring connector(s). Check for battery voltage at the white wire terminal(s) in the loom side of the relevant wiring connector (where there is more than one) with the ignition ON. There should be battery voltage – note that some models have two white wires in different connectors, test both. Also check for battery voltage at the grey/black wire on LX and LXV models, and at the red/blue wire on all other models except S models – there should be permanent voltage, i.e. with the ignition OFF. If there is no voltage, refer to the wiring diagrams and check the wire between the connector and the relevant fuse for loose or broken connections or a damaged wire.

3 Check for continuity to earth in the black wire(s) in the loom side of the connector(s).

4 If the speedometer does not work, first check the cable then check the drive gear in the front wheel hub (Section 17).

5 The temperature gauge and sensor are covered in Chapter 4.

6 The fuel gauge and level sensor are covered in Chapter 5.

7 Referring to *Electrical System Fault Finding* in Section 2 and to the *Wiring Diagrams* at the end of this Chapter for your model, check the wiring and connectors between the relevant instrument or bulb and its source for continuity and security.

Removal and installation

8 Remove the handlebar covers or instrument housing as required according to model (see Chapter 9).

9 Undo the instrument cluster screws and lift it out of the cover/housing **(see illustration)**.

10 If required remove the clear cover from the instrument housing **(see illustration)**.

11 Installation is the reverse of removal. Make sure all wiring is correctly routed and all connectors are secure.

16 Instrument and warning lights

1 Remove the instrument cluster (see Section 15).

2 On LXV and S models, conventional bulbs are fitted. Twist the bulbholder anti-clockwise to release it, then pull the bulb out of the holder and replace it with a new one **(see illustrations)**.

3 All other models have LED instrument and warning lights. Before assuming that an LED has failed, check the cause is not due to the source that supplies its signal, and that all wiring and connectors between the source

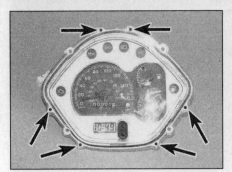

15.10 Front cover is secured by screws (arrowed)

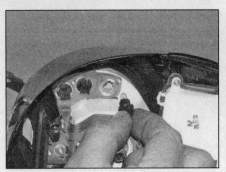

16.2a Twist and remove the bulbholder . . .

16.2b . . . then pull the bulb out

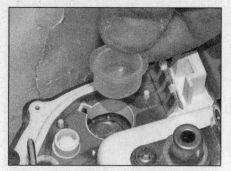

16.4a Remove the plug . . .

16.4b . . . release the cap . . .

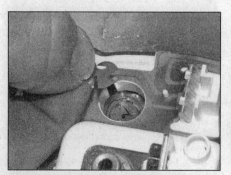

16.4c . . . and remove the contact plate . . .

16.4d . . . and the clock battery (arrowed)

17.2a Unscrew the bolt and detach the cable

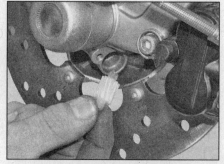

17.2b Withdraw the drive gear

and the instrument cluster are good, a new instrument cluster may have to be fitted – individual LEDs are not available (excess perhaps from an electronics specialist).

4 Where a clock is fitted, to fit a new battery remove the plastic plug, then turn the cap anti-clockwise using a screwdriver and remove the cap, the contact plate and the battery, noting which way up it fits **(see illustrations)**. Fit the new battery, making sure it is the correct way up, then refit the contact plate, cap and plug.

17 Speedometer cable

Removal

1 Remove the front handlebar cover or displace the instrument housing as required according to model (see Chapter 9). Remove the kick panel (see Chapter 9).
2 Unscrew the cable retaining bolt, then draw the cable out **(see illustration)**. Withdraw the drive gear for re-greasing **(see illustration)**.
3 Unscrew the knurled ring or release the clips and detach the cable from the instrument cluster **(see illustrations)**.
4 Free the cable from any guides. Withdraw the cable, noting its routing.

Installation

5 Route the cable up through its guides to the back of the instrument cluster.
6 Connect the cable upper end to the speedometer and tighten the retaining ring or push it up until the clips engage, according to model **(see illustration 17.3a or b)**.
7 Clean and re-grease the drive gear, then fit the gear into the housing **(see illustration 17.2b)**. Fit the cable, locating the end of the inner cable in the drive gear, and tighten the bolt **(see illustration 17.2a)**.
8 Check that the cable doesn't restrict steering movement or interfere with any other components.
9 Install the front handlebar cover or instrument housing (see Chapter 7).

17.3a Either unscrew the ring (arrowed) . . .

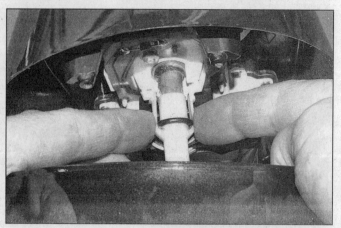

17.3b . . . or press and release the clips, according to model

18.6 Unclip the receiver from the switch

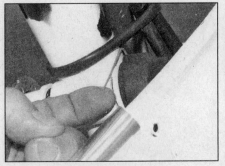

18.7a Release the clip . . .

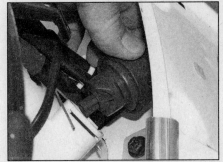

18.7b . . . withdraw the plate . . .

18 Ignition switch

⚠️ **Warning: To prevent the risk of short circuits, disconnect the battery negative (–) lead before making any ignition (main) switch checks.**

Check

1 If there is no power first check the battery, then check the main fuse (see Sections 3 and 5).
2 Next remove the kick panel (see Chapter 9). Disconnect the ignition switch wiring connector (see Step 7).
3 Using an ohmmeter or a continuity tester, check there is continuity between the wire terminals in the switch side of the connector with the ignition switch ON, and there is no continuity with it OFF. If the switch fails the test, replace it with a new one.
4 If it is good, check for battery voltage at the red/black wire terminal on the loom side of the connector. If there is none, check the main fuse (Section 5), then check for continuity in the red/black wire to the fuse, and in the wire from the fuse to the battery. If there is voltage, check the orange wire from the connector to the other circuit fuses, referring to Section 2 and to the wiring diagram for your model at the end of the Chapter.

Removal

5 Remove the front panel grille and the kick panel (see Chapter 9).
6 Where fitted, displace the immobiliser receiver from around the front of the switch – it is a clip-fit **(see illustration)**.
7 To remove the contact plate from the back of the switch, lift up the spring clip and withdraw the plate, noting how it fits **(see illustrations)**. Disconnect the wiring connector **(see illustration)**.
8 To remove the barrel of the switch, insert a small screwdriver into the hole in the housing behind the front of the switch. Push on the retaining tongue with the screwdriver and draw the barrel out of its housing.

Installation

9 Fit the key into the switch and turn it to the ON position. Offer the switch up to its housing, making sure the anchor tang faces down. Insert the switch about half-way into the housing, then simultaneously turn the key to the OFF position and push the switch fully in until the anchor tang is felt to locate.
10 Install the contact plate and immobiliser receiver (where fitted), making sure the wiring connector is secure, the contact plate locates correctly and is secured by the spring clip **(see illustrations 18.7c, b and a, and 18.6)**.

19 Handlebar switches

Check

1 Generally speaking, the switches are reliable and trouble-free. Most troubles, when they do occur, are caused by dirty or corroded contacts, but wear and breakage of internal parts is a possibility that should not be overlooked. If breakage does occur, the entire switch and related wiring harness will have to be replaced with a new one, as individual parts are not available.
2 The switches can be checked for continuity using an ohmmeter or a continuity test light. Always disconnect the battery negative (–) cable, which will prevent the possibility of a short circuit, before making the checks.
3 On LX, S and GTS models remove the front handlebar cover (see Chapter 9). Disconnect the wiring from the switch being tested – if required for better access remove the rear handlebar cover.
4 On LXV, GTV and GT models remove the kick panel (see Chapter 9). Trace the wiring from the relevant switch and disconnect the wiring connector.
5 Check for continuity between the terminals of the switch connector with the switch in the various positions (i.e. switch off – no continuity, switch on – continuity) – see the wiring diagrams at the end of this Chapter. Continuity should exist between the terminals connected by a solid line on the diagram when the switch is in the indicated position.

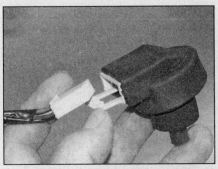

18.7c . . . and disconnect the wiring connector

6 If the continuity check indicates a problem exists, on LXV, GTV and GT models displace the switch housing (see below). On all models spray the switch contacts with electrical contact cleaner (there is no need to remove the switch completely). If they are accessible, the contacts can be scraped clean with a knife or polished with crocus cloth. If switch components are damaged or broken, it will be obvious. If necessary replace the switch or switch housing assembly (according to model) with a new one.

Removal

LX, S and GTS models

7 Remove the handlebar covers (see Chapter 9).
8 Release the switch tabs or undo the screws, according to switch, and withdraw it from the cover **(see illustration)**.

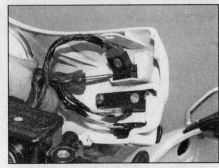

19.8 Switches are retained by tabs or screws

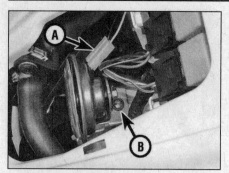

20.2 Horn wiring connectors (A) and mounting bolt (B)

21.7a Pull the boot back and disconnect the connector

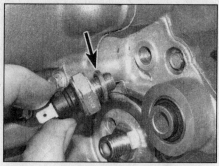

21.7b Unscrew the switch and discard the sealing washer (arrowed)

LXV, GTV and GT models

9 Remove the handlebar cover/instrument housing and the kick panel (see Chapter 9). Disconnect the brake light switch wiring connectors **(see illustration 14.3b)**. Trace the wiring from the relevant switch and disconnect the wiring connector. Feed the wiring back to the switch, freeing it from any clips and ties and noting its routing.

10 Displace the front brake master cylinder assembly from the handlebar (see Chapter 8).

11 To remove the right-hand switch, follow the procedure in Chapter 5, Section 8, for detaching the throttle cables from the pulley – there is no need to detach them from the throttle body.

12 To remove the left-hand switch, undo the switch housing screws and detach the switch face. Undo the clamp bolts and detach the back of the switch.

Installation

13 Installation is the reverse of removal.

14 On LX, S and GTS models make sure the switch tabs locate correctly in the cover **(see illustration 19.8)**.

15 On LXV, GTV and GT models make sure the locating pin in the back of each switch locates in the hole in the handlebar. To fit the right-hand switch refer to Chapter 5, Section 8.

16 Check the operation of the switches and where necessary the throttle cable(s) before riding the scooter.

20 Horn

Check

1 If the horn does not work first check the fuse (see Section 5).

2 If the fuse is good remove the front panel grille (see Chapter 9). Disconnect the wiring connectors from the horn **(see illustration)**. Check them for loose wires.

3 Remove the horn. Using two jumper wires, apply voltage from a fully-charged 12V battery directly to the terminals on the horn.

If the horn doesn't sound, replace it with a new one.

4 If the horn works check for voltage at the grey/black (LX, LXV and S models) or yellow/pink wire connector with the ignition ON and the horn button pressed. If voltage is present, check the black wire for continuity to earth.

5 If no voltage was present, check the light grey/black or yellow/pink wire for continuity between the horn and the horn button, and the wire from the button to the fuse (see the *Wiring Diagrams* at the end of this Chapter). With the ignition switch ON, check that there is voltage at the wire to the horn button in the left-hand handlebar switch.

6 If all the wiring and connectors are good, check the button contacts in the switch (see Section 19).

Replacement

7 Remove the front panel grille (see Chapter 9).

8 Disconnect the wiring connectors from the horn **(see illustration 20.2)**. Unscrew the bolt securing the horn.

9 Install the horn and connect the wiring. Check that it works.

21 Oil pressure switch

Check

1 The oil pressure warning light should come on when the ignition switch is turned ON and go out a few seconds after the engine is started. If it doesn't come on first check the bulb in the instrument cluster (see Section 16) on LXV and S models; other models use an LED warning light which is unlikely to fail. If the oil pressure warning light does not go out or comes on whilst the engine is running, stop the engine immediately and carry out an oil level check, and if the level is correct, an oil pressure check (see Chapter 2A , 2B or 2C).

2 If the oil pressure warning light does not come on when the ignition is turned ON,

disconnect the wiring connector (see Steps 5 and 7). With the ignition switched ON, earth (ground) the wire on the crankcase and check that the warning light comes on. If the light comes on, the switch is defective and must be replaced with a new one.

3 If the light still does not come on, check the relevant fuse (see Section 5), then check for voltage at the wire terminal. If there is no voltage present, check the wire between the switch, the instrument cluster and fusebox for continuity (see the *Wiring Diagrams* at the end of this Chapter).

4 If the warning light does not go out when the engine is started or comes on whilst the engine is running, yet the oil pressure is satisfactory, detach the wire from the oil pressure switch (see above). With the wire detached and the ignition switched ON the light should be out. If it is illuminated, the wire between the switch and instrument cluster is earthed (grounded) at some point. If the wiring is good, the switch must be assumed faulty and replaced with a new one.

Removal

5 The oil pressure switch is screwed into the crankcase on the right-hand side. On LX, LXV and S models remove the alternator cover (see Chapter 2A or 2B). On GTS, GTV and GT models remove the right-hand side panel (see Chapter 9).

6 Drain the engine oil (see Chapter 1).

7 Disconnect the oil pressure switch wiring connector **(see illustration)**. Unscrew the switch using a deep socket **(see illustration)**. Discard the sealing washer – a new one must be fitted on reassembly.

Installation

8 Fit a new sealing washer to the switch and tighten it using a deep socket **(see illustration 21.7b)**. Connect the wiring connector and fit the boot over it **(see illustration 21.7b)**.

9 Refill the engine with oil (see Chapter 1).

10 On LX, LXV and S models install the alternator cover (see Chapter 2A or 2B). On GTS, GTV and GT models install the right-hand side panel (see Chapter 9).

11 Run the engine and check that the switch operates correctly and without leakage.

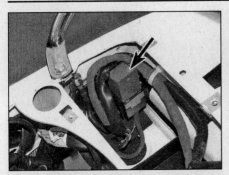

22.2a Starter relay (arrowed) – LX model shown

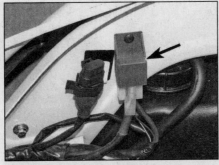

22.2b Starter relay (arrowed) – GTS shown

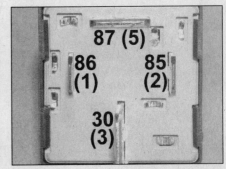

22.5 Terminal identification numbers are marked on the relay

22.11a Pull the relay out of the connector – LX model shown

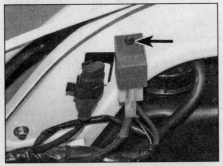

22.11b Undo the screw (arrowed) and displace the relay . . .

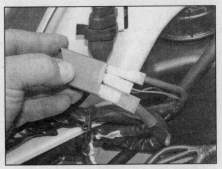

22.11c . . . then disconnect the wiring connectors

22 Starter relay

Check

1 If the starter circuit is faulty, first check the relevant fuses (see Section 5).

2 To access the relay, on LX, LXV and S models remove the battery cover (see Section 3) – the relay is located on the right-hand side of the battery **(see illustration)**. On GTS, GTV and GT models remove the storage compartment (see Chapter 9) **(see illustration)**.

3 With the ignition switch ON, and a brake lever pulled in, press the starter switch. The relay should be heard to click.

4 If the relay doesn't click, switch off the ignition, remove the relay as described below, and test it as follows.

5 Set a multimeter to the ohms x 1 scale and connect it between the 87 and 30 terminals on the relay **(see illustration)**. There should be no continuity (infinite resistance). Using a fully-charged 12 volt battery and two insulated jumper wires, connect the positive (+) terminal of the battery to the 86 terminal, and the negative (–) terminal to the 85 terminal. At this point the relay should be heard to click and the multimeter read 0 ohms (continuity). If this is the case the relay is proved good. If the relay does not click when battery voltage is applied and still indicates no continuity (infinite resistance) across its terminals, it is faulty and must be replaced with a new one.

6 If the relay is good, check for continuity in the main lead from the battery to the relay. Also check that the terminals and connectors at each end of the lead are tight and corrosion-free.

7 Next check for battery voltage at the orange/white wire terminal on the relay wiring connector with the ignition ON, a brake lever pulled in, and the starter button pressed. If there is no voltage, check the wiring and connectors between the relay wiring connector and the starter button, and then from the starter button back to the fuse via the brake light switches. Next check the switches themselves.

8 If voltage is present, check that there is continuity in the orange/blue wire to the ECU.

Removal and installation

9 Disconnect the battery (see Section 3).

23.2 Bench testing a starter motor

10 To access the relay, on LX, LXV and S models remove the battery (see Section 3) and the battery panel (see Chapter 9). On GTS, GTV and GT models remove the storage compartment (see Chapter 9).

11 On LX, LXV and S models, unclip the relay wiring connector then pull the relay out **(see illustration)**. On GTS, GTV and GT models, release the relay and disconnect the wiring connectors **(see illustrations)**.

12 Installation is the reverse of removal.

23 Starter motor

Check

1 Remove the starter motor. Cover the body in some rag and clamp the motor in a soft-jawed vice – do not over-tighten it.

2 Using a fully-charged 12 volt battery and two insulated jumper wires, connect the negative (–) terminal to one of the motor's mounting lugs, then touch the positive (+) terminal of the battery to the protruding terminal on the starter motor – at this point the starter motor should spin **(see illustration)**. If this is the case the motor is proved good. If the motor does not spin, replace it with a new one – individual components are not available.

Removal

3 Disconnect the battery negative (–) lead (see Section 3).

23.5 Peel back the terminal cover then unscrew the nut (arrowed) and detach the lead

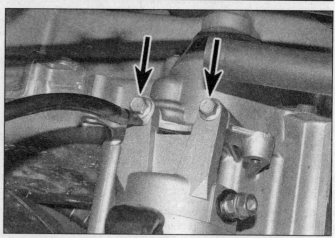

23.6a Unscrew the two bolts (arrowed), noting the earth lead . . .

23.6b . . . and remove the starter motor

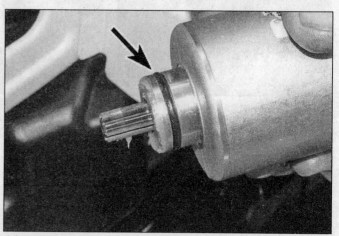

23.8 Fit a new O-ring (arrowed) and lubricate it

4 The starter motor is mounted on the top of the crankcase. Remove the throttle body assembly (see Chapter 5).

5 Peel back the rubber terminal cover on the starter motor **(see illustration)**. Undo the screw or nut securing the starter lead to the motor and detach the lead – if the terminal is corroded spray it with some penetrating fluid and leave it for a while before attempting to undo it.

6 Unscrew the two bolts securing the starter motor to the crankcase, noting the earth lead **(see illustration)**. Slide the starter motor out and remove it **(see illustration)**.

7 Remove the O-ring on the end of the starter motor and discard it as a new one must be used **(see illustration 23.8)**.

Installation

8 Fit a new O-ring onto the end of the starter motor, making sure it is seated in its groove **(see illustration)**. Apply a smear of engine oil to the O-ring.

9 Manoeuvre the motor into position and slide it into the crankcase **(see illustration 23.6b)**.

Install the mounting bolts, not forgetting to secure the earth lead, and tighten them **(see illustration 23.6a)**.

10 Connect the starter lead to the motor and secure it with the screw or nut **(see illustration 23.5)**. Fit the rubber cover over the terminal.

11 Install the throttle body assembly (see Chapter 5).

12 Connect the battery negative (–) lead (see Section 3).

24 Charging system testing

1 If the performance of the charging system is suspect, the system as a whole should be checked first, followed by testing of the individual components. **Note:** *Before beginning the checks, make sure the battery is fully charged and that all system connections are clean and tight.*

2 Checking the output of the charging system and the performance of the various components within the charging system requires the use of a multimeter (with voltage, current, resistance checking facilities). If a multimeter is not available, the job of checking the charging system should be left to a Vespa dealer.

3 When making the checks, follow the procedures carefully to prevent incorrect connections or short circuits resulting in irreparable damage to electrical system components.

Leakage test

Caution: Always connect an ammeter in series, never in parallel with the battery, otherwise it will be damaged. Do not turn the ignition ON or operate the starter motor when the ammeter is connected – a sudden surge in current will blow the meter's fuse.

4 Ensure the ignition is OFF, then disconnect the battery negative (–) lead (see Section 3).

5 Set the multimeter to the Amps function and connect its negative (–) probe to the battery negative (–) terminal, and positive (+) probe to the disconnected negative (–) lead

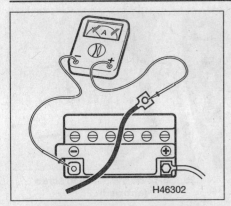

24.5 Checking the charging system leakage rate – connect the meter as shown

(see illustration). Always set the meter to a high amps range initially and then bring it down to the mA (milli Amps) range; if there is a high current flow in the circuit it may blow the meter's fuse.

6 Battery current leakage should not exceed the maximum limit (see Specifications). If a higher leakage rate is shown there is a short circuit in the wiring, although if an after-market immobiliser or alarm is fitted, its current draw should be taken into account. Disconnect the meter and reconnect the battery negative (–) lead.

7 If leakage is indicated, refer to *Wiring Diagrams* at the end of this Chapter to systematically disconnect individual electrical components and repeat the test until the source is identified.

Regulated output test

8 Start the engine and warm it up. Remove the maintenance access panel to the battery/fusebox/starter relay (see Chapter 9).

9 To check the regulated (DC) voltage output, allow the engine to idle with the headlight main beam (HI) turned ON. Connect a multimeter set to the 0-20 volts DC scale across the terminals of the battery with the positive (+) meter probe to battery positive (+) terminal and the negative (–) meter probe to battery negative (–) terminal (see Section 3) **(see illustration).**

10 Slowly increase the engine speed to 5000 rpm and note the reading obtained.

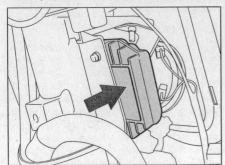

25.7 Regulator/rectifier location on LX, LXV and S models

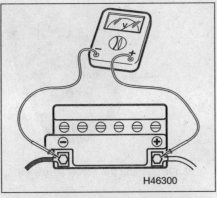

24.9 Checking regulated voltage output – connect the meter as shown

Compare the result with the Specification at the beginning of this Chapter. If the regulated voltage output is outside the specification, check the alternator and the regulator (see Section 25).

  HAYNES HINT *Clues to a faulty regulator are constantly blowing bulbs, with brightnessvaryingconsiderably with engine speed, and battery overheating.*

25 Regulator/rectifier

Check

1 Refer to the removal procedure for your model below for access to the regulator/rectifier wiring connectors and disconnect them. Check the connector terminals for corrosion and security.

2 Set the multimeter to the 0-20 DC volts setting. Connect the meter positive (+) probe to the red/black wire terminal on the loom side of the connector and the negative (–) probe to a suitable ground (earth) and check for voltage. Full battery voltage should be present. On models with two red/black wires check for battery voltage at each one. If there is no voltage check the main fuse (see Section 5), and the wiring to it, and then to the battery.

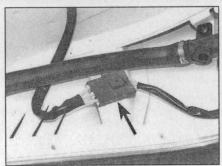

25.12a Disconnect the wiring connector (arrowed) on the floor . . .

3 Switch the multimeter to the resistance (ohms) scale. Check for continuity between the black wire terminal(s) on the loom side of the connector and ground (earth). There should be continuity.

4 Set the multimeter to the ohms x 1 (ohmmeter) scale and measure the resistance between each of the yellow wires on the loom side of the connector, taking a total of three readings, then check for continuity between each terminal and ground (earth). The three readings should be within the range shown in the Specifications for the alternator stator coil at the start of this Chapter, and there should be no continuity (infinite resistance) between any of the terminals and ground (earth).

5 If the above checks do not provide the expected results check the wiring and connectors between the battery, regulator/rectifier and alternator, for shorts, breaks, and loose or corroded terminals (see the wiring diagrams at the end of this chapter).

6 If the wiring checks out, the regulator/rectifier unit is probably faulty. Vespa provide no test data for the unit itself. Take it to a Vespa dealer for confirmation of its condition before replacing it with a new one.

HAYNES HINT *Clues to a faulty regulator are constantly blowing bulbs, with brightnessvaryingconsiderably with engine speed, and battery overheating.*

Removal and installation
LX, LXV and S models

7 Remove the kick panel (see Chapter 9). Remove the horn (see Section 20) – the regulator/rectifier is mounted behind it **(see illustration).**

8 Trace the wiring from the regulator/rectifier and disconnect it at the connectors.

9 Unscrew the two bolts and remove the regulator/rectifier.

10 Installation is the reverse of removal.

GTS, GTV and GT models

11 Remove the kick panel and the floor panel (see Chapter 9).

12 Trace the wiring from the regulator/rectifier and disconnect it at the connectors **(see illustrations).** Release the wiring from any ties.

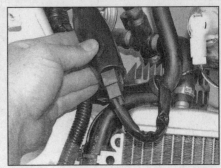

25.12b . . . and the wiring connector inside the rubber boot

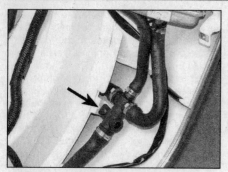

25.13a Undo the screw (arrowed) . . .

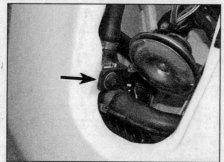

25.13b . . . and the screw (arrowed)

25.13c Undo the nuts and screw
(arrowed) . . .

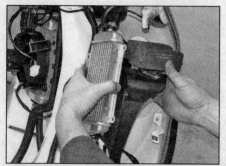

25.13d . . . then displace the radiator and
draw the shroud out . . .

25.14 . . . to access the regulator/rectifier
bolts (arrowed)

13 Undo the coolant hose guide screws below the right-hand radiator at the 4-way joint and above it next to the horn (see illustrations). Displace the right-hand radiator and draw the shroud out until the regulator/rectifier bolts are accessible (see illustrations).

14 Unscrew the two bolts and remove the regulator/rectifier, noting the routing of the wiring (see illustration).

15 Installation is the reverse of removal.

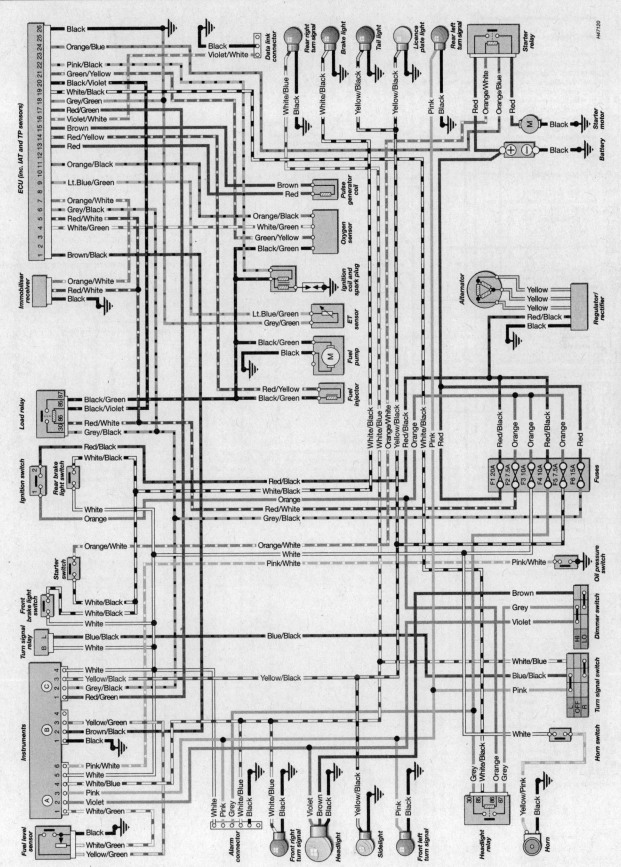

Vespa LX125ie and LX150ie (2009 to 2012 models)

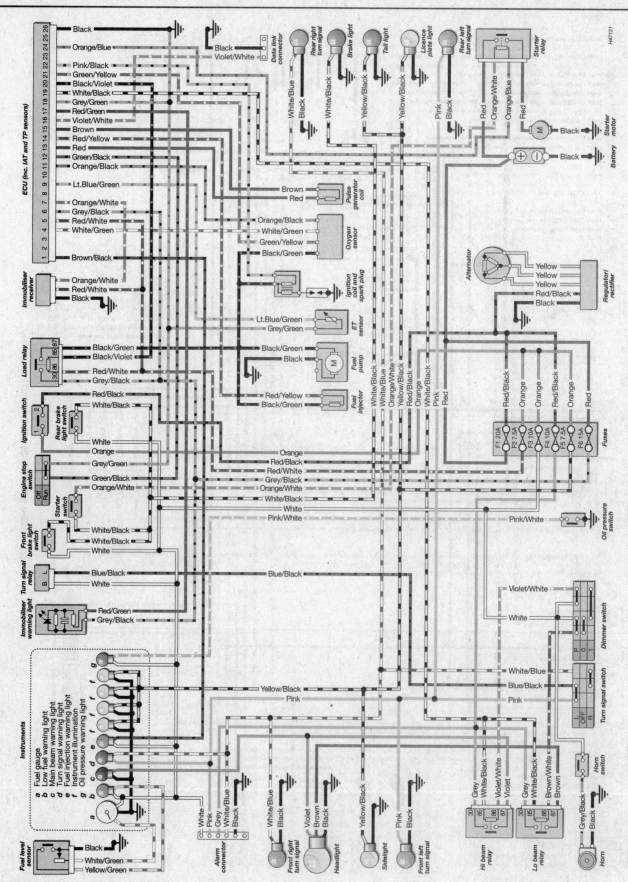

Vespa LXV125ie and LXV150ie (2009 to 2012 models)

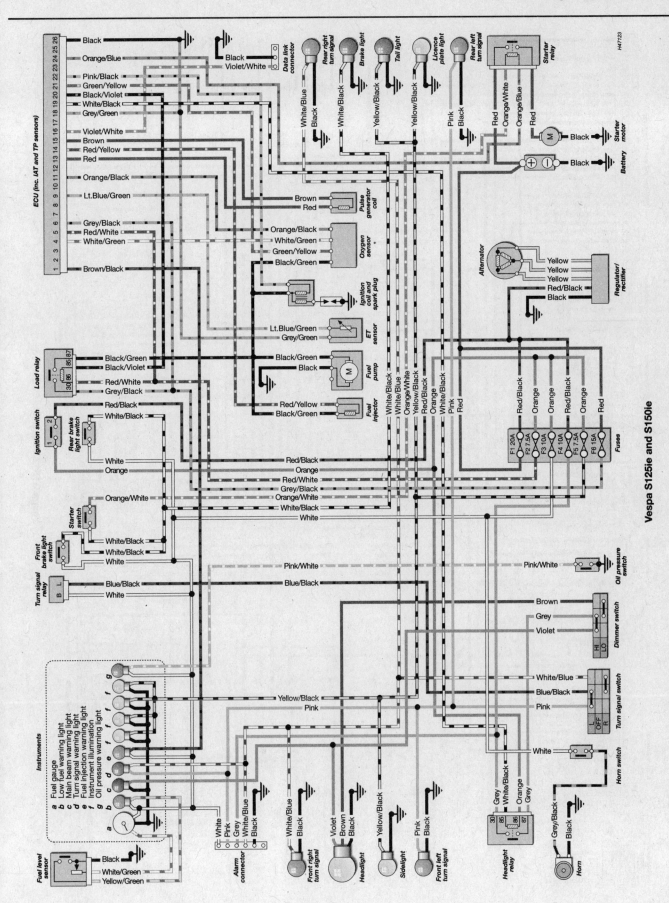

Vespa S125ie and S150ie

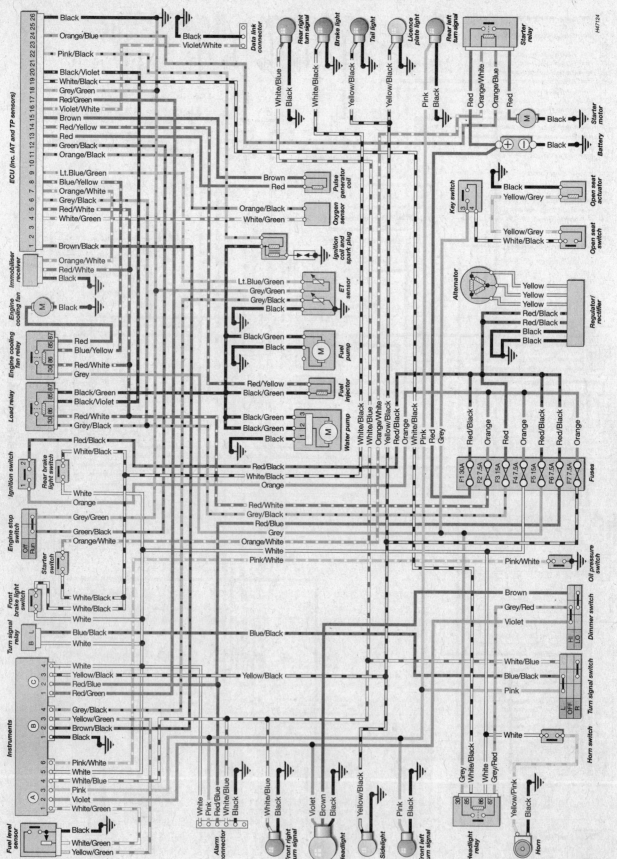

Vespa GTS125ie Super

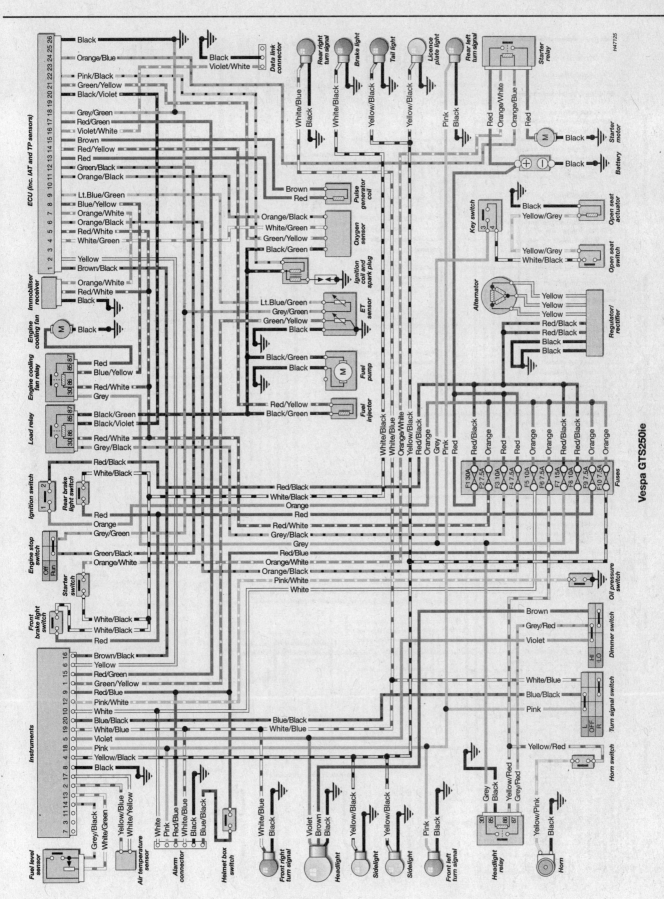

Vespa GTS250ie

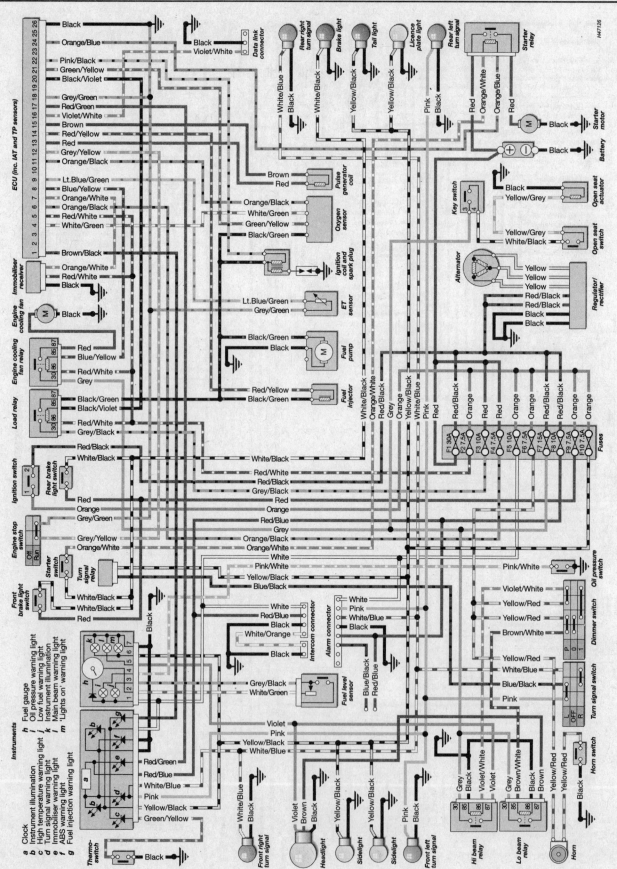

Vespa GTV250ie

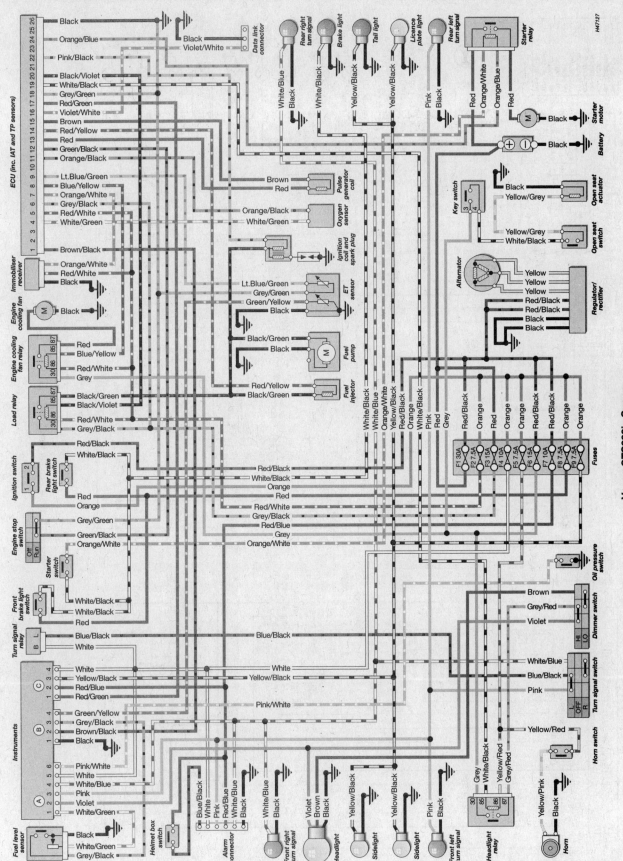

Vespa GTS300ie Super

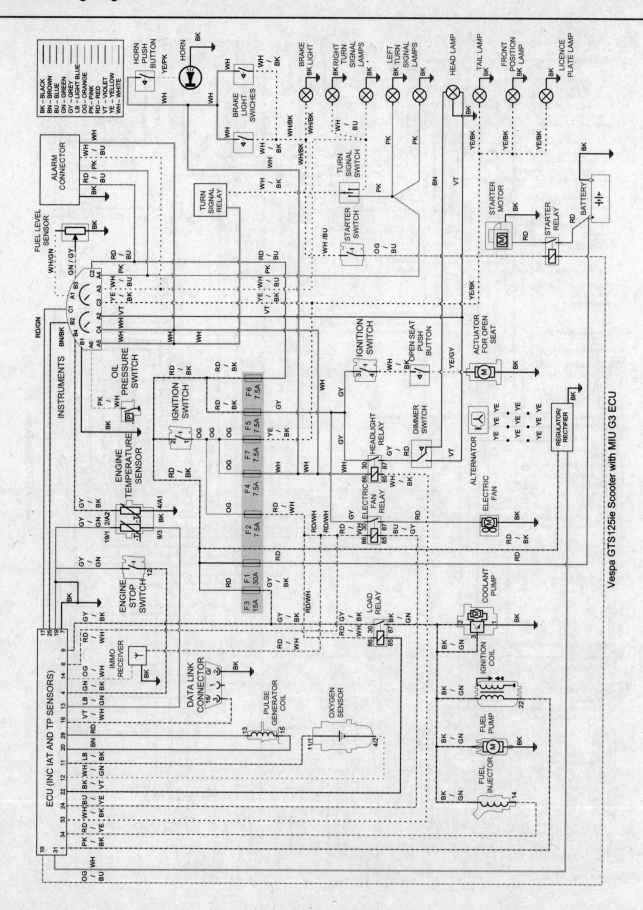

Vespa GTS125ie Scooter with MIU G3 ECU

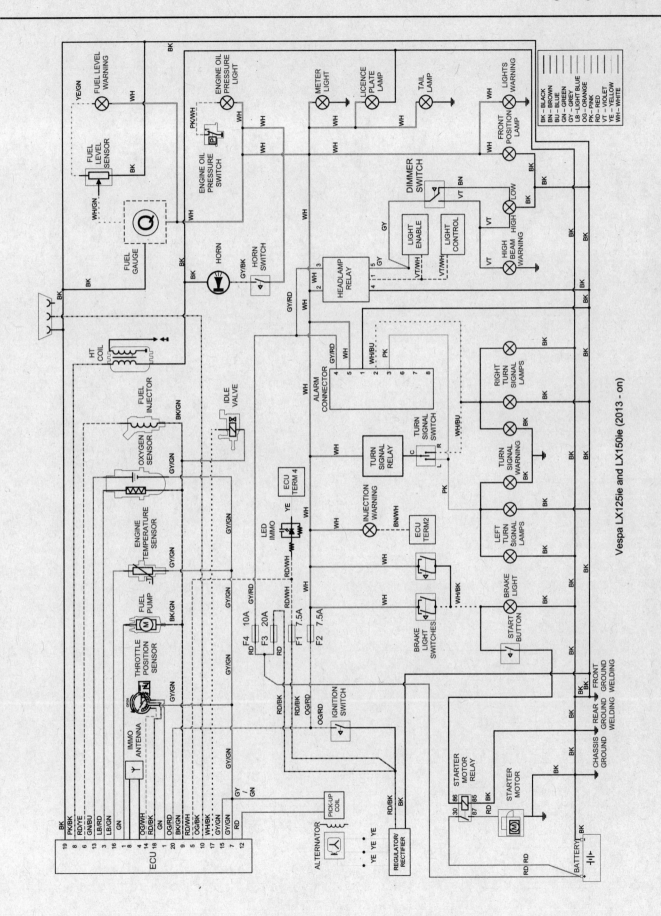

Vespa LX125ie and LX150ie (2013 - on)

Reference

Tools and Workshop Tips

Buying tools

A toolkit is a fundamental requirement for servicing and repairing a scooter. Although there will be an initial expense in building up enough tools for servicing, this will soon be offset by the savings made by doing the job yourself. As experience and confidence grow, additional tools can be added to enable the repair and overhaul of the scooter. Many of the specialist tools are expensive and not often used so it may be preferable to hire them, or for a group of friends or scooter club to join in the purchase.

As a rule, it is better to buy more expensive, good quality tools. Cheaper tools are likely to wear out faster and need to be renewed more often, nullifying the original saving.

 Warning: To avoid the risk of a poor quality tool breaking in use, causing injury or damage to the component being worked on, always aim to purchase tools which meet the relevant national safety standards.

The following lists of tools do not represent the manufacturer's service tools, but serve as a guide to help the owner decide which tools are needed for this level of work. In addition, items such as an electric drill, hacksaw, files, soldering iron and a workbench equipped with a vice, may be needed. Although not classed as tools, a selection of bolts, screws, nuts, washers and pieces of tubing always come in useful.

For more information about tools, refer to the Haynes *Motorcycle Workshop Practice Techbook* (Bk. No. 3470).

Manufacturer's service tools

Inevitably certain tasks require the use of a service tool. Where possible an alternative tool or method of approach is recommended, but sometimes there is no option if personal injury or damage to the component is to be avoided. Where required, service tools are referred to in the relevant procedure.

Service tools can usually only be purchased from a scooter dealer and are identified by a part number. Some of the commonly-used tools, such as rotor pullers, are available in aftermarket form from mail-order motorcycle tool and accessory suppliers.

Maintenance and minor repair tools

- ☐ Set of flat-bladed screwdrivers
- ☐ Set of Phillips head screwdrivers
- ☐ Combination open-end and ring spanners
- ☐ Socket set (3/8 inch or 1/2 inch drive)
- ☐ Set of Allen keys or bits
- ☐ Set of Torx keys or bits
- ☐ Pliers, cutters and self-locking grips (Mole grips)
- ☐ Adjustable spanners
- ☐ C-spanners
- ☐ Tread depth gauge and tyre pressure gauge
- ☐ Cable oiler clamp
- ☐ Feeler gauges
- ☐ Spark plug gap measuring tool
- ☐ Spark plug spanner or deep plug sockets
- ☐ Wire brush and emery paper
- ☐ Calibrated syringe, measuring vessel and funnel

- ☐ Oil filter adapters (4-stroke engines)
- ☐ Oil drainer can or tray
- ☐ Pump type oil can
- ☐ Grease gun
- ☐ Straight-edge and steel rule
- ☐ Continuity tester
- ☐ Battery charger
- ☐ Hydrometer (for battery specific gravity check)
- ☐ Anti-freeze tester (for liquid-cooled engines)

Repair and overhaul tools

- ☐ Torque wrench (small and mid-ranges)
- ☐ Conventional, plastic or soft-faced hammers
- ☐ Impact driver set
- ☐ Vernier gauge
- ☐ Circlip pliers (internal and external, or combination)
- ☐ Set of cold chisels and punches
- ☐ Selection of pullers
- ☐ Breaker bars
- ☐ One-man brake bleeder kit
- ☐ Wire stripper and crimper tool
- ☐ Multimeter (measures amps, volts and ohms)
- ☐ Stroboscope (for dynamic timing checks)
- ☐ Hose clamp
- ☐ Clutch holding tool

Specialist tools

- ☐ Micrometers (external type)
- ☐ Telescoping gauges
- ☐ Dial gauge
- ☐ Stud extractor
- ☐ Screw extractor set
- ☐ Bearing driver set
- ☐ Valve spring compressor (4-stroke engines)
- ☐ Piston pin drawbolt tool
- ☐ Piston ring clamp

1.1 Hydraulic motorcycle ramp

1.2 Use an approved can only for storing petrol (gasoline)

1.3 A fire extinguisher, goggles, mask and protective gloves should be at hand in the workshop

1 Workshop equipment and facilities

The workbench

● Work is made much easier by raising the scooter up on a ramp – components are much more accessible if raised to waist level. The hydraulic or pneumatic types seen in the dealer's workshop are a sound investment if you undertake a lot of repairs or overhauls (**see illustration 1.1**).
● If raised off ground level, the scooter must be supported on the ramp to avoid it falling. Most ramps incorporate a front wheel locating clamp which can be adjusted to suit different diameter wheels. When tightening the clamp, take care not to mark the wheel rim or damage the tyre – use wood blocks on each side to prevent this.

Fumes and fire

● Refer to the Safety first! page at the beginning of the manual for full details. Make sure your workshop is equipped with a fire extinguisher suitable for fuel-related fires (Class B fire – flammable liquids) – it is not sufficient to have a water-filled extinguisher.
● Always ensure adequate ventilation is available. Unless an exhaust gas extraction system is available for use, ensure that the engine is run outside of the workshop.
● If working on the fuel system, make sure the

workshop is ventilated to avoid a build-up of fumes. This applies equally to fume build-up when charging a battery. Do not smoke or allow anyone else to smoke in the workshop.

Fluids

● If you need to drain fuel from the tank, store it in an approved container marked as suitable for the storage of petrol (gasoline) (**see illustration 1.2**). Do not store fuel in glass jars or bottles.
● Use proprietary engine degreasers or solvents which have a high flash-point, such as paraffin (kerosene), for cleaning off oil, grease and dirt – never use petrol (gasoline) for cleaning. Wear rubber gloves when handling solvent and engine degreaser. The fumes from certain solvents can be dangerous – always work in a well-ventilated area.

Dust, eye and hand protection

● Protect your lungs from inhalation of dust particles by wearing a filtering mask over the nose and mouth. Many frictional materials still contain asbestos which is dangerous to your health. Protect your eyes from spouts of liquid and sprung components by wearing a pair of protective goggles (**see illustration 1.3**).
● Protect your hands from contact with solvents, fuel and oils by wearing rubber gloves. Alternatively apply a barrier cream to your hands before starting work. If handling hot components or fluids, wear suitable gloves to protect your hands from scalding and burns.

What to do with old fluids

● Old cleaning solvent, fuel, coolant and oils should not be poured down domestic drains or onto the ground. Package the fluid up in old oil containers, label it accordingly, and take it to a garage or disposal facility. Contact your local authority for location of such sites.

2 Fasteners – screws, bolts and nuts

Fastener types and applications
Bolts and screws

● Fastener head types are either of hexagonal, Torx or splined design, with internal and external versions of each type (**see illustrations 2.1 and 2.2**); splined head fasteners are not in common use on scooters. The conventional slotted or Phillips head design is used for certain screws. Bolt or screw length is always measured from the underside of the head to the end of the item (**see illustration 2.11**).
● Certain fasteners on the scooter have a tensile marking on their heads, the higher the marking the stronger the fastener. High tensile fasteners generally carry a 10 or higher marking. Never replace a high tensile fastener with one of a lower tensile strength.

Washers (see illustration 2.3)

● Plain washers are used between a fastener

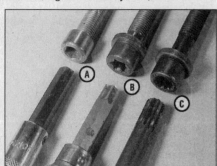

2.1 Internal hexagon/Allen (A), Torx (B) and splined (C) fasteners, with corresponding bits

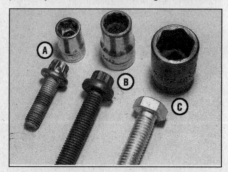

2.2 External Torx (A), splined (B) and hexagon (C) fasteners, with corresponding sockets

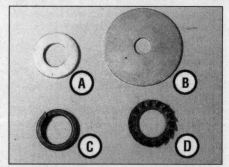

2.3 Plain washer (A), penny washer (B), spring washer (C) and serrated washer (D)

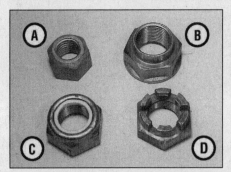

2.4 Plain nut (A), shouldered locknut (B), nylon insert nut (C) and castellated nut (D)

2.5 Bend split pin (cotter pin) arms as shown (arrows) to secure a castellated nut

2.6 Bend split pin (cotter pin) arms as shown to secure a plain nut

head and a component to prevent damage to the component or to spread the load when torque is applied. Plain washers can also be used as spacers or shims in certain assemblies. Copper or aluminium plain washers are often used as sealing washers on drain plugs.

● The split-ring spring washer works by applying axial tension between the fastener head and component. If flattened, it is fatigued and must be renewed. If a plain (flat) washer is used on the fastener, position the spring washer between the fastener and the plain washer.

● Serrated star type washers dig into the fastener and component faces, preventing loosening. They are often used on electrical earth (ground) connections to the frame.

● Cone type washers (sometimes called Belleville) are conical and when tightened apply axial tension between the fastener head and component. They must be installed with the dished side against the component and often carry an OUTSIDE marking on their outer face. If flattened, they are fatigued and must be renewed.

● Tab washers are used to lock plain nuts or bolts on a shaft. A portion of the tab washer is bent up hard against one flat of the nut or bolt to prevent it loosening. Due to the tab washer being deformed in use, a new tab washer should be used every time it is disturbed.

● Wave washers are used to take up endfloat on a shaft. They provide light springing and prevent excessive side-to-side play of a component. Can be found on rocker arm shafts.

Nuts and split pins

● Conventional plain nuts are usually six-sided (see illustration 2.4). They are sized by thread diameter and pitch. High tensile nuts carry a number on one end to denote their tensile strength.

● Self-locking nuts either have a nylon insert, or two spring metal tabs, or a shoulder which is staked into a groove in the shaft – their advantage over conventional plain nuts is a resistance to loosening due to vibration. The nylon insert type can be used a number of times, but must be renewed when the friction of the nylon insert is reduced, ie when the nut spins freely on the shaft. The spring tab type

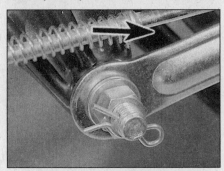

2.7 Correct fitting of R-pin. Arrow indicates forward direction

can be reused unless the tabs are damaged. The shouldered type must be renewed every time it is disturbed.

● Split pins (cotter pins) are used to lock a castellated nut to a shaft or to prevent slackening of a plain nut. Common applications are wheel axles and brake torque arms. Because the split pin arms are deformed to lock around the nut a new split pin must always be used on installation – always fit the correct size split pin which will fit snugly in the shaft hole. Make sure the split pin arms are correctly located around the nut **(see illustrations 2.5 and 2.6)**.

● R-pins (shaped like the letter R), or slip pins as they are sometimes called, are sprung and can be reused if they are otherwise in good condition. Always install R-pins with their closed end facing forwards **(see illustration 2.7)**.

Caution: If the castellated nut slots do not align with the shaft hole after tightening to the torque setting, tighten the nut until

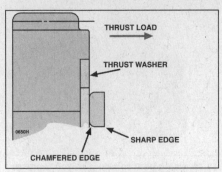

2.9 Correct fitting of a stamped circlip

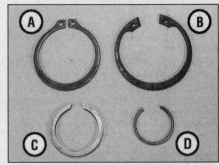

2.8 External stamped circlip (A), internal stamped circlip (B), machined circlip (C) and wire circlip (D)

the next slot aligns with the hole – never slacken the nut to align its slot.

Circlips (see illustration 2.8)

● Circlips (sometimes called snap-rings) are used to retain components on a shaft or in a housing and have corresponding external or internal ears to permit removal. Parallel-sided (machined) circlips can be installed either way round in their groove, whereas stamped circlips (which have a chamfered edge on one face) must be installed with the chamfer facing away from the direction of thrust load **(see illustration 2.9)**.

● Always use circlip pliers to remove and install circlips; expand or compress them just enough to remove them. After installation, rotate the circlip in its groove to ensure it is securely seated. If installing a circlip on a splined shaft, always align its opening with a shaft channel to ensure the circlip ends are well supported and unlikely to catch **(see illustration 2.10)**.

● Circlips can wear due to the thrust of components and become loose in their

THRUST LOAD

THRUST WASHER

SHARP EDGE

CHAMFERED EDGE

0650H

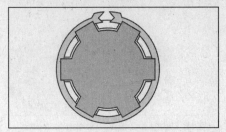

2.10 Align circlip opening with shaft channel

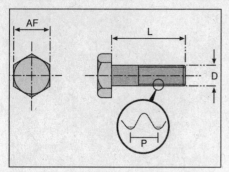

2.11 Fastener length (L), thread diameter (D), thread pitch (P) and head size (AF)

2.12 Using a thread gauge to measure pitch

2.13 A sharp tap on the head of a fastener will often break free a corroded thread

grooves, with the subsequent danger of becoming dislodged in operation. For this reason, renewal is advised every time a circlip is disturbed.

● Wire circlips are commonly used as piston pin retaining clips. If a removal tang is provided, long-nosed pliers can be used to dislodge them, otherwise careful use of a small flat-bladed screwdriver is necessary. Wire circlips should be renewed every time they are disturbed.

Thread diameter and pitch

● Diameter of a male thread (screw, bolt or stud) is the outside diameter of the threaded portion (see illustration 2.11). Most scooter manufacturers use the ISO (International Standards Organisation) metric system expressed in millimetres, eg M6 refers to a 6 mm diameter thread. Sizing is the same for nuts, except that the thread diameter is measured across the valleys of the nut.

● Pitch is the distance between the peaks of the thread (see illustration 2.11). It is expressed in millimetres, thus a common bolt size may be expressed as 6.0 x 1.0 mm (6 mm thread diameter and 1 mm pitch). Generally pitch increases in proportion to thread diameter, although there are always exceptions.

● Thread diameter and pitch are related for conventional fastener applications and the accompanying table can be used as a guide. Additionally, the AF (Across Flats), spanner or socket size dimension of the bolt or nut (see illustration 2.11) is linked to thread and pitch specification. Thread pitch can be measured with a thread gauge (see illustration 2.12).

● The threads of most fasteners are of the right-hand type, ie they are turned clockwise to tighten and anti-clockwise to loosen. The reverse situation applies to left-hand thread fasteners, which are turned anti-clockwise to tighten and clockwise to loosen. Left-hand threads are used where rotation of a component might loosen a conventional right-hand thread fastener.

AF size	Thread diameter x pitch (mm)
8 mm	M5 x 0.8
8 mm	M6 x 1.0
10 mm	M6 x 1.0
12 mm	M8 x 1.25
14 mm	M10 x 1.25
17 mm	M12 x 1.25

Seized fasteners

● Corrosion of external fasteners due to water or reaction between two dissimilar metals can occur over a period of time. It will build up sooner in wet conditions or in countries where salt is used on the roads during the winter. If a fastener is severely corroded it is likely that normal methods of removal will fail and result in its head being ruined. When you attempt removal, the fastener thread should be heard to crack free and unscrew easily – if it doesn't, stop there before damaging something.

● A smart tap on the head of the fastener will often succeed in breaking free corrosion which has occurred in the threads (see illustration 2.13).

● An aerosol penetrating fluid (such as WD-40) applied the night beforehand may work its way down into the thread and ease removal.

Depending on the location, you may be able to make up a Plasticine well around the fastener head and fill it with penetrating fluid.

● If you are working on an engine internal component, corrosion will most likely not be a problem due to the well lubricated environment. However, components can be very tight and an impact driver is a useful tool in freeing them (see illustration 2.14).

● Where corrosion has occurred between dissimilar metals (eg steel and aluminium alloy), the application of heat to the fastener head will create a disproportionate expansion rate between the two metals and break the seizure caused by the corrosion. Whether heat can be applied depends on the location of the fastener – any surrounding components likely to be damaged must first be removed (see illustration 2.15). Heat can be applied using a paint stripper heat gun or clothes iron, or by immersing the component in boiling water – wear protective gloves to prevent scalding or burns to the hands.

● As a last resort, it is possible to use a hammer and cold chisel to work the fastener head unscrewed (see illustration 2.16). This will damage the fastener, but more importantly extreme care must be taken not to damage the surrounding component.

Caution: Remember that the component being secured is generally of more value than the bolt, nut or screw – when the fastener is freed, do not unscrew it with force, instead work the fastener back and forth when resistance is felt to prevent thread damage.

2.14 Using an impact driver to free a fastener

2.15 Using heat to free a seized fastener

2.16 Using a hammer and chisel to free a seized fastener

2.17 Using a stud extractor tool to remove a broken crankcase stud

2.18 Two nuts can be locked together to unscrew a stud from a component

2.19 When using a screw extractor, first drill a hole in the fastener . . .

Broken fasteners and damaged heads

● If the shank of a broken bolt or screw is accessible you can grip it with self-locking grips. The knurled wheel type stud extractor tool or self-gripping stud puller tool is particularly useful for removing the long studs which screw into the cylinder mouth surface of the crankcase or bolts and screws from which the head has broken off **(see illustration 2.17)**. Studs can also be removed by locking two nuts together on the threaded end of the stud and using a spanner on the lower nut **(see illustration 2.18)**.

● A bolt or screw which has broken off below or level with the casing must be extracted using a screw extractor set. Centre punch the fastener to centralise the drill bit, then drill a hole in the fastener **(see illustration 2.19)**. Select a drill bit which is approximately half to three-quarters the diameter of the fastener and drill to a depth which will accommodate the extractor. Use the largest size extractor

possible, but avoid leaving too small a wall thickness otherwise the extractor will merely force the fastener walls outwards wedging it in the casing thread.

● If a spiral type extractor is used, thread it anti-clockwise into the fastener. As it is screwed in, it will grip the fastener and unscrew it from the casing **(see illustration 2.20)**.

 Warning: Stud extractors are very hard and may break off in the fastener if care is not taken – ask an engineer about spark erosion if this happens.

● If a taper type extractor is used, tap it into the fastener so that it is firmly wedged in place. Unscrew the extractor (anti-clockwise) to draw the fastener out.

● Alternatively, the broken bolt/screw can be drilled out and the hole retapped for an oversize bolt/screw or a diamond-section thread insert. It is essential that the drilling is carried out squarely and to the correct depth, otherwise the casing may be ruined – if in

doubt, entrust the work to an engineer.

● Bolts and nuts with rounded corners cause the correct size spanner or socket to slip when force is applied. Of the types of spanner/socket available always use a six-point type rather than an eight or twelve-point type – better grip is obtained. Surface drive spanners grip the middle of the hex flats, rather than the corners, and are thus good in cases of damaged heads **(see illustration 2.21)**.

● Slotted-head or Phillips-head screws are often damaged by the use of the wrong size screwdriver. Allen-head and Torx-head screws are much less likely to sustain damage. If enough of the screw head is exposed you can use a hacksaw to cut a slot in its head and then use a conventional flat-bladed screwdriver to remove it. Alternatively use a hammer and cold chisel to tap the head of the fastener around to slacken it. Always replace damaged fasteners with new ones, preferably Torx or Allen-head type.

2.20 . . . then thread the extractor anti-clockwise into the fastener

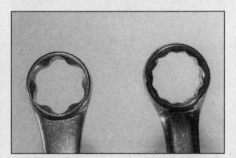

2.21 Comparison of surface drive ring spanner (left) with 12-point type (right)

A dab of valve grinding compound between the screw head and screw-driver tip will often give a good grip.

2.22 A thread repair tool being used to correct an internal thread

2.23 A thread repair tool being used to correct an external thread

Thread repair

● Threads (particularly those in aluminium alloy components) can be damaged by overtightening, being assembled with dirt in the threads, or from a component working loose and vibrating. Eventually the thread will fail completely, and it will be impossible to tighten the fastener.

● If a thread is damaged or clogged with old locking compound it can be renovated with a thread repair tool (thread chaser) **(see illustrations 2.22 and 2.23)**; special thread

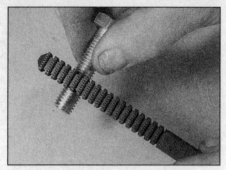

2.24 Using a thread restorer file

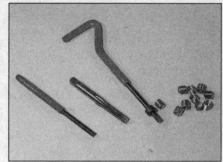

2.25 Obtain a thread insert kit to suit the thread diameter and pitch required

2.26 To install a thread insert, first drill out the original thread . . .

chasers are available for spark plug hole threads. The tool will not cut a new thread, but clean and true the original thread. Make sure that you use the correct diameter and pitch tool. Similarly, external threads can be cleaned up with a die or a thread restorer file **(see illustration 2.24)**.

● It is possible to drill out the old thread and retap the component to the next thread size. This will work where there is enough surrounding material and a new bolt or screw can be obtained. Sometimes, however, this is not possible – such as where the bolt/screw passes through another component which must also be suitably modified, also in cases where a spark plug or oil drain plug cannot be obtained in a larger diameter thread size.

● The diamond-section thread insert (often known by its popular trade name of Heli-Coil)

is a simple and effective method of renewing the thread and retaining the original size. A kit can be purchased which contains the tap, insert and installing tool **(see illustration 2.25)**. Drill out the damaged thread with the size drill specified **(see illustration 2.26)**. Carefully retap the thread **(see illustration 2.27)**. Install the insert on the installing tool and thread it slowly into place using a light downward pressure **(see illustrations 2.28 and 2.29)**. When positioned between a 1/4 and 1/2 turn below the surface withdraw the installing tool and use the break-off tool to press down on the tang, breaking it off **(see illustration 2.30)**.

● There are epoxy thread repair kits on the market which can rebuild stripped internal threads, although this repair should not be used on high load-bearing components.

Thread locking and sealing compounds

● Locking compounds are used in locations where the fastener is prone to loosening due to vibration or on important safety-related items which might cause loss of control of the scooter if they fail. It is also used where important fasteners cannot be secured by other means such as lockwashers or split pins.

● Before applying locking compound, make sure that the threads (internal and external) are clean and dry with all old compound removed. Select a compound to suit the component being secured – a non-permanent general locking and sealing type is suitable for most applications, but a high strength type is needed for permanent fixing of studs in castings. Apply a drop or two of the compound to the first few threads of the fastener, then thread it into place and tighten to the specified torque. Do not apply excessive thread locking compound otherwise the thread may be damaged on subsequent removal.

● Certain fasteners are impregnated with a dry film type coating of locking compound on their threads. Always renew this type of fastener if disturbed.

● Anti-seize compounds, such as copper-based greases, can be applied to protect threads from seizure due to extreme heat and corrosion. A common instance is spark plug threads and exhaust system fasteners.

3 Measuring tools and gauges

Feeler gauges

● Feeler gauges (or blades) are used for measuring small gaps and clearances **(see illustration 3.1)**. They can also be used to measure endfloat (sideplay) of a component on a shaft where access is not possible with a dial gauge.

● Feeler gauge sets should be treated with care and not bent or damaged. They are etched with their size on one face. Keep them clean and very lightly oiled to prevent

2.27 . . . tap a new thread . . .

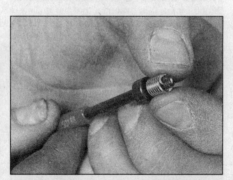

2.28 . . . fit insert on the installing tool . . .

2.29 . . . and thread into the component . . .

2.30 . . . break off the tang when complete

3.1 Feeler gauges are used for measuring small gaps and clearances – thickness is marked on one face of gauge

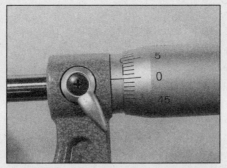

3.2 Check micrometer calibration before use

corrosion build-up.

● When measuring a clearance, select a gauge which is a light sliding fit between the two components. You may need to use two gauges together to measure the clearance accurately.

Micrometers

● A micrometer is a precision tool capable of measuring to 0.01 or 0.001 of a millimetre. It should always be stored in its case and not in the general toolbox. It must be kept clean and never dropped, otherwise its frame or measuring anvils could be distorted resulting in inaccurate readings.

● External micrometers are used for measuring outside diameters of components and have many more applications than internal micrometers. Micrometers are available in different size ranges, eg 0 to 25 mm, 25 to 50 mm, and upwards in 25 mm steps; some large micrometers have interchangeable anvils to allow a range of measurements to be taken. Generally the largest precision measurement you are likely to take on a scooter is the piston diameter.

● Internal micrometers (or bore micrometers) are used for measuring inside diameters, such as valve guides and cylinder bores. Telescoping gauges and small hole gauges are used in conjunction with an external micro-meter, whereas the more expensive internal micrometers have their own measuring device.

External micrometer

Note: *The conventional analogue type instrument is described. Although much easier to read, digital micrometers are considerably more expensive.*

● Always check the calibration of the micrometer before use. With the anvils closed (0 to 25 mm type) or set over a test gauge (for the larger types) the scale should read zero **(see illustration 3.2)**; make sure that the anvils (and test piece) are clean first. Any discrepancy can be adjusted by referring to the instructions supplied with the tool. Remember that the micrometer is a precision measuring tool – don't force the anvils closed, use the ratchet (4) on the end of the micrometer to close it. In this way, a measured force is always applied.

● To use, first make sure that the item being

measured is clean. Place the anvil of the micrometer (1) against the item and use the thimble (2) to bring the spindle (3) lightly into contact with the other side of the item **(see illustration 3.3)**. Don't tighten the thimble down because this will damage the micrometer – instead use the ratchet (4) on the end of the micrometer. The ratchet mechanism applies a measured force preventing damage to the instrument.

● The micrometer is read by referring to the linear scale on the sleeve and the annular scale on the thimble. Read off the sleeve first to obtain the base measurement, then add the fine measurement from the thimble to obtain the overall reading. The linear scale on the sleeve represents the measuring range of the micrometer (eg 0 to 25 mm). The annular scale on the thimble will be in graduations of 0.01 mm (or as marked on the frame) – one full revolution of the thimble will move 0.5 mm on the linear scale. Take the reading where the datum line on the sleeve intersects the thimble's scale. Always position the eye directly above the scale otherwise an inaccurate reading will result.

In the example shown the item measures 2.95 mm **(see illustration 3.4)**:

Linear scale	2.00 mm
Linear scale	0.50 mm
Annular scale	0.45 mm
Total figure	**2.95 mm**

Most micrometers have a locking lever (6) on the frame to hold the setting in place, allowing the item to be removed from the micrometer.

● Some micrometers have a vernier scale on their sleeve, providing an even finer measurement to be taken, in 0.001 increments of a millimetre. Take the sleeve and thimble measurement as described above, then check which graduation on the vernier scale aligns with that of the annular scale on the thimble **Note:** *The eye must be perpendicular to the scale when taking the vernier reading – if necessary rotate the body of the micrometer to ensure this.* Multiply the vernier scale figure by 0.001 and add it to the base and fine measurement figures.

In the example shown the item measures

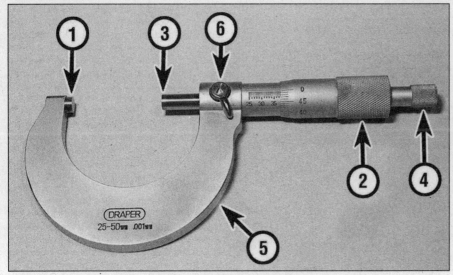

3.3 Micrometer component parts

1	Anvil	3	Spindle	5	Frame
2	Thimble	4	Ratchet	6	Locking lever

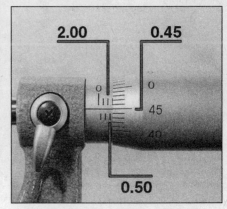

3.4 Micrometer reading of 2.95 mm

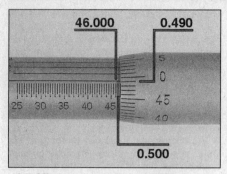

3.5 Micrometer reading of 46.99 mm on linear and annular scales . . .

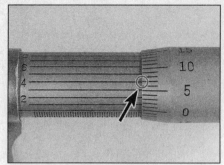

3.6 . . . and 0.004 mm on vernier scale

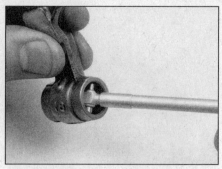

3.7 Expand the telescoping gauge in the bore, lock its position . . .

3.8 . . . then measure the gauge with a micrometer

3.9 Expand the small hole gauge in the bore, lock its position . . .

3.10 . . . then measure the gauge with a micrometer

46.994 mm (see illustrations 3.5 and 3.6):

Linear scale (base)	46.000 mm
Linear scale (base)	00.500 mm
Annular scale (fine)	00.490 mm
Vernier scale	00.004 mm
Total figure	**46.994 mm**

Internal micrometer

● Internal micrometers are available for measuring bore diameters, but are expensive and unlikely to be available for home use. It is suggested that a set of telescoping gauges and small hole gauges, both of which must be used with an external micrometer, will suffice for taking internal measurements on a scooter.
● Telescoping gauges can be used to measure internal diameters of components. Select a gauge with the correct size range, make sure its ends are clean and insert it into the bore. Expand the gauge, then lock its position and withdraw it from the bore **(see illustration 3.7)**. Measure across the gauge ends with a micrometer **(see illustration 3.8)**.
● Very small diameter bores (such as valve guides) are measured with a small hole gauge. Once adjusted to a slip-fit inside the component, its position is locked and the gauge withdrawn for measurement with a micrometer **(see illustrations 3.9 and 3.10)**.

Vernier caliper

Note: *The conventional linear and dial gauge type instruments are described. Digital types are easier to read, but are far more expensive.*
● The vernier caliper does not provide the precision of a micrometer, but is versatile in being able to measure internal and external diameters. Some types also incorporate a depth gauge. It is ideal for measuring clutch plate friction material and spring free lengths.
● To use the conventional linear scale vernier, slacken off the vernier clamp screws (1) and set its jaws over (2), or inside (3), the item to be measured **(see illustration 3.11)**. Slide the jaw into contact, using the thumb-wheel (4) for fine movement of the sliding scale (5) then tighten the clamp screws (1). Read off the main scale (6) where the zero on the sliding scale (5) intersects it, taking the whole number to the left of the zero; this provides the base measurement. View along the sliding scale and select the division which lines up exactly with any of the divisions on the main scale, noting that the divisions usually represents 0.02 of a millimetre. Add this fine measurement to the base measurement to obtain the total reading.

In the example shown the item measures

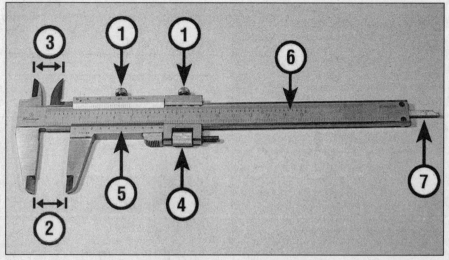

3.11 Vernier component parts (linear gauge)

1 *Clamp screws*	3 *Internal jaws*	5 *Sliding scale*
2 *External jaws*	4 *Thumbwheel*	6 *Main scale*

7 *Depth gauge*

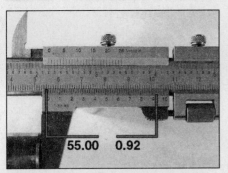

3.12 Vernier gauge reading of 55.92 mm

55.92 mm **(see illustration 3.12)**:

Base measurement	55.00 mm
Fine measurement	00.92 mm
Total figure	**55.92 mm**

● Some vernier calipers are equipped with a dial gauge for fine measurement. Before use, check that the jaws are clean, then close them fully and check that the dial gauge reads zero. If necessary adjust the gauge ring accordingly. Slacken the vernier clamp screw (1) and set its jaws over (2), or inside (3), the item to be measured **(see illustration 3.13)**. Slide the jaws into contact, using the thumbwheel (4) for fine movement. Read off the main scale (5) where the edge of the sliding scale (6) intersects it, taking the whole number to the left of the zero; this provides the base measurement. Read off the needle position on the dial gauge (7) scale to provide the fine measurement; each division represents 0.05 of a millimetre. Add this fine measurement to the base measurement to obtain the total reading.

In the example shown the item measures 55.95 mm **(see illustration 3.14)**:

Base measurement	55.00 mm
Fine measurement	00.95 mm
Total figure	**55.95 mm**

Dial gauge or DTI (Dial Test Indicator)

● A dial gauge can be used to accurately measure small amounts of movement. Typical uses are measuring shaft runout or shaft endfloat (sideplay) and setting piston position for ignition timing on two-strokes. A dial gauge set usually comes with a range of

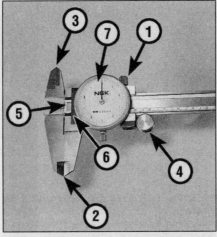

3.13 Vernier component parts (dial gauge)

1	Clamp screw	5	Main scale
2	External jaws	6	Sliding scale
3	Internal jaws	7	Dial gauge
4	Thumbwheel		

different probes and adapters and mounting equipment.

● The gauge needle must point to zero when at rest. Rotate the ring around its periphery to zero the gauge.

● Check that the gauge is capable of reading the extent of movement in the work. Most gauges have a small dial set in the face which records whole millimetres of movement as well as the fine scale around the face periphery which is calibrated in 0.01 mm divisions. Read off the small dial first to obtain the base measurement, then add the measurement from the fine scale to obtain the total reading.

In the example shown the gauge reads 1.48 mm **(see illustration 3.15)**:

Base measurement	1.00 mm
Fine measurement	0.48 mm
Total figure	**1.48 mm**

● If measuring shaft runout, the shaft must be supported in vee-blocks and the gauge mounted on a stand perpendicular to the shaft. Rest the tip of the gauge against the centre of the shaft and rotate the shaft slowly whilst watching the gauge reading **(see illustration 3.16)**. Take several measurements along the length of the shaft and record the maximum

3.14 Vernier gauge reading of 55.95 mm

gauge reading as the amount of runout in the shaft. **Note:** *The reading obtained will be total runout at that point – some manufacturers specify that the runout figure is halved to compare with their specified runout limit.*

● Endfloat (sideplay) measurement requires that the gauge is mounted securely to the surrounding component with its probe touching the end of the shaft. Using hand pressure, push and pull on the shaft noting the maximum endfloat recorded on the gauge **(see illustration 3.17)**.

● A dial gauge with suitable adapters can be used to determine piston position BTDC on two-stroke engines for the purposes of ignition timing. The gauge, adapter and suitable length probe are installed in the place of the spark plug and the gauge zeroed at TDC. If the piston position is specified as 1.14 mm BTDC, rotate the engine back to 2.00 mm BTDC, then slowly forwards to 1.14 mm BTDC.

4 Torque and leverage

What is torque?

● Torque describes the twisting force about a shaft. The amount of torque applied is determined by the distance from the centre of the shaft to the end of the lever and the amount of force being applied to the end of the lever; distance multiplied by force equals torque.

● The manufacturer applies a measured torque to a bolt or nut to ensure that it will not

3.15 Dial gauge reading of 1.48 mm

3.16 Using a dial gauge to measure shaft runout

3.17 Using a dial gauge to measure shaft endfloat

4.1 Set the torque wrench index mark to the setting required, in this case 12 Nm

4.2 Angle tightening can be accomplished with a torque-angle gauge . . .

4.3 . . . or by marking the angle on the surrounding component

slacken in use and to hold two components securely together without movement in the joint. The actual torque setting depends on the thread size, bolt or nut material and the composition of the components being held.

● Too little torque may cause the fastener to loosen due to vibration, whereas too much torque will distort the joint faces of the component or cause the fastener to shear off. Always stick to the specified torque setting.

Using a torque wrench

● Check the calibration of the torque wrench and make sure it has a suitable range for the job. Torque wrenches are available in Nm (Newton-metres), kgf m (kilograms-force metre), lbf ft (pounds-feet), lbf in (inch-pounds). Do not confuse lbf ft with lbf in.

● Adjust the tool to the desired torque on the scale (see illustration 4.1). If your torque wrench is not calibrated in the units specified, carefully convert the figure (see Conversion Factors). A manufacturer sometimes gives a torque setting as a range (8 to 10 Nm) rather than a single figure – in this case set the tool midway between the two settings. The same torque may be expressed as 9 Nm ± 1 Nm. Some torque wrenches have a method of locking the setting so that it isn't inadvertently altered during use.

● Install the bolts/nuts in their correct location and secure them lightly. Their threads must be clean and free of any old locking compound. Unless specified the threads and flange should be dry – oiled threads are necessary in certain circumstances and the manufacturer will take

this into account in the specified torque figure. Similarly, the manufacturer may also specify the application of thread-locking compound.

● Tighten the fasteners in the specified sequence until the torque wrench clicks, indicating that the torque setting has been reached. Apply the torque again to double-check the setting. Where different thread diameter fasteners secure the component, as a rule tighten the larger diameter ones first.

● When the torque wrench has been finished with, release the lock (where applicable) and fully back off its setting to zero – do not leave the torque wrench tensioned. Also, do not use a torque wrench for slackening a fastener.

Angle-tightening

● Manufacturers often specify a figure in degrees for final tightening of a fastener. This usually follows tightening to a specific torque setting.

● A degree disc can be set and attached to the socket (see illustration 4.2) or a protractor can be used to mark the angle of movement on the bolt/nut head and the surrounding casting (see illustration 4.3).

Loosening sequences

● Where more than one bolt/nut secures a component, loosen each fastener evenly a little at a time. In this way, not all the stress of the joint is held by one fastener and the components are not likely to distort.

● If a tightening sequence is provided, work in the REVERSE of this, but if not, work from

the outside in, in a criss-cross sequence (see illustration 4.4).

Tightening sequences

● If a component is held by more than one fastener it is important that the retaining bolts/nuts are tightened evenly to prevent uneven stress build-up and distortion of sealing faces. This is especially important on high-compression joints such as the cylinder head.

● A sequence is usually provided by the manufacturer, either in a diagram or actually marked in the casting. If not, always start in the centre and work outwards in a criss-cross pattern (see illustration 4.5). Start off by securing all bolts/nuts finger-tight, then set the torque wrench and tighten each fastener by a small amount in sequence until the final torque is reached. By following this practice, the joint will be held evenly and will not be distorted. Important joints, such as the cylinder head and big-end fasteners often have two- or three-stage torque settings.

Applying leverage

● Use tools at the correct angle. Position a socket wrench or spanner on the bolt/nut so that you pull it towards you when loosening. If this can't be done, push the spanner without curling your fingers around it (see illustration 4.6) – the spanner may slip or the fastener loosen suddenly, resulting in your fingers being crushed against a component.

● Additional leverage is gained by extending the length of the lever. The best way to do this is to use a breaker bar instead of the regular length tool, or to slip a length of tubing over the end of the spanner or socket wrench.

● If additional leverage will not work, the fastener head is either damaged or firmly corroded in place (see Fasteners).

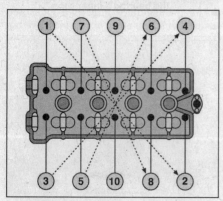

4.4 When slackening, work from the outside inwards

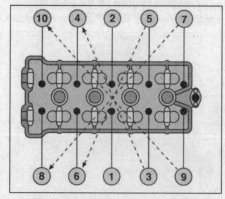

4.5 When tightening, work from the inside outwards

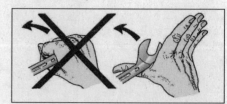

4.6 If you can't pull on the spanner to loosen a fastener, push with your hand open

5.1 Using a bearing driver against the bearing's outer race

5.2 Using a large socket against the bearing's outer race

5.3 This bearing puller clamps behind the bearing and pressure is applied to the shaft end to draw the bearing off

5 Bearings

Bearing removal and installation

Drivers and sockets

● Before removing a bearing, always inspect the casing to see which way it must be driven out – some casings will have retaining plates or a cast step. Also check for any identifying markings on the bearing and if installed to a certain depth, measure this at this stage. Some roller bearings are sealed on one side – take note of the original fitted position.

● Bearings can be driven out of a casing using a bearing driver tool (with the correct size head) or a socket of the correct diameter. Select the driver head or socket so that it contacts the outer race of the bearing, not the balls/rollers or inner race. Always support the casing around the bearing housing with wood blocks, otherwise there is a risk of fracture. The bearing is driven out with a few blows on the driver or socket from a heavy mallet. Unless access is severely restricted (as with wheel bearings), a pin-punch is not recommended unless it is moved around the bearing to keep it square in its housing.

● The same equipment can be used to install bearings. Make sure the bearing housing is supported on wood blocks and line up the bearing in its housing. Fit the bearing as noted on removal – generally they are installed with their marked side facing outwards. Tap the bearing squarely into its housing using a driver or socket which bears only on the bearing's outer race – contact with the bearing balls/rollers or inner race will destroy it **(see illustrations 5.1 and 5.2)**.

● Check that the bearing inner race and balls/rollers rotate freely.

Pullers and slide-hammers

● Where a bearing is pressed on a shaft a puller will be required to extract it **(see illustration 5.3)**. Make sure that the puller clamp or legs fit securely behind the bearing and are unlikely to slip out. If pulling a bearing off a gear shaft for example, you may have to locate the puller behind a gear pinion if there is no access to the race and draw the gear pinion off the shaft as well **(see illustration 5.4)**.

Caution: Ensure that the puller's centre bolt locates securely against the end of the shaft and will not slip when pressure is applied. Also ensure that puller does not damage the shaft end.

● Operate the puller so that its centre bolt exerts pressure on the shaft end and draws the bearing off the shaft.

● When installing the bearing on the shaft, tap only on the bearing's inner race – contact with the balls/rollers or outer race with destroy the bearing. Use a socket or length of tubing as a drift which fits over the shaft end **(see illustration 5.5)**.

● Where a bearing locates in a blind hole in a casing, it cannot be driven or pulled out as described above. A slide-hammer with knife-edged bearing puller attachment will be required. The puller attachment passes through the bearing and when tightened expands to fit firmly behind the bearing **(see illustration 5.6)**. By operating the slide-hammer part of the tool the bearing is jarred out of its housing **(see illustration 5.7)**.

● It is possible, if the bearing is of reasonable weight, for it to drop out of its housing if the casing is heated as described opposite. If this method is attempted, first prepare a work surface which will enable the casing to be tapped face down to help dislodge the bearing – a wood surface is ideal since it will not damage the casing's gasket surface.

5.4 Where no access is available to the rear of the bearing, it is sometimes possible to draw off the adjacent component

5.5 When installing a bearing on a shaft use a piece of tubing which bears only on the bearing's inner race

5.6 Expand the bearing puller so that it locks behind the bearing . . .

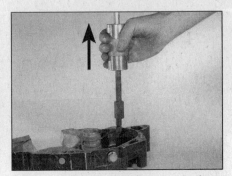

5.7 . . . attach the slide hammer to the bearing puller

5.8 Tapping a casing face down on wood blocks can often dislodge a bearing

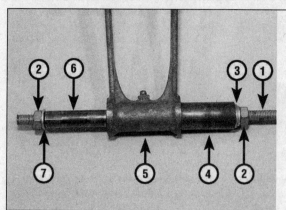

1 Bolt or length of threaded bar
2 Nuts
3 Washer (external diameter greater than tubing internal diameter)
4 Tubing (internal diameter sufficient to accommodate bearing)
5 Suspension arm with bearing
6 Tubing (external diameter slightly smaller than bearing)
7 Washer (external diameter slightly smaller than bearing)

5.9 Drawbolt component parts assembled on a suspension arm

Wearing protective gloves, tap the heated casing several times against the work surface to dislodge the bearing under its own weight (see illustration 5.8).

● Bearings can be installed in blind holes using the driver or socket method described above.

Drawbolts

● Where a bearing or bush is set in the eye of a component, such as a suspension linkage arm or connecting rod small-end, removal by drift may damage the component. Furthermore, a rubber bushing in a shock absorber eye cannot successfully be driven out of position. If access is available to a engineering press, the task is straightforward. If not, a drawbolt can be fabricated to extract the bearing or bush.

● To extract the bearing/bush you will need a long bolt with nut (or piece of threaded bar with two nuts), a piece of tubing which has

an internal diameter larger than the bearing/ bush, another piece of tubing which has an external diameter slightly smaller than the bearing/ bush, and a selection of washers (see illustrations 5.9 and 5.10). Note that the pieces of tubing must be of the same length, or longer, than the bearing/bush.

● The same kit (without the pieces of tubing) can be used to draw the new bearing/bush back into place (see illustration 5.11).

Temperature change

● If the bearing's outer race is a tight fit in the casing, the aluminium casing can be heated to release its grip on the bearing. Aluminium will expand at a greater rate than the steel bearing outer race. There are several ways to do this, but avoid any localised extreme heat

(such as a blow torch) – aluminium alloy has a low melting point.

● Approved methods of heating a casing are using a domestic oven (heated to 100°C) or immersing the casing in boiling water (see illustration 5.12). Low temperature range localised heat sources such as a paint stripper heat gun or clothes iron can also be used (see illustration 5.13). Alternatively, soak a rag in boiling water, wring it out and wrap it around the bearing housing.

⚠ **Warning: All of these methods require care in use to prevent scalding and burns to the hands. Wear protective gloves when handling hot components.**

● If heating the whole casing note that plastic components, such as the oil pressure switch, may suffer – remove them beforehand.

● After heating, remove the bearing as described above. You may find that the expansion is sufficient for the bearing to fall out of the casing under its own weight or with a light tap on the driver or socket.

● If necessary, the casing can be heated to aid bearing installation, and this is sometimes the recommended procedure if the scooter manufacturer has designed the housing and bearing fit with this intention.

● Installation of bearings can be eased by placing them in a freezer the night before installation. The steel bearing will contract slightly, allowing easy insertion in its housing. This is often useful when installing steering head outer races in the frame.

Bearing types and markings

● Plain bearings, ball bearings, needle roller bearings and tapered roller bearings will all be found on scooters (see illustrations 5.14 and 5.15). The ball and roller types are usually caged between an inner and outer race, but uncaged variations may be found.

● Plain bearings are sometimes found at the crankshaft main and connecting rod big-end where they are good at coping with high loads. They are made of a phosphor-bronze material and are impregnated with self-lubricating properties.

5.10 Drawing the bearing out of the suspension arm

5.11 Installing a new bearing (1) in the suspension arm

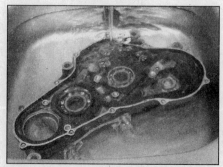

5.12 A casing can be immersed in a sink of boiling water to aid bearing removal

5.13 Using a localised heat source to aid bearing removal

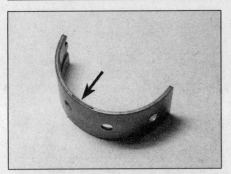

5.14 Bearings are either plain or grooved. They are usually identified by colour code (arrow)

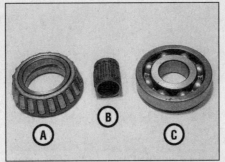

5.15 Tapered roller bearing (A), needle roller bearing (B) and ball journal bearing (C)

5.16 Typical bearing marking

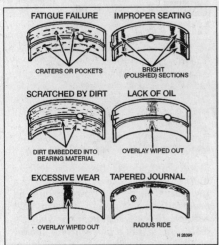

5.17 Typical bearing failures

5.18 Example of ball journal bearing with damaged balls and cages

5.19 Hold outer race and listen to inner race when spun

● Ball bearings and needle roller bearings consist of a steel inner and outer race with the balls or rollers between the races. They require constant lubrication by oil or grease and are good at coping with axial loads. Tapered roller bearings consist of rollers set in a tapered cage set on the inner race; the outer race is separate. They are good at coping with axial loads and prevent movement along the shaft – a typical application is in the steering head.

● Bearing manufacturers produce bearings to ISO size standards and stamp one face of the bearing to indicate its internal and external diameter, load capacity and type **(see illustration 5.16)**.

● Metal bushes are usually of phosphor-bronze material. Rubber bushes are used in suspension mounting eyes. Fibre bushes have also been used in suspension pivots.

Bearing fault finding

● If a bearing outer race has spun in its housing, the housing material will be damaged. You can use a bearing locking compound to bond the outer race in place if damage is not too severe.

● Plain bearings will fail due to damage of their working surface, as a result of lack of lubrication, corrosion or abrasive particles in the oil **(see illustration 5.17)**. Small particles

of dirt in the oil may embed in the bearing material whereas larger particles will score the bearing and shaft journal. If a number of short journeys are made, insufficient heat will be generated to drive off condensation which has built up on the bearings.

● Ball and roller bearings will fail due to lack of lubrication or damage to the balls or rollers. Tapered roller bearings can be damaged by overloading them. Unless the bearing is sealed on both sides, wash it in paraffin (kerosene) to remove all old grease then allow it to dry. Make a visual inspection looking to dented balls or rollers, damaged cages and worn or pitted races **(see illustration 5.18)**.

● A ball bearing can be checked for wear by listening to it when spun. Apply a film of light oil to the bearing and hold it close to the ear – hold the outer race with one hand and spin the inner race with the other hand **(see illustration 5.19)**. The bearing should be almost silent when spun; if it grates or rattles it is worn.

6 Oil seals

Oil seal removal and installation

● Oil seals should be renewed every time a component is dismantled. This is because the seal lips will become set to the sealing surface and will not necessarily reseal.

● Oil seals can be prised out of position using a large flat-bladed screwdriver (see

illustration 6.1). In the case of crankcase seals, check first that the seal is not lipped on the inside, preventing its removal with the crankcases joined.

● New seals are usually installed with their marked face (containing the seal reference code) outwards and the spring side towards the fluid being retained. In certain cases, such as a two-stroke engine crankshaft seal, a double lipped seal may be used due to there being fluid or gas on each side of the joint.

● Use a bearing driver or socket which bears only on the outer hard edge of the seal to install it in the casing – tapping on the inner edge will damage the sealing lip.

Oil seal types and markings

● Oil seals are usually of the single-lipped type. Double-lipped seals are found where a liquid or gas is on both sides of the joint.

6.1 Prise out oil seals with a large flat-bladed screwdriver

6.2 These oil seal markings indicate inside diameter, outside diameter and seal thickness

● Oil seals can harden and lose their sealing ability if the scooter has been in storage for a long period – renewal is the only solution.
● Oil seal manufacturers also conform to the ISO markings for seal size – these are moulded into the outer face of the seal **(see illustration 6.2)**.

7 Gaskets and sealants

Types of gasket and sealant

● Gaskets are used to seal the mating surfaces between components and keep lubricants, fluids, vacuum or pressure contained within the assembly. Aluminium gaskets are sometimes found at the cylinder joints, but most gaskets are paper-based. If the mating surfaces of the components being joined are undamaged the gasket can be installed dry, although a dab of sealant or grease will be useful to hold it in place during assembly.
● RTV (Room Temperature Vulcanising) silicone rubber sealants cure when exposed to moisture in the atmosphere. These sealants are good at filling pits or irregular gasket faces, but will tend to be forced out of the joint under very high torque: They can be used to replace a paper gasket, but first make sure that the width of the paper gasket is not essential to the shimming of internal components. RTV sealants should not be used on components containing petrol (gasoline).
● Non-hardening, semi-hardening and hard

7.1 If a pry point is provided, apply gently pressure with a flat-bladed screwdriver

setting liquid gasket compounds can be used with a gasket or between a metal-to-metal joint. Select the sealant to suit the application: universal non-hardening sealant can be used on virtually all joints; semi-hardening on joint faces which are rough or damaged; hard setting sealant on joints which require a permanent bond and are subjected to high temperature and pressure. **Note:** *Check first if the paper gasket has a bead of sealant impregnated in its surface before applying additional sealant.*
● When choosing a sealant, make sure it is suitable for the application, particularly if being applied in a high-temperature area or in the vicinity of fuel. Certain manufacturers produce sealants in either clear, silver or black colours to match the finish of the engine.
● Do not over-apply sealant. That which is squeezed out on the outside of the joint can be wiped off, whereas an excess of sealant on the inside can break off and clog oilways.

Breaking a sealed joint

● Age, heat, pressure and the use of hard setting sealant can cause two components to stick together so tightly that they are difficult to separate using finger pressure alone. Do not resort to using levers unless there is a pry point provided for this purpose **(see illustration 7.1)** or else the gasket surfaces will be damaged.
● Use a soft-faced hammer **(see illustration 7.2)** or a wood block and conventional hammer to strike the component near the mating surface. Avoid hammering against cast extremities since they may break off. If this method fails, try using a wood wedge between the two components.

7.2 Tap around the joint with a soft-faced mallet if necessary – don't strike cooling fins

Most components have one or two hollow locating dowels between the two gasket faces. If a dowel cannot be removed, do not resort to gripping it with pliers – it will almost certainly be distorted. Install a close-fitting socket or Phillips screwdriver into the dowel and then grip the outer edge of the dowel to free it.

Caution: If the joint will not separate, double-check that you have removed all the fasteners.

Removal of old gasket and sealant

● Paper gaskets will most likely come away complete, leaving only a few traces stuck on the sealing faces of the components. It is imperative that all traces are removed to ensure correct sealing of the new gasket.
● Very carefully scrape all traces of gasket away making sure that the sealing surfaces are not gouged or scored by the scraper **(see illustrations 7.3, 7.4 and 7.5)**. Stubborn

7.3 Paper gaskets can be scraped off with a gasket scraper tool . . .

7.4 . . . a knife blade . . .

7.5 . . . or a household scraper

7.6 Fine abrasive paper is wrapped around a flat file to clean up the gasket face

7.7 A kitchen scourer can be used on stubborn deposits

deposits can be removed by spraying with an aerosol gasket remover. Final preparation of the gasket surface can be made with very fine abrasive paper or a plastic kitchen scourer **(see illustrations 7.6 and 7.7).**

● Old sealant can be scraped or peeled off components, depending on the type originally used. Note that gasket removal compounds are available to avoid scraping the components clean; make sure the gasket remover suits the type of sealant used.

8 Hoses

Clamping to prevent flow

● Small-bore flexible hoses can be clamped to prevent fluid flow whilst a component is worked on. Whichever method is used, ensure that the hose material is not permanently distorted or damaged by the clamp.

a) A brake hose clamp available from auto accessory shops **(see illustration 8.1).**
b) A wingnut type hose clamp **(see illustration 8.2).**
c) Two sockets placed each side of the hose and held with straight-jawed self-locking grips **(see illustration 8.3).**
d) Thick card each side of the hose held between straight-jawed self-locking grips **(see illustration 8.4).**

Freeing and fitting hoses

● Always make sure the hose clamp is moved well clear of the hose end. Grip the hose with your hand and rotate it whilst pulling it off the union. If the hose has hardened due to age and will not move, slit it with a sharp knife and peel its ends off the union **(see illustration 8.5).**

● Resist the temptation to use grease or soap on the unions to aid installation; although it helps the hose slip over the union it will equally aid the escape of fluid from the joint. It is preferable to soften the hose ends in hot water and wet the inside surface of the hose with water or a fluid which will evaporate.

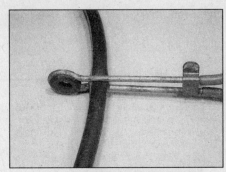

8.1 Hoses can be clamped with an automotive brake hose clamp . . .

8.2 . . . a wingnut type hose clamp . . .

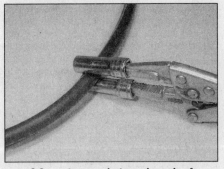

8.3 . . . two sockets and a pair of self-locking grips . . .

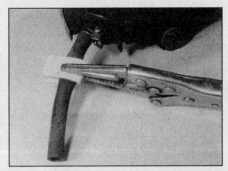

8.4 . . . or thick card and self-locking grips

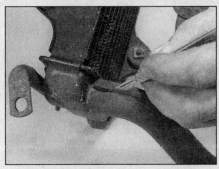

8.5 Cutting a coolant hose free with a sharp knife

About the MOT Test

In the UK, all vehicles more than three years old are subject to an annual test to ensure that they meet minimum safety requirements. A current test certificate must be issued before a machine can be used on public roads, and is required before a road fund licence can be issued. Riding without a current test certificate will also invalidate your insurance.

For most owners, the MOT test is an annual cause for anxiety, and this is largely due to owners not being sure what needs to be checked prior to submitting the scooter for testing. The simple answer is that a fully roadworthy scooter will have no difficulty in passing the test.

This is a guide to getting your scooter through the MOT test. Obviously it will not be possible to examine the scooter to the same standard as the professional MOT tester, particularly in view of the equipment required for some of the checks. However, working through the following procedures will enable you to identify any problem areas before submitting the scooter for the test.

It has only been possible to summarise the test requirements here, based on the regulations in force at the time of printing. Test standards are becoming increasingly stringent, although there are some exemptions for older vehicles. More information about the MOT test can be obtained from the TSO publications, *How Safe is your Motorcycle* and *The MOT Inspection Manual for Motorcycle Testing*.

Many of the checks require that one of the wheels is raised off the ground. Additionally, the help of an assistant may prove useful.

Check that the frame number is clearly visible.

Electrical System

Lights, turn signals, horn and reflector

● With the ignition on, check the operation of the following electrical components. **Note:** *The electrical components on certain small-capacity machines are powered by the generator, requiring that the engine is run for this check.*

a) Headlight and tail light. Check that both illuminate in the low and high beam switch positions.
b) Position lights. Check that the front position (or sidelight) and tail light illuminate in this switch position.
c) Turn signals. Check that all flash at the correct rate, and that the warning light(s) function correctly. Check that the turn signal switch works correctly.
d) Hazard warning system (where fitted). Check that all four turn signals flash in this switch position.

e) Brake stop light. Check that the light comes on when the front and rear brakes are independently applied. Models first used on or after 1st April 1986 must have a brake light switch on each brake.
f) Horn. Check that the sound is continuous and of reasonable volume.

● Check that there is a red reflector on the rear of the machine, either mounted separately or as part of the tail light lens.
● Check the condition of the headlight, tail light and turn signal lenses.

Headlight beam height

● The MOT tester will perform a headlight beam height check using specialised beam setting equipment **(see illustration 1)**. This equipment will not be available to the home mechanic, but if you suspect that the headlight is incorrectly set or may have been maladjusted in the past, you can perform a rough test as follows.
● Position the scooter in a straight line facing a brick wall. The scooter must be off its stand, upright and with a rider seated. Measure the height from the ground to the centre of the headlight and mark a horizontal line on the wall at this height. Position the scooter 3.8 metres from the wall and draw a vertical line up the wall central to the centreline of the scooter. Switch to dipped beam and check that the beam pattern falls slightly lower than the horizontal line and to the left of the vertical line **(see illustration 2)**.

Headlight beam height checking equipment

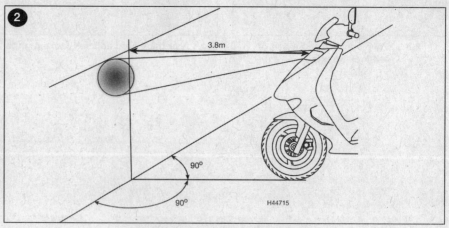

Home workshop beam alignment check

Exhaust System

Exhaust

● Check that the exhaust mountings are secure and that the system does not foul any of the rear suspension components.
● Start the scooter. When the revs are increased, check that the exhaust is neither holed nor leaking from any of its joints. On a linked system, check that the collector box is not leaking due to corrosion.
● Note that the exhaust decibel level ("loudness" of the exhaust) is assessed at the discretion of the tester. If the scooter was first used on or after 1st January 1985 the silencer must carry the BSAU 193 stamp, or a marking relating to its make and model, or be of OE (original equipment) manufacture. If the silencer is marked NOT FOR ROAD USE, RACING USE ONLY or similar, it will fail the MOT.

Steering and Suspension

Steering

● With the front wheel raised off the ground, rotate the steering from lock to lock. The handlebar or switches must not contact anything. Problems can be caused by damaged lock stops on the lower yoke and frame, or by the fitting of non-standard handlebars.
● When performing the lock to lock check, also ensure that the steering moves freely without drag or notchiness. Steering movement can be impaired by poorly routed cables, or by overtight head bearings or worn bearings. The tester will perform a check of the steering head bearing lower race by mounting the front wheel on a surface plate, then performing a lock to lock check with the weight of the machine on the lower bearing (see illustration 3).
● Grasp the fork sliders (lower legs) and attempt to push and pull on the forks (see illustration 4). Any play in the steering head bearings will be felt. Note that in extreme cases, wear of the front fork bushes can be misinterpreted for head bearing play.
● Check that the handlebars are securely mounted.
● Check that the handlebar grip rubbers are secure. They should by bonded to the bar left end and to the throttle twistgrip on the right end.

Front suspension

● With the scooter off the stand, hold the front brake on and pump the front suspension up and down (see illustration 5). Check that the movement is adequately damped.
● Inspect the area above and around the front fork oil seals (see illustration 6). There should be no sign of oil on the fork tube (stanchion) nor leaking down the slider (lower leg).
● On models with leading or trailing link front suspension, check that there is no freeplay in the linkage when moved from side to side.

Front wheel mounted on a surface plate for steering head bearing lower race check

Checking the steering head bearings for freeplay

Hold the front brake on and pump the front suspension up and down to check operation

Inspect the area around the fork dust seal for oil leakage

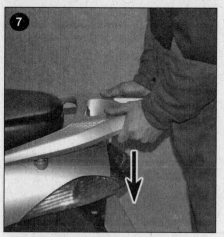

Bounce the rear of the scooter to check rear suspension operation

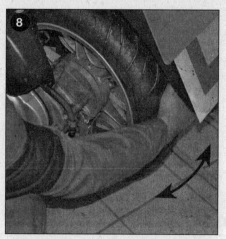

Grasp the rear wheel to check for play in the engine-to-frame mountings

● With the scooter off the stand and an assistant supporting the scooter by its handlebars, bounce the rear suspension (see illustration 7). Check that the suspension components do not foul the bodywork and check that the shock absorber(s) provide adequate damping.

● Visually inspect the shock absorber(s) and check that there is no sign of oil leakage from its damper.

● With the rear wheel raised off the ground, grasp the wheel as shown and attempt to move it from side to side (see illustration 8). Any play in the engine-to-frame mountings will be felt as movement.

Brakes, Wheels and Tyres

Brakes

● With the wheel raised off the ground, apply the brake then free it off, and check that the wheel is about to revolve freely without brake drag.

● On disc brakes, examine the disc itself. Check that it is securely mounted and not cracked.

● On disc brakes, view the pad material through the caliper mouth and check that the pads are not worn down beyond the limit (see illustration 9).

● On drum brakes, check that when the brake is applied the angle between the operating lever and cable or rod is not too great (see illustration 10). Check also that the operating lever doesn't foul any other components.

● On disc brakes, examine the flexible hoses from top to bottom. Have an assistant hold the brake on so that the fluid in the hose is under pressure, and check that there is no sign of fluid leakage, bulges or cracking. If there are any metal brake pipes or unions, check that these are free from corrosion and damage.

● The MOT tester will perform a test of the scooter's braking efficiency based on a calculation of rider and scooter weight. Although this cannot be carried out at home, you can at least ensure that the braking systems are properly maintained. For hydraulic disc brakes, check the fluid level, lever/ pedal feel (bleed of air if its spongy) and pad material. For drum brakes, check adjustment, cable or rod operation and shoe lining thickness.

Brake pad wear can usually be viewed without removing the caliper. Some pads have wear indicator grooves (arrow)

On drum brakes, check the angle of the operating lever with the brake fully applied. Most drum brakes have a wear indicator pointer and scale

Wheels and tyres

● Check the wheel condition. Cast wheels should be free from cracks and if of the built-up design, all fasteners should be secure.

● With the wheel raised off the ground, spin the wheel and visually check that the tyre and wheel run true. Check that the tyre does not foul the suspension or mudguards.

● With the wheel raised off the ground, grasp the wheel and attempt to move it about the axle (see illustration 11). Any play felt here indicates wheel bearing failure.

● Check the tyre tread depth, tread condition and sidewall condition (see illustration 12).

● Check the tyre type. Front and rear tyre types must be compatible and be suitable for

Check for wheel bearing play by trying to move the wheel about the axle (spindle)

Checking the tyre tread depth

Tyre direction of rotation arrow can be found on tyre sidewall

Two straight-edges are used to check wheel alignment

road use. Tyres marked NOT FOR ROAD USE, COMPETITION USE ONLY or similar, will fail the MOT.

● If the tyre sidewall carries a direction of rotation arrow, this must be pointing in the direction of normal wheel rotation **(see illustration 13)**.

● Check that the wheel axle nuts (where applicable) are properly secured. A self-locking nut or castellated nut with a split-pin or R-pin can be used.

● Wheel alignment is checked with the scooter off the stand and a rider seated. With the front wheel pointing straight ahead, two

perfectly straight lengths of metal or wood and placed against the sidewalls of both tyres **(see illustration 14)**. The gap each side of the front tyre must be equidistant on both sides. Incorrect wheel alignment may be due to a cocked rear wheel or in extreme cases, a bent frame.

General checks and condition

● Check the security of all major fasteners, bodypanels, seat and mudguards.

● Check that the pillion footrests, handlebar levers and stand are securely mounted.

● Check for corrosion on the frame or any load-bearing components. If severe, this may affect the structure, particularly under stress.

Conversion Factors

Length (distance)

Inches (in)	x 25.4	= Millimetres (mm)	x 0.0394	= Inches (in)
Feet (ft)	x 0.305	= Metres (m)	x 3.281	= Feet (ft)
Miles	x 1.609	= Kilometres (km)	x 0.621	= Miles

Volume (capacity)

Cubic inches (cu in; in^3)	x 16.387	= Cubic centimetres (cc; cm^3)	x 0.061	= Cubic inches (cu in; in^3)
Imperial pints (Imp pt)	x 0.568	= Litres (l)	x 1.76	= Imperial pints (Imp pt)
Imperial quarts (Imp qt)	x 1.137	= Litres (l)	x 0.88	= Imperial quarts (Imp qt)
Imperial quarts (Imp qt)	x 1.201	= US quarts (US qt)	x 0.833	= Imperial quarts (Imp qt)
US quarts (US qt)	x 0.946	= Litres (l)	x 1.057	= US quarts (US qt)
Imperial gallons (Imp gal)	x 4.546	= Litres (l)	x 0.22	= Imperial gallons (Imp gal)
Imperial gallons (Imp gal)	x 1.201	= US gallons (US gal)	x 0.833	= Imperial gallons (Imp gal)
US gallons (US gal)	x 3.785	= Litres (l)	x 0.264	= US gallons (US gal)

Mass (weight)

Ounces (oz)	x 28.35	= Grams (g)	x 0.035	= Ounces (oz)
Pounds (lb)	x 0.454	= Kilograms (kg)	x 2.205	= Pounds (lb)

Force

Ounces-force (ozf; oz)	x 0.278	= Newtons (N)	x 3.6	= Ounces-force (ozf; oz)
Pounds-force (lbf; lb)	x 4.448	= Newtons (N)	x 0.225	= Pounds-force (lbf; lb)
Newtons (N)	x 0.1	= Kilograms-force (kgf; kg)	x 9.81	= Newtons (N)

Pressure

Pounds-force per square inch (psi; lbf/in^2; lb/in^2)	x 0.070	= Kilograms-force per square centimetre (kgf/cm^2; kg/cm^2)	x 14.223	= Pounds-force per square inch (psi; lbf/in^2; lb/in^2)
Pounds-force per square inch (psi; lbf/in^2; lb/in^2)	x 0.068	= Atmospheres (atm)	x 14.696	= Pounds-force per square inch (psi; lbf/in^2; lb/in^2)
Pounds-force per square inch (psi; lbf/in^2; lb/in^2)	x 0.069	= Bars	x 14.5	= Pounds-force per square inch (psi; lbf/in^2; lb/in^2)
Pounds-force per square inch (psi; lbf/in^2; lb/in^2)	x 6.895	= Kilopascals (kPa)	x 0.145	= Pounds-force per square inch (psi; lbf/in^2; lb/in^2)
Kilopascals (kPa)	x 0.01	= Kilograms-force per square centimetre (kgf/cm^2; kg/cm^2)	x 98.1	= Kilopascals (kPa)
Millibar (mbar)	x 100	= Pascals (Pa)	x 0.01	= Millibar (mbar)
Millibar (mbar)	x 0.0145	= Pounds-force per square inch (psi; lbf/in^2; lb/in^2)	x 68.947	= Millibar (mbar)
Millibar (mbar)	x 0.75	= Millimetres of mercury (mmHg)	x 1.333	= Millibar (mbar)
Millibar (mbar)	x 0.401	= Inches of water (inH$_2$O)	x 2.491	= Millibar (mbar)
Millimetres of mercury (mmHg)	x 0.535	= Inches of water (inH$_2$O)	x 1.868	= Millimetres of mercury (mmHg)
Inches of water (inH$_2$O)	x 0.036	= Pounds-force per square inch (psi; lbf/in^2; lb/in^2)	x 27.68	= Inches of water (inH$_2$O)

Torque (moment of force)

Pounds-force inches (lbf in; lb in)	x 1.152	= Kilograms-force centimetre (kgf cm; kg cm)	x 0.868	= Pounds-force inches (lbf in; lb in)
Pounds-force inches (lbf in; lb in)	x 0.113	= Newton metres (Nm)	x 8.85	= Pounds-force inches (lbf in; lb in)
Pounds-force inches (lbf in; lb in)	x 0.083	= Pounds-force feet (lbf ft; lb ft)	x 12	= Pounds-force inches (lbf in; lb in)
Pounds-force feet (lbf ft; lb ft)	x 0.138	= Kilograms-force metres (kgf m; kg m)	x 7.233	= Pounds-force feet (lbf ft; lb ft)
Pounds-force feet (lbf ft; lb ft)	x 1.356	= Newton metres (Nm)	x 0.738	= Pounds-force feet (lbf ft; lb ft)
Newton metres (Nm)	x 0.102	= Kilograms-force metres (kgf m; kg m)	x 9.804	= Newton metres (Nm)

Power

Horsepower (hp)	x 745.7	= Watts (W)	x 0.0013	= Horsepower (hp)

Velocity (speed)

Miles per hour (miles/hr; mph)	x 1.609	= Kilometres per hour (km/hr; kph)	x 0.621	= Miles per hour (miles/hr; mph)

Fuel consumption*

Miles per gallon, Imperial (mpg)	x 0.354	= Kilometres per litre (km/l)	x 2.825	= Miles per gallon, Imperial (mpg)
Miles per gallon, US (mpg)	x 0.425	= Kilometres per litre (km/l)	x 2.352	= Miles per gallon, US (mpg)

Temperature

Degrees Fahrenheit = (°C x 1.8) + 32   Degrees Celsius (Degrees Centigrade; °C) = (°F - 32) x 0.56

It is common practice to convert from miles per gallon (mpg) to litres/100 kilometres (l/100km), where mpg x l/100 km = 282

1 Engine doesn't start or is difficult to start

- [ ] Starter motor doesn't rotate
- [ ] Starter motor rotates but engine does not turn over
- [ ] Starter works but engine won't turn over (seized)
- [ ] No fuel flow
- [ ] Engine flooded
- [ ] No spark or weak spark
- [ ] Compression low
- [ ] Stalls after starting
- [ ] Rough idle

2 Poor running at low speed

- [ ] Spark weak
- [ ] Fuel/air mixture incorrect
- [ ] Compression low
- [ ] Poor acceleration

3 Poor running or no power at high speed

- [ ] Firing incorrect
- [ ] Fuel/air mixture incorrect
- [ ] Compression low
- [ ] Knocking or pinking
- [ ] Miscellaneous causes

4 Overheating

- [ ] Engine overheats
- [ ] Firing incorrect
- [ ] Fuel/air mixture incorrect
- [ ] Compression too high
- [ ] Engine load excessive
- [ ] Lubrication inadequate

5 Transmission problems

- [ ] No drive to rear wheel
- [ ] Vibration
- [ ] Poor performance
- [ ] Clutch not disengaging completely

6 Abnormal engine noise

- [ ] Knocking or pinking
- [ ] Piston slap or rattling
- [ ] Valve noise
- [ ] Other noise

7 Abnormal frame and suspension noise

- [ ] Front end noise
- [ ] Shock absorber noise
- [ ] Brake noise

8 Excessive exhaust smoke

- [ ] White smoke
- [ ] Black smoke
- [ ] Brown smoke

9 Poor handling or stability

- [ ] Handlebar hard to turn
- [ ] Handlebar shakes or vibrates excessively
- [ ] Handlebar pulls to one side
- [ ] Poor shock absorbing qualities

10 Braking problems – disc brakes

- [ ] Brakes are ineffective
- [ ] Brake lever pulsates
- [ ] Brakes drag

11 Braking problems – drum brakes

- [ ] Brakes are ineffective
- [ ] Brake lever pulsates
- [ ] Brakes drag

12 Electrical problems

- [ ] Battery dead or weak
- [ ] Battery overcharged

1 Engine doesn't start or is difficult to start

Starter motor doesn't rotate

- [ ] Fuse blown. Check fuse and starter circuit (Chapter 10).
- [ ] Battery voltage low. Check and recharge battery (Chapter 10).
- [ ] Starter motor defective. Make sure the wiring to the starter is secure. Make sure the starter relay clicks when the start button is pushed. If the relay clicks, then the fault is in the wiring or motor.
- [ ] Starter relay faulty. Check it (Chapter 10).
- [ ] Starter button on handlebar not contacting. The contacts could be wet, corroded or dirty. Disassemble and clean the switch (Chapter 10).
- [ ] Wiring open or shorted. Check all wiring connections and harnesses to make sure that they are dry, tight and not corroded. Also check for broken or frayed wires that can cause a short to earth.
- [ ] Ignition switch defective. Check the switch according to the procedure in Chapter 10. Fit a new switch if it is defective.
- [ ] Starter safety circuit fault. Check brake light switches/inhibitor switches and wiring (Chapter 10).

Starter motor rotates but engine does not turn over

- [ ] Starter clutch defective. Inspect and repair or renew (Chapter 2A, 2B or 2C).
- [ ] Damaged starter gears. Inspect and renew the damaged parts (Chapter 2A, 2B or 2C).

Starter works but engine won't turn over (seized)

- [ ] Seized engine caused by one or more internally damaged components. Failure due to wear, abuse or lack of lubrication. Damage can include piston, cylinder, connecting rod, crankshaft and bearings (Chapter 2A, 2B or 2C).

No fuel flow

- [ ] No fuel in tank.
- [ ] Fuel tank vent in filler cap blocked. Clean and blow through or replace with a new one.
- [ ] Fuel hose pinched – check the hose and its routing.
- [ ] Fuel hose clogged. Remove the fuel hose and carefully blow through it.
- [ ] Fuel pump circuit fault – check all components in the circuit (Chapter 5).
- [ ] Fuel pump defective – problems could include a faulty pump motor, faulty pressure regulator or blocked filter or strainer. In all cases replace the pump with a new one (Chapter 5).
- [ ] Fuel injection system fault. See Chapter 5.

Engine flooded

- [ ] The fuel injector could be stuck open, or there could be too much pressure in the system. Check the injector first, then check fuel pressure (Chapter 5).
- [ ] Starting technique incorrect. Under normal circumstances the machine should start with no throttle, whatever the temperature.

1 Engine doesn't start or is difficult to start (continued)

No spark or weak spark

☐ Battery voltage low. Check and recharge the battery as necessary (Chapter 10).

☐ Spark plug dirty, defective or worn out. Locate reason for fouled plug using spark plug condition chart at the end of this manual and follow the plug maintenance procedures (Chapter 1).

☐ Spark plug cap or lead faulty. Check condition (Chapter 6).

☐ Spark plug cap not making good contact. Make sure that the plug cap fits snugly over the plug end.

☐ Electronic control unit (ECU) defective. Check the unit, referring to Chapter 6 for details.

☐ Pulse generator coil defective. Check it, referring to Chapter 6 for details.

☐ Ignition coil defective. Check the coil, referring to Chapter 6.

☐ Wiring shorted or broken. Make sure that all wiring connections are clean, dry and tight. Look for chafed and broken wires (Chapters 6 and 10).

Compression low

☐ Spark plug loose (Chapter 1).

☐ Cylinder head not sufficiently tightened down. If the cylinder head is suspected of being loose, then there's a chance that the gasket or head is damaged if the problem has persisted for any length of time. The head nuts/bolts should be tightened to the proper torque in the correct sequence (Chapter 2A, 2B or 2C).

☐ Cylinder and/or piston worn. Excessive wear will cause compression pressure to leak past the rings. This is usually accompanied by worn rings as well. A top-end overhaul is necessary (Chapter 2A, 2B or 2C).

☐ Piston rings worn, weak, broken, or sticking. Broken or sticking piston rings usually indicate a lubrication or fuelling problem that causes excess carbon deposits to form on the pistons and rings. Top-end overhaul is necessary (Chapter 2A, 2B or 2C).

☐ Piston ring-to-groove clearance excessive. This is caused by excessive wear of the piston ring lands. Piston renewal is necessary (Chapter 2A, 2B or 2C).

☐ Cylinder head gasket damaged. If the head is allowed to become loose, or if excessive carbon build-up on the piston crown and combustion chamber causes extremely high compression, the head gasket may leak. Retorquing the head is not always sufficient to restore the seal, so gasket renewal is necessary (Chapter 2A, 2B or 2C).

☐ Cylinder head warped. This is caused by overheating or improperly tightened head nuts/bolts. Machine shop resurfacing or head renewal is necessary (Chapter 2A, 2B or 2C).

☐ Incorrect valve clearance. If a valve is not closing completely then engine pressure will leak past the valve. Check and adjust the valve clearances (Chapter 1).

☐ Valve not seating properly. This is caused by a bent valve (from over-revving or improper valve adjustment), burned valve or seat (improper combustion) or an accumulation of carbon deposits on the seat (from combustion or lubrication problems). The valves must be cleaned and/or renewed and the seats serviced if possible (Chapter 2A, 2B or 2C).

☐ Valve spring broken or weak. Caused by component failure or wear; the springs must be renewed (Chapter 2A, 2B or 2C).

Stalls after starting

☐ Ignition malfunction (Chapter 6).

☐ Fuel injection system fault (Chapter 5).

☐ Fuel contaminated. The fuel can be contaminated with either dirt or water, or can change chemically if the machine is allowed to sit for several months or more. Drain the tank (Chapter 5).

☐ Inlet air leak. Check for loose inlet manifold connection (Chapter 5).

Rough idle

☐ Ignition malfunction (Chapter 6).

☐ Idle speed incorrect (Chapter 1).

☐ Fuel injection system fault (Chapter 5).

☐ Fuel contaminated. The fuel can be contaminated with either dirt or water, or can change chemically if the machine is allowed to sit for several months or more. Drain the tank and fuel system components (Chapter 5).

☐ Intake air leak. Check for loose intake manifold connection (Chapter 5).

☐ Air filter clogged. Clean or renew the air filter element (Chapter 1).

2 Poor running at low speeds

Spark weak

☐ Battery voltage low. Check and recharge battery (Chapter 10).

☐ Spark plug fouled, defective or worn out. Refer to Chapter 1 for spark plug maintenance.

☐ Spark plug cap or HT wiring defective. Refer to Chapter 6 for details on the ignition system.

☐ Spark plug cap not making contact.

☐ Incorrect spark plug. Wrong type, heat range or cap configuration. Check and install correct plug listed in Chapter 1.

☐ Electronic control unit (ECU) defective (Chapter 6).

☐ Pulse generator coil defective (Chapter 6).

☐ Ignition coil defective (Chapter 6).

Fuel/air mixture incorrect

☐ Fuel injector clogged or fuel injection system fault (see Chapter 5).

☐ Air filter clogged, poorly sealed or missing (Chapter 1).

☐ Air filter housing poorly sealed. Look for cracks, holes or loose clamps and renew or repair defective parts.

☐ Intake air leak. Check for loose throttle body-to-intake manifold connections or a leaking gasket (Chapter 4).

☐ Fuel tank vent in filler cap blocked. Clean and blow through or replace with a new one.

Compression low

☐ Spark plug loose (Chapter 1).

☐ Cylinder head not sufficiently tightened down. If the cylinder head is suspected of being loose, then there's a chance that the gasket or head is damaged if the problem has persisted for any length of time. The head nuts/bolts should be tightened to the proper torque in the correct sequence (Chapter 2A, 2B or 2C).

☐ Cylinder and/or piston worn. Excessive wear will cause compression pressure to leak past the rings. This is usually accompanied by worn rings as well. A top-end overhaul is necessary (Chapter 2A, 2B or 2C).

☐ Piston rings worn, weak, broken, or sticking. Broken or sticking piston rings usually indicate a lubrication or fuelling problem that causes excess carbon deposits to form on the pistons and rings. Top-end overhaul is necessary (Chapter 2A, 2B or 2C).

☐ Piston ring-to-groove clearance excessive. This is caused by excessive wear of the piston ring lands. Piston renewal is necessary (Chapter 2A, 2B or 2C).

☐ Cylinder head gasket damaged. If the head is allowed to become loose, or if excessive carbon build-up on the piston crown and combustion chamber causes extremely high compression, the head

2 Poor running at low speeds (continued)

gasket may leak. Retorquing the head is not always sufficient to restore the seal, so gasket renewal is necessary (Chapter 2A, 2B or 2C).

☐ Cylinder head warped. This is caused by overheating or improperly tightened head nuts/bolts. Machine shop resurfacing or head renewal is necessary (Chapter 2A, 2B or 2C).

☐ Incorrect valve clearance. If a valve is not closing completely then engine pressure will leak past the valve. Check and adjust the valve clearances (Chapter 1).

☐ Valve not seating properly. This is caused by a bent valve (from over-revving or improper valve adjustment), burned valve or seat (improper combustion) or an accumulation of carbon deposits on the seat (from combustion or lubrication problems). The valves must be cleaned and/or renewed and the seats serviced if possible (Chapter 2A, 2B or 2C).

☐ Valve spring broken or weak. Caused by component failure or wear; the springs must be renewed (Chapter 2A, 2B or 2C).

Poor acceleration

☐ Fuel injection system fault (Chapter 5).

☐ Timing not advancing. The pulse generator coil or the electronic control unit (ECU) may be defective (Chapter 6).

☐ Brakes dragging. On disc brakes, usually caused by debris which has entered the brake piston seals, or from a warped disc or bent axle, or cable out of adjustment where appropriate. On drum brakes, cable out of adjustment, shoe return spring broken. Repair as necessary (Chapter 8).

☐ Clutch slipping, drive belt worn, or variator faulty (Chapter 3).

3 Poor running or no power at high speed

Firing incorrect

☐ Air filter clogged. Clean or renew filter (Chapter 1).

☐ Spark plug fouled, defective or worn out (Chapter 1).

☐ Spark plug cap or HT lead defective. See Chapter 6 for details of the ignition system.

☐ Spark plug cap not in good contact (Chapter 6).

☐ Incorrect spark plug. Wrong type, heat range or cap configuration. Check and install correct plug listed in Chapter 1.

☐ Electronic control unit (ECU) or ignition coil defective (Chapter 5 and 6).

Fuel/air mixture incorrect

☐ Fuel injector clogged or fuel injection system fault (see Chapter 5).

☐ Air filter clogged, poorly sealed or missing (Chapter 1).

☐ Air filter housing poorly sealed. Look for cracks, holes or loose clamps and renew or repair defective parts.

☐ Intake air leak. Check for loose throttle body-to-intake manifold connections or a leaking gasket (Chapter 5).

☐ Fuel tank vent in filler cap blocked. Clean and blow through or replace with a new one.

Compression low

☐ Spark plug loose (Chapter 1).

☐ Cylinder head not sufficiently tightened down. If the cylinder head is suspected of being loose, then there's a chance that the gasket or head is damaged if the problem has persisted for any length of time. The head nuts/bolts should be tightened to the proper torque in the correct sequence (Chapter 2A, 2B or 2C).

☐ Cylinder and/or piston worn. Excessive wear will cause compression pressure to leak past the rings. This is usually accompanied by worn rings as well. A top-end overhaul is necessary (Chapter 2A, 2B or 2C).

☐ Piston rings worn, weak, broken, or sticking. Broken or sticking piston rings usually indicate a lubrication or fuelling problem that causes excess carbon deposits to form on the pistons and rings. Top-end overhaul is necessary (Chapter 2A, 2B or 2C).

☐ Piston ring-to-groove clearance excessive. This is caused by excessive wear of the piston ring lands. Piston renewal is necessary (Chapter 2A, 2B or 2C).

☐ Cylinder head gasket damaged. If the head is allowed to become loose, or if excessive carbon build-up on the piston crown and combustion chamber causes extremely high compression, the head gasket may leak. Retorquing the head is not always sufficient to restore the seal, so gasket renewal is necessary (Chapter 2A, 2B or 2C).

☐ Cylinder head warped. This is caused by overheating or improperly tightened head nuts/bolts. Machine shop resurfacing or head renewal is necessary (Chapter 2A, 2B or 2C).

☐ Incorrect valve clearance. If a valve is not closing completely then engine pressure will leak past the valve. Check and adjust the valve clearances (Chapter 1).

☐ Valve not seating properly. This is caused by a bent valve (from over-revving or improper valve adjustment), burned valve or seat (improper combustion) or an accumulation of carbon deposits on the seat (from combustion or lubrication problems). The valves must be cleaned and/or renewed and the seats serviced if possible (Chapter 2A, 2B or 2C).

☐ Valve spring broken or weak. Caused by component failure or wear; the springs must be renewed (Chapter 2A, 2B or 2C).

Knocking or pinking

☐ Carbon build-up in combustion chamber. Use of a fuel additive that will dissolve the adhesive bonding the carbon particles to the crown and chamber is the easiest way to remove the build-up. Otherwise, the cylinder head will have to be removed and decarbonised (Chapter 2A, 2B or 2C).

☐ Incorrect or poor quality fuel. Old or improper grades of fuel can cause detonation. This causes the piston to rattle, thus the knocking or pinking sound. Drain old fuel and always use the recommended fuel grade.

☐ Spark plug heat range incorrect. Uncontrolled detonation indicates the plug heat range is too hot. The plug in effect becomes a glow plug, raising cylinder temperatures. Install the proper heat range plug (Chapter 1).

☐ Improper air/fuel mixture. This will cause the cylinder to run hot, which leads to detonation. A fuel injection system fault or an air leak can cause this imbalance (Chapter 5).

Miscellaneous causes

☐ Throttle valve doesn't open fully. Check the action of the twistgrip, and check the cable for kinks and incorrect routing. Adjust the throttle twistgrip freeplay (Chapter 1).

☐ Clutch slipping, drive belt worn, or variator faulty (Chapter 3).

☐ Timing not advancing (Chapter 6).

☐ Brakes dragging. On disc brakes, usually caused by debris which has entered the brake piston seals, or from a warped disc or bent axle. On drum brakes, cable out of adjustment, shoe return spring broken. Repair as necessary (Chapter 8).

4 Overheating

Air-cooled models

☐ Engine cowling sections broken, missing or poorly fitted. Check and refit or replace with new ones (Chapter 2A or 2B).
☐ Cooling fan vanes broken (Chapter 2A or 2B).

Liquid-cooled models

☐ Coolant level low. Check and add coolant (*Pre-ride checks*).
☐ Leak in cooling system. Check cooling system hoses and radiator for leaks and other damage. Repair or renew parts as necessary (Chapter 4).
☐ Thermostat sticking open or closed (Chapter 4).
☐ Coolant passages clogged. Drain and flush the entire system, then refill with fresh coolant (Chapter 4).
☐ Air lock in system – usually follows draining and refilling of the system. If less than the specified amount of coolant could be added when filling, drain the system again, then refill adding the coolant slowly, and tip the scooter from side to side to dislodge any trapped air (Chapter 4).
☐ Water pump defective. Check the pump (Chapter 4).
☐ Clogged radiator fins. Clean them by blowing compressed air through the fins from the back of the radiator.

Firing incorrect

☐ Air filter clogged. Clean or renew filter (Chapter 1).
☐ Spark plug fouled, defective or worn out (Chapter 1).
☐ Spark plug cap or HT lead defective. See Chapter 6 for details of the ignition system.
☐ Spark plug cap not in good contact (Chapter 6).
☐ Incorrect spark plug. Wrong type, heat range or cap configuration. Check and install correct plug listed in Chapter 1.
☐ Electronic control unit (ECU) or ignition coil defective (Chapter 5 and 6).

Fuel/air mixture incorrect

☐ Fuel injector clogged or fuel injection system fault (see Chapter 5).
☐ Air filter clogged, poorly sealed or missing (Chapter 1).
☐ Air filter housing poorly sealed. Look for cracks, holes or loose clamps and renew or repair defective parts.
☐ Intake air leak. Check for loose throttle body-to-intake manifold connections or a leaking gasket (Chapter 5).
☐ Fuel tank vent in filler cap blocked. Clean and blow through or replace with a new one.

Compression too high

☐ Carbon build-up in combustion chamber. Use of a fuel additive that will dissolve the adhesive bonding the carbon particles to the piston crown and chamber is the easiest way to remove the build-up. Otherwise, the cylinder head will have to be removed and cleaned (Chapter 2A, 2B or 2C).
☐ Improperly machined head surface or installation of incorrect size cylinder base gasket during engine assembly.

Engine load excessive

☐ Clutch slipping, drive belt worn, or variator faulty (Chapter 3).
☐ Brakes dragging. On disc brakes, usually caused by debris which has entered the brake piston seals, or from a warped disc or bent axle. On drum brakes, cable out of adjustment, shoe return spring broken. Repair as necessary (Chapter 8).

Lubrication inadequate

☐ Engine oil level too low. Friction caused by intermittent lack of lubrication or from oil that is overworked can cause overheating. The oil provides a definite cooling function in the engine. Check the oil level (*Pre-ride checks*).
☐ Poor quality engine oil or incorrect viscosity or type. Oil is rated not only according to viscosity but also according to type. Some oils are not rated high enough for use in this engine. Check the Specifications section and change to the correct oil (Chapter 1).

5 Transmission problems

No drive to rear wheel

☐ Drive belt broken (Chapter 3).
☐ Clutch not engaging (Chapter 3).
☐ Clutch or drum excessively worn (Chapter 3).

Transmission noise or vibration

☐ Bearings worn. Also includes the possibility that the shafts are worn. Overhaul the gearbox (Chapter 3).
☐ Gears worn or chipped (Chapter 3).
☐ Clutch drum worn unevenly (Chapter 3).
☐ Worn bearings or bent shaft (Chapter 3).
☐ Loose clutch nut or drum nut (Chapter 3).

Poor performance

☐ Variator worn or damaged (Chapter 3).
☐ Weak or broken clutch pulley spring (Chapter 3).
☐ Clutch shoes or drum excessively worn (Chapter 3).
☐ Grease on clutch friction material (Chapter 3).
☐ Drive belt excessively worn (Chapter 3).

Clutch not disengaging completely

☐ Weak or broken clutch shoe springs (Chapter 3).
☐ Engine idle speed too high (Chapter 1).

6 Abnormal engine noise

Knocking or pinking

- [ ] Carbon build-up in combustion chamber. Use of a fuel additive that will dissolve the adhesive bonding the carbon particles to the piston crown and chamber is the easiest way to remove the build-up. Otherwise, the cylinder head will have to be removed and decarbonised (Chapter 2A, 2B or 2C).
- [ ] Incorrect or poor quality fuel. Old or improper fuel can cause detonation. This causes the piston to rattle, thus the knocking or pinking sound. Drain the old fuel and always use the recommended grade fuel (Chapter 5).
- [ ] Spark plug type incorrect. Uncontrolled detonation indicates that the plug heat range is too hot. The plug in effect becomes a glow plug, raising cylinder temperatures. Install the proper plug (Chapter 1).
- [ ] Improper air/fuel mixture. This will cause the cylinder to run hot and lead to detonation. A fuel injection system fault or an air leak can cause this imbalance (Chapter 5).

Piston slap or rattling

- [ ] Cylinder-to-piston clearance excessive. Caused by improper assembly. Inspect and overhaul top-end parts (Chapter 2A, 2B or 2C).
- [ ] Connecting rod bent. Caused by over-revving, trying to start a badly flooded engine or from ingesting a foreign object into the combustion chamber. Renew the damaged parts (Chapter 2A, 2B or 2C).

- [ ] Piston pin or piston pin bore worn or seized from wear or lack of lubrication. Renew damaged parts (Chapter 2A, 2B or 2C).
- [ ] Piston ring(s) worn, broken or sticking. Overhaul the top-end (Chapter 2A, 2B or 2C).
- [ ] Piston seizure damage. Usually from lack of lubrication or overheating. First find and cure the cause of the problem (Chapters 2 and 4), then rebore the cylinder and fit an oversize piston and rings on 125/150 cc 2-valve engines or renew the piston and cylinder on all other engines (Chapter 2A, 2B or 2C).
- [ ] Connecting rod small or big end clearance excessive. Caused by excessive wear or lack of lubrication. Renew worn parts (Chapter 2A, 2B or 2C).

Other noise

- [ ] Exhaust pipe leaking at cylinder head connection. Caused by improper fit of pipe or damaged gasket. All exhaust fasteners should be tightened evenly and carefully (Chapter 5).
- [ ] Crankshaft runout excessive. Caused by a bent crankshaft (from over-revving) or damage from an upper cylinder component failure (Chapter 2A, 2B or 2C).
- [ ] Engine mounting bolts loose. Tighten all engine mounting bolts (Chapter 2A, 2B or 2C).
- [ ] Crankshaft bearings worn (Chapter 2A, 2B or 2C).

7 Abnormal frame and suspension noise

Front end noise

- [ ] Steering head bearings loose or damaged. Clicks when braking. Check and adjust or replace as necessary (Chapters 1 and 7).
- [ ] Bolts loose. Make sure all bolts are tightened to the specified torque (Chapter 7).
- [ ] Front suspension damaged. Good possibility if machine has been in a collision. Check and replace any damaged components with new ones (Chapter 7).
- [ ] Front hub nut or wheel bolts loose. Tighten to the specified torque (Chapter 8).
- [ ] Loose or worn wheel bearings. Check and renew as needed (Chapter 8).

Shock absorber noise

- [ ] Fluid level low due to leakage from defective seal. Shock will be covered with oil. Renew the shock (Chapter 7).
- [ ] Defective shock absorber with internal damage. Renew the shock (Chapter 7).
- [ ] Bent or damaged shock body. Renew the shock (Chapter 7).
- [ ] Loose or worn rear suspension swingarm components. Check and renew as necessary (Chapter 7).

Brake noise

- [ ] Squeal caused by dust on brake pads or shoes. Usually found in combination with glazed pads or shoes. Renew the pads/shoes (Chapter 8).
- [ ] Contamination of brake pads or shoes. Oil or brake fluid causing brake to chatter or squeal. Renew pads or shoes (Chapter 8).
- [ ] Pads or shoes glazed. Caused by excessive heat from prolonged use or from contamination. Do not use sandpaper, emery cloth, carborundum cloth or any other abrasive to roughen the pad surfaces as abrasives will stay in the pad material and damage the disc or drum. A very fine flat file can be used, but pad or shoe renewal is advised (Chapter 8).
- [ ] Disc or drum warped. Can cause a chattering, clicking or intermittent squeal. Usually accompanied by a pulsating lever and uneven braking. Check the disc runout and the drum ovality (Chapter 8).
- [ ] Loose or worn wheel (front) or transmission (rear) bearings. Check and renew as needed (Chapter 8).

8 Excessive exhaust smoke

White smoke

- [ ] Piston oil ring worn. The ring may be broken or damaged, causing oil from the crankcase to be pulled past the piston into the combustion chamber. Replace the rings with new ones (Chapter 2A, 2B or 2C).
- [ ] Cylinder worn, cracked, or scored. Caused by overheating or oil starvation. First find and cure the cause of the problem, then rebore the cylinder and fit an oversize piston and rings on 125/150 cc 2-valve engines, or fit new parts on all other engines (Chapter 2A, 2B or 2C).
- [ ] Valve stem seal damaged or worn. Remove valves and replace seals with new ones (Chapter 2A, 2B or 2C).
- [ ] Valve guide worn. Perform a complete valve job (Chapter 2A, 2B or 2C).
- [ ] Engine oil level too high, which causes the oil to be forced past the rings. Drain oil to the proper level (Pre-ride checks).
- [ ] Head gasket broken between oil return and cylinder. Causes oil to be pulled into the combustion chamber. Renew the head gasket and check the head for warpage (Chapter 2A, 2B or 2C).
- [ ] Abnormal crankcase pressurisation, which forces oil past the rings. Clogged breather is usually the cause.

Black smoke (rich mixture)

- [ ] Air filter clogged. Clean or renew the element (Chapter 1).
- [ ] Fuel injection system malfunction (Chapter 5).
- [ ] Fuel pressure too high. Check the fuel pressure (Chapter 5).

Brown smoke (lean mixture)

- [ ] Fuel pump faulty or pressure regulator stuck open (Chapter 5).
- [ ] Throttle body clamp or intake duct bolts loose (Chapter 5).
- [ ] Air filter poorly sealed or not installed (Chapter 1).
- [ ] Fuel injection system malfunction (Chapter 5).

9 Poor handling or stability

Handlebar hard to turn

- ☐ Steering head bearing adjuster nut too tight. Check adjustment as described in Chapter 1.
- ☐ Bearings damaged. Roughness can be felt as the bars are turned from side-to-side. Replace bearings and races (Chapter 7).
- ☐ Races dented or worn. Denting results from wear in only one position (e.g. straight ahead), from a collision or hitting a pothole or from dropping the machine. Renew races and bearings (Chapter 7).
- ☐ Steering stem lubrication inadequate. Causes are grease getting hard from age or being washed out by high pressure car washes. Disassemble steering head and repack bearings (Chapter 7).
- ☐ Steering stem bent. Caused by a collision, hitting a pothole or by dropping the machine. Renew damaged part. Don't try to straighten the steering stem (Chapter 7).
- ☐ Front tyre air pressure too low (Pre-ride checks).

Handlebar shakes or vibrates excessively

- ☐ Tyres worn (Pre-ride checks).
- ☐ Suspension worn. Renew worn components (Chapter 7).
- ☐ Wheel rim(s) warped or damaged. Inspect wheels for runout (Chapter 8).
- ☐ Wheel bearings worn. Worn wheel bearings (front) or transmission bearings (rear) can cause poor tracking. Worn front bearings will cause wobble (Chapter 8).

- ☐ Handlebar mounting loose (Chapter 7).
- ☐ Front suspension bolts loose. Tighten them to the specified torque (Chapter 7).
- ☐ Engine mounting bolts loose. Will cause excessive vibration with increased engine rpm (Chapter 2A, 2B or 2C).

Handlebar pulls to one side

- ☐ Frame bent. Definitely suspect this if the machine has been in a collision. May or may not be accompanied by cracking near the bend. Renew the frame.
- ☐ Wheels out of alignment. Caused by improper location of axle spacers or from bent steering stem or frame (Chapter 8).
- ☐ Steering stem bent. Caused by impact damage or by dropping the machine. Renew the steering stem (Chapter 7).
- ☐ Fork tube bent. Disassemble the front suspension and renew the damaged parts (Chapter 7).

Poor shock absorbing qualities

Too hard:
- a) Suspension bent. Causes a harsh, sticking feeling (Chapter 7).
- b) Shock absorber internal damage (Chapter 7).
- c) Tyre pressure too high (Pre-ride checks).

Too soft:
- a) Shock absorber spring(s) weak or broken (Chapter 7).
- b) Shock absorber internal damage or leakage (Chapter 7).

10 Braking problems – disc brake

Brake is ineffective

- ☐ Air in brake hose. Caused by inattention to master cylinder fluid level (Pre-ride checks) or by leakage. Locate problem and bleed brake (Chapter 8).
- ☐ Pads or disc worn (Chapters 1 and 8).
- ☐ Brake fluid leak. Locate problem and rectify (Chapter 8).
- ☐ Contaminated pads. Caused by contamination with oil, grease, brake fluid, etc. Renew pads. Clean disc thoroughly with brake cleaner (Chapter 8).
- ☐ Brake fluid deteriorated. Fluid is old or contaminated. Drain system, replenish with new fluid and bleed the system (Chapter 8).
- ☐ Master cylinder or caliper internal parts worn or damaged (Chapter 8).
- ☐ Master cylinder bore scratched by foreign material or broken spring. Renew master cylinder (Chapter 8).
- ☐ Disc warped. Renew disc (Chapter 8).

Brake lever pulsates

- ☐ Disc warped. Renew disc (Chapter 8).
- ☐ Axle bent. Renew axle (Chapter 8).
- ☐ Brake caliper bolts loose (Chapter 8).
- ☐ Wheel warped or otherwise damaged (Chapter 8).
- ☐ Wheel or hub bearings damaged or worn (Chapter 8).

Brake drags

- ☐ Master cylinder piston seized. Caused by wear or damage to piston or cylinder bore (Chapter 8).
- ☐ Lever balky or stuck. Check pivot and lubricate (Chapter 7).
- ☐ Brake caliper piston seized in bore. Caused by wear or ingestion of dirt past deteriorated seal (Chapter 8).
- ☐ Brake pads damaged. Pad material separated from backing plate. Usually caused by faulty manufacturing process or from contact with chemicals. Renew pads (Chapter 8).
- ☐ Caliper slider pins sticking (sliding caliper). Clean the slider pins and apply a smear of silicone grease (Chapter 8).
- ☐ Pads improperly installed (Chapter 8).

11 Braking problems – rear drum brake

Brake is ineffective

☐ Cable incorrectly adjusted. Check cable (Chapter 1).
☐ Shoes or drum worn (Chapter 8).
☐ Contaminated shoes. Caused by contamination with oil, grease etc. Renew shoes. Clean drum thoroughly with brake cleaner (Chapter 8).
☐ Brake arm incorrectly positioned, or cam excessively worn (Chapter 8).

Brake lever pulsates

☐ Drum warped. Renew drum (Chapter 8).
☐ Wheel warped or otherwise damaged (Chapter 8).
☐ Gearbox output shaft bearings worn (Chapters 8 and 3).

Brake drags

☐ Cable incorrectly adjusted or requires lubrication. Check cable (Chapters 1 and 8).
☐ Shoe return springs broken (Chapter 8).
☐ Lever balky or stuck. Check pivot and lubricate (Chapter 7).
☐ Brake arm or cam binds. Caused by inadequate lubrication or damage (Chapter 8).
☐ Brake shoe damaged. Friction material separated from shoe. Usually caused by faulty manufacturing process or from contact with chemicals. Renew shoes (Chapter 8).
☐ Shoes improperly installed (Chapter 8).

12 Electrical problems

Battery dead or weak

☐ Battery faulty. Caused by sulphated plates which are shorted through sedimentation. Also, broken battery terminal making only occasional contact (Chapter 10).
☐ Battery leads making poor electrical contact (Chapter 10).
☐ Load excessive. Caused by addition of high wattage lights or other electrical accessories.
☐ Ignition switch defective. Switch either earths internally or fails to shut off system. Renew the switch (Chapter 10).
☐ Regulator/rectifier defective (Chapter 10).

☐ Alternator stator coil open or shorted (Chapter 10).
☐ Wiring faulty. Wiring either shorted to earth or connections loose in ignition, charging or lighting circuits (Chapter 10).

Battery overcharged

☐ Regulator/rectifier defective. Overcharging is noticed when battery gets excessively warm (Chapter 10).
☐ Battery defective. Renew battery (Chapter 10).
☐ Battery amperage too low, wrong type or size. Install manufacturer's specified amp-hour battery to handle charging load (Chapter 10).

Note: *References throughout this index are in the form* **"Chapter number"** • **"Page number"**. *So, for example, 2A•15 refers to page 15 of Chapter 2A.*

Note: *References throughout this index are in the form "Chapter number" • "Page number". So, for example, 2A•15 refers to page 15 of Chapter 2A.*

*Note: References throughout this index are in the form "**Chapter number**" • "**Page number**". So, for example, 2A•15 refers to page 15 of Chapter 2A.*

Haynes Motorcycle Manuals – The Complete List

Title		Book No
APRILIA RS50 (99 – 06) & RS125 (93 – 06)		4298
Aprilia RSV1000 Mille (98 – 03)	♦	4255
Aprilia SR50		4755
BMW 2-valve Twins (70 -96)	♦	0249
BMW F650	♦	4761
BMW K100 & 75 2-valve models (83 - 96)	♦	1373
BMW F800 (F650) Twins (06 – 10)	♦	4872
BMW R850, 1100 & 1150 4-valve Twins (93 – 06)	♦	3466
BMW R1200 (04 – 09)	♦	4598
BMW R1200 dohc Twins (10 – 12)	♦	4925
BSA Bantam (48 – 71)		0117
BSA Unit Singles (58 – 72)		0127
BSA Pre-unit Singles (54 – 61)		0326
BSA A7 & A10 Twins (47 – 62)		0121
BSA A50 & A65 Twins (62 – 73)		0155
CHINESE, Taiwanese & Korean Scooters		4768
Chinese, Taiwanese & Korean 125cc motorcycles		4781
DUCATI 600, 620, 750 & 900 2-valve V-twins (91 – 05)	♦	3290
Ducati Mk III & Desmo singles (69 – 76)	◊	0445
Ducati 748, 916 & 996 4-valve V-twins (94 – 01)	♦	3756
GILERA Runner, DNA, Ice & SKP/Stalker (97 – 11)		4163
HARLEY-DAVIDSON Sportsters (70 – 10)	♦	2534
Harley-Davidson Shovelhead & Evolution Big Twins (70 -99)	♦	2536
Harley-Davidson Twin Cam 88, 96 & 103 models (99 – 10)	♦	2478
HONDA NB, ND, NP & NS50 Melody (81 -85)	◊	0622
Honda NE/NB50 Vision & SA50 Vision Met-in (85-95)	◊	1278
Honda MB, MBX, MT & MTX50 (80 – 93)		0731
Honda C50, C70 & C90 (67 – 03)		0324
Honda XR50/70/80/100R & CRF50/70/80/100F (85 – 07)		2218
Honda XL/XR 80, 100, 125, 185 & 200 2-valve models (78 – 87)		0566
Honda H100 & H100S Singles (80 – 92)	◊	0734
Honda 125 Scooters (00 – 09)		4873
Honda ANF125 Innova Scooters (03 -12)	♦	4926
Honda CB/CD125T & CM125C Twins (77 – 88)	◊	0571
Honda CBF125 (09 – 12)	♦	5540
Honda CG125 (76 – 07)	◊	0433
Honda NS125 (86 – 93)	◊	3056
Honda CBR125R (04 – 10)		4620
Honda MBX/MTX125 & MTX200 (83 – 93)	◊	1132
Honda XL125V & VT125C (99 – 11)		4899
Honda CD/CM185 200T & CM250C 2-valve Twins (77 – 85)		0572
Honda CMX250 Rebel & CB250 Nighthawk Twins (85 – 09)	◊	2756
Honda XL/XR 250 & 500 (78 – 84)		0567
Honda XR250L, XR250R & XR400R (86 – 03)		2219
Honda CB250 & CB400N Super Dreams (78 – 84)	◊	0540
Honda CR Motocross Bikes (86 – 07)		2222
Honda CRF250 & CRF450 (02 – 06)		2630
Honda CBR400RR Fours (88 – 99)	◊♦	3552
Honda VFR400 (NC30) & RVF400 (NC35) V-Fours (89 – 98)	◊♦	3496
Honda CB500 (93 – 02) & CBF500 (03 – 08)	◊	3753
Honda CB400 & CB550 Fours (73 – 77)		0262
Honda CX/GL500 & 650 V-Twins (78 – 86)		0442
Honda CBX550 Four (82 – 86)	◊	0940
Honda XL600R & XR600R (83 – 08)	♦	2183
Honda XL600/650V Transalp & XRV750 Africa Twin (87 – 07)	♦	3919
Honda CB600 Hornet, CBF600 & CBR600F (07 – 12)	♦	5572
Honda CBR600F1 & 1000F Fours (87 – 96)	♦	1730
Honda CBR600F2 & F3 Fours (91 – 98)	♦	2070
Honda CBR600F4 (99 – 06)	♦	3911
Honda CB600F Hornet & CBF600 (98 – 06)	◊♦	3915
Honda CBR600RR (03 – 06)	♦	4590
Honda CBR600RR (07 -12)	♦	4795
Honda CB650 sohc Fours (78 – 84)		0665
Honda NTV600 Revere, NTV650 & NT650V Deauville (88 – 05)	◊♦	3243
Honda Shadow VT600 & 750 (USA) (88 – 09)		2312
Honda NT700V Deauville & XL700V Transalp (06 -13)	♦	5541
Honda CB750 sohc Four (69 – 79)		0131
Honda V45/65 Sabre & Magna (82 – 88)		0820
Honda VFR750 & 700 V-Fours (86 – 97)	♦	2101
Honda VFR800 V-Fours (97 – 01)	♦	3703
Honda VFR800 V-Tec V-Fours (02 – 09)	♦	4196
Honda CB750 & CB900 dohc Fours (78 – 84)		0535
Honda CBF1000 (06 -10) & CB1000R (08 – 11)	♦	4927
Honda VTR1000 Firestorm, Super Hawk & XL1000V Varadero (97 – 08)	♦	3744
Honda CBR900RR Fireblade (92 – 99)	♦	2161
Honda CBR900RR Fireblade (00 – 03)	♦	4060
Honda CBR1000RR Fireblade (04 – 07)	♦	4604
Honda CBR1100XX Super Blackbird (97 – 07)	♦	3901
Honda ST1100 Pan European V-Fours (90 – 02)	♦	3384
Honda ST1300 Pan European (02 -11)	♦	4908

Title		Book No
Honda Shadow VT1100 (USA) (85 – 07)		2313
Honda GL1000 Gold Wing (75 – 79)		0309
Honda GL1100 Gold Wing (79 – 81)		0669
Honda Gold Wing 1200 (USA) (84 - 87)		2199
Honda Gold Wing 1500 (USA) (88 – 00)		2225
Honda Goldwing GL1800	♦	2787
KAWASAKI AE/AR 50 & 80 (81 – 95)		1007
Kawasaki KC, KE & KH100 (75 – 99)		1371
Kawasaki KMX125 & 200 (86 – 02)	◊	3046
Kawasaki 250, 350 & 400 Triples (72 – 79)		0134
Kawasaki 400 & 440 Twins (74 – 81)		0281
Kawasaki 400, 500 & 550 Fours (79 – 91)		0910
Kawasaki EN450 & 500 Twins (Ltd/Vulcan) (85 – 07)		2053
Kawasaki ER-6F & ER-6N (06 -10)	♦	4874
Kawasaki EX500 (GPZ500S) & ER500 (ER-5) (87 – 08)	♦	2052
Kawasaki ZX600 (ZZ-R600 & Ninja ZX-6) (90 – 06)	♦	2146
Kawasaki ZX-6R Ninja Fours (95 – 02)	♦	3451
Kawasaki ZX-6R (03 – 06)	♦	4742
Kawasaki ZX600 (GPZ600R, GPX600R, Ninja 600R & RX) & ZX750 (GPX750R, Ninja 750R) (85 – 97)	♦	1780
Kawasaki 650 Four (76 – 78)		0373
Kawasaki Vulcan 700/750 & 800 (85 – 04)	♦	2457
Kawasaki Vulcan 1500 & 1600 (87 – 08)	♦	4913
Kawasaki 750 Air-cooled Fours		0574
Kawasaki ZR550 & 750 Zephyr Fours (90 – 97)	♦	3382
Kawasaki Z750 & Z1000 (03 – 08)	♦	4762
Kawasaki ZX750 (Ninja ZX-7 & ZXR750) Fours (89 – 96)	♦	2054
Kawasaki Ninja ZX-7R & ZX-9R (94 – 04)	♦	3721
Kawasaki 900 & 1000 Fours (73 – 77)		0222
Kawasaki ZX900, 1000 & 1100 Liquid-cooled Fours (83 – 97)	♦	1681
KTM EXC Enduro & SX Motocross (00 – 07)	♦	4629
LAMBRETTA Scooters (58 – 00)	♦	5573
MOTO GUZZI 750, 850 & 1000 V-Twins (74 – 78)		0339
MZ ETZ models (81 – 95)	◊	1680
NORTON 500, 600, 650 & 750 Twins (57 – 70)		0187
Norton Commando (68 – 77)		0125
PEUGEOT Speedfight, Trekker & Vivacity Scooters (96 – 08)	◊	3920
PIAGGIO (Vespa) Scooters (91 – 09)	◊	3492
SUZUKI GT, ZR & TS50 (77 – 90)	◊	0799
Suzuki TS50X (84 – 00)	◊	1599
Suzuki 100, 125, 185 & 250 Air-cooled Trail bikes (79 – 89)		0797
Suzuki GP100 & 125 Singles (78 – 93)	◊	0576
Suzuki GS, GN, GZ & DR125 Singles (82 – 05)	◊	0888
Suzuki Burgman 250 & 400 (98 – 11)	♦	4909
Suzuki GSX-R600/750 (06 – 09)	♦	4790
Suzuki 250 & 350 Twins (68 – 78)		0120
Suzuki GT250X7, GT200X5 & SB200 Twins (78 – 83)	◊	0469
Suzuki DR-Z400 (00 – 10)	♦	2933
Suzuki GS/GSX250, 400 & 450 Twins (79 – 85)		0736
Suzuki GS500 Twin (89 – 08)	♦	3238
Suzuki GS550 (77 – 82) & GS750 Fours (76 – 79)		0363
Suzuki GS/GSX550 4-valve Fours (83 – 88)		1133
Suzuki SV650 & SV650S (99 – 08)	♦	3912
Suzuki GSX-R600 & 750 (96 – 00)	♦	3553
Suzuki GSX-R600 (01 – 03), GSX-R750 (00 – 03) & GSX-R1000 (01 – 02)	♦	3986
Suzuki GSX-R600/750 (04 – 05) & GSX-R1000 (03 – 06)	♦	4382
Suzuki GSF600, 650 & 1200 Bandit Fours (95 – 06)	♦	3367
Suzuki Intruder, Marauder, Volusia & Boulevard (85 – 09)	♦	2618
Suzuki GS850 Fours (78 – 88)		0536
Suzuki GS1000 Four (77 – 79)		0484
Suzuki GSX-R750, GSX-R1100 (85 – 92) GSX600F, GSX750F, GSX1100F (Katana) Fours (88 – 96)	♦	2055
Suzuki GSX600/750F & GSX750 (98 – 02)	♦	3987
Suzuki GS/GSX1000, 1100 & 1150 4-valve Fours (79 – 88)		0737
Suzuki TL1000S/R & DL V-Strom (97 – 04)	♦	4083
Suzuki GSF650/1250 (07 – 09)	♦	4798
Suzuki GSX1300R Hayabusa (99 – 04)	♦	4184
Suzuki GSX1400 (02 – 08)	♦	4758
TRIUMPH Tiger Cub & Terrier (52 – 68)		0414
Triumph 350 & 500 Unit Twins (58 – 73)		0137
Triumph Pre-Unit Twins (47 – 62)		0251
Triumph 650 & 750 2-valve Unit Twins (63 – 83)		0122
Triumph 675 (06 – 10)	♦	4876
Triumph 1050 Sprint, Speed Triple & Tiger (05 -13)	♦	4796
Triumph Trident & BSA Rocket 3 (69 – 75)		0136
Triumph Bonneville (01 – 12)	♦	4364
Triumph Daytona, Speed Triple, Sprint & Tiger (97 – 05)	♦	3755
Triumph Triples & Fours (carburetor engines) (91 – 04)	♦	2162
VESPA P/PX125, 150 & 200 Scooters (78 – 12)		0707
Vespa GTS125, 250 & 300 (05 – 10)		4898

Title		Book No
Vespa Scooters (59 – 78)		0126
YAMAHA DT50 & 80 Trail Bikes (78 – 95)	◊	0800
Yamaha T50 & 80 Townmate (83 – 95)	◊	1247
Yamaha YB100 Singles (73 – 91)	◊	0474
Yamaha RS/RXS 100 & 125 Singles (74 – 95)		0331
Yamaha RD & DT125LC (82 – 87)	◊	0887
Yamaha TZR125 (87 – 93) & DT125R (88 – 07)	◊	1655
Yamaha TY50, 80, 125 & 175 (74 – 84)	◊	0464
Yamaha XT & SR125 (82 – 03)	◊	1021
Yamaha YBR125 & XT125R/X (05 – 13)		4797
Yamaha YZF-R125 (08 – 11)	♦	5543
Yamaha Trail Bikes (81 – 00)		2350
Yamaha 2-stroke Motocross Bikes (86 – 06)		2662
Yamaha YZ & WR 4-stroke Motorcross Bikes (98 – 08)		2689
Yamaha 250 & 350 Twins (70 – 79)		0040
Yamaha XS250, 360 & 400 sohc Twins (75 – 84)		0378
Yamaha RD250 & 350LC Twins (80 – 82)		0803
Yamaha RD350 YPVS Twins (83 – 95)		1158
Yamaha RD400 Twin (75 – 79)		0333
Yamaha XT, TT & SR500 Singles (75 – 83)		0342
Yamaha XZ550 Vision V-Twins (82 – 85)		0821
Yamaha FJ, FX, XY & YX600 Radian (84 – 92)		2100
Yamaha XT660 & MT-03 (04 – 11)	♦	4910
Yamaha XJ600S (Diversion, Seca II) & XJ600N Fours (92 – 03)	♦	2145
Yamaha YZF600R Thundercat & FZS600 Fazer (96 – 03)	♦	3702
Yamaha FZ-6 Fazer (04 – 08)	♦	4751
Yamaha YZF-R6 (99 – 02)	♦	3900
Yamaha YZF-R6 (03 – 05)	♦	4601
Yamaha YZF-R6 (06 – 13)	♦	5544
Yamaha 650 Twins (70 – 83)		0341
Yamaha XJ650 & 750 Fours (80 – 84)		0738
Yamaha XS750 & 850 Triples (76 – 85)		0340
Yamaha TDM850, TRX850 & XTZ750 (89 – 99)	◊♦	3450
Yamaha YZF750R & YZF1000R Thunderace (93 – 00)	♦	3720
Yamaha FZR600, 750 & 1000 Fours (87 – 96)	♦	2056
Yamaha XV (Virago) V-Twins (81 – 03)	♦	0802
Yamaha XVS650 & 1100 Drag Star/V-Star (97 – 05)	♦	4195
Yamaha XJ900F Fours (83 – 94)	♦	3239
Yamaha XJ900S Diversion (94 – 01)	♦	3739
Yamaha YZF-R1 (98 – 03)	♦	3754
Yamaha YZF-R1 (04 – 06)	♦	4605
Yamaha FZS1000 Fazer (01 – 05)	♦	4287
Yamaha FJ1100 & 1200 Fours (84 – 96)	♦	2057
Yamaha XJR1200 & 1300 (95 – 06)	♦	3981
Yamaha V-Max (85 – 03)	♦	4072
ATV's		
Honda ATC 70, 90, 110, 185 & 200 (71 – on)		0565
Honda Rancher, Recon & TRX250EX ATVs		2553
Honda TRX300 Shaft Drive ATVs (88 – 00)		2125
Honda Foreman (95 – 11)		2465
Honda TRX300EX, TRX400EX & TRX450R/ER ATVs (93 – 06)		2318
Kawasaki Bayou 220/250/300 & Prairie 300 ATVs (86 – 03)		2351
Polaris ATVs (85 – 97)		2302
Polaris ATVs (98 – 07)		2508
Suzuki/Kawasaki/Artic Cat ATVs (03 – 09)		2910
Yamaha YFS200 Blaster ATV (88 – 06)		2317
Yamaha YFM350 & YFM400 (ER & Big Bear) ATVs (87 – 09)		2126
Yamaha YFZ450 & YFZ450R (04 – 10)		2899
Yamaha Banshee and Warrior ATVs (87 – 10)		2314
Yamaha Kodiak and Grizzly ATVs (93 – 05)		2567
ATV Basics		10450
TECHBOOK SERIES		
Twist and Go (automatic transmission) Scooters Service and Repair Manual		4082
Motorcycle Basics Techbook (2nd edition)		3515
Motorcycle Electrical Techbook (3rd edition)		3471
Motorcycle Fuel Systems Techbook		3514
Motorcycle Maintenance Techbook		4071
Motorcycle Modifying		4272
Motorcycle Workshop Practice Techbook (2nd edition)		3470

◊ = not available in the USA ♦ = Superbike

The manuals on this page are available through good motorcycle dealers and accessory shops.
In case of difficulty, contact: **Haynes Publishing**
(UK) **+44 1963 442030** (USA) **+1 805 498 6703**
(SV) **+46 18 124016**
(Australia/New Zealand) **+61 2 8713 1400**

MCL 30.09.13

Haynes Manuals – The Complete UK Car List

Title	Book No.
ALFA ROMEO Alfasud/Sprint (74 - 88) up to F *	0292
Alfa Romeo Alfetta (73 – 87) up to E *	0531
AUDI 80, 90 & Coupe Petrol (79 – Nov 88) up to F	0605
Audi 80, 90 & Coupe Petrol (Oct 86 – 90) D to H	1491
Audi 100 & A6 Petrol & Diesel (May 91 – May 97) H to P	3504
Audi A3 Petrol & Diesel (96 – May 03) P to 03	4253
Audi A3 Petrol & Diesel (June 03 – Mar 08) 03 to 08	4884
Audi A4 Petrol & Diesel (95 – 00) M to X	3575
Audi A4 Petrol & Diesel (01 – 04) X to 54	4609
Audi A4 Petrol & Diesel (Jan 05 – Feb 08) 54 to 57	4885
AUSTIN A35 & A40 (56 – 67) up to F *	0118
Mini (59 – 69) up to H *	0527
Mini (69 – 01) up to X	0646
Austin Healey 100/6 & 3000 (56 – 68) up to G *	0049
BEDFORD/Vauxhall Rascal & Suzuki Supercarry (86 – Oct 94) C to M	3015
BMW 1-Series 4-cyl Petrol & Diesel (04 – Aug 11) 54 to 11	4918
BMW 316, 320 & 320i (4-cyl)(75 – Feb 83) up to Y *	0276
BMW 3- & 5- Series Petrol (81 – 91) up to J	1948
BMW 3-Series Petrol (Apr 91 – 99) H to V	3210
BMW 3-Series Petrol (Sept 98 – 06) S to 56	4067
BMW 3-Series Petrol & Diesel (05 – Sept 08) 54 to 58	4782
BMW 5-Series 6-cyl Petrol (April 96 – Aug 03) N to 03	4151
BMW 5-Series Diesel (Sept 03 – 10) 53 to 10	4901
BMW 1500, 1502, 1600, 1602, 2000 & 2002 (59 – 77) up to S *	0240
CHRYSLER PT Cruiser Petrol (00-09) W to 09	4058
CITROEN 2CV, Ami & Dyane (67 – 90) up to H	0196
Citroen AX Petrol & Diesel (87- 97) D to P	3014
Citroen Berlingo & Peugeot Partner Petrol & Diesel (96 – 10) P to 60	4281
Citroen C1 Petrol (05 – 11) 05 to 11	4922
Citroen C3 Petrol & Diesel (02 – 09) 51 to 59	4890
Citroen C4 Petrol & Diesel (04 – 10) 54 to 60	5576
Citroen C5 Petrol & Diesel (01 – 08) Y to 08	4745
Citroen C15 Van Petrol & Diesel (89 – Oct 98) F to S	3509
Citroen CX Petrol (75 – 88) up to F	0528
Citroen Saxo Petrol & Diesel (96 – 04) N to 54	3506
Citroen Visa Petrol (79 – 88) up to F	0620
Citroen Xantia Petrol & Diesel (93 – 01) K to Y	3082
Citroen XM Petrol & Diesel (89 – 00) G to X	3451
Citroen Xsara Petrol & Diesel (97 – Sept 00) R to W	3751
Citroen Xsara Picasso Petrol & Diesel (00 – 02) W to 52	3944
Citroen Xsara Picasso (Mar 04 – 08) 04 to 58	4784
Citroen ZX Diesel (91 – 98) J to S	1922
Citroen ZX Petrol (91 – 98) H to S	1881
FIAT 126 (73 – 87) up to E *	0305
Fiat 500 (57 – 73) up to M *	0090
Fiat 500 & Panda (04 – 12) 53 to 61	5558
Fiat Bravo & Brava Petrol (95 – 00) N to W	3572
Fiat Cinquecento (93 – 98) K to R	3501
Fiat Panda (81 – 95) up to M	0793
Fiat Punto Petrol & Diesel (94 – Oct 99) L to V	3251
Fiat Punto Petrol (Oct 99 – July 03) V to 03	4066
Fiat Punto Petrol (03 – 07) 03 to 07	4746
Fiat Punto Petrol (Oct 99 – 07) V to 07	5634
Fiat X1/9 (74 – 89) up to G *	0273
FORD Anglia (59 – 68) up to G *	0001
Ford Capri II (& III) 1.6 & 2.0 (74 – 87) up to E *	0283
Ford Capri II (& III) 2.8 & 3.0 V6 (74 – 87) up to E	1309
Ford C-Max Petrol & Diesel (03 – 10) 53 to 60	4900
Ford Escort Mk I 1100 & 1300 (68 – 74) up to N *	0171
Ford Escort Mk I Mexico, RS 1600 & RS 2000 (70 – 74) up to N *	0139
Ford Escort Mk II Mexico, RS 1800 & RS 2000 (75 – 80) up to W *	0735
Ford Escort (75 – Aug 80) up to V *	0280
Ford Escort Petrol (Sept 80 – Sept 90) up to H	0686
Ford Escort & Orion Petrol (Sept 90 – 00) H to X	1737
Ford Escort & Orion Diesel (Sept 90 – 00) H to X	4081
Ford Fiesta Petrol (Feb 89 – Oct 95) F to N	1595
Ford Fiesta Petrol & Diesel (Oct 95 – Mar 02) N to 02	3397
Ford Fiesta Petrol & Diesel (Apr 02 – 08) 02 to 58	4170
Ford Fiesta Petrol & Diesel (08 – 11) 58 to 11	4907
Ford Focus Petrol & Diesel (98 – 01) S to Y	3759
Ford Focus Petrol & Diesel (Oct 01 – 05) 51 to 05	4167
Ford Focus Petrol (05 – 09) 54 to 09	4785
Ford Focus Diesel (05 – 09) 54 to 09	4807
Ford Fusion Petrol & Diesel (02 – 11) 02 to 61	5566
Ford Galaxy Petrol & Diesel (95 – Aug 00) M to W	3984
Ford Galaxy Petrol & Diesel (00 – 06) X to 06	5556
Ford Granada Petrol (Sept 77 – Feb 85) up to B *	0481
Ford Ka (96 – 08) P to 58	5567
Ford Mondeo Petrol (93 – Sept 00) K to X	1923
Ford Mondeo Petrol & Diesel (Oct 00 – Jul 03) X to 03	3990
Ford Mondeo Petrol & Diesel (July 03 – 07) 03 to 56	4619
Ford Mondeo Petrol & Diesel (Apr 07 – 12) 07 to 61	5548
Ford Mondeo Diesel (93 – Sept 00) L to X	3465
Ford Sierra V6 Petrol (82 – 91) up to J	0904
Ford Transit Connect Diesel (02 – 11) 02 to 11	4903
Ford Transit Diesel (Feb 86 – 99) C to T	3019
Ford Transit Diesel (00 – Oct 06) X to 56	4775
Ford 1.6 & 1.8 litre Diesel Engine (84 – 96) A to N	1172
HILLMAN Imp (63 – 76) up to R *	0022
HONDA Civic (Feb 84 – Oct 87) A to E	1226
Honda Civic (Nov 91 – 96) J to N	3199
Honda Civic Petrol (Mar 95 – 00) M to X	4050
Honda Civic Petrol & Diesel (01 – 05) X to 55	4611
Honda CR-V Petrol & Diesel (02 – 06) 51 to 56	4747
Honda Jazz (02 to 08) 51 to 58	4735
JAGUAR E-Type (61 – 72) up to L *	0140
Jaguar Mk I & II, 240 & 340 (55 – 69) up to H *	0098
Jaguar XJ6, XJ & Sovereign, Daimler Sovereign (68 – Oct 86) up to D	0242
Jaguar XJ6 & Sovereign (Oct 86 – Sept 94) D to M	3261
Jaguar XJ12, XJS & Sovereign, Daimler Double Six (72 – 88) up to F	0478
JEEP Cherokee Petrol (93 – 96) K to N	1943
LAND ROVER 90, 110 & Defender Diesel (83 – 07) up to 56	3017
Land Rover Discovery Petrol & Diesel (89 – 98) G to S	3016
Land Rover Discovery Diesel (Nov 98 – Jul 04) S to 04	4606
Land Rover Discovery Diesel (Aug 04 – Apr 09) 04 to 09	5562
Land Rover Freelander Petrol & Diesel (97 – Sept 03) R to 53	3929
Land Rover Freelander (97 – Oct 06) R to 56	5571
Land Rover Series II, IIA & III 4-cyl Petrol (58 – 85) up to C	0314
Land Rover Series II, IIA & III Petrol & Diesel (58 – 85) up to C	5568
MAZDA 323 (Mar 81 – Oct 89) up to G	1608
Mazda 323 (Oct 89 – 98) G to R	3455
Mazda B1600, B1800 & B2000 Pick-up Petrol (72 – 88) up to F	0267
Mazda MX-5 (89 – 05) G to 05	5565
Mazda RX-7 (79 – 85) up to C *	0460
MERCEDES-BENZ 190, 190E & 190D Petrol & Diesel (83 – 93) A to L	3450
Mercedes-Benz 200D, 240D, 240TD, 300D & 300TD 123 Series Diesel (Oct 76 – 85) up to C	1114
Mercedes-Benz 250 & 280 (68 – 72) up to L *	0346
Mercedes-Benz 250 & 280 123 Series Petrol (Oct 76 – 84) up to B *	0677
Mercedes-Benz 124 Series Petrol & Diesel (85 – Aug 93) C to K	3253
Mercedes-Benz A-Class Petrol & Diesel (98 – 04) S to 54	4748
Mercedes-Benz C-Class Petrol & Diesel (93 – Aug 00) L to W	3511
Mercedes-Benz C-Class (00 – 07) X to 07	4780
Mercedes-Benz Sprinter Diesel (95 – Apr 06) M to 06	4902
MGA (55 – 62)	0475
MGB (62 – 80) up to W	0111
MGB 1962 to 1980 (special edition) *	4894
MG Midget & Austin-Healey Sprite (58 – 80) up to W *	0265
MINI Petrol (July 01 – 06) Y to 56	4273
MINI Petrol & Diesel (Nov 06 – 13) 56 to 13	4904
MITSUBISHI Shogun & L200 Pick-ups Petrol (83 – 94) up to M	1944
MORRIS Minor 1000 (56 – 71) up to K	0024
NISSAN Almera Petrol (95 – Feb 00) N to V	4053
Nissan Almera & Tino Petrol (Feb 00 – 07) V to 56	4612
Nissan Micra (83 – Jan 93) up to K	0931
Nissan Micra (93 – 02) K to 52	3254
Nissan Micra Petrol (03 – Oct 10) 52 to 60	4734
Nissan Primera Petrol (90 – Aug 99) H to T	1851
Nissan Qashqai Petrol & Diesel (07 – 12) 56 to 62	5610
OPEL Ascona & Manta (B-Series) (Sept 75 – 88) up to F *	0316
Opel Ascona Petrol (81 – 88)	3215
Opel Ascona Petrol (Oct 91 – Feb 98)	3156
Opel Corsa Petrol (83 – Mar 93)	3160
Opel Corsa Petrol (Mar 93 – 97)	3159
Opel Kadett Petrol (Oct 84 – Oct 91)	3196
Opel Omega & Senator Petrol (Nov 86 – 94)	3157
Opel Vectra Petrol (Oct 88 – Oct 95)	3158
PEUGEOT 106 Petrol & Diesel (91 – 04) J to 53	1882
Peugeot 107 Petrol (05 – 11) 05 to 11	4923
Peugeot 205 Petrol (83 – 97) A to P	0932
Peugeot 206 Petrol & Diesel (98 – 01) S to X	3757

* Classic reprint

Title	Book No.
Peugeot 206 Petrol & Diesel (02 – 06) 51 to 06	4613
Peugeot 207 Petrol & Diesel (06 – July 09) 06 to 09	4787
Peugeot 306 Petrol & Diesel (93 – 02) K to 02	3073
Peugeot 307 Petrol & Diesel (01 – 08) Y to 58	4147
Peugeot 308 Petrol & Diesel (07 – 12) 07 to 12	5561
Peugeot 405 Diesel (88 – 97) E to P	3198
Peugeot 406 Petrol & Diesel (96 – Mar 99) N to T	3394
Peugeot 406 Petrol & Diesel (Mar 99 – 02) T to 52	3982
Peugeot 407 Diesel (04 -11) 53 to 11	5550
PORSCHE 911 (65 – 85) up to C	0264
Porsche 924 & 924 Turbo (76 – 85) up to C	0397
RANGE ROVER V8 Petrol (70 – Oct 92) up to K	0606
RELIANT Robin & Kitten (73 – 83) up to A *	0436
RENAULT 4 (61 – 86) up to D *	0072
Renault 5 Petrol (Feb 85 – 96) B to N	1219
Renault 19 Petrol (89 – 96) F to N	1646
Renault Clio Petrol (91 – May 98) H to R	1853
Renault Clio Petrol & Diesel (May 98 – May 01) R to Y	3906
Renault Clio Petrol & Diesel (June 01 – 05) Y to 55	4168
Renault Clio Petrol & Diesel (Oct 05 – May 09) 55 to 09	4788
Renault Espace Petrol & Diesel (85 – 96) C to N	3197
Renault Laguna Petrol & Diesel (94 – 00) L to W	3252
Renault Laguna Petrol & Diesel (Feb 01 – May 07) X to 07	4283
Renault Megane & Scenic Petrol & Diesel (96 – 99) N to T	3395
Renault Megane & Scenic Petrol & Diesel (Apr 99 – 02) T to 52	3916
Renault Megane Petrol & Diesel (Oct 02 – 08) 52 to 58	4284
Renault Scenic Petrol & Diesel (Sept 03 – 06) 53 to 06	4297
Renault Trafic Diesel (01 – 11) Y to 11	5551
ROVER 216 & 416 Petrol (89 – 96) G to N	1830
Rover 211, 214, 216, 218 & 220 Petrol & Diesel (Dec 95 – 99) N to V	3399
Rover 25 & MG ZR Petrol & Diesel (Oct 99 – 06) V to 06	4145
Rover 414, 416 & 420 Petrol & Diesel (May 95 – 99) M to V	3453
Rover 45 / MG ZS Petrol & Diesel (99 – 05) V to 55	4384
Rover 618, 620 & 623 Petrol (93 – 97) K to P	3257
Rover 75 / MG ZT Petrol & Diesel (99 – 06) S to 06	4292
Rover 820, 825 & 827 Petrol (86 – 95) D to N	1380
Rover 3500 (76 – 87) up to E *	0365
Rover Metro, 111 & 114 Petrol (May 90 – 98) G to S	1711
SAAB 95 & 96 (66 – 76) up to R *	0198
Saab 90, 99 & 900 (79 – Oct 93) up to L	0765
Saab 900 (Oct 93 – 98) L to R	3512
Saab 9000 4-cyl (85 – 98) C to S	1686
Saab 9-3 Petrol & Diesel (98 – Aug 02) R to 02	4614
Saab 9-3 Petrol & Diesel (92 – 07) 52 to 57	4749
Saab 9-3 Petrol & Diesel (07-on) 57 on	5569
Saab 9-5 4-cyl Petrol (97 – 05) R to 55	4156
Saab 9-5 (Sep 05 – Jun 10) 55 to 10	4891
SEAT Ibiza & Cordoba Petrol & Diesel (Oct 93 – Oct 99) L to V	3571
Seat Ibiza & Malaga Petrol (85 – 92) B to K	1609
Seat Ibiza Petrol & Diesel (May 02 – Apr 08) 02 to 08	4889

Title	Book No.
SKODA Fabia Petrol & Diesel (00 – 06) W to 06	4376
Skoda Felicia Petrol & Diesel (95 – 01) M to X	3505
Skoda Octavia Petrol (98 – April 04) R to 04	4285
Skoda Octavia Diesel (May 04 – 12) 04 to 61	5549
SUBARU 1600 & 1800 (Nov 79 – 90) up to H *	0995
SUNBEAM Alpine, Rapier & H120 (68 – 74) up to N *	0051
SUZUKI SJ Series, Samurai & Vitara 4-cyl Petrol (82 – 97) up to P	1942
Suzuki Supercarry & Bedford/Vauxhall Rascal (86 – Oct 94) C to M	3015
TOYOTA Avensis Petrol (98 – Jan 03) R to 52	4264
Toyota Aygo Petrol (05 – 11) 05 to 11	4921
Toyota Carina E Petrol (May 92 – 97) J to P	3256
Toyota Corolla (80 – 85) up to C	0683
Toyota Corolla (Sept 83 – Sept 87) A to E	1024
Toyota Corolla (Sept 87 – Aug 92) E to K	1683
Toyota Corolla Petrol (Aug 92 – 97) K to P	3259
Toyota Corolla Petrol (July 97 0 Feb 02) P to 51	4286
Toyota Corolla Petrol & Diesel (02 – Jan 07) 51 to 56	4791
Toyota Hi-Ace & Hi-Lux Petrol (69 – Oct 83) up to A	0304
Toyota RAV4 Petrol & Diesel (94 – 06) L to 55	4750
Toyota Yaris Petrol (99 – 05) T to 05	4265
TRIUMPH GT6 & Vitesse (62 0 74) up to N *	0112
Triumph Herald (59 – 71) up to K *	0010
Triumph Spitfire (62 – 81) up to X	0113
Triumph Stag (70 – 78) up to T *	0441
Triumph TR2, TR3, TR3A, TR4 & TR4A (52 – 67) up to F *	0028
Triumph TR5 & TR6 (67 – 75) up to P *	0031
Triumph TR7 (75 – 82) up to Y *	0322
VAUXHALL Astra Petrol (Oct 91 – Feb 98) J to R	1832
Vauxhall/Opel Astra & Zafira Petrol (Feb 98 – Apr 04) R to 04	3758
Vauxhall/Opel Astra & Zafira Diesel (Feb 98 – Apr 04) R to 04	3797
Vauxhall/Opel Astra Petrol (04 – 08)	4732
Vauxhall/Opel Astra Diesel (04 – 08)	4733
Vauxhall/Opel Astra Petrol & Diesel (Dec 09 – 13) 59 to 13	5578
Vauxhall/Opel Calibra (90 – 98) G to S	3502
Vauxhall Cavalier Petrol (Oct 88 0 95) F to N	1570
Vauxhall/Opel Corsa Diesel (Mar 93 – Oct 00) K to X	4087
Vauxhall Corsa Petrol (Mar 93 – 97) K to R	1985
Vauxhall/Opel Corsa Petrol (Apr 97 – Oct 00) P to X	3921
Vauxhall/Opel Corsa Petrol & Diesel (Oct 03 – Aug 06) 53 to 06	4617
Vauxhall/Opel Corsa Petrol & Diesel (Sept 06 – 10) 56 to 10	4886
Vauxhall/Opel Corsa Petrol & Diesel (00 – Aug 06) X to 06	5577
Vauxhall/Opel Frontera Petrol & Diesel (91 – Sept 98) J to S	3454
Vauxhall/Opel Insignia Petrol & Diesel (08 – 12) 08 to 61	5563
Vauxhall/Opel Meriva Petrol & Diesel (03 – May 10) 03 to 10	4893
Vauxhall/Opel Omega Petrol (94 – 99) L to T	3510
Vauxhall/Opel Vectra Petrol & Diesel (95 – Feb 99) N to S	3396

Title	Book No.
Vauxhall/Opel Vectra Petrol & Diesel (Mar 99 – May 02) T to 02	3930
Vauxhall/Opel Vectra Petrol & Diesel (June 02 – Sept 05) 02 to 55	4618
Vauxhall/Opel Vectra Petrol & Diesel (Oct 05 – Oct 08) 55 to 58	4887
Vauxhall/Opel Vivaro Diesel (01 – 11) Y to 11	5552
Vauxhall/Opel Zafira Petrol & Diesel (05 -09) 05 to 09	4792
Vauxhall/Opel 1.5, 1.6 & 1.7 litre Diesel Engine (82 – 96) up to N	1222
VW Beetle 1200 (54 – 77) up to S	0036
VW Beetle 1300 & 1500 (65 – 75) up to P	0039
VW 1302 & 1302S (70 – 72) up to L *	0110
VW Beetle 1303, 1303S & GT (72 – 75) up to P	0159
VW Beetle Petrol & Diesel (Apr 99 – 07) T to 57	3798
VW Golf & Jetta Mk 1 Petrol 1.1 & 1.3 (74 – 84) up to A	0716
VW Golf, Jetta & Scirocco Mk 1 Petrol 1.5, 1.6 & 1.8 (74 – 84) up to A	0726
VW Golf & Jetta Mk 1 Diesel (78 – 84) up to A	0451
VW Golf & Jetta Mk 2 Petrol (Mar 84 – Feb 92) A to J	1081
VW Golf & Vento Petrol & Diesel (Feb 92 – Mar 98) J to R	3097
VW Golf & Bora Petrol & Diesel (Apr 98 – 00) R to X	3727
VW Golf & Bora 4-cyl Petrol & Diesel (01 – 03) X to 53	4169
VW Golf & Jetta Petrol & Diesel (04 – 09) 53 to 09	4610
VW LT Petrol Vans & Light Trucks (76 – 87) up to E	0637
VW Passat 4-cyl Petrol (May 88 – 96) E to P	3498
VW Passat 4-cyl Petrol & Diesel (Dec 96 – Nov 00) P to X	3917
VW Passat Petrol & Diesel (Dec 00 – May 05) X to 05	4279
VW Passat Diesel (June 05 – 10) 05 to 60	4888
VW Polo Petrol (Nov 90 – Aug 94) H to L	3245
VW Polo Hatchback Petrol & Diesel (94 – 99) M to S	3500
VW Polo Hatchback Petrol (00 – Jan 02) V to 51	4150
VW Polo Petrol & Diesel (02 – May 05) 51 to 05	4608
VW Transporter 1600 (68 – 79) up to V	0082
VW Transporter 1700, 1800 & 2000 (72 – 79) up to V *	0226
VW Transporter (air cooled) Petrol (79 – 82) up to Y *	0638
VW Transporter (water cooled) Petrol (82 – 90) up to H	3452
VW Type 3 (63 – 73) up to M *	0084
VOLVO 120 & 130 Series (& P1800) (61 – 73) up to M *	0203
Volvo 142, 144 & 145 (66 – 74) up to N *	0129
Volvo 240 Series Petrol (74 – 93) up to K	0270
Volvo 440, 460 & 480 Petrol (87 – 97) D to P	1691
Volvo 740 & 760 Petrol (82 – 91) up to J	1258
Volvo 850 Petrol (92 – 96) J to P	3260
Volvo 940 Petrol (90 – 98) H to R	3249
Volvo S40 & V40 Petrol (96 – Mar 04) N to 04	3569
Volvo S40 & V50 Petrol & Diesel (Mar 04 – Jun 07) 04 to 07	4731
Volvo S60 Petrol & Diesel (01 – 08) X to 09	4793
Volvo S70, V70 & C70 Petrol (96 – 99) P to V	3573
Volvo V70 / S80 Petrol & Diesel (98 – 07) S to 07	4263
Volvo V70 Diesel (June 07 – 12) 07 to 61	5557
Volvo XV60 / 90 Diesel (03 – 12) 52 to 62	5630

* Classic reprint

CL 27.08.1

Preserving Our Motoring Heritage

< The Model J Duesenberg Derham Tourster. Only eight of these magnificent cars were ever built – this is the only example to be found outside the United States of America

Almost every car you've ever loved, loathed or desired is gathered under one roof at the Haynes Motor Museum. Over 300 immaculately presented cars and motorbikes represent every aspect of our motoring heritage, from elegant reminders of bygone days, such as the superb Model J Duesenberg to curiosities like the bug-eyed BMW Isetta. There are also many old friends and flames. Perhaps you remember the 1959 Ford Popular that you did your courting in? The magnificent 'Red Collection' is a spectacle of classic sports cars including AC, Alfa Romeo, Austin Healey, Ferrari, Lamborghini, Maserati, MG, Riley, Porsche and Triumph.

A Perfect Day Out

Each and every vehicle at the Haynes Motor Museum has played its part in the history and culture of Motoring. Today, they make a wonderful spectacle and a great day out for all the family. Bring the kids, bring Mum and Dad, but above all bring your camera to capture those golden memories for ever. You will also find an impressive array of motoring memorabilia, a comfortable 70 seat video cinema and one of the most extensive transport book shops in Britain. The Pit Stop Cafe serves everything from a cup of tea to wholesome, home-made meals or, if you prefer, you can enjoy the large picnic area nestled in the beautiful rural surroundings of Somerset.

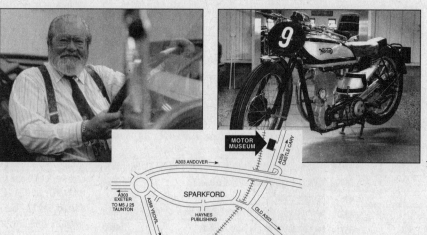

> John Haynes O.B.E., Founder and Chairman of the museum at the wheel of a Haynes Light 12.

< The 1936 490cc sohc-engined International Norton – well known for its racing success

The Museum is situated on the A359 Yeovil to Frome road at Sparkford, just off the A303 in Somerset. It is about 40 miles south of Bristol, and 25 minutes drive from the M5 intersection at Taunton.
Open 9.30am - 5.30pm (10.00am - 4.00pm Winter) 7 days a week, *except Christmas Day, Boxing Day and New Years Day*
Special rates available for schools, coach parties and outings Charitable Trust No. 292048